ENERGY FINANCE
AND ECONOMICS

The *Robert W. Kolb Series in Finance* provides a comprehensive view of the field of finance in all of its variety and complexity. It covers all major topics and specializations in finance, ranging from investments, to corporate finance, to financial institutions. Each volume is written or edited by a specialist (or specialists) in a particular area of finance and is intended for practicing finance professionals, graduate students, and advanced undergraduate students. The goal of each volume is to encapsulate the current state of knowledge in a particular area of finance so that the reader can quickly achieve a mastery of that discipline.

Please visit www.wiley.com/go/kolbseries to learn about recent and forthcoming titles in the Kolb Series.

ENERGY FINANCE AND ECONOMICS

Analysis and Valuation, Risk Management, and the Future of Energy

Editors

Betty J. Simkins
Russell E. Simkins

The Robert W. Kolb Series in Finance

WILEY

John Wiley & Sons, Inc.

Published by John Wiley & Sons, Inc., Hoboken, New Jersey.
Published simultaneously in Canada.

For general information on our other products and services or for technical support, please contact our Customer Care Department within the United States at (800) 762-2974, outside the United States at (317) 572-3993 or fax (317) 572-4002.

Wiley also publishes its books in a variety of electronic formats. Some content that appears in print may not be available in electronic books. For more information about Wiley products, visit our web site at www.wiley.com.

Library of Congress Cataloging-in-Publication Data:

Energy finance and economics : analysis and valuation, risk management, and the future of energy / Betty J. Simkins and Russell E. Simkins, editors.
    p. cm. – (The Robert W. Kolb series in finance)
  Includes index.
  ISBN 978-1-118-01712-8 (cloth); ISBN 978-1-118-22190-7 (ebk); ISBN 978-1-118-26056-2 (ebk); ISBN 978-1-118-23598-0 (ebk)
  1. Energy industries–Finance.   2. Energy policy.   3. Renewable natural resources.
  I. Simkins, Betty J., 1957–   II. Simkins, Russell E.
  HD9502.A2E54385 2013
  333.79–dc23
                                                                                    2012034409

Printed in the United States of America

V10002629_071818

To our family:
Luke and his future bride, Stephanie;
Walt and his wife, Lauren;
our daughter, Susan
and her long-time boyfriend, Jason;
our other daughter, April.

Contents

PART FOUR   Case Studies

Acknowledgments

We appreciate the contributions of the authors in this volume, who shared their valuable insights into the complex topic of energy finance and economics. Without them, this book would not have been possible. We also thank the Natural Gas and Energy Association of Oklahoma (NGEAO) for inspiring us to publish a book about energy and economics. We would like to also thank Emilie Herman, Tiffany Charbonier, Kevin Commins, and Melissa Lopez at John Wiley & Sons for their patience and hard work in the publication of this book. In addition, we appreciate Bob Kolb for his encouragement and contributions to this volume of the *Kolb Series in Finance*.

ENERGY FINANCE AND ECONOMICS

CHAPTER 1

An Introduction to Energy Finance and Economics

BETTY J. SIMKINS
Williams Companies Professor of Business and Professor of Finance,
Oklahoma State University

RUSSELL E. SIMKINS
Manager of Proposal Services, College of Engineering, Architecture,
and Technology, Oklahoma State University

> He who loves practice without theory is like the sailor who boards ship without a
> rudder and compass and never knows where he may be cast.
> —Leonardo da Vinci, 1452–1519

> An investment in knowledge always pays the best interest.
> —Benjamin Franklin

SO WHY A BOOK ON ENERGY FINANCE AND ECONOMICS?

The purpose of this book is to provide the latest information and insights into the finance and economics of energy, based on contributions written by academics and practitioners who are experts in various areas of energy finance and economics. We strive to bridge the theory–practice gap, as the quote from Leonardo da Vinci emphasizes, between the scientific and technological foundations of energy and the real-world applications in the fields of finance and economics. Theory and practice go hand in hand, so that students and practitioners can better understand the what, why, and how of energy finance and economics to aid them in performing at a higher level no matter where "they may be cast." Likewise, investing in knowledge will lead to success for anyone working in the energy industry or a related area, as the Benjamin Franklin quote suggests.

The book is intended to be useful to both educators and executives interested in the broad topic of energy finance and economics, but it will be relevant to energy users in general. To our knowledge, this is the first book to provide this breadth of coverage on this topic. We strive to provide accurate and nonbiased information by experts in each of the subject areas. Surveys, an example of

1

which is described in Chapter 7, have shown that, in general, the public is very misinformed about what influences the prices of energy in our society. This is indeed unfortunate because learning the basics is fundamental to both citizens and politicians who make important decisions regarding energy. There is a desperate need for more education on energy, and we believe this book is a step in the right direction.

What do we mean by energy finance and economics? By this, we mean the finance and economics of energy involving the principles and tools necessary to conduct sound decision making and analysis. This also includes a broad understanding of the complex topics related to energy for a solid foundation. By linking both the economics and finance of energy in the book, we are striving to break down the silo mentality that sometimes separates two fields, especially in education, so that the knowledge flows freely between these two areas.[1]

This leads to the **learning objectives** of the book, which are:

1. To gain basic knowledge and key concepts of energy supply and demand, terminology, industry structure, and related concepts.
2. To analyze geopolitics and world energy use and learn about the outlook for the U.S. and global energy needs over the next 30 years and beyond.
3. To understand energy applications that all professionals should know for best practices in financial analysis. These include understanding the basics such as accounting standards that apply to oil and gas companies, financial statement analysis, capital budgeting and risk analysis for energy projects, valuation, financing, and related topics including renewable energy.
4. To explore value creation and decision making in the energy industry.
5. To learn about the types of energy derivatives and markets and utilize key hedging techniques that are useful for energy risk management.
6. To provide a firm understanding of the importance of the energy industry and the role that alternative energy sources can provide (and not provide) in meeting our future energy needs.
7. To analyze case studies related to energy financial analysis, such as the economics of buying a hybrid vehicle, Southwest Airlines' decision to retrofit their fleet of Boeing jets with blended winglets to save on fuel costs, and the economics of a wind energy project, among others.
8. More broadly, to achieve a strong foundation in leading best practices that apply to the field of energy finance and economics.

THE CHALLENGES OF ENERGY TRANSITIONS AND THE TRICKY TRADEOFFS

Past energy transitions to inherently attractive fossil fuels took half a century; moving the world to cleaner fuels could be harder and slower.
—Richard A. Kerr (2010)

There has been a large push for renewable energy (wind, solar, etc.) worldwide with the corresponding Chicken Little warnings that we are running out of oil. Contrary to what most people believe, peak oil has not happened, and there is no

Exhibit 1.1 Future Global Energy Demand

Consumption	2008 Actual		2035		
	Quad BTU	% Share	Quad BTU	% Share	% Change
Liquid fuels	173.0	34.3	225.2	29.3	30.2
Coal	139.0	27.5	209.1	27.2	50.5
Natural gas	114.3	22.6	174.7	22.7	52.8
Renewables	51.3	10.2	109.5	14.2	113.5
Nuclear power	27.2	5.4	51.2	6.7	88.6
Total	504.7	100.0%	769.8	100.0%	52.5
Oil and natural gas	287.3	56.9	399.9	52.0	39.2
Oil, natural gas, and coal	426.3	84.4	609.1	79.1	42.9

braking point in sight.[2] Oil and natural gas supply capacity is growing worldwide at an unprecedented level that may outpace consumption, according to Maugeri (2012). As later discussed in Chapter 3 of the book, most forecasts of future global energy demand through the year 2035 show that sustaining even modest economic growth worldwide will require massive new investments in energy, particularly oil and natural gas (see for example, EIA 2012 and API 2012).[3] The latest projections of global energy needs in the year 2035 by the Energy Information Administration (EIA) indicate the energy mix shown in Exhibit 1.1.[4] This forecast assumes a 3.4 percent annual rate of growth in the global economy. As shown, oil, natural gas, and coal should still dominate the energy mix by providing 79.1 percent of global energy needs, as compared to 84.4 percent in 2008. Renewable energy is expected to grow from 10.2 percent in 2008 to 14.2 percent by 2035.

The good news is that having an increasing supply of oil and natural gas helps give us time to do the research and development necessary to shift to a more renewable-based economy. It also gives us time to solve a major challenge of renewables—building the infrastructure necessary to get the renewable energy where it is needed. It took the United States almost a century to build the system we have today to transport oil and gas efficiently throughout our country. It can easily take a similar time period to build new systems to take advantage of renewables.

Another challenge for renewables is that for the first time in the history of the world, we are attempting to move to new energy sources that are "less useful and convenient than the currently dominant sources: fossil fuels" (Kerr 2010). Historically, we have always moved to a more convenient and economic fuel, which makes the transition easier. In the 1800s, we shifted from wood to coal and then in the 1900s, from coal to oil. Shifting to renewables will require behavioral changes by all consumers of energy.

Another challenge for renewables lies largely with their inconvenience relative to fossil fuels and lack of infrastructure to get the energy from where it is produced to where it is needed. Whereas oil and natural gas can be transported easily by truck, rail, or pipeline to the point of use, wind and solar power do not have that flexibility. There is also a large difference in the energy density. Liquid

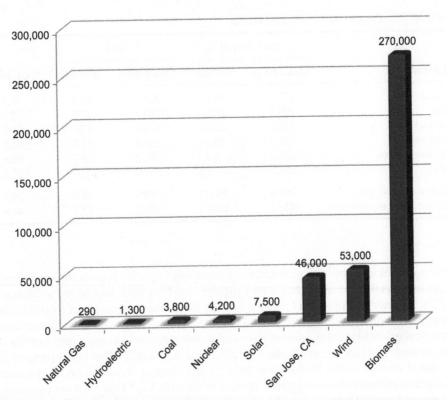

Exhibit 1.2 Land Area Needed to Provide Energy Sources in San Jose, California, Compared to Land (in Hectares) the City Occupies
Source: Based on research by Cho (2010), D. Spitzley, and the University of Michigan Center for Sustainable Systems, National Academy of Sciences, Department of Energy.

hydrocarbons have very high energy content per volume, or what we call "high energy density," compared to renewables. On a weight basis, oil has three times the energy of biomass and almost five times as much on a volume basis. In addition, wind and solar production is intermittent, whereas fossil fuel power plants operate 75 to 90 percent of the time. To make these renewables more attractive, they have been pushed hard with government tax incentives and subsidies to encourage their development.

Another challenge involves land. When the amount of land used to produce energy is considered, oil yields from 5 to 50 times as much power as a solar facility. Wind and solar farms have large land footprints as does planting crops for biofuels. This is illustrated in Exhibit 1.2, which compares the amount of land that the city of San Jose occupies in comparison to the amount of land needed for various energy sources to provide San Jose's power (see Cho 2010).

Clearly, there are many challenges ahead in energy but also many opportunities. This book is structured to cover core concepts and applications to help educate us for this journey.

SUMMARY OF THE BOOK CHAPTERS

As described earlier, the purpose of this book is to provide a broad coverage of energy finance and economics in order to educate practitioners and students alike. To achieve this goal, the book is organized into the following four sections:

Part One   An Overview of Energy Finance and Economics
Part Two   Financial and Economic Analysis in the Energy Industry
Part Three Energy Risk Management and Related Topics
Part Four   Case Studies

Next, we provide a brief description of the author(s) and the chapters in the book.

Part One: An Overview of Energy Finance and Economics

Chapters 2 through 7 provide an excellent background by covering core topics: geopolitics, energy economics, myths and realities about sustainable energy, an introduction to the petroleum industry, the economics of renewables, and a survey of consumers' understanding of what drives energy prices.

Chapter 2, "Geopolitics and World Energy Markets," by Robert W. Kolb, provides insights into the story of energy, which is intertwined with international politics, all with dramatic effect on energy markets. Given the crucial nature of geopolitics, this chapter is a must-read for anyone interested in energy finance and economics. The author eloquently discusses geopolitics and world energy markets and describes threats to these markets. He illustrates how the effect of an oil supply disruption that affects only a single small country can be quite large and how the world nexus of energy supply draws many nations into simultaneous interaction. Kolb concludes by pointing out that the future of world energy is as likely to be determined by the interaction of nations as by the fluctuations in world supply of and demand for energy.

"Energy Economics: Past, Present, and Prospects for the Future" is presented in Chapter 3 by James L. Williams (owner of WTRG Economics) and Betty J. Simkins (Williams Companies Professor of Business and Professor of Finance, Oklahoma State University). James Williams, a leading authority on energy economics, has published the globally distributed newsletter, "The Energy Economist," for many years. Betty Simkins collaborates with James to provide a brief overview of the past, the present, and the prospects for the future of energy with a focus on the demand side: energy consumption, particularly petroleum. Their discussion begins with a brief history of energy usage in the United States, followed by coverage of energy consumption in the five primary sectors: transportation, power, residential, commercial, and industrial. The authors then move to a global viewpoint and investigate recent trends in world energy consumption and also discuss what influences oil prices. Finally, they peer into their crystal ball and examine future forecasts of energy demand before presenting their conclusion.

Five authorities on sustainable energy have co-authored Chapter 4, "Sustainable Energy: Myths and Realities." In this chapter, Olamide Shadiya, Jane

Talkington, John Mowen, Karen High, and Josh Wiener, all with Oklahoma State University, investigate the myths and realities of sustainable energy. They begin by providing a definition of sustainable energy. Implied in the term *sustainable* is the concept of time. When an energy source is said to be sustainable, what time period does this involve—25 years, 50 years, 200 years? Their analysis indicates that at current and expected future rates of depletion, the conventional energy sources (while nonrenewable) will continue to be used for at least 50 years. The authors also identify a series of alleged sustainable energy myths that have been proposed by various pundits and organizations. Of course, implied in these myths is the supposed reality. The authors also present the results of a survey of 900 consumers on their perceptions of various aspects of nine energy sources and identify four potential myths held by consumers about sustainable energy. They present a model for identifying the sustainability of energy sources and then apply it to the production of electricity in the United States. Their analysis identifies that it is critical to consider economics when establishing the sustainability of energy sources. This chapter finishes with a set of conclusions and a brief discussion of the importance of setting a time frame when identifying the myths and realities of sustainable energy.

In Chapter 5, "A Brief Introduction to the Petroleum Industry: From Crude Oil and Natural Gas to Petrochemicals," Russell Simkins, co-editor of this book, and Ken Borokhovich, Lecturer in Finance at Miami University of Ohio, discuss the properties of crude oil and natural gas, the refining and processing methods, the end products, and the connection with the petrochemical industry. Throughout the discussion, the various end products, both from the refinery and the petrochemical industry, are highlighted with examples of end-use goods. The chapter also explains how an understanding of this topic is crucial to financial and economic analysis in the energy industry.

Chapter 6, "The Economics of Renewable Energy," by Brad Carson (Director of the National Energy Policy Institute at the University of Tulsa, Associate Professor of Entrepreneurship and Business Law, and General Counsel of the U.S. Army), critically examines the prevailing method of evaluating renewable energy projects and investigates alternative methodologies. The foremost method of estimating the cost of electricity, known as *levelized cost*, is discussed, and comparisons are made among different energy technologies. Altering assumptions are discussed including the tremendous impact these can make on levelized cost estimates, including the bedrock assumptions about what discount rate to use.

It is surprising how many people are misinformed on what drives energy prices. Sheridan Titman (Walter W. McAllister Centennial Chair in Financial Services and Professor of Finance, University of Texas at Austin) conducted a survey that shows just this. In Chapter 7, "How Our Political Views Affect Our View of Energy Prices," he summarizes the results of the inaugural University of Texas at Austin (UT) Energy Poll. In this poll, UT asked participants to identify the factors influencing energy pricing. Surprisingly, poll participants, who speak for a broad representative cross-section of the U.S. population, have it exactly backwards in what influences energy prices. They do not understand that supply and demand for oil, natural gas, and electricity are the most important determinants of energy prices. A closer look at the data reveals significant differences in the opinions of Democrats and Republicans. They are equally misinformed, but misinformed in

very different ways. This chapter highlights the importance of educating the general public on energy economics.

Part Two: Financial and Economic Analysis in the Energy Industry

Part Two of the book, Chapters 8 through 14, provides detailed financial and economic analyse, which are crucial topics for anyone desiring a strong foundation. To fully understand energy finance and economics and to correctly interpret financial statements of oil and gas companies, a background in accounting standards for oil and gas is essential. For this reason, Part Two of the book starts with Chapter 8, "Oil and Gas Accounting," authored by L. Charles Evans III (Partner, Grant Thornton) who has many years of oil and gas accounting experience. The oil and gas industry is unique in that there are two fundamentally different acceptable methods to account for its activities—successful efforts and full cost. Charles Evans discusses these methods in detail and how they impact the financial statements. The chapter includes coverage of required accounting disclosures, impairment, and conveyances, among other topics, concluding with a discussion of the current status for integrating U.S. accounting standards with International Financial Reporting Standards (IFRS).

"Financial Statement Analysis for Oil and Gas Companies and Competitive Benchmarking" is presented in Chapter 9. This chapter is co-authored by Siamak Javadi, a PhD Candidate at Oklahoma State University (OSU), Betty J. Simkins, Williams Companies Professor of Business and Professor of Finance, Oklahoma State University, and Mary E. Wicker, a PhD student at OSU. This chapter discusses how to analyze the financial statements of oil and gas companies and competitive benchmarking. Analyzing an oil and gas company is very different from any other type of financial statement analysis because it involves an in-depth analysis of the 10-K report notes. In this chapter, standard financial ratios are covered together with an in-depth analysis of the nine most important energy ratios that are used to analyze the upstream operations of oil and gas companies: production ratio, reserve life index, reserve replacement ratios, the cost of replacing reserves including finding cost and lifting cost, and the reserve value added ratios.

In Chapter 10, "Petroleum Economics, Risk, and Opportunity Analysis: Some Practical Perspectives," David Wood (a consultant with more than 30 years of international oil and gas experience spanning technical and commercial exploration and production operations, contract evaluation, and senior corporate management) presents an overview of financial analysis in petroleum. In energy finance, discounted cash flow analysis is one of the main methods employed in valuing projects, companies, and assets based upon their future cash flow forecasts. Wood presents practical analysis and perspective on petroleum economics, risk, and opportunities.

"Real Options and Applications in the Energy Industry" are defined and discussed in Chapter 11. What are real options? Kris Kemper (Assistant Professor, University of Wisconsin–Eau Claire) and Betty Simkins (co-editor of the book) explain that real options are option-like opportunities, such as business decisions and flexibilities, where the underlying assets are real assets, hence the term *real options*.

These opportunities are based on managerial flexibility and are commonly found in the operation of many corporate assets. Examples include the choice to expand into new markets and product lines when growth opportunities are available in the marketplace; the option to wait until more information is available (such as to delay investment and operating decisions in response to uncertainty in the marketplace); the option to switch between inputs, outputs, or processes (such as a dual-fired power plant that operates on two types of fuel and can switch from one fuel to another); the option to abandon or temporarily shut down operations when losses are being occurred; and hybrid options. The remainder of the chapter provides a brief history of real options, discusses the differences between financial and real options, describes the types of real options together with examples from the energy industry, and lists ways real options are valued.

Chapter 12, "International Petroleum Fiscal System Design and Analysis" was written by David Johnston, an engineer from the University of Rochester and an engineering and petroleum industry consultant who has worked and lectured internationally on the subjects of energy and technology for many years. The design and analysis of international petroleum fiscal systems is relatively new, although many of the principles of fiscal system design date back hundreds of years to early agricultural production sharing. Governments must at once design fiscal systems that maximize revenues and provide investors with incentives to explore for and develop hydrocarbons as efficiently as possible. Investors are looking to recover investments and share in the profits produced—with as little grief as possible. This chapter is a primer on fiscal system design and analysis, and exploration acreage allocation from the perspectives of host governments and investors.

Financing in the energy industry is a complex topic because many projects cost in the billions of dollars. In Chapter 13, "Financing Large Capital Projects," the optimal financing of large energy projects focusing on the oil and gas (O&G) industry is examined. There are two important issues that arise at the very outset. First, how important are large projects in the oil and gas industry, and what are their notable features? Second and more importantly, why do these projects merit special attention; that is, why can one not simply apply the standard corporate finance framework to finance these projects? This chapter was written by two experts on this topic: Stephen V. Arbogast (Executive Professor of Finance at the University of Houston) and Praveen Kumar (Texas Commerce Bank/Tenneco Professor of Finance and Chair, Department of Finance in the C. T. Bauer College of Business from the University of Houston).

No book is complete on energy finance without coverage of bio-fuels. In Chapter 14, "Financing Bio-Fuels Projects: Case Study Lessons," Stephen Arbogast, now at the University of Houston, discusses this topic. Stephen served from 1999 to 2004 as the Treasurer of ExxonMobil Chemical Company and has more than 30 years of experience in finance working with Exxon Corporation and Exxon-Mobil Chemical. His vast experience in the petroleum and petrochemical industries makes him uniquely qualified to author this chapter. Bio-fuels projects have been a growing factor in U.S. energy markets for over a decade. Today, corn-based ethanol plants deliver over 12 billion gallons per year into America's gasoline pool. Bio-diesel also exists, though on a much smaller scale. Rapid expansion of domestic bio-fuels manufacturing is now an official U.S. public policy objective. The Energy Independence and Security Act (EISA) of 2007 established aggressive

mandates for 2022. By that year, the U.S. gasoline pool is required to include 36 billion gallons of assorted bio-fuels. Only 15 billion gallons of corn-based ethanol is incorporated into this mandate. The rest is expected to come from "cellulosic-based bio-fuels (CBFs)" and other "advanced bio-fuels (ABFs)." What exactly are these new bio-fuels, and what is going to determine whether they appear on time or not? We encourage you to read this chapter to learn the answers to these questions.

Part Three: Energy Risk Management and Related Topics

With the high volatility in energy prices, managing this source of risk is a topic of great concern to both users and producers of energy. We begin Part Three, which focuses on energy risk management and related subjects, with five informative chapters.

Chapter 15, "Energy Derivatives and Markets," focuses on explaining the nature of derivative securities traded on energy commodities. Furthermore, the reader can learn about the history of energy derivatives, different instruments available for risk management, global perspective of the market, and how the exchanges deal with derivative instruments in energy. Craig Pirrong, who is Professor of Finance and Energy Markets Director for the Global Energy Management Institute at the University of Houston, and Mohsen Mollagholamali, a PhD student in finance at Oklahoma State University, co-author this chapter to give an insightful coverage on this topic.

In Chapter 16, "Introduction to Energy Risk Management," Ivilina Popova, Associate Professor at Texas State University–San Marcos, and Betty Simkins (co-editor of this book), join forces to provide an introduction on to how to manage energy risk using derivatives. Both authors, who received their doctorates from Case Western Reserve University and wrote their dissertations on aspects of derivatives, have spent many years working in the area. In this chapter, they explain the basics of hedging using different types of derivatives including futures contracts, options (both calls and puts), collars, and swaps. Many examples are provided to show how both users of energy and producers of energy can manage price risk. Ivilina and Betty also explain the unique aspects of energy markets where forward prices can be in either contango or backwardation. This chapter is a must-read for anyone interested in energy risk management.

Continuing on the topic of energy risk management, in Chapter 17, "Risks in Trading Energy Commodities," Divya Krishnan, formerly Market Risk Analyst with CITGO and now Senior Financial Analyst at Laureate Education Inc., discusses the major risks inherent in the trading of energy commodities. This chapter provides an excellent continuation of the previous chapter. As the author explains, there has been high volatility in the energy industry over the past few years, especially with regard to commodity prices. The key factors that drive energy price volatility are structural and are likely to have a long-term impact. Furthermore, significant events such as natural disasters, political uncertainty, and corporate misconduct have spurred instability in the energy markets. Increasing volatility and complexity of the energy commodities have made it an attractive market for financial players including hedge funds. Corporations use various hedging strategies to minimize or eliminate their exposure to risks. The goal of hedging is not to

make a profit, but to eliminate unwanted risk, which may be done by locking in a profit. This chapter examines the various types of risk and means of minimizing the risk.

"Carbon Management and Environment Issues," the title of Chapter 18, may sound like a topic from the past right now. The author, Evgenia Golubeva, is an RRT Assistant Professor of Finance and Adjunct Lecturer in Energy Management at the Michael F. Price College of Business, University of Oklahoma. Evgenia has an undergraduate degree in Oil and Gas Exploration Geophysics from Moscow State Academy of Oil and Gas (Russia), and worked several years in the oil and gas industry prior to obtaining her PhD in Finance from the University of Utah. Evgenia points out that while the cap-and-trade legislation in the United States has run aground, climate exchanges have closed, and emission allowance contracts have delisted, there are still important environmental issues that need to be addressed. The efforts of the international community, public pressure, and regulatory developments all shape the profile of environmental risks and opportunities that businesses in all industries will continue to face with increasing intensity. To understand the nature of the issues and the related uncertainties, costs, benefits, risks, and opportunities is important regardless of the regulatory status *du jour*. This chapter's objective is to provide an overview of these issues and discuss the past and the present challenges and realities.

"Hedging and Value in the U.S. Airline Industry," Chapter 19, is co-authored by three academics who are well known for their research on hedging in the airline industry. The co-authors are David Carter, Professor of Finance and Greg Massey Professor of Finance at Oklahoma State University, Daniel A. Rogers, Associate Professor of Finance at Portland State University, and Betty J. Simkins. The authors conducted a study of the fuel price hedging of 28 airlines from 1992 to 2003. This research paper, on which this chapter is based, was published in *Financial Management* (2006) and won the Addison-Wesley Best Paper in *Financial Management*. The chapter summarizes that work and is a reprint of an article previously published in the *Journal of Applied Corporate Finance*. In recent years, a growing number of companies have devoted major resources to implementing risk management programs designed to hedge financial risks such as interest rate, currency, and commodity price risk. Because of the increasing reliance on such programs, it is important to ask, "Does hedging add value to corporations?" And if it does, the obvious follow-up question is "How does it add value?"

Part Four: Case Studies

In Part Four of the book, we include six excellent cases that involve challenging analysis in different areas of energy finance and economics. In our opinion, any book on energy is not complete without case studies.

Chapter 20, "PKO Resources, Inc.: Valuing a Producing Oil and Gas Property," is a case study about the evaluation of a new exploration and production (E&P) project for PKO Resources, Inc. This case is co-authored by three experts in the field, John D. Martin (Carr P. Collins Chair in Finance in the Hankamer School of Business at Baylor University), J. Douglas Ramsey (Vice President and Chief Finance Officer of EXCO Resources, Inc.), and Sheridan Titman (Walter W. McAllister Centennial Chair in Financial Services and Professor of Finance, University of Texas at Austin). The analysis involves constructing a hypothetical example project to test

understanding of the cash flows generated by an E&P investment. The case also covers the implications of the use of hedging and the forward price curve for valuing oil and gas properties. The reader learns to construct and execute a simulation of the value of an oil and gas property where oil and gas prices are simulated using geometric Brownian motion with parameter estimates taken from historical price changes for oil and gas. The case also considers the impact of the option to abandon in the evaluation of unproved reserves.

Do you own a hybrid car or are you considering buying one? If so, you will want to read Chapter 21. This case study, "Financial Analysis of the Purchase of a Hybrid Consumer Vehicle," is co-authored by Don M. Chance (James C. Flores Endowed Chair of MBA Studies and Professor of Finance at Louisiana State University), Pratik Dhar (Financial Controls Analyst at The Shaw Group Inc.), and Betty Simkins. This case analyzes the incremental cost and financial benefits of 15 hybrid vehicles in relationship to their standard counterparts. For most consumers, hybrids cannot be justified on a purely financial basis, with an incremental all-in present value cost ranging from $1,600 to $3,500 for standard-size vehicles. Standard-size vehicles can, however, likely be justified for businesses that drive a large number of miles in a city. In contrast, large SUVs do provide clear financial benefits for consumers but not because of mileage improvement. Rather, these vehicles are costly even in the standard version, and the manufacturer is reluctant to mark them up as much as it does smaller vehicles.

It is important to cover the topic of relative valuation in energy mergers and acquisition in the book. We pick our favorite recent energy acquisition and publish a case about it in Chapter 22, "ExxonMobil Corp.'s Acquisition of XTO Energy, Inc.: An Exercise in Valuation." Allissa Lee (Visiting Assistant Professor of Finance at the Spears School of Business at Oklahoma State University) and Betty Simkins collaborate to provide an insightful tutorial on relative valuation. As the title implies, this chapter covers ExxonMobil's acquisition of XTO Energy, with the purpose of illustrating to the reader how to conduct relative valuation of an energy company and determine if the acquisition price is justified. Was XTO worth the $41 billion offered by ExxonMobil? The case addresses five questions: (1) What should the acquisition price for XTO shares have been? (2) Which comparable firm is the best comparison firm for XTO? (3) Why did ExxonMobil want to acquire XTO? (4) Based on the analysis, did ExxonMobil overpay for XTO or get a bargain? And (5) What additional information could help with this analysis?

Chapter 23, "Southwest Airlines: The Blended Winglet Project," examines Southwest Airlines' decision to retrofit part of their fleet with blended winglets to save on jet fuel costs. The blended winglet project was a proposed technology that would cost Southwest Airlines approximately $762,000 per aircraft to install and promised to provide improved range, greater fuel savings, and reduced noise and emissions. The project was aimed at providing Southwest with an additional cost advantage over its competitors, an important source of competitive advantage for the company. One of the most interesting elements of the case is the illustration of the teamwork necessary to analyze a complex capital budgeting project. The winglet project required analyses conducted by the engineering, facilities, and flight operations groups before the economics could be fully assessed. The process lasted approximately one year, and the first blended winglet technology could be seen on a Southwest flight in early October 2003. This case provides an excellent

example of how to analyze a project involving energy savings and is co-authored by Aaron Martin with Sempra Energy, Daniel Rogers, Associate Professor at Portland State University, and Betty Simkins.

A book on energy finance and economics is not complete without a case study analyzing the economics of wind energy. In Chapter 24, "Wind Energy Power Company, Inc. (A): Analyzing a Wind Energy Investment," the three authors of Chapter 20, John Martin, Doug Ramsey, and Sheridan Titman, come together again to write another excellent case. This case presents the reader with the decision as to whether or not it is economical to invest in a wind energy project. The time period is the summer of 2008, when dramatic increases in the cost of fossil fuels and concerns over greenhouse gases and global warming have made the development of alternative energy sources increasingly attractive. At this time, natural gas prices rose to $13 per MMBtu, which made wind power generation very attractive, and huge investment projects were undertaken. Most notably, Boone Pickens announced plans for the largest wind power generation farm in the United States. In the case, the Wind Energy Company (TWEPCO) announced its plans to build a 2,500 MW wind generation farm near Vernon, Texas, in July 2008 when natural gas prices were at their peak. By October 2008, the price of natural gas had dropped to $6 per MMBtu, and TWEPCO is reconsidering its plan to build the new wind farm. Chapter 24 raises questions about whether the wind energy project economically viable and what TWEPCO's next steps might be.

There is no doubt that speculators can sometimes exert significant influence on energy markets. Before ending the book, we include our favorite case on this subject: Chapter 25, "A Case Study on Risk Management: Lessons from the Collapse of Amaranth Advisors L.L.C." This chapter is authored by Ludwig B. Chincarini, an Assistant Professor at Pomona College, who has studied the forensics on this hedge fund collapse. Ludwig, who received his PhD from the Massachusetts Institute of Technology, provides a detailed and insightful coverage of what went wrong at Amaranth Advisors. In September 2006, the activities of Amaranth Advisors, a large-sized Connecticut hedge fund, sent menacing ripples through the natural gas market. By September 21, 2006, Amaranth had lost roughly $4.942 billion over a three-week period, or one-half of its assets primarily due to its activities in natural gas futures and options. Shortly thereafter, Amaranth funds were being liquidated. This case study uses data obtained from the Senate Subcommittee on Investigations, energy exchanges, and other sources to analyze exactly what caused this spectacular hedge fund failure. This case also analyzes Amaranth's trading activities within a standard risk management framework to understand to what degree reasonable measures of risk measurement could have captured the potential for the dramatic declines that occurred in September. Even by very liberal measures, Amaranth was engaging in highly risky trades. This chapter provides insight into this fascinating debacle.

Instructors can find additional material on www.wiley.com.

WHAT DOES THE FUTURE HOLD FOR ENERGY?

When one door closes another door opens; but we often look so long and so regretfully upon the closed door that we do not see the ones which open for us.
—Alexander Graham Bell, inventor of the telephone

Current trends show a resurgence in fossil fuels with the innovations in fracking and other engineering advances in hydrocarbon recovery. For example, the August 2012 issue of *SmartMoney* boasts the headline on the cover of the issue: "The Return of Fossil Fuels."[5] But at some point, we will be out of the age of fossil fuels. If your time frame is 1 million years, fossil fuels are renewable. Our time frame is much shorter, so the trillion-dollar question is: "What is behind the next door?" Will the fuel of the future be a mix of the alternatives we are currently developing or will there be a new invention or discovery of a totally new source of energy we have not envisioned yet? Daniel Yergin forecasts that higher oil prices will produce "a great bubbling of innovation" across the energy spectrum.[6] There may also be a game changer out there we have not even envisioned yet.

It is impossible to know the answer at this point in time, but it is exciting to ponder. In the short run, we will see enormous new oil and gas discoveries in the United States, which will have a very positive impact on the U.S. economy. These same technological breakthroughs in harvesting conventional energy will have a global impact, too. This is good news. Regardless, alternative energy sources have big shoes to fill and challenges to overcome to supply our future energy needs. Fossil fuels are finite resources, so at some point, even if it is gradual, we will be forced to see what is behind the next door.

CHAPTER QUESTIONS

1. List and describe advantages and disadvantages of renewable fuels and renewable energy sources.
2. This question requires you to think outside the box. What types of alternative fuels or energy sources can you think of that are not discussed in the chapter? Disregard economic or practical considerations and brainstorm possible future sources of energy. Use the Internet, if you wish, to assist in your answer.
3. Using the Internet, research the history of energy usage. What were the great transition points and what drove those transitions?
4. What is peak oil, and who came up with that theory? (You will have to do a little research for this.)
5. What topic would you like to see included in this book that is not covered? Why?

NOTES

1. Silo mentality is an attitude found in some organizations that occurs when several departments or groups do not freely share information or knowledge with other individuals or groups in the same organization. A silo mentality reduces efficiency and hurts innovation.
2. A braking point is where social and economic progress is halted due to a lack of energy (Stansberry and Reimbold 2008). As the name implies, peak oil is the point in time when world production of crude oil reaches a maximum, after which the rate of production is expected to enter terminal decline.
3. For the latest forecasts, the API report is available at www.api.org/energyzingamerica, and EIA reports are available at eia.doe.gov. Other energy forecasts are available from the IEA (www.iea.org and www.iea.org/weo/ for the world energy outlook), BP (www.bp.com/energyoutlook), and ExxonMobil (www.exxonmobil.com/Corporate/energy outlook.aspx). All reports are available for free.

4. See EIA (2011).
5. See the August 2012 issue of *SmartMoney* published by the *Wall Street Journal*.
6. See Yergin (2012).

REFERENCES

American Petroleum Institute (API). 2012. *Energizing America: Facts for Addressing Energy Policy*, available at www.api.org/energizingamerica.

Carter, David A., Daniel A. Rogers, and Betty J. Simkins. 2006. "Does Hedging Affect Firm Value? Evidence from the U.S. Airline Industry," *Financial Management* 35:2, 53–86.

Carter, David A., Daniel A. Rogers, and Betty J. Simkins. 2006. "Hedging and Value in the U.S. Airline Industry," *Journal of Applied Corporate Finance* 18:4, 31–43.

Cho, Adrain. 2010. "Energy's Tricky Tradeoffs," *Science* 329:5993, 786–787.

Energy Information Administration (EIA). 2012. *Annual Energy Outlook 2012 with Projections to 2035*. Report Number DOE/EIA-0383 (June).

Energy Information Administration (EIA). 2012. *International Energy Outlook 2011 with Projections to 2035*. Report Number DOE/EIA-0484 (September).

Kapadia, Reshma, et al. 2012. "The Return of Fossil Fuels." *SmartMoney* (August).

Kerr, Richard A. 2010. "Do We Have the Energy for the Next Transition?" *Science* 329:5993, 780–781.

Maugeri, Leonardo. 2012. *Oil: The Next Revolution: The Unprecedented Upsurge of Oil Production Capacity and What It Means for the World*. Cambridge, MA: Harvard Kennedy School of Government.

Stansberry, Mark A., and Jason P. Reimbold. 2008. *The Braking Point: America's Energy Dreams and Global Economic Realities*. Tulsa, OK: Hawk Publishing Group.

Yergin, Daniel. 2012. "Daniel Yergin on the Future of Global Energy," *McKinsey Quarterly* (March). Interview conducted at the World Economic Forum, video available at http://www.mckinseyquarterly.com/.

ABOUT THE EDITORS

Betty J. Simkins, PhD, is the Williams Companies Professor of Business and a Professor of Finance in the Department of Finance at Oklahoma State University's (OSU) Spears School of Business, where she teaches energy finance, corporate finance, and enterprise risk management, among other courses. Dr. Simkins received her PhD from Case Western Reserve University (CWRU), her MBA from OSU, and her BS in chemical engineering from the University of Arkansas. She has more than 50 publications in academic finance journals and book chapters and has won awards for her research, most recently in risk management. In addition, Betty has won several teaching awards including the Regents Distinguished Teaching Award. She has taught Energy Finance, a course she created, at both the undergraduate and graduate levels for over 12 years and teaches executive education courses on energy finance for companies around the world. She is also very active in the finance profession and currently serves on the Board of Directors for the Financial Management Association, as co-editor of the *Journal of Applied Finance*, as past president of the Eastern Finance Association, and on the editorial boards of several prestigious finance journals. Prior to academia, she worked in the energy industry for Williams Companies and Conoco (now ConocoPhillips). In addition to being co-editor of this book, in 2010 she co-edited *Enterprise Risk Management:*

Insights and Analysis on Today's Leading Research and Best Practices, also published by John Wiley & Sons.

Russell E. Simkins, PE, is Manager of Proposal Services in the College of Engineering, Architecture, and Technology at Oklahoma State University (OSU) and is a licensed Professional Engineer in the state of Oklahoma. He has more than 30 years of engineering experience working in many different areas including project management, research and development, marketing and sales, and field testing. Simkins has previously worked for ConocoPhillips, Fractionation Research Institute, Lubrizol Corporation, Southwest Research Institute, and the U.S. Department of Energy (DOE). At the DOE, he managed the alternative fuels database, among other responsibilities. He has also been active in the engineering profession as a member of various working groups in the Society of Automotive Engineers (SAE), Coordinating Research Council (CRC), and American Society of Testing Materials (ASTM) dealing with fuels and lubricants. Russell holds three engineering degrees: a Masters Degree in industrial engineering and management from OSU with a focus in energy management, a Bachelor of Science degree in chemical engineering from the University of Arkansas, and a Bachelor of Science degree in Mechanical Power Technology from OSU.

Biographies and Summaries of Authors, Keynote Speakers, and Panelists, Alphabetical by Interviewee (cont.)

Russell E. Thomas, PE, is an associate of Research Services at the College of Engineering, Architecture, and Technology at CEI Moore State University (CEI) and has held such positions. He received his doctorate in the state of Oklahoma. He has more than 20 years of applied engineering experience working in many different areas, including project management, and has represented many different firms and institutions over the past twenty-seven years. He joined CEI after working with the Southwest Research Institute, the Institute for Civil Construction, Southwest Research Institute, and the U.S. Department of Energy (DOE). At the DOE, he managed the alternative fuels program. He has represented various organizations. He has authored the engineering for the subject of wind energy production projects in the fields of Architecture, Engineering, Surveying, Research Construction Management and Maintenance of Air and American Society of Test and Materials (ASTM) dealing with fuels and materials. Since then his interest in energy projects has focused on the field of industrial engineering and management. He holds CEI, with a focus in energy management, a bachelor of science degree in the art of engineering from the University of ASTM and has had a bachelor of science degree in mechanical power technology from CEI.

An Overview of Energy Finance and Economics

CHAPTER 2

Geopolitics and World Energy Markets*

ROBERT W. KOLB
Professor of Finance and Considine Chair of Applied Ethics at Loyola
University Chicago

INTRODUCTION

In early 2011, the price of crude oil rose by 62 percent in a single month, rocketing from $75 to $120 per barrel as protests and revolts shook an arc of Arab countries. The price of crude jumped 6 percent on a single day, February 21, in response to sudden and dramatic unrest in Libya. This strong price reaction occurred even though Libya accounts for only about 2 percent of annual world oil production. The large influence of troubles in this relatively minor producer stemmed from two main sources. First, already-occurring unrest across the oil-producing countries of the Middle East, accompanied by fears that other nations would soon be inflamed, raised market doubts about the ability of other producers to surge their production to compensate for the withdrawal of Libyan oil from the market. Second, Libya produces a light sweet (low sulfur) crude that is particularly suited to certain refineries and is especially valued in some market segments. Saudi Arabia, the main supplier thought to be capable of a surge in production, pumps a heavier more sour (higher sulfur) crude. With many refineries in Europe and Asia being poorly equipped to handle higher-sulfur crude, an expansion of Saudi production could not adequately substitute for the missing Libyan contribution. In 2012, continuing sanctions against Iran and the fear of an imminent strike against Iranian nuclear capabilities contributed to near-record world oil prices and extremely high gasoline pump prices in the United States and around the world.

Energy prices have always been subject to shocks from events that occur in single countries, and this will remain true as long as major sources of energy are concentrated in relatively few countries. However, looking back as well as forward, larger geopolitical considerations go beyond the impact of any single nation, and those transnational and more enduring factors are the focus of this chapter.

---

*This chapter is a revised, updated, and extended version of Robert W. Kolb, "Geopolitical Threats to World Energy Markets," which first appeared in *The Journal of Social, Political, and Economic Studies* 36:2 (Summer 2011), 154–196.

ENERGY GEOPOLITICS FOR THE NEXT GENERATIONS: DEMAND, MIX, AND INTERNATIONAL MOVEMENTS

The overall contours of energy geopolitics are rather straightforward and understood by most people at least on a casual level. First, there are several basic types of energy sources: fossil fuels (including coal, oil, and natural gas), nuclear energy, and renewables (including hydroelectric power, wind energy, biomass, waste products, and solar). Each of these resources is best suited to particular uses. For example, hydroelectric power can generate electricity quite well, but it would be a poor choice for a transportation fuel.

Further, these various energy resources are distributed across the world in a way that does not match the point of most likely or beneficial consumption. The response to this situation is twofold. First, one can adapt a geographically convenient energy source to a use for which it less well suited. For example, near the end of World War II, the almost-defeated axis powers were driven to near-desperate expedients. Oil-starved Japan converted some automobiles to burn wood as fuel. After failing to capture oil fields in Romania and in the Caucasus, Germany, having developed the world's first jet-propelled aircraft, used oxen to tow planes onto the runway in order to conserve jet fuel.[1]

As a second approach, one can move a fuel from its source to where it will be used. The contemporary world economy, built on fossil fuel, has developed and elaborated this model for almost a century, starting with the conversion of the British Navy from coal to oil in the first decades of the twentieth century.[2] The mismatch between the geographical location of energy resources and their points of consumption drives the geopolitics of oil. If oil must be transported from the nations where it originates to the countries where it will be consumed, the energy must cross national boundaries, international waters, and sometimes-contested borderlands as well.

Three more general factors complete the geopolitical stage setting. First, virtually all experts expect worldwide energy demand to increase markedly over the next generation or so, focusing on a horizon out to 2030–2050. Energy demand will grow faster in some regions (most notably China and India according to most expectations) while demand in other regions may stagnate or expand at a much slower rate (North America and the European Community). On balance, the world will demand sharply increasing energy supplies. Second, the energy mix—the proportion of fossil fuels, nuclear, and renewables—will change only slowly. Thus, the energy mix of today is essentially the energy mix of 2030–2050. Third, the largest energy-consuming regions of the next generation will gather an increasing portion of their energy from outside their own borders. We consider each of these main features in turn.

Exhibit 2.1 shows ExxonMobil's analysis of energy consumption in the recent past, the present, along with the anticipated situation in 2040, with total energy demand being broken into six categories. Every category shows substantial growth, except for coal and biomass. Measured from 2000 to 2040, ExxonMobil anticipates that energy consumption will surge by more than two-thirds, and from 2010 to 2040 by more than 30 percent. British Petroleum (BP) presents a similar analysis in "BP Energy Outlook 2030," key elements of which appear in

Exhibit 2.1 ExxonMobil's Analysis of World Energy by Type (Quadrillion BTUs)

	2000	2010	2040	% Change 2000 to 2040	% Change 2010 to 2040
Oil	156	177	220	41.03	24.29
Gas	89	115	186	108.99	61.74
Coal	90	128	130	44.44	1.56
Nuclear	27	29	55	103.70	89.66
Biomass/Waste	41	48	53	29.27	10.42
Hydroelectric	9	12	18	100.00	50.00
Renewables	3	7	30	900.00	328.57
Total	**414**	**525**	**692**	**67.15**	**31.81**

Source: ExxonMobil, "2012 The Outlook for Energy: A View to 2040" (2012).

Exhibit 2.2.[3] From 2000 to 2030, BP forecasts total growth in energy consumption of 80 percent and for the 2010–2030 subperiod a growth of 41 percent in consumption. In its analysis covering 2001–2030, Deloitte also foresees rapidly increasing demand for energy, with total use increasing by two-thirds.[4] If these analyses are even approximately correct, we will witness a tremendous increase in worldwide energy consumption in the next 20 years.

Exhibit 2.3 also draws on estimates for 2030 by ExxonMobil and BP, and shows the percentage of each type of energy source prevailing in 2010 and the distribution that these energy firms expect to hold in 2030. Interestingly, there are some distinct differences in the assessment of the 2010 situation by these two firms. Some apparent disagreements stem from slight differences in energy classifications, but others appear to be more substantial. For example, the two predictions for the role of hydroelectricity differ by a factor of at least 100 percent. Even with some important differences, however, the two forecasts are in broad agreement, especially regarding the categories that are likely to be most important from a geopolitical perspective. They both agree that oil will provide 25–30 percent of all energy in 2030 and

Exhibit 2.2 BP's Analysis of World Energy Consumption by Type (Million Metric Tons of Oil or Equivalent)

	2000	2010	2030	% Change 2000 to 2030	% Change 2010 to 2030
Fossil fuel liquids	3,562.1	3,943.3	4,671.1	31.1	18.5
Natural gas	2,175.5	2,828.3	4,312.4	98.2	52.5
Coal	2,337.6	3,496.1	4,411.9	88.7	26.2
Nuclear energy	584.3	613.9	1,096.8	87.7	78.7
Hydroelectricity	600.1	772.8	1,144.0	90.6	48.0
Renewables	658.9	985.2	2,174.9	230.1	120.8
Totals	**9,918.5**	**12,639.7**	**17,811.1**	**79.6**	**40.9**

Fossil fuel liquids include oil, gas-to-liquids, and coal-to-liquids.
Source: BP, "BP Energy Outlook 2030," January 2011, London. Data are available at www.bp.com. Accessed April 16, 2011.

Exhibit 2.3　Percentage of Consumption by Fuel Types, Estimates of ExxonMobil and BP

	Exxon		BP	
	2010	**2030**	**2010**	**2030**
Oil and derivatives	34.19	32.08	31.20	26.23
Natural gas	22.13	25.79	22.38	24.21
Coal	25.30	21.07	27.66	24.77
Nuclear energy	5.53	7.86	4.86	6.16
Hydroelectricity	2.17	2.52	6.11	6.42
Renewables	10.67	10.69	7.79	12.21
Totals	**100.00**	**100.00**	**100.00**	**100.00**
Oil + Gas + Coal	81.62	78.93	81.23	75.21

Categories were adjusted slightly to make them congruent. Note that ExxonMobil has a category "Biomass/Waste," which BP does not. This exhibit combines "Biomass/Waste" as a part of "Renewables." Included here in "Oil and derivatives" for BP are their subcategories gas-to-liquid and coal-to-liquid.
Source: BP, "BP Energy Outlook 2030," January 2011, London. Data are available at www.bp.com (accessed April 16, 2011), and ExxonMobil, "The Outlook for Energy: A View to 2030," 2010, 53.

that natural gas will contribute about 25 percent, with fossil fuels all considered (coal, oil, and natural gas) together accounting for 75–80 percent of all energy the world will consume in 2030. Further, in a subsequent analysis, Exxon extended its forecast to 2040 in which it forecasts that oil will still account for more than 30 percent of world energy and that hydrocarbons will also constitute 77 percent of world energy, with renewables rising to what will still be a less than 5 percent share.[5]

Of the six categories of energy shown in Exhibit 2.3, some types are consumed where they originate, while large portions of other types of energy are shipped great distances. Hydroelectricity, energy produced from renewables, and nuclear energy have virtually no shipping or transmission across national boundaries.[6] Not only has this been true historically, but it is projected to remain true for the next generation. Thus, the principal energy sources that are shipped transregionally are all fossil fuels—oil, natural gas, and coal—as Exhibit 2.4 shows. Of these, not all three are shipped equally. For example, in 2010, North America, Asia Pacific, Europe, and Eurasia imported 1,296 million metric tons of oil, but total world imports of coal in 2010 totaled only 91 million tons. This difference is perhaps not surprising for three reasons: Oil has much more value per unit of weight, oil is easier to ship, and coal deposits are more widely distributed than oil, so that coal is consumed near its point of production. BP, as also shown in Exhibit 2.4, expects transregional shipments of oil to increase by about 50 percent by 2030, with those of coal remaining essentially unchanged.

Natural gas occupies a middle ground between oil and coal in terms of shipments. Traditionally, natural gas moved only through pipelines, with an almost negligible shipment of gas in the form of liquefied natural gas (LNG). However, shipments of LNG have become more cost competitive with other energy transportation methods recently, and LNG shipments have accelerated rapidly in recent years.

Exhibit 2.4 Fossil Fuel Demanded for Import and Available for Export, 2010 and 2030, Projected

		Percentage of Consumption Demanded for Import (negative values indicate proportion of consumption available for export)		Millions of Metric Tons of Oil or Equivalent Demanded for Import (negative values indicate tons available for export)	
		2010	2030	2010	2030
Oil	North America	37.53	30.55	387	291
	Asia Pacific	68.37	82.88	854	1475
	Europe and Eurasia	6.07	6.84	55	59
	Middle East	−235.51	−229.58	−829	−1153
	Africa	−226.58	−166.71	−333	−345
	South and Central America	−37.77	−29.29	−97	−105
Natural Gas	North America	2.19	1.53	17	13
	Asia Pacific	14.19	19.56	70	204
	Europe and Eurasia	7.20	11.76	72	145
	Middle East	−22.98	−13.28	−80	−98
	Africa	−102.94	−141.52	−97	−263
	South and Central America	−9.63	−8.17	−13	−20
Coal	North America	−4.62	−11.39	−26	−52
	Asia Pacific	1.72	2.36	40	79
	Europe and Eurasia	9.04	−1.38	43	−6
	Middle East	89.64	85.18	8	8
	Africa	−35.81	−29.66	−38	−48
	South and Central America	−116.60	−105.15	−29	−37

Source: BP. "BP Energy Outlook 2030," January 2011, London. Data are available at www.bp.com, accessed April 16, 2011.

To ship LNG requires that natural gas be liquefied by cooling the gas to −260 degrees Fahrenheit. In this process, natural gas is first transported by pipeline to a liquefaction facility, typically located at or near a port or railhead. After liquefaction, the LNG is pumped onto a ship or into railroad tank cars, which then carry the LNG to its destination, a facility at which it can be re-gasified and shipped on via a natural gas pipeline. Obviously this transmission cycle requires the development of an elaborate infrastructure, which has been developing quite rapidly.[7] The growth of LNG is one of the reasons that consumption of natural gas is expected to grow more rapidly than either coal or oil (see Exhibits 2.1 and 2.2). In addition, natural gas is increasingly popular as a fuel for electrical generation, due in no small measure to its lower emission of greenhouse gases.[8]

With the advance of LNG as a method for shipping natural gas, one might expect the long-term result to be a world in which both oil and natural gas in the form of LNG have a similar pattern of international shipment. Previously, with no way to transport natural gas across great ocean distances, much of it was stranded. With the development of a robust LNG infrastructure, natural gas seems poised to fully enter the world energy market.

Natural gas may one day be traded around the world with a facility matching that of oil. However, a potentially extremely important development for the availability and geopolitical significance of natural gas lies in the future of shale gas—gas trapped in deep sedimentary layers of shale that has been unrecoverable in a commercially viable manner until quite recently. Massive shale gas deposits around the world, including the United States, promise to make natural gas much more abundant near the point of ultimate consumption. Thus, the future of shale gas can dramatically affect the future geopolitical significance of natural gas and even have a dramatic effect on markets for other forms of energy. These issues are addressed specifically in a later section of this chapter.

The argument of this chapter thus far lays a foundation for the critical importance of oil and natural gas. Even setting aside the emerging importance of shale gas, oil and natural gas are the two forms of the world's energy that dominate international energy shipments. As a result, the geopolitical implications of energy turn on the acquisition of oil and natural gas from abroad and the shipment of oil and gas around the world. Thus, the balance of this chapter focuses primarily on these two forms of energy and their geopolitical implications for energy finance.[9]

THE WORLD MARKET FOR ENERGY

Oil today trades in a mature worldwide market, which has developed from a longstanding and mostly successful U.S. policy.[10] Metaphorically at least, recent decades have seen the *financialization* of oil. With the operation of this worldwide market, oil has become essentially fungible, with oil in one location being readily convertible into oil in another. Of course, not all oil is the same. This chapter has already noted the importance of Libyan oil and sweet versus sour types of crude oil, so oil may be largely fungible, but different kinds of oil are not quite as fungible as cash.

Nonetheless, to a large extent, the old accounting law that "all sources support all uses" has become true of oil in the world market, and the promise of LNG may soon make the same true of natural gas. This is an extremely important geopolitical dimension of the world energy market. Speaking of the diversity of supply, Winston Churchill noted almost 100 years ago, "Safety and certainty in oil lie in variety and variety alone,"[11] and the same remains true today. That variety of supply depends on robust world energy markets. Further, it seems evident that talk of "energy independence" for the United States is a fanciful notion, in spite of longstanding claims by a succession of presidents that we are working toward such energy autarky. As Exhibit 2.4 makes clear, the location of supply and demand for energy makes evident the future of an interdependent world of energy.[12] For the United States, the best outcome is for energy to be traded in a free worldwide

market, with the hope that new technologies can lessen dependence on foreign energy sources.

OPEC AND THE FUTURE ROLE OF A CARTEL

While the preceding section described the development of a world energy market, it is hardly a free market or one that is likely to remain free of noncompetitive influences and disruptions to the current market structure. The creation, survival, and effectiveness of the Organization of Petroleum Exporting Countries (OPEC) have long demonstrated the market power of key suppliers of crude oil. According to OPEC's own estimates, shown in Exhibit 2.5, the cartel currently supplies slightly over one-third of the world's oil, a proportion anticipated to remain essentially stable over the next 20 years, even as world demand increases. BP sees an even more dominant role for OPEC, saying: "The importance of OPEC is expected to grow. On our projections, OPEC's share of global production would increase from 40% in 2010 to 46% in 2030 (a level not reached since 1977)."[13]

Over its history of almost half a century, OPEC has been one of the most effective cartels in any major market in the world. Although OPEC has had periods when oil prices sank despite its efforts, notably after the Asian financial crisis of the late 1990s, it has enjoyed spectacular successes. OPEC first brought the world the oil shock, price spike, and long gas lines of the 1970s, and today OPEC appears to be meeting with great success as crude oil is currently priced well about $100 per barrel. Edward Morse and Amy Jaffe summarize the situation: "OPEC has been one of the most remarkable success stories and also one of the most extraordinary anomalies in the global economy for over forty years. It is a success story because, despite persistent forecasts that it is doomed to fail, it has not simply managed to survive but can be credited with succeeding in its basic objectives: defending and supporting the income and revenue aims of its members, and forcing any burden of adjustment to higher oil prices on other countries."[14]

OPEC manages supply to manage price—OPEC has not fundamentally increased its supply capacity in any meaningful way for more than a decade.[15] Not surprisingly, restricting capacity aids OPEC members in respecting its self-imposed production targets. In addition, OPEC sometimes cuts production to support higher prices, such as in 2006 and 2007.[16]

Exhibit 2.5 OPEC and the Future of the World's Supply of Oil

	2010	2015	2020	2025	2030
World oil demand	85.5	91	96.2	100.9	105.5
Non-OPEC supply	51.9	53.9	55.7	56.6	57.5
OPEC crude supply	29.3	30.8	33.2	36	38.7
Percentage supplied by OPEC	34.27	33.85	34.51	35.68	36.68

Source: Adapted from OPEC, 2010, "World Oil Outlook." See p. 10.

There can be no doubt that OPEC adjusts its productive capacity as a function of its efforts to control prices and in response to prices. Any business will respond to a market environment with lower prices by adjusting its production schedule. But a cartel does not merely respond to external market developments. It is not a price taker, but rather functions to control prices. OPEC effectively acknowledges this by speaking of its concern with *security of demand*: "Recent behaviour has shown that oil prices continue to matter for supply. The low prices witnessed at the end of 2008 led to a revision in investment plans; and if prices had remained that low, the implications for supply moving forward, both in OPEC and non-OPEC countries, could have been substantial. This, in turn, is a reflection of the lesson that low oil prices can sow the seeds of higher ones, and that security of supply is improved by security of demand."[17] Thus, OPEC would like high and stable demand and a high and stable price, but this gives rise to a tension between price maintenance and expanding production. As Amy Jaffe makes the point, "OPEC's joint desires to garner maximum revenues for its oil and its long term aim to attain energy security of demand are at odds with each other."[18] And as Abdalla el-Badri, the secretary general of OPEC said, speaking in 2007: "If we [OPEC] are unable to see security of demand . . . we may revisit investment in the long term."[19]

Most predictions see expanding demand for oil over the next decades, with OPEC's share of the market remaining fairly steady. Indeed, this is the official position of OPEC as Exhibit 2.5 shows. This relatively steady state envisioned by most observers implies a stable role for OPEC in the oil market going forward. As John Deutch, James Schlesinger, and David Victor note, "The potential market power of OPEC will not decline in future years, partly because the market share of oil production by OPEC is not expected to decline."[20]

Contrary to the narrative developed in this section, there is the prospect of a market disruption that might substantially weaken the role of OPEC and curb its market power. If shale gas develops as fully as some believe, and if LNG becomes as robust a transport mechanism as many hope, these developments could curb the demand for OPEC's oil significantly. This possibility is covered in a later section, as is the recent effort of some natural gas suppliers to develop a natural gas cartel.

THE RISE OF NATIONAL OIL COMPANIES AND BILATERAL CONTRACTS

From the end of World War II into the late 1970s, seven of the larger international oil companies—the so-called Seven Sisters—collectively controlled 85 percent of known world oil reserves.[21] In more recent years, the Seven Sisters have given way to the "Big Five" international oil companies (IOCs) of Exhibit 2.6.[22] Over this same period, many of the largest petroleum producing nations have cast off their colonial encumbrances and gained control of their own oil resources.[23] Today, nationally owned oil companies (NOCs) control over 90 percent of world oil reserves. Excluding production of the OPEC nations, the countries formerly constituting the Soviet Union account for 25 percent of the balance, and the Big Five produce 20 percent, with the next 20 largest U.S. firms accounting for only 4 percent of non-OPEC production. Chinese firms contribute 8 percent, and Mexico's Pemex 7 percent.[24] The pursuit of wealth, rather than geopolitical advantage,

Exhibit 2.6 Major Oil Companies of the World

Supermajors, the "Big Five" International Oil Companies (IOCs)

BP	United Kingdom
ChevronTexaco	United States
Conoco Phillips	United States
ExxonMobil	United States
Royal Dutch Shell	Netherlands and United Kingdom

Key National Oil Companies (NOCs) (includes nationally owned firms focused mainly on natural gas)

Abu Dhabi	Abu Dhabi National Oil Company
Algeria	Sonatrach
Brazil	Petrobras
China	China National Offshore Oil Company (CNOOC)
China	China National Petroleum Corporation (CNPC)
China	Sinopec
Iran	National Iranian Oil Company (NIOC)
Iraq	Oil Ministry
India	ONGC
Indonesia	Pertamina
Kazakhstan	Kazmunaigaz
Kuwait	Kuwait Petroleum Company
Libya	Libya National Oil Company
Malaysia	Petronas
Mexico	Pemex
Nigeria	Nigerian National Petroleum Corporation (NNPC)
Norway	Statoil
Qatar	Qatar General Petroleum Corporation
Russia	Gasprom
Russia	Rosneft
Saudi Arabia	Saudi Aramco
Venezuela	Petroleos de Venezuela, S. A. (PDVSA)

Note: These companies are also referred to as investor-owned companies in this same context, because they are all publicly held, unlike NOCs.

primarily motivates OPEC's NOCs. However, to many, the ascendance of Russian and Chinese NOCs carries ominous geopolitical overtones. Some fear that these powerful and populous nations may use their state-owned enterprises as instruments of foreign policy.

For its part, Russia appears to be concerned mostly with maintaining (or regaining) influence over its *near abroad*, those nations that were formerly part of the Soviet Union. It seeks this control or influence largely by managing its pipeline connections with these countries, drawing oil and gas into Russia, before shipping it on via pipeline to western Europe. By occupying the key nodal points in this vast pipeline network, Russia has been able to exercise considerable influence over these now-independent nations. A later section addresses the geopolitical aspects of pipelines explicitly.

Chinese NOCs have recently garnered a great deal of attention, much of it unwelcome. The three Chinese NOCs—China National Petroleum Corporation (CNPC), China Petroleum and Chemical Corporation (Sinopec), and China

National Offshore Oil Corporation (CNOOC)—all emerged from Chinese government ministries. CNPC is China's largest oil producer; Sinopec is the largest refiner; and CNOOC owns the most service stations. These NOCs also hold controlling shares in Chinese petroleum companies listed on stock exchanges.[25] The national government and communist part of China exert control over these NOCs through the power "...to appoint, dismiss, and promote the companies' general managers."[26] The Chinese government has directed all three companies to become full vertically integrated oil companies. In 1998, to facilitate this expansion, the Chinese government directed CNPC to grant oilfields to Sinopec in exchange for Sinopec's refineries.[27]

In 2005, CNOOC brought these Chinese NOCs to wider public attention when it attempted to acquire the U.S. firm UNOCAL for $18.5 billion, with a portion of the financing being derived from the Chinese government.[28] This merger attempt stimulated widespread fear in the United States that Chinese would be gaining control of U.S. energy assets and transferring the product of those assets to China. In the face of strong public and congressional opposition, CNOOC abandoned its overtures. Part of this outrage may have been due to the $7 billion in financing that the Chinese government provided to CNOOC to facilitate the merger, whereas U.S.-based Chevron, which also sought to capture UNOCAL, had no supporting government financing. In the West, concern over Chinese NOCs perhaps reflects the general anxiety regarding the rapid economic and political development of China.

Faced with the imperative to develop into fully vertically integrated oil companies, China's three NOCs all need to acquire upstream resources. However, China's oil in place is extremely limited. As a result, China's NOCs have been extremely active in securing resources not only in China but in a variety of other countries. For example, CNPC has acquired oil and gas assets in at least 23 countries, including Sudan, Algeria, Ecuador, Nigeria, Chad, and Kazakhstan. For its part, Sinopec acquired a stake in Iran's Yadavaran oil field. CNOOC purchased a significant stake in the Akpo field in the Niger Delta. All in all, the Middle East yields about 50 percent of China's imports, and Africa contributes 25 percent.[29] Taking China's three NOCs together, they operate in at least 31 countries, with equity oil holdings concentrated in Kazakhstan, Sudan, Venezuela, and Angola. Also, these NOCs are participating in transnational pipeline projects to bring oil and gas from North, Central, and Southeast Asia to China.[30]

For IOCs and NOCs, the holy grail of oil investment has been the direct or equity ownership of upstream oil assets. Before the oil-producing nations gained greater sway over their own resources and developed their NOCs, IOCs enjoyed considerable equity stakes around the world. Now, most nations restrict equity participation to their own NOCs. However, a number of African countries make exceptions to this general rule, and the chance for equity participation is one of the factors that have made Africa particularly attractive to Chinese NOCs. Most of the equity oil holdings of CNPC, Sinopec, and CNOOC in Africa are concentrated in Sudan, but these firms are currently diversifying into Angola and Nigeria.[31]

To sustain their thrust into Africa, China's NOCs have broadened their relationship with host countries to extend far beyond narrow oil interests by investing in oil infrastructure and non-energy development projects. For instance, in the Sudan, China invested more than $8 billion in Sudan's oil industry. Included

in this investment was the construction of a 900-mile pipeline from Sudan's oil field to the Red Sea.[32] Beyond Sudan, China has participated in infrastructure projects in Angola, Nigeria, Congo, and Gabon, in tandem with advancing its oil interests.[33]

The thrust of China's NOCs into Africa has raised both fears and criticisms. First, there is the concern that the NOCs' acquisition of equity oil in Africa will sew up supplies and make the oil of these nations unavailable to the wider market. Thus, some fear that these bilateral arrangements between China on the one hand and various African nations on the other will both subvert the world market and divert Africa's oil directly to China. A second major concern is China's apparently happy acquiescence in bonding with some regimes that the West regards as the most oppressive and illegitimate, giving rise to the view that China's friendship with these regimes undermines efforts to make them comply with Western ideals. Henry Lee and Dan Shalmon make the point quite trenchantly:

> From the political perspective, Western nongovernmental organizations have accused China of using its investments to support some of the more abusive, corrupt, and violent governments in the world. The poster child for this argument has been China's support for the Sudanese government and its unwillingness to condemn publicly the genocidal practices of the janjaweed militias operating in Darfur. China's repeated contention that it does not get involved in domestic politics and that its relationships with African governments [are] strictly commercial is perceived by many as hollow. Critics argue that without China's investments and tacit support, African governments, such as the Sudan's, would be forced to amend their behavior.[34]

Sudan provides China with the second-greatest supply of oil of any foreign country, and CNPC holds a 40 percent stake in the Greater Nile Petroleum Operating Company there.[35]

Aside from undermining international efforts to bring human rights pressure on governments such as Sudan's, China seems to be aiming at creating multidimensional relationships with oil-supplying nations. The general strategy seems to be that China seeks equity interests in oil where possible and establishes bilateral contracts to gain secure supplies of oil that it regards as more secure than merely acquiring oil in the open market. In addition, by helping oil-supplying nations entrench their governments and improve their infrastructure, China seeks to solidify its influence over these nations in the service of its broader geopolitical interests. While most observers deny that China's NOCs are directly controlled by the Chinese government, there can be no doubt that their business strategies are more coordinated with overall Chinese foreign policy than is the case for the IOCs and their respective host nations.[36]

The fear that China's efforts to secure equity oil and to establish bilateral supply contracts at the expense of the world oil market is presently unfounded. China has come to the African continent in search of oil long after IOCs secured the best tracts, and the proportion of African oil that is under contract with China is actually quite small. Further, some of the oil that China acquires in Africa under these equity and bilateral arrangements actually winds up in the world market through Chinese sales.[37] Further, oil that China helps to develop in Africa under equity or

bilateral agreement actually expands the world's supply of oil, thereby strengthening the present oil market structure. If the world oil market really operates within a context in which "all sources fund all uses," then China's development of African oil actually increases world supply.

Contrary to the optimistic outlook just considered, it is possible to imagine a situation in which burgeoning Chinese control of oil could actually diminish the supply to the world market. Consider a situation in which a market disruption significantly reduces the world supply. This situation could arise from OPEC holding oil off the market, or from disruptions to major energy infrastructure, such as the pipeline network, or through a disruption of oil market commerce over various sea lanes. Such a development would almost instantly diminish the total world supply of oil. In such a context, China's effective control over the output of particular nations could alleviate its own supply concerns while exacerbating those of other nations. In sum, as long as the size of the world market is robust relative to demand, China's foray into Africa holds little threat, but that could change if world supplies become smaller relative to demand, and such a supply-demand imbalance could occur through natural growth in demand relative to supply or from reduction of the size of the world market through some untoward events such as embargoes, terrorist attacks, or interruptions of the physical distribution system.

PIPELINES

The world's network of transnational oil and gas pipelines is already vast, yet it is expanding rapidly. The construction and routing of pipelines is fraught with geopolitical implications. Once established, a pipeline is too expensive to reroute or duplicate, so any transnational pipeline route establishes clear and enduring geopolitical costs and benefits.[38]

The pipeline network established over the decades of the Soviet Union provides the clearest example of the geopolitical dimensions of pipeline routings. The Russian system is currently the world's largest and is operated by the Russian NOC, Gazprom.[39] The Caucasus or the Caspian region consists of newly independent countries that were former Soviet republics: Turkmenistan, Kazakhstan, Azerbaijan, Georgia, Armenia, Tajikistan, Kyrgyzstan, and Uzbekistan. The Soviet-era pipeline system links all of these new nations as providers and consumer of energy. The Soviet-era pipeline network was designed to run from these central Asian regions into Russia. From there, the pipeline network connected with Russia's own huge supply sources and then fanned westward toward other eastern European Soviet republics and on to nations of western Europe—the vast majority of Russian natural gas transits Ukraine. In this pipeline web, Russia continues to occupy the key central nodes.[40]

This arrangement redounds to Russian advantage. Because most of these central Asian nations are landlocked and have no other means of distribution, all or most of their international sales must transit Russia via the pipeline network, leaving these nations somewhat under the control of a single customer. Similarly, European nations to the west of Russia, whether former Soviet satellites (Ukraine, Moldavia, Byelorussia, Latvia, Estonia, Lithuania, East Germany) or countries that were always outside the Soviet bloc (e.g., West Germany, France, and Italy),

rely on the Russian-controlled pipeline for a substantial portion of their natural gas supplies.[41]

For years since the demise of the Soviet Union, Russia has maintained geopolitical sway over its former republics to the west by providing gas at below-market prices. However, in a price dispute, Russia cut off Ukraine's supply of natural gas on January 1, 2006. This could have been extremely serious to Ukraine, as Michael Klare notes: "Ukraine would have been plunged into an immediate (and possibly lethal) energy crisis except for one thing—Gazprom's main gas pipeline to Western Europe ran through its territory, and the Ukrainians promptly responded to the Russian cutoff by siphoning off gas meant for Europe to satisfy their own requirements."[42]

Both supplying and consuming nations on the Gazprom pipeline network would like to escape the Russian embrace. The United States, of course, also supports initiatives to reduce Russian energy influence. Accordingly, there is widespread interest in the development of new pipelines that evade Russian control. For example, the recently-constructed Baku-Tbilisi-Ceyhan (BTC) pipeline runs from Baku, Azerbaijan, to Tbilisi, Georgia, and on to Ceyhan, Turkey, on the Mediterranean, thereby providing Azerbaijan with an outlet to the west. Planners dubbed another contemplated pipeline "Nabucco," after some pipeline planners happened to see a Viennese performance of the Verdi opera in 2002.[43] Nabucco is planned to originate in Baku on the Caspian Sea and run to Tbilisi on the route of the BTC pipeline and then to continue across Turkey, transit from Asia to Europe across the Bosporus, and terminate in Vienna after crossing Bulgaria, Rumania, and Hungary. This pipeline remains merely contemplated, in part because it is not free of its own geopolitical limitations, as it crosses some countries that may not be reliably stable.

The energy-producing nations of central Asia also seek Russia-free outlets to the east, and these have their own geopolitical complications. For instance, there is a planned pipeline to run from Turkmenistan through Afghanistan, across Pakistan, and into India, the TAPI pipeline. While such a route would help Turkmenistan escape Russian energy control, it is difficult to imagine a more geopolitically hostile and unstable set of countries to traverse.[44]

Geopolitical contention also arises from competitors for a given supply. Russia would like to develop alternative markets to its European outlets. To that end, Russia is developing a pipeline to link Siberian oil to East Asian outlets, notably China and Japan. This Eastern Siberia-Pacific Ocean (ESPO) pipeline originates in Taishet, in Russia's far eastern regions, and should eventually reach the Pacific coast at Perevoznaya Bay. En route to the Pacific, the pipeline passes within thirty miles of the Chinese-Russian border. From there, a spur already runs to Daqing, China, and deliveries to China along this spur started in early 2011. Japan would be a primary customer for oil that reaches the Pacific, and some oil will flow to the Pacific via rail, pending completion of the last portion of the pipeline. Russia plans a similar route for a natural gas pipeline. Thus, China and Japan are placed in possible contention for supply of eastward-bound energy, in addition to competing with Europe as well.[45]

Building a pipeline establishes a permanent route with a dual geopolitical potential. The pipeline may contribute to geopolitical stability by increasing the supply of globally available energy, or it may exclude portions of the world's

supply from general accessibility. Further, the establishment of new transnational pipelines and the routes they follow will almost always be a geopolitical issue. In a certain sense, pipelines with an origination and termination point resemble a bilateral contract between an energy surplus and an energy deficit state. They have the potential to both expand market supply, but also the capacity to shunt a portion of the world's energy supply to a particular nation and away from the general price-driven market as the result of a relationship that is both economic and geopolitical.

SEA LANES

In contrast to unidimensional pipelines or bilateral contracts, the open sea offers a fully two-dimensional sphere of maneuver in which ships can chart a course to connect any two points. In this respect, the United States benefits from the sourcing of its oil imports. Almost 58 percent of U.S. oil imports are drawn from North and South America, with Canada and Mexico together accounting for more than one-third of all U.S. imported oil. The next-largest regional source is the coast of Africa, from Nigeria, Algeria, and Angola, with transport lanes across the expanses of the Atlantic Ocean. The United States draws only 20 percent of its oil imports from the Persian Gulf region (Saudi Arabia, Iraq, and Kuwait).[46] This distribution of supplies makes it relatively easy for the U.S. Navy to defend its vital oil import sea lanes. In peace, this distribution is less important as normal energy markets constitute an environment in which "all sources support all uses." The real problem with any distribution of energy imports arises when normal world markets are threatened in some way, or when transport avenues are disturbed or closed.

In contrast with the wide-open Atlantic from the coast of Africa to the East Coast of the United States, much of the sea is not open. Instead, the distribution of the land interacts with the sea to create a number of critical chokepoints, which are distributed in a manner that seemingly purposefully complicates the geopolitical dimension of energy markets. Three of the most critical chokepoints lie near the mother lode of the world's oil supply in the Middle East. They are the Strait of Hormuz (controlling the opening of the Persian Gulf into the Indian Ocean), the Strait of Bab el-Mandab (lying at the junction of the Red Sea and its juncture with the Gulf of Aden and on to the Indian Ocean), and the Suez Canal (connecting the Mediterranean and the Red Sea). (See Exhibit 2.7.) The Strait of Hormuz witnesses the passage of almost 20 million barrels of oil per day, which ultimately amounts to about two-thirds of all ship-borne oil and about 20 percent of the world's total daily consumption.[47] Further, most of the world's surge capacity of oil must transit the Strait of Hormuz as well.

The Strait of Bab el-Mandeb are somewhat less strategically important, even though about 4 million barrels a day of crude oil transit this passage, which runs along the shores of Yemen, one of the world's least stable countries. Further, inter-diction of shipments in the Bab el-Mandeb would also choke off the Suez Canal from the south. The Suez Canal carries about 2 million barrels per day, even though it is too small to accommodate Very Large Crude Carriers (VLCCs). The associated Suez-Mediterranean (SUMED) pipeline runs from the western shore of the Red Sea across Egypt to the Mediterranean west of Alexandria and has a capacity of 2.3 million barrels per day. Blockage of the Red Sea passageway would require ships from the Persian Gulf to sail an additional 6,000 miles around the Cape of Good Hope

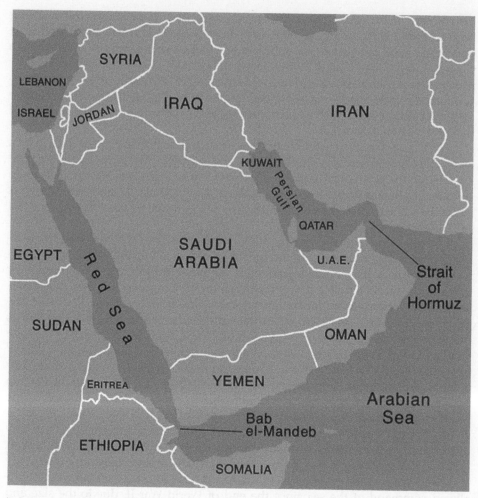

Exhibit 2.7 Energy Chokepoints: The Straits of Hormuz and the Bab el-Mandeb

to reach Europe and the Mediterranean, disrupting supplies and increasing costs. These chokepoints almost literally lie under the guns of regimes that are clearly hostile to western interests, even though the economic lifeblood of those hostile powers depends largely on sales to western nations.

The Strait of Malacca, lying just along the western shore of Malaysia, down to Singapore and running north of Indonesia, is the most critical constricted passageway in the Indian Ocean. At Phillips Channel is only 1.7 miles wide, yet more than 60,000 ships transit the strait annually.[48] Japan and China are the large energy consumers that are most vulnerable to problems in the Strait of Malacca. Interdiction of the strait would require a journey around the southern coast of Indonesia before heading north toward the South China Sea through the Lombok or Sunda Strait. Somewhat less critical are additional sea lane choke points in the Bosporus, the Panama Canal, and the Danish Straits.

Interruption of tanker traffic through any of these passages could cause severe disruption of the world's oil markets, with sudden shifts in the quantity and

distribution of supply. Perhaps not surprisingly, then, the Persian Gulf has long been regarded as an American lake, with the U.S. Sixth Fleet being based athwart the Persian Gulf in Bahrain. Nonetheless, some of these chokepoints are subject to closure through the threat of asymmetric warfare, such as swarming speedboats or missile attacks, perhaps being launched from Iran.[49] While the effect of such disruptions on world energy markets would certainly be large, it is difficult to estimate their magnitude without some indication as to the thoroughness or persistence of the interruption in traffic.

For China, the most vital energy sea lanes follow an arc from eastern Africa along the northern coast of the Indian Ocean, past Iran, Pakistan, and India, and on through the Strait of Malacca, and into the South China Sea. Much of this route is within a short distance from land making it fairly easy for land-based powers along the route to project power southward across these sea lanes that are so vital to Chinese energy supply.

Perhaps more than anyone else, Robert D. Kaplan has emphasized the increasing geopolitical consequence of the Indian Ocean, most notably in his book, *Monsoon*, as well as in his other publications.[50] While the Indian Ocean is important for much of the world's trade, it is critically important for energy. Further, the importance of the Indian Ocean for energy shipments has been heightened by the emergence of China as a key participant in world trade. Much of China's oil comes from the Persian Gulf and the east coast of Africa, from where it must make the long journey past the southern shores of many nations that range from the unruly to hostile. From this point of view, China's sourcing leaves it in a particularly vulnerable position, because its key oil imports come from East Africa and the Persian Gulf region. Further, this critical route of China's energy supply is subject to the naval might of the United States.

As Kaplan emphasizes, China is working assiduously to strengthen its ability to secure its path of energy supplies through the Indian Ocean and also to thwart U.S. naval dominance in this region. As military dominance depends on capacity and need not require the exercise of might, the United States has enjoyed unparalleled command of the sea since the end of World War II, due to the size and sophistication of its naval resources, most particularly a large blue-water navy led by a suite of nuclear aircraft carriers. According to some, China is pursuing a *sea-denial strategy* to counterbalance U.S. naval dominance in traditional resources. For example, rather than trying to match the United States in developing a fleet of nuclear-powered aircraft carriers, China appears to be developing antiship missiles capable of sinking ships, or at least keeping them far out to sea far away from China's vital sea lanes.[51]

Partially in response to their naval vulnerability, many see the Chinese as developing a *string-of-pearls strategy* of securing access to bases and harbors where Chinese ships can resupply and refit. For example, China is working with Pakistan to build a port facility in Gwadar, Pakistan, and it is helping establish a fueling station in Sri Lanka. Other potential pearls include Hainan Island, Woody Island in the Paracel Archipelago, a container port in Chittagong, Bangladesh, and a deep-water port in Sittwe, Myanmar. While the idea of this string of pearls has garnered considerable attention, there is a persistent debate about whether China itself has conceived these moves as developing a necklace of pearls to wreath the south Asian littoral. Nonetheless, the establishment of numerous naval "places and

bases" of resupply along the route from the oil-rich regions of Africa and the Middle East would give China the means to project power over that route in order to protect its own peaceful acquisition of supplies or to dominate the route upon which other nations, most notably Japan, must rely.[52]

Beyond establishing a network of facilities for ships, China appears to be concentrating on developing other means to secure its access to oil resources in the region. For example, China in cooperation with other nations is exploring the establishment of pipelines to link the Bay of Bengal with Yunnan, a canal across the Isthmus of Kra in Thailand, as well as rail links to bring oil overland from the coast of the Indian Ocean directly into China, thus avoiding some sea lane chokepoints.

While U.S. naval might has long been instrumental in keeping the sea lanes open for energy shipments and other forms of commerce, a strong Chinese naval power would have the potential to either secure or obstruct these sea lanes. Both alternatives have dramatic implications for energy markets over the next several decades. The United States has long demonstrated its resolve to maintain open seas, and China may well be expected to have similar interests, at least in normal circumstances. Thus, the presence of two guarantors of open seas, may help to stabilize energy markets. However, with a still strong United States and a strengthening China, any confrontation between the two powers could imply a very significant disruption to the transport of energy across the seas. In some year not too distant, one can easily imagine a situation in which the United States and China are both strong and have conflicting interests in sustaining or in impeding energy shipments to other nations. In such an event, both nations may have the power to interdict normal shipments of oil from the Middle East, and any such disruption would generate cataclysmic price increases and price volatility in energy markets.

THE NEW WORLD OF NATURAL GAS

Recent technological innovations for transporting and developing natural gas threaten a technological disruption that may radically alter the world's energy landscape in the next two decades. A previous section of this chapter briefly alluded to the emergence of economically feasible LNG systems, which by itself has large implications for energy geopolitics. However, as soon as the importance of LNG started to become clear, shale gas began to become a force. In fact, shale gas has the potential to swamp the already large importance of LNG. This section focuses on the interplay of LNG and shale gas and the vast potential that shale gas holds for changing world energy markets.

Without liquefaction, natural gas was essentially transportable only via pipeline. When it is liquefied, natural gas can move by train or ship. Thus, the advent of LNG gives natural gas a transport and market potential much more like crude oil. Even without shale gas, LNG transportability has been anticipated to drive an expansion of natural gas in the world's energy mix. In the EU, for example, predictions suggested in 2005 that natural gas consumption would grow by 67 percent in 30 years, even in the face of declining EU production. That increase was to be fed in large part by LNG imports.[53] Similarly, Exxon's "Energy Outlook to 2030" showed an increase in natural gas consumption of 60 percent from 2005 to 2030 as shown in Exhibit 2.1, and BP's estimates show that natural gas should provide as much of the world's energy as oil by the same time, as Exhibit 2.2 shows.

Because LNG technology transforms natural gas into an energy commodity similar to crude oil, one can expect natural gas to eventually have the same strengths and weaknesses as the market for crude oil. As recently as 2005, LNG accounted for only one-third of worldwide gas shipments, with two-thirds moving by pipeline.[54] But the further maturation of LNG infrastructure promises to change those proportions. For example, South Korea, Taiwan, and Japan have virtually no natural gas resources and together accounted for two-thirds of global LNG demand in 2003. As LNG matures, such nations can meet an increasing portion of their energy needs by natural gas imported as LNG. Further, as LNG technology continues to improve, such nations can diversify their supplies of LNG more fully than at present.

However, just as the worldwide market for crude oil—with major supplies concentrated in just a few countries—eventually gave rise to OPEC, there is fear that worldwide use of LNG could lead to a cartel in natural gas (ignoring for a moment the promise of shale gas, which is explored below). Fifteen natural gas–exporting nations have already banded together to form the Gas Exporting Countries Forum (GECF), which many regard as an incipient cartel. Iran and Russia are clear leaders in this movement.[55]

In contrast to crude oil, however, natural gas is much more widely distributed across the world, and much of the world's resources of natural gas occur in the form of shale gas. Previously not exploitable because of inadequate technology and high costs, shale gas promises to vastly increase the world's resources of usable natural gas, with a geographical distribution that will help to frustrate the formation of any cartel. For example, North America may have as much as one quadrillion cubic feet of shale gas, while Europe may have almost 200 trillion cubic feet.[56] Exhibit 2.8 shows the distribution of shale gas "plays" in the lower 48 of the United

Exhibit 2.8 Shale Gas "Plays" in the United States

States. (One barrel of oil is equivalent to about 6,000 cubic feet of natural gas.) The Energy Information Association puts the importance of shale gas into perspective: "Thus, adding the identified shale gas resources to other gas resources increases total world technically recoverable gas resources by over 40 percent to 22,600 trillion cubic feet."[57]

The geographical distribution of these shale basins that hold so much natural gas is extremely important for the future of the world's energy market. Major shale gas formations lie in North America, southern South America, South Africa, Europe, Central Asia, and throughout the Maghreb. For the United States, with its already well-developed and extensive gas pipeline network, the advent of shale gas promises to move the nation markedly closer to the elusive goal of energy independence. Over the next decades, the United States should be self-sufficient in natural gas production. This at least temporary abundance of natural gas may retard the necessity for ever-increasing oil imports if natural gas is used to generate electricity and electricity becomes a more important energy source of the transportation fleet.

While the shale gas resources of Europe are not as well explored as those in the United States, it is now clear that Europe possesses substantial shale gas resources. From a geopolitical point of view, the development of European shale gas can reduce reliance on natural gas imports from Russia, with all of the geopolitical leverage that might provide. China's shale gas lies mainly in its western regions, but there are apparently large shale gas basins in the northeast that have yet to be assessed.[58] Pipelines from these regions may prove to make an important contribution to China's ever-growing energy budget. Key countries in the global economy of east Asia—Japan, Taiwan, Singapore, South Korea—have not yielded any new discoveries of shale gas, so they are left with no improvement in their own resources. However, they are quite likely to benefit indirectly. With the prospect of much more natural gas production, these nations stand to benefit from a greater diversity of LNG suppliers and, perhaps, costs that are lower than they otherwise would be.

While shale gas has great promise, it is not free of serious risks and concerns. Shale gas is produced by forcing a mixture of water and chemicals into the shale formation to create small fissures in the rock—the process of hydraulic fracturing or *fracking*. These cracks allow the gas to flow up through the rock to be collected. The shale deposits are typically quite deep, lying well below aquifers. The great fear is that fracking may lead to contamination of the aquifers, thereby destroying a considerable portion of the water supply for wide geographical regions.

The potential dangers of fracking are entering the public consciousness. The documentary film *Gasland* was nominated for an Academy Award in 2011 and features water from a kitchen sink that bursts into flames. Similarly, the ProPublica.org website has published an account of Louis Meeks's problems with his water supply in "Hydrofracked? One Man's Mystery Leads to a Backlash Against Natural Gas Drilling."[59] Beyond destruction of an aquifer, the fracking process also creates wastewater that is laced with the chemicals added to the hydraulic fracturing mix. This second potential environmental hazard is probably not as serious as the possibility of destroying an aquifer. One of the earliest and perhaps largest shale formations that has been exploited is the Barnett Shale, which lies across 5,000 square miles and at least 17 Texas counties, including the city of Fort Worth.

Major aquifer damage in such a heavily populated region has truly dramatic potential.

To date, hydraulic fracturing operations have been largely unregulated. Different drillers use different proprietary mixtures of chemicals to add to the water forced into the shale, and the composition of the various chemical mixtures is not public information. It is clear that hydraulic fracturing will be subject to increased regulation. France is contemplating a ban on even the exploration for shale gas that would use hydraulic fracturing.[60] In addition to its sudden and unexpected abundance, one big advantage for natural gas is that it is cleaner than alternatives, especially coal. However, some are questioning whether natural gas produced by fracking is really so clean. Some accounts even suggest that it could generate more greenhouse gas emissions than coal.[61] Already some states are moving to strengthen their regulatory control over hydraulic fracturing and the environmental threats it may pose.[62] While shale gas has the potential to enlarge the world's energy supply and increase the diversity of sources, the ultimate future of shale gas remains unclear due to uncertainty over its environmental impacts.

NUCLEAR POWER

Nuclear power has been and will continue to be generated and consumed entirely within the borders of the producing country. As such, conventional thinking has held that nuclear power presents few geopolitical issues. The March 2011 earthquake-tsunami-nuclear disaster in Japan has already highlighted potential international consequences of nuclear power to great public consciousness. Shortly after the disruption at the Fukushima-Daiichi nuclear power plant, elevated radiation levels were detected in California and in milk produced in nearby regions near the plant. The United States banned milk, vegetables, and fruits from affected regions of Japan in the aftermath of the disaster.[63] While the dispersion of nuclear material from the Fukushima-Daiichi plant was relatively small, it suggests the possible consequences of a much more extensive radiation emission more proximate to other nations and their population centers. For example, France relies extensively on nuclear power generation, and a major radiation emission from France would certainly have large geopolitical implications.

At the very least, the Fukushima-Daiichi disaster clouds the future of nuclear power. It has already caused the cancellation of some plans for building new nuclear capacity.[64] If nuclear power is a smaller portion of the energy mix in the future, it will affect the resulting allocation of demand for other sources of energy. This shifting demand will have its own geopolitical, price, and market volatility consequences.

CLIMATE CHANGE AND ENVIRONMENTAL CONSIDERATIONS

The acquisition of energy in any form imposes some environmental burden. The overriding problem for energy and the environment is whether a growing world population with intensifying energy use can acquire sufficient energy to sustain an enriched way of life at an acceptable environmental cost. One of the greatest issues in this domain is the question of climate change. But we have seen that even such optimistic plans as the development of shale gas and the enlargement

of nuclear power generation are subject to changing assessments of their environmental impact.

This chapter has barely touched on environmental considerations, perhaps the largest and most dramatic of these being a fear of anthropogenic destruction of the environment through the emission of greenhouse gases. To date, much of the world has made no serious efforts to change energy consumption to constrain greenhouse gases. Nonetheless, the future of world energy will continue to be affected by environmental concerns. But those issues lie beyond the scope of this chapter and deserve their own thorough treatment.

THE FUTURE OF ENERGY GEOPOLITICS AND ENERGY FINANCE

From the development of a worldwide network of coaling stations to service the British fleet, to the beginning of the age of oil, and through the present day, the story of energy has been intertwined with international politics, all with dramatic effect on energy markets. The aftermath of World War II led to a bipolar world dominated by the Soviet Union and the United States, which briefly gave way to a unipolar world with the demise of the Soviet Union. Today, a multipolar world appears to be developing. This world of many significant powers and increasing energy demand will necessarily engender geopolitical tensions, and these potential conflicts will continue to have a dramatic effect on energy markets.

For energy finance, geopolitical understanding is necessary. We have seen that the effect of an oil supply disruption that affects only a single small country can be quite large. But the world nexus of energy supply draws many nations into simultaneous interaction. This requires participants in energy finance to be students of energy geopolitics, because the future of world energy is as likely to be determined by the interaction of nations as by the fluctuations in world supply of and demand for energy.

DISCUSSION QUESTIONS

1. Explain the difference between geopolitical threats within the current framework of energy markets and geopolitical threats to that framework. What are the events or developments associated with each type of threat?

2. Many energy market observers expect shale gas to be an increasingly important energy source over the next few decades. Explain the geopolitical impact of different future developments for shale gas. For example, what are the likely geopolitical impacts of the problem of groundwater pollution and its potential severity?

3. By most accounts, China should have a continuing enormous surge in GDP over the next few decades. Opposed to that scenario stands much of Chinese history with repeated failures to achieve potential that seemed available due to changes in government or an inward-turning of society. From a geopolitical perspective, and with a focus on energy markets, what scenarios for China seem most probable and what do those scenarios imply for energy geopolitics?

4. The United States currently possesses a blue water navy that appears to dominate the naval forces of all other nations. If that changes to a condition more closely approximating parity, how might such developments affect the geopolitics of energy?

5. The Japanese tsunami followed by the Fukushima nuclear disaster has changed the world's perception of nuclear energy. For example, shortly after the disaster in Japan, Germany announced that it would phase out its reliance on nuclear power generation. Yet nuclear energy may not be abandoned to the extent that now seems probable. Explain how these alternative futures for nuclear energy might affect the geopolitics of energy and energy markets.

6. Most large energy companies expect the world's distribution of energy sources to be approximately the same in 2030 as they were in 2010, or as they are today, with various forms of renewable energy gaining only a few percentage points in the world's energy mix. By contrast, others think that more environmentally friendly forms of energy may develop much more quickly. What are the likely geopolitical dimensions of a rapid improvement in the economics of environmentally friendly energy sources? How might such developments affect markets?

NOTES

1. Daniel Yergin, "Energy Security and Markets," in Jan H. Kalicki and David L. Goldwyn, *Energy and Security: Toward a New Foreign Policy Strategy*, Baltimore: Johns Hopkins University Press, 2005, 60.
2. See Erik J. Dahl, "Naval Innovation: From Coal to Oil," *Joint Forces Quarterly*, Winter 2000–2001, 50–56; and F. William Engdahl, "Oil and the Origins of the 'War to Make the World Safe for Democracy,'" June 22, 2007, available at www.engdahl.oilgeopolitics.net/.
3. BP, "BP Energy Outlook 2030," January 2011, London.
4. Deloitte, "Globalization and Energy Supply: Strategic Risk in the 21st Century," 2004.
5. ExxonMobil, "2012 The Outlook for Energy: A View to 2040," 2012.
6. BP, "BP Energy Outlook 2030," January 2011, London.
7. For assessments of the importance of LNG, see: Baker Institute, "The Geopolitics of Natural Gas," March 2005; Baker Institute, "Natural Gas in North America: Markets and Security," January 2008; Cindy Hurst, "Liquefied Natural Gas: The Next Prize?" in Gail Luft and Anne Korin, eds., *Energy Security Challenges for the 21st Century: A Reference Handbook*, Santa Barbara, CA: ABC-Clio, 2009, 271–281; and Donald A. Juckett and Michelle Michot Foss, "Can a 'Global' Natural Gas Market Be Achieved?" in Jan H. Kalicki and David L. Goldwyn, *Energy and Security: Toward a New Foreign Policy Strategy*, Baltimore: Johns Hopkins University Press, 2005, 531–552.
8. See Baker Institute Policy Report, "The G8, Energy Security, and Global Climate Issues," Number 37, July 2008; International Energy Agency, "World Energy Outlook 2010: Fact Sheet," 2010; and Robert A. Hefner III, "The Age of Energy Gases: The Importance of Natural Gas in Energy Policy," in Kurt M. Campbell and Jonathon Price, *The Global Politics of Energy*, Washington, DC: The Aspen Institute, 2008, 149–182.
9. Contrary to the thrust of this chapter, some offer a radically different vision. The National Intelligence Council, in "Global Trends 2025: A Transformed World," November 2008, foresees a technological breakthrough in the energy field by 2025 ". . . that will provide an alternative to oil and natural gas." However, even this radically different vision of the world's energy future maintains that ". . . implementation will lag because of the necessary infrastructure costs and need for longer replacement time" (see pp. 45–51, especially p. 46).
10. For the foreign policy dimension of the international energy market, see John Deutch, James R. Schlesinger, and David G. Victor, "National Security Consequences of U.S. Oil Dependency," Council on Foreign Relations, Independent Task Force Report No. 58; Donald A. Juckett and Michelle Michot Foss, "Can a 'Global'

Natural Gas Market Be Achieved?" in Jan H. Kalicki and David L. Goldwyn, *Energy and Security: Toward a New Foreign Policy Strategy*, Baltimore: Johns Hopkins University Press, 2005, 531–552; Loyola de Palacio, "Reforming the Gas Market," in Jan H. Kalicki and David L. Goldwyn, *Energy and Security: Toward a New Foreign Policy Strategy*, Baltimore: Johns Hopkins University Press, 2005, 175–194; and Daniel Yergin, "Energy Security and Markets," in Jan H. Kalicki and David L. Goldwyn, *Energy and Security: Toward a New Foreign Policy Strategy*, Baltimore: Johns Hopkins University Press, 2005, 51–64.

11. Parliamentary Debates, Commons, July 17, 1913, 1474–1477, quoted in Daniel Yergin, "Energy Security and Markets," in Jan H. Kalicki and David L. Goldwyn, *Energy and Security: Toward a New Foreign Policy Strategy*, Baltimore: Johns Hopkins University Press, 2005, 51–64. See p. 52.

12. For the unlikelihood of energy independence for the United States, see John Deutch, James R. Schlesinger, and David G. Victor, "National Security Consequences of U.S. Oil Dependency," Council on Foreign Relations, Independent Task Force Report No. 58; Peter M. Jackson, "The Future of Global Oil Supply: Understanding the Building Blocks," Cambridge Energy Research Associates, November 2009; Clifford Krauss, "Can We Do Without the Mideast?" *New York Times*, March 30, 2011; and Philip K. Verleger Jr., "Forty Years of Folly: The Failure of U.S. Energy Policy," *International Economy*, Winter 2011, 49–66 passim.

13. See "BP Energy Outlook 2030," January 2011, London, 37. www.bp.com/sectiongenericarticle800.do?categoryId=9037134&contentId=7068677.

14. Edward L. Morse and Amy Myers Jaffe, "OPEC in Confrontation with Globalization," in Jan H. Kalicki and David L. Goldwyn, *Energy and Security: Toward a New Foreign Policy Strategy*, Baltimore: Johns Hopkins University Press, 2005, 65–95, especially 68.

15. See, for instance, Amy Myers Jaffe, "OPEC: An Anatomy of a Cartel," in Gail Luft and Anne Korin, eds., *Energy Security Challenges for the 21st Century: A Reference Handbook*, Santa Barbara, CA: ABC-Clio, 2009, 78–90, especially 83.

16. See Christof Rühl, "Global Energy After the Crisis," *Foreign Affairs*, March-April 2010.

17. OPEC, *World Oil Outlook, 2010*, 125–126.

18. Amy Myers Jaffe, "OPEC: An Anatomy of a Cartel," in Gail Luft and Anne Korin, eds., *Energy Security Challenges for the 21st Century: A Reference Handbook*, Santa Barbara, CA: ABC-Clio, 2009, 78–90. See p. 86.

19. Quoted in Amy Myers Jaffe and Ronald Soligo, "Militarization of Energy: Geopolitical Threats to the Global Energy System," Baker Institute for Public Policy, May 2008, 8.

20. John Deutch, James R. Schlesinger, and David G. Victor, "National Security Consequences of U.S. Oil Dependency," Council on Foreign Relations, Independent Task Force Report No. 58, 2006, 16.

21. *Time*, "The Seven Sisters Still Rule," September 11, 1978, available at www.time.com/time/magazine/article/0,9171,946053,00.html, accessed April 20, 2011. The Seven Sisters were Standard Oil of New Jersey, Standard Oil Company of New York, Standard Oil of California, Gulf Oil, Texaco, Royal Dutch Shell, and Anglo-Persian Oil Company. A succession of name changes and mergers has led largely to the Big Five of Exhibit 2.6.

22. IOC serves as an abbreviation for both "international oil companies" and "investor-owned companies," but both refer to the same set of corporations.

23. For an account of the transition from oil dominance by IOCs to control by NOCs, see Daniel Yergin, *The Prize: The Epic Quest for Oil, Money and Power*, New York: Free Press, 1991, especially Chapter 28, "The Hinge Years: Countries Versus Companies."

24. Amy Myers Jaffe and Ronald Soligo, "The International Oil Companies," Baker Institute for Public Policy, November 2007. See p. 12.

25. CNPC holds 86.3 percent of PetroChina; Sinopec owns 75.8 percent of Sinopec Corp; and CNOOC controls 66.4 percent of CNOOC Ltd. See Erica S. Downs, "Who's Afraid of China's Oil Companies?" in Carlos Pascual and Jonathan Elkind, eds., *Energy Security: Economics, Politics, Strategies, and Implications*, Washington, DC: Brookings Institution Press, 2010, 73–102.
26. Erica S. Downs, "Who's Afraid of China's Oil Companies?" in Carlos Pascual and Jonathan Elkind, eds., *Energy Security: Economics, Politics, Strategies, and Implications*, Washington, DC: Brookings Institution Press, 2010, 73–102. See p. 75.
27. Steven W. Lewis, "Chinese NOCs and World Energy Markets: CNPC, Sinopec, and CNOOC," Baker Institute, March 2007. See pp. 3–4.
28. Erica S. Downs, "The Fact and Fiction of Sino-African Energy Relations," *China Security*, 3:3, Summer 2007, 42–68. See p. 55.
29. Steven W. Lewis, "Chinese NOCs and World Energy Markets: CNPC, Sinopec, and CNOOC," Baker Institute, March 2007. See pp. 22–23.
30. Julie Jiang and Jonathan Sinton, "Overseas Investments by Chinese National Oil Companies: Assessing the Drivers and Impacts," International Energy Agency, February 2011. See pp. 9–10.
31. Erica S. Downs, "The Fact and Fiction of Sino-African Energy Relations," *China Security*, 3:3, Summer 2007, 42–68. See p. 44.
32. Steven W. Lewis, "Chinese NOCs and World Energy Markets: CNPC, Sinopec, and CNOOC," Baker Institute, March 2007. See p. 20.
33. Serge Michael and Michel Beuret, *China Safari: On the Trail of Beijing's Expansion in Africa*, New York: Nation Books, 2009.
34. Henry Lee and Dan Shalmon, "Searching for Oil: China's Oil Strategy in Africa," in Robert I. Rotberg, *China into Africa: Trade, Aid, and Influence*, Washington, DC: Brookings Institution Press, 2008, 109–136. See p. 109.
35. Jeffrey A. Bader, "Rising China and Rising Oil Demand: Real and Imagined Problems for the International System," in Kurt M. Campbell and Jonathon Price, *The Global Politics of Energy*, Washington, DC: The Aspen Institute, 2008, 97–113. See p. 107.
36. For the range of economic contacts and between Chinese and their African hosts, along with the tensions these developments have engendered, see "The Chinese in Africa: Trying to Pull Together," and "Africa and China: Rumble in the Jungle," *The Economist*, April 20, 2011.
37. Julie Jiang and Jonathan Sinton, "Overseas Investments by Chinese National Oil Companies: Assessing the Drivers and Impacts," International Energy Agency, February 2011. See p. 17.
38. Gal Luft, "The Pipeline Paradox: Why Is the United States Helping Iran Sell Natural Gas?" *Foreign Policy*, April 12, 2011, discusses the unintended consequences of American foreign policy regarding Iran in this context.
39. Michael T. Klare, *Rising Powers, Shrinking Planet*, New York: Henry Holt and Company, LLC, 2008. See p. 91.
40. However, Russia is anxious to bypass the Ukraine. It recently opened a direct pipeline from Russia to Germany, Nord Stream, which transits the Baltic Sea. It also is striving to complete South Stream, a line from Russia under the Black Sea that also bypasses Ukraine.
41. For various perspectives on the pipelines of the Soviet era, see Mehdi Parvizi Amineh and Henk Houweling, "Global Energy Security and Its Geopolitical Impediments—The Case of the Caspian Region," *Perspectives on Global Development and Technology*, 6, 2007, 365–388; Gawdat Bahgat, "The Geopolitics of Energy in Central Asia and the Caucasus," *Journal of Social, Political, and Economic Studies*, 34:2, Summer 2009, 139–153; Baker Institute Policy Report, "Russia and the Caspian States in the Global Energy Balance," May 2009; Daniel Freifeld, "The Great Pipeline Opera," *Foreign Policy*,

September-October 2009, 120–127; Pinar Ipek, "Azerbaijan's Foreign Policy and Challenges for Energy Security," *Middle East Journal*, 63:2, Spring 2009, 227–239; Jeff Smith and Ilan Berman, "Central Asia's Energy Bazaar," *Real Clear World*, January 27, 2011, www.realclearworld.com/articles/2011/01/27/central_asias_energy_bazaar_99372.html; and Marat Terterov, John Van Pool, and Sergiy Nagornyy, "Russian Geopolitical Power in the Black and Caspian Seas Region: Implications for Turkey and the World," *Insight Turkey*, 12:3, 2010, 191–203.

42. Michael T. Klare, *Rising Powers, Shrinking Planet*, New York: Henry Holt and Company, LLC, 2008. See p. 109.

43. Daniel Freifeld, "The Great Pipeline Opera," *Foreign Policy*, September-October 2009, 120–127. See p. 123.

44. John Foster, "Afghanistan, the TAPI Pipeline, and Energy Geopolitics," March, 23, 2010, available at: tp://www.ensec.org/. The four participating nations recently reached agreement to build the pipeline. See *Pipelines International*, "Agreement Paves Way for TAPI Pipeline," http://pipelinesinternational.com/news/agreement_paves_way_for_tapi_pipeline/053838/, accessed April 23, 2011.

45. Regarding the ESPO pipeline particularly, see Steven W. Lewis, "Chinese NOCs and World Energy Markets: CNPC, Sinopec, and CNOOC," Baker Institute, March 2007; Robert Morley, "How Russia Is About to Dramatically Change the World," Trumpet.com, January 5, 2010; and Richard Weitz, "Chinese Pipe Dreams," *The Diplomat*, January 3, 2011.

46. U.S. Energy Information Administration, "Crude Oil and Total Petroleum Imports Top 15 Countries," March 30, 2011, www.eia.doe.gov/pub/oil_gas/petroleum/data_publications/company_level_imports/current/import.html.

47. "The G8, Energy Security, and Global Climate Issues," Baker Institute Policy Report, Number 37, July 2008. See p. 9. See also Daniel Brumberg, Jareer Elass, Amy Myers Jaffe, and Kenneth B. Medlock III, "Iran, Energy, and Geopolitics," Baker Institute for Public Policy, May 2008.

48. Energy Information Administration, "World Oil Transit Chokepoints," February 2011. See p. 3. This document provides an excellent general discussion of these chokepoints. See also Michael T. Klare, *Rising Powers, Shrinking Planet*, New York: Henry Holt and Company, LLC, 2008; and Daniel Brumberg, Jareer Elass, Amy Myers Jaffe, and Kenneth B. Medlock, III, "Iran, Energy, and Geopolitics," Baker Institute for Public Policy, May 2008.

49. Daniel Brumberg, Jareer Elass, Amy Myers Jaffe, and Kenneth B. Medlock, III, "Iran, Energy, and Geopolitics," Baker Institute for Public Policy, May 2008. See p. 14.

50. Robert D. Kaplan, *Monsoon: The Indian Ocean and the Future of American Power*, New York: Random House, 2010. See also three other works by Robert D. Kaplan: "Center Stage for the 21st Century: Power Plays in the Indian Ocean," *Foreign Affairs*, March-April 2009; "The Geography of Chinese Power," *Foreign Affairs*, May-June 2010, 22–41; and "Lost at Sea," *New York Times*, September 21, 2007.

51. See Andrew S. Erickson and David D. Yang, "Using the Land to Control the Sea? Chinese Analysis Consider the Antiship Ballistic Missile," *Naval War College Review*, 62:4, Autumn 2009, 53–86; Michael T. Klare, "The New Geopolitics of Energy," *The Nation*, May 1, 2008; and Robert D. Kaplan, "Lost at Sea," *New York Times*, September 21, 2007.

52. This metaphor of a string of pearls apparently derives from a Pentagon report developed in 2004 and leaked to the press in early 2005. For an extended geopolitical treatment, see Robert D. Kaplan, *Monsoon: The Indian Ocean and Future of American Power*, New York: Random House, 2010. Christopher J. Pehrson, "String of Pearls: Meeting the Challenge of China's Rising Power Across the Asian Littoral," Strategic Studies Institute, July 2006, provides a more technical military assessment. Of those concerned with this issue, some take the string of pearls strategy as a clear part of conscious Chinese policy. Others are

less sure. Intellibrief, "China: 'String of Pearls' Strategy," April 1, 2007, sums up the situation quite nicely: "The development of the 'String of Pearls' may not, in fact, be a strategy explicitly guided by China's central government. Rather, it may be a convenient label applied by some in the United States to describe an element of China's foreign policy." See also Andrew S. Erickson and David D. Yang, "Using the Land to Control the Sea? Chinese Analysts Consider the Antiship Ballistic Missile," *Naval War College Review*, 62:4, Autumn 2009, 53–86; Michael T. Klare, "The New Geopolitics of Energy," *The Nation*, May 1, 2008; Robert D. Kaplan, "Lost at Sea," *New York Times*, September 21, 2007; Robert D. Kaplan, "Center Stage for the 21st Century: Power Plays in the Indian Ocean," March-April 2009, *Foreign Affairs*; and Daniel J. Kostecka, "Places and Bases: The Chinese Navy's Emerging Support Network in the Indian Ocean," *Naval War College Review*, 64:1, Winter 2011, 59–78.

53. Loyola de Palacio, "Reforming the Gas Market," in Jan H. Kalicki and David L. Goldwyn, *Energy and Security: Toward a New Foreign Policy Strategy*, Baltimore: Johns Hopkins University Press, 2005, 175–194. See p. 176.

54. Donald A. Juckett and Michelle Michot Foss, "Can a 'Global' Natural Gas Market Be Achieved?" in Jan H. Kalicki and David L. Goldwyn, *Energy and Security: Toward a New Foreign Policy Strategy*, Baltimore: Johns Hopkins University Press, 2005, 531–552. See p. 534.

55. For discussion of the possibilities of a cartel in natural gas, see Gawdat Bahgat, "The Geopolitics of Energy in Central Asia and the Caucasus," *Journal of Social, Political, and Economic Studies*, 34:2, Summer 2009, 139–153; "Russia and the Caspian States in the Global Energy Balance," Baker Institute Policy Report, May 2009; Cindy Hurst, "Liquefied Natural Gas: The Next Prize?" in Gail Luft and Anne Korin, eds., *Energy Security Challenges for the 21st Century: A Reference Handbook*, Santa Barbara, CA: ABC-Clio, 2009, 271–281; Amy Myers Jaffe, "Shale Gas Will Rock the World," *Wall Street Journal*, May 10, 2010; and Donald A. Juckett and Michelle Michot Foss, "Can a 'Global' Natural Gas Market Be Achieved?" in Jan H. Kalicki and David L. Goldwyn, *Energy and Security: Toward a New Foreign Policy Strategy*, Baltimore: Johns Hopkins University Press, 2005, 531–552.

56. Amy Myers Jaffe, "Shale Gas Will Rock the World," *Wall Street Journal*, May 10, 2010.

57. U.S. Energy Information Administration, "World Shale Gas Resources: An Initial Assessment of 14 Regions Outside the United States," April 2011. See p. 3.

58. For an assessment of world resources, see U.S. Energy Information Administration, "World Shale Gas Resources: An Initial Assessment of 14 Regions Outside the United States," April 2011, and especially the map on pp. 1–7.

59. Abrahm Lustgarten, "Hydrofracked? One Man's Mystery Leads to a Backlash Against Natural Gas Drilling," ProPublica.org, February 25, 2011, available at www.propublica.org/article/hydrofracked-one-mans-mystery-leads-to-a-backlash-against-natural-gas-drill, accessed April 27, 2011. This short account is also available as a free publication on Kindle.

60. Max Colchester and Geraldine Amiel, "France Mills Banning Shale Exploration," *Wall Street Journal*, April 19, 2011.

61. Abrahm Lustgarten, "More Reasons to Question Whether Gas Is Cleaner than Coal," ProPublica.org, April 12, 2011, available at: www.propublica.org/article/more-reasons-to-question-whether-gas-is-cleaner-than-coal, accessed April 27, 2011.

62. Pennsylvania is already moving to regulate the disposal of wastewater from hydraulic fracturing. See Robbie Brown, "Gas Drillers Asked to Change Method of Waste Disposal," *New York Times*, April 19, 2011.

63. ABC News, "FDA Bans Milk, Vegetable, Fruits from Nuclear Plant Crisis-Affected Areas in Japan," March 22, 2011.

64. Rebecca Smith, "NRG Drops Plan for Texas Reactors," *Wall Street Journal*, April 20, 2011.

REFERENCES

ABC News. 2011. "FDA Bans Milk, Vegetable, Fruits from Nuclear Plant Crisis-Affected Areas in Japan." March 22.

Amineh, Mehdi Parvizi, and Henk Houweling. 2007. "Global Energy Security and Its Geopolitical Impediments—The Case of the Caspian Region." *Perspectives on Global Development and Technology* 6, 365–388.

Bader, Jeffrey A. 2008. "Rising China and Rising Oil Demand: Real and Imagined Problems For the International System." In Kurt M. Campbell and Jonathon Price, eds. *The Global Politics of Energy*, 97–113. Washington, DC: The Aspen Institute.

Bahgat, Gawdat. 2009. "The Geopolitics of Energy in Central Asia and the Caucasus." *Journal of Social, Political, and Economic Studies*, 34:2, 139–153.

Bahgat, Gawdat. 2008. "Gas OPEC? Rhetoric Versus Reality. *Journal of Social, Political and Economic Studies* 33:3, 281–294.

Baker Institute Policy Report. 2008. "The G8, Energy Security, and Global Climate Issues," Number 37. July.

Baker Institute Policy Report. 2005. "The Geopolitics of Natural Gas." March.

Baker Institute Policy Report. 2008. "Natural Gas in North America: Markets and Security." January.

Baker Institute Policy Report. 2009. "Russia and the Caspian States in the Global Energy Balance." May.

"BP Energy Outlook 2030." 2011. London. January.

Brumberg, Daniel, Jareer Elass, Amy Myers Jaffe, and Kenneth B. Medlock III. 2008. "Iran, Energy, and Geopolitics." Baker Institute for Public Policy. May.

Brown, Robbie. 2011. "Gas Drillers Asked to Change Method of Waste Disposal." *New York Times*, April 19.

Colchester, Max, and Geraldine Amiel. 2011. "France Mills Banning Shale Exploration." *Wall Street Journal*, April 19.

Dahl, Erik J. 2000–2001. "Naval Innovation: From Coal to Oil." *Joint Forces Quarterly*. Winter. 50–56.

Deloitte. 2004. "Globalization and Energy Supply: Strategic Risk in the 21st Century."

Deutch, John, James R. Schlesinger, and David G. Victor. 2006. "National Security Consequences of U.S. Oil Dependency." Council on Foreign Relations, Independent Task Force Report No. 58.

Downs, Erica S. 2007. "The Fact and Fiction of Sino-African Energy Relations." *China Security* 3:3, 42–68.

Downs, Erica S. 2010. "Who's Afraid of China's Oil Companies?" In Carlos Pascual and Jonathan Elkind, eds., 73–102. *Energy Security: Economics, Politics, Strategies, and Implications*. Washington, DC: Brookings Institution Press.

The Economist. 2011. "Africa and China: Rumble in the Jungle." April 20.

The Economist. 2011. "The Chinese in Africa: Trying to Pull Together." April 20.

Engdahl, F. William. 2007. "Oil and the Origins of the 'War to Make the World Safe for Democracy.'" June 22. Available at www.engdahl.oilgeopolitics.net/.

Erickson, Andrew S. and David D. Yang. 2009. "Using the Land to Control the Sea? Chinese Analysis Consider the Antiship Ballistic Missile." *Naval War College Review*, 62:4, 53–86.

Foster, John. 2010. "Afghanistan, the TAPI Pipeline, and Energy Geopolitics." March, 23. Available at: tp://www.ensec.org/.

Freifeld, Danie. 2009. "The Great Pipeline Opera." *Foreign Policy*, September/October, 120–127.

Hefner III, Robert A. 2008. "The Age of Energy Gases: The Importance of Natural Gas in Energy Policy." In Kurt M. Campbell and Jonathon Price, eds., 149–182. *The Global Politics of Energy*, Washington, DC: The Aspen Institute.

Holmes, James, and Tashi Yoshihara. 2011. "Is China Planning String of Pearls?" *The Diplomat*. February 21.

Hurst, Cindy. 2009. "Liquefied Natural Gas: The Next Prize?" In Gail Luft and Anne Korin, eds., 271–281. *Energy Security Challenges for the 21st Century: A Reference Handbook*. Santa Barbara, CA: ABC-Clio.

Intellibrief. 2007. "China: 'String of Pearls' Strategy." April 1.

International Energy Agency. 2010. "World Energy Outlook 2010: Fact Sheet."

Ipek, Pinar. 2009. "Azerbaijan's Foreign Policy and Challenges for Energy Security." *Middle East Journal* 63:2, 227–239.

Jackson, Peter M. 2009. "The Future of Global Oil Supply: Understanding the Building Blocks." Cambridge Energy Research Associates. November.

Jaffe, Amy Myers. 2009. "OPEC: an anatomy of a cartel." In Gail Luft and Anne Korin eds., *Energy Security Challenges for the 21st Century: A Reference Handbook*, 78–90. Santa Barbara, CA: ABC-Clio.

Jaffe, Amy Myers, and Ronald Soligo. 2007. "The International Oil Companies." Baker Institute for Public Policy. November.

Jaffe, Amy Myers, and Ronald Soligo. 2008. "Militarization of Energy: Geopolitical Threats to the Global Energy System." Baker Institute for Public Policy. May.

Jaffe, Amy Myers. 2010. "Shale Gas Will Rock the World." *Wall Street Journal*, May 10, 2010.

Jiang, Julie, and Jonathan Sinton. 2011. "Overseas Investments by Chinese National Oil Companies: Assessing the Drivers and Impacts." International Energy Agency. February.

Juckett, Donald A., and Michelle Michot Foss. 2005. "Can a 'global' natural gas market be achieved?" In Jan H. Kalicki and David L. Goldwyn, eds. *Energy and Security: Toward a New Foreign Policy Strategy*, 531–552. Baltimore: Johns Hopkins University Press.

Kaplan, Robert D. 2009. "Center Stage for the 21st Century: Power Plays in the Indian Ocean." *Foreign Affairs*, 88:2.

Kaplan, Robert D. 2010. "The Geography of Chinese Power." *Foreign Affairs*, 89:3, 22–41.

Kaplan, Robert D. 2007. "Lost at Sea." *New York Times*, September 21.

Kaplan, Robert D. 2010. *Monsoon: The Indian Ocean and the Future of American Power*. New York: Random House.

Klare, Michael T. 2008. "The New Geopolitics of Energy." *The Nation*. May 1.

Klare, Michael T. 2008. *Rising Powers, Shrinking Planet*. New York: Henry Holt and Company, LLC.

Kostecka, Daniel J. 2011. "Places and Bases: The Chinese Navy's Emerging Support Network in the Indian Ocean." *Naval War College Review* 64:1, 59–78.

Krauss, Clifford. 2011. "Can We Do Without the Mideast?" *New York Times*, March 30.

Lee, Henry, and Dan Shalmon. 2008. "Searching for Oil: China's Oil Strategy in Africa." In Robert I. Rotberg, *China Into Africa: Trade, Aid, and Influence*, 109–136. Washington, DC: Brookings Institution Press.

Lewis, Steven W. 2007. "Chinese NOCs and World Energy Markets: CNPC, Sinopec, and CNOOC." Baker Institute. March.

Luft, Gal. 2011. "The Pipeline Paradox: Why Is the United States Helping Iran Sell Natural Gas?" *Foreign Policy*, April 12.

Lustgarten, Abrahm. 2011. "More Reasons to Question Whether Gas Is Cleaner than Coal." ProPublica.org. April 12. Available at www.propublica.org/article/more-reasons-to-question-whether-gas-is-cleaner-than-coal. Accessed April 27, 2011.

Lustgarten, Abrahm. 2011. "Hydrofracked? One Man's Mystery Leads to a Backlash Against Natural Gas Drilling." ProPublica.org. February 25. Available at www.propublica.org/article/hydrofracked-one-mans-mystery-leads-to-a-backlash-against-natural-gas-drill. Accessed April 27, 2011.

Michael, Serge, and Michel Beuret. 2009. *China Safari: On the Trail of Beijing's Expansion in Africa*. New York: Nation Books.

Morley, Robert. 2010. "How Russia Is About to Dramatically Change the World." Trumpet.com. January 5.

Morse, Edward L, and Amy Myers Jaffe. 2005. "OPEC in confrontation with globalization." In Jan H. Kalicki and David L. Goldwyn, eds., *Energy and Security: Toward a New Foreign Policy Strategy*, 65–95. Baltimore: Johns Hopkins University Press.

National Intelligence Council, "Global Trends 2025: A Transformed World." November 2008.

OPEC. 2010. *World Oil Outlook, 2010*.

Palacio, Loyola de. 2005. "Reforming the Gas Market." In Jan H. Kalicki and David L. Goldwyn, eds., *Energy and Security: Toward a New Foreign Policy Strategy*, 175–194. Baltimore: The Johns Hopkins University Press, 2005.

Pehrson, Christopher J. 2006. "String of Pearls: Meeting the Challenge of China's Rising Power Across the Asian Littoral." Strategic Studies Institute. July.

Pipelines International. 2011. "Agreement Paves Way for TAPI Pipeline." http://pipelines international.com/news/agreement_paves_way_for_tapi_pipeline/053838/. Accessed April 23, 2011.

Rühl, Christof. 2010. "Global Energy After the Crisis." *Foreign Affairs*, 89: 2.

Smith, Jeff, and Ilan Berman. 2011. "Central Asia's Energy Bazaar." Realclear world.com. January 27. Available at www.realclearworld.com/articles/2011/01/27/central_asias_energy_bazaar_99372.html.

Smith, Rebecca. 2011. "NRG Drops Plan for Texas Reactors." *Wall Street Journal*. April 20.

Terterov, Marat, John Van Pool and Sergiy Nagornyy. 2010. "Russian Geopolitical Power in the Black and Caspian Seas Region: Implications for Turkey and the World." *Insight Turkey* 12:3, 191–203.

Time. 1978. "The Seven Sisters Still Rule." September 11. Available at www.time.com/time/magazine/article/0,9171,946053,00.html. Accessed April 20, 2011.

U.S. Energy Information Administration. 2011. "Crude Oil and Total Petroleum Imports Top 15 Countries." March 30.

U. S. Energy Information Administration. 2011. "World Oil Transit Chokepoints." February.

U.S. Energy Information Administration. 2011. "World Shale Gas Resources: An Initial Assessment of 14 Regions Outside the United States." April.

Verleger, Jr., Philip K. 2011. "Forty Years of Folly: The Failure of U.S. Energy Policy." *International Economy*, 25: 1, 49–66 passim.

Weitz, Richard. 2011. "Chinese Pipe Dreams." *The Diplomat*. January 3.

Victor, David G. 2006. "National Security Consequences of U.S. Oil Dependency." Council on Foreign Relations, Independent Task Force Report No. 58.

Yergin, Daniel. 2005. "Energy Security and Markets." In Jan H. Kalicki and David L. Goldwyn, eds., *Energy and Security: Toward a New Foreign Policy Strategy*, 51–64. Baltimore: Johns Hopkins University Press, 2005.

Yergin, Daniel. 1991. *The Prize: The Epic Quest for Oil, Money and Power*. New York: Free Press.

ABOUT THE CONTRIBUTOR

Robert W. Kolb holds two PhDs from the University of North Carolina at Chapel Hill (philosophy 1974, finance 1978) and has been a finance professor at five universities. He is currently a professor of finance at Loyola University Chicago, where he also holds the Considine Chair of Applied Ethics.

Kolb's recent writings include *Futures, Options, and Swaps*, 5th ed., and *Understanding Futures Markets*, 6th ed., both co-authored with James A. Overdahl. Recent edited volumes are *Lessons from the Financial Crisis: Causes, Consequences, and Our Economic Future; Sovereign Debt: From Safety to Default*; and *Financial Contagion: The Viral Threat to the Wealth of Nations*, both forthcoming from John Wiley & Sons. Kolb's most recent books are *The Financial Crisis of Our Time* (2011), and *Too Much Is Not Enough: Incentives in Executive Compensation* (2012), both published by Oxford University Press and both selected for the Financial Management Association's Survey and Synthesis Series.

CHAPTER 3

Energy Economics

Past, Present, and Prospects for the Future

JAMES L. WILLIAMS
Energy Economist and Owner, WTRG Economics

BETTY J. SIMKINS
Williams Companies Professor of Business and Professor of Finance, Oklahoma
State University

> Prediction is very difficult, especially if it's about the future.
> —Niels Bohr (1885–1962), Nobel Laureate in Physics

There are three rules for forecasting oil prices:

(1) Never mention a price and a date in the same talk;
(2) If you can't forecast well, forecast often; and
(3) If you are ever lucky enough to get it right, don't let anyone forget it.

> —James Williams, WTRG Economics

INTRODUCTION

The petroleum price shocks that began in the 1970s made the world quickly realize the risk of uncertain energy supply and the importance of energy in economic development. In fact, energy economics did not develop as a specialized branch of economics until after the 1973 oil price shock (Edwards 2003). Today, energy economics is a recognized field with degree programs at the bachelor's, master's, and doctoral levels.

In this chapter we provide a brief overview of the past, the present, and the prospects for the future of energy with a focus on the demand side: energy consumption, particularly petroleum. As discussed in Chapter 2, the story of energy intertwines with international politics that have a dramatic effect on energy markets. We will see the impact of price shocks on petroleum demand. Our discussion begins with a brief history of energy usage in the United States, followed by coverage of energy consumption in the five primary sectors: transportation, power, residential, commercial, and industrial. We move on to a global viewpoint

and investigate recent trends in world energy consumption. We then focus on petroleum supply and pricing. Finally, we peer into our crystal ball and examine future forecasts of energy demand before providing a conclusion.

A BRIEF HISTORY OF ENERGY USAGE IN THE UNITED STATES

Most of the major changes in the history of energy span the history of the United States. This history is rather short when you realize that it only spans four life-times and that each of the four would see a very different picture in terms of the source of energy used. The U.S. Energy Information Administration (EIA) recently published historical estimates of U.S. energy use since 1775. It fails to estimate any sources of energy except wood before 1850. We will mention a few.

Until 1850, wood dominated U.S. energy use both for heat and later to gen-erate steam to power ships and factories. However, there were other sources of energy besides wood. Coal was just beginning its rise. In 1850, the total horse-power of all prime movers in the United States was 8.495 million, of which 5.960 million was provided by horses and other work animals. That year Mark Twain (Samuel Langhorne Clemens) was a lad of 15. Merchant ships had a total estimated horsepower of 725,000 of which 325,000 used wood and in some cases coal, but 400,000 horsepower was from sailing vessels still powered by wind. Factories used about 1.150 million horsepower, and windmills generated roughly 14,000 horse-power that year. Also missing in the oldest EIA data is energy from water-powered gristmills and factories. It was not uncommon for a single water-powered wheel to provide mechanical energy to several factories spinning yarn and thread or to power sawmills.

In 1859, Colonel E. L. Drake struck oil in the tiny village of Titusville, Pennsylvania. This event marked the beginning of the oil industry in the United States. However, it was another 60 years before oil became a major player in sup-plying energy in the United States.[1]

As shown in Exhibit 3.1, by 1885 coal was making inroads into wood's mar-ket share and made up 50.3 percent of estimated energy consumption followed by wood at 47.5 percent, with natural gas and petroleum at 1.5 percent and 0.75 per-cent respectively. Thirty years later in 1915, coal was king with 75.0 percent market share followed by wood at 9.5 percent, petroleum at 8.0 percent, and natural gas at 3.3 percent. The developing hydroelectric industry attained 3.3 percent of the market.

Exhibit 3.2 shows U.S. energy consumption by primary fuel based on quadrillion Btu.[2] Coal use peaked at 15.5 quadrillion Btu (Quads) in 1920 before declining during the Great Depression to 10.6 Quads in 1930. With World War II came an end to the Great Depression and a second peak in coal use at 16.0 Quads. Coal did not achieve this level again until the mid-1950s.

Petroleum use grew throughout most of the Depression. Increased use of petroleum for transportation, power generation, and heating along with the use of natural gas for heat and power caused coal's share of the market to drop from almost 60 percent to below 20 percent. Natural gas and petroleum burned cleaner

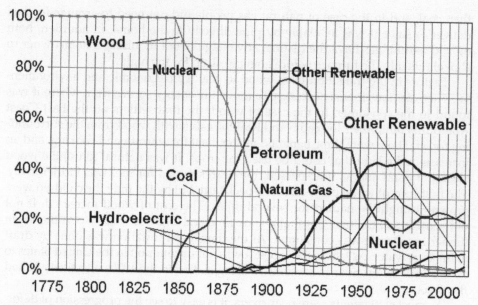

Exhibit 3.1   Market Share—Consumption by Primary Fuel from 1775 to 2011
Source: WTRG Economics and the EIA.

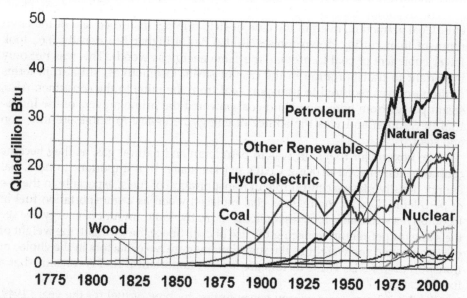

Exhibit 3.2   Estimated U.S. Energy Consumption by Primary Fuel from 1775 to 2011
Source: WTRG Economics and the EIA.

than coal, and in the case of natural gas people did not need to arrange for fuel deliveries since it was available by pipe directly to the home. In addition, both oil and natural gas have the distinct advantage of not requiring a homeowner to shovel fuel into the furnace before going to sleep for the night.

Factors in the transition from wood to coal were economic and environmental. Then, as now, it was necessary to move the energy source from where it was found to the consumer. In the case of wood, the first settlers on the East Coast would first build their log cabin and heat the cabin with wood from the surrounding forest. There were three benefits: shelter, heat for warmth and cooking, and an increase in the land that could be used for crops. It was natural to use the wood closest at hand and as time passed, the nearest wood for fuel was farther away. The first cord of wood came from the backyard, but by the time the children were grown, it might be hauled for several miles. The cost of wood increased. It not only cost to fell the tree, but it also took time and expense to transport the fallen timber to where it was consumed. At the time, transportation was done by draft animals or water. As late as the 1950s, it was not uncommon in the United States to float timber down river to sawmills, but legislation in the 1970s effectively halted the practice.

As most settlements were near rivers, it is easy to see the progression of deforestation. The natural tendency would be to use the forest closest to the water. When Samuel Clemens was riding paddle wheelers on the Mississippi, the wood for the boilers usually came from timber closest to the Mississippi. The effect of removing the timber near the river increased runoff, which caused the river to widen, become more shallow and thus, less navigable.

The transition from wood to coal provided economic and environmental benefits. Coal extraction, even in the case of strip mining, disturbed less of the environment than cutting down forests. It also had a higher Btu density (i.e., took fewer cubic feet of coal to provide the same energy as wood). This was not only important to transportation in the case of steam locomotives, but also in terms of the resources required to transport coal from the mine to the consumer. Also, steam power from both wood and coal powered the prime movers of the Industrial Revolution and was the source of energy necessary to refine ore into iron and steel.

The next major fuel shift was to petroleum and natural gas, as they became central in the erosion of King Coal's market share. It is important to note that energy density plays a central role in transportation of fuels, especially in the use of petroleum. One of the reasons coal replaced wood as a transportation fuel in locomotives was that it took less space to carry the same amount of energy. We see the same for petroleum replacing the use of coal. Space, fuel weight, the weight of the engine, and the weight of the fuel container are major factors in the choice of transportation fuels. These factors are far less important if fuel is consumed at a fixed location.

Exhibit 3.3 compares energy consumption by type of fuel for the years 1949, 1978, 1998, and 2010 in the United States.[3] In 1949, shortly after World War II, petroleum consumption was roughly 37 percent of total U.S. energy consumption. By 1978, at 48 percent petroleum was the source of almost half of U.S. energy production. By 1983 (just five years later), the percentage dropped to 41 percent as a result of the oil price shocks in the 1970s. In 1998, petroleum consumption was at

Exhibit 3.3 A Comparison of Energy Consumption by Fuel: 1949, 1978, 1998, and 2010 (in %; numbers may not sum to 100% due to rounding)

Fuel	1949	1978	1998	2010
Coal	37.46	17.26	22.83	21.24
Petroleum	37.15	47.60	38.81	36.70
Natural gas	16.09	25.08	24.07	25.15
Nuclear	0.00	3.79	7.45	8.61
Renewable fuels				
Biomass	4.84	2.55	3.09	4.38
Hydroelectric	4.45	3.68	3.48	2.56
Solar	0.00	0.00	0.07	0.11
Wind	0.00	0.00	0.03	0.94
Geothermal	0.00	0.04	0.18	0.22

Source: WTRG Economics and the EIA.

39 percent of energy use and by 2010, it was down to 37 percent. Of the renewable fuels, solar, wind, and geothermal are the only ones to provide a greater percentage of energy consumption between 1949 and 2010.

Exhibit 3.4 shows total U.S. energy consumption by primary fuel over the period 1949 through 2011 based on quadrillion Btu. Over the last thirty years, the rate of growth in energy consumption was far slower than it was before 1978.

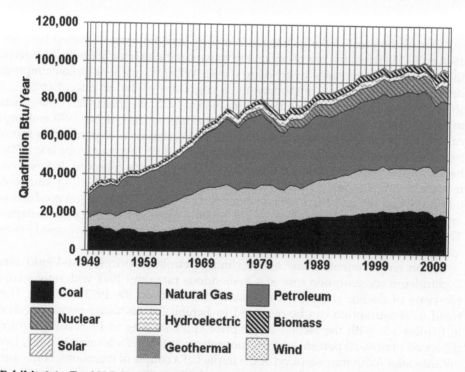

Exhibit 3.4 Total U.S. Energy Consumption by Primary Fuel from 1949 to 2011
Source: WTRG Economics and the EIA.

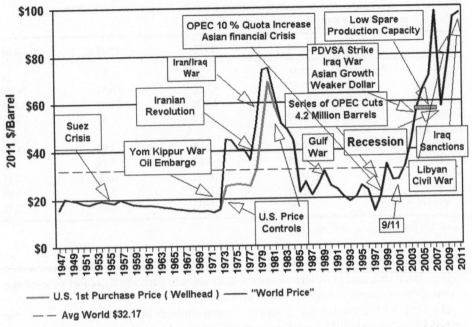

Exhibit 3.5   World Crude Oil Price since 1947 in 2011 Dollars from 1947 to June 2011
Source: WTRG Economics and the EIA.

One of the most striking changes in energy consumption happened between 1948 and 1958 when the use of coal in the transportation sector fell from 20 percent to zero when locomotives switched to diesel. Why? As we look at consumption detail for petroleum, it is important to be cognizant of the oil price. Exhibit 3.5 shows the price of oil in 2011 dollars. From 1948 to 1972, the price in real dollars was in decline and often below $20 per barrel in real terms. The October 1973 embargo caused the price to more than double, and the combination of production losses from the Iranian Revolution and the Iraq-Iran War, which followed in the late 1970s, had a similar impact. The price collapse of the early 1980s followed. Prices were moderate until the early 2000s when the PDVSA[4] strike and the Iraq War took oil off the market, and there was an extended period of low spare oil production capacity. In 2008, the financial crisis and ensuing recession led to a price collapse. The Libyan civil war in 2011 and the drop in production that followed caused prices to return to the level of 2008.

In an environment of low and declining petroleum prices, post–World War II petroleum consumption rose at a tremendous rate until 1978 with only a couple years of decline during the recession that followed the 1973 embargo. This trend in consumption can be observed in Exhibit 3.4 discussed previously and in Exhibit 3.5. With the second major price spike starting in 1978, consumption collapsed almost 20 percent and did not return to the 1978 level until 1998, two decades later. With the exception of the impact of a couple of recessions, consumption increased through 2007 when it reached 20.6 million barrels per day (b/d). Largely because of the financial crisis, recession, and weak recovery, consumption

declined and is currently at about the same level as 1978. In almost 34 years, net growth in petroleum consumption is essentially zero.

U.S. ENERGY CONSUMPTION BY SECTOR

Next, we discuss U.S. energy consumption trends by sector with a focus on petroleum. We begin with transportation, followed by power, commercial, residential, and industrial. There are a few lessons from the 20 percent decline in overall U.S. petroleum consumption between 1978 and 1983 that apply today; we will discuss these trends by sector. Exhibit 3.6 shows U.S. petroleum consumption by sector in thousands of barrels per day for the period 1949 to 2011. As shown, the largest overall growth and greatest changes have occurred in the transportation sector.

Consumption in the Transportation Sector

Because of the current price advantage, natural gas is under consideration as a replacement for petroleum in the transportation sector. If successful, it would not be the first time for a major shift in fuels. In 1949, petroleum's market share of transportation was only 77 percent with coal representing almost 22 percent of the market. It only took a decade for petroleum to replace coal in locomotives. Most of the change took place within a five-year period. The movement away from coal took place at a time when energy use for transportation was on the rise, diesel was replacing coal for locomotives, and petroleum was providing additional energy

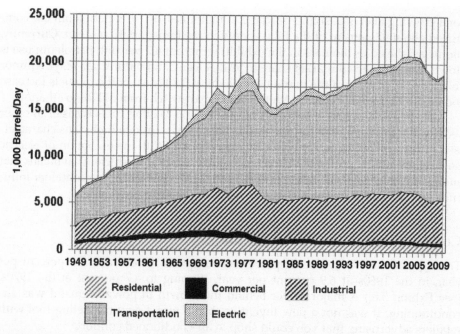

Exhibit 3.6 U.S. Petroleum Consumption by sector from 1949 to 2011
Source: WTRG Economics and the EIA.

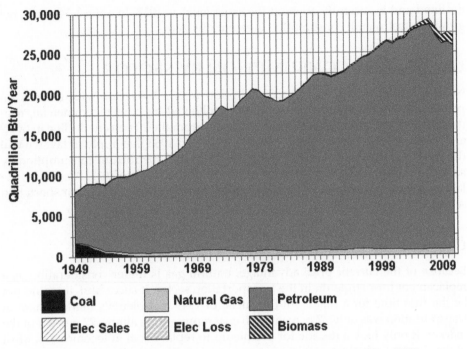

Exhibit 3.7   Transportation Sector Consumption by Fuel Type from 1949 to 2011
Source: WTRG Economics and the EIA.

for a growing fleet of gasoline-powered automobiles. By 1978, petroleum use comprised about 97 percent of the total energy in the transportation sector. Currently, biofuels (labeled as biomass in the exhibit) represent 4.2 percent, petroleum use is down from 97 percent market share to 92.8 percent, and natural gas plays a minor role with 2.7 percent of the market. (See Exhibit 3.7.) Most of the biofuels increase took place in the last decade with the mandated switch from MTBE to ethanol.

As we will see, fuel switching from petroleum to other fuels is easier in other sectors. Energy use in the transportation sector has a unique if obvious characteristic. Consumption does not occur in a fixed place. With the exception of electric rail systems, fuel for transportation is carried onboard the vehicle. That means that energy density and the weight and size of the tank or other energy container influence fuel choice. These are not major factors in the other sectors.

Consumption in the Power Sector

Throughout the 1950s, electric power consumption increased at 5.9 percent per year, in the 1960s at 6.9 percent per year, slipping to 4.7 percent in the 1970s. (See Exhibit 3.8.) A major driver behind the growth in power demand was air-conditioning. It was not a new invention, but it was a new marketing tool with retailers advertising that you could shop in air-conditioned comfort.

Until the mid-1960s, petroleum use by the electric power sector was less than a quarter of a million barrels per day. (See Exhibit 3.9.) From the mid-1960s

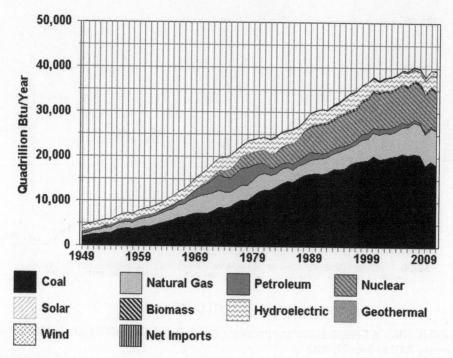

Exhibit 3.8 Energy Consumption by the Electric Power Sector from 1949 to 2011
Source: WTRG Economics and the EIA.

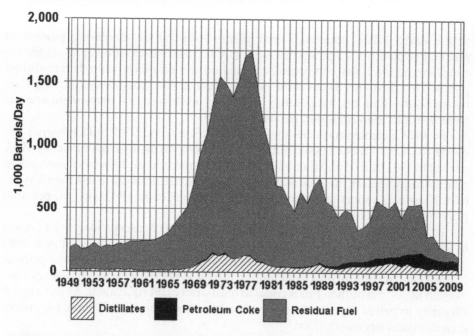

Exhibit 3.9 U.S. Petroleum Consumption by the Electric Power Sector from 1949 to 2011
Source: WTRG Economics and the EIA.

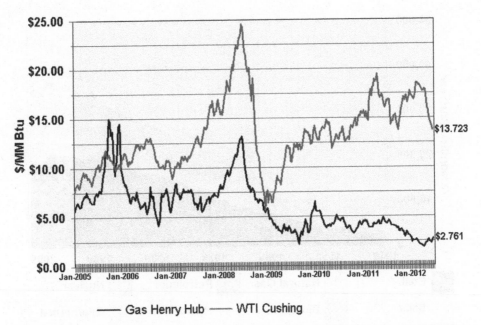

Exhibit 3.10 A Comparison of the Prices of Crude Oil and Natural Gas on a Btu Basis from January 2005 to June 27, 2012
Source: WTRG Economics and the EIA.

to the early 1970s, petroleum-fired plants supplied an increasing portion of power. Petroleum-fired plants are especially suited to service power needs for air-conditioning loads since they can be cycled on and off much faster than coal-fired plants. This flexibility is desirable as the power needed for air-conditioning fluctuates hourly with the temperature. They require less capital investment and are faster to build than coal-fired plants.

By 1978, petroleum use by power companies reached 1.747 million barrels per day (b/d), which was a 1.506 million b/d (625 percent) increase over 1960. By 1985, use fell to 478,000 b/d and fluctuated near that number until 2006 when high prices relative to competing fuels like natural gas and coal reduced use to less than 200,000 b/d. There was a short-lived increase in the latter half of the 1980s after the nominal price of crude fell to $10 in 1986.

In 2011, use only averaged 129,000 b/d. Since 2005, except for a brief period in the winter of 2008–2009, the price of petroleum was too high to compete with natural gas. This is clearly illustrated in Exhibit 3.10, which compares the price of natural gas to crude oil on a $ per million Btu (MM Btu) basis using the energy conversion factor: 5.8 million Btu is equal to one barrel of oil equivalent. As shown, the disparity in prices is evident, and crude oil has been consistently more expensive on a Btu basis since early 2006.

Even if oil prices drop to $60 and natural gas prices more than double to $5.00, there will be no financial incentive to switch from natural gas to petroleum for the foreseeable future. The outlook for petroleum consumption in the power sector is

for consumption to stay below 200,000 b/d and more likely approach 100,000. In 2011, it provided less than 1 percent of the fuel consumed to generate electricity.

The lesson from the use of fuel in the power sector is that major shifts can occur in as little as five years. As shown in Exhibit 3.9, in the two-decade period beginning in 1963, petroleum consumption went from 250,000 b/d to 1.7 million b/d and back to 500,000 b/d. The rise was slower than the fall because it required the construction of new petroleum-fired power plants. In a sense, it served as a bridge to the increased use of nuclear energy and natural gas, but the collapse was primarily driven by price.

Consumption in the Commercial and Residential Sectors

Residential and commercial use of petroleum is relatively small and currently accounts for only 5.4 percent of petroleum usage as shown earlier in Exhibit 3.4. These sectors' share of the petroleum market steadily declined since the peak of 17.7 percent in 1961.

Residential Sector

In the residential sector, consumption does not include gasoline or diesel for vehicle use, which are instead included in the transportation sector, but rather those fuels consumed on premises. As illustrated in Exhibit 3.11, from 1949 to 1979 petroleum accounted for 20 percent or more of the energy consumed by households. In 1973, the year of the oil embargo and first price spike, petroleum represented 26.8 percent

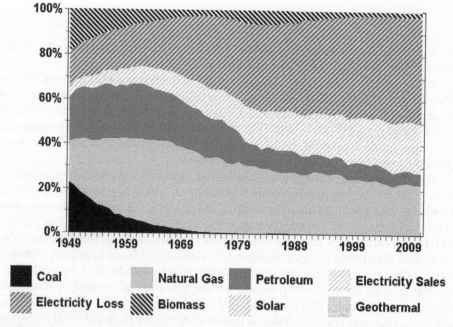

Exhibit 3.11 Residential Energy Consumption by Fuel from 1949 to 2011
Source: WTRG Economics and the EIA.

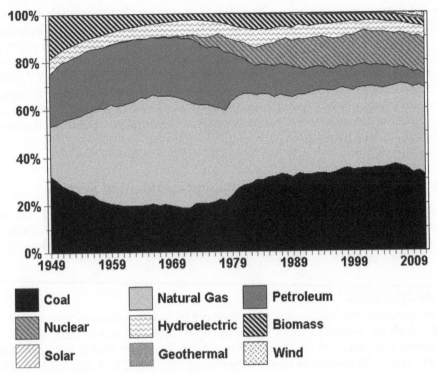

Exhibit 3.12   Residential Energy Consumption by Primary Fuel from 1949 to 2011
Source: WTRG Economics and the EIA.

of total residential consumption. By that year coal, which provided over 20 percent of household energy in 1949, had virtually disappeared.

Until the late 1970s, most petroleum for residential use was heating oil. The price spike of the late 1970s resulted in many residences switching from heating oil to natural gas as shown in Exhibit 3.11. Consumption of heating oil fell from 938,000 barrels per day to 435,000 b/d in 1983. Another contributor to lower consumption was better home insulation. It was mandated in new homes, and consumers were given tax subsidies to insulate existing structure.

By 2011, the use of coal by the residential sector disappeared, and petroleum is minimal. By far the greatest source of energy is electricity, and only a third of the energy that goes into the generation of the power is delivered to the consumer. Exhibit 3.12 shows the energy consumed by the residential sector by the primary fuel. In this exhibit, the fuel used by the power plants replaces the delivered electricity and the system losses in Exhibit 3.11. Exhibit 3.12 leads to entirely different conclusions, but more accurate than those implied by Exhibit 3.11. Instead of disappearing from the residential sector, we see that over 30 percent of residential energy use still comes from coal. That is the same percentage as in 1949. The main difference between 1949 and today is that in 1949 most of the residential consumption of coal occurred at the residence. Today, the residential sector consumes its coal indirectly at the power generation plant.

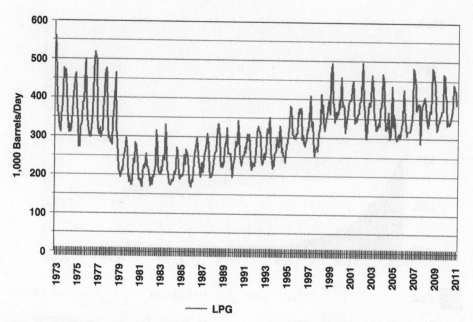

Exhibit 3.13 Liquid Petroleum Gas (LPG) Consumption in the Residential Sector from January 1973 to March 2012
Source: WTRG Economics and the EIA.

Residential use of petroleum is predominately for heating as evidenced by the seasonal variation in heating oil use. Some of the winter consumption shows up in the summer as people fill up their tanks ahead of winter use or to replenish inventory. This is a good strategy when crude oil prices are stable, as the price spread between distillates (heating oil and diesel) and crude oil tends to be lower in the summer because of low demand.

Residential use of propane (see Exhibit 3.13) also felt the impact of fuel switching and the effect of more efficient insulation and furnaces. Consumption fell from 396,000 b/d in 1978 to 224,000 b/d in 1982. Unlike heating oil, propane consumption in the residential sector increased from 1982 through 2000 to a peak of 427,000 b/d and remained relatively flat at 378,000 b/d in 2011. In areas where natural gas is not available, propane replaced heating oil in many cases.

Why did propane use remain strong and not decline like heating oil? The answer is twofold. First propane is more versatile than heating oil. It is used for cooking and in hot water heaters as well as for heating. Second, like heating oil it is ideal for rural applications where natural gas lines are not available and may reflect the large number of families who want to live farther out than the suburbs.

Commercial Sector

The commercial sector is a broad category including stores, office buildings, government offices, hospitals, and universities. Compared to the residential sector energy, use by the commercial sector showed similar but more extreme changes as shown in Exhibit 3.14. In 1949, coal accounted for 42 percent of energy use in the

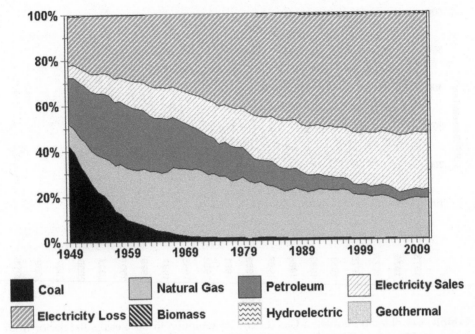

Exhibit 3.14 Commercial Sector Energy Consumption by Fuel from 1949 to 2011
Source: WTRG Economics and the EIA.

commercial sector, but by 1978 coal use was under 2 percent. Petroleum moved from a 20 percent to a 14 percent market share in the same period and is under 4 percent today.

Electricity's share of the market increased significantly in the early years. It was responsible for most of the commercial sector's energy consumption growth in the 1950s and 1960s. Much of the change was due to increased use of air-conditioning in commercial buildings. Coal and petroleum were primarily for heating while natural gas was also used in restaurants, hospitals, and schools for cooking.

As shown in Exhibit 3.14, coal was phased out and later petroleum. There were two major factors: air pollution and price. The old coal furnaces covered cities with soot. Petroleum-fired plants also created pollution problems, but these were not as great as coal. With the second oil price spike in the late 1970s, commercial buildings found petroleum to be too expensive, leading to fuel switching from oil to natural gas and electricity.

Residual fuel oil, which is more viscous and contains more sulfur than distillate fuel oil, lost more of the market than the distillates in the late 1970s price spike. Between 1978 and 1983, residual fuel oil use in this sector fell to 91,000 b/d from 311,000 b/d in 1978 and currently stands at 32,000 b/d. In the past 35 years, residual fuel oil consumption fell almost 90 percent. A chart of the primary fuels used to supply the commercial sector would show different results with coal having a significant market share.

Overall, we see similar patterns in the nontransportation sectors we examined. Petroleum use fell with high prices, partially due to increased efficiency, but primarily because of fuel switching. The changes are more or less permanent. These

three sectors share a common characteristic with the industrial sector in that consumption in all of these sectors takes place at a fixed location.

Consumption in the Industrial Sector

Approximately 21 percent of total U.S. energy consumption was in the industrial sector in 2011. The largest user of energy is the bulk chemicals industry, which represented 21 percent of total energy consumption in the industrial sector in 2011. According to data published by the EIA, collectively, energy-intensive manufacturing industries (e.g., bulk chemicals, refining, paper products, iron and steel, aluminum, food, glass, and cement) produce slightly more than one-quarter of the total dollar value of industrial shipments while accounting for nearly two-thirds of industrial delivered energy consumption. Over the 2008 to 2009 recession, we attribute most of the decline in petroleum consumption in the industrial sector to a weaker economy with some fuel switching to natural gas.

Overall, there are several lessons to be learned about energy consumption from 30 years ago and the recent recession. Every sector except transportation has significant declines in petroleum consumption compared to 30 years ago. The industrial sector declined the least because it uses petroleum as a feedstock for raw material for the products it manufactures.

So why has transportation been the only sector to continually increase petroleum consumption? The fundamental difference between the transportation sector and the others is that it does not consume petroleum in a fixed place. Automobiles, trucks, trains, airplanes, and ships all carry their energy with them. Liquid fuels have a high Btu density and are an efficient way with respect to volume and weight to carry your energy with you. To compete, alternative fuels and their containers need to have comparable size and weight to a gasoline tank and be able to deliver enough energy to travel 350–400 miles without refueling. Until then, fuel switching is very limited. With over 70 percent of petroleum consumption for transportation, this sector must be the point of focus for reducing dependence on imported petroleum.

Next, we turn our focus to world petroleum consumption.

OVERVIEW OF WORLD PETROLEUM CONSUMPTION, SUPPLY, AND PRICES

Following the depth of the 2007–2009 recession, world demand returned to a growth path until 2011 when the rate of increase began to slow (see Exhibit 3.15). Consumption only increased 780,000 barrels per day in 2011 compared to an average annual gain of 1.3 million b/d from 1995 to 2007. Growth is expected to average between 900,000 and a million b/d in 2012 assuming Europe's recession does not spread to the United States.

Exhibit 3.16 presents petroleum consumption in developed countries (OECD).[5] Consumption has not recovered from the recession, averaging 45.6 million b/d in 2011, which is down 540,000 b/d from the prior year. Consumption will likely fall an average of 300,000–400,000 b/d in 2012 unless the economies recover.

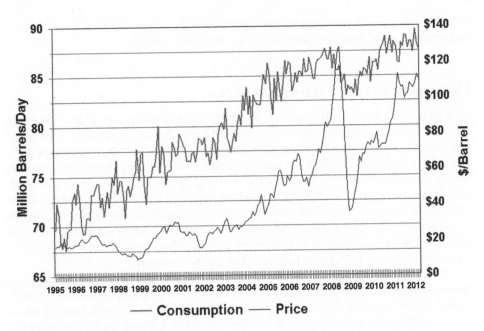

Exhibit 3.15   World Petroleum Consumption from January 1995 to April 2012
Source: WTRG Economics and the EIA.

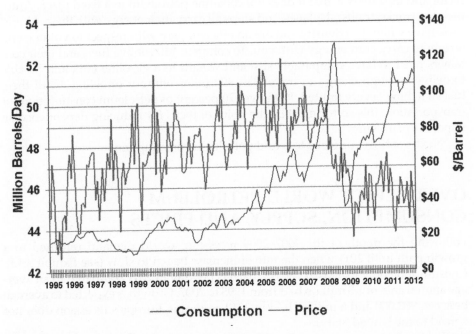

Exhibit 3.16   Petroleum Consumption in OECD Countries from January 1995 to April 2012
Source: WTRG Economics and the EIA.

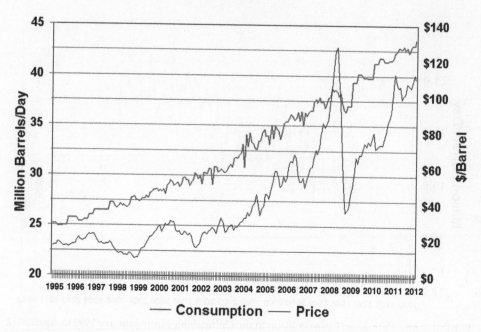

Exhibit 3.17 Petroleum Consumption in Non-OECD Countries from January 1995 to April 2012
Source: WTRG Economics and the EIA.

The post-recession gains in world petroleum use are concentrated in the non-OECD countries as shown in Exhibit 3.17. After the dip in 2008 and early 2009, non-OECD use returned to what is almost a trend line. In the past eight years, the average increase was 1.4 million b/d per year compared with an average annual decline in the OECD countries of 400,000 b/d over the same period.

OECD Petroleum Consumption Detail

As shown in Exhibit 3.18, U.S. demand peaked in 2006 and 2007, and has declined every year since with the exception of a small increase in 2010. Demand declined 300,000 b/d in 2011 and continues to slide in 2012.

In contrast, consumption in Canada has been relatively flat since the recession and will likely stay near 2.2 million b/d in 2012 as well. As a net exporter of petroleum, Canada sees benefits from higher oil prices. Canadian exports would be greater with the XL pipeline from Canada to the Gulf Coast. European OECD demand continues down with the weak European economy. It was down 300,000 b/d in 2011 and should match 2012 as well (see Exhibit 3.19).

The only country really breaking the pattern is Japan. In its drive for efficiency, Japanese consumption has declined by a little over 10,000 b/d every year in recent years. Because of the need to use oil-fired power plants to replace electricity from the tsunami-damaged nuclear facilities, petroleum use was up marginally in 2011 and should be a few thousand b/d higher in 2012.

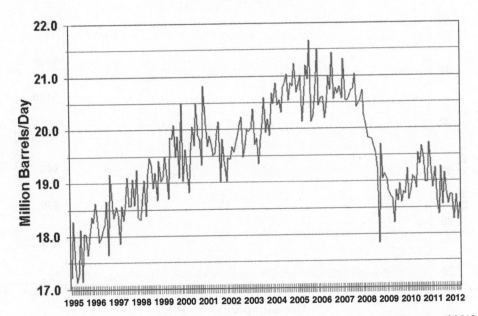

Exhibit 3.18   Petroleum Consumption in the United States from January 1995 to April 2012
Source: WTRG Economics and the EIA.

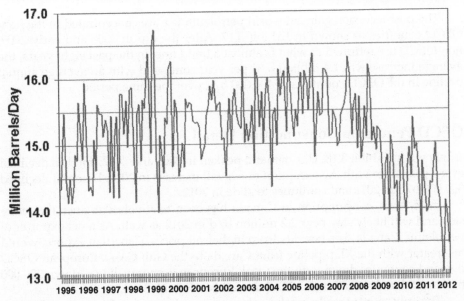

Exhibit 3.19   Petroleum Consumption in OECD European Countries from January 1995 to April 2012
Source: WTRG Economics and the EIA.

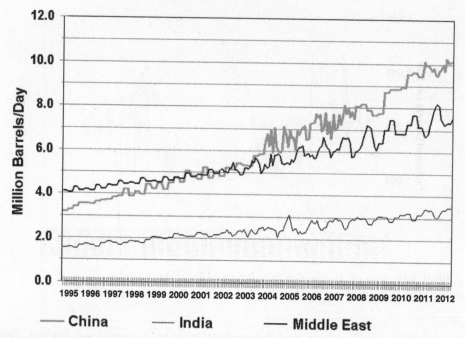

Exhibit 3.20 Petroleum Consumption in China, India, and the Middle East from January 1995 to April 2012
Source: WTRG Economics and the EIA.

Non-OECD Petroleum Consumption Detail

Petroleum consumption in China, India, and the Middle East continued to grow as shown in Exhibit 3.20 over the period 1995 to 2012. Consumption in China was up almost a half million b/d in 2011 following 850,000 b/d in 2010, and the 2012 overall increase is expected to be one-half million.

India's consumption continues to grow and was up about 160,000 b/d in 2011 with estimates of 100,000 b/d growth in 2012. The Middle East may soon see abatement in its rate of growth as countries seek alternatives to generating electric power from petroleum. In 2011, consumption only increased 240,000 b/d, and the gains may be slightly lower by the end of 2012.

Supply and Prices

Exhibit 3.5, presented earlier, illustrates oil prices in 2011 dollars with some of the major events that caused price movements. In particular, we see that major supply interruptions lead to spikes in oil prices. The October 1973 embargo was a response by many Muslim countries to embargo shipments of crude oil to the United States and other nations that supported Israel in the Yom Kippur war. The price run-up of the late 1970s was a result of two supply interruptions. The first was a drop in Iranian production due to the Iranian revolution. While production dropped dramatically two-thirds was restored within a few months. Before it could fully

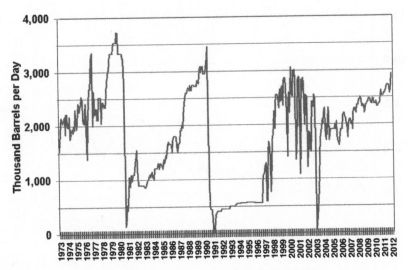

Exhibit 3.21 Iraq Oil Production from January 1973 to April 2012
Source: WTRG Economics and the EIA.

recover, Iraq attacked Iran, and the production of both countries collapsed. This drove prices to the highest level in current dollars since 1859. See Exhibits 3.21 and 3.22. The next price spike comes with the Gulf War when Iraq invades Kuwait in 1990. Once again Iraqi production and exports collapse, but this time with Kuwaiti production (Exhibit 3.23) instead of Iran. The PDVSA strike from December 2002 through February 2003 and the invasion of Iraq in 2003 were the proximate causes of the next major upward move in prices. See Exhibits 3.24 and 3.21.

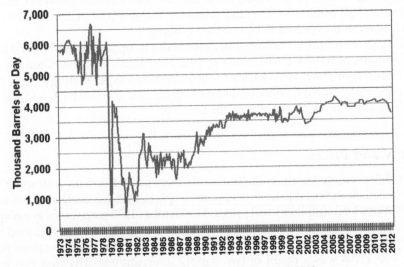

Exhibit 3.22 Iran Oil Production from January 1973 to April 2012
Source: WTRG Economics and the EIA.

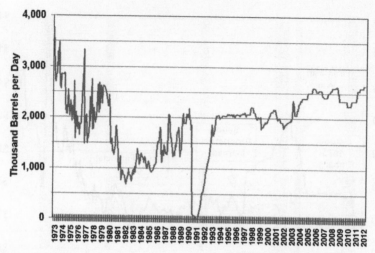

Exhibit 3.23   Kuwait Oil Production from January 1973 to April 2012
Source: WTRG Economics and the EIA.

As shown in Exhibit 3.25, major supply interruptions lead to price spikes, and sharply higher oil prices can be a major contributor to recessions. However, that same exhibit indicates that recessions lead to lower oil prices. For example, the rising prices in the late 1970s and the back-to-back recessions of the early 1980s led to a drop of almost 20 percent in U.S. consumption between 1978 and 1983. There was a similar reaction in other developed countries. It took the United States two decades to return to the 1978 level of consumption. The situation was similar but not as extreme in most developed countries. The lower level of consumption led to a price collapse. The 2008 recession with its anemic recovery has had a similar impact on OECD consumption and with European weakness, this has put downward pressure on oil prices in the second quarter of 2012.

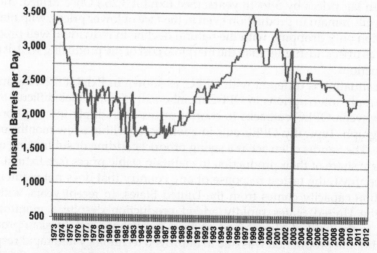

Exhibit 3.24   Venezuela Oil Production from January 1973 to April 2012
Source: WTRG Economics and the EIA.

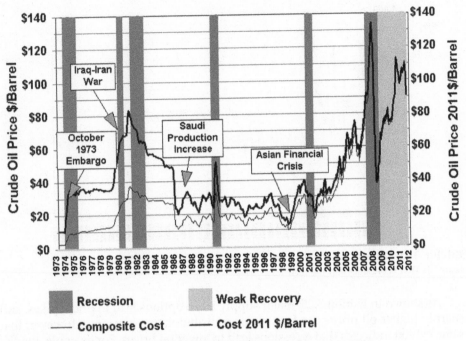

Exhibit 3.25 Recessions and Oil Prices from January 1973 to June 2012
Sources: NBER, EIA, St. Louis Fed, WTRG Economics.

Oil production in all countries lags prices to varying degrees. Rising prices attract more exploration and drilling, but new discoveries may take years to come on line. By the time the wells are in production and connected to the infrastructure, the price environment is often different. Peaks and troughs in non-OPEC production often lag prices by 5 to 10 years. (See Exhibit 3.26.) Once drilled, most non-OPEC wells remain in production even in the face of lower prices, with non-OPEC production only dropping with the natural decline in individual well production. As long as prices are higher than the marginal cost of the producing well, it remains in production.

The situation is different with OPEC, as shown in Exhibit 3.27. Because of so many supply interruptions in OPEC members, it is sometimes difficult to distinguish between OPEC cutbacks to control prices and supply interruptions in the overall graph. Typically, OPEC cuts in quota occur within a few months of a price collapse. The Saudis often act as a swing producer adding or subtracting a disproportionate share of their production to maintain stable prices (see Exhibit 3.28).

In contrast, the fastest response of any country that does not maintain spare production capacity comes from the United States. In recent years, with higher prices the United States rapidly added production despite a moratorium on drilling in the Gulf of Mexico and declines in offshore and Alaskan production. The additional production was due to improved technology and rapid response to higher prices. All of the gains were onshore in the lower 48 states (see Exhibit 3.29), primarily in shale or other tight formations.

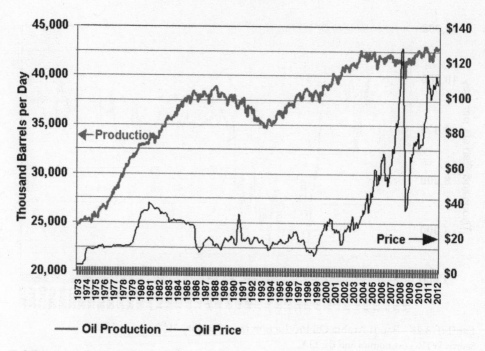

Exhibit 3.26 Non-OPEC Oil Production from January 1973 to April 2012
Source: WTRG Economics and the EIA.

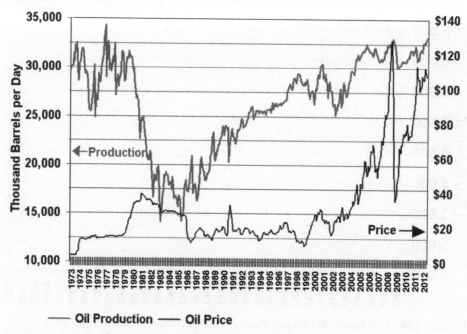

Exhibit 3.27 OPEC Oil Production from January 1973 to April 2012
Source: WTRG Economics, OPEC, and the EIA.

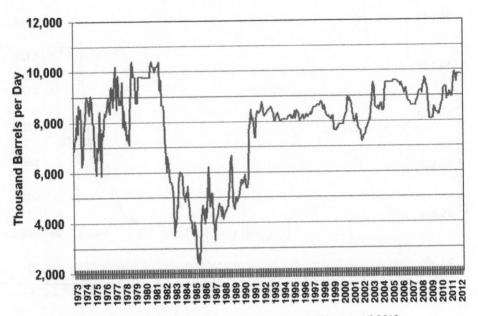

Exhibit 3.28 Saudi Arabia Oil Production from January 1973 to April 2012
Source: WTRG Economics and the EIA.

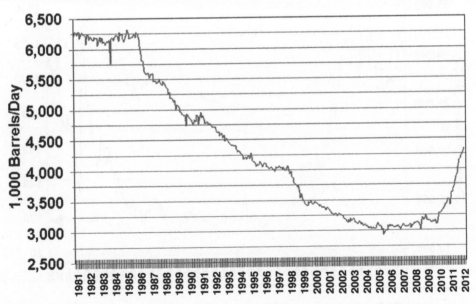

Exhibit 3.29 U.S. Lower 48 Onshore Production from January 1981 to April 2012
Source: WTRG Economics and the EIA.

For more information on past and present energy supply, there are a number of good sources. One excellent source is the International Energy Agency (IEA), which publishes the *Oil Market Report,* a vital analytical tool for analyzing the fundamentals (the true balance of supply and demand) in the market. Exhibit 3.30 shows the world oil supply and demand published by the IEA as of June 2012. Two more resources that provide a short-term energy outlook on a monthly basis are the EIA's *Short-Term Energy Outlook* and OPEC's *Monthly Oil Report* available at www.eia.gov and www.opec.org respectively.[6]

PROSPECTS FOR THE FUTURE

Most forecasts of future global energy demand show that sustaining even modest economic growth worldwide will require massive new investments in energy, particularly oil and natural gas (see OPEC 2011, EIA 2012b, API 2012, ExxonMobil 2012, and BP 2012).[7] This topic is also discussed in Chapter 2, "Geopolitical and World Energy Markets." Panels A and B of Exhibit 3.31 contain forecasts for future U.S. and world energy demand published in the most recent EIA report (see EIA 2012b). These forecasts by the EIA and the API (see API 2012) for the year 2035 can be briefly summarized as follows:

- The rate of growth in energy use slows over the projection period, reflecting moderate population growth, an extended economic recovery, and increasing energy efficiency in end-use applications.
- Natural gas production increases throughout the projection period, allowing the United States to transition from a net importer to a net exporter of natural gas.
- Total energy-related emissions of carbon dioxide in the United States remain below their 2005 level through 2035.
- Sustaining a 3.4 percent annual rate of growth in the global economy will require about 26.5 million more barrels per day in global oil supplies. This is equivalent to more than doubling the current consumption of North America.
- Although the share of non-fossil fuels is growing, oil, natural gas, and coal will continue to play leading roles and are expected to supply approximately 77 percent of U.S. energy needs and 79 percent of world energy needs by 2035.
- Approximately 8 percent of U.S. energy needs were supplied by renewable energy sources in 2010, and this is expected to grow to 14 percent by 2035. For the various renewable fuels, the amounts of U.S. energy supplied are (2010 versus 2035): solar energy (0.01 percent versus 0.2 percent), hydroelectric (2.62 percent versus 2.8 percent), geothermal energy (0.2 percent versus 0.5 percent), biomass (4.4 percent versus 9.4 percent), and wind energy (0.9 percent versus 1.7 percent).

CONCLUSION

This chapter has focused on the past, the present, and the prospects for the future of energy, with an emphasis on consumption. As discussed in the chapter, oil and

Exhibit 3.30 World Oil Supply and Demand

	(Million Barrels per Day)				
	2008	2009	2010	2011	2012E
OECD DEMAND					
North America	24.2	23.3	23.8	23.5	23.3
Europe	15.4	14.7	14.7	14.3	13.9
Pacific	8.1	7.7	7.8	7.9	8.0
Total OECD	47.6	45.6	46.2	45.6	45.2
NON-OECD DEMAND					
FSU	4.2	4.1	4.3	4.6	4.7
Europe	0.8	0.7	0.7	0.8	0.8
China	7.7	7.9	9.0	9.4	9.7
Other Asia	9.8	10.3	10.6	10.9	11.1
Latin America	6.0	6.0	6.4	6.6	6.8
Middle East	7.2	7.4	7.7	7.9	8.1
Africa	3.3	3.4	3.4	3.4	3.5
Total Non-OECD	39.0	39.9	42.1	43.4	44.7
Total Demand[1]	86.7	85.5	88.4	89.1	89.9
OECD SUPPLY					
North America[4]	13.3	13.6	14.1	14.5	15.4
Europe	4.8	4.5	4.1	3.8	3.5
Pacific	0.6	0.6	0.6	0.5	0.5
Total OECD	18.7	18.8	18.8	18.8	19.5
NON-OECD SUPPLY					
FSU	12.8	13.3	13.5	13.6	13.7
Europe	0.1	0.1	0.1	0.1	0.1
China	3.8	3.9	4.1	4.1	4.2
Other Asia[2]	3.7	3.6	3.7	3.6	3.6
Latin America[2,4]	3.7	3.9	4.1	4.2	4.3
Middle East	1.7	1.7	1.7	1.6	1.4
Africa[2]	2.6	2.6	2.5	2.5	2.3
Total Non-OECD	28.4	29.1	29.8	29.8	29.6
Processing Gains[3]	2.0	2.0	2.1	2.2	2.3
Global Biofuels[4]	1.4	1.6	1.9	1.9	1.9
Total Non-OPEC[5]	50.6	51.5	52.6	52.7	53.4
Non-OPEC Historical Composition[2]	49.6	51.5	52.6	52.7	53.4
OPEC					
Crude[6]	31.6	29.1	29.2	29.8	
NGLs	4.5	4.9	5.4	5.8	6.2
Total OPEC	36.1	34.0	34.6	35.6	
OPEC Historical Composition[2]	37.1	34.0	34.6	35.6	
Total Supply[6]	86.7	85.5	87.2	88.3	

[1]Measured as deliveries from refineries and primary stocks, comprises inland deliveries, international marine bunkers, refinery fuel, crude for direct burning, oil from non-conventional sources and other sources of supply.

[2]Other Asia includes Indonesia throughout. Latin America excludes Ecuador throughout. Africa excludes Angola throughout.

Total Non-OPEC excludes all countries that were members of OPEC at 1 January 2009.

Total OPEC comprises all countries which were OPEC members as of 1 January 2009.

[3]Net volumetric gains and losses in the refining process (excludes net gain/loss in former USSR, China, and non-OECD Europe) and marine transportation losses.

[4]As of the July 2010 OMR, Global Biofuels refer to all world biofuel production including fuel ethanol from the US and Brazil.

[5]Non-OPEC supplies include crude oil, condensates, NGL, and non-conventional sources of supply such as synthetic crude, ethanol, and MTBE.

[6]Comprises crude oil, condensates, NGLs, oil from non-conventional sources, and other sources of supply.

Exhibit 3.31 Forecast for Future U.S. and World Energy Demand by the EIA

Panel A: U.S. Energy Demand Forecast

Consumption	2010 Actual		2035		
	Quad Btu	% Share	Quad Btu	% Share	% Change
Oil	36.11	36.8	34.05	31.5	−5.7
Ethanol, biodiesel, and green liquids	1.14	1.2	3.95	3.7	246.5
Natural gas	24.71	25.2	27.11	25.1	9.7
Coal	20.76	21.1	21.57	20.0	3.9
Nuclear power	8.44	8.6	9.35	8.7	10.8
Hydropower	2.51	2.6	3.06	2.8	21.9
Biomass and renewables	4.22	4.3	8.65	8.0	105.0
Other*	0.29	0.3	0.24	0.2	−17.2
Total	98.18	100.0	107.98	100.0	10.0
Oil and natural gas	60.82	61.9	61.16	56.6	0.6
Oil, natural gas, and coal	81.58	83.1	82.73	76.6	1.4

Panel B: World Energy Demand Forecast

Consumption	2008 Actual		2035		
	Quad Btu	% Share	Quad Btu	% Share	% Change
Liquid fuels	173.0	34.3	225.2	29.3	30.2
Coal	139.0	27.5	209.1	27.2	50.5
Natural gas	114.3	22.6	174.7	22.7	52.8
Renewables	51.3	10.2	109.5	14.2	113.5
Nuclear power	27.2	5.4	51.2	6.7	88.6
Total	504.7	100.0	769.8	100.0	52.5
Oil and natural gas	287.3	56.9	399.9	52.0	39.2
Oil, natural gas, and coal	426.3	84.4	609.1	79.1	42.9

*Includes nonbiogenic municipal solid waste and net electricity imports.
Source: EIA (2012b), International Energy Outlook 2011.

natural gas are crucial to the world economy for many years to come, and ours is a hydrocarbon society. We are, in the language of anthropologists and as Yergin (1992) put it: "hydrocarbon man." Other forms of energy are also critical components to meeting demand and are crucial to economies globally. An examination of the history of U.S. energy consumption gives us insight into this complex topic and helps us better understand where to place emphasis in managing our future energy needs. Not only in the United States but also globally, we have observed that energy consumption decreases come from improving efficiency, fuel substitution, conservation, and weak economies.

Going forward, oil, gas, and coal will still play an important role through 2035. In the United States, petroleum independence can most likely be achieved through

a combination of increased domestic production and a decrease in consumption through increased efficiency, conservation, and fuel switching. It is important to promote all sources of energy production and encourage investment in advanced technologies, not just in the United States, but globally. We cannot remain passive to developing our future energy needs.

CHAPTER QUESTIONS

1. Discuss U.S. energy consumption trends by sector (i.e., transportation, power, commercial, residential, and industrial).

2. The largest energy consumption sector in the United States is ___, and the fastest-growing energy consumption sector is ___.

3. For the residential sector, why has propane use remained strong and not declined like heating oil?

4. For the period 1949 through 2011 for the transportation sector, why has overall petroleum use continued to remain strong while other sectors have seen more declines?

5. What event marked the beginning of the oil industry in the United States?

6. How does energy demand growth in OECD countries compare to non-OECD countries? Which two non-OECD countries have the fastest growing demand?

7. According to the forecast for 2035 described in this chapter, what is the fastest growing renewable energy source?

8. Go to the API website at www.api.org and download the latest "Energizing America" report. What are the current energy forecasts for the United States and world future energy needs (both in terms of additional new energy needed and percentage change)? How much is expected to be supplied by oil, natural gas, coal, and renewables?

9. From the API report listed above, list the largest oil companies based on proven reserves. How many of the top 15 are national oil companies, and how many are investor-owned companies?

10. Go to the International Energy Agency (IEA) website and download the latest *Oil Market Report*, which should be available at http://www.iea.org/publications/oilmarketreport/. Investigate the latest supply and demand fundamentals and describe your observations. Describe the main highlights that the report covers. (Note: Go to the IEA main website at www.iea.org if the previous link has changed.)

11. Go to the Energy Information Administration (EIA) website at http://www.eia.gov/ and download the latest *Short-Term Energy Outlook* research report. Skim the report and answer the following questions:
    a. Summarize the energy outlook for the short term.
    b. What is the current supply and demand outlook?
    c. Are there any areas of concern for supply, demand, geopolitics?
    d. What are the current forecasts for gasoline prices, crude oil prices, and natural gas prices for both the United States and globally over the next year? Are prices forecast to increase or decrease? Why?
    e. What are the forecasts for U.S. renewable fuels?

12. What impact did the Iraq-Iran War and the two Gulf wars have on oil supply in Iraq and Kuwait? What happened to oil prices?

13. Discuss whether higher oil prices are a cause of recessions or whether recessions lead to lower oil prices. Describe historical events as examples.

14. In the graphs of real petroleum prices, we used the GDP deflator. Download the composite refiner acquisition price from the EIA website, obtain the GDP deflator and the consumer price index (CPI) and producer prices, then show the real prices of oil in current dollars using each of the price indicators. Discuss the difference in the results and identify the most appropriate deflator to use. (Hints: Do consumers use crude oil? Which producers make up the producer price index, or PPI?)

NOTES

1. Native Americans had known of the oil in western Pennsylvania before this. Like many ancient societies, petroleum seeps were used since prehistoric times. For example, Homer describes petroleum in the *Iliad*, and the Byzantines used it as a major component of Greek fire (Yergin 1992). Petroleum became a major industry following the oil discovery in Titusville. The United States became the largest oil-producing country in the world for a large part of the nineteenth and twentieth centuries, but now is in third place.
2. Btu stands for British thermal unit and is the amount of energy needed to heat 1 pound of water by one degree F. This is an extremely small unit of heat, so more often, it is expressed in the therm which is 100,000 Btu, in million Btu (MM Btu), or the Quad (a quadrillion Btu or 10^{15} Btu).
3. Data has been obtained from WTRG Economics (see www.wtrg.com) and the Energy Information Administration (see http://eia.doe.gov).
4. PDVSA is Petróleos de Venezuela, S.A., the Venezuelan state-owned petroleum company.
5. The Organisation for Economic Co-operation and Development (OECD) is an international economic organization of 34 countries founded in 1961 to stimulate economic progress and world trade. For a list of OECD countries, see www.oecd.org/document/58/0,3746,en_2649_201185_1889402_1_1_1_1,00.html.
6. The OPEC Monthly Oil Market Report covers major issues affecting the world oil market and provides an outlook for crude oil market developments for the coming year. The report provides a detailed analysis of key developments impacting oil market trends in world oil demand, supply, and the oil market balance.
7. For the latest forecasts, the API report is available at www.api.org/energyzingamerica and EIA reports are available at eia.doe.gov. Other energy forecasts are available from the IEA (www.iea.org and www.iea.org/weo/ for the world energy outlook), BP (www.bp.com/energyoutlook) and ExxonMobil (www.exxonmobil.com/Corporate/energy_outlook.aspx). All reports are available for free.

REFERENCES

American Petroleum Institute (API). 2012. "Energizing America: Facts for Addressing Energy Policy." Available at www.api.org/energizingamerica.

Edwards, Brian K. 2003. *The Economics of Hydroelectric Power*. Cheltenham, UK: Edward Elgar Publishing.

Energy Information Administration, Department of Energy. Available at www.eia.gov.

Energy Information Administration (EIA). 2012a. *Annual Energy Outlook 2012 with Projections to 2035*. Report Number DOE/EIA-0383 (June).

Energy Information Administration (EIA). 2012b. *International Energy Outlook 2011 with Projections to 2035*. Report Number DOE/EIA-0484 (September).

Energy Information Administration (EIA). 2012c. *Short-Term Energy Outlook*. Published monthly and available at www.eia.gov.

International Energy Agency (IEA). 2012. *Oil Market Report*. Available at www.iea.org/publications/oilmarketreport/.

International Energy Agency (IEA). Available at www.iea.org.

Organization of Petroleum Exporting Countries (OPEC). 2011. *World Oil Outlook*. Available at www.opec.org.

WTRG Economics. Available at www.wrtg.com.

Yergin, Daniel. 1992. *The Prize: The Epic Quest for Oil, Money, and Power*. New York: Simon & Schuster.

ABOUT THE CONTRIBUTORS

James "Jim" L. Williams is an energy economist and the owner of WTRG Economics, which publishes WTRG's *Energy Economist Newsletter*. Williams started analyzing the energy industry when he forecast petrochemicals as Senior Economist for El Paso's petrochemical division. He has over 30 years of experience using sophisticated economic, statistical, and financial analysis tools to assist clients in analyzing the petroleum and natural gas industries. His current focus is on country risk and the potential for supply interruptions and the impact that new drilling and production technologies will have in mitigating U.S. dependence on imports. Jim has an MS in mathematics from the University of Arkansas and additional graduate studies in abstract mathematics and economics. He taught mathematics at the undergraduate level and economics and finance at the both the undergraduate and graduate levels. He is frequently quoted in the press internationally regarding his expertise about the oil and gas industry and has published in the *Oil and Gas Journal*, *MEER*, as well as several academic publications. His clients and newsletter subscribers include independent and major producers, consumers of energy products, financial intuitions, governments, and the energy trading community.

Betty J. Simkins, PhD, is the Williams Companies Professor of Business and a Professor of Finance in the Department of Finance at Oklahoma State University's Spears School of Business where she teaches energy finance, corporate finance, and enterprise risk management, among other courses. Dr. Simkins received her PhD from Case Western Reserve University (CWRU), MBA from Oklahoma State University, and BS in chemical engineering from the University of Arkansas. She has over 40 publications in academic finance journals and has won awards for her research, most recently in risk management. In addition, Dr. Simkins has won several teaching awards including the Regents Distinguished Teaching Award. She is also very active in the finance profession and currently serves on the Board of Directors for the Financial Management Association, as co-editor of the *Journal of Applied Finance*, as past president of the Eastern Finance Association, and on the editorial boards of several prestigious finance journals. Prior to academia, she worked in the corporate world for Williams Companies and Conoco (now ConocoPhillips). In addition to being co-editor of this book, in 2010 she co-edited *Enterprise Risk Management: Insights and Analysis on Today's Leading Research and Best Practices*, also published by John Wiley & Sons.

CHAPTER 4

Sustainable Energy: Myths and Realities

OLAMIDE O. SHADIYA
Chemical Engineer

JANE A. TALKINGTON
PhD Candidate in Environmental Science, Oklahoma State University

JOHN MOWEN
Emeritus Regents Professor, Spears School of Business, Oklahoma State University

KAREN HIGH
Associate Professor, Department of Chemical Engineering, Oklahoma State University

JOSH L. WIENER
Carson Professor, Department Head, and Director of the Center for Social and Services Marketing at Oklahoma State University

> Wind and wind-generated hydrogen will shape not only the energy sector of the global economy but the global economy itself.
>
> —Lester Brown (Brown 2003)

> ... except for relatively small regions, [wind] cannot become the single largest source, even less so the dominant mode of generation.
>
> —Vaclav Smil (2010, p. 132)

INTRODUCTION

The above quotes were made by two authorities on sustainable energy, yet they are diametrically opposed. Indeed, each guru would call the other's statement a myth. How can two "experts" develop such opposing views? Which is a myth? Or can both statements be true?

The word *myth* swirls around the field of sustainable energy. As used in articles and books, the term connotes a false belief held by a large number of people. Myths can be promulgated by true believers or by individuals and organizations

for purely self-serving reasons. False statements can also be communicated when scientists and pundits fall prey to the confirmation bias—a phenomena in which people gather and recall information in a selective manner so as to confirm a previously held position (Plous 1993).

In this chapter, we investigate the myths and realities of sustainable energy. We begin with an introduction in which we provide a definition of sustainable energy. The next section identifies a series of alleged sustainable energy myths that have been proposed by various pundits and organizations. Of course, implied in these myths is the supposed reality. In the subsequent section, we present the results of a survey of 900 consumers on their perceptions of various aspects of 9 energy sources. From this survey, we identify four potential myths held by consumers about sustainable energy. Then, in the next section we present a model for identifying the sustainability of energy sources. We then apply it to the production of electricity in the United States. This chapter finishes with a set of conclusions and a brief discussion of the importance of setting a time frame when identifying the myths and realities of sustainable energy.

A DEFINITION OF SUSTAINABLE ENERGY

What do we mean by sustainable energy? Numerous definitions can be found in the academic and journalistic literatures. Many are based upon the idea that a sustainable source of energy must be efficient and renewable. Indeed, efficiency and renewability have been called the twin pillars of sustainable energy policy (Prindle and Eldrige 2007).

The Environmental Protection Agency (EPA) does not provide a definition of sustainable energy, but it does identify two broad types of energy—conventional and renewable. Conventional energy sources include oil, natural gas, nuclear, and coal. In contrast, renewable energy sources restore themselves over short periods of time and do not diminish. They include sun, wind, moving water, organic plant and waste material (biomass), and the earth's heat (geothermal). Green energy is a subset of renewable energy and is represented by those renewable energy sources that provide the greatest environmental benefit.

In contrast to previous approaches for defining sustainable energy, we believe that its definition must allow for the continued use of conventional energy sources such as oil, natural gas, and coal. While these resources are finite, they are also the current pillars of the world's economies and, as we will argue, will continue so for the foreseeable future. Because these resources are finite, they will have to be gradually replaced by renewable energy sources over the next 25-plus years. However, they will be sustainable over this time period. Based upon these ideas, we propose the following definition of sustainable energy.

Sustainable energy represents the ability of the world's societies to evolve and grow the mix of resources needed to meet the world's energy needs for present and future generations while also enhancing the environment, the economic viability of the world's nations, and the equitable treatment of people.

This definition fulfills several goals. First, we sought to include in the definition the principles of the triple bottom line: protecting the environment, creating social equity, and enhancing the economies of nations. Second, we wanted to recognize the fact that many of the world's nations are seeking to grow their economies so that their people can achieve a higher standard of living, which inevitably implies increased energy usage. Third, we suggest that the energy sources of the foreseeable future will continue to include the conventional sources presently in use. Fourth, the definition implicitly recognizes that different nations will employ divergent and indigenous sources of energy to meet their needs.

Finally, the definition recognizes that we must not only avoid harming the environment, but also take proactive steps to restore and improve it.

SUSTAINABLE ENERGY MYTHS

In this section, we first identify myths proposed by individuals and organizations. We then present a study that was performed to investigate 900 consumers' perceptions of energy sources.

Myths Identified by Individuals and Organizations

A variety of organizations and individuals have proposed lists of energy myths. Perhaps the most notable are ideas proposed by Vaclav Smil; he identified eight myths in his book, *Energy Myths and Realities*. The myths that he identified are found in Exhibit 4.1. Another effort to identify energy myths is summarized in Exhibit 4.2, which presents 10 energy myths that were identified in a book published by Drew Thornley, *Energy & the Environment: Myths & Factors*. These myths were derived from a survey of 1,000 consumers conducted in January 2009.

As can be seen in Exhibit 4.2, some of the ideas overlap with those of Vaclav Smil. Thus similar points are made on issues related to the likelihood of running out of fossil fuels and to sustainable energy sources having a major impact. In addition, Smil also noted that employment levels are unlikely to increase with a move toward renewable energy sources and that conservation and energy gains will meet future energy needs. Other myths identified by Thornley are highly specific, such as the finding that the majority of his respondents believed that the United States gets most of its oil from the Middle East, that our air is becoming more polluted, and that U.S. forests and landfills are shrinking. Finally, some of the ideas that Thornley identified as myths held by the public are inconsistent with current scientific knowledge as well as current events. These include myths 8, 9, and 10. Recent events reveal that offshore drilling often causes significant environmental damage, that science reveals that the earth is warming at a steady rate, and that science reveals that humans are the main drivers of the greenhouse effect. More will be said about these "myths" in the next section of the chapter.

The organizations that published the books by Smil and by Thornley are both known as fitting on the conservative side of the political spectrum. As one would expect, one finds substantial differences when myths are identified by individuals and organizations on the more liberal side of the political spectrum.

Exhibit 4.1　Energy Myths Identified by Vaclav Smil

1. The future belongs to electric cars. "It will be decades, rather than years, before we can judge to what extent electric cars offer a real substitute for vehicles powered by internal combustion engines . . ." (p. 30).
2. Nuclear electricity will be too cheap to meter. "[I]t would be naïve to think that it could be (as some suggest) the single most effective component of this challenge during next 10 to 30 years"(p. 43).
3. Soft-energy illusions. Various pundits argue that soft energy—various types of renewable energy sources—can meet future energy needs. "The overall energy supply draws a bit more on renewable flows, but hardly on the small, decentralized units of the soft vision. The verdict is clear: Soft and small has not worked as predicted" (p. 54).
4. Peak oil is here. Oil's "declining share of the global commercial primary energy supply spells no imminent end of the oil era; given the very large remaining conventional and nonconventional resources, oil will continue as a major contributor to the world market during the first half of the twenty-first century" (p. 77).
5. Carbon dioxide can be sequestered. Carbon capture sequestration "cannot provide enough storage in time to avoid further substantial increase in emissions; it will be a major consumer of energy, erasing half a century of efficiency gains in electricity generation; there will always be concerns regarding the safety of long-term storage and the possibilities of leaks; it will be an expensive undertaking; and it will carry significant liability risks" (p. 96).
6. Biofuels can replace refined oil for transportation. "More important than the fact that liquid biofuels *cannot* displace refined oil products in transportation is that they *should not*" (p. 115).
7. Electricity from wind is the solution. "[E]xcept for relatively small regions, [wind] cannot become the single largest source, even less so the dominant mode of generation" (p. 132).
8. Energy transitions will occur rapidly. "A world without fossil fuel combustion is highly desirable. . . . Coming energy transitions will unfold, as the past ones have done, across decades, not years."

Source: Vaclav Smil, *Energy Myths and Realities,* Washington DC: American Enterprise Institute for Public Policy, 2010.

Exhibit 4.2　Ten Energy Myths Identified by Drew Thornley

1. The United States gets the largest share of its oil imports from the Middle East.
2. The United States is rapidly running out of fossil fuels, but within 10 years, we can replace them with alternative fuels and renewable energies.
3. Moving toward renewable energies and away from fossil fuels will likely increase national employment levels.
4. Conservation and efficiency gains alone can meet our future energy needs.
5. U.S. forests and landfill space are shrinking.
6. Our air is becoming more polluted.
7. Nuclear power is unsafe.
8. Offshore oil drilling has often caused significant environmental damage.
9. The earth is warming at a steady rate.
10. Humans are the main drivers of the greenhouse effect, which is likely to cause global warming.

Source: Drew Thornley, *Energy & the Environment: Myths & Factors,* Manhattan Institute. Available at www.manhattan-institute.org/energymyths/index.htm.

Exhibit 4.3   Myths Identified by Henning Thomsen

1. Solar power is too expensive to be of much use.
2. Wind power is too unreliable.
3. Marine energy is a dead end.
4. Nuclear power is cheaper than other low-carbon sources of electricity.
5. Electric cars are slow and ugly.
6. Biofuels are always destructive to the environment.
7. Climate change means we need more organic agriculture.
8. Zero carbon homes are the best ways of dealing with greenhouse gas emissions from buildings.
9. The most efficient power stations are big.
10. All proposed solutions to climate change need to be big.

Source: Henning Thomsen, Sustainable Cities blog (2008).

Exhibit 4.3 presents the myths identified by Henning Thomsen, which were found in a Sustainable Cities blog.

Clearly, the myths identified by Henning Thomsen are quite different from those listed by Thornely and Smil. For example, Thomsen listed a myth that "Wind power is too expensive." On the other hand, Smil states: ". . . except for relatively small regions, [wind] cannot become the single largest source, even less so the dominant mode of generation." Indeed, the statements made by Smil and Thomsen are not necessarily in disagreement; they just focus on different aspects of the use of wind as an energy source and on differences in their time horizon. More will be said about this in the concluding section when results of our sustainability analysis can provide a glimpse of reality to our discussion.

Consumer Perceptions of Energy Sources

In March of 2011, 900 members of a consumer panel who were broadly representative of the U.S. population completed an online survey administered by Oklahoma State University. Exhibit 4.4 presents the results from five key questions.

In interpreting the results found in Exhibit 4.4, one of the immediate findings is that a halo effect occurred. That is, the respondents had a highly positive view of solar and wind as energy sources, which influenced all of their answers. Thus, the respondents viewed solar and wind as sustainable far into the future, as the preferred routes to energy independence for the United States, as the least costly, as the most preferred approaches to increasing domestic production, and overall as the most preferred. From these results, four myths emerge.

Myth 1: Solar and Wind Energy Are Less Costly than Other Forms of Energy
Reality. To investigate Myth 1, data from Morgan and the Nuclear Energy Institute are presented in Exhibit 4.5. The cost is presented in cents per kilowatt hour (cents/kwh). It is important to note that the total cost is the sum of construction, production, and decommissioning costs. (Only nuclear energy has decommissioning costs, which are the expenses associated with dismantling the nuclear power plant.) As shown in Exhibit 4.5, solar energy is actually the most expensive form

Exhibit 4.4　Consumer Energy Perception Results

	Q1	Q2	Q3	Q4	Q5
Oil	3.06	2.93	4.31	3.52	2.98
Natural gas	3.64	3.41	3.83	3.82	3.54
Nuclear	3.70	3.84	4.02	3.87	3.44
Coal	3.22	3.08	3.87	3.41	2.95
Wind	4.39	4.44	3.53	4.38	4.41
Bioenergy non-food	4.16	4.14	4.07	4.17	4.11
Bioenergy from food	3.93	3.92	4.11	3.95	3.82
Hydroelectric	4.30	4.31	3.70	4.28	4.29
Solar	4.46	4.51	3.52	4.47	4.50

Q1: Expanding the emphasis on _____ is a route to energy independence of the United States.

Q2: The use of _____ as an energy source is sustainable far into the future.

Q3: Currently, for consumers the use of _____ as an energy source is very costly.

Q4: I believe that the United States can increase the domestic production of energy from _____.

Q5: Overall, I am extremely in favor of using _____ as a major energy source in the United States.

*Scale: 1 = strongly disagree and 5 = strongly agree.

of energy, costing 22 cents/kwh. Hydroelectric is the cheapest form, costing about 3 cents/kwh; and wind energy is about 8 cents/kwh. Coal and nuclear energy are among the cheapest forms of energy, costing about 4 cents/kwh. Hence it can be concluded that wind and solar energy are currently more expensive compared to nuclear, coal, and hydroelectric energy. Importantly, however, over the next 25 years, one can anticipate that the cost of nonrenewable energy sources will increase as they become depleted. Conversely, it is likely that the costs of wind and solar energy will decrease because of economies of scale. Thus, over the long term the myth may become reality.

Myth 2: Expanding the Emphasis on Renewable Energy Is the Route to Energy Independence of the United States

Reality: Expanding the emphasis on renewable energy (i.e., biofuels, solar, wind, and hydroelectric) so that it replaces the oil imported from foreign countries is simply not feasible within a 25-year time frame. The main route to creating independence is to minimize the importation of petroleum products from foreign countries because they are used predominantly for transportation. In 2010, the United States used 19.1 million barrels of petroleum products. Of this amount, 11.8 million barrels were imported. Interestingly, however, we exported 2.3 million barrels. Thus, the net percentage of imported petroleum products in 2010 was 49.2 percent.

Dramatically increasing the production of biofuels will likely be the dominant approach for replacing petroleum products for transportation. In fact, biofuel supporters claim that it could be a solution to energy security in the United States.

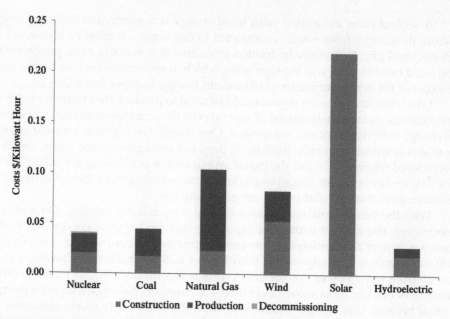

Exhibit 4.5 Comparison of Costs for Various Forms of Energy
Source: J. Morgan, "Comparing Energy Costs of Nuclear, Coal, Gas, Wind and Solar," 2010. Available at
nuclearfissionary.com/2010/04/02/comparing-energy-costs-of-nuclear-coal-gas-wind-and-solar.

However, these pundits have not looked at the numerous issues associated with
biofuels. The production of biofuel is currently almost twice as expensive as gasoline (Wright 2007). Indeed, Pimentel and Patzek (2005) concluded that the energy
output from biofuel is much less than the energy input to create the fuel.

Can wind energy assist in the United States in becoming energy independent? If a substantial portion of the transportation needs of the United States could
be supplied by electrical vehicles, the electricity produced by wind power could
reduce the need to import foreign oil. There are two main challenges associated
with dramatically increasing the use of wind energy. First, except for natural gas
and solar energy, it is very expensive compared to other forms of energy (American
Energy Independence 2011). The cost involved in the manufacturing, installing,
and shipping of wind turbines requires huge up-front capital; and most of the
technology and equipment is imported, at least 55 percent from countries like
Denmark, Germany, China, and India (Tanton 2009). One issue to remember about
wind is that if the wind speed is not high, the technology is ineffective. To convert as little as 20 percent of electrical energy generation in the United States to
wind energy, 180,000 to 200,000 wind turbines must be installed (U.S. Department of Energy 2007). The task is herculean. As of 2011, 41,400 megawatts of wind
power were installed in the United States. With each turbine producing on average
1.24 megawatts of electricity, the results suggest that about 33,000 turbines are producing electricity (U.S. Wind Industry First Quarter 2011 Market Report). Thus, the
fleet of wind turbines will need to be increased by roughly 600 percent to achieve
the goal of replacing only 20 percent of U.S. electrical energy.

A second issue associated with wind energy is transmission and road costs. Before the energy from wind is connected to our homes, it must be connected to an electrical grid that might be located in an area that is not in close proximity to the wind turbine. This will increase costs, which in some cases become higher than the cost of the wind turbine itself (American Energy Independence 2011).

Like wind energy, solar power could be used to produce the electricity for electric vehicles. Solar panels consist of several cells that contain semiconductors used to charge batteries or power equipment. One strong driving force for solar energy is that it is environmentally friendly: it does not emit greenhouse gases, and it is considered renewable. After the initial investment of purchasing the solar panels, the day-to-day costs are almost negligible because energy from the sun is free. The maintenance costs of solar energy are also quite low.

With the benefits offered by solar energy, why is it not meeting demands for electricity? The answer is that the capital investment for solar energy due to the costly nature of the semiconductors (mostly purified silicon) used in manufacturing the panels is very expensive. It costs over $.20 to produce a kilowatt of electricity from solar power (Yarow 2009). This is significantly higher than the other sources of electricity, as shown in Exhibit 4.5. Another challenge with solar energy is that because this energy is generated from the sun, it only works efficiently in areas with high sunlight. Clouds and air pollution can affect the efficiency of solar energy. The rate at which solar rays are converted to electricity is also quite low and hence might never be sufficient to meet our ever-increasing energy demand.

Other issues to keep in mind are that alternative sources of energy such as wind, solar, and bioenergy have been highly subsidized for years by the U.S. government. Even though billions of dollars have been invested towards these alternative forms of energy, collectively they only meet 7 percent of U.S. energy demand (see Exhibit 4.6).

Until groundbreaking technology has been developed to improve the efficiency of renewable energy in general, it will be impossible for it to allow the United States to become energy independent.

Myth 3: The Use of Oil and Coal Are Not Sustainable Far into the Future

Reality. The evidence strongly indicates that the use of oil and coal is sustainable at least for the next 50 years. In the authors' opinions, this meets the test of being sustainable far into the future. How can we make this statement when scientists have projected that if we continue at our present rate, energy from fossil fuels will not be able to sustain us in the future? Well, is this a myth?

The world is dependent on fossil fuel. In the United States, 74 percent of the electricity generated is provided from coal, oil, and natural gas (see Exhibit 4.7). But the use of fossil fuels creates several challenges. One of the issues with fossil fuel is that it is a nonrenewable resource that will eventually be depleted. Another issue is that the use of fossil fuel contributes to pollution due to sulfur dioxide, nitrogen oxides, CO_2, methane, and volatile organic compound emissions during the burning processes. These emissions result in negative environmental impacts such as acid deposition, photochemical smog, other air pollution issues, and global warming. Fossil fuels also contribute to hazardous wastes from petroleum products such as motor oil and gasoline. It could also lead to underground water contamination from chemicals such as benzene, xylene, and MTBE due to leaking

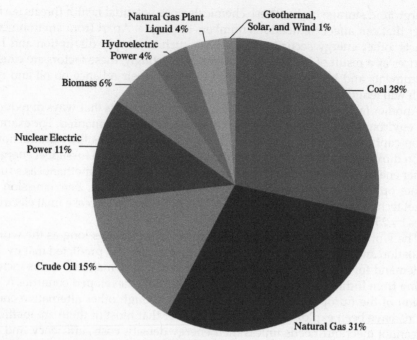

Exhibit 4.6 United States Primary Energy Sources

Source: U.S. Energy Information Administration, "Annual Energy Review 2009," Washington, DC: National Energy Information Center, 2010.

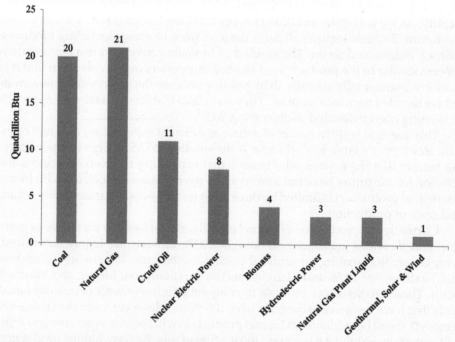

Exhibit 4.7 Energy Generated from Different Sources

Source: U.S. Energy Information Administration, "Annual Energy Review 2009," Washington, DC: National Energy Information Center, 2010.

underground storage tanks. These chemicals pose potential health threats such as cancer that can affect tremendous numbers of people. Apart from environmental impacts, other energy security issues exist, such as supply disruption and high oil prices as a result of increasing demand. Interestingly, these factors are causing governments and businesses to attempt to reduce their reliance on oil and coal, which will lengthen their useful life prior to depletion.

Another factor that will extend the use of oil and coal is that ways of reducing their environmental impact are being developed and implemented. For example, carbon capture technology has been developed that reduces the introduction of carbon dioxide into the atmosphere. Converting conventional fossil fuel energy to cleaner energy sources such as hydrogen, dimethyl ether, and methanol as a fuel is another option that has been considered to address this issue. Zero emission fossil fuel technology is being developed and is projected to increase final electricity prices by 25 to 50 percent (Tanton 2009).

The world's energy demand will continue to increase as long as the world's population and standard of living continue to increase. It is predicted that by 2030 the demand for coal will increase by 70 percent with the majority of this increase coming from India and China and 10 percent from the developed countries (Commission of the European Communities 2007). Although other alternative energy options have been explored, we must remember that most of them are inefficient and cannot meet our needs unless their energy density, costs, efficiency, and sustenance are improved. Hence it can be concluded that fossil fuels, if available, will be needed for the next 25-plus years.

Myth 4: Energy from Biofuels Is Sustainable Far into the Future

Reality. As we will show, obtaining energy from food crops is not sustainable into the future. Biofuels include all fuels derived from biomass, including biodiesel, ethanol, biogas, and so on. The method of biomass conversion is a fermentation process similar to the production of alcohol. Supporters of biofuels claim that it is more environmentally friendly than gasoline because the greenhouse gases emitted are recycled back into biomass. They also claim that it is a sustainable approach to meeting energy demand (Goldemberg 2007).

This question is still a matter of debate as different experts have different opinions on whether a large biofuel sector is the solution to U.S. energy independence. We believe that the experts who believe that expanding the biofuel sector is the solution for the future have not looked at the overall issues associated with biofuels. Biofuel production is limited by three main factors—costs, sustainability issues, and scale of production.

Currently, the production of biofuel is costly, almost twice as expensive as gasoline, and therefore uneconomical (Wright 2007). Biofuels are highly subsidized, with tax credits creating an artificial pricing mechanism. Tax credits for ethanol and biodiesel are $0.56 and $1.20, respectively (Thompson, Meyer, and Westhoff 2010). These credits allow biofuels to compete effectively with petroleum-based fuels that have been in business for over 100 years. However, once the credits are removed, it will be evident that biofuel production will become expensive and difficult to sustain. Exhibit 4.8 is a good illustration of this. As seen, biofuel production has been increasing since 2005. However, we notice a sharp decrease in production in 2010 when the U.S. Senate allowed a biofuels tax credit program to lapse (Biodiesel.org 2010). Several biodiesel production facilities shut down because they

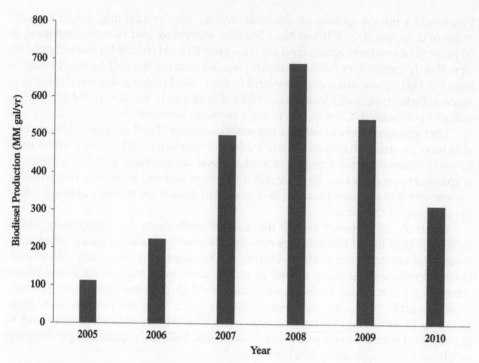

Exhibit 4.8 United States Biodiesel Production
Source: Estimated U.S. Biodiesel Production, 2011, www.biodiesel.org.

could not afford to operate at a loss. The 2010 incident shows that the biofuel industry relies heavily on tax credits, and hence it is difficult to sustain when government incentives are not available. Another problem is that ethanol cannot be transported via pipeline because of its corrosive nature; it must be trucked to fueling stations, which further increases its cost and its environmental footprint.

Limited yield poses another challenge to the biofuel industry. As shown in Exhibit 4.9, one bushel of corn only makes 2.74 gallons of ethanol (U.S. Wind Industry First Quarter 2011); thus 600 pounds of corn results in 480 gallons of ethanol. To produce 1 billion gallons of ethanol from corn, 1,736 square miles (1.43 times the size of Rhode Island) is required. In order to meet the oil demand of the United

Exhibit 4.9 2.74 Gallons Produced from One Bushel of Corn

States—23.4 billion gallons of ethanol—would require planting 406,250 square miles of corn, the size of Texas, New Mexico, Maryland, and Hawaii combined, or 55 percent of available arable land for corn growth used strictly for biofuel production. If only corn stover (stalks of maize) is used to avoid the fuel-for-food swap, at least 920,000 square miles of arable land in the United States is required (the size of Alaska, California, and Florida); the United States only has about 734,375 square miles of arable land. Clearly, this is not a possible scenario.

This question leads to another big issue coined as "Food for Fuel." Using valuable food products to make biofuels leads to important social issues. Corn is used to make numerous food products and as feed for animals. If it is increasingly employed to produce fuel, its price will increase as demand increases. This will ultimately result in increased hunger and malnourishment for millions of low-income people around the world.

Contrary to popular belief, the use of biofuels is not completely clean. Although burning of biofuel does not directly emit greenhouse gases, other environmental concerns are at stake. During the biomass conversion step, the chemical plant releases emissions as well as accumulates huge amounts of waste water. Apart from that, fossil fuels are also consumed during the production process, which contributes to air pollution. Also, in order to grow the biomass, large amounts of fertilizers, herbicides, and pesticides are needed, which can lead to ground and surface water pollution. In addition, fuels are required to produce the fertilizer, herbicides, and pesticides.

Finally, the growing of the biomass can degrade the limited amount of arable land available as multinational corporations and farmers plant as much biomass as possible to meet the demand needed for biofuel production (Banholzer, Watson, and Jones 2008). Importantly, efforts are being made to increase the amount of arable land available for farming by cutting down forests, wetlands, and grasslands. Unfortunately, these resources are critical to the storage of carbon (U.S. EIA 2011). Deforestation, which accounts for 20 percent of carbon emissions, has become rampant in countries like Indonesia, Brazil, and Malaysia as they try to support their biofuel industries with the growth of palm oils and sugarcanes. Ecologist David Tilman from the University of Minnesota conducted a study to investigate the effect of carbon emission as a result of clearing land to grow palm oil and corn (U.S. EIA 2011). His study revealed that the ecosystem will recover from palm oil and corn deforestation only after 400 and 93 years, respectively. These challenges must be addressed before this energy source can be considered sustainable.

In conclusion, unless technological breakthroughs occur (e.g., using algae for fuel), the idea that biofuels are sustainable far into the future is a myth because they are not sustainable in the present.

A MODEL FOR DETERMINING THE SUSTAINABILITY OF ENERGY SOURCES

In this section, we present a set of evaluation criteria that are employed to assess each energy source's ability to meet the electricity demands for this and future generations. We chose electricity generation because its production is likely to rise substantially in the future because of its use to power electric autos. It is important

Exhibit 4.10   Aspects of Sustainable Energy

Economic Concerns	Environmental Concerns	Social Concerns
Direct	Usage Impact	Quality of Life
• Raw material cost	• Land usage	• Energy security
• Labor cost	• Water usage	• Job creation
• Capital cost	• Energy usage	• Lost-time injuries
• Profitability	• Renewability	• Mortality risks
Potentially Hidden	• Efficiency	• Risks of illness
• Lawsuits	Environmental Burden	• Use restrictions
• Liability	• Smog creation	• Reported Deaths
• Employee injury costs	• Acid rain	Perception and Peace of Mind
• Government subsidies	• Biodiversity reduction	• Perceived risk
	• Eutrophication	• Complaints
	• Global warming	• Risk of terrorist attack

then to evaluate the ability of the various energy sources as fuel stocks for electricity production. Thus, we first present the evaluative criteria and then apply them to electricity generation.

The Evaluative Criteria

The evaluative criteria are based upon three main dimensions of sustainable energy, which are economic, environmental, and social. Each characteristic listed in Exhibit 4.10 is used to assess whether each energy source is sustainable.

The first impact is economic, and this measures the profitability of any energy source. No energy source should be developed that has an overall economic loss to society. There are two subcategories under the economic dimension of sustainable energy.

1. **Direct Costs:** These costs include capital, operating, and labor costs required to install, manufacture, or produce this energy source.
2. **Potential Hidden Costs:** These are liability costs associated with producing any energy source. For example, lawsuit costs due to environmental spills and employee injury or fines imposed by the U.S. government for not meeting discharge limits. Government subsidies could also impact the economics of an energy source. If the subsidies are removed, the energy source may no longer be sustainable.

The second impact category, environmental impact, evaluates the ecological risks of any energy source. There are two subcategories under the environmental dimension of sustainable energy.

1. **Usage Impact:** This environmental category measures land, water, and energy impacts from producing and using the energy source. It also evaluates whether the energy source is renewable.

2. **Environmental Burden:** This category evaluates the environmental concerns such as smog creation, acid rain, global warming, eutrophication, and biodiversity reduction associated with producing, using, and implementing any energy source.

The last impact category, social impact, evaluates the impact of any energy source on society. There are two subcategories under the social dimension of sustainable energy.

1. **Quality of Life:** This social impact evaluates whether an energy source will lead to energy security and job creation. It also evaluates any health and safety risks associated with a particular type of energy source.
2. **Perception and Peace of Mind:** This category evaluates societal views about an energy source. It also looks at other risks, such as risks of terrorist attack.

Sustainability Assessment of Electricity Generated from Various Energy Sources

In the United States, 39 percent of energy produced is used for electricity generation (U.S. Environmental Protection Agency 2009). Therefore, a sustainability assessment of electricity-generation systems is important. A sustainability assessment of electricity generation from the following energy sources is presented: solar energy, wind energy, hydroelectric energy, geothermal energy, coal, and natural gas. The assessment is categorized according to the three major dimensions of sustainability. The results of the economic, environmental, and social assessment are presented in the next sections.

Economic Assessment

Any electricity-generation system must be economical in order to be sustainable. The economics of any electricity-generation system is highly reflective of its levelized costs. The levelized costs include capital cost, operating costs, performance, and fuel cost. The levelized costs of different electricity generating systems obtained from the Energy Information Administration are shown in Exhibit 4.11. As shown in the exhibit, solar energy is the most expensive electricity-generation

Exhibit 4.11 Levelized Cost of Electricity from Various Sources (U.S. EIA 2011)

Energy Source	Price (¢/mwh)
Biomass	113
Coal	95
Geothermal	102
Hydro	86
Natural gas	66
Nuclear	114
Solar	211
Wind	97

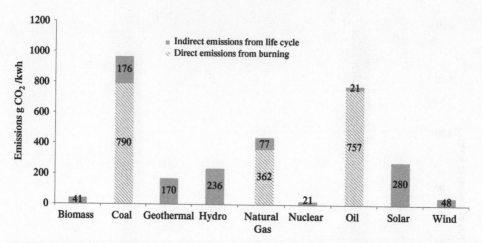

Exhibit 4.12 CO_2 Emissions (g/kwh) for Various Energy Generating Sources
Source: World Nuclear Association, "Comparative Carbon Dioxide Emissions from Power Generation." 2011, available at www.world-nuclear.org/education/comparativeco2.html; B. K. Sovacool, "Valuing the Greenhouse Gas Emissions from Nuclear Power: A Critical Survey," *Energy Policy* 36:8, 2008, 2950–2963.

source, costing around 211 cents per megawatt hour (mwh). The cheapest energy-generation sources are natural gas, geothermal, hydroelectric, and wind.

Environmental Assessment

The environmental impact of the various electricity generating sources were also examined. The following six metrics are discussed: carbon dioxide (CO_2), sulfur oxide (SO_2), and nitrogen oxides (NO_x) emissions, water impact, land impact, and energy ratio. Electricity generation by various sources emits carbon dioxide (CO_2), sulfur oxide (SO_2), and nitrogen oxides (NO_x) directly or indirectly during its life cycle. The CO_2, SO_2, and NO_x emissions from various sources used in electricity generation are shown in Exhibits 4.12, 4.13, and 4.14. As shown in Exhibit 4.12, coal-generated electricity has the highest CO_2 emissions at about 966g/kwh, while nuclear energy has the lowest emissions per kwh. Exhibit 4.13 shows that electricity generated by coal has the highest SO_2 emissions; electricity generated by nuclear, geothermal, hydro, and natural gas have negligible emissions as electricity generation from these energy sources does not discharge SO_2. Emissions are, however, generated indirectly during its life cycle. As shown in Exhibit 4.14, electricity generation by coal, natural gas, and biomass have the highest NO_x emissions. While electricity generated by nuclear and hydro does not discharge NO_x, emissions are generated indirectly during its life cycle.

CO_2, SO_2, and NO_x emissions contribute to several environmental concerns. CO_2 emissions result in depletion of stratospheric ozone, which protects us from ultraviolet rays from the sun. SO_x, NO_x, and CO_2 emissions from electricity-generation systems lead to smog formation, which involves the reaction of these pollutants with combustive material resulting in a smoke-like appearance of the environment. The last environmental concern is atmospheric acidification. The

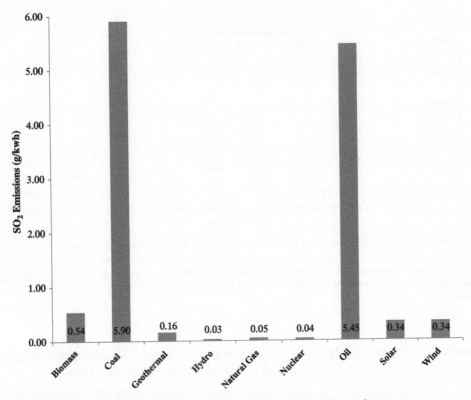

Exhibit 4.13   SO$_2$ Emissions g/kwh for Various Energy Generating Sources

Source: United States Environmental Protection Agency, "How Does Electricity Affect the Environment?" 2009, available at www.epa.gov/cleanenergy/energy-and-you/affect/index.html; Geothermal Energy Association, "Geothermal Basics—Environment," 2011, available at www .geoenergy.org/geo_basics_environment.aspx; Edvard, "Renewables and the Impact on Environment," 2011, available at http://electrical-engineering-portal.com/renewables-and-the-impact-on-environment; A. Vob, "Energy and Sustainability—An Outlook," 2006, Institute for Energy Economics and the Rational Use of Energy, Universität Stuttgart: International Materials Forum 2006, Bayreuth, Germany.

emissions of SO$_2$ and NO$_x$ lead to the increase of acid in the atmosphere, which leads to acid rain.

Water impact for various electric-generation systems was also evaluated. Large volumes of water are required to produce electricity. This could be a concern as water is a vital resource for human life. Water usage information for various energy sources was obtained from a report by the World Economic Forum (2009). For energy sources that had a water usage value given in ranges, average values were calculated, and the results are presented in Exhibit 4.15, which shows that oil has the greatest water usage. For example, production of oil from unconventional resources such as heavy oil requires huge volumes of water for the steam-generation process, which reduces the viscosity of the oil. Biomass also requires a significant amount of water, mostly used in growing biofuel crops. Wind, solar, natural gas, and coal use negligible amounts of water.

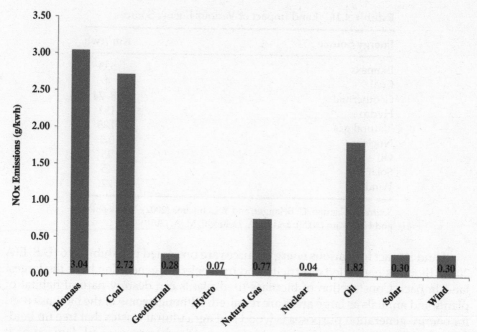

Exhibit 4.14 NOx Emissions g/kwh for Various Energy Generating Sources

Source: United States Environmental Protection Agency, "How Does Electricity Affect the Environment?" 2009, available at www.epa.gov/cleanenergy/energy-and-you/affect/index.html; Geothermal Energy Association, "Geothermal Basics—Environment," 2011, available at www .geoenergy.org/geo_basics_environment.aspx; Edvard, "Renewables and the Impact on Environment," 2011, available at http://electrical-engineering-portal.com/renewables-and-the-impact-on-environment; A. Vob, "Energy and Sustainability—An Outlook," 2006, Institute for Energy Economics and the Rational Use of Energy, Universität Stuttgart: International Materials Forum 2006, Bayreuth, Germany.

Exhibit 4.15 Water Impact of Various Energy Sources

Energy Source	L/kwh
Biomass	196.0
Coal	0.4
Geothermal	5.3
Hydro	17.0
Natural gas	0.2
Nuclear	0.4
Solar PV	0.0
Wind	0.0
Oil	9300.0

Source: World Economic Forum, "Thirsty Energy: Water and Energy in the 21st Century," World Economic Forum in partnership with Cambridge Energy Research Associates, 2009.

Exhibit 4.16 Land Impact of Various Energy Sources

Energy Source	Km²/twh
Biomass	533
Coal	4
Geothermal	18–74
Hydro	152
Natural gas	0.35
Nuclear	0.5
Oil	45
Solar PV	45
Wind	72

Source: L. Gagnon, C. Bélanger, and Y. Uchiyama (2002); V. Fthenakis and H. C. Kim (2009); and M. A. Delucchi, M. A. (2010).

Land impact for various energy sources are presented in Exhibit 4.16 (U.S. EIA 2011). Biomass-generated electricity and hydroelectric generation have the largest land impact. Construction of biomass-fired plants can destroy natural habitat of plants and animals as large areas are required. Although some of the biomass used for energy-generation purposes is wood and agricultural wastes that free up land-fill space, growing crops used for biomass can lead to severe soil damage as it requires several acres of land and affects soil nutrients. It also can lead to issues such as erosion of wildlife habitat. Soil contamination occurs at coal-fired plant sites, taking several years for the land to recover even after shutdown. Coal mining and extraction also pose land impact risks. Construction of dams used in hydro-electricity generation results in issues such as erosion and flooding. These problems can also affect the ecosystem of aquatic and wildlife populations.

Nuclear and natural gas have the lowest land-impact value, as shown in Exhibit 4.16. Construction of nuclear power plants can destroy natural habitat of plants and animals. Radioactive waste can contaminate land, preventing its future reuse. Construction of natural gas-fired plants can destroy natural habitat of plants and animals. Production can lead to erosion, landslides, and loss of productivity. In comparison to fossil-fuel-fired plants, less land is required by geothermal power plants. There is, however, a high risk of land sinking if water is not reinjected to maintain pressure. Construction of oil-fired power plants can destroy natural habi-tats of plants and animals, and wastes from these plants, if not handled appropri-ately, can contaminate land. Oil spills can also degrade soil and land.

Solar power requires small land spaces, as photovoltaic systems are usually placed on existing structures. Although turbines used for wind power require large areas of land, the space can also be used for multiple purposes such as animal graz-ing. There is no long-term environmental impact such as land contamination after wind turbines are dismantled. However, erosion risks are associated with wind turbine removal. Bird and bat mortality have been a major issue of concern for wind farms.

The energy ratio (defined as the total energy produced during a system's life-time divided by the energy required to build, maintain, and fuel various electric-ity generating systems) was also investigated from various sources, the results of which are shown in Exhibit 4.17. Energy ratio is a good gauge of the environmental

Exhibit 4.17   Energy Ratio of Various Energy Sources

Energy Source	Energy Ratio
Biomass	5–27
Coal	1.6–29
Geothermal	31
Hydro	43–280
Natural gas	1.5–10.6
Nuclear	10.5–59
Oil	0.7–17
Solar PV	3–12
Wind	6–35.3

Source: L. Gagnon, "Electricity Generation Options: Energy Payback Ratio," 2005, available at www.hydroquebec.com/sustainable-development/documentation/pdf/options_energetiques/rendement_investissement.pdf; S. Husebye, "Environmental and Health Impact of Electricity Generation," The International Energy-Implementing Agreement for Hydropower Technologies and Programmes 2002, 2011, available at www.ieahydro.org/reports/ST3-020613b.pdf.

performance of any electricity-generating system. Systems that have an energy ratio close to or less than 1 should not be developed—they use up as much energy as they generate. As shown in the exhibit, hydroelectric power (hydro) has the highest energy ratio, with natural gas and coal having the lowest energy ratios.

Social Assessment

In March 2011, the authors completed a 900-member consumer survey that questioned public perceptions of various forms of energy. Five pertinent questions that the survey investigated are presented in Exhibit 4.18. Survey participants were

Exhibit 4.18   Results of Energy Survey

Energy Source	Q1	Q2	Q3	Q4	Q5	Average
Oil	4.04	4.00	3.89	4.03	4.05	4.00
Natural gas	3.52	3.46	3.57	3.53	3.54	3.52
Nuclear	3.70	3.66	4.14	3.74	3.52	3.75
Coal	4.02	4.01	3.71	4.02	4.20	3.99
Wind	2.62	2.21	2.45	2.37	2.23	2.38
Bio food	3.36	3.32	3.37	3.47	3.33	3.37
Hydroelectric	3.06	2.81	3.02	3.09	2.67	2.93
Solar	2.44	2.19	2.42	2.37	2.25	2.33

1. Use of _____ as an energy source has a negative effect on birds, mammals, reptiles, and other wildlife.
2. The use of _____ as an energy source harms the environment.
3. The use of _____ as an energy source can lead to catastrophic events.
4. The use of _____ as an energy source has a negative effect on water quality in our rivers.
5. The use of _____ as an energy source has a negative effect on quality of the air we breathe.

Exhibit 4.19   Death Rates for Various Energy Sources

Energy Source	Death/twh
Biomass	12.00
Coal	26.00
Hydro	0.10
Natural gas	4.00
Nuclear	0.04
Oil	36.00
Solar PV	0.44
Wind	0.15

Source: N. Starfelt and C. Wikdahl, "Economic Analysis of Various Options of Electricity Generation—Taking into Account Health and Environmental Effects," 2011 available at http://manhaz.cyf.gov.pl/manhaz/strona_konferencja_EAE-2001/15%20-%20Polenp~1.pdf.

asked to select their perceptions from a list of various energy sources, and they were asked to rank them based on six choices: strongly disagree (5), disagree (4), neutral (3), agree (2), strongly agree (1), don't know (0). As shown in the Exhibit 4.18, it can be concluded that solar and wind power are the most favored forms of energy, with positive reviews from consumers who were asked questions relating to ecological concerns, risk of catastrophe, and quality of life. Coal and oil had the most negative reviews when asked the same questions.

The death rate caused by various energy sources was also investigated, and the results are presented in Exhibit 4.19 from a report (Starfelt and Wikdahl 2011) aimed at investigating the health and environmental effects of various electricity-generating sources. As shown in the exhibit, nuclear power has the lowest death rate while petroleum oil production has the highest death rate.

A University of Berkley study (Wei, Patadia, and Kammen 2010) was conducted to investigate job creation of various energy sources; results of the study are shown in Exhibit 4.20. The key conclusions of the study are that renewable energies provide more jobs than fossil-fuel-based sources; and among all the renewable forms of energy, solar energy has the highest job-creation rate/gwh.

Exhibit 4.20   Job-Creation Rates of Various Energy Sources

Energy Source	Total Job-Years/gwh
Biomass	0.21
Coal	0.11
Geothermal	0.25
Hydro	0.27
Natural gas	0.11
Nuclear	0.14
Oil	0.11
Solar PV	0.87
Wind	0.17

Source: M. Wei, S. Patadia, and D. M. Kammen, "Putting Renewables and Energy Efficiency to Work: How Many Jobs Can the Clean Energy Industry Generate in the U.S.?" *Energy Policy* 38:2, 2010, 919–931.

Exhibit 4.21 Sustainability Ranking of Various Energy Sources

Evaluation Parameter	Biomass	Coal	Natural Gas	Geothermal	Hydro	Nuclear	Oil	Solar	Wind
Price	2	2	1	2	2	2	1	4	2
CO_2 emissions	1	4	3	2	3	1	4	3	1
SO_2 emissions	2	4	1	2	1	1	4	2	2
NO_x emissions	4	3	2	1	1	1	2	1	1
Water impact	4	1	1	2	1	1	4	1	1
Land impact	4	1	1	1	3	1	2	2	1
Energy ratio	2	2	3	2	1	1	3	3	2
Public perception	3	4	3	2	2	3	4	1	1
Death rate	3	4	2	1	1	1	4	1	1
Job creation	3	4	4	3	3	4	4	1	3
Economic impact	2	2	1	2	2	2	1	4	2
Environmental impact	2.8	2.5	1.8	1.7	1.7	1.0	3.2	2.0	1.5
Social impact	3.0	4.0	3.0	2.0	2.0	2.7	4.0	1.0	1.7
Overall impact value	7.8	8.5	5.8	5.7	5.7	5.7	8.2	7.0	5.2

Overall Evaluation

Ten different quantifiable metrics were selected for the evaluation of various electricity-generating energy sources. For every selected indicator, each technology was assigned an index ranging from 1 to 4 (see the Appendix). The indices are assigned according to the corresponding value of their respective indicators so that each energy source can be ranked. The results of this ranking exercise are shown in Exhibit 4.21. The lower the index value, the more sustainable the process. The corresponding ranking range for each metric can be found in the Appendix. An overall impact value ranging from 5.2 to 7.8 was obtained by normalizing the metrics for each of the three dimensions of sustainability. In general natural-gas- and oil-generated electricity had the lowest economic impact values as they had the lowest levelized costs, while solar power was the most expensive electricity-generating source. Nuclear-generated electricity has the least environmental concerns, while oil-generated electricity has the most. Lastly, coal- and oil-generated electricity had the highest social impact value, while solar-generated electricity had the lowest social impact value. In conclusion, the most sustainable electricity-generating energy source is wind energy as it had the lowest overall sustainability impact value of 5.2.

CONCLUSION

Implied in the term *sustainable* is the concept of time. When an energy source is said to be sustainable, over what time period are we thinking—25 years, 50 years, 200 years? Our analysis indicates that at current and expected future rates of depletion, the conventional energy sources (while nonrenewable) will continue to be used for at least 50 years. Thus, if our definition of sustainable goes to 50 years in the future, conventional energy sources are sustainable. Indeed, because of the effects of financial markets, as the cost of conventional fuel increases because of its depletion, we can anticipate that its extraction will slow as it is replaced by renewable energy sources. Thus we can readily see the continued use of conventional fuels for the next 100 years—barring some type of unexpected scientific breakthrough.

These ideas bring us back to the two quotes that introduced the chapter. There is a likelihood that Lester Brown is right and that "wind and wind-generated hydrogen will shape . . . the energy sector . . ." if you look 25 to 50 years into the future. Similarly, there is a likelihood that Vaclav Smil is right when he said that "it cannot be said wind cannot be a dominant mode of energy generation . . ." if one looks at a time horizon of less than 25 years. In sum, what is a myth and what is reality depends in large part upon one's time horizon.

We can, however, take our analysis in the previous section and make several generalizations. As described in the section, Sustainable Energy Myths, Thompson listed as a myth that "wind power is too expensive," and Smil stated, "except for relatively small regions, [wind] cannot become the single largest source, even less so the dominant mode of generation." The real problem with these statements is that overall sustainability was not evaluated. From our sustainability analysis in the section, A Model for Determining the Sustainability of Energy Sources, wind becomes one of the most preferred sources of energy due to its low environmental and social impact. While the economic impact of wind energy is moderate, it has less of an impact than solar power has.

The fact that nuclear power has a low impact is also noteworthy. There are a number of public challenges to the use of nuclear power, particularly considering the recent tsunami damage at the Fukushima nuclear plant in Japan. Public perception of nuclear power may hinder the rapid acceptance of increased use of this resource.

Our analysis shows that it is critical to consider economics when establishing the sustainability of energy sources. Without an economic consideration, sources such as solar appear to be sustainable when in fact they are not, based on our analysis. Solar energy is a very expensive source. It is important to make decisions about energy usage that are grounded in economic and scientific reality, not based on ignorant acceptance of political or societal views.

APPENDIX

Index Scores Used in Evaluating the Sustainability of Various Energy Sources

The index scores are presented in Exhibits 4.22 through 4.31 for the following sustainability metrics: price, CO_2 emissions, SO_2 emissions, NO_X emissions, water impact, land impact, energy ratio, public perception, death rate, and job creation. Based on the value of each metric, each energy source is assigned an index score. The index scores for the 10 selected metrics range from 1 to 4, with 1 being the most sustainable and 4 being the least sustainable. Each metric is classified into the three dimensions of sustainability. There is only one economic metric, and thus the value of the economic index shown in Exhibit 4.21 is exactly equal to the price metric value shown in Exhibit 4.22. There are six environmental metrics; thus the environmental impact is the average of the index values assigned to CO_2 emissions, SO_2 emissions, NO_X emissions, water impact, land impact, and energy ratio as shown in Exhibit 4.21. There are three social metrics; thus the social index is the average of the index values assigned to public perception, death rate, and job creation as shown in Exhibit 4.21. The overall impact value is the sum of economic, environmental, and social indices values as presented in Exhibit 4.21.

Exhibit 4.22 Index Score for Levelized Cost of Electricity from Various Energy Sources

Levelized Cost (¢/mwh)	Score
<90	1
91–120	2
121–150	3
>151	4

Exhibit 4.23 Index Score for CO_2 Emissions (g/kwh) for Various Energy Sources

CO_2 Emission (g/kwh)	Score
<80	1
81–199	2
200–499	3
>500	4

Exhibit 4.24 Index Score for SO_2 Emissions (g/kwh) for Various Energy Sources

SO_2 Emission (g/kwh)	Score
<0.05	1
0.06–1	2
1–3	3
>3	4

Exhibit 4.25 Index Score for NO_x Emissions (g/kwh) for Various Energy Sources

NO_x Emission (g/kwh)	Score
<0.5	1
0.5–2	2
2.1–3	3
>3	4

Exhibit 4.26 Index Score for Water Impact for Various Energy Sources

Water Impact (l/kwh)	Score
<10	1
11–50	2
51–100	3
>101	4

Exhibit 4.27   Index Score for Land Impact for Various Energy Sources

Land Impact (km²/twh)	Score
<10	1
11–100	2
101–200	3
>201	4

Exhibit 4.28   Index Score for Energy Ratio for Various Energy Sources

Energy Ratio	Score
>50	1
20–49	2
10–19	3
<9	4

Exhibit 4.29   Index Score for Public Perception for Various Energy Sources

Public Perception	Score
<2.5	1
2.6–3.1	2
3.2–3.6	3
>3.7	4

Exhibit 4.30   Index Score for Death Rate (Death/twh) for Various Energy Sources

Death Rate (Death/twh)	Score
<1	1
2–10	2
11–20	3
>21	4

Exhibit 4.31   Index Score for Job Creation (Total Job-Years/gwh) for Various Energy Sources

Job Creation (Total Job-Years/gwh)	Score
>0.71	1
0.4–0.7	2
0.16–0.39	3
<0.15	4

DISCUSSION QUESTIONS

1. List and discuss five energy myths.
2. How many wind turbines would it take to produce 100 percent of electric power used in the United States in 2011?
3. How many years, at a minimum, will current supplies of fossil fuels last? Discuss.
4. If all transportation fuel needs were met by ethanol (biofuel), how many acres would be needed, and what percentage of arable farmable land in the United States is that?
5. Are biofuels a sustainable energy source? Why or why not?
6. The chapter discusses the results of a survey of 900 consumers on their perceptions of various aspects of nine energy sources. From this survey, the authors identify four potential myths held by consumers about sustainable energy. Based on your ideas, suggest ways in which consumers can be educated on energy so that they understand the differences between energy myths and realities.

REFERENCES

American Energy Independence. 2011. "Trouble Is Blowing in the Wind." Available at http://americanenergyindependence.com/windenergy.aspx.

Banholzer, W., K. Watson, and M. Jones. 2008. "How Might Biofuels Impact the Chemical Industry?" *Chemical Engineering Progress* by American Institute of Chemical Engineers, 104:3, S7–S14.

Biodiesel.org. 2010. "Tax Credit Lapse Cripples Biodiesel Industry 2010." Available at www.biodiesel.org/news/bulletin/2010/ 20100301.htm.

Biodiesel.org. 2011. "Estimated U.S. Biodiesel Production." Available at www.biodiesel.org.

Brown, Lester. 2003. "Wind Power Set to Become World's Leading Energy Source." Earth Policy Institute. Available at www.earth-policy.org/updates/update24.htm. Accessed April 11, 2011.

Commission of the European Communities. 2007. "Sustainable Power Generation from Fossil Fuels: Aiming for Near-Zero Emissions from Coal after 2020." Communication from the Commission to the Council and the European Parliament. Brussels.

Delucchi, M. A. 2010. "Impacts of Biofuels on Climate Change, Water Use, and Land Use." *Annals of the New York Academy of Sciences* 1195:1, 28–45.

Edvard. 2011. "Renewables and the Impact on Environment." Available at http://electrical-engineering-portal.com/renewables-and-the-impact-on-environment.

Fthenakis, V., and H. C. Kim. 2009."Land Use and Electricity Generation: A Life-Cycle Analysis." *Renewable and Sustainable Energy Reviews* 13:6–7, 1465–1474.

Gagnon, L. 2005. "Electricity Generation Options: Energy Payback Ratio." Available at www.hydroquebec.com/sustainable-development/documentation/pdf/options_energetiques/rendement_investissement.pdf.

Gagnon, L., C. Bélanger, and Y. Uchiyama. 2002. "Life-Cycle Assessment of Electricity Generation Options: The Status of Research in Year 2001." *Energy Policy* 30:14, 1267–1278.

Geothermal Energy Association. 2011. "Geothermal Basics—Environment." Available at www.geo-energy.org/geo_basics_environment.aspx.

Goldemberg, J. 2007. "Ethanol for a Sustainable Energy Future." *Science* 315:5813, 808–810.

Husebye, S. 2011. "Environmental and Health Impact of Electricity Generation." The International Energy-Implementing Agreement for Hydropower Technologies and Programmes 2002. Available at www.ieahydro.org/reports/ST3-020613b.pdf.

Morgan, J. 2010. "Comparing Energy Costs of Nuclear, Coal, Gas, Wind and Solar." Available at nuclearfissionary.com/2010/04/02/comparing-energy-costs-of-nuclear-coal-gas-wind-and-solar/.

Pimentel, D., and T. W. Patzek. "2005. "Ethanol Production Using Corn, Switchgrass, and Wood: Biodiesel Production Using Soybean and Sunflower." *Natural Resources Research* 14:1, 65–76.

Plous, Scott. 1993. *The Psychology of Judgment and Decision Making.* New York: McGraw-Hill.

Prindle, Bill, and Maggie Eldridge. 2007. *The Twin Pillars of Sustainable Energy: Synergies between Energy Efficiency and Renewable Energy Technology and Policy.* American Council for an Energy-Efficient Economy, Report Number E074.

Smil, Vaclav. 2010. *Energy Myths and Realities.* Washington, DC: American Enterprise Institute for Public Policy.

Sovacool, B. K. 2008. "Valuing the Greenhouse Gas Emissions from Nuclear Power: A Critical Survey." *Energy Policy* 36:8, 2950–2963.

Starfelt, N., and C. Wikdahl. 2011. "Economic Analysis of Various Options of Electricity Generation—Taking into Account Health and Environmental Effects." Available at http://manhaz.cyf.gov.pl/manhaz/strona_konferencja_EAE-2001/15%20-%20Polenp~1.pdf.

Tanton, T. 2009. *Top Ten Energy Myths.* San Francisco: Pacific Research Institute.

Thompson, W., S. Meyer, and P. Westhoff. 2010. "The New Markets for Renewable Identification Numbers." *Applied Economic Perspectives and Policy* 32:4, 588–603.

Thornley, Drew. 2009. *Energy & the Environment: Myths & Factors,* Manhattan Institute. Available at www.manhattan-institute.org/energymyths/index.htm.

U.S. Department of Energy. 2007. "Office of Energy Efficiency and Renewable Energy, 20% Wind Energy by 2030: Increasing Wind Energy's Contribution to U.S. Electricity Supply." DOE/GO-102008-2567.

U.S. Energy Information Administration. 2010. *Annual Energy Review 2009.* Washington, DC: National Energy Information Center.

U.S. Energy Information Administration. 2011. *Annual Energy Outlook.* Department of Energy/EIA-0383(2010).

U.S. Energy Information Administration. 2011. "Land Resource Use." Available at www.epa.gov/cleanenergy/energy-and-you/affect/land-resource.html.

U.S. Environmental Protection Agency. 2009. "How Does Electricity Affect the Environment?" Available at www.epa.gov/cleanenergy/energy-and-you/affect/index.html.

U.S. Environmental Protection Agency. 2012. "Green Power Market." Available at www.epa.gov/greenpower/gpmarket/index.htm.

"U.S. Electricity Production Costs and Components (1995–2011)." *Nuclear Energy Institute.* 29 Sept. 2012. http://www.nei.org/resourcesandstats/documentlibrary/reliableandaffordableenergy/graphicsandcharts/uselectricityproductioncostsandcomponents/.

U.S. Wind Industry First Quarter. 2011. "Market Report," April.

Vob, A. 2006. "Energy and Sustainability—An Outlook." Institute for Energy Economics and the Rational Use of Energy. Universität Stuttgart: International Materials Forum 2006. Bayreuth, Germany.

Wake, David B., and Vance T. Vredenburg. 2008. "Are We in the Midst of the Sixth Mass Extinction? A View from the World of Amphibians." *Proceedings of the National Academy of Science* 105:Supplement 1, 11466–11473. Available at 10.1073/pnas.0801921105.

Wei, M., S. Patadia, and D. M. Kammen. 2010. "Putting Renewables and Energy Efficiency to Work: How Many Jobs Can the Clean Energy Industry Generate in the U.S.?" *Energy Policy* 38:2, 919–931.

World Economic Forum. 2009. "Thirsty Energy: Water and Energy in the 21st Century." World Economic Forum in partnership with Cambridge Energy Research Associates.

World Nuclear Association. 2011. "Comparative Carbon Dioxide Emissions from Power Generation." Available at www.world-nuclear.org/education/comparativeco2.html.

Wright, R. 2007 *Environmental Science: Toward a Sustainable Future*, 10th ed. Upper Saddle River, NJ: Prentice Hall.

Yarow, J. 2009. "Solar Still Can't Compete on Efficiency or Price." *Business Insider*. Available at http://articles.businessinsider.com/2009-02-09/green_sheet/30062159_1_thin-film-panels-first-solar-solar-power.

ABOUT THE CONTRIBUTORS

Olamide O. Shadiya received her BS degree from Iowa State University and her PhD degree in chemical engineering from Oklahoma State University. Her area of specialty was sustainable process design. As a graduate student, Shadiya was awarded the Yarborough Distinguished Graduate Fellowship for outstanding academic performance. She has authored several academic publications, technical reports, and presented at numerous conferences. Shadiya recently received an outstanding Graduate Research Award at the International Congress on Sustainability Science and Engineering Conference. She currently works in the oil and gas industry as a chemical engineer.

Jane A. Talkington, is a Stillwater, Oklahoma, native who is pursuing a PhD in Oklahoma State University's Environmental Science Graduate Program with a specialization in sustainability. Talkington also holds an MBA. She has worked as a sustainability researcher-writer-consultant in green building, building science, green chemistry, and urban planning. Maintaining industry collaborations has provided opportunities for her to develop evidence-based teaching curriculum for a variety of sustainability classes at Oklahoma State University, University of Oklahoma, and University of California–Berkeley Extension.

John Mowen, PhD, is an Emeritus Regents Professor in the Spears School of Business at Oklahoma State University where he held the Noble Foundation Chair of Marketing Strategy. Dr. Mowen received a PhD in social psychology from Arizona State University, where he also did post-doctoral work in marketing. He is a fellow and past president of the Society for Consumer Psychology. He and his colleagues have published over 70 refereed articles in the fields of managerial/consumer decision making and personality (e.g., *Journal of Behavioral Finance, Journal of Marketing Research, Journal of Marketing, Journal of Personality and Social Psychology, Journal of Applied Psychology, Journal of the Academy of Marketing Sciences*, and *Journal of Consumer Psychology*). Dr. Mowen has published nine books, including *The Art of High-Stakes Decision Making* (John Wiley & Sons), *Judgment Calls: High Stakes Decisions in a Risky World* (Simon & Schuster), *The 3M Model of Motivation and Personality* (Kluwer Academic Press), and six editions of his textbook *Consumer Behavior* with various publishers.

Karen High, PhD, has been an Associate Professor at Oklahoma State University since 1991. Dr. High received her BS from the University of Michigan in 1985, her

MS from Penn State in 1988, and her PhD in 1991. Since coming to Oklahoma, Dr. High has been involved primarily with process design, optimization, and control projects. These have had an environmental bent (how to minimize waste while maximizing profit), a catalytic focus (how to do refinery operations better with new catalysts), and a control aspect (how to control to economic optimums as opposed to a set point). Dr. High is also very interested in creativity and entrepreneurial skills and how they apply to engineering education. This includes product design and development of new technologies and all issues that get them commercialized from cradle to grave.

Josh L. Wiener is the Carson Professor, department head, and director of the Center for Social and Services Marketing at Oklahoma State University; and an associate editor of the *Journal of Public Policy and Marketing*. He has co-chaired both the AMA-Sheth Doctoral Consortium and the marketing and society SIG, national conference, Doctoral Workshop. Wiener's research has been published in outlets such as the *Journal of Marketing*, *Journal of Marketing Research*, and *Journal of Consumer Research*. Over the years he has been the Principal Investigator (PI) or Co-PI on projects from federal agencies such as the National Science Foundation, Department of Defense, and National Institute for Drug Abuse; as well as from state agencies. His current research interests include both understanding why (and how to influence) people who are engaged in self/socially destructive behaviors (inertia); and why people support or oppose specific types of public policy interventions. His PhD is in economics from the University of North Carolina at Chapel Hill.

CHAPTER 5

A Brief Introduction to the Petroleum Industry

From Crude Oil and Natural Gas to Petrochemicals and Their Products

RUSSELL E. SIMKINS
Manager of Proposal Services in the College of Engineering, Architecture, and Technology, Oklahoma State University

KENNETH A. BOROKHOVICH
Department of Finance, Miami University

Oil is not in short supply. From a purely physical point of view, there are huge volumes of conventional and unconventional oils still to be developed, with no "peak-oil" in sight. The real problems concerning future oil production are above the surface, not beneath it, and relate to political decisions and geopolitical instability.

—Leonardo Maugeri, Harvard Kennedy School (2012)

INTRODUCTION

The petroleum industry is complex. Its range begins by locating the required petroleum natural resources through exploration. These natural resources, which provide the raw materials for the industry, fall within the broad categories of oil and natural gas, but they do not all have the same characteristics. The raw materials are then extracted with varying degrees of difficulty depending upon their characteristics and location. Once extracted, they are transported by a number of different means to facilities where they are refined employing an array of processes either singly or in combination. The processes used depend on the characteristics of the raw materials and the desired relative quantities of resulting products. The broad array of resulting products, some non-energy related, are then transported to market. As the quote at the beginning of the chapter emphasizes (Maugeri 2012), oil and natural gas are not in short supply and will be major players in supplying energy needs for years to come.

The industry is dynamic and constantly responding to market demands. Since the same raw materials can be transformed into a number of different products or

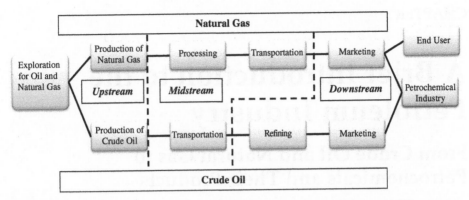

Exhibit 5.1 Structure of the Petroleum Industry: Upstream, Midstream, and Downstream through Petrochemicals

even different quantities of the same products, the markets for the different products are actually in competition. Markets for energy-related products compete with each other as well as with the non-energy-related products made from the same raw materials. To understand energy finance and economics it is crucial to not only understand the dynamics of the energy industry, but also all sectors of the oil and gas industry.

This chapter describes the chemical engineering aspects of that industry from the natural resources that provide the raw materials to the end products. It identifies the heterogeneous types of petroleum and the qualities that make them more or less desirable for processing into specific intermediate and end products. A discussion of the methods for processing oil and natural gas follows. It also demonstrates how the goal quantities of intermediate and end products dictate the choice of processes individually and in combination. From a financial standpoint, the end result is a view of the petroleum industry that may be categorized as a portfolio of complex real options. A basic knowledge of this industry is necessary in order to understand the financial and economic implications that are discussed in the following chapters.

Before discussing the details, we first describe the broad structure of the industry, from upstream through the petrochemical industry, as illustrated in Exhibit 5.1. *Upstream* is a term that describes the exploration and production sectors within the oil and natural gas industry. *Midstream* is a term often used to describe the processing, storage, and transportation sectors within the industry and defines the processes that occur between the upstream and downstream sectors. *Downstream*, in the context of the oil and gas industry, applies to the refining and marketing sectors of the industry. The chemical industry is further downstream but is part of the downstream sector.

Origin of Petroleum

Crude oil is made up of hydrocarbons that take shape in many sizes and forms. A hydrocarbon is made up, just like it sounds, from hydrogen and carbon atoms. Panel A of Exhibit 5.2 illustrates the chemical structure of common hydrocarbons.

Panel A: The Chemical Structure of Common Hydrocarbons

Hydrocarbon	Chemical Structure	Boiling Point
Methane	CH_4	−260°F
Ethane	C_2H_6	−125°F
Propane	C_3H_8	−50°F
Butane	C_4H_{10}	30°F
Pentane	C_5H_{12}	100°F
Hexane	C_6H_{14}	160°F
Heptane	C_7H_{16}	210°F
Octane	C_8H_{18}	260°F

Panel B: Ethylene Production

Ethane, CH_3CH_3

Cracking

Ethylene—the carbon atoms share four electrons in a double bond.

Exhibit 5.2   The Chemical Structure of Common Hydrocarbons and Ethylene Production

The smallest hydrocarbon is methane, made from one carbon atom and four hydrogen atoms (CH_4). Methane is the primary molecule in natural gas.[1] Four of the hydrocarbons shown in the exhibit (methane, ethane, propane, and butane) are gases under normal conditions. In this hydrocarbon series, as the number of carbon atoms in the chemical structure increases, the hydrocarbons become heavier liquids and eventually waxy solids. At the end of the spectrum are very heavy molecules that can consist of hundreds of carbon atoms and thousands of hydrogen atoms.

Hydrocarbon reserves develop naturally and are derived from the decomposition of organic matter, algae, and bacteria trapped and preserved in sedimentary deposits. Burial of these deposits and the corresponding increase in heat and pressure cooks the organic matter. This breaks down the complex hydrogen and carbon molecules and converts them into solid, liquid, or gaseous hydrocarbons known as fossil fuels. Natural gas can be formed from almost any marine or terrestrial organic material.

The hydrocarbon reserves form in permeable reservoir rocks, usually sandstone or chalk, and are trapped by an impermeable layer of rock known as the cap or seal. These petroleum reservoirs have distinctive shapes, or configurations, that prevent the escape of hydrocarbons that migrate into the trap. Geologists classify reservoir traps into two types: structural traps and stratigraphic traps. Exhibit 5.3 illustrates two types of structural traps: fault traps and anticlinal traps. These structural traps form because of a deformation in the rock layer. To be commercially productive, the reservoir must have adequate porosity (a measure of the openings in the rock that can hold the petroleum) and permeability (a measure of the ability of the petroleum to flow through the rock from one pore space to another) in addition to having sufficient reserves.

A new source of natural gas and crude oil is from shale formations, previously not commercially viable. With the advent of hydraulic fracturing ("fracking") and

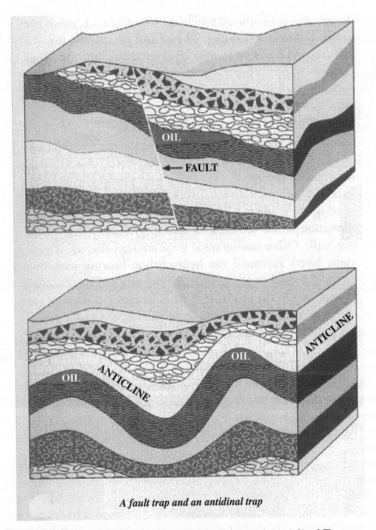

A fault trap and an antidinal trap

Exhibit 5.3 Examples of Petroleum Traps: Fault Traps and Anticlinal Traps
Source: Blue Ridge Group, available at www.blueridgegroup.com/primer.html.

horizontal drilling, shale gas is quickly becoming a large contributor to natural gas reserves worldwide. This is discussed in detail in Chapter 2 under the heading of "The New World of Natural Gas."

THE CHEMISTRY OF PETROLEUM AND THE REFINING PROCESS

In this section, we will discuss a little basic chemistry and some background on crude oil types so that readers will know a little about how products are made from oil. There are many products that come from crude that are seemingly unrelated to oil, and it takes several processing steps to make them.[2]

Crude oil is not a uniform material and there are many different types. Its physical appearance varies from a light, almost colorless liquid to a heavy viscous black/brown sludge. Density (light/medium/heavy) is classified by the American Petroleum Institute (API). API gravity is defined in terms of density at 20 degrees centigrade. The higher the API gravity is numerically, the lighter the crude oil. Light crudes generally exceed 38 degrees API, and heavy crudes are generally those with an API gravity of 22 degrees or less. Crude oil is also classified by sulfur content. Sweet crude oil, such as West Texas Intermediate or Bonny Light, has less than 1 percent sulfur content, whereas sour crude oils have greater than 1 percent sulfur (such as Arab Light and West Texas Sour). Crude prices vary depending on the oil's density (API gravity), sulfur content, and other physical characteristics, as well as the oil's proximity to markets.

In addition to API gravity and sulfur content, the type of hydrocarbon molecules and other natural characteristics may affect the cost of processing or restrict a crude oil's suitability for specific uses. The presence of heavy metal contaminants (such as vanadium and cadmium) is one example. The molecular structure of a crude oil also dictates whether a crude stream can be used for the manufacture of specialty products, such as lubricating oils, or of petrochemical feedstocks.

Refining and Crude Oil Fractions

The difference in refineries is critical to what yields can be obtained, and refineries are categorized by size and configuration (complexity). Exhibit 5.4 illustrates the types of yields that can be produced from Arab Light crude oil, depending on four different refinery complexities (simple, Rotterdam, U.S. Gulf Coast, and Highly Complex). In a simple refinery, only 11.7 percent of the Arab Light crude oil will be refined as light ends (the most desirable being gasoline for the transportation industry), whereas in the highly complex refinery, 59 percent will be light ends. Likewise, 45 percent will be residue (residuum) in a simple refinery whereas in the

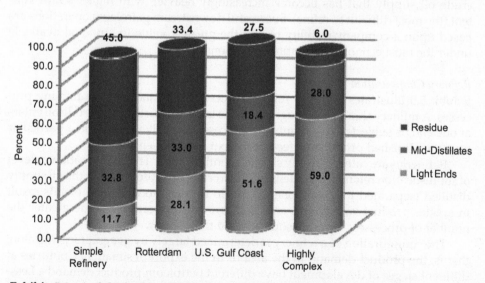

Exhibit 5.4 Arab Light Crude Oil Refining Values for Four Types of Refineries
Source: Energy Intelligence Research 2011.

highly complex refinery, only a small fraction (6 percent) is residue. The quality of the crude oil dictates the level of processing necessary to achieve the optimal combination of product output. Therefore, price and price differentials between crude oils also reflect the relative ease of refining. A premium crude oil like West Texas Intermediate, the U.S. benchmark, has a relatively high natural yield of desirable naphtha and straight-run gasoline. Another premium crude oil, Nigeria's Bonny Light, has a high natural yield of middle distillates such as kerosene and diesel fuel. However, even West Texas Intermediate and Bonny Light have a yield of about one-third residuum after the simple distillation process. Heavier crudes require more processing (refining) and usually produce more heavier products, such as asphalt, used to pave roads. Additionally, very heavy fuel oil, used in large engines such as those that power ships, is also made from the heavier crudes and as by-products of some of the lighter crudes.

Crude Oil Fractions

Crude oil is divided into fractions, roughly divided up by the boiling points. The lightest fractions have the lowest boiling points, and the heaviest have the highest. Methane boils at −263°F (−164°C) at atmospheric pressure. Heavier fractions can boil at temperatures as high as 400 to 500°F, and crudes containing solids, such as tars, boil upward of 850°F. Other techniques, such as putting a vacuum on the product while distilling, will reduce the boiling temperature but require extra processing equipment. Essentially, the more equipment required and the more heat required, the more it costs to process the crude oil.

Refiners therefore strive to run the optimal mix (or slate) of crudes through their refineries, depending on the refinery's equipment, the desired output mix, and the relative price of available crudes. In recent years, refiners have confronted two opposite forces—consumers' needs and government mandates that increasingly require light products of higher quality (the most difficult to produce), and crude oil supply that has become increasingly heavier, with higher sulfur content (the most difficult to refine). Successful downstream petroleum operations are based upon a company's ability to add the greatest value to crude oil available under the most economic operating conditions.

Refinery Configuration

Exhibit 5.5 illustrates a typical refinery process flow chart and the refining processes. A refinery should be thought of as one large production line: crude oil enters at one end, is subjected to a number of processes that alter its state in a particular way, then finished products or feedstocks exit the other end.

Refineries are categorized by size and configuration. The configuration or level of sophistication refers to the extent to which crude oil is processed: Is the oil simply distilled (separated into components), or do further processes and blends result in greater product variety and enhanced product performance? The greater the number of processes, the more sophisticated the refinery.

The configuration of a refinery is determined largely by geographical location; that is, the product demand in the area or in the export destination. Countries at different stages of development have different petroleum product demands. Less-developed countries in the early stages of industrialization require more heavy fuel oils. Developed countries have more advanced technology requiring lighter, more efficient, and less polluting fuels.

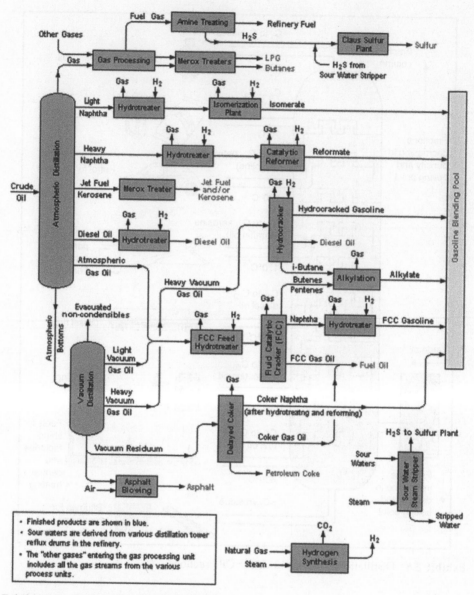

Exhibit 5.5 Typical Refinery Process Flow Chart
Source: http://en.wikipedia.org/wiki/Refinery.

Refining Processes

Primary refining units fall into three processing categories: separation, conversion and treatment.

Step 1: Simple Distillation The core refining process is simple distillation, as shown in the left-hand side of Exhibit 5.5. Because crude oil is made up of a mixture of hydrocarbons, this first and basic refining process is intended to separate the crude oil into its *fractions*, the broad categories of its component hydrocarbons. This distillation process and the resulting crude oil fractions are illustrated in more

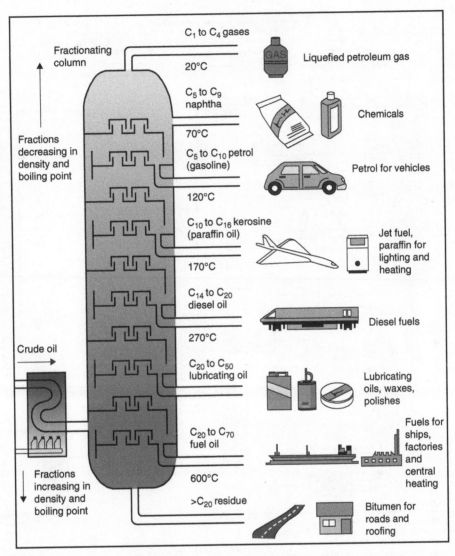

Exhibit 5.6   Distillation Process and Crude Oil Fractions

detail in Exhibit 5.6. Crude oil is heated and put into a distillation column. The different products boil off and can be recovered at different temperatures since various crude components have different boiling points. As crude is gradually heated, the gases (methane, ethane, propane, and butane) evaporate first and rise to the top of the distillation column. These are followed by naphtha, which is used in the blending of motor and aviation gasoline and as a petrochemical feedstock. The medium distillates, which have a higher boiling point, are converted to jet fuel, diesel oil, and feedstocks for secondary conversion units. Finally, the heaviest products (residuum or residual fuel oil) are recovered, sometimes at temperatures over 1,000°F. The simplest refineries stop at this point. However, many refineries

reprocess the heavier fractions into lighter products to maximize the output of the most desirable products, as discussed below.

Refining Step 2: Conversion Processes—Cracking Cracking is a volumetrically expansive conversion process, which can employ heat, pressure, chemical catalysts, and hydrogen individually, or in unison, and is used to promote chemical change and break down the structure of the hydrocarbon molecules. These steps are illustrated in the center area of Exhibit 5.5. The cracking process essentially breaks up heavier high boiling-range feedstocks like heavy gas oils and residue into lighter products such as gasoline, liquefied petroleum gas (LPG), and light distillates. There are three main cracking processes: catalytic cracking, hydrocracking, and thermal cracking (coking).

Catalytic Cracking

The fluid catalytic cracker (FCC) utilizes heat, pressure, and a metallic catalyst to convert heavy straight-run gas oils and vacuum gas oils into gasoline. Cat crackers are used extensively in the gasoline-intensive markets of North America and Western Europe. Cat crackers are also a primary source of olefins (chemical feedstocks). A major problem with cat gasoline is its high sulfur content. New sulfur regulations in Europe and the United States require significant and potentially expensive hydrotreating of either the cat gasoline itself or some of the gas oil streams that are fed into the front end of the unit.

Hydrocracking

Catalytic cracking is a very hydrogen-deficient operation, which generates highly sulfuric and aromatic products. These harmful compounds require further blending and treatment for environmental compliance. The hydrocracker addresses this problem through the introduction of hydrogen to the cracking process. In addition to producing cleaner final products, hydrocrackers offer much greater processing flexibility than do standard FCCs. A hydrocracker can be optimized for gasoline production (yielding 110 percent of feed), jet fuel production (70 percent), or diesel production (85 percent). This flexibility comes at a price: the high expense of a standalone hydrocracker and its associated hydrogen-generating infrastructure, generally make it the costliest facility in a refinery (hundreds of millions of dollars).

Thermal Cracking: Coking

The coking process reduces the yield of low-value heavy products. Coking is the most severe form of thermal cracking, and can eliminate 100 percent of the residual oil feed. The process employs great heat at moderate pressure to convert fuel oil into naphtha, gas oils, and coke. The process is designed to produce maximum yields of transportation fuels and can be used where there is little or no fuel oil demand. However, the coking process is very expensive, and can increase overall plant operating costs by up to 20 percent.

Non-Cracking Conversion Processes

Catalytic Reforming

Reformers are primarily designed to convert low-octane naphthas into high-octane blending components. Reforming actually rearranges molecules rather than cracking them, so there is no yield gain in this procedure. The process yields hydrogen and reformate, a highly aromatic gasoline feedstock. The catalytic reformer is a minimum requirement for simple refineries required to produce gasoline with sufficient octane content. Such refineries are referred to as hydroskimmers due to the excess hydrogen produced during the catalytic reforming process.

Alkylation/Isomerization

Unlike cracking, alkylation and isomerization actually increase the size of the molecules processed. Alkalization and isomerization often work in tandem, converting naturally occurring and cracked gaseous by-products into high-quality-gasoline blending components. Alkylate is, in fact, almost the perfect blending component due to its high octane rating (89–97) and low vapor pressure. Alkylation units utilize either sulfuric acid or hydrofluoric acid catalysts and are therefore very dangerous to operate.

Refining Step 3: Treatment/Blending   As shown on the right-hand side of Exhibit 5.5, treatment is the final stage of finished product development. The primary treatment method is blending. Blending processes are generally designed to bring different constituent streams together in an attempt to achieve minimum product quality standards. Unlike conversion, the blending process does not alter a specific product's chemical composition, but rather enhances it through addition or dilution. One of the best examples of gasoline blending is the introduction of alcohols (oxygenates) such as ethanol. The addition of ethanol raises the octane level of gasoline while simultaneously promoting more complete combustion from the additional oxygen contained in the alcohol.

Finished Petroleum Products

The most important crude oil products are transportation fuels. Indeed, as much as 84 percent of crude oil products are transportation fuels. However, this still leaves a large portion of the crude for other products.

We list products that are the finished or almost finished output from a refinery. The products will not be divided as those that come from light crudes versus heavier crudes because that is outside the scope of this chapter. In many instances, the same products are made from both types of crude oil but require additional processing depending on the quality of the crude.

1. Natural gas—The lightest of the hydrocarbons is methane.[3]
2. Petrochemical feedstocks, LPG—The output of finished products at the lightest end of the distillation range can vary greatly, depending on the design of the refinery. The gaseous products at the upper end of the distillation curve can be processed into high-quality gasoline components, sold as

heating or transportation fuels, upgraded into higher-value petrochemical products, or simply burned as a refinery fuel source. Propane and butane are both termed liquefied petroleum gas (LPG), and can also be produced from reforming and cracking. Once distilled, LPGs are liquefied and either sold in bottles, used for gasoline blending, or as ethylene steam cracker feedstock to manufacture base chemicals. Heavier products such as naphtha (essentially untreated gasoline) are primary feedstocks for the European petrochemical industry.

3. Gasoline (also called petrol, mogas)—Gasoline, the primary transportation fuel of the OECD (Organisation for Economic Co-operation and Development), is favored in developed nations for its superior combustion and low pollution characteristics. Finished gasoline is composed of straight-run gasoline (from the distillation column), treated naphtha (reformer), treated cracked gas oil (cat cracker, hydrocracker), alkylate, isomerate, and blending components (primarily ethers). These gasoline pool constituents are blended together to achieve the desired balance of engine performance and emission reductions. Increasingly stringent European and North American gasoline specifications require a growing degree of complexity among gasoline producing refiners.

4. Kerosene and jet fuel—Kerosene, the original refined product, falls within the lightest of the distillate class products, with a boiling range of approximately 320 to 518°F (160 to 270°C). Kerosene was originally used to replace whale oil[4] as a fuel for lamps, and over time, its use was adapted for cooking and space heating needs. Today, kerosene is primarily consumed in jet and turbine engines. Kerosene's volatility and pour point fall between that of gasoline and diesel fuel. It is important for jet fuel to maintain very consistent ignition and physical flow characteristics over a broad range of atmospheric conditions. A high flash-point prevents premature explosions in overheated airplane tanks (and bullet-compromised tanks in military aircraft) while a low pour point ensures that the jet fuel flows to the engines under subzero temperatures at high altitude. The purity and low smoke requirements of jet fuel necessitate extensive hydrotreating. Primary sources of finished jet fuel are hydro-treated straight-run kerosene and hydrocracked gas oil.

5. Distillate fuel oil (gas oil/diesel/heating oil)—These medium distillates have a boiling range of 375 to 644°F (190 to 340°C). Different grades are used for transportation, residential heating, light industrial and commercial uses, and as a feedstock for secondary processing units and petrochemical plants. Mid-range diesel fuels are primarily differentiated by ignition quality (cetane number) and sulfur content. On-road diesel fuel has a higher cetane number (low self-ignition temperature) and lower sulfur content than heating oil. Higher cetane grades offer better cold-starting characteristics and reduced smoke emissions. Sulfur reduction is the primary focus of environmental regulation for middle distillates. Sulfur reduction is primarily achieved through hydrotreating.

6. Residual fuel oil (fuel oil, bunker fuel)—Residual oil, often referred to simply as resid, is the heaviest, most contaminated constituent of crude oil. In fact, it is the only cut that isn't vaporized in the distillation column. Resid is

the heavy *residual* liquid drained off from the bottom of the distillation tower at the tail end of the distillation process. Residual fuel reigned supreme during the early periods of centralized, pollution-insensitive industrial development. Heavy industry, utilities, and shipping concerns valued resid for its high caloric content, low volatility, and ease of transportation and storage. Unfortunately, the majority of crude oil's sulfur and heavy metals reside within the residual boiling range, being concentrated by the distillation process as the lighter products are boiled off. These contaminants, along with resid's inherently low hydrogen-to-carbon ratio, combine to make residual fuel the most polluting of all petroleum products, making its combustion undesirable in most developed economies. Over the last two decades, U.S. residual fuel oil consumption has diminished by over 70 percent. In the world's more sophisticated energy markets, most residual fuel is reprocessed in cokers or converted into asphalt. Power plants and large industrial customers still burn significant volumes of treated or naturally occurring low-sulfur resid, and shipping demand accounts for the balance of high-sulfur residual consumption (bunkers).

7. Asphalt/bitumen and road oil—Produced from residual oil, these products are used for road construction and roofing material. Asphalt paving is prolific in North America, and the product can be quite profitable to produce. There are many small, unsophisticated refineries in the United States that are solely dedicated to asphalt production.

8. Petroleum coke—This black solid residue is obtained mainly by thermally cracking residue feedstock, tar, and pitches. It mostly consists of carbon and is used as a feedstock in coke ovens for the steel industry, for heating purposes, for electrode manufacture, and for the production of chemicals. In some markets, like the U.S. West Coast, there is no local demand for coke, and regional refiners are occasionally forced to pay foreign buyers to remove the product off-shore.

As we show in the section about petrochemicals, there are many other products that come from oil and natural gas that people do not associate with being derived from petroleum.

The Refining Crack Spread

An important measure of the profitability of a refinery is the margin it realizes. A refinery's gross margin (also referred to as the crack spread as a rough estimate) is the difference in dollars per barrel between its product revenue (sum of the barrels of each product times the price of each product) minus the cost of raw materials (primarily crude oil). A common calculation is the 3-2-1 crack spread that assumes three barrels of a given crude can produce two barrels of gasoline and one barrel of distillate. In other words, the 3-2-1 crack spread is equal to:

$$= 2/3 \text{ cost of a barrel of gasoline} + 1/3 \text{ cost of barrel of distillate}$$
$$- \text{cost of crude oil per barrel}$$

Data on refining margins and the crack spread are available in many places including Bloomberg and the *Oil and Gas Journal* (in the Statistics section). As of

May 25, 2012, the OGJ Crack Spread was $11.01 per barrel (product value $119.01—Brent crude oil value $108.00).[5] Derivatives contracts are also traded on the crack spread (see www.cmegroup.com/trading/energy/).

Crack spreads can be very volatile because product prices, especially on the spot market, do not always move in tandem with oil prices. These observations lead to perhaps one of the best-known truisms in the downstream industry: quickly rising crude oil prices consistently erode refining margins and almost eliminate retail margins in the short term, while falling crude prices sometimes benefit refining margins but invariably expand retail spreads (see UBS 2004). Even over longer time periods, price differentials between different qualities of crude oils can shift dramatically. As Maples (2000) notes, some refineries were designed to process heavy crude such as Arab Heavy (which is less expensive than Bonny Light) to take advantage of the higher differential between light and heavy crudes, only to find that they were not competitive when the differential shrank.

PETROCHEMICALS

The oil industry's interaction with the chemical industry began in the 1920s when refiners sought uses for the growing number of by-products from the refining process (principally naphtha) as the economics of the industry necessitated that every conceivable bit of crude be converted into a usable product. As a result, when crude oil is processed, there are many by-products that form the basic building blocks of the petrochemical industry. These petrochemicals are used to make end products such as textiles, plastics, and pharmaceuticals. Today, chemical operations account for approximately 5 percent of global integrated oil company earnings and account for 39 percent of the world's chemical market. This makes oil companies some of the largest chemical companies in the world. Crude oil produces a large quantity of these petrochemical feedstocks, along with natural gas. When natural gas comes out of the ground, it contains roughly 95 percent methane and 5 percent other hydrocarbons known as natural gas liquids (NGLs).[6]

Let's look at a few examples of petrochemical products that many people use in everyday life and may not realize that the product is mainly derived from crude oil and natural gas.

- Do you drive a car? About 600 pounds of petrochemical-derived plastics, composites, rubber, coating, and textile products are used in the average car accounting for about 15 percent of the total car weight. Some of the components can include the seat belts, instrument panel, wire and cable covers, valve cover, bumpers, tires, interior panels, seat cushions, seat covers, gas tanks, cooling fan, wheel covers, suspension bushings, and gaskets. Some manufacturers have used plastic body panels for weight reduction and resiliency.
- Do you use a cell phone? Electronics and appliances contain up to 40 percent or more of plastics derived from oil and natural gas. A partial listing includes cell phones, televisions, air conditioners, fans, washing machines, water heaters, insulation, refrigerators and freezers, dishwashers, computers, DVD and CD players, television screens.
- Do you use a laptop, tablet, or iPad? Most of the components are made from various plastics derived from petrochemicals.

- Are you using detergent to wash your clothes or dishes? (We hope so!) Many detergents are made from the petrochemical, ethylene.
- Do you use an ink pen? The ink is derived from petrochemicals (butylenes) and so is the plastic casing (which is made from acetal resins derived from methane).
- Are you wearing athletic shoes? Most likely, 100 percent of your shoe is made from petrochemicals such as nylon, which is derived from propylene, and butadiene.
- Have you taken an aspirin or other pain relief medication recently? Aspirin is derived from ethylene and other medications are derived from other petrochemicals.
- Did you put on deodorant, perfume, or cologne today? A large portion of these products are derived from petrochemicals such as ethylene and propylene.
- Do you have carpet in your home or apartment? Most carpets are made from petrochemicals such as nylon, polyester fibers, and so on.
- Many plastic laminates such as countertops and furniture surfaces are derived from petroleum.
- SAP, superabsorbent polymers, can hold over 100 percent of their own weight in water-based liquids and are used primarily in baby diapers.

Naphtha, natural gas, and NGLs are the principal feedstocks for the petrochemical industry, all of which are derived from crude oil and natural gas.[7] Other feedstocks include gas oil, wax, kerosene, and fuel oil. These feedstocks undergo a cracking process involving treatment with heat and pressure to produce the first generation petrochemicals (the building blocks), specifically: olefins (ethylene, propylene, butylenes, and butadiene) and aromatics (benzene, toluene, and xylenes).

Ethylene is one of the primary building blocks in the chemical industry and is used to make two of the most widely used plastics, which are polyvinyl chloride (PVC) and polyethylene. For example, PVC is used in pipes, siding, clothing, cable insulation, and inflatable products. Polyethylene is used for bags, plastic bottles (such as for detergent, oil, shampoo, milk cartons, and so on), and plastic film just to name a few. The olefins are generally used for the production of their respective polymers: polyethylene, polypropylene, or polybutylene. The major uses of aromatics are as intermediates for other chemicals such as solvents or in motor fuel to raise the octane number.

These primary petrochemicals can be further treated and upgraded to produce derivative chemicals and petrochemical end products. Of these derivative chemicals produced, 75 percent are based on ethylene, propylene, and benzene, which can be viewed as the three most important building blocks of the industry. These building blocks are discussed in more detail in the next section.

Some typical petrochemical intermediates are:

- Vinyl acetate for paint, paper, and textile coatings.
- Vinyl chloride for polyvinyl chloride (PVC) resin manufacture.
- Ethylene glycol for polyester textile fibers.
- Styrene, which is important in rubber and plastic manufacturing.
- Polymers.

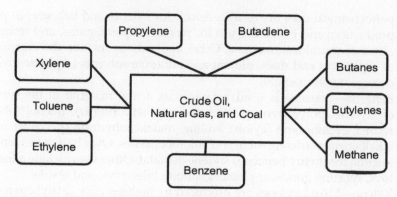

Exhibit 5.7 Nine Basic Petrochemical Feedstocks

The process by which many of the primary and intermediate petrochemicals are converted into synthetic resins, plastics, and fibers is known as polymerization. In polymerization, the basic units (monomers) react in the presence of a catalyst, with or without the application of heat, to form a long chain compound or polymer.

Next, we describe the base chemicals (i.e., the primary building blocks), the intermediates, and the end-use plastics.

The Base Chemicals That Are the Building Blocks

Exhibit 5.7 illustrates the nine basic petrochemical feedstocks that are the building blocks used in the chemical industry that are produced from crude oil, natural gas, and NGLs. For brevity, we will focus on five of these in our discussion.[8]

1. Ethylene—Ethylene is the most-widely used hydrocarbon in the chemical industry, and one of the primary building blocks is ethane as illustrated in Exhibit 5.2 Panel B. By itself, ethylene has almost no end-use, but it is a basic raw material for a variety of industrial products, either alone (polyethylene) or after reaction with other chemicals (vinyls such as polyvinyl chloride—PVC, polyester, etc.). Of the world's ethylene demand, 59 percent is consumed in polyethylene production. Other major derivatives are ethylene oxide/glycol (13 percent), ethylene dichloride (13 percent), and ethylbenzene/styrene (6 percent). Ethylene is produced commercially by steam cracking a wide range of hydrocarbon feedstocks.

2. Propylene—Propylene is an important chemical used in the manufacture of plastics. It is used to manufacture many common household items such as food storage containers, diapers, and children's toys. Propylene consumption is dominated by polypropylene (PP), which accounts for 60 percent of demand and is one of the fastest-growing derivatives. Other important derivatives are propylene oxide (7 percent), acrylonitrile (9 percent), cumene (6 percent) and oxo-alcohols (9 percent). The primary source of propylene is from cracking naphtha and other liquids, such as gas oil and condensates, to produce ethylene.

3. Toluene—Toluene is used in large quantities as an octane booster in gasoline, but most of that portion is never removed from refinery streams. Its

petrochemical uses are as a feedstock for xylenes and benzene; in phenol production; and in solvent use for paints, lacquers, gums, and resins. It is also a chemical intermediate. Other applications include the manufacture of explosives and dyes, diluent and adhesive solvents in plastic toys, and detergent manufacture.

4. Benzene—Benzene is used primarily as a raw material in the synthesis of styrene (polystyrene plastics and synthetic rubber), phenol (phenolic resins), cyclohexane (nylon), aniline, maleic anhydride (polyester resins), alkylbenzenes (detergents), and chlorobenzenes. Over half of benzene production feeds ethylbenzene/styrene demand. Other uses include adhesives, toys, sporting goods, appliances, automobiles, tires, and textiles.

5. Xylene—Mixed xylenes are produced by high-severity catalytic reforming of naphtha. Xylenes are also obtained from the pyrolysis gasoline stream in a naphtha steam cracker and by toluene disproportionation (oxidation and reduction). This building block is used as a solvent in the printing, rubber, and leather industries. It is also used as a cleaning agent, as paint thinner, and in paints and varnishes. Together with toluene, it is also a key ingredient in unleaded gasoline. There are three commercial isomers of xylene (metaxylene, paraxylene, and orthoxylene), which are used to produce such products as higher-quality unsaturated polyesters, PET resins, polyester fiber, resin and film, bactericides, soybean herbicides, and lube oil additives.

The Intermediates and Derivatives That Lead to the End Products

Ethylene glycol—Its principal applications are as an intermediate in the production of polyesters and as automotive antifreeze. Around 55 percent of world production is used in polyester fibers, 16 percent in PET (polyethylene terephthalate) resin, 15 percent in antifreeze, 6 percent in other applications such as de-icing fluid and surface coatings, and 3 percent in other polyesters. There are three grades of ethylene glycol: fiber grade, industrial grade, and antifreeze grade. Specific applications include its use as a heat-transfer fluid in aircraft and runway de-icing mixtures, to provide freeze-thaw stabilization to latex coatings, to improve flexibility and drying time of oil-based paints containing alkyd resins, as a dehydrating agent for natural gas, in motor oil additives, and as an additive in the formulation of inks, pesticides, wood stains, adhesives, and other products.

Phenol—The primary chemical intermediates and derivatives of phenol include phenolic resins, bisphenol-A (BPA), caprolactam, adipic acid, and plasticizers. Phenolic resins are used for adhesives, binders for insulation, and for molding compounds. Phenol is also used as a slimicide, which is a chemical toxic to bacteria and fungi; as a disinfectant; and as an anaesthetic in medicinal preparations including ointments, ear and nose drops, cold sore lotions, throat lozenges, and antiseptic lotions.

Acrylic acid—Acrylic acid has traditionally been used to produce solvent-based acrylic resins. However, environmental concerns over solvent use led to the development of water-based acrylics. Applications for water-based acrylics are primarily in decorative, masonry, and industrial

coatings. Since the mid-1980s, two new applications—superabsorbent polymers (SAPs) and detergent polymers—have emerged, and now account for nearly 40 percent of world acrylic acid consumption. SAPs are cross-linked polyarcylates with the ability to absorb and retain more than 100 times their own weight in liquid. They have experienced very strong growth, primarily in baby diapers.

Acetic acid—Principal uses are as a chemical intermediate and solvent in chemical reactions. Its main use is in vinyl acetate monomer, used to make protective coatings, adhesives, and plastics, and accounts for about 44 percent of the consumption. PTA (purified terephthalic acid) production accounts for around 18 percent, solvent esters 14 percent, and acetic anhydride, used primarily in cigarette filters, about 13 percent.

Styrene—Styrene is mainly used in the manufacture of homopolymers and copolymers. Its predominant use is in polystyrene (66 percent), of which 50 percent is in the manufacture of general purpose (GP) and high-impact (HI) polystyrene (PS), and 16 percent in expanded polystyrene. Other uses include styrene-butadiene rubber and latex (11 percent) as well as ABS/SAN (acrylonitrile butadiene styrene/styrene-acrylonitrile) resins (14 percent). There is a wide range of end uses for styrene's derivatives including packaging, construction materials, automotive parts including tires, household goods, electrical appliances and electronic cases, and drinking cups and other food use items.

End-Products: The Plastics

Polyethylene—This is one of the two most widely used plastics in the world. The manufacture of most resins or plastics begins with the polymerization or linking of the basic compound (monomer), usually a gas or liquid, into high-molecular-weight noncrystalline solids. The manufacture of the basic monomer is not considered part of the plastics industry and is usually carried out at a chemical or petroleum plant. The manufacture of most plastics involves an enclosed reaction or polymerization step, a drying step, and a final treating and forming step. Treatment of the resin after polymerization varies with the proposed use. Resins for moldings are dried and crushed or ground into molding powder. Resins, such as the alkyd to be used for protective coatings, are usually transferred to an agitated thinning tank, where they are thinned with some type of solvent and then stored in large steel tanks equipped with water-cooled condensers to prevent loss of solvent to the atmosphere. Other resins are stored in latex form as they come from the kettle. Three types of polyethylene are discussed next—HDPE, LDPE, and LLDPE.

HDPE—High Density Polyethylene: HDPE refers to a plastic used to make bottles for milk, juice, water, and laundry products. Unpigmented HDPE bottles are translucent and have good barrier properties and stiffness. They are well suited for packaging products with short shelf life such as milk, margarine, and yogurt containers. Because HDPE has good chemical resistance, it is used for packaging many household products as well as industrial chemicals such as detergents and bleach. Pigmented HDPE bottles

generally have better stress crack and chemical resistance than bottles made from unpigmented HDPE.

LDPE—Low Density Polyethylene: A plastic employed predominately in film applications due to its toughness, flexibility, and relative transparency, making it popular in applications where heat sealing is necessary. LDPE is also used to manufacture some flexible lids and bottles and in wire and cable applications because of its properties and processing characteristics. LDPE is also used in sheathing for electrical and communication cables, the extrusion coating of paper and board for the packaging of liquids, and in moisture barrier applications.

LLDPE—Linear Low Density Polyethylene is a thermoplastic, which, in many applications, replaces its predecessor—low-density polyethylene (LDPE)—or is used in blends with LDPE. In particular, LLDPE's short chain branching gives it higher tensile strength, puncture, and anti-tear properties, making it particularly suitable for film applications. Other outlets include injection-molding products and wire and cable. Metallocene-based LLDPE resins are penetrating the film and packaging markets due to their enhanced physical properties, while catalyst developments should improve their processability.

Polyvinyl chloride (PVC)—This is one of the two most widely used plastics in the world. There are two types of PVC homopolymers: rigid resins that are inflexible and hard; and flexible resins that contain a large proportion of plasticizer to make them soft and stretchable. In addition to its stable physical properties, PVC has good chemical resistance, good weatherability, flow characteristics, and stable electrical properties. The diverse slate of vinyl products can be broadly divided into rigid and flexible materials. Bottles and packaging sheets are the major rigid markets, but vinyl is also widely used in the construction market for applications such as pipes and fittings, siding, carpet backing, and windows. Flexible vinyl is used in wire and cable insulation, film and sheet floor coverings, synthetic leather products, coatings, blood bags, medical tubing, and many other applications.

Polypropylene (PP)—Polypropylene has good chemical resistance, is strong, and is the lowest-density plastic used in packaging. It has a high melting point, making it ideal for hot-fill liquids. PP is found in flexible and rigid packaging products, fibers, and large molded parts for automotive and consumer products.

Polystyrene (PS)—Polystyrene is a very versatile plastic that can be rigid or foamed. Typical applications include protective packaging, containers, lids, cups, bottles, and trays. Extruded polystyrene foam (Styrofoam) sheets are formed into egg carton containers, meat and poultry trays, and fast-food containers requiring hot or cold insulation. Solid polystyrene sheets are formed into drinking cups and lids, and disposable food packaging. Durable goods, including housewares and furniture, are also made of polystyrene.

Polyethylene terephthalate (PET or PETE)—PET is transparent and tough, and has good gas and moisture barrier properties. This plastic is commonly used in soft drink bottles and many other injection-molded consumer product containers. Other applications include strapping, molding

compounds, and both food and nonfood containers. Demand for cleaned and recycled PET flakes and pellets is high in the areas of spinning fiber for carpet yarns and producing fiberfill and geotextiles.

Purified terephthalic acid (PTA)—This is primarily used in polyester production, with polyester fiber consuming a large proportion of global output. However, polyethylene terephthalate (PET) resin production for packaging and film applications is growing rapidly due to its success in penetrating the soft drink and water bottle market. A smaller proportion of PTA is utilized in the production of polyester film, which had, until recently, been the material of choice for the audio recording industry. The remaining PTA is used to manufacture other plastic derivatives.

CONCLUSION

Financial and economic analyses are embedded in all aspects of this complex industry. As discussed in the chapter, petroleum products impact all areas of our life every single day, and many people do not realize that these everyday items are derived from fossil fuels. Without the products made from petroleum, we would be back in the dark ages.

When performing financial analysis in this industry, some of the heterogeneous factors are obvious. Drilling a well in Oklahoma or Kazakhstan may be similar because the platforms for the wells are situated on dry ground. Building a rig in the North Sea to provide a platform for the well is obviously different from these other two cases. Also, the logistics involved in getting the oil or natural gas to a refinery is quite different when the well is located in Kazakhstan rather than in Oklahoma. These differences are important.

Equally as important are the considerations of the density of the oil and the intermediate and end products demanded by the market. These products are competing against each other for the raw materials in a very real sense. Getting from the raw materials to the ultimate products requires processing, which can be done, as has been demonstrated here, in a variety of ways. In some cases, more than one process may fulfill the need, but only one will most efficiently provide the products to the market based on the characteristics of the raw materials. In other cases, only one process or sequence of processes can produce the proper quantities of products. As is the case in any financial analysis, the final distribution of products will be determined by the combination of specific products and quantities that maximize value. It is necessary for anyone involved in energy finance and economics to understand how these factors are interrelated. As this chapter demonstrates, it is imperative that the process be matched to the characteristics of the raw materials to gain the desired results as efficiently as possible. These are real options of a very complex order that financial analysts have to recognize in their entirety. They can only do so through an understanding of the petroleum industry as a whole.

DISCUSSION QUESTIONS

1. List and describe the three segments of the oil and natural gas industry.
2. List and describe the three main processing steps of refineries.

3. What are the major finished petroleum products from the refining process? List in order from lighter to heavier.

4. Assuming a 3-2-1 crack spread, what is the crack spread if gasoline is $125.00 per barrel, distillate is $119.00 per barrel, and the cost of crude oil is $113.68 per barrel.

5. List and describe five of the petrochemical building blocks that are the primary feedstocks for the chemical industry.

6. You just purchased a bottle of your favorite soft drink at the convenience store. This bottle is most likely made from which of the following plastics?
   a. Polyvinyl chloride
   b. Low-density polyethylene
   c. High-density polyethylene
   d. Polyethylene terephthalate

7. What is a SAP? What type of polymer is it? What is its main use?

8. You just ordered a meal from your favorite fast food restaurant. Look around at the items you are using and what other people are using in the restaurant. What petroleum products are you and other people using? More specifically, list the items you and other customers are using that are derived from petrochemicals and which of the petrochemicals are used.

9. Look around your home. List five goods made from plastics and explain which plastics make up the good along with describing the good. Use five different plastics examples.

10. ____ is a system of classifying crude oil based on its specific gravity, whereby the greater the gravity, the lighter the oil.
    a. Full cost
    b. API
    c. FASB
    d. Sweet
    e. Sour

11. What is a hydrocarbon?
    a. A chemical containing water
    b. A molecule with carbon and hydrogen
    c. A non-polluting fossil fuel
    d. A compound produced at hydroelectric plants

NOTES

1. Natural gas is a combustible mixture of hydrocarbon gases. While natural gas is formed primarily of methane (70 to 90 percent), before processing it can also include ethane, propane, butane, and pentane (up to 20 percent in total of these four hydrocarbons), and very small amounts of carbon dioxide, oxygen, nitrogen, and hydrogen sulphide. The composition of natural gas can vary widely.

2. This chapter utilizes many sources for the discussion and also knowledge from working in the refining industry. Part of the discussion on the refining industry and petrochemicals is based on UBS (2004) and Maples (2000). For more information on the energy industry, also refer to Raymond and Leffler (2006), Hefner III (2009), Energy Intelligence Research (2011), among others.

3. Liquefied natural gas, or LNG, is natural gas that has been condensed into a liquid by cooling it to minus 260 degrees Fahrenheit or by pressure for storage and transportation purposes. Liquefied natural gas is colorless, odorless, non-corrosive, and non-toxic.

4. The use of kerosene in place of whale oil has been credited with saving some whale species from being hunted to extinction.

5. See *Oil and Gas Journal*, June 4, 2012, 112.
6. Natural gas liquids are those portions of reservoir gas that are separated from natural gas and liquefied in a gas-processing plant during upstream processing. Natural gas liquids include ethane, propane, butane, and condensate.
7. Naphtha is a broad term covering among the lightest and most volatile fractions of the liquid hydrocarbons in crude oil.
8. For more information on the petrochemical industry, refer to Burdick and Leffler (2001).

REFERENCES

Burdick, Donald L., and William L. Leffler. 2001. *Petrochemicals in Nontechnical Language*, 3rd ed. Tulsa, OK: Pennwell Corporation.
Energy Intelligence Research. 2011. *Energy Fundamentals: Understanding the Oil & Gas Industry*, 5th ed. New York: Energy Intelligence Group, Inc.
Hefner III, Robert A. 2009. *The Grand Energy Transition: The Rise of Energy Gases, Sustainable Life and Growth, and the Next Great Economic Expansion*. Hoboken, NJ: John Wiley & Sons.
Maples, Robert E. 2000. *Petroleum Refinery Process Economics*, 2nd ed. Tulsa, OK: Pennwell Corporation.
Maugeri, Leonardo. 2012. *Oil: The Next Revolution: The Unprecedented Upsurge of Oil Production Capacity and What It Means for the World*. Cambridge: Harvard Kennedy School.
PennWell Corporation. 2012. *Oil and Gas Journal* 110:6 (June).
Raymond, Martin S., and William L. Leffler. 2006. *Oil and Gas Production in Nontechnical Language*. Tulsa, OK: Pennwell Corporation.
UBS Investment Research. 2004. *Introduction to the Oil Industry*. London: UBS, Inc.

ABOUT THE CONTRIBUTORS

Russell E. Simkins, PE, is Manager of Proposal Services in the College of Engineering, Architecture, and Technology at Oklahoma State University (OSU) and is a licensed Professional Engineer (PE) in the state of Oklahoma. He has over 30 years of engineering experience working in many different areas including project management, research and development, marketing and sales, and field testing. He has previously worked for ConocoPhillips, Fractionation Research Institute, Lubrizol Corporation, Southwest Research Institute, and the U.S. Department of Energy. He has also been active in the engineering profession as a member of various working groups in the Society of Automotive Engineers (SAE), Coordinating Research Council (CRC), and American Society of Testing Materials (ASTM) dealing with fuels and lubricants. Simkins holds three engineering degrees: a Master's Degree in Industrial Engineering and Management from Oklahoma State University with a focus in energy management, a Bachelor of Science degree in Chemical Engineering from the University of Arkansas, and a Bachelor of Science degree in Mechanical Power Technology from OSU.

Kenneth A. Borokhovich, PhD, is a Lecturer in Finance at Miami University. Prior to his current appointment, he had over 20 years of experience as a member of the faculty at Case Western Reserve University and Cleveland State University. He has also been a visiting faculty member at Lehigh University and Wayne State University. He holds a doctoral degree is in finance as well as an MBA from Ohio State University. In addition, he is a lieutenant colonel, U.S. Army, retired. Borokhovich has published many articles in leading finance journals.

CHAPTER 6

The Economics of Renewable Energy*

BRAD CARSON
Director of the National Energy Policy Institute and Associate Professor of
Entrepreneurship and Business Law, University of Tulsa and also General Counsel
of the U.S. Army

INTRODUCTION

Baseload electricity generation from thermal plants—plants fueled by coal, nuclear
fission, or natural gas—has many advantages to system operators: it is reliable, predictable, and historically quite inexpensive. For all of its promise in mitigating climate change and in promoting energy security, renewable energy will not become
widespread unless it offers system operators similar advantages. Yet renewable
energy—particularly wind power and solar power—is intermittent; its availability
cannot be predicted with precision (Trainer 2010). When available, many renewable sources—again wind power and solar power are particular examples—are
variable; the speed of the wind or the intensity of solar irradiation for any particular day cannot be known in advance (ISONE 2010; NERC 2009). Renewable energy
is often site-dependent and located far from population centers where power is
in greatest demand; solar energy in the deserts of the American Southwest and
wind turbines in the Great Plains require transmission that will be both costly
and involve efficiency losses (Elliott 2000). Biomass production provokes land use
change; increased carbon emissions are possible with their careless cultivation, and
the food supply is very possibly diminished as agriculture turns to energy production (Searchinger et al. 2008; Tilman et al. 2009). But the most significant problem facing renewable energy is cost (Lloyd and Forest 2010; Trainer 1995, 2010).
While many of the obstacles confronting renewable energy can arguably be sur-
mounted through innovative grid management or improved planning, the relative
expense of renewable energy—as typically calculated—will limit its use in electricity production (Denholm and Hand 2011; Ibrahim, Ghandour, Dimitrova, Ilinca,
and Perron 2011; ISONE 2010; NERC 2009). This chapter critically examines the

*I would like to thank Mary Haddican and Doreen Griffiths for research assistance, Mike
Pfeiff for many insights into energy markets, and Sharon Showalter of OnLocation, Inc., for
invaluable technical help. I would also like to thank the National Energy Policy Institute at
the University of Tulsa for sponsoring this work.

prevailing method of evaluating renewable energy projects and looks, too, at alternative methodologies.

MEASURING RENEWABLE ENERGY'S VALUE

Electricity is a unique market, characterized by a constantly fluctuating demand and supply, difficult storage, and the practical inability to ration or queue. Servicing this market in the United States are two broad classes of providers. There are more than 3,000 traditional electric utilities (EIA 2011a). These utilities can be investor-owned, publicly owned, or cooperatives, and they are regulated by local, state, and federal authorities. Traditional utilities have designated franchise territories and are often vertically integrated, including generation, transmission, and distribution facilities among their assets. There are also nearly 2,000 nonutility power producers in the country. This class of producers includes Qualifying Facilities established under the Public Utility Regulatory Policies Act of 1978 (PURPA); independent power producers that sell electricity at market-based rates; and combined heat and power plants co-located at industrial sites.

Calculating Levelized Costs

The foremost method of estimating the cost of electricity is known as *levelized cost*. The levelized cost of electricity is the present value of the total cost of building and operating a power plant over its economic life, converted to equal amounts per watt-hour of electricity generated by the plant (Heptonstall 2007). In other words, the levelized cost is that price which equates the net present value of revenue from the plant with the net present value of the cost (Borenstein 2012; EIA 2010). It is the equivalent of average cost in microeconomics (Rothwell 2010). As these definitions suggest, an essential input in the calculation of levelized cost is total lifetime plant costs—the sum of capital expenditures, operating and maintenance costs, and fuel costs. Once the total lifetime cost of a plant is established, it is but a short step to determine the levelized cost of electricity.

Before proceeding too far in the method itself, it should be noted that levelized cost can be expressed in either real or nominal values or, to use slightly different but more confusing terms, in level current-dollars or level constant-dollars. As the level nominal (or current-dollar) price will always be higher than the level real (or constant-dollar) price, this distinction is very important, even though more honored in the breach than in fact (Black and Veatch 2011). Part of the prevalent confusion rests in the befuddling terms *current-dollar* and *constant-dollar*. But returning to a familiar example assists in understanding the difference. Home mortgage payments are usually made in equal installments over the life of the debt, with the payment amount set at the time the home is purchased and never varying thereafter. This ubiquitous arrangement is the paradigmatic type of level current-dollar payment, as each installment has the same face value (set at the beginning in current dollars), even though a uniform payment every month for 15 years or 30 years will have ever-diminishing real value. This mortgage payment is but one species of annuity, a genus almost always calculated in level nominal or current-dollar values, although it should be noted that this is not strictly necessary. By contrast, a constant-dollar or real levelized cost will increase with inflation over time, ensuring that the real value of the payment never declines although its face value will

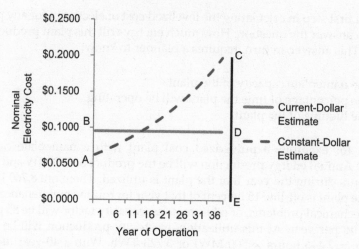

Exhibit 6.1 Lifetime Nominal Costs of Current-Dollar and Constant-Dollar Levelized Cost

change. This is illustrated in Exhibit 6.1. Assuming that each year of operations produces the same quantity of electricity, the rectangle mapped by the origin and points B, D, and E has the same present value as the area marked by the origin and points A, C, and E.

This graphic shows the levelized cost of a supercritical coal plant whose constant-dollar levelized cost is $0.0624 and whose current-dollar levelized cost is $0.0951. The *x* axis measures years of plant operations, while the Y axis is the nominal price of electricity. A constant-dollar estimate will maintain its real value over time, meaning that its nominal value must grow. This increase is the curve AC. The current-dollar levelized cost does not increase over time. Assuming that the quantity of electricity produced is the same for each year, the area underneath the curve AC and the rectangle bounded by the line BD will have the same present value.

As Black and Veatch (2011) observe, a real or constant-dollar levelized cost is analogous to the Year 1 price of electricity in a power purchase agreement or feed-in tariff that increases with inflation each and every year; the nominal or current-dollar levelized cost would be equivalent to a flat and unchanging price in each year of the project's life. Either method is intellectually sound and finds widespread use. Governments and policymakers typically state levelized cost in real terms, while developers and project owners seem to prefer nominal levelized cost, as these will mirror values appearing in financial statements. In the end, much depends on the purpose of the analysis (Short, Packey, and Holt 2005). A choice of current-dollar or nominal levelized cost will make future actual cash flows easier to determine, and is often used in short-term studies. A constant-dollar levelized cost provides clear insight into cost trends. Most importantly, though, comparisons among energy technologies should use a consistent and well-communicated approach, making the choice of current-dollars or constant-dollars explicit.

Plant Utilization

Plant utilization (or *capacity factor* as it is usually termed in renewable energy discussions) is a driver of variable operating costs, fuel cost, and revenues. So an

important first step in calculating the levelized cost of electricity for any particular plant is to answer the question: How much energy will this plant produce over its lifetime? This answer, in turn, requires a planner to know:

1. The nameplate capacity of the plant.
2. The percentage of time the plant will be operating.
3. The lifetime of the plant.

Take, for example, a pulverized coal plant with a nameplate capacity of 500 MW.[1] Annual energy production will be the product of 500 MW and the number of hours during the year that the plant is utilized. There are 8,760 hours in a year; if the plant is off-line 15 percent of that year for routine maintenance, unanticipated mechanical problems, or other reasons, capacity factor will be 85 percent or 7,446 hours per year. At this utilization, electricity production will be 3.723 billion kWh (= 7,446 hours × 500 MW) or 3.723 TWh. With a 40-year life, the 500 MW plant will produce a total of 148.92 billion kWh (= 40 × 3.723 TWh) of energy before decommissioning. This level of utilization would not be uncommon for a 500 MW coal, combined-cycle natural gas, or nuclear power plant.

Geothermal energy and biomass energy have capacity factors that can rival traditional, baseload power plants. But most sources of renewable energy suffer from much lower utilization. This is not too surprising; the sun does not always shine, the wind does not always blow, and the tide's strength quite literally ebbs and flows. Lower capacity factors will, all else being equal, increase levelized cost both by reducing annual generation (and its attendant revenues) and by lowering the amount of energy over which fixed costs can be amortized. Indeed, it is not much of an exaggeration to say that the utilization rate (capacity factor) is the prime mover in levelized cost calculations, at least for renewables. It is the technologies with the lowest utilization—solar and wind, notably—that levelized cost invariably finds the most expensive. The combination of higher capacity factor and longer lives gives traditional power plants a large advantage in levelized cost comparisons. Consequently, assumptions about annual utilization and plant life should be carefully scrutinized.

Capital Expenditures

Construction costs are the lion's share of capital expenditures, and it is a convention to state the construction costs of power plants in *dollars per installed kilowatt*. This estimate is not only frequently reported in governmental publications, but is also to be found in many energy reports that do not otherwise calculate a technology's levelized cost. Almost always, the construction costs are given as *overnight capital costs*, a term of art unique to energy economics, and meaning that the cost estimates are as if the plant were to be built in a single day. Regrettably, the locution obscures more than enlightens; the most important question to be asked about any quoted overnight cost is: What is to be included among its accounts? Items rightfully considered are not only structural material and installation, mechanical equipment and installation, and supply and installation of electrical instrumentation and controls, but also engineering fees, contractor fees, scaffolding costs, and various so-called owner's costs, such as development costs, permitting and legal fees, insurance costs, and property taxes, just to name a few. Exhibit 6.2 shows

Exhibit 6.2 Costs of Various Generating Technologies

Technology	Size (mW)	Lead time (yrs)	Base Overnight Cost in 2009 (2008 $/kW)	Project Contingency Factor	Total Overnight Cost in 2009 (2008 $/kW)	Variable O&M (Operating & Maintenance) (2008 mills/kWh)	Fixed O&M (2008 $/kW)	Heat Rate in 2009 (Btu/kWh)
Scrubbed Coal New	600	4	2,078	1.07	2,223	4.69	28.15	9,200
Conv Gas/Oil Comb Cycle	250	3	937	1.05	984	2.11	12.76	7,196
Adv Gas/Oil Comb Cycle (CC)	400	3	897	1.08	968	2.04	11.96	6,752
Conv Comb Turbine	160	2	653	1.05	685	3.65	12.38	10,788
Adv Comb Turbine	230	2	617	1.05	648	3.24	10.77	9,289
Fuel Cells	10	3	4,744	1.05	5,478	49.00	5.78	7,930
Adv Nuclear	1,350	6	3,308	1.10	3,820	0.51	92.04	10,488
Biomass	80	4	3,414	1.07	3,849	6.86	65.89	9,451
Geothermal	50	4	1,666	1.05	1,749	0.00	168.33	32,969
MSW—Landfill Gas	30	3	2,430	1.07	2,599	0.01	116.80	13,648
Conventional Hydropower	500	4	2,084	1.10	2,291	2.49	13.93	9,884
Wind	50	3	1,837	1.07	1,966	0.00	30.98	9,884
Wind Offshore	100	4	3,492	1.10	3,937	0.00	86.92	9,884
Solar Thermal	100	3	4,798	1.07	5,132	0.00	58.05	9,884
Photovoltaic	5	2	5,879	1.05	6,171	0.00	11.94	9,884

Source: Adapted from EIA 2010.

133

estimates by the U.S. Energy Information Administration of, among other things, overnight capital costs, with all of the aforementioned costs concealed within. This estimate is updated annually by the EIA, and includes a fudge factor for "Project Contingency" costs; this is added to the base overnight cost to arrive at the total overnight cost.

By definition, overnight construction costs are in current dollars. So it would not be erroneous to say that, if the plant was going to be built immediately, the total capital costs of the plant would be roughly equal to the overnight costs:

$$TLKC_{pv} = O_k \tag{6.1}$$

where $TLKC_{pv}$ = the present value of the total lifetime capital costs of the plant. If construction does not start for several months or years, due to permitting requirements, financing difficulties, or other logistical challenges, only a few accommodations to the calculation are needed. Specifically, overnight construction cost must account for the time value of money and also for inflation. In other words, the construction costs—when construction finally starts—will be equal to the overnight construction cost today—as shown by sources such as Exhibit 6.2—multiplied by $\left[\frac{1+i}{1+r}\right]^{t-1}$ where i is the inflation rate; r is the nominal discount rate; and t is the number of years until commencement of construction. Exhibit 6.2, above, provides estimates of construction lead times, too.

If construction costs will occur over several years but in equal installments, the present value of the construction costs will be:

$$TLKC_{pv} = \frac{O_k}{t} * \sum_{n=0}^{t-1} \left[\frac{1+i}{1+r}\right]^n \tag{6.2}$$

where $TLKC_{pv}$ = present value of lifetime capital costs
         O_k = overnight capital cost
         t = the number of periods for construction
         i = the inflation rate per period
         r = the nominal discount rate per period

As the summation of a geometric series, equation (6.2) can be restated:

$$TLKC_{pv} = \frac{O_k}{t} * \frac{1 - R^t}{1 - R} \tag{6.3}$$

with $R = \frac{1+i}{1+r}$.

On the other hand, if construction costs are not in equal annual amounts, the only solution is to abandon shortcuts and add together each year's capital costs, accounting for inflation and then discounting accordingly. This should not be a laborious task. Rework and other intermittent capital costs can be treated similarly.

Determination of base present value construction costs, even when broadly defined as was done in Exhibit 6.1, is not tantamount to a determination of lifetime capital costs. At a minimum, there will be additional capital expenditures over the lifetime of the plant; inverters in solar PV plants must be replaced every few years, wind turbines experience mechanical problems, and thermal plants will

require the occasional overhaul. There are other possible expenditures that should also not be overlooked. Land may need to be purchased, and sometimes royalties must be prepaid. Capital may also be devoted to fuel inventory, and, in any event, additional construction of balance-of-plant facilities—water tanks, break rooms, security shacks, business offices—must be undertaken. And, perhaps most significantly, there is a financing cost for doing all of these things—this would include the interest on debt or, for equity, the opportunity cost, and the longer the construction period, the more biting these financing costs become. For nuclear plants, admittedly among the most capital-intensive of technologies and also likely to have long lead times, Rothwell (2010) estimates that financing costs could equal more than one-third of the overnight cost alone. The exact amount of these costs—termed *indirect* by Rothwell (2010) and more frequently called *allowance for funds used during construction* (EPRI 2010)—will be a function of the discount rate, the construction lead time, and the distribution of capital expenditures. For short lead times of one to two years, capitalized finance costs may only be 5 to 10 percent of base construction costs; for lead times of four years or more, the cost will be much more painful. Exhibit 6.1, for all of its comprehensiveness, does not include financing costs in its overnight capital cost estimates.

Operating and Maintenance Costs

As with construction costs, operating and maintenance (O&M) costs are usually estimated on a *dollars per installed kilowatt* basis. Often, too, as shown in Exhibit 6.2, the O&M costs will be broken down into fixed and variable components. (Alternatively, planners sometimes take the O&M costs of a plant of similar size and technology as the basis for estimations.) Direct labor is the most important of fixed O&M costs, along with overhead; variable O&M would cover the costs of water, wastewater disposal, consumables, and similar items. No matter what expenses are classified as fixed or variable O&M, the same procedures as used with capital costs are to be followed in calculating levelized cost. The only significant difference is that, while base capital costs are given in overnight terms and will in any event be of comparatively short duration, O&M costs are annual expenditures over the life of the power plant, which could be many decades. Another difference is that O&M costs, while known as of today, will not start until construction is complete and the plant is actually operational, which could be several years hence.

Fuel Costs

Fuel costs are an important component of the levelized cost of thermal plants, such as those fired by natural gas, coal, and nuclear fission. For most renewable sources of energy, fuel costs are not significant and are, in fact, often zero. A coal plant with a capacity of 500MW and a utilization rate of 85 percent will have an annual energy output of 3.723 billion kWh (= 8,760 hours/year × 85% × 500MW) or 3.723 TWh. How much coal will be required to generate 3.723 TWh of electricity? It depends on the heat rate of the plant—the efficiency in converting the chemical energy of a fuel source into electrical energy. Most coal-fired power stations have an efficiency ranging from 33 percent to 45 percent (Franco and Diaz 2009). If the plant's efficiency is in the middle of that range—and the EIA's estimates in Exhibit 6.2 assume

an efficiency of 37 percent for a new coal plant—then 3.723 TWh of annual electricity generation will require 10.04 TWh of coal (= 3.723 TWh/.37). Assuming that a ton of bituminous coal has a net heat value of about 26 million BTUs and making some simple conversions—such as the fact that a watt-hour of energy is equivalent to 3.412 BTU—reveals that an annual requirement of 10.04 TWh of energy from coal is equivalent to 34.25 trillion BTUs (= 10.04 TWh × 3.412 BTU/Wh) or, 1.32 million short tons of bituminous coal (= 34.25 trillion/26 million). If the price of coal today is, say, $70 per delivered short ton, then this year's fuel bill will be $92.2 million (= $70 × 1.32 million tons).

WACC and Inflation

In levelized cost estimates, all future costs and revenues are discounted back to the present through a choice of discount rate, usually the *weighted average cost of capital*, or WACC. The WACC is a function of the return on debt and the return on equity, measured in proportion to the contribution of each to the firm's capital structure. In many studies of levelized cost, the WACC is, alas, frequently obscured. And even in those reports that do make clear this important input, some state the WACC in real values and others in nominal terms, with the WACC ranging from 5 to 15 percent (nominal). In the most recent version of its influential projections of levelized cost, EIA (2011a) adopts an after-tax nominal WACC of 10 percent. In setting this figure, the EIA assumes that the fraction of debt financing for an energy project will be 45 percent, with equity obviously having the remainder. EIA (2011b) sees the cost of debt approximated by the industrial Baa bond rate, while the rate of the 10-year U.S. Treasury note is taken as the risk-free rate for determining the cost of equity. With the equity risk-premium assumed to be 6 percent and the beta (for utility projects) estimated to be 1.25, the EIA projects a cost of equity of 13 percent for most technologies. It should be noted that, as interest on debt is tax deductible, the actual cost of debt is $(1 - x)$ the actual required return, where x is the tax rate of the obligee. In 2011, the EIA added another 3 percent to the cost of debt and equity for new coal plants without carbon capture and sequestration; this increase reflects the greater risk of this greenhouse-gas-intensive technology relative to alternatives.

Balancing Costs and Revenues

Levelized cost is that price of electricity perfectly equilibrating the lifetime revenues and lifetime costs of the plant:

$$TLR_{pv} = TLKC_{pv} + TLOMC_{pv} + TLFC_{pv} \qquad (6.4)$$

where TLR_{pv} = present value of lifetime revenues from the sale of the plant's electricity
         $TLKC_{pv}$ = present value of lifetime capital costs
         $TLOMC_{pv}$ = present value of lifetime operating and maintenance costs
         $TLFC_{pv}$ = present value of lifetime fuel costs

Revenues will not be earned until the plant is operational, of course, just as O&M and fuel costs will not be incurred until that date.

The present value of lifetime revenue can be restated:

$$TLR_{pv} = D_0 * R^t * \frac{1 - R^p}{1 - R}$$ (6.5)

with $R = \frac{1+i}{1+r}$.

where TLR_{pv} = present value of total lifetime revenues
Su D_0 = revenues per period, as known today
t = the number of periods for construction
p = lifetime of the plant in periods
i = the inflation rate per period
r = the nominal discount rate per period

Substituting into equation (6.4) results in equation (6.5):

$$D_0 * R^t * \frac{1 - R^p}{1 - R} = \left[\frac{O_k}{t} * \frac{1 - R^t}{1 - R} \right] + \left[OM_0 * R^t * \frac{1 - R^p}{1 - R} \right] + \left[FC_0 * R^t * \frac{1 - R^p}{1 - R} \right]$$

There are many common terms on both sides of equation (6.5). Simplifying provides:

$$D_0 = \left[\frac{O_k}{t} * \frac{1 - R^t}{1 - R^p} * \frac{1}{R^t} \right] + OM_0 + FC_0$$ (6.6)

Equation (6.6) has isolated the annual revenue in dollars as of today, D_0, that would over the life of the plant exactly offset the lifetime costs. D_0 is, of course, the product of the average revenue per unit of electricity and the number of units generated:

$$D_0 = COE_L * G_t$$ (6.7)

where COE_L = levelized cost of energy per unit
G_t = plant output in per period t

And rewriting equation (6.7) in light of equation (6.6):

$$COE_L = \frac{1}{G_t} \left[\left[\frac{O_k}{t} * \frac{1 - R^t}{1 - R^p} * \frac{1}{R^t} \right] + OM_0 + FC_0 \right]$$ (6.8)

This is the formula to calculate the real or constant-dollar levelized cost. The levelized cost, COE_L, will be denominated in the same units as are the various costs on the right-hand side of equation (6.8). In other words, COE_L will be in dollars if the capital, fuel, and operating costs are also expressed in dollars. And, importantly, the unit of electricity will be expressed in the same unit as G_t. If G_t, the annual energy output of the plant, is expressed in MWh, then COE_L will be per MWh and, similarly, if G_t is in kWh, then COE_L will be per kWh. In many cases, the various costs of the plant will be given in dollars, and the levelized cost per kWh will be

sought, an answer that is most frequently given in cents/kWh. To solve this, ensure that G_t is expressed in kWh, and the result of equation (6.8) will be the levelized cost in dollars per kWh. Simply multiply this by 100 to convert the levelized cost into cents per kWh.

A Simple Example

It has already been shown that a typical 500 MW pulverized coal plant will produce 3.7234 billion kWh annually, or, over its 40-year life, nearly 150 billion kWh. While the 500 MW coal plant might easily produce close to 4 TWh of energy each year, the 250 MW concentrating solar plant, with a capacity factor of 25 percent (due to cloud cover, night, varying solar irradiation over the day), will only produce 500 GWh of energy (= 8,760 hours/year × .25 × 250 MW).

According to Exhibit 6.2, the base cost per installed kilowatt of a new pulverized coal plant is $2,223 (in 2008 dollars). This estimate includes $2,078 per kW in base costs and a contingency fund equal to 7 percent of total capital costs. A concentrating solar plant has much higher base capital costs, $5,134 per installed kW, or 230 percent more than the coal plant. A 500 MW coal plant, if constructed overnight, would have a base cost of $1.1 billion (= 500 MW × $2,223/kW). The concentrating solar plant would cost about the same, $1.28 billion (= 250 MW × $5,134/kW), but would offer only one-half the capacity of the coal plant (and much lower utilization to boot!). Exhibit 6.1 estimates the lead time on a new coal plant at four years, while only three years of lead time is necessary for the concentrating solar plant. Given these construction estimates, and assuming that an inflation rate of 3 percent and a discount rate of 12 percent apply to both projects, the present value of base construction costs can be calculated: the new pulverized coal plant has a total construction cost of $984.8 million; the present value base construction cost of the solar facility is $1.18 billion. For the 500 MW coal plant with a utilization rate of 85 percent and a life of 40 years, construction costs (on a constant-dollar or real basis) will contribute only $0.031 per kWh to levelized cost. For a 250 MW concentrating solar plant with a capacity factor of 25 percent and a life of 30 years, base construction costs are going to be a constant-dollar (or real) levelized $0.1215 per kWh, four times that of the coal plant.

In the case of the 500 MW pulverized coal plant, there is a fixed and variable component to O&M costs. For fixed O&M costs, the EIA's estimates for a new coal plant, shown in Exhibit 6.1, are $28.15 annually per installed kW. For a 500 MW facility, this sums to slightly more than $14 million per year. Variable O&M is dependent on output; at 4.69 mills per kWh of generation (or $0.00469 per kWh), and with an annual expected generation of 3.723 billion kWh, variable O&M for the coal plant amounts to $17.46 million a year. Together, lifetime fixed and variable O&M for the coal plant, at an annual cost of $31.53 million in current dollar (= $14.07 million + $17.46 million), has a present value of $294.5 million. In the case of the 250 MW concentrating solar facility, there are no variable O&M costs, but there is fixed O&M. And, for a concentrating solar plant, fixed O&M is estimated at $58.05 per installed kW or $14.51 million each year for the 250 MW plant. O&M costs over the 30-year life of the solar plant have a present total value of $140.37 million.

Fuel costs for the solar plant will be zero. In the example of the 500 MW coal plant, the annual fuel bill as of today was found to be $92.21 million per year. If

construction lasts for four years, and inflation is 3 percent and the discount rate is 12 percent, the present value of lifetime fuel costs for the coal plant—with a life-time of 40 years—will be $861.27 million. This expense, while seemingly large, is responsible for $0.027 per kWh of the plant's levelized cost on a real constant-dollar basis.

To recap, the lifetime cost of the representative 500 MW pulverized coal plant is, in present value terms, a little more than $2.14 billion. This can be disaggregated into a lifetime present value capital cost of $984.76 million, a lifetime present value O&M cost of $294.49 million, and a lifetime present value fuel cost of $861.27 million. With a construction period of four years, an assumed 40-year life, inflation of 3 percent, a discount rate of 12 percent, and 85 percent utilization (among other plausible if contestable assumptions), the levelized cost of energy from the plant is, in real (constant-dollar) terms, $0.067/kWh. To this total levelized cost, the con-tribution of capital costs is 3.08 cents/kWh in real terms. Fuel costs add, in real terms, 2.69 cents/kWh to the levelized cost. The contribution of O&M costs is .92 cents per kWh in real terms. The capital costs drive 46 percent of levelized cost, with fuel and O&M charged with 40 percent and 14 percent respectively. On the other hand, the present value lifetime cost of the 250 MW concentrating solar plant is $1.32 billion. For this facility, lifetime construction costs amount, in present value terms, to $1.18 billion of the total; O&M costs contribute the slim remainder, $140 million. But with a construction time of 3 years, a life of 30 years, and likely utilization of 25 percent (along with otherwise similar financial assumptions as with the 500 MW coal plant), the levelized cost of electricity from the solar facil-ity is 13.59 cents/kWh in real or constant-dollar terms. Of this, capital costs, at 12.15 cents/kWh in constant-dollar terms, drive 89 percent of the results.

Extensions to the Calculation

It is not difficult to extend equation (6.8) with more inputs. A more realistic estimate of levelized cost should include increases or decreases in real operating and fuel costs over the life of the plant. Environmental taxes should also be factored into lifetime costs. Income taxes and depreciation are often ignored, but can be pow-erful drivers of plant economics. Subsidies and incentives abound for renewable energy. Degradation of annual output should also be expected. With only modest manipulation, levelized cost calculations can incorporate all of these.

Weaknesses of Levelized Cost

Despite its ubiquity in the economics literature, the method of levelized cost is not without weaknesses. Levelized cost is notoriously sensitive to inputs. The choice of discount rate is critical to the calculation. Capital costs change rapidly. Fuel costs are unpredictable. Levelized cost omits indirect costs. Land must be acquired. Transmission must be built out. Levelized cost also ignores externalities. Many technologies emit pollutants whose environmental damage is hard to quantify but is nonetheless rarely considered. While all of these problems can be solved with adequate algebraic manipulation, levelized cost estimates rarely do so, and the costs of complexity can become quite high.

OPTIONS APPROACHES

The options revolution in finance has spread to the valuation of real assets, including those involved in energy production. This migration was pushed by widespread discounted cash flow techniques (Martínez-Ceseña and Mutale 2011). Fuel prices may vary from the predicted path, as can capital costs; regulations change, technology evolves, opportunities vanish, alternatives arise. To contain, if not eliminate, these and many other types of uncertainty is exactly why options theory was developed, and then extended. The option to abandon a project; the option to defer investment; the option to change or modify the scope of a project; the option to alter operating scale; the option to switch output; the option to enter or expand into a new market: all of these are a means of grappling with an uncertain, possibly unknowable future, for options buy time, time gives information, and information reveals truth. Despite their practical complexities, there can be little doubt that real options highlight the value of managerial flexibility in a powerful way that unlocks the attractiveness of business ideas in a way that DCF (discounted cash flow) cannot approach (Boer 2002). Real options have found particular application in the energy sector, where they have been used by oil and gas companies to evaluate drilling prospects and by utilities in deciding on power plants. A full review of the growing use of real options for energy evaluation can be found in Fernandes, Cunha, and Ferreira (2011). As the electricity market becomes less regulated, it is likely that real options will gain more favor still.

When quantified, the value of a financial option depends on six factors: the value of the underlying asset; the exercise price of the option; the time to expiration of the option; the volatility in the value of the underlying asset; the risk-free rate of interest; and any dividends that might be paid during the option period. Each of these six factors has an analogue in the valuation of real assets. Exhibit 6.3 maps the comparison, and a simple example can explain and illustrate both the nature of option valuation in general, its intuitive basis, and also its application to renewable energy. To start, take a company that is contemplating the development of a wind farm, for which a particular revenue per kWh generated has been predicted. The revenue forecast could be based on a known feed-in tariff, the going rate in local power purchase agreements, or the likely allowance from a regulatory body. With a known cost structure and anticipated revenue stream, the company's financial

Exhibit 6.3 Analogy between Project Characteristics of a Real Asset and Inputs into Valuation of Financial Options

Project Characteristics	Option Value Inputs
Present value of expected cash flows	Stock price
Present value of plant investment	Exercise price
Length of deferral time	Time to maturity
Time value of money	Risk-free rate
Volatility of project's returns	Variance of stock returns
Interim returns on project	Dividends paid

Source: Fernandes, Cunha, and Ferreira (2011) and Venetsanos, Angelopoulos, and Tsoutsos (2002).

analysts could determine the net present value of cash flows from the wind project. This is covered in basic finance textbooks, and the textbook gives the company a simple decision rule: if the net present value of the cash flows is positive, build; otherwise, abort.

CONCLUSION

Renewable energy faces many barriers to greater use in the production of electricity, but foremost among these is its perceived expense. As levelized cost is the predominant method for determining and comparing the cost of generation technologies, it is an important subject of study and critique. Since its development in the late nineteenth century, the electricity industry has struggled with basic issues of pricing. Most of the work on electricity pricing was done not by economists, but by engineers, who often incorporated the work of engineers from other regulated industries, such as railroads. In the 1970s, as nuclear power and renewable energy challenged the hegemony of coal-fired, oil-fired, and hydroelectric power plants, some benchmark for comparing new and old technologies was needed, and levelized cost became the widely-adopted standard. But despite its recent vintage, levelized cost is paradoxically already outdated. Levelized cost finds it hard to incorporate the many different regulatory policies that increasingly affect energy production. Levelized cost also ignores or misapplies the techniques of modern finance. The result is that typical comparisons between renewable energy and thermal generation are unsatisfactory. Omitting the effect of taxes and depreciation creates a bias against capital-intensive green technologies, as does failure to include tax. The riskiness of fuel costs creates uncertainty for thermal plants that is unknown to renewable energy. This riskiness is likely going to only grow as more externalities are priced into fossil fuels. Altering assumptions can make a tremendous difference in the calculation of levelized cost, including the bedrock assumptions about what discount rate to use. Perhaps most basically, the notion that revenues can be entirely disregarded is no longer tenable in an increasingly deregulated electricity market. Better techniques to compare electricity generation are desperately needed.

DISCUSSION QUESTIONS

1. What is *levelized cost*, and how is it calculated?
2. Levelized cost can be expressed in either real or nominal values. This statement is:
   a. True
   b. False
3. What is the formula to calculate the real or constant-dollar levelized cost? Create a simple example to illustrate the equation.
4. Explain how extensions can be applied to the formula given in Question 3 such as using more inputs.
5. Describe the weaknesses of levelized costs.
6. Exhibit 6.2 shows the costs of various generating technologies. Answer the following questions using Exhibit 6.2.
   a. Which technology has the longest lead time? The shortest lead time?

  b. Which two technologies have the highest and next-to-highest Total Overnight Costs in 2009 as shown in the exhibit?

  c. Which two technologies have the lowest and next-to-lowest Total Overnight Costs in 2009 as shown in the exhibit?

NOTE

1. MW stands for megawatts, a unit of power, and is 106 watts. Other common abbreviations used in this chapter are k for kilo (103), G for giga (109), and T for tera (1,012). The terms for power and energy are often confused. Power is the rate at which energy is generated or consumed and is expressed in the unit, watts, which is joules per second. A unit of energy is kilowatt hour, kWh and is a unit of energy equal to 1,000, or 103, watt hours. For constant power, energy in watt hours is the product of power in watts and time in hours. (Note: The kilowatt hour is most commonly known as a billing unit for energy delivered to consumers by electric utilities.) Refer to the appendix at the end of this book for common conversion factors.

REFERENCES

Black & Veatch (Producer). 2011. "1: Levelized Cost of Energy Calculation: Methodology and Sensitivity [Powerpoint Slides]." Available at http://www.efchina.org/csepupfiles/report/20112844913435.70772110666485.pdf/Levelized%20Cost%20of%20Energy%20Calculation_BV_EN.pdf.

Boer, F. P. 2002. *The Real Options Solution: Finding Total Value in a High-Risk World*. Vol. 110. Hoboken, NJ: John Wiley & Sons.

Borenstein, S. 2012. "The Private and Public Economics of Renewable Electricity Generation," *Journal of Economic Perspectives, American Economic Association* vol. 26(1), 67–92.

Denholm, P., and M. Hand. 2011. "Grid Flexibility and Storage Required to Achieve Very High Penetration of variable Renewable Electricity." *Energy Policy* 39:3, 1817–1830.

Elliott, D. (2000). Renewable energy and sustainable futures. *Futures*, 32:3-4, 261–274.

EIA. 2010. *Annual Energy Outlook 2010*. Available at www.eia.gov/oiaf/aeo/pdf/0383(2010).pdf.

EIA. 2011a. *Electric Power Monthly*. Available at http://205.254.135.7/electricity/monthly/index.cfm.

EIA. 2011b. *The Electricity Market Module of the National Energy Modeling System Model Documentation Report*.

EPRI. 2010. *Technical Assessment Guide*.

Fernandes, B., J. Cunha, and P. Ferreira. 2011. "The Use of Real Options Approach in Energy Sector Investments." *Renewable and Sustainable Energy Reviews* 15:9, 4491–4497.

Franco, A., and A. R. Diaz. 2009. "The Future Challenges for 'Clean Coal Technologies': Joining Efficiency Increase and Pollutant Emission Control." *Energy* 34:3, 348–354.

Heptonstall, P. 2007. "A Review of Electricity Unit Cost Estimates." UK Energy Research Centre Working Paper.

Ibrahim, H., M. Ghandour, M. Dimitrova, A. Ilinca, and J. Perron. 2011. "Integration of Wind Energy into Electricity Systems: Technical Challenges and Actual Solutions." *Energy Procedia* 6, 815–824.

ISONE. 2010. *New England Wind Integration Study*. Available at www.iso-ne.com/committees/comm_wkgrps/prtcpnts_comm/pac/mtrls/2010/jan212010/newis.pdf.

Lloyd, B., and A. S. Forest. 2010. "The Transition to Renewables: Can PV Provide an Answer to the Peak Oil and Climate Change Challenges?" *Energy Policy* 38:11, 7378–7394.

Martínez-Ceseña, E. A., and J. Mutale. 2011. "Application of an Advanced Real Options Approach for Renewable Energy Generation Projects Planning."*Renewable and Sustainable Energy Reviews* 15:4, 2087–2094.

NERC. 2009. *Accommodating High Levels of Variable Generation.* Princeton, NJ:NERC.

Rothwell, G. 2010. *New U.S. Nuclear Generation: 2010–2030.* Washington, DC: Resources for the Future and National Energy Policy Institute.

Searchinger, T., R. Heimlich, R.A. Houghton, F. Dong, A. Elobeid, J. Fabiosa, et al. 2008. "Use of US Croplands for Biofuels Increases Greenhouse Gases through Emissions from Land-Use Change." *Science* 319:5867, 1238–1240.

Short, W., D. J. Packey, and T. Holt. 2005. *A Manual for the Economic Evaluation of Energy Efficiency and Renewable Energy Technologies.* Honolulu, Hawaii: University Press of the Pacific.

Tilman, D., R. Socolow, J. A. Foley, J. Hill, E. Larson, L. Lynd, et al. 2009. "Beneficial Biofuels—The Food, Energy, and Environment Trilemma." *Science* 325:5938, 270–271.

Trainer, F. E. 1995. "Can Renewable Energy Sources Sustain Affluent Society?" *Energy Policy* 23:12, 1009–1026.

Trainer, F. E. 2010. Can Renewables Etc. Solve the Greenhouse Problem? The Negative Case. *Energy Policy* 38:8, 4107–4114.

Venetsanos, K., P. Angelopoulou, and T. Tsoutsos. 2002. "Renewable Energy Sources Project Appraisal under Uncertainty: The Case of Wind Energy Exploitation within a Changing Energy Market Environment." *Energy Policy* 30:4, 293–307.

ABOUT THE CONTRIBUTOR

Brad Carson is the Director of the National Energy Policy Institute at the University of Tulsa, where he also is as an associate professor of entrepreneurship and business law. Carson is also General Counsel of the U.S. Army, a position to which he was confirmed by the United States Senate in December 2011. Carson graduated from Baylor University with honors and was elected a Rhodes Scholar. After receiving his MA from Oxford University in the United Kingdom, he received his law degree from the University of Oklahoma. In 2000, he was elected to represent the Second District of Oklahoma in the United States House of Representatives. After leaving office in 2004, he was a fellow at the Kennedy School of Government at Harvard University, and, later, Chief Executive Officer of Cherokee Nation Businesses, LLC. From 2009 to 2010, he served in Iraq on active military duty, for which he was awarded the Bronze Star. He has contributed journalism to the *Weekly Standard, Blueprint, The New Republic,* and *Democracy: A Journal of Ideas.*

CHAPTER 7

How Our Political Views Affect Our View of Energy Prices

SHERIDAN TITMAN
Walter W. McAllister Centennial Chair in Financial Services and Professor of Finance in the Department of Finance at the McCombs School of Business, at the University of Texas at Austin

INTRODUCTION

In our inaugural University of Texas Energy Poll in 2011, we asked participants to identify the factors influencing energy pricing. Of the approximately 3,000 respondents, 36 percent thought that the pricing power of energy companies and/or electric utilities had the most impact on prices, 21 percent thought that global politics had the most important impact, government regulation was next at 18 percent, while demand (15 percent) and supply (9 percent) were viewed as having the least impact. See Exhibit 7.1.

These poll participants, who represent a broad representative cross-section of the U.S. population, have it exactly backwards. The supply and demand for oil, natural gas, and electricity are the most important determinants of energy prices.

To further explore this issue, we conducted an informal, anonymous survey asking energy industry experts[1] the same question about factors influencing pricing. It is important to note that the majority of these industry experts were not energy producers, but academics, bankers, consultants, accountants, private equity investors, and so on. Although the sample size is small (21 respondents) and the results were not statistically validated, the responses indicate that the industry experts believe basic economics drive pricing, not companies' pricing power; 71 percent of industry experts selected demand/supply as having the most impact on energy prices. None of the industry experts believed companies' pricing power had the most impact.

Recent events in Asia, as well as the United States, illustrate how supply and demand factors influence energy prices. The past decade has seen a substantial *increase in demand* for transportation fuel in developing markets like China and India. This increase in demand, combined with a *diminishing supply* of cheap and easy-to-produce oil, has led to an *increase in oil prices*, which has in turn led to an increase in more difficult, and more expensive, oil production from oil sands, shale rock, and offshore deep-water drilling.

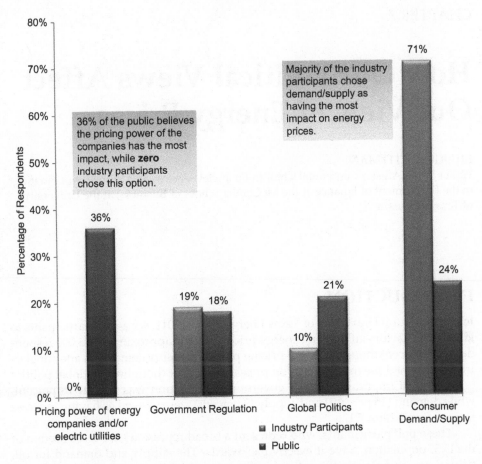

Exhibit 7.1 Which Factor Has the Most Impact on Energy Prices?

The dynamics of the natural gas market have been very different. During the past four years we have seen a substantial *increase in the supply* of natural gas extracted from shale, and because of this, a substantial *decline in natural gas prices*. This decline in natural gas prices, in turn, leads to relatively inexpensive electricity prices. In comparison to supply and demand, regulation and the pricing power of energy companies have only modest effects on prices.

While regulation is sometimes misguided, it can potentially influence prices because of its effect on supply. However, thus far the effect seems to be relatively modest. If regulation encourages offshore drilling in the Gulf of Mexico, or off the coast of Florida or California, this will increase supply, which may reduce the price of oil. Oil is a large global market, however, and the increase in supply from the United States is likely to have a modest effect on total global supply and be somewhat offset by supply cuts in other parts of the world. Similarly, the supply of natural gas is currently constrained by low prices rather than regulation. And yet there is the potential for draconian regulations on hydraulic fracturing, which I think are unlikely, to have an important influence on natural gas prices, particularly on the East Coast.

The pricing powers of energy companies and utilities probably have the least important influence on prices. In short, the oil and gas industries are extremely competitive, and the individual firms have very little influence on prices. Indeed, the profits of these firms, which are quite large because they are very large firms, are not particularly big as a percentage of the oil and gas that they produce. Some electrical utilities are monopolists in their regions and therefore have pricing power; however, they are regulated and cannot get away with overcharging their customers. It should also be noted that while some mistakes during the deregulation process opened opportunities for price manipulation, such as in California at the turn of the millennium, I am not aware of any evidence of pervasive manipulation.

CONCLUSION

A closer look at the data reveals significant differences in the opinions of Democrats and Republicans. They are equally misinformed, but misinformed in very different ways. Democrats tend to believe that the pricing power of energy firms has the most important impact on energy prices while Republicans tend to believe that regulation has the most impact. Beliefs about the lack of importance of supply and demand considerations seem to enjoy bipartisan support.

It's not surprising that Democrats tend to distrust large corporations and that Republicans tend to think that regulation does more harm than good. However, a casual evaluation of the recent political discourse suggests that politicians, in their pandering to the world view of their base, slant information in ways that reinforce misperceptions. Democracy requires an educated and informed electorate. A political process that encourages misinformation can't be a good thing.

DISCUSSION QUESTIONS

1. What is the biggest factor in energy pricing? Discuss.
2. Why would you think that the political party of the respondent gave the results presented?

NOTE

1. For more information on oil and gas prices, please see my interview with Deloitte personnel regarding the dynamics of oil and gas prices and implications for the U.S. economy. Available at https://texasenterprise.org/article/effects-cheap-natural-gas-us-economy.

ABOUT THE CONTRIBUTOR

Sheridan Titman holds the Walter W. McAllister Centennial Chair in Financial Services and is a professor of finance in the Department of Finance at the McCombs School of Business, University of Texas at Austin. He is also a research associate of the National Bureau of Economics. He is serving as president of the American Finance Association in 2012. He is also the Executive Director of the Energy Management and Innovation Center (EMIC) at the University of Texas at Austin and has a blog, Energy Insights, which focuses primarily on energy.

Financial and Economic Analysis in the Energy Industry

CHAPTER 8

Oil and Gas Accounting

L. CHARLES EVANS III[1]
Partner in the Accounting Principles Group, Grant Thornton

INTRODUCTION

The oil and gas industry is unique in that there are two fundamentally different acceptable methods to account for its activities—successful efforts and full cost. Both methods have been widely used by oil and gas companies since the 1960s.

The Financial Accounting Standards Board (FASB) unsuccessfully attempted at one time to require a single accounting method for oil and gas companies. In December 1977, after years of heated debate, the FASB issued Statement 19, *Financial Accounting and Reporting by Oil and Gas Producing Companies*, which required the successful efforts method. Before Statement 19 became effective, the Securities and Exchange Commission (SEC), under intense pressure, decided that oil and gas producing companies subject to its reporting requirements could follow either the successful efforts method as provided by Statement 19 or the full cost method specified by the SEC in ASR 258, *Oil and Gas Producers—Full Cost Accounting Practices*. In response to the SEC's action, the FASB issued Statement 25, *Suspension of Certain Accounting Requirements for Oil and Gas Producing Companies—An Amendment of FASB Statement No. 19*. Statement 25 suspended the requirements of Statement 19 related to the successful efforts method of accounting, permitting oil and gas producing companies not subject to SEC reporting requirements to continue their present methods of accounting. One outcome of the tumultuous standard-setting debate is that public oil and gas entities have a choice between two accounting methods that can yield widely different results, and private companies have no mandatory guidance with respect to accounting methods. Exhibit 8.1 provides a summary of the differences between full cost and successful efforts accounting.

Exhibit 8.1   Differences between Full Cost and Successful Efforts Accounting

Type of Activity	Full Cost	Successful Efforts
Acquisition Costs		
Leasehold costs		
• Proved reserves found	Capitalize	Capitalize
• No proved reserves found	Capitalize	Expense
Exploration Costs		
Geological and geophysical costs	Capitalize	Expense
Costs of carrying unproved properties (delay rentals)	Capitalize	Expense
Exploratory drilling costs (equipment and intangible drilling costs):		
• Proved reserves are found	Capitalize	Capitalize
• Dry hole	Capitalize	Expense
Development Costs		
Developmental drilling costs		
• Successful	Capitalize	Capitalize
• Dry hole	Capitalize	Capitalize

SUCCESSFUL EFFORTS ACCOUNTING

Accounting for Costs at the Time They Are Incurred

Under the successful efforts method, the initial accounting for costs depends on which of the following oil and gas activity phases the costs are incurred:

- Acquisition of properties
- Exploration
- Development
- Production

Acquisition of Mineral Interests

In the United States, oil and gas entities typically acquire rights to drill wells and produce oil and gas through lease agreements with the holder of a property's mineral rights.[2] An oil and gas lease grants a working interest in the property to the oil and gas entity. As a working interest holder, the oil and gas entity bears most of the costs related to drilling and equipping wells and producing any oil and gas that is found. In most cases, the working interest in an oil and gas property will be shared among several oil and gas entities in order to spread the risk of exploration and development.

Lease agreements have a primary term, which is the maximum period that the oil and gas entity is allowed to begin drilling on the property. If drilling has not commenced during the primary term, the lease terminates. Once a successful well has been drilled and production begins, the lease remains in effect as long as there is production. Normally, the holder of the mineral rights of the property will receive

a royalty interest in the leased properties, entitling it to receive a percentage of the value (net of production or severance taxes) of the oil and gas produced, without having to bear any costs.

Most lease agreements require the oil and gas entity to pay a lease bonus at the inception of the lease. This payment is capitalized, along with other costs of acquiring mineral interests such as brokers' fees, legal costs, and recording fees.

International contractual agreements may differ from those in the United States as mineral interests are often owned by the government. Typical agreement types include:

- Concessions, which are similar to a lease in the United States with the concession participant having title to the oil and gas.
- Production-sharing contracts, which specify the sharing of costs and the allocation of any production.
- Service contracts, which typically provide that the entity bears the risk of oil and gas activities and is paid a fee for recovery of costs and profits, normally in production.

Exploration

Exploration activities include identifying broad areas that may have oil and gas reserves, and then further examining specific areas that are considered promising enough to justify drilling. Exploration costs may occur before and after the oil and gas entity acquires a specific property.

The principal types of exploration costs include geological and geophysical (G&G) costs, carrying and retention costs of undeveloped properties, and costs of drilling and equipping exploratory wells.

Oil and gas entities perform G&G activities to obtain information about subsurface geological conditions that can be evaluated in determining if oil and gas reserves exist in a certain area. Some oil and gas entities conduct their own studies; many utilize an outside contractor. Additionally, oil and gas entities may acquire nonproprietary seismic data from oil industry service entities. G&G costs include, among other costs, topographical, geological and geophysical studies, including seismic surveys, access rights to properties to conduct the studies, and the salaries and related expenses of the geologists, geophysical crews, or others that conduct the studies. G&G costs are expensed as incurred.

Oil and gas entities incur certain costs to carry and retain undeveloped oil and gas properties. For instance, some lease agreements require the oil and gas entity to pay a fee called a *delay rental* to defer drilling activities for each additional year after the lease's first year during its primary term. Other costs of carrying undeveloped properties include ad valorem taxes, legal costs for title defenses, and maintenance costs of land and lease records. Costs of carrying undeveloped oil and gas properties should be expensed as incurred.

Typically, the largest exploration cost is the drilling and equipping of exploratory oil and gas wells. An exploratory well is one drilled to look for oil or gas in a stratum that is not known to contain proved oil and gas reserves. Prior to the determination of whether a well has found proved reserves, it is capitalized as an uncompleted well. Whether these costs ultimately remain capitalized or are expensed depends on the success of the well. Costs of exploratory wells that find

proved reserves are capitalized as part of an oil and gas well and related equipment asset. Costs of exploratory wells that do not find proved reserves are expensed as dry hole costs.

Evaluating if an exploratory well has found proved reserves is critical in the ultimate accounting for the well. Proved oil and gas reserves are defined as the quantities of oil and gas that can be estimated with reasonable certainty to be economically producible prior to the expiration of contracts providing the right to operate (unless evidence indicates that renewal is reasonably certain). To meet the *economic producibility* criterion, future expected sales of oil and gas must exceed the expected costs of extraction. The SEC has indicated that existing economic conditions should be used in this evaluation and has required oil and gas entities to use the unweighted average of the prices on the first day of each month within the 12-month period prior to the end of the reporting period in determining economic producibility.

Development

In most situations, a single well does not sufficiently develop a reservoir. Additional wells, known as development wells, are required to economically extract the reserves proved by an exploratory well. Also, certain production facilities such as storage tanks, natural gas cycling and processing plants, and utility and waste disposal system may be necessary. Development costs are capitalized.

Development wells, unlike exploratory wells, are capitalized regardless of their success. Development wells are effectively evaluated as part of a larger asset that comprises the system of wells and necessary equipment and facilities required to produce known reserves. Since development wells are drilled to proved areas and proved depths, the vast majority of the wells are successful.

Production

Once an oil and gas well is completed, production activities begin. Production costs include costs that an oil and gas entity incurs to operate and maintain its wells and related equipment and facilities. Examples of production costs (which are often referred to as lifting costs or lease operating expenses) include the following:

- Depreciation and operating costs of support equipment and facilities.
- Salary costs of employees who operate the wells and related equipment and facilities.
- Repairs and maintenance.
- Property taxes and insurance.
- Severance taxes.

Production costs and depreciation, depletion, and amortization (DD&A) of capitalized acquisition, exploration, and development costs are included in the cost of oil and gas produced. As many oil and gas entities sell all production in the same period it is lifted and do not carry inventory, production costs are typically expensed in the period they are incurred.

DISPOSITION OF CAPITALIZED COSTS

Unproved Properties

Oil and gas entities assess unproved properties periodically for impairment. Impairment exists when the carrying amount of a property exceeds its fair value. Entities evaluate individually significant unproved properties on a property-by-property basis. Some of the factors that may be considered include:

- The entity's intent and ability to commence drilling on the lease.
- Dry holes that have been drilled on the lease or on nearby leases.
- The remaining lease term.

Individual leases may be partially or totally impaired. Any loss is recognized in the income statement, with a valuation allowance reducing the carrying value of the unproved property.

Entities may aggregate or group individually insignificant properties and amortize the cost of the properties based on the entity's historical experience.

If a lease is surrendered or expires without the oil and gas entity finding proved reserves, the cost is charged against the valuation allowance established either individually or in the aggregate. Any excess is charged to the income statement.

Oil and gas entities reclassify costs from unproved to proved properties when proved reserves are discovered. For leases covering extremely large areas, the entity may transfer only a portion of the unproved property costs to proved. For properties individually assessed for impairment, the net carrying amount is classified to proved properties; for properties that a valuation allowance was determined on a group basis, the gross acquisition cost is reclassified.

Depreciation, Depletion, and Amortization

Oil and gas entities deplete, depreciate, and amortize the capitalized acquisition, exploratory, and development costs related to proved reserves using the unit-of-production method. This results in each barrel of oil or thousand cubic feet (mcf) of gas produced being assigned a pro rata portion of the unamortized costs. Depreciation, depletion, and amortization (DD&A) is computed either on a property-by-property (lease) basis or on the basis of some reasonable grouping of properties with a common geological structural feature or stratigraphic condition, such as a reservoir or field.

The DD&A rate for acquisition costs of proved properties is computed based on total estimated proved oil and gas reserves. The rate for proved exploration and development costs is computed using total estimated proved *developed* reserves, rather than on the basis of all proved reserves.

If an oil and gas entity incurs significant development costs (such as the cost of an off-shore production platform) in connection with a planned group of development wells before all of the planned wells have been drilled, the entity excludes a portion of those development costs in calculating the DD&A rate until the additional development wells are drilled. Similarly, the entity would exclude from the DD&A rate computation those proved developed reserves that will be produced

only after significant additional development costs are incurred. Future development costs cannot be anticipated in computing the DD&A rate.

Companies revise DD&A rates at least annually, but also whenever there are circumstances that indicate a need for revision. Revisions are accounted for prospectively as changes in accounting estimates.

Many properties include both oil and gas reserves. In these situations, the oil and gas entity converts both the reserves and production to a common unit of measure using the approximate relative energy content of the oil and gas. The conversion rate commonly used is 6,000 cubic feet (mcf) of gas to one barrel of oil. However, if either oil or gas dominates both the current production or reserves, or the relative proportion of oil and gas produced in the current period is expected to remain constant throughout the remaining life of the property, an oil and gas entity may compute its DD&A rate on the basis of one of the two minerals only, using the dominant mineral in the first instance.

In some cases, an oil and gas entity may conclude it is more appropriate to depreciate natural gas cycling and processing plants by a method other than the unit-of-production method.

Impairment of Proved Properties

An entity is required to test a long-lived asset group to be held and used for recoverability whenever events or changes in circumstances indicate that the carrying amount may not be recoverable. Possible indicators that an oil and gas entity should evaluate proved properties and related equipment and facilities for recoverability include:

- Lower expected oil and/or gas prices.
- Significant increase in expected future development costs.
- Significant downward revisions to reserve estimates.
- Adverse change in the legislative or regulatory climate.
- More likely than not expectation that the property will be sold significantly before the end of its useful life.

If an oil and gas entity qualitatively determines that the carrying amount of an asset group may not be recoverable, it applies a two-step impairment model. In the first step, an entity tests for recoverability by comparing the asset or asset group's carrying amount to its undiscounted expected future cash flows. If the undiscounted cash flows exceed the carrying amount, then the asset group would not be considered impaired, and no further analysis is required. However, if the undiscounted cash flows are less than the carrying amount, then the entity moves to the second step of the impairment model. In step 2, an impairment loss is measured as the amount by which the field's pre-tax carrying amount exceeds its fair value.

An oil and gas entity will typically test impairment using the same asset grouping that it uses to compute DD&A. As previously discussed, this is either on a property-by-property (lease) basis or on the basis of some reasonable grouping of properties with a common geological structural feature or stratigraphic condition, such as a reservoir or field.

In testing recoverability in the first step, the oil and gas entity's principal inputs in calculating an asset group's undiscounted cash flows are future production volumes, selling prices, and costs. Volumes are normally based on oil and gas reserve reports from external or internal petroleum engineers. An oil and gas entity uses proved, probable, and possible reserves in its undiscounted cash flow analysis, although the latter two categories are discounted for risk. Prices reflect the oil and gas entity's best estimate of future prices, and may often be determined based on observable market future pricing curves. Costs contained in the estimated future cash flow estimate include development (both development drilling and facilities costs) and operating costs.

If an asset group fails the first step of the impairment test, the oil and gas entity must estimate the group's fair value in order to measure the amount of the impairment. In many instances, the oil and gas entity estimates fair value by applying an appropriate discount rate to the undiscounted cash flows computed in the first step of the impairment test. The entity should use a discount rate that is consistent with observed oil and gas sales of reserves and that is commensurate with the risks of the related property.

Asset Retirement Obligations

Oil and gas entities are required to recognize a liability for legal obligations related to the retirement of long-lived assets in the period that the liability is incurred if a reasonable estimate of the fair value of the liability can be made. Asset retirement obligations (ARO) are initially recorded as liabilities at fair value, with a corresponding amount recorded as an increase in the related asset. Any subsequent change in the estimated undiscounted cash outflows originally estimated adjust the recorded liability and capitalized asset retirement cost. Upward revisions should be discounted using the current credit-adjusted risk-free rate; downward revisions should be discounted using the credit-adjusted risk-free rate that was used when the liability was initially recorded.

Oil and gas entities commonly have ARO associated with plugging and abandoning wells and with the dismantlement of offshore platforms. The amount recorded as an asset is recognized in expense as the oil and gas entity records DD&A.

Conveyances

A conveyance is the assignment or transfer of a mineral interest from one entity to another. Since most conveyances involve working interests, conveyances often involve the transfer of all or some part of the rights and responsibilities to develop an oil and gas property. Oil and gas entities often enter into conveyance transactions in order to spread the risks related to exploration and also to generate sufficient capital to undertake exploration and development activities.

Conveyances include a number of types of transactions. The accounting question related to conveyances is whether a gain or loss should be recorded for the conveyance transaction. Generally, a gain or loss is recognized (unless there are aspects of the transaction that would not permit recognition under generally accounting

principles applicable to non-oil and gas entities), except that gains cannot be recognized at the time of the following types of conveyances:

- Pooling of assets in a joint undertaking intended to find, develop, or produce oil or gas (losses are also not reflected at the inception of these types of conveyance).
- Part of an interest owned is sold and substantial uncertainty exists about recovery of costs applicable to the interest that is retained.
- Part of an interest owned is sold and the seller has substantial future performance obligations, for instance, an obligation to drill a well without proportional reimbursement for costs applicable to the interest sold.

FULL COST ACCOUNTING

Accounting for Costs at the Time They Are Incurred

As discussed earlier in this chapter, the guidance for applying the full cost method was developed by the SEC. This guidance is included in Rule 4-10(c) of Regulation S-X.

The fundamental concept of the full cost method is that costs of unsuccessful acquisition and exploration efforts are required for the discovery of reserves, even though a specific cost incurred may not actually result in the finding or development of oil and gas reserves. Accordingly, all acquisition, exploration, and development costs are capitalized under the full cost method, including G&G costs, carrying costs of unproved properties, and dry hole exploratory well costs. An oil and gas entity can also capitalize internal costs if they are directly identified with acquisition, exploration, and development activities.

Depreciation, Depletion, and Amortization

Under the full cost method, entities establish cost centers or full cost pools on a country-by-country basis. An oil and gas entity will have a separate DD&A calculation for each country in which it conducts oil and gas activities—a much higher level of aggregation than the field basis typically used by an entity using the successful efforts method.

The full cost pool that will be amortized for each country includes:

- All net capitalized costs, other than certain excludable costs.
- Estimated future development costs.
- Estimated dismantlement and abandonment costs, net of salvage values, that have not been recorded as asset retirement costs.

An oil and gas entity is permitted to exclude all costs directly associated with the acquisition and evaluation of unproved properties from its DD&A computation until it determines whether proved reserves can be assigned to the properties. Unevaluated properties are assessed at least annually to determine if impairment

has occurred, with individually significant properties assessed on a separate basis. Properties that are not individually significant may be grouped for purposes of assessing impairment. Impairment is estimated using the factors previously discussed in the successful efforts section of this chapter. The impairment assessed under either of these methods is added to the costs to be amortized.

The costs of exploratory dry holes are included in the full cost pool immediately after the entity determines that the well is dry.

If an entity cannot directly associate G&G costs with specific unevaluated properties, then the entity must include those costs in the appropriate full cost pool as incurred. Upon complete evaluation of a property, an entity would include the total remaining excluded cost (net of any impairment) in the full cost pool.

An entity may also exclude costs of major development projects involving significant costs to ascertain the quantities of proved reserves. Examples of such projects include the installation of an offshore drilling platform from which development wells are to be drilled, the installation of improved recovery programs, and similar major projects for which an entity expects significant additions to proved reserves. Excluded costs and the related proved reserves are transferred into the full cost pool on well-by-well or property-by-property basis as the project is evaluated and proved reserves established or impairment determined. Once an entity establishes proved reserves, it can no longer exclude the related costs from the full cost pool even if there are delays in production or marketing.

Oil and gas entities using the full cost method, like those using successful-efforts, compute DD&A on the basis of physical units, with oil and gas converted to a common unit of measure on the basis of their approximate relative energy content. However, economic circumstances may indicate that an entity should use units of revenue in computing DD&A. In this situation, an entity computes DD&A on the basis of current gross revenues (excluding royalty payments and net profits disbursements) from production in relation to future estimated gross revenues. In some cases, it may be more appropriate for an entity to depreciate natural gas cycling and processing plants, using a method other than the unit-of-production method. Entities using the full cost method compute DD&A on a consolidated basis, including investees accounted for on a proportionate consolidation basis.

Refer to Exhibit 8.2 for an illustrative example of how drilling costs are treated under successful efforts as compared to full cost accounting.

Impairment

An oil and gas entity that uses the full cost method is subject to much more restrictive impairment testing requirements than those that use the successful efforts method. While a company using the successful efforts method is required to perform detailed impairment tests only if events or changes in circumstances indicate that the carrying amount may not be recoverable, entities using the full cost method must test for impairment every quarter. Additionally, the full cost ceiling (the maximum amount of carrying value that a cost center can have without recording impairment) is computed using only proved reserves priced at the average sales price.

Exhibit 8.2   Example of the Differences in Accounting for Drilling Costs under the
Successful Efforts and Full Cost Methods

XYZ Exploration is an oil and gas exploration company that began operations in 20X0.
XYZ drilled successful wells in late 20X0 but did not begin production until 20X1.

At the beginning of 20X1, XYZ has the following net investment by field, all located in the
United States.

Field	Costs (in millions)	Beginning of the Year—Reserves Equivalent Barrels
A	$10	500,000
B	$12	800,000
C	$15	500,000

The following activity takes place during 20X1:

- XYZ incurs G&G costs of $1 million and drills a dry exploration well costing $4 million,
  both in Field D, a new field in 20X1.
- XYZ drills a dry development well in Field B costing $3 million, then subsequently
  drills another development well for $5 million, which is a producing well.
- XYZ incurs $1 million of delay rental costs to retain certain leases in Field B.

The following analyzes the differences between accounting for these costs under the
successful efforts and full cost methods.

Dry Hole Costs: Under successful efforts, XYZ would expense exploratory dry hole costs,
but would capitalize the costs of the development dry hole of Field B, increasing the costs
subject to DD&A in Field B by $3 million.

Under full cost, both exploratory and development dry hole costs would be capitalized
and included in the full cost pool to be amortized.

G&G costs, lease carrying (delay rental) costs: these costs are expensed under successful
efforts, but capitalized and subject to DD&A under the full cost method.

DD&A: XYZ has chosen to compute DD&A on a field basis. XYZ's computation of DD&A
under successful efforts would be as follows:

	Costs Subject to Amortization (in millions)	BOY Reserves (in equivalent barrels)	DD&A Rate	Production (in equivalent barrels)	DD&A (in millions)
Field A	$10	500,000	$20/equivalent barrel	50,000	$1
Field B	20[(a)]	800,000	$25/equivalent barrel	80,000	2
Field C	15	500,000	$30/equivalent barrel	100,000	3
	$45	1,800,000		230,000	$6

(a) $12 million beginning of the period costs, plus development well costs of $8 million
drilled during the year.

Under the full cost method, DD&A is computed on a country-by-country basis. Since all of
XYZ's oil and gas interests are located in the United States, it would have a single full cost
pool.

Exhibit 8.2 Example of the Differences in Accounting for Drilling Costs under the Successful Efforts and Full Cost Methods (*Continued*)

	In Millions
Costs, beginning of period	$37

Additions:

Field B	Development wells	8
Field D	G&G costs	1
Field D	Dry hole costs	4
Field B	Delay rental costs	1
		14
	Future development costs	—
		$51

DD&A rate: $51 million/1.8 million equivalent barrel reserves = $28.33/equivalent barrel

DD&A expense: $28.33 × 230,000 equivalent barrels = $6,515,900

Summary	Successful Efforts	Full Cost
G&G expense	$ 1.0	$ –
Dry hole cost	$ 4.0	–
Delay rentals	$ 1.0	–
DD&A	$ 6.0	6.5
Total oil and gas expenses	$12.0	$6.5

Under the full cost method, G&G, exploratory dry hole costs, and lease carrying costs (delay rentals) are capitalized and depreciated/depleted/amortized, subject to impairment testing. Provided no impairment occurs, the full cost method provides for more stable earnings in periods of high exploration costs and unsuccessful exploratory drilling.

An entity using the full cost method must, for each cost center, compare the capitalized costs, less accumulated amortization and related deferred income taxes, to the full cost ceiling, which is the sum of:

- The present value of estimated future net revenues. This is computed by multiplying the unweighted average of the prices on the first day of each month within the 12-month period prior to the end of the reporting period of oil and gas reserves (with consideration of price changes only to the extent provided by contractual arrangements) to estimated future production of proved oil and gas reserves as of the date of the latest balance sheet presented, less estimated future expenditures (based on current costs) to be incurred in developing and producing the proved reserves computed using a discount factor of 10 percent and assuming continuation of existing economic conditions, less related deferred income taxes.

- The cost of properties not being amortized, net of income tax effects.
- The lower of cost or estimated fair value of unproven properties included in the costs being amortized, net of income tax effects.

Exhibit 8.3 illustrates an impairment test for a company that uses the full cost method of accounting and has operations in two countries. If unamortized costs capitalized within a full cost pool, less related deferred income taxes, exceed the pool's full cost ceiling, the oil and gas entity should expense the excess. The amount of the impairment is separately disclosed during the period in which it occurs. Amounts that are written off cannot be reinstated in subsequent periods for increases in the full cost pool's ceiling.

Conveyances

Oil and gas entities using the full cost method generally follow the same accounting for conveyances as used by successful efforts entities, with one significant exception. An oil and gas entity using the full cost method accounts for a sale of oil and gas properties as an adjustment of the full cost pool, with no gain or loss recognized, unless the sale substantially alters the relationship between a cost center's capitalized costs and proved reserves. In Rule 4-10 of Regulation S-X, the SEC has indicated that they would not expect a significant alteration to have occurred unless more than 25 percent of a cost center's reserves were sold.

Asset Retirement Obligations

Like conveyances, the accounting requirements for asset retirement obligations, ARO, are similar for the successful efforts and full cost methods, with one exception. It is unclear in the full cost rules whether an oil and gas entity using the full cost method should recognize a gain or loss on the settlement of ARO, or whether the amount should increase or decrease the capitalized costs of the related full cost pool. The Financial Reporting Executive Committee of the AICPA (American Institute of Certified Public Accountants) has indicated that either accounting method is acceptable.

Production Revenue

There is no difference in the accounting for revenues from the production and sale of oil and gas between the successful efforts and full cost methods.

In general, recognition of oil and gas revenues is relatively straightforward as compared to many other industries. Revenues are recognized when title passes to the customer, the price is determinable, and collectability is reasonably assured. For properties for which an oil and gas entity is not the operator, the entity may have to estimate revenues at the end of a period for production sold for which it has not yet received payment.

One complicating issue related to recognizing revenue may occur when an oil and gas entity does not take its proportionate share of oil and gas sold. This results in a need to balance production consistent with each owner's proportionate interest. In such situations, provided that the imbalance does not meet the definition

Exhibit 8.3 Example of an Impairment Test for a Company That Uses the Full Cost Method of Accounting

---

ABC Exploration uses the full cost method of accounting and operates in two countries, the United Stated States and Canada.

Prior to performing its fourth quarter full cost impairment test on December 31, 201X, ABC has the following costs:

	United States	Canada
Capitalized Costs	$ 85	$ 40
Accumulated DD&A	(20)	(15)
	$ 65	$ 25

Other information needed to perform the impairment test included the following:

- The tax basis of the U.S. and Canadian capitalized costs are $25 million and $10 million, respectively. The tax rate in each jurisdiction is 40 percent. Deferred tax liabilities are $16 million and $6 million, respectively.
- ABC has $4 million of Canadian properties that are not being amortized as they are unevaluated, unproved properties. Tax and book basis for the properties are the same. There are no excluded costs from the U.S. cost center.
- ABC has no properties that have been included in either cost base that have not been evaluated.
- The present value of future net revenues is $35 million for the United States and $30 million for Canada.

ABC would calculate its ceiling for each of its two full cost pools as follows:

	United States (in millions)	Canada (in millions)
Present value of future net revenues	$ 35	$ 30
Cost of properties not being amortized	–	4
Lower of cost or fair value of unevaluated properties included in amortization base	–	–
Unproved properties being amortized	$ 35	$ 34
Income tax effect*	4	9.6
Ceiling	$ 31	$ 25.4

*Computed as follows:

	United States (in millions)	Canada (in millions)
Value before taxes	$ 35	$ 34
Less: Tax basis	(25)	(10)
	10	24
Tax rate	40%	40%
	$ 4	$ 9.6

Impairment would be calculated as follows:

	United States (in millions)	Canada (in millions)
Capitalized costs	$ 65	$ 29
Deferred tax liability	(16)	(6)
Capitalized costs	49	23
Ceiling	31	25.4
Impairment	$ 18	$ –

of a derivative, the entity can recognize revenue either on the basis of its working interest (entitlement method) or on the basis of actual oil and gas sold (sales method). If the entitlement method is used, the entity should record a receivable for an undertaken position and a payable for an overtaken position. The SEC staff has indicated that for gas imbalances, the receivable or payable should be measured using the lower of:

- The price at the time of production.
- Current market value.
- If applicable, the contract price.

No explicit guidance exists for measuring crude oil imbalances using the entitlement method, so practice has included market value, actual sales proceeds, and production cost.

If the sale method is used, then an entity would not record a receivable or payable unless the entity has taken production that exceeds its estimated allocable production for the life of the property. In that instance, the entity reflects a liability for the excess volumes it has taken. The SEC has indicated that if insufficient sales volumes are available to offset a gas imbalance, then the liability recognized should be valued at the current market price, unless a different price is specified in a contract between the entity and the other owners.

The accounting method used for imbalances should be disclosed. The SEC has stated that the same method should be used for all gas imbalances.

An oil and gas entity may not sell all the oil and gas it produces in a period and may have inventory at the end of the period. Oil and gas inventoried at a balance sheet date are recorded at the lower of cost or market.

Disclosure Requirements

Oil and gas entities are subject to extensive disclosure requirements. For many investors, these disclosures provide essential information that is critical in their evaluation of the performance of an oil and gas entity. The appendix at the end of this chapter provides an example of the financial statement disclosures that are discussed in this section including:

- Example disclosure of reserve quantities.
- Example disclosure of capitalized costs.
- Example disclosure of costs incurred for property acquisition, exploration, and development activities
- Example disclosure of result of operations for oil and gas producing activities.
- Example disclosure of standardized measure of discounted future cash flows and changes in standardized discounted cash flows.

In developing the disclosures to be required, the FASB acknowledged that the historical cost-based financial statements of oil and gas entities lack information to assess the predictive value of the entity—especially of assessing the entity's amounts, timing, and risk related to the entity's future cash flows. Since there is

not necessarily a direct relationship between an entity's costs and the value of its oil and gas reserves and the costs of finding specific reserves are unique, the costs of existing reserves are not indicators of cash inflows from the production and sale of the reserves or of the cash flows required to replace those reserves. The board's objective in developing oil and gas entity disclosures was to close the informational gap of the financial statement reporting and provide additional information that would allow users to:

- Assess future cash flows.
- Estimate the value or replacement cost of reserves.
- Better compare financial information of entities in the oil and gas exploration industry.

The FASB ultimately decided on a disclosure framework that consists of historical cost information, reserve quantity information, and information relating to the future net cash flows related to oil and gas reserves. As the discovery of reserves is the critical event in oil and gas exploration, information about those reserves and changes in them were considered to be an essential disclosure. However, the board considered that historical cost and reserve information alone did not provide complete information for predictive analytical analysis as reserves can have significantly different values due to factors such as location, qualitative properties, development status, and tax characteristics. Additionally, historical production trends could differ significantly from the entity's future plans. As a result of these considerations, the board decided that information about future cash flows in the form of a standardized measure of discounted cash flows should be required.

Disclosures Applicable to All Companies

All oil and gas entities, both public and private, are required to disclose the method of accounting for costs incurred in oil and gas producing activities and the manner of disposing those costs that are capitalized.

Additionally, all entities applying the successful efforts method must disclose capitalized exploratory well costs that are pending the determination of proved reserves. For each annual period that an income statement is disclosed, changes in those costs from the following must be disclosed:

- Additions.
- Reclassifications to proved costs.
- Charges to expense.

Amounts that were initially capitalized and then expensed in the same fiscal year are not to be included in the above amounts.

The oil and gas entity must also disclose the amount of exploratory well costs that have been capitalized for more than one year, an aging of those amounts by year (or a range of years), and the number of projects to which the costs relate, both in total and by aging category. Additionally, the oil and gas entity must include a description of each of these projects, including the activities to date and the remaining activities required to classify the related reserves as proved.

Disclosures Applicable to Public Companies Only

Publicly traded oil and gas entities with significant oil and gas activities are required to disclose information about the following as supplementary information outside the financial statements:

- Proved oil and gas reserve quantities.
- Capitalized costs of oil and gas producing activities.
- Costs incurred in oil and gas–property acquisition, exploration, and development activities.
- Results of operations for oil and gas producing activities.
- A standardized measure of discounted future net cash flows relating to proved oil and gas reserve quantities, with changes during the period in that measure.

These disclosures are required on a consolidated basis. Unless certain conditions are met, an oil and gas entity should make separate disclosure for its equity method investments.

Proved Oil and Gas Reserve Quantities

An oil and gas entity is required to disclose the net quantities of its interests in proved reserves and proved developed reserves of crude oil (including condensate and, unless significant, natural gas liquids; if significant, separate disclosure of the natural gas liquids amounts is required), natural gas, synthetic oil, synthetic gas, and other nonrenewable natural resources that are intended to be converted to synthetic oil and gas as of the beginning and the end of the year. "Net" quantities of reserves include those relating to the entity's operating and nonoperating interests in properties. Reserves relating to royalty interests held by the entity are included if the information is available to the entity; if the information is unavailable, the oil and gas entity must disclose that fact, along with the enterprise's share of oil and gas produced for those royalty interests that are disclosed for the year. "Net" quantities exclude reserves relating to the interests of others in properties owned by the oil and gas entity. As illustrated in the appendix in this chapter, an oil and gas entity must disclose the changes in the net quantities of its proved reserves of oil and of gas during the year using the following categories:

- *Revisions of previous estimates.* Revisions represent upward or downward changes in previous estimates of proved reserves, resulting from new information typically obtained through development drilling and production history. Changes in reserves resulting from a change in economic factors are also included in this category.
- *Improved recovery.* Changes in reserve estimates resulting from application of improved recovery techniques are shown separately, if significant. If the amounts are not significant, they are included in revisions of previous estimates.
- *Purchases of minerals in place.*
- *Extensions and discoveries.*

- *Production.*
- *Sales of minerals in place.*

An oil and gas entity is required to disclose proved reserves and the related changes in total and separately for each geographic area in which significant reserves are located. A geographic area can be an individual country, a group of countries within a continent, or a continent as appropriate for meaningful disclosure. An oil and gas entity should consider all facts and circumstances, and not only the quantity of reserves, in deciding whether reserves are significant. At a minimum, reserves must be presented separately for each country that contains 15 percent or more, on an equivalent barrel basis, of an entity's proved reserves. If an oil and gas entity's proved oil and gas reserves are located entirely within its home country that fact has to be disclosed.

Net reserves disclosed cannot include oil or gas subject to purchase under long-term supply, purchase, or similar agreements and contracts, including those agreements with foreign governments or authorities. However, quantities of oil or gas that are subject to such agreements with foreign governments or authorities as of the end of the year, and the net quantity of oil or gas received under the agreements during the year, are separately disclosed if the entity participates in the operation of the properties in which the oil or gas is located or serves as the "producer" of those reserves.

If the oil and gas entity issues consolidated financial statements, 100 percent of the net reserve quantities attributable to the parent company and 100 percent of the net reserve quantities attributable to its consolidated subsidiaries (regardless of whether the subsidiary is wholly owned) are included. If a significant amount of the proved reserve quantities at the end of the year are attributable to a consolidated subsidiary with a significant noncontrolling interest, that fact and the approximate portion is disclosed.

An oil and gas entity should explain important economic factors or significant uncertainties that may affect its proved reserves. This would include unusually high expected development or production costs, the need to build a major facility such as a pipeline before production can begin, and contractual commitments to sell production at below-market prices.

In some instances, a foreign government may prohibit disclosing reserves in that country, or the government may prohibit disclosing reserves in a particular field and disclosing reserves in that country would effectively disclose reserves of that particular field. In these circumstances, an oil and gas entity is not required to disclose the proved reserves by country. However, if the government allows the disclosure of the reserves as part of a more aggregated total (such as a group of countries within a continent or a continent), then an oil and gas entity should disclose the reserves for the most disaggregated geographic area that does not violate the government restriction.

Capitalized Costs of Oil and Gas Producing Activities

An oil and gas entity is required to disclose the cumulative capitalized costs relating to its producing activities and the cumulative related accumulated DD&A and valuation allowances as of the end of the year. Refer to the appendix for an

example disclosure. An entity typically will separately disclose capitalized costs for the following asset categories or a combination of these categories:

- Mineral interests in properties.
- Wells and related equipment and facilities.
- Support equipment and facilities.
- Uncompleted wells, equipment, and facilities.

Additionally, if significant, the entity should separately disclose the capitalized costs of unproved properties.

Costs Incurred in Oil and Gas Property Acquisition, Exploration, and Development Activities

As illustrated in the appendix, an oil and gas entity must disclose each of the following types of costs annually, regardless of whether the costs are capitalized or charged to expense when incurred:

- Property acquisition costs
- Exploration costs
- Development costs

If some or all of those costs are incurred in foreign countries, an entity must separately disclose the amounts for each of the geographic areas for which reserve quantities are disclosed. If an entity has incurred significant costs to acquire mineral interests that have proved reserves, it must disclose those costs separately from the costs of acquiring unproved properties.

These disclosures are important in helping a financial statement user assess the oil and gas entity's efforts to replace its reserves through finding new reserves as well as its efforts to develop existing reserves.

Disclosure of the Results of Operations for Oil and Gas Producing Activities

An oil and gas entity is required to disclose its results of operations for oil and gas producing activities for the year. Refer to the appendix for an example. That information is disclosed in total and for each geographic area for which reserve quantities are disclosed. The results of operations should include the following information:

- Revenues.
- Production (lifting) costs.
- Exploration expenses (generally only applicable to the entity's using the successful efforts method as those using the full cost method would capitalize exploration costs).
- Depreciation, depletion, and amortization, and valuation provisions.
- Income tax expense.
- Results of operations for oil and gas producing activities (excluding corporate overhead and interest costs).

Results of operations for oil and gas producing activities are defined as revenues less production (lifting) costs, exploration expenses, depreciation, depletion, and amortization, valuation provisions, and income tax expenses. An oil and gas entity should include general corporate overhead and interest costs as expenses in determining the results of operations for its oil and gas producing activities. However, entities must analyze expenses incurred at a central administrative office as some of those expenses may be operating expenses of oil and gas producing activities and not general corporate expenses.

In disclosing revenues, the oil and gas entity should include sales to third parties and sales or transfers to the entity's other operations (such as refineries or chemical plants). Sales to third-party enterprises and sales or transfers to the entity's other operations are disclosed separately. Sales or transfers to the entity's other operations are based on market prices that approximate those that could be obtained in an arm's length transaction. Royalty payments and net profits disbursements are not included in gross revenues.

An oil and gas entity should compute income tax expense using the statutory tax rate for the period, applied to revenues less the other expenses used to calculate the results of operations for oil and gas producing activities. The calculation of income tax expense reflects tax deductions and tax credits and allowances relating to the oil and gas producing activities.

If an oil and gas entity has an oil and gas investment accounted for using the equity method, the entity's share of the investees' results of operations for oil and gas producing activities accounted should be separately disclosed for the year, in the aggregate and by each geographic area for which reserve quantities are disclosed. The investee's results of operations for oil and gas producing activities are not included in the oil and gas entity's results of operations for oil and gas producing activities.

The FASB viewed the separate disclosure of oil and gas operations important to understanding of the nature of future cash flows for an integrated oil and gas entity as the risks associated with exploration activities are significantly different from those of other aspects of the entity, such as refining and marketing.

Disclosure of a Standardized Measure of Discounted Future Net Cash Flows Relating to Proved Oil and Gas Reserve Quantities

An oil and gas entity is required to disclose a standardized measure of discounted future net cash flows relating to the entity's proved oil and gas reserves and oil and gas subject to purchase under long-term supply, purchase, or similar agreements and contracts in which the entity participates in the operation of the properties on which the oil or gas is located or otherwise serves as the producer of those reserves as of the end of the year. The appendix at the end of this chapter contains an example disclosure of the standardized measure of discounted future net cash flows. The following information is disclosed in the aggregate and for each geographic area for which reserve quantities are required to be disclosed:

- *Future cash inflows*, computed by multiplying the prices used to estimate the entity's proved reserves to the year-end quantities of those reserves.

Future price changes are only considered if they are provided by contractual arrangements that exist at year end.

- *Future development and production costs,* computed by estimating the expenditures to be incurred in developing and producing the year-end proved oil and gas reserves, based on year-end costs and assuming that existing economic conditions will continue. If an entity's development expenditures are significant, the entity should presented them separately from estimated production costs.
- *Future income tax expenses,* computed by applying the year-end statutory tax rates, with consideration of changes in future tax rates that have already been enacted, to the future pre-tax net cash flows relating to the entity's proved oil and gas reserves, less the tax basis of the related properties. The computation of the tax expense should also consider tax deductions, credits, and allowances relating to the entity's proved oil and gas reserves.
- *Future net cash flows,* computed by subtracting future development and production costs and future income tax expenses from future cash inflows.
- *Discount,* computed by applying an annual 10 percent discount rate to reflect the timing of the future net cash flows.
- *Standardized measure of discounted future net cash flows,* which is the future net cash flows less the computed discount.

The standardized measure of discounted net cash flows is not fair value as, among other things, only proved reserves (and not probable or possible reserves) are used in the computation, pricing is based on a historical average of the year as opposed to estimated future prices, and an arbitrary discount rate is used that may not be indicative of the rate that would be used in a fair value estimate. However, the FASB intended the standardized measure to achieve some of the characteristics of a fair value measure without the extreme subjectivity that would be inherent in either a direct estimation of market value or entity-specific discounted net cash flows. The standardized measure of discounted net cash flows is typically responsive to some of the key variables that affect fair value, including changes in reserve quantities, selling prices, production costs, and tax rates, and serves as a point of comparison between different oil and gas entities.

If a significant portion of the economic interest in the consolidated entity's standardized measure of discounted future net cash flows reported is attributable to a consolidated subsidiary, in which there is a significant noncontrolling interest, that fact and the approximate portion shall be disclosed.

The aggregate change in the standardized measure of discounted future net cash flows is required to be disclosed for the year. If individually significant, the following sources of change are required to be presented separately:

- Net change in sales and transfer prices and in production costs related to future production.
- Changes in estimated future development costs.
- Sales and transfers of oil and gas produced during the period.
- Net change due to extensions, discoveries, and improved recovery.
- Net change due to purchases and sales of minerals in place.
- Net change due to revisions in quantity estimates.

- Previously estimated development costs incurred during the period.
- Accretion of discount.
- Other—unspecified.
- Net change in income taxes.

In computing the amounts for each of the above categories, an oil and gas entity should consider the effects of changes in prices and costs before the effects of changes in quantities. As a result, changes in quantities are reflected at the prices used to estimate reserves and year-end costs. The net change in income taxes is computed considering the effect of income taxes incurred during the period as well as the change in future income tax expenses. Therefore, all changes except income taxes are reported pre-tax.

Additionally, an oil and gas entity should disclose additional information needed to keep the disclosure of the standardized measure of discounted future net cash flows and the related changes from being misleading.

Full Cost Disclosures

Public oil and gas entities that apply the full cost method must disclose, for each of its cost centers for each year that an income statement is required, the total amount of amortization expense (per equivalent unit of production if DD&A is computed using physical units or per dollar of gross revenue from production if DD&A is computed using gross revenues).

Also, an entity must separately indicate on the face of the balance sheet the amount of costs of unproved properties and major development projects that have been excluded from the capitalized costs being amortized. Additionally, the entity has to include in the footnotes a description of the significant properties or projects involved, and indicate the anticipated timing of when the costs would be included in the DD&A computation. Certain detailed information about the nature and aging of the costs is also required to be presented in the footnotes.

INTERNATIONAL FINANCIAL REPORTING STANDARDS

As of the writing of this chapter in late 2011, the SEC is determining if, when, and how it will integrate international financial reporting standards (IFRS) in the United States for public filing companies.[3] Generally, IFRS lacks specific accounting guidance for many extractive activities. Although IFRS 6, *Exploration for and Evaluation of Mineral Resources*, addresses the accounting for exploration and evaluation costs, it was primarily developed as a stopgap measure to allow entities adopting IFRS to continue to apply their existing accounting policies for these costs. Concerns have been raised about the lack of comparability in international financial reporting of extractive industries because of the absence of comprehensive guidance. As a result, the International Accounting Standards Board has issued a discussion paper, *Extractive Industries*, which proposes a framework for financial reporting for extractive industries.

The 183-page document discusses how to estimate and classify reserves and resources and what information about extractive activities should be disclosed,

as well as an accounting model for asset recognition and measurement. The proposed accounting framework, which would apply to both the mining and oil and gas industries, would be based on historical cost, as opposed to fair value. Upon the acquisition of legal rights, entities would begin capitalizing costs. All subsequent costs that provide information about the property, regardless of the phase of activity (exploration, development, or production) in which they occur, would be considered enhancements of the property and would be capitalized as part of the oil and gas asset. For instance, under the proposed framework, geological and geophysical costs and exploratory dry hole costs would be capitalized.

Additionally, the proposed framework's unit of account (level of detail/aggregation at which assets would be recognized) would initially be based on the exploration rights received, with contraction of that unit of account as exploration and evaluation occurs so that once development and production begin, the unit of account would be an area or group of contiguous areas that are managed separately and generate largely independent cash flows. Impairment of properties that are in the development and production phases would be assessed under current IFRS requirements, which require a one-step impairment test that compares the higher of the property's value in use (future discounted cash flows) and fair value less costs to sell to the carrying value. However, properties in the exploration phase would require impairment charges only if, in management's judgment, there is a high likelihood that the carrying amount will not be recoverable in full.

The proposed framework has some significant differences as compared to the existing U.S. successful efforts and full cost rules. A U.S. successful efforts company would capitalize more costs under the proposal. U.S. full cost companies would face a much smaller unit of account than the country basis they currently use. The proposed impairment rules would be different from either the current successful efforts or full cost rules.

The FASB has received over 140 comment letters concerning the discussion paper. It is currently evaluating those comment letters in deciding whether to add a project to its agenda to address extractive industries accounting.

DISCUSSION QUESTIONS

1. Describe the differences between full cost and successful efforts accounting.
2. Go to the Securities and Exchange Commission (SEC) website at www.sec.gov and download the latest 10-K report for ExxonMobil. Locate and read the oil and gas disclosures in the footnotes of the financial statements and locate the specific disclosures described in the appendix of this chapter. Describe your observations.
3. What is impairment, and how is the impairment test performed using a two-step impairment model? Is impairment testing more restrictive for full cost or successful efforts accounting? Why?
4. Discuss if expenses are either capitalized or expensed in the exploration, development, and production stages for oil and gas companies.
5. Why are oil and gas entities subject to extensive disclosure requirements? Include in your answer how the historical costs provided in financial statements lack information and how the FASB additional disclosure requirements help provide essential information to investors.

APPENDIX

Example Disclosure of Reserve Quantities

Reserve Quantity Information[a][d]
For the Year Ended December 31, 20X1

	Total (Optional Disclosure)	Total—by Product		Continent A		Continent B—Country A		Other Countries In Continent B		Other Continents/Countries	
	All Products	Oil	Synthetic Oil	Oil	Synthetic Oil	Oil	Synthetic Oil	Oil	Synthetic Oil	Oil	Synthetic Oil
Proved developed and undeveloped reserves (consolidated entities only):											
Beginning of year	9,292	5,521	3,771	939	713	673	1,510	2,058	821	1,851	727
Revisions of previous estimates	635	202	433	(70)	79	39	274	253	23	(20)	57
Improved recovery	26	11	15	–	15	–	–	–	–	11	–
Purchase of minerals in place	13	13	–	10	–	–	–	3	–	–	–
Extensions and discoveries	191	103	88	29	–	4	68	65	18	5	2
Production	(775)	(582)	(193)	(84)	(27)	(155)	(115)	(239)	(32)	(104)	(19)
Sales of minerals in place	(118)	(34)	(84)	(2)	(52)	(28)	–	–	(8)	(4)	(24)
End of year	9,264[b]	5,234	4,030	822	728	533	1,737	2,140	822	1,739	743
Entity's share of proved developed and undeveloped reserves of investees accounted for by the equity method											
Beginning of year	1,950	1,250	700	400	200	300	100	250	200	300	200
Revisions of previous estimates	45	20	25	(20)	–	35	5	(5)	20	10	–
Improved recovery	20	10	10	8	2	2	1	–	5	–	2
Purchase of minerals in place	25	20	5	–	–	20	–	–	–	–	5
Extensions and discoveries	110	80	30	20	5	50	–	10	5	10	20
Production	(145)	(65)	(80)	(30)	(40)	(20)	(5)	(10)	(25)	(5)	(10)
Sales of minerals in place	(35)	(14)	(21)	(2)	(4)	(7)	(2)	–	(10)	(5)	(5)
Entity's share of reserves of investees accounted for by the equity method-end of year	1,970	1,301	669	376	163	380	99	245	195	300	212

Reserve Quantity Information[a][d]
For the Year Ended December 31, 20X1

	Total (Optional Disclosure)	Total—by Product		Continent A		Continent B— Country A		Other Countries In Continent B		Other Continents/ Countries	
	All Products	Oil	Synthetic Oil	Oil	Synthetic Oil	Oil	Synthetic Oil	Oil	Synthetic Oil	Oil	Synthetic Oil
Total consolidated and equity interests in reserves—end of the year (*optional disclosure*)	11,234	6,535	4,699	1,198	891	913	1,836	2,385	1,017	2,039	955
Proved developed reserves (consolidated entities only):											
Beginning of the year	5,599	3,529	2,070	682	520	518	900	1,202	400	1,127	250
End of the year	5,771	3,531	2,240	580	540	410	1,050	1,384	430	1,157	220
Proved undeveloped reserves (consolidated entities only):											
Beginning of the year	3,693	1,992	1,701	257	193	155	610	856	421	724	477
End of the year	3,493	1,703	1,790	242	188	123	687	756	392	582	523
Oil and gas subject to long-term supply, purchase, or similar agreements with governments or authorities in which the entity participates in the operation of the properties where the oil and gas is located or otherwise serves as the producer of those reserves (consolidated entities only)[c]											
Total under contract (quantity subject to agreement)—end of the year	309	174	135	150	—	20	35	4	100	—	—
Received during the year	71	41	30	30	—	10	5	1	25	—	—

[a]Oil and synthetic oil reserves stated in barrels.

[b]Includes reserves of 250 barrels attributable to a consolidated subsidiary in which there is a 5 percentage noncontrolling interest.

[c]If applicable, this information should be disclosed for the entity's share of reserves of investees accounted for by the equity method.

[d]If applicable, reserve quantity information is required for gas and synthetic gas reserves, and other products.

Example Disclosure of Capitalized Costs

Capitalized Costs Relating to Oil and Gas Producing Activitiesat December 31, 20X1

	Consolidated	Entity's Share of Equity Method Investees
Unproved oil and gas properties	$ 68,000	$ 40,000
Proved oil and gas properties	490,000	100,000
Accumulated depreciation, depletion, and amortization, and valuation allowances	(140,000)	(38,000)
Net capitalized costs	$ 418,000	$ 102,000

Example Disclosure of Costs Incurred for Property Acquisition, Exploration, and Development Activities

Costs Incurred in Oil and Gas Property Acquisition, Exploration, and Developmentfor the Year Ended December 31, 20X1

	Total	Continent A	Continent B—Country A	Continent B—Other Countries	Other Continents/ Countries
Consolidated entities:					
Acquisition of properties					
Proved	$60,000	$40,000	$10,000	$7,000	$3,000
Unproved	57,000	45,000	7,000	4,000	1,000
Exploration costs	1,400	400	500	350	150
Development costs	86,000	72,000	8,000	4,500	1,500
Entity's share of equity method investees:					
Acquisition of properties					
Proved	$20,000	$12,000	$ 5,500	$2,000	$ 500
Unproved	20,000	15,000	3,000	1,000	1,000
Exploration costs	600	250	150	150	50
Development costs	29,000	22,000	1,000	4,000	2,000

Example Disclosure of Result of Operations for Oil and Gas Producing Activities

Results of Operations for Oil and Gas Producing Activities for the Year Ended December 31, 20X1

	Total	Continent A	Continent B—Country A	Continent B—Other Countries	Other Continents/ Countries
Consolidated entities:					
Revenues					
Sales	$27,000	$ 4,000	$ 4,500	$11,000	$ 7,500
Transfers	52,000	8,500	3,500	10,800	29,200
Total	79,000	12,500	8,000	21,800	36,700
Production costs	(9,500)	(2,100)	(1,700)	(2,600)	(3,100)
Exploration expenses	(1,400)	(400)	(500)	(350)	(150)

Results of Operations for Oil and Gas Producing Activities for the Year Ended December 31, 20X1

	Total	Continent A	Continent B—Country A	Continent B—Other Countries	Other Continents/ Countries
Depreciation, depletion, and amortization, and valuation provisions	(8,000)	(1,300)	(900)	(2,500)	(3,300)
	60,100	8,700	4,900	16,350	30,150
Income tax expenses	(37,000)	(5,200)	(1,500)	(11,700)	(18,600)
Results of operations from producing activities (excluding corporate overhead and interest costs)	$ 23,100	$ 3,500	$ 3,400	$ 4,650	$ 11,550
Entity's share of equity method investees:					
Revenues					
Sales	$ 10,000	$ 3,000	$ 3,500	$ 2,000	$ 1,500
Transfers	18,000	9,000	6,000	1,000	2,000
Total	28,000	12,000	9,500	3,000	3,500
Production costs	(6,000)	(3,000)	(2,000)	(400)	(600)
Exploration expenses	(600)	(250)	(150)	(150)	(50)
Depreciation, depletion, and amortization, and valuation provisions	(8,000)	(4,000)	(1,800)	(1,000)	(1,200)
	13,400	4,750	5,550	1,450	1,650
Income tax expenses	(4,000)	(1,600)	(1,900)	(400)	(100)
Results of operations from producing activities (excluding corporate overhead and interest costs)	$ 9,400	$ 3,150	$ 3,650	$ 1,050	$ 1,550
Total consolidated and equity method investees results of operations for producing activities (excluding corporate overhead costs) *(optional disclosure)*	$ 32,500	$ 6,650	$ 7,050	$ 5,700	$ 13,100

Example Disclosure of Standardized Measure of Discounted Future Cash Flows and Changes in Standardized Discounted Cash Flows

Standardized Measure of Discounted Future Net Cash Flows at December 31, 20X1

	Total	Continent A	Continent B—Country A	Continent B—Other Countries	Other Continents/ Countries
Consolidated entities:					
Future cash inflows[a]	$ 749,000	$ 536,000	$186,000	$21,000	$ 6,000
Future production and development costs[a]	(301,000)	(252,000)	(41,000)	(5,000)	(3,000)
Future income tax expenses[a]	(47,000)	(38,000)	(7,000)	(600)	(1,400)
Future net cash flows	401,000	246,000	138,000	15,400	1,600
10 percent annual discount for estimated timing of cash flows	(140,000)	(84,000)	(53,000)	(2,500)	(500)
Standardized measure of discounted future net cash flows	$ 261,000[b]	$ 162,000	$ 85,000	$12,900	$ 1,100
Entity's share of equity method investees:					
Future cash inflows[a]	11,000	4,000	3,000	1,000	3,000
Future production and development costs[a]	(3,000)	(1,000)	(500)	(400)	(1,100)
Future income tax expenses[a]	(1,000)	(500)	(100)	(100)	(300)
Future net cash flows	7,000	2,500	2,400	500	1,600
10 percent annual discount for estimated timing of cash flows	(2,000)	(700)	(700)	(150)	(450)
Standardized measure of discounted future net cash flows	$ 5,000	1,800	$ 1,700	$ 350	$ 1,150
Total consolidated and equity interests in the standardized measure of discounted future cash flows *(optional disclosure)*	$ 266,000	$ 163,800	$ 86,700	$13,250	$ 2,250

[a]Future net cash flows were computed using prices used in estimating the entity's (or the investee's) proved oil and gas reserves, year-end costs, and statutory tax rates (adjusted for tax deductions) that relate to existing proved oil and gas reserves. These include those mineral interests related to long-term supply arrangements with governments for which entity (or the investee) participates in the operation of the related properties or otherwise serves as the producer of the reserves, but does not include other supply arrangements or contracts that represent the right to purchase (as opposed to extract) oil and gas.

[b]Includes $20,000 attributable to a consolidated subsidiary in which there is a 5 percent noncontrolling interest.

Changes in the Standardized Measure for Discounted Cash Flows for the Year Ended December 31, 20X1

	Consolidated	Entity's Share of Equity Method Investees	Total (optional disclosure)
Net change in sales and transfer prices and in production (lifting) costs related to future production	$(228,000)	$(1,000)	$(229,000)
Changes in estimated future development costs	(32,000)	(1,000)	(33,000)
Sales and transfers of oil and gas produced during the period	(149,000)	(900)	(149,900)
Net change due to extensions, discoveries, and improved recovery	78,000	500	78,500
Net change due to purchase and sales of minerals in place	67,000	3,000	70,000
Net change due to revisions in quantity estimates	(44,000)	(150)	(44,150)
Previously estimated development costs incurred during the period	20,000	200	20,200
Accretion of discount	40,000	100	40,100
Net change in income taxes	102,000	900	102,900
Other	7,700	400	8,100
Aggregate change in the standardized measure of discounted future net cash flows for the year	$(138,300)	$ 2,050	$(136,250)

NOTES

1. I would like to thank Brandon Sear and Kevin Schroeder for their contributions to this chapter. Brandon Sear, CPA, is a partner in the Audit Department of the Houston office of Grant Thornton and is the leader of our National Energy Industry Practice Partners. Brandon has 20 years of public accounting experience and specializes in providing audit services primarily to energy companies. Kevin Schroeder, CPA, is a partner and oil and gas practice leader for the Oklahoma City office of Grant Thornton. Kevin has extensive experience in the energy and natural resources industry where he has audited and advised fully integrated, exploration and production, marketing and trading, transportation and field services companies.
2. For more information about international petroleum drilling agreements, see Chapter 12 in this book, titled "International Petroleum Fiscal System Design and Analysis."
3. For the latest information on IFRS and the SEC guidelines, refer to the websites of these organizations at www.ifrs.org and www.sec.gov.

REFERENCES

Financial Accounting Standards Board (FASB). Statement 19. *Financial Accounting and Reporting by Oil and Gas Producing Companies.*

Financial Accounting Standards Board (FASB). Statement 25. *Suspension of Certain Accounting Requirements for Oil and Gas Producing Companies.*

International Financial Reporting Standards (IFRS). 6. *Exploration for and Evaluation of Mineral Resources.*

Securities and Exchange Commission (SEC). ASR 258. Oil and Gas Producers—Full Cost Accounting Practices.
Securities and Exchange Commission (SEC). Rule 4-10(c) of Regulation S-X.

ABOUT THE CONTRIBUTOR

L. Charles "Chuck" Evans III, CPA, is a partner in the Accounting Principles Group of Grant Thornton's National Professional Standards Group. He has over 25 years of public accounting experience with expertise in manufacturing and distribution, energy, and financial services. He has worked at the Securities and Exchange and has served on Working Groups for Emerging Issues Task Force at the Financial Accounting Standards Board. Evams is a Certified Public Accountant, member of the American Institute of Certified Public Accountants and their Accounting Standards Executive Committee, and a member of the Texas Society of Certified Public Accountants. He graduated summa cum laude from Texas A&M University.

CHAPTER 9

Financial Statement Analysis for Oil and Gas Companies and Competitive Benchmarking

SIAMAK JAVADI
PhD Candidate, Oklahoma State University

BETTY J. SIMKINS
Williams Companies Professor of Business and Professor of Finance,
Oklahoma State University

MARY E. WICKER
PhD Student, Oklahoma State University

INTRODUCTION

One of the most famous hostile takeover attempts of an oil company was of Gulf Oil, one of the seven sisters, in 1984 by Boone Pickens of Mesa Petroleum.[1] At the time, the attempt was audacious and unprecedented, and it made Boone Pickens and Mesa Petroleum famous overnight. While Gulf Oil was slightly underperforming industry peers in the standard financial ratios, careful investigation of the oil and gas operations through energy ratio analysis revealed a very poor exploration and production operation that was destroying shareholder value. Uncovering these key insights requires scrutinizing the upstream operations in the notes of the financial statements. This chapter will provide the reader with the solid background for such scrutiny.

In this chapter, we explain how to analyze oil and gas companies and compare them to their industry peers. We provide a comprehensive coverage that includes not only the standard financial ratios that apply to all companies but also the energy ratios. The energy ratios are a unique set of ratios that analyze the upstream oil and gas operations. The financial statements of oil and gas companies operating in exploration and production (E&P) contain extensive disclosures of vital reserve and cost information that is unique to this industry. Any analysis of E&P companies that does not include the energy ratios is grossly inadequate and incomplete. Unique features of the E&P industry, which must be kept in mind, are as follows:

- The most important tangible assets of upstream oil and gas firms are the reserves in the ground, a depleting asset. The value of these assets on the

balance sheet is not an accurate reflection of their true economic value. Therefore, it is necessary to analyze the 10-K notes.

- As discussed in Chapter 8, accounting standards for E&P companies are complex and result in extensive disclosures in the notes. Understanding the accounting standards is crucial to financial statement analysis. In the United States, there are two widely different accounting methods that are allowed: full cost accounting and successful efforts accounting. The analyst must be aware of which reporting method a company uses when conducting ratio analysis.
- The value of oil and gas reserves added each year typically has much greater value to the company than the oil and gas produced during the same period. For this reason, the quantity of reserves is a more important measure of success than the earnings reported on the income statement. Hence, analyzing energy ratios is a must.
- The E&P sector is very high risk, requiring high capital investment that may not be successful. Even if it is successful, it may not produce a cash inflow for many years. There is typically a long lag between investment and cash flow.

This chapter covers various ratios that are used by finance practitioners in assessing the performance of oil and gas companies. This chapter attempts to give a more insightful exposition of financial data and accounting information through the use of real-world examples. We will get behind the numbers and dig deep into the accounting disclosures to uncover how well an E&P company is actually performing by analyzing the energy ratios. We will use ConocoPhillips's 10-K (2011) report to illustrate the calculations. Furthermore, we will conduct competitive benchmarking by comparing ConocoPhillips' performance to peer companies. Hereafter, we will refer to ConocoPhillips as COP, which is the firm's stock ticker symbol.

Financial statement analysis is an important way to gauge the overall financial health of a company. Ratio analysis can be viewed in this way. When you go to the physician to get a complete checkup, the physician will take your blood pressure, listen to your heart and lungs, check your ears, test your reflexes, and so on. Samples of your blood and urine will be sent to the medical lab for analysis. The physician then examines all of this information to make an overall assessment of your health. If there are still questions or concerns after this set of tests, the physician will most likely do more examinations and schedule more frequent visits if necessary. Financial statement analysis is similar. All ratio categories must be analyzed to make an overall determination of the financial fitness of the company. Just as the physician cannot only listen to your heart to determine if you are healthy, a financial analyst cannot just look at just one area of ratios to make a judgment on the company's financial health. If there are warning signs from the ratio analysis, then more research should be done, and the company should be monitored more closely over time.

A wealth of financial information is available on the internet about publicly traded companies. We encourage the reader to investigate other sources of information to gain additional insights to supplement their research. See the insert "Examples of Financial Information on the Internet."

> ## Examples of Financial Information on the Internet
>
> Bloomberg (Bloomberg.com)
> CNN Money (money.cnn.com)
> Google Finance (google.com/finance)
> Reuters (reuters.com)
> SmartMoney (smartmoney.com)
> Yahoo! Finance (finance.yahoo.com)
> Value Line Investment Survey (valueline.com)
> *Wall Street Journal* (online.wsj.com)

If you are already familiar with basic financial statement analysis, you may wish to skip to the section titled Energy Ratios for a detailed discussion on how to analyze upstream operations.

FINANCIAL STATEMENTS

Financial statements are like fine perfume; to be sniffed but not swallowed.
—Abraham Brilloff[2]

Before getting started, we need to introduce terminology that will be used frequently throughout this chapter.

Annual Report and Form 10-K: The appendix at the end of this chapter contains a summary of information found in the Form 10-K report. International companies that have stock traded on U.S. exchanges file a Form 20-F, which contains similar disclosures to the 10-K report. These reports disclose the firm's performance during the past fiscal year, provide snapshots of the firm's operations and financial position, and discuss new improvements and projects that will affect future operations. These reports are available for free. Annual reports are published on the company website (see Investor Relations), and the 10-K report can be downloaded from the SEC website.[3] These reports contain four major financial statements: the Balance Sheet, the Income Statement, the Statement of Cash Flows, and the Statement of Retained Earnings. Next, we will describe these statements one by one.

Balance Sheet: This financial statement represents a snapshot of the firm's position as it stood on a specific date and at a specific time. It gives a breakdown of the firm's assets and how those assets are financed, whether by debt or by equity, as well as whether the assets are financed with short-term capital or long-term capital.[4] Exhibit 9.1 shows the Consolidated Balance Sheet for COP. From the Balance Sheet we can determine the size of the firm, the book value of the company, the company's real (market) value, the amount of working capital, the degree of leverage, whether the company is growing, and so on.

Exhibit 9.1   ConocoPhillips' Consolidated Balance Sheets

($ millions, except per-share data)	At December 31 2011	2010
Assets		
Cash and cash equivalents	5,780	9,454
Short-term investments	581	973
Accounts and notes receivable	14,648	13,787
Accounts and notes receivable—related parties	1,878	2,025
Investment in LUKOIL	–0–	1,083
Inventories	4,631	5,197
Prepaid expenses and other current assets	2,700	2,141
Total Current Assets	30,218	34,660
Investments and long-term receivables	32,108	31,581
Loans and advances—related parties	1,675	2,180
Net properties, plants, and equipment	84,180	82,554
Goodwill	3,332	3,633
Intangibles	745	801
Other assets	972	905
Total Assets	153,230	156,314
Liabilities		
Accounts payable	17,973	16,613
Accounts payable—related parties	1,680	1,786
Short-term debt	1,013	936
Accrued income and other taxes	4,220	4,874
Employee benefit obligations	1,111	1,081
Other accruals	2,071	2,129
Total Current Liabilities	28,068	27,419
Long-term debt	21,610	22,656
Asset retirement obligations and accrued environmental costs	9,329	9,199
Joint venture acquisition obligation—related party	3,582	4,314
Deferred income taxes	18,055	17,335
Employee benefit obligations	4,068	3,683
Other liabilities and deferred credits	2,784	2,599
Total Liabilities	87,496	87,205
Equity		
Common stock Issued (2011—1,749,550,587 sh; 2010—1,740,529,279 sh)		
Par value	17	17
Capital in excess of par	44,725	44,132
Grantor trusts (at cost: 2010—36,890,375 shares)	–0–	−633
Treasury stock (at cost: 2011—463,880,628 shares; 2010—272,873,537 shares)	−31,787	−20,077
Accumulated other comprehensive income	3,086	4,773
Unearned employee compensation	−11	−47
Retained earnings	49,194	40,397
Total Common Stockholders' Equity	65,224	68,562
Noncontrolling interests	510	547
Total Equity	65,734	69,109
Total Liabilities and Equity	153,230	156,314

Source: ConocoPhillips 2011 10-K Report, p. 83.

Income Statement: This financial statement captures the results of the business operations over a specified length of time (i.e., a year, a quarter, or a month). It summarizes the generated revenues and the incurred expenses. From the Income Statement, we can see whether the firm is profitable and to what extent it has the capacity to honor its financial obligations. Income Statement analysis usually helps answer questions about the firm's level of sales, profitability, revenue growth rate, earnings, net income, and so on. Exhibit 9.2 illustrates the Consolidated Income Statement for COP.

Statement of Cash Flows: This financial statement describes how the firm's operating, investing, and financing activities have impacted the cash

Exhibit 9.2 ConocoPhillips' Consolidated Income Statement

($ millions, except per-share data)	At December 31		
	2011	2010	2009
Revenues and Other Income			
Sales and other operating revenues*	244,813	189,441	149,341
Equity in earnings of affiliates	4,077	3,133	2,531
Gain on dispositions	2,007	5,803	160
Other income	329	278	358
Total Revenues and Other Income	251,226	198,655	152,390
Costs and Expenses			
Purchased crude oil, natural gas, and products	185,867	135,751	102,433
Production and operating expenses	10,770	10,635	10,339
Selling, general, and administrative expenses	2,078	2,005	1,830
Exploration expenses	1,066	1,155	1,182
Depreciation, depletion, and amortization	7,934	9,060	9,295
Impairments	792	1,780	535
Taxes other than income taxes*	18,307	16,793	15,529
Accretion on discounted liabilities	455	447	422
Interest and debt expense	972	1,187	1,289
Foreign currency transaction (gains) losses	−16	92	−46
Total Costs and Expenses	228,225	178,905	142,808
Income before income taxes	23,001	19,750	9,582
Provision for income taxes	10,499	8,333	5,090
Net income	12,502	11,417	4,492
Less: net income attributable to noncontrolling interests	−66	−59	−78
Net Income Attributable to ConocoPhillips	12,436	11,358	4,414
Net Income Attributable to ConocoPhillips per Share of Common Stock (*dollars*)			
Basic	9.04	7.68	2.96
Diluted	8.97	7.62	2.94
Average Common Shares Outstanding (*in thousands*)			
Basic	1,375,035	1,479,330	1,487,650
Diluted	1,387,100	1,491,067	1,497,608
*Includes excise taxes on petroleum products sales:	13,954	13,689	13,325

Source: ConocoPhillips 2011 10-K Report, p. 81.

position over a specified length of time. The Statement of Cash Flows reveals the investment decisions (uses of cash) and financing decisions (sources of cash). This statement categorizes information about the company's cash into three different groups: Operating Activities, Investing Activities, and Financing Activities. Using the Statement of Cash Flows, we can determine the amount of cash generated (or lost), the firm's cash generation ability, whether the firm has a successful investment strategy, and the effectiveness of the firm's financial strategy. Exhibit 9.3 shows COP's Statement of Cash Flows.

Statement of Retained Earnings: This financial statement shows the changes in the common equity accounts between balance sheet dates. As Brigham and Houston (2013) state: " ... retained earnings as reported on the balance sheet do not represent cash and are not 'available' for dividends or anything else."

A QUICK LOOK AT CONOCOPHILLIPS AND COMPETITIVE BENCHMARKING

Let's take a quick look at COP and other firms operating in the industry before calculating the ratios. COP is known as an integrated oil company because they are involved in exploration and production (E&P) and also at least one of the other industry segments. An independent oil company is only involved primarily in E&P. (*Note:* We are analyzing COP at 2011 year end, before they separated the upstream and downstream parts of COP in a spin-off. On April 30, 2012, COP completed the spin-off of the downstream operations, Phillips 66, as a separate company and the E&P segment remained as COP.) For more information about the structure of the oil and gas industry, refer to Chapter 5: "A Brief Introduction to the Petroleum Industry: From Crude Oil and Natural Gas to Petrochemicals and Their Products."

COP's business is organized into six operating segments:

1. Exploration and Production (E&P)—This segment primarily explores for, produces, transports, and markets crude oil, bitumen, natural gas, liquefied natural gas (LNG), and natural gas liquids on a worldwide basis.
2. Midstream—This segment gathers, processes, and markets natural gas produced by COP and others, and fractionates and markets natural gas liquids.
3. Refining and Marketing (R&M)—This segment purchases, refines, markets, and transports crude oil and petroleum products, mainly in the United States, Europe and Asia (now Phillips 66).
4. LUKOIL Investment—This segment consists of past investment in the ordinary shares of OAO LUKOIL, an international, integrated oil and gas company headquartered in Russia. This was divested in the first quarter of 2011.
5. Chemicals—This segment manufactures and markets petrochemicals and plastics on a worldwide basis.
6. Emerging Businesses—This segment represents investment in new technologies or businesses outside the normal scope of operations.

Exhibit 9.3 ConocoPhillips' Consolidated Statement of Cash Flows

($ millions)	For Years Ended December 31		
	2011	2010	2009
Cash Flows from Operating Activities			
Net income	12,502	11,417	4,492
Adjustments to reconcile net income to net cash provided by operating activities			
Depreciation, depletion, and amortization	7,934	9,060	9,295
Impairments	792	1,780	535
Dry hole costs and leasehold impairments	470	477	606
Accretion on discounted liabilities	455	447	422
Deferred taxes	1,287	−878	−1,115
Undistributed equity earnings	−1,077	−1,073	−1,254
Gain on dispositions	−2,007	−5,803	−160
Other	−359	−249	196
Working capital adjustments			
Decrease (increase) in accounts and notes receivable	−1,169	−2,427	−1,106
Decrease (increase) in inventories	556	−363	320
Decrease (increase) in prepaid expenses and other current assets	−306	43	282
Increase (decrease) in accounts payable	1,290	2,887	1,612
Increase (decrease) in taxes and other accruals	−722	1,727	−1,646
Net Cash Provided by Operating Activities	**19,646**	**17,045**	**12,479**
Cash Flows from Investing Activities			
Capital expenditures and investments	−13,266	−9,761	−10,861
Proceeds from asset dispositions	4,820	15,372	1,270
Net sales (purchases) of short-term investments	400	−982	−0−
Long-term advances/loans—related parties	−9	−313	−525
Collection of advances/loans—related parties	648	115	93
Other	392	234	88
Net Cash Provided by (Used in) Investing Activities	**−7,015**	**4,665**	**−9,935**
Cash Flows from Financing Activities			
Issuance of debt	−0−	118	9,087
Repayment of debt	−961	−5,320	−7,858
Issuance of company common stock	96	133	13
Repurchase of company common stock	−11,123	−3,866	−0−
Dividends paid on company common stock	−3,632	−3,175	−2,832
Other	−685	−709	−1,265
Net Cash Used in Financing Activities	−16,305	−12,819	−2,855
Effect of Exchange Rate Changes on Cash and Cash Equivalents	−0−	21	98
Net Change in Cash and Cash Equivalents	−3,674	8,912	−213
Cash and cash equivalents at Beginning of Year	9,454	542	755
Cash and Cash Equivalents at End of Year	5,780	9,454	542

Source: ConocoPhillips 2011 10-K Report, p. 84.

Exhibit 9.4   ConocoPhillips' Net Income Attributed to Each Business Segment

	Millions of Dollars		
Years Ended December 31	2011	2010	2009
E&P	$ 8,242	9,198	3,604
Midstream	458	306	313
R&M	3,751	192	37
LUKOIL investment	239	2,503	1,219
Chemicals	745	498	248
Emerging businesses	(26)	(59)	3
Corporate and other	(973)	(1,280)	(1,010)
Net income attributable to ConocoPhillips	$12,436	11,358	4,414

Source: ConocoPhillips 2011 10-K report, p. 44.

A summary of COP's net income attributable to each business segment is listed in Exhibit 9.4. As shown, COP's upstream operations (E&P) are the largest business segment, accounting for 66.3 percent of net income in 2011 (i.e., 8,242/12,436), followed by R&M at 30.2 percent. In 2011, ConocoPhillips employed approximately 29,800 people.

As shown in Exhibit 9.5, Largest Oil Companies (Percent of Worldwide Proved Reserves), national oil companies owned by the country's government clearly dominate the exploration and production segment (referred to as upstream) of the industry based on worldwide proved reserves. Saudi Aramco ranks first with 17.7 percent of global proved reserves, followed by Petroleos de Venezuela with 14.37 percent, and then National Iranian Oil at 9.32 percent. In fact, no investor-owned company (publicly held) is in the top 10 worldwide. Where does a U.S. company rank on this list? ExxonMobil is the 18th-largest oil company in the world

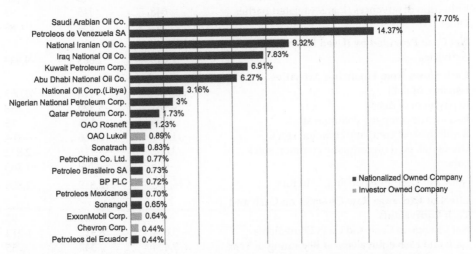

Exhibit 9.5   2010 Largest Oil Companies (Percent of Worldwide Proved Reserves)
Source: Calculated from World Reserves of 1.5 trillion barrels as of January 1, 2011, according to the *Oil & Gas Journal*, December 5, 2011, and leading companies, according to *Oil & Gas Journal*, October 3, 2011.

based on reserves. Only four public companies are in the top 20—OAO Lukoil, BP, ExxonMobil, and Chevron.

Exhibit 9.6, World's Top 20 Oil Companies in 2011, shows another way to view the top oil companies in the world based on other metrics in addition to reserves, as determined by *Petroleum Intelligence Weekly* and Standard & Poor's (2012). They rank the top oil companies based on their assets and other measures. Using this ranking, it is clear that state-owned firms still dominate the upstream, while publicly owned companies dominate the refining and marketing industry segment (known as downstream).

Competitive benchmarking is an important part of ratio analysis and involves comparing how well a company is doing relative to other companies—its peers. This involves selecting comparable companies to use in benchmarking. This information is useful to individual investors, institutional investors, employees or people seeking employment, the company itself for self-appraisal, and to mergers and acquisitions (M&A) experts.

Based on the rankings in Exhibits 9.5 and 9.6, we select ExxonMobil, Chevron, BP (British Petroleum), and Royal Dutch Shell, to conduct competitive benchmarking with COP, in addition to the industry medians for "Oil & Gas Exploration, Production & Petroleum Refining." Competitive benchmarking results are presented in the following exhibits:

- Exhibit 9.7 Summary of Financial Ratios for ConocoPhillips and E&P Industry
- Exhibit 9.8 Key Financial Ratios for Selected Energy Sectors
- Exhibit 9.9 Competitive Benchmarking with Peer Firms

USING THE FINANCIAL STATEMENTS

All calculations are shown in millions of dollars unless otherwise indicated.

Operating Cash Flow: This is the amount of cash available to the firm for investment in assets if it has no debt. This means COP would have generated $18, 260 million in cash flow if it had no debt in its capital structure.

$$\text{Operating Cash Flow} = \text{NOI}(1 - \text{Tax Rate})$$

$$+ \text{Depreciation and Amortization Expense}$$

$$= \text{Net Operating Profit After Taxes}$$

$$+ \text{Depreciation and Amortization Expense} \quad (9.1)$$

where:

$$\text{NOI} = \text{Net Operating Income}$$

$$= \text{Earnings Before Interest and Taxes (EBIT)} \quad (9.2)$$

Exhibit 9.6 World's Top 20 Oil Companies in 2011

PIW* Rank	Company	Country	State Ownership (%)	Reserves		Output		Refinery Product	
				Liquids (MMBbl)	Gas (Bcf)	Liquids (M B/D)	Gas MMcf/Day)	Capacity (M B/D)	Sales (M B/D)
1	Saudi Aramco	Saudi Arabia	100	264,500	283,100	10,007	8,121	2,423	2,962
2	NIOC	Iran	100	151,821	1,168,599	4,292	13,292	1,741	2,117
3	ExxonMobil	United States	(public)	11,673	78,815	2,422	12,148	6,260	6,414
4	PDV	Venezuela	100	296,501	195,095	2,970	4,003	3,035	2,534
5	CNPC	China	100	25,682	116,814	2,840	8,018	3,142	2,106
6	BP	UK	(public)	10,709	42,700	2,374	8,401	2,667	5,927
7	Royal Dutch Shell	UK/Netherlands	(public)	6,146	47,135	1,709	9,305	3,594	6,460
8	Chevron	United States	(public)	6,503	24,251	1,923	5,040	2,160	3,113
9	Total	France	(public)	5,987	25,788	1,340	5,648	2,363	3,776
10	Gazprom	Russia	50	9,452	670,700	870	49,188	1,091	816
11	Pemex	Mexico	100	11,394	12,494	2,901	4,633	1,710	1,668
12	ConocoPhillips	United States	(public)	4,691	21,716	1,268	4,860	2,657	3,040
13	KPC	Kuwait	100	101,548	64,007	2,556	1,464	1,136	1,039
14	Lukoil	Russia	(public)	13,319	23,615	1,942	2,063	1,436	2,165
15	Petrobras	Brazil	32.2	10,766	11,953	2,150	2,570	2,107	2,753
16	Sonatrach	Algeria	100	11,300	159,100	1,538	7,547	456	652
17	Adnoc	United Arab Emirates	100	52,812	115,002	1,538	2,665	500	371
18	Petronas	Malaysia	100	8,568	117,180	577	5,178	448	837
19	Rosneft	Russia	75.2	18,110	27,922	2,322	1,193	1,019	989
20	Qatar Petroleum	Qatar	100	10,363	643,846	1,285	7,014	216	438

Abbreviations used are as follows: Bbl—barrels, B/D—Barrels per day, M B/D—thousand barrels per day, MMBbl—million barrels, BCF—billion cubic feet, MMcf/D—Million cubic feet per day.
Source: Petroleum Intelligence Weekly's ranking as of December 2011, based on 2010 fiscal year-end operating results and Standard & Poor's (2012).

Exhibit 9.7 Summary of Financial Ratios for ConocoPhillips and E&P Industry (million $)

Ratio	Formula for Calculation	Calculation	Ratio	Ind. Median	Comment
Liquidity					
Current	$= \dfrac{\text{Current Assets}}{\text{Current Liabilities}}$	$= \dfrac{\$30,218}{\$28,068}$	$= 1.07\times$	$1.19\times$	Fair
Quick	$= \dfrac{\text{Current Assets} - \text{Inventories}}{\text{Current Liabilities}}$	$= \dfrac{\$25,587}{\$28,068}$	$= 0.91\times$	$0.94\times$	Fair
Asset Management					
Inventory Turnover	$= \dfrac{\text{Costs of Goods Sold}}{\text{Inventories}}$	$= \dfrac{\$200,990}{\$4,631}$	$= 43.40\times$	$16.46\times$	Excellent
Day Sales Outstanding (DSO)	$= \dfrac{\text{Accounts Receivable}}{\text{Annual Sales}/360}$	$= \dfrac{\$16,526}{\dfrac{\$230,859}{360}}$	$= 25.77\times$	$46.71\times$	Excellent
Total Assets Turnover	$= \dfrac{\text{Sales}}{\text{Total Assets}}$	$= \dfrac{\$230,859}{\$153,230}$	$= 1.51\times$	$0.43\times$	Excellent
EBITDA to Capital Expenditures	$= \dfrac{\text{EBITDA}}{\text{Capital Expenditures}}$	$= \dfrac{\$26,725}{\$13,266}$	$= 2.01\times$	$1.12\times$	Excellent
Debt Mgmt					
Debt to Equity	$= \dfrac{\text{Total Liabilities}}{\text{Net Worth}}$	$= \dfrac{\$87,496}{\$65,734}$	$= 1.33\times$	$1.15\times$	Fair
Times Interest Earned (TIE)	$= \dfrac{\text{EBIT}}{\text{Interest Charges}}$	$= \dfrac{\$18,564}{\$972}$	$= 19.10\times$	$6.04\times$	Excellent
Market Value Price/Earnings (P/E)	$= \dfrac{\text{Market Price per Share}}{\text{Earnings per Share}}$	$= \dfrac{\$72.92}{\$9.04}$	$= 8.06\times$	$11.14\times$	Fair to Poor
Price/Cash Flow (P/CF)	$= \dfrac{\text{Market Price per Share}}{\text{Cash Flow per Share}}$	$= \dfrac{\$72.92}{\$13.27}$	$= 5.49\times$	$5.04\times$	Good
Market/Book (M/B)	$= \dfrac{\text{Market Price per Share}}{\text{Book Value per Share}}$	$= \dfrac{\$72.92}{\$47.81}$	$= 1.52\times$	$1.46\times$	Average

(Continued)

Exhibit 9.7 *(Continued)*

Ratio	Formula for Calculation	Calculation	Ratio	Ind. Median	Comment
Payoff Policy					
Dividend Yield	$= \dfrac{\text{Most Recent Dividend per Share}}{\text{Market Price per Share}}$	$= \dfrac{\$2.64}{\$72.92}$	$= 3.62\%$	1.50%	Excellent
Dividend Payout	$= \dfrac{\text{Total Dividends Paid}}{\text{Net Income}}$	$= \dfrac{\$3,632}{\$12,436}$	$= 29.21\%$	15.81%	—
Profitability					
Net Profit Margin	$= \dfrac{\text{Net Profit}}{\text{Sales}}$	$= \dfrac{\$12,436}{\$230,859}$	$= 5.38\%$	9.32%	Fair
Return on Assets (ROA)	$= \dfrac{\text{Net Income}}{\text{Total Assets}}$	$= \dfrac{\$12,436}{\$153,230}$	$= 8.11\%$	5.46%	Good
Return on Equity (ROE)	$= \dfrac{\text{Net Income}}{\text{Common Equity}}$	$= \dfrac{\$12,436}{\$65,734}$	$= 18.91\%$	11.42%	Excellent
Return on Capital Employed (ROCE)	$= \dfrac{\text{Net Operating Profit After Tax}}{\text{Capital Employed}}$	$= \dfrac{\$10,099}{\$125,162}$	$= 8.07\%$	7.21%	Good

Exhibit 9.8 Key Financial Ratios for Selected Energy Industry Sectors

NAICS Code(s) Line of Business (Number of Firms)	Current Ratio (×)	Quick Ratio (×)	Debt-to-Equity Ratio (×)	TIE Ratio (×)	DSO (days)	Inventory Turnover (×)	Total Assets Turnover (×)	Profit Margin (%)	Return on Assets (%)	Return on Equity (%)
211111, 211112, 324110 Oil & Gas Exploration Production & Petroleum Refining (98; restricted to firms with TA >$1 billion)	1.19 (1.40)	0.94 (1.20)	1.15 (1.12)	6.04 (14.99)	46.71 (53.59)	16.46 (65.48)	0.43 (0.74)	9.32 (1.13)	5.46 (4.79)	11.42 (10.12)
213111, 213112 Oil & Gas Field Services (including Well Drilling) (45)	1.83 (1.90)	1.56 (1.65)	0.84 (1.13)	3.90 (18.33)	82.10 (88.27)	13.84 (38.44)	0.61 (0.73)	8.80 (4.16)	3.63 (3.26)	9.07 (5.91)
221210, 486210 Natural Gas Distribution & Marketing (46)	0.88 (0.96)	0.69 (0.76)	2.04 (1.96)	3.47 (3.78)	39.82 (46.44)	12.41 (30.85)	0.37 (0.51)	7.33 (9.92)	3.50 (3.43)	9.98 (9.62)
324121, 324122, 324191, 324199 Petroleum & Coal Products Manufacturing (9)	2.43 (3.62)	1.73 (3.18)	0.60 (1.79)	0.36 (−8.55)	73.15 (78.35)	8.90 (10.58)	0.79 (0.76)	−39.10 (−51.70)	−14.06 (−21.32)	6.48 (−66.66)
424710, 424720, 454311, 454312 Petroleum & Petroleum Products Wholesalers (28)	1.47 (1.48)	1.11 (1.11)	1.60 (1.85)	2.30 (153.30)	30.76 (88.41)	15.80 (29.21)	1.57 (2.71)	1.32 (−15.10)	3.23 (2.47)	8.40 (9.30)
486110, 486190 Oil & Gas Transportation & Storage (4)	1.06 (1.11)	0.75 (0.73)	2.12 (2.31)	3.80 (3.82)	25.17 (36.08)	31.98 (30.84)	0.68 (0.94)	6.38 (9.67)	5.34 (5.71)	21.72 (19.09)
325xxx (34 different NAICS codes) Chemical Manufacturing (288)	2.27 (2.85)	1.60 (2.26)	0.72 (0.81)	5.25 (14.77)	55.89 (74.51)	3.50 (14.93)	0.73 (0.86)	4.81 (−291.69)	4.31 (−23.15)	12.73 (13.06)

The primary data provided are industry medians while the industry averages are given below them in parentheses.
Source: Calculated using Compustat data.

Exhibit 9.9 Competitive Benchmarking with Peer Firms

Ratio	COP	XOM	CVX	BP	RDS	Comment
Liquidity						
Current	1.07×	0.94×	1.58×	1.16×	1.17×	Average
Quick, or Acid Test	0.91×	0.75×	1.42×	0.85×	0.88×	Average
Asset Management						
Inventory Turnover	43.4×	23.08×	32.31×	12.53×	13.68×	Excellent
DSO	25.77×	32.09×	33.20×	42.19×	45.74×	Good
Total Assets Turnover	1.51×	1.31×	1.13×	1.28×	1.36×	Good
EBITDA /CapEx	2.01×	2.25×	1.93×	2.16×	2.13×	Average
Debt Management						
Debt to Equity	1.33×	1.06×	0.71×	1.61×	1.02×	Fair
Times Interest Earned (TIE)	19.1×	64.41×	132.98×	25.38×	20.87×	Fair
Market Value						
Price/Earnings (P/E)	8.06×	10.05×	7.86×	5.24×	7.34×	Fair
Price/Cash Flow (P/CF)	5.49×	8.83×	6.10×	4.56×	6.11×	Fair
Market/Book (M/B)	1.52×	2.60×	1.74×	1.21×	1.35×	Average
Payoff Policy						
Dividend Yield	3.62%	2.18%	2.90%	3.93%	4.60%	Average
Dividend Payout	29.21%	21.97%	22.83%	15.85%	33.82%	Average
Profitability						
Net Profit Margin	5.38%	9.47%	11.38%	6.84%	6.58%	Fair
Return on Total Assets (ROA)	8.11%	12.40%	12.84%	8.77%	8.96%	Fair
Return on Equity (ROE)	18.91%	25.54%	22.01%	22.85%	18.08%	Fair
Return on Capital Employed (ROCE)	8.07%	12.29%	12.35%	8.80%	9.86%	Fair
Energy Ratios (3-year averages)						
Reserves Ratios						
Production	8.92%	7.10%	10.52%	7.47%	8.52%	Average
Reserve Life Index (years)	11.27	14.10	9.53	13.44	11.74	Average
Production Replacement	97.20%	239.38%	123.99%	54.63%	280.15%	Fair
F&D Reserve Replacement	114.85%	152.31%	116.32%	76.85%	228.93%	Fair
Reserve Cost Ratios						
Reserve Replacement Cost ($/BOE)	$13.90	$14.51	$29.02	$28.48	$14.81	Good to Excellent
Finding Costs ($/BOE)	$7.18	$3.45	$7.88	$15.21	$7.60	Good
Lifting Costs ($/BOE)	$8.16	$10.59	$11.20	$7.53	$11.31	Good
Reserve Value Ratios						
Value of Proved Res. Addn. ($/BOE)	$10.77	$7.58	$24.45	−$19.99	$20.26	Average
Value Added	0.79	0.53	0.80	−0.44	1.47	Good
Successful Efforts Accounting	Yes	Yes	Yes	Yes	Yes	—
% Reserves Oil (Gas)	53 (47)	57 (43)	51 (49)	46 (54)	43 (57)	—

Financial ratios are calculated for 2011 and energy ratios are calculated as three-year averages (2009–2011). The firms are listed by ticker symbol. Ratings assigned based on five categories: Excellent, Good, Average, Fair, and Poor.

Using COP's Income Statement (Exhibit 9.2), we have:[5]

NOI = EBIT = Sales − Cost of Goods Sold

− Selling, General, and Administrative Expenses

− Exploration Expenses − Depreciation and Amortization

= ($244,813 − $13,954) − ($185,867 + $10,770 + ($18,307 − $13,954))

− $2,078 − $1,066 − $8,156 = $18,564

Operating Cash Flow = Net Operating Profit After Taxes

+ Depreciation and Amortization Expense

= $10,099 + $8,161 = $18,260

Free Cash Flow: It is the cash flow with which the firm is able to pay the financiers after taking into account the cash investments needed to keep operations running. This would include investments in fixed assets, working capital, and other projects that would increase the stock price. As Brigham and Houston (2013) state, this is "the amount of cash that could be withdrawn without harming a firm's ability to operate and to produce future cash flows."

FCF = Operating Cash Flow − Investments

= Operating Cash Flow − (Δ in fixed assets + ΔNOWC)   (9.3)

where:

NOWC is defined as Net Operating Working Capital:

$$\text{NOWC} = \left(\begin{array}{c} \text{Current Assets} \\ \text{Required for Operation} \end{array} \right) - \left(\begin{array}{c} \text{Non-Interest-Bearing} \\ \text{Current Liabilities} \end{array} \right) \quad (9.4)$$

Looking at the Balance Sheet in Exhibit 9.1, we see that COP's current assets include cash and equivalents, account receivables, inventories, and other current assets that are part of their day-to-day operations. Short-term debt in the liabilities portion of the balance sheet represents an interest-bearing item, and thus it must be excluded from the total current liability when computing NOWC. So, to find the change in NOWC we have to compute the NOWC for each year:

Year 2010: NOWC = $34,660 − ($27,419 − $936) = $8,177

Year 2011: NOWC = $30,218 − ($28,068 − $1,013) = $3,163

ΔNOWC = $8,177 − $3,163 = $5,014

To find the changes in the fixed assets, we have to use the Balance Sheet in Exhibit 9.1:

Year 2010: Fixed Assets = $82,554

Year 2011: Fixed Assets = $84,180

ΔFixed Assets = $84,180 − $82,554 = $1,626

Now we have all the necessary elements to calculate free cash flow:

$$FCF = \text{Operating Cash Flow} - (\Delta\text{Fixed Assets} + \Delta NOWC)$$

$$= \$18,260 - (\$1,626 + \$5,014) = \$11,620$$

RATIO ANALYSIS

Ratios are merely accounting numbers translated into relative values. Financial analysis involves the interaction between different pieces of information provided in the financial statements. Ratios are designed to show relationships between financial statement accounts both *within* firms and *between* firms. The purpose of ratio analysis is to get an idea of how well a company is running. These ratios are standardized numbers which facilitate comparisons, and thus, they can be used to highlight weaknesses and strengths.

It is important to understand the potential problems and limitations of ratio analysis. For example, the choice of accounting methods and convention has a great impact on ratios since the inputs for these ratios come from accounting information. You may hear the term "GIGO" in reference to ratio analysis. GIGO simply stands for "Garbage In, Garbage Out," and it means that if the numbers you use to compute ratios are not consistent or comparable, then the ratios computed using them will not be consistent or comparable either. Before analyzing the energy ratios, in the next subsection we conduct ratio analysis for COP and compare each ratio with its industry counterpart. These results are summarized in Exhibits 9.7, 9.8 and 9.9. In Exhibit 9.7, we evaluate the financial ratios using the ratings of excellent, good, average, fair, and poor.

In this analysis, we use industry medians rather than means, unless otherwise specified. This is because the distribution of each ratio in our industry representative sample is not normally distributed to warrant the use of the mean, and moreover, these ratios appear to be very sensitive to outliers. Our representative sample of the industry is comprised of any energy company with assets more than 1 billion USD or CAD. It includes 98 energy companies worldwide.

There are six major categories of financial ratios. They are discussed next.

Liquidity Ratios

Liquidity ratios provide a fast and easy-to-use measure of liquidity by linking the level of cash and other current assets (liquid assets) to the firm's current liabilities. Two commonly used liquidity ratios are the Current Ratio and the Quick Ratio.

Current Ratio: It is defined as the division of current assets by current liabilities. It shows how well the company is able to meet its short-term financial obligations; a higher ratio is better and indicates the company has greater liquidity. Current assets are the most liquid of a firm's assets. Refer to Exhibit 9.1 for the values.

$$\text{Current Ratio} = \frac{\text{Current Assets}}{\text{Current Liabilities}} = \frac{\$30,218}{\$28,068} = 1.07 \text{ times}$$

$$\text{Industry Median} = 1.19 \text{ times} \qquad (9.5)$$

This ratio tells us that in case of financial difficulty, COP's liquid assets can cover only 7 percent more than its current short-term financial obligations. Going strictly by the accounting numbers, COP has a safety cushion of about 7 percent of the size of their short-term liabilities. In other words, this means that with a current ratio of 1.07, if COP can liquidate its current assets even at 92.9 percent of their book value, it is still able to pay its creditors in full without experiencing financial distress.[6] Since COP's current ratio is below the industry median, their liquidity position is slightly weaker than the median firm in the industry, so we give a rating of "fair" as indicated in Exhibit 9.7.

Quick (or Acid Test) Ratio: Because Inventory is the least liquid of current assets, subtracting it from Current Assets and then dividing the result by Current Liabilities gives a better measure of the firm's capacity to convert liquid assets to cash to pay off short-term liabilities.

$$\text{Quick Ratio} = \frac{\text{Current Assets} - \text{Inventory}}{\text{Current Liabilities}} = \frac{\$30,218 - \$4,631}{\$28,068} = 0.91 \text{ times}$$

$$\text{Industry Median} = 0.94 \text{ times} \tag{9.6}$$

If a company carries significant inventories, the quick ratio will always indicate a lower liquidity position for a firm. For COP, current assets are 107 percent of the short-term liabilities from the current ratio, and roughly about 16.5 percent of that is due to potentially illiquid inventory. Thus, adjusting the current ratio to account for the potentially illiquid inventory reveals a slightly weaker liquidity position in the quick ratio. Comparing the industry median for the quick ratio with that of COP, we see that again, the liquidity position is slightly below the industry median, and we assign a rating of "fair."

It is worthwhile to mention that a significant deviation from the industry median (or mean) requires a judgment call from the analyst. If a firm does not hold a sufficient level of liquid assets, they can be in danger of not having sufficient resources to cover their short-term liabilities as they come due. Moreover, having too many liquid assets (hence a very high current or quick ratio) is also an indication of poor investment decision making. This is because liquid assets earn a lower rate of return (or even no return) than long-term investments, and thus maintaining excess liquidity would also not be in line with maximizing shareholders' wealth. Firms with more aggressive working capital management policy such as Chesapeake Energy or Walmart often have liquidity ratios below 1.0. Chesapeake Energy's current ratios for 2009, 2010, and 2011 are 0.91, 0.73, and 0.44, respectively, whereas Walmart's are 0.86, 0.89, and 0.88. For Chesapeake Energy, the current ratio shows a declining liquidity position over the three-year period, and news indicates the firm is experiencing financial distress. Trends like this should always be monitored for companies and illustrate why it is important to do ratio analysis over a minimum of three- to five-year windows.

Net Working Capital: This is defined as the difference between current assets and current liabilities. It is the amount of capital needed above and beyond the current liabilities to finance current assets.

$$\text{NWC} = \text{Current Assets} - \text{Current Liabilities} \tag{9.7}$$

Using the Balance Sheet in Exhibit 9.1 we have:

$$\begin{cases} \text{Current Assets} & = \$30,218 \\ \text{Current Liabilities} & = \$28,068 \end{cases}$$

$$\text{NWC} = \$30,218 - \$28,068 = \$2,150$$

Asset Management Ratios

These ratios measure the firm's effectiveness in managing its assets. They basically attempt to deal with questions about the level of assets given the current and projected status of the corporation. On the one hand, having too many assets that are used ineffectively would adversely affect the firm since the cost of financing these assets is probably higher than cash flow generated by them. On the other hand, a low level of assets might hinder the firm's ability to produce (provide) enough goods (services) to meet demand, and consequently the firm could lose its market share and competitive edge.

Days Sales Outstanding (DSO) Ratio: In order to maintain their customer base, some firms offer credit sales to their customers. These sales are reflected in accounts receivable in the balance sheet. The effectiveness of firms (specified in days) to collect their money is captured by this ratio. Days Sales Outstanding ratio (DSO), which is also sometimes referred to as Average Collection Period (ACP), expresses in days the average period of time it takes a firm to collect its cash after making a credit sale.[7]

$$\text{Days Sales Outstanding} = \frac{\text{Accounts Receivable}}{\left(\dfrac{\text{Annual Sales}}{360}\right)}$$

$$\text{Days Sales Outstanding} = \frac{\$14,648 + \$1,878}{\left(\dfrac{\$244,813 - \$13,954}{360}\right)} = 25.77 \text{ days}$$

$$\text{Industry Median} = 46.71 \text{ days} \tag{9.8}$$

We can conclude that it takes COP about 26 days to collect its receivables whereas the industry median DSO is roughly 47 days. This means COP collects its cash 1.8 times faster than the median corporation in the industry. This is a very strong ratio relative to the industry average, so we give a rating of "excellent."

Inventory Turnover Ratio: This ratio specifies how many times in a year inventory is sold and replenished, or *turned over*. For COP, this ratio is 43.4 times, which is dramatically higher than the industry median, indicating that COP is turning over its inventory roughly about every eight days (43.4 times in a year). In other words, COP is selling and replenishing its inventory almost 2.6 times faster than the median firm in the industry. This suggests that COP does not hold excess inventory (rating is "excellent"). It should be noted that this ratio is less

meaningful for firms in the oil and gas industry but for a retailer, it can be extremely important.

$$\text{Inventory Turnover Ratio} = \frac{\text{Cost of Goods Sold}}{\text{Inventory}}$$

$$\text{Inventory Turnover Ratio} = \frac{\$185,867 + \$10,770 + (\$18,307 - \$13,954)}{\$4,631}$$

$$= 43.40 \text{ times}$$

$$\text{Industry Median} = 16.46 \text{ times} \tag{9.9}$$

Total Asset Turnover Ratio: This ratio measures the firm's ability to generate sales per dollar of total assets. It is computed by the following formula:

$$\text{Total Assets Turnover Ratio} = \frac{\text{Sales}}{\text{Total Assets}}$$

$$\text{Total Assets Turnover Ratio} = \frac{(\$244,813 - \$13,954)}{\$153,230} = 1.51 \text{ times}$$

$$\text{Industry Median} = 0.43 \text{ times} \tag{9.10}$$

This ratio shows that every dollar COP spends on total assets helps to generate about $1.51 of sales, whereas the industry median suggests that a dollar investment in total assets would help generate 43 cents of sales. COP's ratio is more than 3.5 times greater than the industry median, meaning that Conoco is using its total assets to generate sales more effectively than that which is suggested by the industry median (rating of "excellent").

EBITDA (Earnings Before Interest, Taxes, Depreciation, and Amortization) to Capital Expenditures: This ratio indicates the firm's effectiveness in making investment decisions over time and shows how each dollar invested in capital expenditures (CapEx) helps to generate net operating income. An alternative interpretation of this ratio as it pertains to fiscal responsibility is to see if the firm is overinvesting or underinvesting relative to cash flow. This ratio is popular with Wall Street analysts. For example, Nicole Decker, Energy Sector Analyst at UBS, uses this ratio to investigate if an energy company is overly aggressive in capital investments over time or the opposite, depending on current energy prices and a company's unique situation.[8] The energy industry has historically experienced boom and bust cycles where prices can rise or fall quickly (high volatility). If this ratio is consistently below 1.0 times, then this can be a warning sign that the firm is over spending cash flows, especially if the forecast is for weak energy prices. If the ratio is consistently high, then it can indicate the opposite. The following formula is used to compute this ratio.

$$\text{EBITDA to Capital Expenditures Ratio} = \frac{\text{EBITDA}}{\text{CapEx}} \tag{9.11}$$

The EBITDA to Capital Expenditures ratio for COP is calculated below:

$$\text{EBITDA to Capital Expenditures Ratio} = \frac{\$26,725}{\$13,266} = 2.01 \text{ times}$$

$$\text{Industry Median} = 1.12 \text{ times}$$

EBITDA can be garnered from the Income Statement (Exhibit 9.2), and Capital Expenditures can be obtained from the Statement of Cash Flows (Exhibit 9.3). This means that each dollar COP invested in capital expenditures generated $2.01 in net operating income. This is 1.8 times greater than that of the industry median, indicating that Conoco's investment decisions are effective in generating cash flows (rating of "excellent").

Let's look at another example. Chesapeake Energy has invested heavily in shale natural gas plays in recent years with an aggressive capital investment program. Natural gas prices have recently collapsed due to oversupply, and Chesapeake is experiencing financial distress. Chesapeake Energy's EBITDA/CapEx ratios for 2009, 2010, and 2011 are 0.34, 0.34 and –0.99, respectively. This is not a sustainable capital investment program.

Debt Management Ratios

Examining the debt management ratios and understanding the financial leverage of a firm is a crucial part of financial statement analysis. Debt affects the expected rate of return to shareholders and avoids the dilutive effect of equity offerings. However, it increases the riskiness of the firm. During a period of financial distress, since interest payments are contractual and do not change with the firm's economic conditions, they could impose significant burden on the firm. In extreme circumstances, bondholders can force the firm to file for bankruptcy if the firm cannot make interest payments. There are many corporate tombstones reflecting the riskiness of excessive leverage, many from the recent financial crisis.

Debt-to-Equity Ratio: It reflects how extensively a firm is financed by debt relative to their level of equity financing. The following formula is used to compute this ratio.

$$\text{Debt to Equity Ratio} = \frac{\text{Total Liabilities}}{\text{Net Worth}} \tag{9.12}$$

Debt-to-equity ratio for COP is calculated below:

$$\text{Debt to Equity Ratio} = \frac{\$87,496}{\$65,734} = 1.3311$$

$$\text{Industry Median} = 1.15 \text{ times}$$

Total Liabilities can be taken from the Balance Sheet (Exhibit 9.1). Net worth is equal to total equity, which can also be extracted from the balance sheet. This ratio shows that COP is financed by debt roughly 33 percent more than it is by equity. This translates to an almost 60-to-40 breakdown of debt-to-equity. COP is

more leveraged than the median firm in the industry (rating of "fair). This should be reflected in higher interest expenses and probably lower-than-median (average) profit margin, which will be discussed shortly.

Times-Interest-Earned (TIE) Ratio: It is a measure of the available safety cushion provided by net operating income (also called EBIT, earnings before interest and taxes). It is a multiple that indicates how many dollars of EBIT the firm has to cover every dollar of interest expense. In other words, it tells how far earnings could drop before meeting interest expenses becomes a problem. The TIE ratio for COP is 19.10, indicating that for each dollar of interest expense, COP has roughly $19 of EBIT to cover it.

$$\text{Times Interest Earned} = \frac{\text{Earnings Before Interest and Taxes (EBIT)}}{\text{Interest Charges}}$$

$$= \frac{\$18,564}{\$972} = 19.10 \times$$

$$\text{Industry Median} = 6.04 \text{ times} \qquad (9.13)$$

COP's high TIE ratio is very strong relative to the industry (rating of "excellent"), and they have a larger safety cushion. On first glance this might seem contrary to what one would expect from the high debt-equity ratio. One would correctly expect that the use of leverage above the industry median should lead to higher interest expenses and thus to a lower TIE ratio. But we have to keep in mind that COP's investment decisions were very effective as reflected in its 80 percent higher EBITDA to Capital Expenditures ratio. Moreover, COP's leverage is only 15 percent above the industry median ($\frac{1.3311}{1.15} = 1.15$). So, its higher earnings capacity more than offsets higher interest payments, and thus it has a higher TIE ratio. (*Note:* As shown in Exhibit 9.9, the TIE is low compared to peer energy firms.)

Market Valuation Ratios

The market value ratios reflect the perception of investors regarding the future prospects of the corporation. We discuss three ratios in this section: price/earnings ratio, price/cash flow ratio, and market/book ratio.

Price/Earnings Ratio: The price/earnings (P/E) ratio is one of the most widely used market value ratios because it is intuitive and easy to calculate. This ratio measures how much investors are willing to spend for a share of stock relative to each dollar of profit the company generates for its common stockholders.

$$\text{Price/Earnings Ratio} = \frac{\text{Price per Share}}{\text{Net Income per Share}} \qquad (9.14)$$

Price/Earnings ratio for Conoco is calculated below:

$$\text{Price/Earnings Ratio} = \frac{\$72.92}{\$9.04} = 8.06 \text{ times}$$

$$\text{Industry Median} = 11.14 \text{ times}$$

The stock price is available on many websites, one of our favorites being Yahoo!Finance (finance.yahoo.com). Earnings per share, which is net income per share, can be taken from the income statement (Exhibit 9.2). This ratio shows that COP's shares are selling for more than 8 times what the company is generating in profits for its common stockholders. Firms with higher growth potential have higher P/E ratios, *ceteris paribus* (all else being equal). If we know the total number of shares outstanding, we can calculate EPS (earnings per share) by simply diving net income by total number of shares. A lower than industry median P/E ratio is suggestive that investors perceive COP to be riskier than other firms in the industry and/or that they regard the company as having lower growth opportunity. Overall, this ratio does not tell us much about current financial performance, but does indicate what investors believe about future prospects. We assign a rating of "fair to poor."

Price/Cash Flow Ratio: Similar to the P/E ratio, the Price/Cash Flow ratio compares the stock price paid relative to a dollar of cash flow.

$$\text{Price/CashFlow Ratio} = \frac{\text{Price per Share}}{\text{Cash Flow per Share}}$$

$$= \frac{\text{Price per Share}}{\text{Cash Flow/Number of Common Shares Outstanding}}$$

$$(9.15)$$

Price/Cash Flow ratio for COP is calculated below:

$$\text{Price/Cash Flow Ratio} = \frac{\$72.92}{\$18,260,000,000/1,375,035,000} = 5.49 \text{ times}$$

$$\text{Industry Median} = 5.04 \text{ times}$$

Cash flow per share can be found by dividing operating cash flow by the number of common shares outstanding (from the Balance Sheet, Exhibit 9.1). The operating cash flow was computed previously in the section "Using the Financial Statements." This ratio shows that COP's shares are traded roughly 5.49 times more than the cash flow generated for each share and is slightly higher than the industry median, indicating investors are willing to pay slightly more for its shares relative to cash flow.

Market/Book Ratio: This ratio reflects the value of the company's stock in the market relative to the book value of its common equity. Like the previous two market value ratios we have discussed, this ratio captures the perception of the investors about the future prospects of the company. Firms that are regarded as likely to produce high returns are typically traded at high multiples of book value.

$$\text{Market/BookRatio} = \frac{(\text{Market}) \text{ Price per Share}}{\text{Book value per Share}}$$

$$= \frac{(\text{Market}) \text{ Price per Share}}{\text{Common equity/Number of Common Shares Outstanding}} \quad (9.16)$$

Market/Book ratio for COP is calculated below:

$$\text{Market/Book Ratio} = \frac{\$72.92}{\$65,734,000,000/1,375,035,000} = 1.52 \text{ times}$$

Industry Median = 1.46 times

Again, COP's stock price can be gathered from the Internet. Book value per share can be found by dividing the common equity by the number of common shares outstanding, both of which can be found on the Balance Sheet (Exhibit 9.1). This ratio shows that the price for COP's shares in the market is about one and a half times greater than the book value per share, indicating that investors are willing to pay 50 percent more for each dollar of COP's book value. It is slightly greater than the industry median of 1.46 and we assign a rating of "average."

Market value ratios are giving mixed results. On the one hand, we observe the lower P/E ratio, which indicates higher risk or lower growth associated with COP by investors. On the other hand, we observe high P/CF and high MB ratios. This may be due to a number of factors. For example, it may be the result of having higher financial leverage and higher interest expenses than the industry, making the firm riskier than its comparable competitors (lower P/E) while having larger generated cash flow along with more effective asset management (higher P/CF and MB ratios). Once we analyze the remaining ratios including the energy ratios, we will have a full set of information.

Payoff Policy Measures

Any cash payment made to the stockholders from the income of the firm, whether generated from the current fiscal period or previous period, is referred to as dividends. Extensive literature on the effect of dividend policy on the firm's value highlights that this policy appears to have two opposing effects. On the one hand, expressing stock price based on a constant dividend model results in higher stock value if the dividend is increased. On the other hand, increasing the dividend payout would lead to lower available capital for reinvestment, which would slow down firm growth and thus, adversely affect the stock price. More importantly, it is now widely accepted that dividends are *sticky* meaning that once they are initiated, corporations are reluctant to cut them. It should now be quite clear why ratios of payout policy are extremely important.

Dividend Yield: It is the ratio of dividend paid out to current stock price.

$$\text{Dividend Yield} = \frac{D_0}{P_0}$$

$$= \frac{3,632,000,000/1,375,035,000}{72.92} = 0.0362 = 3.62\% \text{ for COP}$$

Industry Median = 1.5%

(9.17)

D_0 is the most recent dividend per share and is calculated by dividing total dividend (from the Statement of Cash Flows, Exhibit 9.3) by the total number of shares

outstanding. This is the current dividend yield. Similarly, one can calculate the expected dividend yield by making a projection about the next dividend payment (D_1).

The current dividend yield of COP is more than twice that of the industry median. For every dollar investment in COP's stock, an investor has received 3.6 cents of dividend. This makes COP more attractive to those investors who are interested in higher dividends and we assign a rating of "excellent" relative to the industry. (*Note:* As shown in Exhibit 9.9, this dividend payout is similar to peer energy firms.)

Dividend Payout: This ratio shows how much of the income generated within the current fiscal year has been retained for future investment and how much has been paid out to shareholders. This ratio can take a value of zero if management retains all earnings and pays no dividend.

$$\text{Payout Ratio} = \frac{\text{Dividend}}{\text{Income}}$$
$$= \frac{\$3,632}{\$12,436} = 0.2921 = 29.21\%$$
$$\text{Industry Median} = 15.8\% \tag{9.18}$$

COP's management team has decided to pay out about 29 percent of the income generated in the 2011 fiscal year to its shareholders. This is about twice as much as the industry median, which is consistent with the previous ratio. Using the payoff policy measures, it seems that COP pays higher dividends than its competitors in the industry.

We have to bear in mind that a very high payout ratio relative to the industry is not necessarily a good attribute. As argued before, dividends are *sticky* in a sense that managers are hesitant to cut them or reduce them, since reduction typically has huge negative impact on the stock price. This is exactly why an increase in the dividend is typically very well received in the market. An increase in dividends indicates that managers are sure about the future prospects of the firm and its earning capacity, and that they believe they can maintain this higher dividend through higher earnings.

During a financial downturn, a very high payout policy could impose a serious burden on the firm. It may force the firm to issue debt in order to pay dividends. Moreover, due to high dividends the firm may not have enough capital for future projects and thus may have to use financial leverage to finance growth and that would increase interest expenses, riskiness of the firm, and possibly hinder profitability.

Profitability Ratios

Now, we get to the bottom-line ratios. The net effect of all the analysis discussed so far is reflected in profitability ratios. In particular, profitability ratios capture the collective effect of all the policies related to liquidity, asset management, and debt management.

(Net) Profit Margin: The net profit margin is the profit generated by each dollar of sales; thus, the higher the better.

$$\text{Net Profit Margin} = \frac{\text{Net Profit}}{\text{Sales}}$$

$$= \frac{\$12,436}{\$230,859} = 0.0538 = 5.38\% \text{ for COP}$$

$$\text{Industry Median} = 9.32\% \tag{9.19}$$

COP's net profit margin is 5.38 percent versus 9.32 percent for the industry (57 percent lower). Various reasons may explain the lower margin such as higher interest expenses due to more leverage, higher exploration and production costs, and so forth. We will have a more comprehensive view once we cover the energy ratios. COP is one of the largest firms in the industry, so size is something we take into consideration. We assign a rating of "fair."

Return on (Total) Assets (ROA): ROA is the percentage profit generated by one dollar of investment in assets. This ratio shows how effective the management team uses the firm's assets to generate profit.

$$\text{ROA} = \frac{\text{Net Income}}{\text{Total Asset}}$$

$$= \frac{\$12,436}{\$153,230} = 0.0811 = 8.11\% \text{ for COP}$$

$$\text{Industry Median} = 5.46\% \tag{9.20}$$

COP's operations are generating 8.11 percent versus 5.46 percent for the industry (48 percent higher). This is consistent with what was found by the asset management ratios, so it is apparent that COP has made effective use of its assets in 2011 relative to the industry (rating of "good").

Return on (Common) Equity (ROE): This is the most common ratio used for measuring the return to shareholders and is a widely published statistic. This indicates how much the firm has earned over the year on common equity.

$$\text{ROE} = \frac{\text{Net Income}}{\text{Common Equity}}$$

$$= \frac{\$12,436}{\$65,734} = 0.1891 = 18.91\% \text{ for COP}$$

$$\text{Industry Median} = 11.42\% \tag{9.21}$$

In 2011, COP realized about 19 cents in net income for every dollar per book value of equity. This ratio is very strong (rating is "excellent") and is about 65 percent higher than the median firm in the industry. Possible reasons are: greater use of financial leverage as reflected in the debt ratio, effectiveness in its investment decisions and asset management as reflected in its high EBITDA/capital expenditures and asset management ratios, wise investment decisions (80 percent higher EBTIDA/CapEx ratio than that of industry), and efficient asset management (3.5 times higher TA turnover than that of industry).

Return on Capital Employed (ROCE): ROCE gives the percentage profit generated by capital employed. In other words, this ratio shows how effective the management team uses the firm's assets to generate profit. ROCE compares earnings with capital invested in the company. It is similar to Return on Assets discussed above, but takes into account sources of financing. Net Operating Profit After Tax (NOPAT) is equal to EBIT * (1 − Tax Rate)—the return on the capital employed should be measured in after-tax terms.[9]

$$ROCE = \frac{\text{Net Operating Profit After Tax}}{\text{Capital Employed}} = \frac{\text{EBIT} \times (1 - \text{Tax Rate})}{\text{Total Assets} - \text{Current Liabilities}}$$

$$ROCE = \frac{\$10,099}{(\$153,230 - \$28,068)} = 0.0807 \text{ or } 8.07\%$$

$$\text{Industry Median} = 7.21\%\% \tag{9.22}$$

COP's ROCE is "good" relative to the industry median but only "fair" compared to the industry peers in Exhibit 9.9.

DuPont Analysis: DuPont analysis is a way to view how a company manages the profit margin, total asset turnover, and the equity multiplier to generate the ROA and ROE. DuPont Analysis was first developed by the management team of the DuPont Corporation, hence the name. The benefit of this approach is that it gives greater detail by showing which key areas impact ROA and ROE and helps the management team analyze different ways to improve the performance of the corporation. In its basic form the **DuPont equation** is as follows:

$$ROA = \text{Net Profit Margin} \times \text{Total Asset Turnover}$$

$$= \frac{\text{Net Income}}{\text{Sales}} \times \frac{\text{Sales}}{\text{Total Assets}} = \frac{\$12,436}{\$251,226} \times \frac{\$251,226}{\$153,230}$$

$$= 4.9\% \times 1.64 = 8.1\% \text{ for COP} \tag{9.23}$$

It is obvious from the discussion thus far that, if Conoco had no debt, ROA and ROE would have been equal. However, because Conoco has debt outstanding (as shown earlier), their equity is less than 100 percent of their capital, and thus, Conoco's ROE should be—and is—higher than their ROA. In fact, as we can see from the calculations earlier, Conoco's ROE is more than twice as its ROA. ROA is lowered by debt (because interest expense lowers net income, which also lowers ROA). However, the use of debt also reduces the need for equity financing, and, if equity is lowered more than net income, then ROE would increase.[10] This is consistent with our earlier calculation of ROE. Thus, to get ROE from ROA we need an equity multiplier. This multiplier is equal to the ratio of total assets to common equity. Then the product of ROA and this multiplier give ROE:

$$ROE = ROA \times \text{Equity Multiplier}$$

$$= ROA \times \frac{\text{Total Assets}}{\text{Common Equity}} = 8.1\% \times \frac{\$153,230}{\$65,734} = 18.9\% \text{ for COP}$$

$$\tag{9.24}$$

We can further combine the last two formulas to obtain an extended version of the DuPont equation:

$$\begin{aligned}\text{ROE} &= \text{Profit Margin} \times \text{Total Assets Turnover} \times \text{Equity Multiplier} \\ &= \frac{\text{Net Income}}{\text{Sales}} \times \frac{\text{Sales}}{\text{Total Assets}} \times \frac{\text{Total Assets}}{\text{Common Equity}} \\ &= \frac{\$12,436}{\$251,226} \times \frac{\$251,226}{\$153,230} \times \frac{\$153,230}{\$65,734} = 18.9\% \text{ for COP}\end{aligned} \qquad (9.25)$$

Interestingly, some companies have utilized significantly more leverage through the equity multiplier to increase return on equity. This is risky because of the higher debt levels required. The recent financial crisis is evidence: Lehman Brothers and Bear Stearns, just to name a few, maintained extremely high debt levels because executives' compensation was benchmarked off of ROE. As long as times were good, these executives earned higher bonuses as a result. Now we have the forensic evidence from many of the books written about the crisis that show some firms took on extra leverage, just to maximize ROE for bonus purposes.

Refer to Exhibit 9.9 for analysis comparing COP to the industry peers: XOM, CVX, BP, and RDS.

ENERGY RATIOS

A crucial component of financial statement analysis for oil and gas companies is evaluation of upstream operations. This involves computing the energy ratios that are specific to extraction industries. Replacing reserves is the lifeblood of an oil and gas company, whether it is integrated (operates in upstream and downstream) or independent (upstream only). The information used to calculate the energy ratios is found in the detailed disclosures of the 10-K report, referred to as the "notes." See Item 8 that includes the supplementary data on the oil and gas operations. As discussed in Chapter 8, "Oil and Gas Accounting," the information necessary to compute the ratios is made available because of the disclosures required by the FASB (Financial Accounting Standards Board) and SEC (Securities and Exchange Commission) for U.S. listed companies and the IASB (International Accounting Standards Board) for international companies.

In this section, we will cover the nine most commonly used energy ratios, and classify the ratios into three areas as shown in Exhibit 9.10, Reserve Ratios, Reserve Cost Ratios, and Reserve Value Ratios.

Reserve Ratios tell us (energy ratios 1 through 4):

- How long will reserves last?
- What percentage of reserves is produced?
- How are reserves replaced, and how much of reserves that were produced have been replaced?

Reserve Cost Ratios answer the questions (energy ratios 5, 6, and 7):

- How much does it cost to find oil?
- How much does it cost to replace reserves either through drilling operations or buying reserves on Wall Street?
- How much does it cost to produce reserves?

Exhibit 9.10 Most Commonly Used Energy Ratios

Energy Ratios	Formula for Calculation
Reserve Ratios	
1. Production Ratio	$= \dfrac{\text{Production}}{\text{Reserves}}$
2. Reserve Life Index	$= \dfrac{\text{Reserves}}{\text{Production}}$
3. Production Replacement Ratio	$= \dfrac{\text{Increase in Reserves} + \text{Production}}{\text{Production}}$
4. Finding and Development (F&D) Reserve Replacement Ratio	$= \dfrac{\text{Extensions and Discoveries} + \text{Improved Recovery} + \text{Reserve Revisions}}{\text{Production}}$
Reserve Cost Ratios	
5. Reserve Replacement Cost Ratio	$= \dfrac{\text{Total Costs Incurred}}{\text{Revisions} + \text{Improved Recovery} + \text{Extensions and Discoveries} + \text{Purchases}}$
6. Finding Costs Ratio	$= \dfrac{\text{Exploration Cost}}{\text{Extensions and Discoveries}}$
7. Lifting Costs Ratio	$= \dfrac{\text{Total Lifting Costs}}{\text{Annual Production}}$
Reserve Value Ratios	
8. Value of Proved Reserve Additions	$= \dfrac{\text{Changes due to Extensions, Discoveries, and Improved Recovery} + \text{Changes due to Revisions} + \text{Changes due to Purchases}}{\text{Reserve Extensions and Discoveries} + \text{Improved Recovery} + \text{Revision} + \text{Purchases of Reserves in Place}}$
9. Value Added Ratio	$= \dfrac{\text{Value of Proved Reserve Additions}}{\text{Reserve Replacement Cost Ratio}}$

Reserve Value Ratios answer questions about the value of reserves (energy ratios 8 and 9):

- What is the value of the reserves additions per BOE?
- What value has been added?

To calculate these ratios, we will use Exhibits 9.11 through 9.15, which contain the disclosures from COP's 10-K report.

- Exhibit 9.11, Proved Reserve Disclosures for Oil and Gas Reserves
- Exhibit 9.12, Costs Incurred in Oil and Gas Acquisition, Exploration and Development
- Exhibit 9.13, Result of Operations from Oil and Gas Activities
- Exhibit 9.14, Standardized Measure of Discounted Future Net Cash Flows Relating to Proved Oil and Gas Reserve Quantities
- Exhibit 9.15, Sources of Change in Discounted Future Net Cash Flows

Exhibit 9.9, Competitive Benchmarking with Peer Firms, contains energy ratio analysis for the five firms: COP, ExxonMobil (XOM), Chevron (CVX), BP, and Royal Dutch Shell (RDS), along with our assessment of COP's performance relative to the peers. These five peer firms will be used to calculate the industry averages for the energy ratios. All of these firms employ successful efforts accounting. For ease of presentation and consistency across comparable analysis, we will exclude equity affiliates in reserve calculations and only use reserves classified as consolidated operations. (*Note:* Reserves for equity affiliates are reported separately for all firms. Comprehensive investigation should include equity affiliates but for brevity, we exclude the analysis here. Equity affiliates are often higher risk because such operations are frequently in countries subject to high political risk. For example, Venezuela nationalized oil company assets in 2007 through 2009, including the equity affiliates COP held there.)

A word about energy conversions: The 10-K reports use the general conversion of one barrel of crude oil is equal to six mcf (thousand cubic feet of natural gas). The "e" is added to the end of each volume unit to indicate there has been a conversion (e.g., BOE indicates "barrel of oil equivalent" and mcfe indicates "thousand cubic feet of natural gas equivalent"). Refer to the Appendix at the end of the book for more energy conversions.

A word about the time period to calculate energy ratios: One of the unique aspects of the oil and gas industry is the long time frame between when exploration expenditures are made and when the reserve's results are known (whether or not oil and gas is found). Production volumes typically fluctuate from year to year, depending on oil and gas price levels and the structure of the company. There is no ideal way to handle this mismatch between investment and reserve additions. In particular, the reserve cost ratios will vary significantly from year to year. Therefore, it is best to compute a moving average of the cost ratios over a period of three to five years. This will make competitive benchmarking more reliable. We will use three-year averages in this section for the benchmarking comparisons.

Exhibit 9.11   Proved Reserve Disclosures for Oil and Gas Reserves

Years Ended December 31	Total Proved Reserves									
	Millions of Barrels of Oil Equivalent									
	Alaska	Lower 48	Total United States	Canada	Europe	Russia	Asia Pacific/ Middle East	Africa	Other Areas	Total
Developed and Undeveloped										
Consolidated operations										
End of 2008	1,617	2,131	3,748	629	936	—	904	448	135	6,800
Revisions	151	22	173	404	32	—	(28)	10	(13)	578
Improved recovery	14	2	16	—	—	—	2	—	—	18
Purchases	—	—	—	—	—	—	—	—	—	—
Extensions and discoveries	14	41	55	186	11	—	35	3	—	290
Production	(112)	(183)	(295)	(89)	(143)	—	(96)	(36)	—	(659)
Sales	—	(1)	(1)	(1)	—	—	—	—	(5)	(7)
End of 2009	1,684	2,012	3,696	1,129	836	—	817	425	117	7,020
Revisions	107	68	175	109	42	—	1	27	—	354
Improved recovery	55	2	57	—	—	—	5	—	—	62
Purchases	—	2	2	—	—	—	—	—	—	2
Extensions and discoveries	17	51	68	18	33	—	11	10	—	140
Production	(101)	(165)	(266)	(82)	(132)	—	(99)	(38)	—	(617)
Sales	—	(52)	(52)	(254)	—	—	—	—	—	(306)
End of 2010	1,762	1,918	3,680	920	779	—	735	424	117	6,655
Revisions	101	48	149	31	8	—	(9)	7	—	186
Improved recovery	14	4	18	1	60	—	13	—	—	92
Purchases	—	2	2	—	—	—	—	—	—	2
Extensions and discoveries	21	97	118	97	128	—	40	—	—	383
Production	(94)	(163)	(257)	(73)	(105)	—	(86)	(25)	—	(546)
Sales	—	(10)	(10)	(12)	—	—	—	—	—	(22)
End of 2011	1,804	1,896	3,700	964	870	—	693	406	117	6,750

Includes 594 million barrels of oil equivalent due to the cessation of equity accounting.
Source: ConocoPhillips 2011 10-K Report, p. 148.

Exhibit 9.12 Costs Incurred in Oil and Gas Acquisition, Exploration, and Development

Costs Incurred

Years Ended December 31

	Alaska	Lower 48	Total U.S.	Canada	Europe	Russia	Asia Pacific/ Middle East	Africa	Other Areas	Total
2011										
Consolidated operations										
Unproved property acquisition	$1	577	578	145	—	—	—	—	—	723
Proved property acquisition	—	10	10	—	—	—	36	—	—	46
	1	587	588	145	—	—	36	—	—	769
Exploration	84	1,031	1,115	269	201	1	226	63	88	1,963
Development	499	2,633	3,132	1,347	2,123	—	949	263	726	8,540
	$584	4,251	4,835	1,761	2,324	1	1,211	326	814	11,272
2010										
Consolidated operations										
Unproved property acquisition	$(26)	286	260	113	9	—	—	—	—	382
Proved property acquisition	—	100	100	1	—	—	—	—	—	101
	−26	386	360	114	9	—	—	—	—	483
Exploration	119	487	606	269	144	3	356	45	143	1,566
Development	588	1,439	2,027	927	1,351	—	858	375	729	6,267
	$681	2,312	2,993	1,310	1,504	3	1,214	420	872	8,316

Amounts in Asia Pacific/Middle East were reclassified between "Unproved property acquisition" and "Proved property acquisition." Total acquisition costs were unchanged.

December 31	Alaska	Lower 48	Total U.S.	Canada	Europe	Russia	Asia Pacific/ Middle East	Africa	Other Areas	Total
2009										
Consolidated operations										
Unproved property acquisition	—	78	78	62	5	—	30	—	55	230
Proved property acquisition	1	6	7	7	—	—	—	—	—	14
	1	84	85	69	5	—	30	—	55	244
Exploration	137	476	613	251	184	4	342	33	90	1,517
Development	790	1,726	2,516	1,114	1,108	—	1,244	240	685	6,907
	928	2,286	3,214	1,434	1,297	4	1,616	273	830	8,668

Source: ConocoPhillips 2011 10-K Report, pp. 159–160.

Exhibit 9.13 Result of Operations from Oil and Gas Activities for 2011

Results of Operations Year Ended December 31, 2011	Alaska	Lower 48	Total United States	Canada	Europe	Russia	Asia Pacific/Middle East	Africa	Other Areas	Total
Consolidated operations										
Sales	4,319	3,513	7,832	2,123	5,233	—	5,901	1,486	—	22,575
Transfers	3,869	3,283	7,152	176	3,854	—	932	54	—	12,168
Other revenues	−46	303	257	138	−16	—	−264	30	16	161
Total revenues	8,142	7,099	15,241	2,437	9,071	—	6,569	1,570	16	34,904
Production costs excluding taxes	1,023	1,286	2,309	781	956	—	742	266	—	5,054
Taxes other than income taxes	2,721	520	3,241	65	4	1	543	23	—	3,877
Exploration expenses	36	368	404	177	201	—	192	51	54	1,079
Depreciation, depletion, and amortization	468	2,113	2,581	1,504	1,407	1	940	188	—	6,621
Impairments	2	71	73	253	−38	—	—	—	—	288
Transportation costs	609	432	1,041	128	273	—	120	27	—	1,589
Other related expenses	49	60	109	55	63	20	87	−7	56	383
Accretion	59	58	117	50	203	—	23	2	1	396
	3,175	2,191	5,366	−576	6,002	−22	3,922	1,020	−95	15,617
Provision for income taxes	1,167	755	1,922	−194	4,355	3	1,844	722	−23	8,629
Results of operations for producing activities	2,008	1,436	3,444	−382	1,647	−25	2,078	298	−72	6,988
Other earnings	−25	−165	−190	−32	248	11	191	11	7	246
Net income (loss) attributable to ConocoPhillips	1,983	1,271	3,254	−414	1,895	−14	2,269	309	−65	7,234

Source: ConocoPhillips 2011 10-K Report, p. 151.

Exhibit 9.14 Standardized Measure of Discounted Future Net Cash Flows Relating to Proved Oil and Gas Reserve Quantities for 2011 (refer to the 10-K report for 2010 and 2009)

Discounted Future Net Cash Flows (values in millions of $)	Alaska	Lower 48	Total United States	Canada	Europe	Russia	Asia Pacific/ Middle East	Africa	Other Areas	Total
2011										
Consolidated operations										
Future cash inflows	143,652	73,807	217,459	40,581	78,250	—	49,936	33,017	11,891	431,134
Less:										
Future production and transportation costs*	75,771	32,766	108,537	19,148	17,166	—	14,380	4,113	3,768	167,112
Future development costs	11,385	7,519	18,904	13,393	16,986	—	3,051	885	2,080	55,299
Future income tax provisions	20,512	11,771	32,283	2,060	29,853	—	11,967	23,825	990	100,978
Future net cash flows	35,984	21,751	57,735	5,980	14,245	—	20,538	4,194	5,053	107,745
10 percent annual discount	19,233	9,643	28,876	4,025	5,372	—	6,649	1,522	3,712	50,156
Discounted future net cash flows	16,751	12,108	28,859	1,955	8,873	—	13,889	2,672	1,341	57,589

*Includes taxes other than income taxes.

Source: ConocoPhillips 2011 10-K Report, pp. 162–164.

Exhibit 9.15 Sources of Change in Discounted Future Net Cash Flows

	Consolidated Operations			Equity Affiliates			Total Company		
	2011	2010	2009	2011	2010	2009	2011	2010	2009
Discounted future net cash flows at the beginning of the year	45,466	30,393	24,548	11,094	11,881	3,033	56,560	42,274	27,581
Changes during the year									
Revenues less production and transportation costs for the year*	−24,223	−22,296	−18,460	−1,962	−3,083	−2,793	−26,185	−25,379	−21,253
Net change in prices, and production and transportation costs*	38,161	39,532	19,208	4,685	3,478	14,386	42,846	43,010	33,594
Extensions, discoveries, and improved recovery, less estimated future costs	8,730	4,517	2,312	832	297	1,342	9,562	4,814	3,654
Development costs for the year	8,428	5,617	6,148	1,488	1,758	1,623	9,916	7,375	7,771
Changes in estimated future development costs	−8,374	−2,917	−7,036	−1,508	−129	−2,197	−9,882	−3,046	−9,233
Purchases of reserves in place, less estimated future costs	19	19	3	—	—	96	19	19	99
Sales of reserves in place, less estimated future costs	−390	−3,729	−75	−234	−5,405	—	−624	−9,134	−75
Revisions of previous quantity estimates**	−1,938	3,062	5,149	491	372	−1,597	−1,447	3,434	3,552
Accretion of discount	7,710	5,000	3,972	1,284	1,404	365	8,994	6,404	4,337
Net change in income taxes	−16,000	−13,732	−5,376	−1,537	521	−2,377	−17,537	−13,211	−7,753
Total changes	12,123	15,073	5,845	3,539	−787	8,848	15,662	14,286	14,693
Discounted future net cash flows at year end	57,589	45,466	30,393	14,633	11,094	11,881	72,222	56,560	42,274

The net change in prices, and production and transportation costs is the beginning-of-year reserve-production forecast multiplied by the net annual change in the per-unit sales price, and production and transportation cost, discounted at 10 percent.

Certain amounts have been restated to remove future development costs related to probable reserves.

*Includes taxes other than income taxes.

**Includes amounts resulting from changes in the timing of production.

Purchases and sales of reserves in place, along with extensions, discoveries and improved recovery, are calculated using production forecasts of the applicable reserve quantities for the year multiplied by the 12-month average sales prices, less future estimated costs, discounted at 10 percent.

The net change in income taxes is the annual change in the discounted future income tax provisions.

Source: ConocoPhillips 2011 10-K Report, p. 165.

A word about why we should care: As S&P (2012) states in their *Global Industry Surveys: Oil & Gas Europe* industry survey: "The fortunes of oil and gas companies are tied to overall supply and demand issues that are reflected in oil and gas prices, though changes affect industry sectors differently. For example, high prices for oil and natural gas benefit the upstream (exploration and production) companies but hurt the downstream (refiners) in the form of higher raw materials costs. For integrated oil companies, the business diversification between the upstream and downstream tends to mitigate the effects of oil and gas price fluctuations. However, because they are usually more leveraged (hold more assets) in the upstream, such companies generally benefit from higher prices for oil and natural gas."

S&P also points out important differences in oil and gas production in North America compared to internationally: "Oil and natural gas production in North America tends to be more sensitive to price than is international production. We believe one reason for this is that North America is dominated by independent exploration and production companies, which tend to work from short-term plans focused on relatively smaller natural gas projects. International oil production, in contrast, is dominated by the supermajors and national oil companies, which tend to work from long-term plans focused on large oil-based projects."

Reserve Ratios

Energy ratios 1 through 4 can be computed using Exhibit 9.11, Proved Reserve Disclosures for Oil and Gas Reserves, which is from page 148 of COP's 2011 10-K report.

Energy Ratio 1: Production to Reserves Ratio
The production to reserves ratio tells us what percentage of the reserves were produced in the year being studied. This ratio can be calculated separately for oil, natural gas liquids (NGLs), and natural gas and/or based on combined total reserves. We will calculate the combined total reserves ratio for COP in 2011 using Exhibit 9.11 (values are in million BOE).

$$\text{Production to Reserves Ratio in 2011} = \frac{\text{Production}}{\text{Reserves}} = \frac{546}{6750}$$

$$= 0.0809 \text{ or } 8.1\% \qquad (9.26)$$

As shown in Exhibit 9.9, Competitive Benchmarking with Peer Firms, COP is in line with the industry. Three-year averages over 2009–2011 are as follows: COP = 8.9 percent, XOM = 7.1 percent, CVX = 10.5 percent, BP = 7.5 percent, RDS = 8.5 percent, industry average = 8.5 percent. More in-depth analysis should include calculating this ratio separately for natural gas and crude oil.

Energy Ratio 2: Reserve Life Index
The *reserve life index* (RLI) is the reciprocal of the production to reserves ratio or simply, Reserves/Production. It provides an indication of how long reserves would last at the current production rate if there were no additions to reserves. This is purely a hypothetical calculation, but it is a useful ratio to analyze. A long RLI is not

always a good sign. It may indicate a lack of production development. For example, in 1999 Norsk Hydro acquired Saga Petroleum and part of the justification was Saga's reserve base of 24 years. Norsk Hydro had the means and intent to produce those reserves.

$$\text{Reserve Life Index in 2011} = \frac{\text{Reserves}}{\text{Production}} = \frac{6750}{546} = 12.4 \text{ years} \qquad (9.27)$$

As shown in Exhibit 9.9, COP again is in line with the industry. Three-year averages over 2009–2011 are as follows: COP = 11.3 years, XOM = 14.1, CVX = 9.5, BP = 13.4, RDS = 11.7, and industry average = 12.0. More in-depth analysis should include calculating this ratio separately for natural gas and crude oil. Often, the RLI is greater for natural gas than for crude oil.

We also need to know if a company is replacing the reserves that are being depleted through production and also if the reserves are being replaced through the drill bit or by acquisition. Energy ratios 3 and 4 answer these questions (i.e., Production Replacement Ratio and Reserve Replacement Ratio).

Energy Ratio 3: Production Replacement Ratio
This ratio measures if a company is replacing the reserves that are being depleted through production and it is a very important ratio. A company replacing the reserves it produces should have a ratio of 1.0 times, which is 100 percent as a minimum. Using the information in Exhibit 9.11 (values are in million BOE):

$$\text{Production Replacement Ratio in 2011} = \frac{\text{Increase in Reserves} + \text{Production}}{\text{Production}}$$

$$= \frac{6750 - 6655 + 546}{546} = 1.174 \text{ or } 117.4\% \qquad (9.28)$$

COP is above the desired level of 100 percent in 2011 but slightly below the three-year average for the group of 159 percent, as shown in Exhibit 9.9. We assign a rating of "fair." Three-year averages over 2009–2011 are as follows: COP = 97.2 percent, XOM = 239.4 percent, CVX = 124.0 percent, BP = 54.6 percent, and RDS = 280.2 percent. As before, more in-depth analysis should include calculating this ratio separately for natural gas and crude oil.

It is also interesting to note that around 2004, we saw an unusual number of reserve writedowns—most likely driven by the Sarbanes-Oxley law.

Energy Ratio 4: Finding and Development Reserve Replacement Ratio
This is the percentage of the company's oil and gas reserves consumed by production during the year that were replaced through improved recovery or new discoveries—Finding and Development (F&D). This ratio measures a company's ability to continue to operate in the future by replacing the reserves it is producing. A firm that is not replacing the reserves it produces will ultimately deplete its pool of resources and cease to do business, unless it purchases new reserves. Since purchasing reserves in-place is typically more expensive than acquisition of reserves through exploration and drilling, it is desirable for a company to consistently add to its reserves at a rate equal to or higher than its rate of production. A ratio greater

than 1 times, which is 100 percent, is desired. The F&D Reserve Replacement Ratio for COP in 2011 is 121.1 percent, calculated as shown in Equation 9.29.

Finding and Development Reserve Replacement Ratio

$$= \frac{\text{Extensions and Discoveries} + \text{Improved Recovery} + \text{Reserve Revisions}}{\text{Production}}$$

$$= \frac{383 + 92 + 186}{546} = 1.211 \text{ or } 121.1\% \tag{9.29}$$

For the three-year period 2009–2011, COP is above the desired level of 100 percent but slightly below the group average of 137.9 percent: COP = 114.9 percent, XOM = 152.3 percent, CVX = 116.3 percent, BP = 76.9, RDS = 228.9, and industry average = 137.9. We give a rating of "fair." As with ratios 1 through 3, this ratio can also be analyzed separately for natural gas and crude oil.

Reserve Cost Ratios

In this section, we examine Energy Ratios 5, 6, and 7, which answer questions about how much it costs to find oil, replace reserves, and produce reserves. As mentioned earlier, the reserve cost ratios will typically vary significantly from year to year. Therefore, it is very important to compute a moving average of the cost ratios over a period of three to five years, to gain any meaningful insights and make comparisons with peer firms. Exhibit 9.12, Costs Incurred in Oil and Gas Acquisition, Exploration, and Development, from pages 159–160 of COP's 10-K report, together with Exhibit 9.11, are used to calculate these ratios. These ratios can only be calculated for oil and gas operations combined since the costs are reported in aggregate, not separately for oil and gas.

Energy Ratio 5: Reserve Replacement Cost
This is a broad definition of replacement costs. It is the average cost of adding one barrel of oil equivalent (BOE) to the company's proven reserves of oil and gas through acquisition or exploration. A lower cost to replace reserves is best. *Note:* The ratio is usually higher if a company uses full cost accounting versus successful efforts (U.S. accounting standards only), because the reported costs will be higher due to the accounting treatment. Refer back to Chapter 8 in the book for a refresher on these accounting treatments.

Reserve Replacement Cost in 2011

$$= \frac{\text{Costs Incurred}}{\text{Revisions} + \text{Imp. Recovery} + \text{Extensions \& Discoveries} + \text{Purchases}}$$

$$= \frac{\$11,272 \text{ million}}{(186 + 92 + 383 + 2) \text{ million BOE}} = \$17.00 \text{ per BOE} \tag{9.30}$$

For the three-year period, COP looks best with the lowest Reserve Replacement Cost per BOE of $13.90 as compared to XOM = $14.51, CVX = $29.02, BP = $28.48, and RDS = $14.81, average = $20.14 (see Exhibit 9.9). We assign a rating of "good to excellent."

Energy Ratio 6: Finding Cost Ratio

Finding costs per BOE is one of the most common performance measures used in evaluating oil and gas exploration operations. Because of this, it is the most frequently cited ratio utilized in evaluating the efficiency of a company in adding new reserves. Similar to Energy Ratio 5, we calculate this ratio for both oil and gas combined, and a lower value is preferred. This ratio cannot be calculated separately since costs are reported in aggregate. Therefore, we use total reserve additions (both oil and gas). The basic ratio consists of the exploration costs divided by the new reserves added, as shown in Equation 9.31:

$$\text{Finding Costs Ratio in 2011} = \frac{\text{Exploration Cost}}{\text{Extensions and Discoveries}}$$

$$= \frac{\$1963 \text{ millions}}{383 \text{ million BOE}} = \$5.13 \text{ per BOE} \quad (9.31)$$

COP is competitive with the industry and slightly lower than the average so we assign a rating of "good." Three-year averages over 2009–2011 are as follows: COP = \$7.18, XOM = \$3.45, CVX = \$7.88, BP = \$15.21, RDS = \$7.60, and industry average = \$8.26. Similar to Energy Ratio 5, this ratio is usually higher if a company uses full cost accounting versus successful efforts. Other factors to consider are the quality of reserves added and the type of drilling program (less expensive onshore drilling versus more costly deepwater drilling).

Energy Ratio 7: Lifting Costs Ratio

The lifting cost ratio is a very popular measure of performance. This ratio is helpful in analyzing the extent to which a company is controlling production costs and indicates how efficiently a company operates. This ratio is basically the costs of getting the oil and gas out of the ground. A lower ratio is preferred and indicates more efficient operations, all else being equal. Similar to ratio 6, there are other factors to take into account when evaluating this ratio. While the ratio is computed for combined oil and gas production, it typically costs more to produce oil than gas. Therefore, if one company has primarily oil production, its ratio will be higher, and it may appear less efficient than another company that has primarily gas production. These factors need to be taken into account. Also, revenues should be considered, along with the quality of crude and production location. Frequently, the terms *lifting costs* and *production costs* are used interchangeably. Production costs are reported in Exhibit 9.13, Result of Operations from Oil and Gas Activities, from page 151 of COP's 10-K report. As always, it is important to compare the results with other companies in the benchmarking group.

$$\text{Lifting Costs Ratio} = \frac{\text{Total Lifting Costs}}{\text{Annual Production}} = \frac{\$5054 \text{ million}}{546 \text{ million BOE}} = \$9.26 \text{ per BOE}$$

$$(9.32)$$

COP compares very favorably (rating of "good") with a lower lifting cost as compared to all peer firms with the exception of BP. Three-year averages over 2009–2011 are as follows: COP = \$8,16, XOM = \$10.59, CVX = \$11.20, BP = \$7.53, RDS = \$11.31, and industry average = \$9.76. Exhibit 9.9 also lists the percentage of reserves in 2011 that are oil and gas for each company.

Reserve Value Ratio

While the preceding ratios tell us about reserve replacement and cost of reserves, it is useful to analyze the value and quality of the reserves added. Reserves can be of high quality and require fewer expenses to produce, transport, and refine—and vice versa. The Reserve Value Ratios help us analyze this: Value of Proved Reserve Additions and Value Added Ratio.

Energy Ratio 8: Value of Proved Reserve Additions

As the name implies, this ratio calculates the value added per BOE of reserve additions. Exhibit 9.15, Sources of Change in Discounted Future Net Cash Flows, which is from page 165 of COP's 10-K report, is used to calculate this ratio. These values are calculated from the changes in the standardized measure of oil and gas reserves. The standardized measure of oil and gas reserves is often referred to as the SMOG; Exhibit 9.14 contains the 2011 SMOG disclosures.

Value of Proved Reserve Additions in 2011

$$= \frac{\begin{array}{c} \text{Changes due to Extensions, Discoveries, and} \\ \text{Improved Recovery} + \text{Changes due to Revisions} + \text{Changes due to Purchases} \end{array}}{\begin{array}{c} \text{Reserve Extensions and Discoveries} \\ + \text{Improved Recovery} + \text{Revisions} + \text{Purchases of Reserves in Place} \end{array}}$$

$$= \frac{8730 + (-1938) + 19 \text{ million \$}}{383 + 92 + 186 + 2 \text{ million BOE}} = \$10.27 \text{ per BOE} \qquad (9.33)$$

There is a wide variation in this ratio for the peer firms as shown in Exhibit 9.9. COP has a higher value than XOM but lower than CVX and RDS, so we assign a rating of "average." (*Note:* BP's ratio is negative due to the Gulf Oil spill and other factors.)

Energy Ratio 9: Value Added Ratio

The objective of this ratio is to investigate the costs of adding reserves in relation to the value of those reserves added. Companies should try to maximize this value added and at a minimum, it should be greater than 1.0. Intuitively, the ratio measures the value of adding reserves in relation to the cost of replacing those reserves. The ratio is calculated as follows for 2011 and the average results over 2009–2011 are presented in Exhibit 9.9:

$$\text{Value Added Ratio} = \frac{\text{Value of Proved Reserve Additions}}{\text{Reserve Replacement Cost Ratio}}$$

$$= \frac{\text{Energy Ratio 8}}{\text{Energy Ratio 5}} = \frac{10.27}{13.00} = 0.60 \qquad (9.34)$$

As shown in Exhibit 9.9, COP compares very favorably (rating of "good") with an average of 0.79 over 2009–2011 as compared to XOM's 0.53 and CVX's 0.80. RDS looks best with the highest value of 1.47.

In summary, COP is performing well as compared to its peers, and we assign an overall rating of "average to good."

Other Ratios

In this chapter, we have presented nine leading energy ratios but there are other useful ratios. Three that we wish to point out are:

1. **Net Wells to Gross Wells Ratio:** The ratio of net wells to gross wells is considered a measure of future profitability (Gallun, Wright, Nichols, and Stevenson 2001). Net wells is the company's total net interest in wells whereas gross wells is the total of wells in which the company has any working interest, even if the interest is very small. A high ratio indicates that a company owns relatively large working interests in the overall wells and a low ratio indicates the opposite. A high ratio is viewed as a better indicator of future profitability because if a company owns a large interest in each well, they are more likely to be the operator. The operator has a greater say in operations. Also, having larger interests in fewer properties is better than having more properties with small interests due to economies of scale.

2. **Recycle Ratio:** This is another type of value added ratio. This ratio consists of profit per barrel (called the netback) divided by the cost of finding that barrel, the F&D costs. Different methods can be used to calculate this ratio; it is also available through Bloomberg. The higher the ratio, the better the operations.

3. **DD&A per BOE:** DD&A (depreciation, depletion, and amortization) per BOE reflects the historical cost of finding and developing reserves (i.e., prior periods) while lifting costs are for the current period. It is another type of reserve cost ratio but provides additional information other ratios do not.

Other Factors to Consider

Other factors to include:

- Structure of the company: integrated oil company, independent, refiner only, etc. The structure of the company will influence the ratios.
- Be aware of the reserve accounting standard used—full cost or successful efforts.
- Has the company had a number of downward reserve revisions over the past several years? This may indicate the company is overly aggressive in booking reserves and it is a negative indication.
- Use of an outside petroleum engineer to verify reserves is desired. Reserves estimation is one of the most essential tasks in the petroleum industry. It is the process by which the economically recoverable hydrocarbons in a field, area, or region are evaluated quantitatively. Downward revisions of U.S. Security and Exchange Commission (SEC)-booked reserves by some oil companies in 2004 brought the topic under public scrutiny. Confidence in reserves disclosures became a public issue, and there were calls from investors and lending institutions for more reliable reserves estimates.
- Make sure that the definition of the ratio you are using is consistent with any comparisons values.

- What are the percentages of developed reserves versus undeveloped reserves? Developed reserves are more valuable.
- These are dramatic times in the far upstream end of the industry, especially given the recent shale boom. Exploration is simply not what it was even a generation ago.
- More companies than ever are competing worldwide, so competition is great.
- The industry is moving into higher-cost environments. It has always been a high-risk industry, but it is getting tougher these days.
- The future of exploration is not dead—but companies must go into deeper water and more remote, inhospitable frontier regions—both geographically and politically. This will increase the importance of financial statement analysis!
- There are limitations of ratio analysis. For example, corporate governance oversight (the quality of the board of directors) and top management's expertise are important to the success of a firm.

CONCLUSION

Analyzing the financial statements of oil and gas companies is extremely complex, as should be clear from this chapter, and involves a detailed analysis of the 10-K report notes. The purpose of this chapter was to provide a comprehensive coverage on evaluating an oil and gas company. Standard financial ratios were covered together with an in-depth coverage of the nine most important energy ratios. Competitive benchmarking is essential to assess how a company performs against its industry peers, as we demonstrated with COP, which we give an overall rating of "average to good" relative to five of the top global energy companies.

Although ratio analysis is very useful, it should always be applied using good judgment. In particular, many factors in upstream operations can influence the various energy ratios. Best practices should always include multiple years of analyses. Just as a physician must conduct many tests to gauge the health of a patient, an analyst must conduct comprehensive financial analysis to assess the health of a company. The analysis is more complex if it is an oil and gas company and involves digging through the notes of the 10-K report. If the patient (company) looks sickly, more frequent analysis should be done and where possible, changes should be made to improve the "health."

APPENDIX: SUMMARY OF INFORMATION FOUND IN THE FORM 10-K ANNUAL REPORT

PART I

Item 1. Business.
Item 1A. Risk Factors.
Item 1B. Unresolved Staff Comments.
Item 2. Properties.
Item 3. Legal Proceedings.
Item 4. Mine Safety Disclosures.

PART II

Item 5. Market for Registrant's Common Equity, Related Stockholder Matters and Issuer Purchases of Equity Securities.

Item 6. Selected Financial Data.

Item 7. Management's Discussion and Analysis of Financial Condition and Results of Operations.

Item 7A. Quantitative and Qualitative Disclosures about Market Risk.

Item 8. Financial Statements and Supplementary Data.

- Report of Management
- Report of Independent Registered Public Accounting Firm on Consolidated Financial Statements
- Report of Independent Registered Public Accounting Firm on Internal Control Over Financial Reporting
- Consolidated Income Statement for three years
- Consolidated Statement of Comprehensive Income for three years
- Consolidated Balance Sheet for two years
- Consolidated Statement of Cash Flows for three years
- Consolidated Statement of Changes in Equity for three years
- Notes to Consolidated Financial Statements
- Supplementary Information
- Oil and Gas Operations
- Selected Quarterly Financial Data
- Condensed Consolidating Financial Information

Item 9. Changes in and Disagreements with Accountants on Accounting and Financial Disclosure.

Item 9A. Controls and Procedures.

Item 9B. Other Information.

PART III

Item 10. Directors, Executive Officers and Corporate Governance.

Item 11. Executive Compensation.

Item 12. Security Ownership of Certain Beneficial Owners and Management and Related Stockholder Matters.

Item 13. Certain Relationships and Related Transactions, and Director Independence.

Item 14. Principal Accounting Fees and Services.

PART IV

Item 15. Exhibits, Financial Statement Schedules.

QUESTIONS

1. Use the 2010 and 2011 Balance Sheets for Anadarko Petroleum Corporation following to answer the following questions.

Anadarko Petroleum Corp: December 31 Balance Sheets (millions of dollars)

Assets	2011	2010	Liabilities and Equity	2011	2010
Cash and Cash Equivalents	$2,697	$3,680	Accounts Payable	$3,299	$2,726
Accounts Receivable, net of allowance	3,259	2,423	Accrued Expenses	1,430	1,097
Inventory	975	572	Current Portion of Long-Term Debt	170	291
Total Current Assets	$6,931	$6,675	Total Current Liabilities	$4,899	$4,114
			Long-Term Debt	15,060	12,722
			Deferred Income Taxes	8,479	9,861
			Asset Retirement Obligations	1,737	1,529
			Other	2,621	1,894
			Total Liabilities (Debt)	$32,796	$30,120
			Common Stock	7,902	7,547
			Retained Earnings	11,619	14,449
			Treasury Stock	(804)	(763)
			Accumulated Other Comprehensive Income (Loss)	(612)	(549)
Net Properties, Plants, and Equipment	37,501	37,957	Total Common Equity	$18,105	$20,684
Other Assets	1,516	1,616	Noncontrolling Interests	878	755
Goodwill and Other Intangible Assets	5,831	5,311	Total Equity	18,983	21,439
Total Assets	$51,779	$51,559	Total Liabilities and Equity	$51,779	$51,559

a. What are Anadarko's current and quick ratios for 2011? What is Anadarko's net working capital in 2011?

b. Anadarko's total sales for 2011 are $13,967 million. What is their total assets turnover ratio?

c. The fixed assets turnover ratio is computed using the following formula:

$$\text{Fixed Assets Turnover Ratio} = \frac{\text{Sales}}{\text{Net Fixed Assets}}$$

If you use "Net Properties, Plants, and Equipment" for Net Fixed Assets, what is Anadarko's fixed assets turnover ratio? How would that compare to ConocoPhillips' fixed assets turnover ratio (using the same assumption regarding fixed assets and the sales figure from part b.)?

d. What is Anadarko's debt-to-equity ratio?

2. Drill-it-Well Inc. currently has $50 million in accounts receivable, and its days sales outstanding (DSO) is 40 days. If accounts receivable constitutes half of the firm's current assets and Drill-it-Well has $100 million in net fixed assets, what is Drill-it-Well's total

assets turnover ratio? Assume Drill-it-Well uses a 360-day accounting year in calculating its financial ratios.

3. The following data apply to Roughneck Petroleum Corp ($ millions):

Cash and equivalents	$4,000
Fixed assets	$9,000
Sales	$20,000
Net income	$2,190
Quick ratio	1.03×
Current ratio	1.46×
DSO	68 days
ROE	27.375%

Roughneck has no preferred stock—only common equity, current liabilities, and long-term debt.

a. Find Roughneck's (1) accounts receivable, (2) current liabilities, (3) current assets, (4) total assets, (5) ROA, (6) common equity, and (7) long-term debt.

b. In part a, you should have found Roughneck's accounts receivable to be $3,750 million. If Roughneck could reduce its DSO from 68 days to 60 days while holding other things constant, how much cash would it generate? If this cash were used to buy back common stock (at book value) and thereby reduce the amount of common equity, how would this action affect the company's (1) ROE, (2) ROA, and (3) total debt/total assets ratio?

4. Fracking Oil Company's ROE (return on equity) last year was only 12 percent, but its management has developed a new operating plan designed to improve things. The new plan calls for a debt-to-equity ratio of 1.50×, which will result in interest charges of $8,640 million per year. Management projects an EBIT of $25,920 million on sales of $108,000 million, and it expects to have a total assets turnover ratio of 1.125. Under these conditions, the average tax rate will be 40 percent. If the changes are made, what return on equity (ROE) will Fracking earn? What is the ROA?

5. Sweet Gas Explorations Inc. expects 2012 sales to be $7,200 million. Operating costs other than depreciation are expected to be 80 percent of sales, and depreciation is expected to be $360 million in 2012. All sales revenues will be collected in cash, and costs other than depreciation must be paid during the year. Sweet Gas's interest expense is expected to be $540 million, and it is taxed at a 40 percent rate.

a. Set up an income statement and a cash flow statement (use two columns on one page) for Sweet Gas. What is the expected operating cash flow?

b. Suppose Congress changed the tax laws so that Sweet Gas's depreciation expenses doubled in 2012, but no other changes occurred. What would happen to the net income and operating cash flow expected in 2012?

c. Suppose that Congress, rather than increasing Sweet Gas's 2012 depreciation, reduced it by 50 percent. How would the net income and operating cash flow be affected in this scenario?

d. If this company belonged to you, would you prefer that Congress increase or decrease the depreciation expense allowed your company? Explain why.

6. What is competitive benchmarking?

7. Why is it so very important to calculate the energy ratios over multiple years and analyze averages of these ratios instead of just looking at annual estimates?

8. How do you interpret the finding costs ratio? Why is this ratio so widely used in financial statement analysis of energy companies? Answer the same two questions for the lifting cost ratio.

9. What are the three classifications (i.e. categories) for energy ratios? List and describe each.

10. Which of the energy ratios gives an estimate of the cost to replace reserves through the "drill bit"?

11. Why is it not recommended for a publicly traded company to have a reserve life index greater than 20 years?

12. Go to the SEC website (www.sec.gov), download the 2011 Form 20-F Report for Total S.A., and calculate the energy ratios as shown in Exhibit 9.10 for the total combined reserves. Use only the consolidated subsidiaries and omit equity affiliates. (*Hint:* See page S-4 of the 2011 20-F Report for Total to calculate the first four energy ratios.)

13. Go to the SEC website (www.sec.gov), download the 2012 10-K Report for Cono-coPhillips, and calculate the energy ratios. Using only the consolidated subsidiaries, compare the 2012 results with the 2009 to 2011 period. What do you find?

14. Using the information from Question 7, conduct competitive benchmarking for Total as compared to the industry peers listed in Exhibit 9.9 for the energy ratios. Give Total S.A. a rating on each ratio and an overall assessment. Explain your answers.

15. What is the value of proved reserve additions ratio attempting to measure? How do you interpret the value of proved reserve additions ratio?

16. What is the value added ratio? What does a high or low value added ratio indicate?

17. Using the disclosure in Appendix 8.A of Chapter 8, calculate the nine energy ratios for the combined company including equity affiliates. List and describe your results.

18. What are the limitations of ratio analysis? In other words, what other factors should be considered?

19. What are not directly reflected on an oil and gas company balance sheet?
    a. Assets
    b. Reserve values
    c. Liabilities
    d. Stockholder's equity
    e. Net property, plant, and equipment

20. What is the world's largest nationalized oil company (NOC)?
    a. Saudi Aramco
    b. British Petroleum
    c. ExxonMobil
    d. Royal Dutch/Shell
    e. Kuwait Oil Company

21. National oil companies (NOCs) do not control the world's oil reserves. Today, world oil reserves are 80 percent owned by investor-owned companies (IOCs), and only 6 percent is held by NOCs. This statement is:
    a. True
    b. False

22. Investors should view proved developed reserves as somewhat higher risk than proved undeveloped reserves. This statement is:
    a. True
    b. False

23. The finding cost ratio for Devon in 2006 was $0.375 per mcfe. In $ per BOE, this is equal to:
    a. $0.625
    b. $0.225
    c. $2.25

    d. $6.25

    e. None of the above

24. At the end of 2007, ConocoPhillips had 3,104 million barrels of oil as proved reserves. In mcfe, this is equal to:

    a. 18,624 mcfe

    b. 18,624,000 mcfe

    c. 517,333 mcfe

    d. 517,333,000 mcfe

    e. 18,624,000,000 mcfe

NOTES

1. The seven sisters were a "Consortium" of major oil companies that prior to the oil crisis of 1973, controlled around 85 percent of the world's petroleum reserves. The group comprised Anglo-Persian Oil Company (now BP), Gulf Oil, Standard Oil of California (Socal), Texaco (now Chevron), Royal Dutch Shell, Standard Oil of New Jersey (Esso), and Standard Oil Company of New York (Socony) (now ExxonMobil). Today, there are four surviving sisters: BP, Chevron, ExxonMobil, and Royal Dutch Shell, and these are known as the "supermajors."

2. We would like to acknowledge that Higgins (1995) made us aware of this interesting quote.

3. See www.sec.gov where the filings are available through the EDGAR system.

4. See Chapters 3 and 4 of Brigham and Houston (2013) for more discussion on financial statement analysis.

5. This Depreciation and Amortization figure is from Compustat, and it differs by $227 million from the Depreciation, Depletion, and Amortization figure given in ConocoPhillips' 2011 10-K. We have used the Compustat figure to maintain consistency with the ratios provided in the tables at the end of this chapter. This Net Operating Profit After Taxes is calculated using ConocoPhillips' effective tax rate of 45.6 percent as given on page 132 at the end of Note 20 in their 2011 10-K. It can be computed by dividing the Provision for Income Taxes by Income Before Income Taxes.

6. They would need to cover $28,068 of current assets to pay all current liabilities, which is 28,068/30,218 = 92.9%.

7. Formula (9.8) assumes that there are 360 days in a year. This convention may differ from one analysis to the other. Some analysts may use 365 while others may use 252, which is a typical convention for the number of trading days in a year.

8. Nicole Decker's presentation to Oklahoma State University students visiting UBS in New York City on May 8, 2012.

9. The EBIT used in the calculations is from Compustat.

10. The denominator of the ROE formula is decreasing more than its numerator, which leads to a higher ROE ratio.

REFERENCES

Brigham, Eugene F., and Joel H. Houston. 2013. *Fundamentals of Financial Management.* Mason, OH: South-Western Cengage Learning.

Gallun, Rebecca A., Charlotte J. Wright, Linda M. Nichols, and John W. Stevenson. 2001. *Fundamentals of Oil & Gas Accounting.* Tulsa, OK: Pennwell Corporation.

Higgins, Robert C. 1995, *Analysis for Financial Management.* Chicago: Irwin.

Johnston, David, and Daniel Johnson. 2006. *Introduction to Oil Company Financial Analysis*. Tulsa, OK: Pennwell Corporation.

Standard & Poor's. 2012. *Global Industry Surveys Oil & Gas: Europe*, February. S&P Capital IQ Industry Surveys.

ABOUT THE CONTRIBUTORS

Siamak Javadi had his early education in his home country, Iran. He received his bachelor's degree in mechanical engineering from Azad University. After working as an engineer for a while he went to Malaysia to pursue an MBA degree. He received his MBA from Multimedia University in Malaysia. He found his calling in finance and came to the United States in 2008 for a master of science degree in Quantitative Financial Economics (MSQFE). He is a PhD candidate at Oklahoma State University in the Department of Finance, Spears School of Business. His research interests include risk management, investment, and empirical asset pricing.

Betty J. Simkins, PhD, is the Williams Companies Professor of Business and a Professor of Finance in the Department of Finance at Oklahoma State University's (OSU) Spears School of Business where she teaches energy finance, corporate finance, and enterprise risk management, among other courses. Dr. Simkins received her PhD from Case Western Reserve University (CWRU), her MBA from OSU, and her BS in chemical engineering from the University of Arkansas. She has over 50 publications in academic finance journals and book chapters and has won awards for her research, most recently in risk management. In addition, Betty has won several teaching awards including the Regents Distinguished Teaching Award. She has taught Energy Finance, a course she created, at both the undergraduate and graduate levels for over 12 years and teaches executive education courses on energy finance for companies around the world. She is also very active in the finance profession and currently serves on the Board of Directors for the Financial Management Association, as co-editor of the *Journal of Applied Finance*, as past president of the Eastern Finance Association, and on the editorial boards of several prestigious finance journals. Prior to academia, she worked in the energy industry for Williams Companies and Conoco (now ConocoPhillips). In addition to being co-editor of this book, in 2010 she co-edited *Enterprise Risk Management: Insights and Analysis on Today's Leading Research and Best Practices*, also published by John Wiley & Sons.

Mary E. Wicker is a PhD Student in finance in the Spears School of Business at Oklahoma State University. Previously, she received her MBA in agriculture business and bachelor's degree in agriculture from Missouri State University. While pursuing her undergraduate degree, Wicker joined the Missouri Army National Guard as an automated logistical specialist. She served one tour of duty in Iraq in 2006–2007, and then she returned to complete her MBA in 2009. Wicker has co-authored a working paper and a book chapter. Her research interests include investment banking, corporate governance, and empirical capital structure.

CHAPTER 10

Petroleum Economics, Risk and Opportunity Analysis: Some Practical Perspectives

DAVID A. WOOD
Principal Consultant, DWA Energy Limited

INTRODUCTION

In energy finance, discounted cash flow (DCF) analysis is one of the main methods employed in valuing projects, companies, and assets based upon their future cash flow forecasts (Brealey, Myers, and Allen 2008). DCF applies the long-established concepts of the time value of money, usually involving quite straightforward calculations. All future cash flows are estimated and discounted to a particular point in time, usually close to the present day or the effective date of a transaction, and give what is termed their present values (PVs). The sum of the PVs of all future cash flow values (FVs), both incoming and outgoing, is the net present value (NPV), which is taken as the value of the cash flows in question in present-day terms. Although the basic calculations are not challenging, in practice issues arise as to how best to integrate DCF with risk analysis and calculate NPV in nominal and real terms. This chapter addresses these specific issues.

DISCOUNTED CASH FLOW (DCF) AND TIME-VALUE CONSIDERATIONS

Energy projects are characterized by high capital investment in early years, without revenue, often followed by many periods or decades of positive net revenue (i.e., the sum of incoming cash flows derived from energy sales less the sum of outgoing cash flows in the form of operating and maintenance—O&M—and overhead costs) after production start-up. This characteristic requires that the future cash flows be adjusted for the time that revenues will be received in order to calculate their value in the money of the day in which the investment decision is being made.

Exhibit 10.1 illustrates the effect of discounting 1,000 monetary units of net revenue earned in each of the next 10 years to the money of today (year zero) following an initial capital investment made in year zero (not shown). In this case, the net present value (NPV) would be the present value of an investment's future net

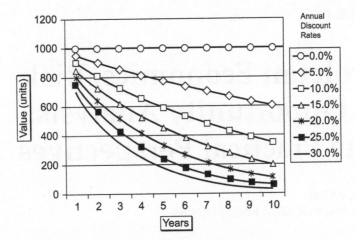

Exhibit 10.1 The Impact of Discounting a Constant Net Revenue Stream over 10 Future Years at Different Discount Rates

Note that at high discount rates the value of money earned in the later years is very low in year zero present value terms. Some organizations advocate increasing the discount rate to adjust for increasing risk. This is poor practice as it inappropriately penalizes the later cash flow periods more severely than the earlier cash flow periods. Discount rates should be used for time value adjustments not risk adjustments.

Source: David A. Wood.

cash flows minus the initial capital investments made. The simplistic decision rule (ignoring risk) usually adopted is that if NPV is positive, the investment should be made (unless an even better investment exists), and otherwise it should not. Note that NPV calculation is not an adjustment for risk, but simply for the timing at which revenues will be received and costs incurred in the future. Clearly, there is often a requirement to further adjust NPV for risk and opportunity to establish a risked discounted value for more meaningful decision analysis. Selecting the appropriate discount rate with which to calculate NPV also requires careful consideration and calculation.

MANIPULATING THE PRESENT VALUE AND FUTURE VALUE FORMULAE

Money to be received at some time in the future is said to have a present value (PV) that is less than the amount received by the interest that could be earned on it in the interim. The PV is the amount that could be invested at an interest rate such that the amount plus the total interest earned equals the future value (FV). In formula terms this is expressed as:

Future value (FV) $= PV + (i * PV)$

Where i is the interest rate for one interest period and FV is the value at the end of that one interest period.

This equation can be rearranged to: $FV = PV(1 + i)$

An example: $FV = (\$6,000,000)(1 + 0.08) = \$6,480,000$

Expressed in words this equation tells us that $480,000 is the simple interest earned in one investment period at an 8 percent interest rate on an initial investment of $6,000,000 (the principal).

PV and FV are related to each other through interest rates and discount factors. For example, if an interest rate (i) of 10 percent applies for one investment period, then a PV of US$10 million has a FV of US$11 million at the end of the investment period, applying the relationship $FV = PV * (1 + i)$. Rather than calculating the future value from the present value in adjusting for cash flow in future periods, in DCF analysis we are interested in calculating PV from FV. We can do this simply by rearranging this equation.

If we know that FV is US$11 million we can apply a 10 percent discount rate to calculate a PV of US$10 million at the start of the investment period using the rearranged equation $PV = FV/(1 + d)$. In this form d is the discount rate for the investment period and $(1 + d)$ is referred to as the discount factor.

As we have cash flows to adjust for many years into the future, we need to also make an adjustment to each cash flow depending upon the period in which that cash flow is realized. The equation used achieves the opposite of a compound interest equation used to calculate how an investment in a deposit account grows over time assuming the interest earned is reinvested in each successive period. The discount equivalent of this process can be expressed by applying the discount factor to the FV to calculate its PV such that:

$$PV = FV * \left[\frac{1}{(1 + d)^n} \right]$$

This can also be expressed as:

$$PV = FV * (1 + d)^{-n}$$

The exponent n is the number of investment periods. For energy projects, the calculation is most often performed in investment periods measured in years, with d being the annual discount rate. However, the calculation can be performed for other period lengths, for instance, in months with d being the monthly discount rate. In this equation n is an exponent, which means as the number of periods increases the discount factor $[(1 + d)^{-n}]$ becomes smaller and smaller.

Hence the PV of an FV of US$6,125,000 to be received at the end of three years based on an annual expected return of 7 percent is $5,000,000.

$$\$5,000,000 = \$6,125,000 \, (1 + 0.07)^{-3}$$

Note that 7 percent is the discount rate. Different organizations will apply different discount rates, usually related to their weighted average cost of capital (WACC, i.e., how much on average it costs them to raise equity and debt). For small companies operating with mainly equity funds, this can be high (e.g., 15 percent or more) and will depend upon where in the world the funding is raised. For large multinational entities (MNEs) using cash from operations plus equity and some debt this is often much lower (e.g., 7.5 percent to 10 percent) and for governments it can be much lower (e.g., 5 percent or less). Hence the same project cash flows

may yield different NPVs for different organizations because they have different WACCs and rightly use different discount rates.

DCF analysis using the formulae described can be calculated easily by calculator or, more usually, by a spreadsheet. Indeed Excel has special functions to make such calculations, which are used to good effect by energy economists. There are several other formulae, or variations on the basic formulas, that are applicable in certain situations, such as continuous discounting for very short periods of investment and reinvestment. Also, it is possible to adjust the basic formulae to deal with discounting back to the end of the first investment period, mid-year or any other date within a particular year. These variations are not discussed further in this chapter, but are important for analysts to apply in practice.

INFLATION, REAL, AND NOMINAL (MONEY-OF-THE-DAY) VALUES

Inflation is said to occur when the prices of most goods and services in the economy are rising by some degree over time—also referred to as "general inflation." Economists believe that inflation is usually caused when there is more demand expressed for goods and services in the economy than there is supply of those same goods and services at current prices. To produce the goods and services needed to meet demand, firms must pay more for the inputs (including labor and raw materials) needed to produce the goods and services.

For example, it might be necessary to pay overtime premiums to existing workers or pay higher wages to attract new workers. These higher costs get passed on to consumers in the form of higher prices for the goods and services produced; consumers in turn seek higher wages to pay for the higher priced goods and services, and so on, in a circular manner.

Economists usually measure inflation by comparing the price of groupings or *market baskets* of goods and services from year to year. The prices of some goods and services in the grouping will go up, the prices of others may go down—it is the overall price level of the grouping that captures the effect of inflation. A price or inflation index is constructed by dividing the price of the grouping in each year by its price in a fixed base year, and multiplying the result by 100. The change in the index value from year to year reveals the trend and scale of inflation.

Just as inflation is encountered in the general economy, the costs of energy projects tend to rise over time as a result of inflation. This is because such projects must compete for many of the same resources (such as labor or steel) that other sectors of the economy require.

Inflation in construction costs is measured by the changes in unit prices from year to year. Several indices are available. Money from one year can be converted into equivalent money of another year (as measured by purchasing power) by using price indices to add or remove the effects of inflation. Money from which the inflation component has been removed is referred to as *real, constant,* or *base year* money. A real dollar is able to buy the same amount of goods and services in a future year as in the base year of the analysis. Money that includes the effects of inflation is referred to as *nominal, current,* or *data year* dollars. A nominal dollar

will typically buy a different amount of goods and services in each year of the analysis period.

In the case of DCF analysis of investments and associated forward-looking cash flows, it is best practice to forecast life cycle costs and benefits of a project without inflation (i.e., in real or base year dollars). Inflation is very hard to predict, particularly for some years into the future. More importantly, if inflation is added to benefits and costs projected for future years, it should be removed again before these benefits and costs can be compared in the form of dollars of any given base year. The essential time to consider inflation is when formulating a project's budget. Future year or multiyear project budgets are often expressed in future year dollars rather than base year dollars. Failure to account for inflation in project budgets will almost always result in too few future year dollars being set aside to complete the project (leading to stakeholder perceptions of cost overruns and mismanagement) and will hurt an organization's reputation and its credibility in budgeting for future projects. Also, if historical cost data are being used to develop base year cost estimates for a project, the historical cost data should be adjusted to base year dollars using an appropriate inflation index.

When adjusting for inflation, an index appropriate for the task should be used. For performing cost or budget estimates, this index should be industry sector–specific. In a few cases, the analyst may believe that a resource's cost has grown or will grow much more rapidly than the rate of inflation. For instance, right-of-way costs may soar due to real estate speculation in anticipation of a new energy facility. In such cases, the analyst needs to determine how much the real cost of the resource will change over time and include this adjusted cost in the DCF analysis.

It is often necessary to be able to adjust between real and nominal values. The formulas described below facilitate such adjustments.

Say inflation is 5 percent per year and you can earn interest for a one-year bond at 5 percent gross returning $1.05 in one year, what is this really worth to you next year when you receive your nominal cash flow of $1.05?

A key issue in answering that question is what can $1.05 buy next year, given that a basket of prices will on average collectively rise by 5 percent?

The real or inflation-adjusted value of $1.05 in one year is:

$$\text{Real Cash Flow} = \text{Nominal Cash Flow}/[(1 + \text{inflation rate})^1]$$
$$= 1.05/(1 + 0.05) = \$1.00$$

In general, at an annual inflation rate for investment periods n:

$$(\text{Real Cash Flow})^n = (\text{Nominal Cash Flow})^n * (1 + \text{inflation rate})^{-n}$$

Nominal interest rates are those typically quoted in the market as investment return rates. Real interest rate (Rreal) is nominal interest rate (Rnominal) adjusted for inflation rate.

Example: $1.00 invested at a 5 percent interest rate grows to $1.05 in next year's dollars. If inflation rate is 3 percent per year, then the real value is $1.05/1.03 = 1.0194. The real return is 1.94 percent.

$$(1 + \text{Rreal}) = (1 + \text{Rnominal}) * (1 + \text{inflation rate})$$

Where Rreal = real interest rate; Rnominal = nominal interest rate and the inflation rate is commonly assigned i

$$(1 + Rreal) = (1 + Rnominal)/(1 + \text{inflation rate})$$

Say you are forecasting next year's revenues from production based on this year's production sales value of $100 million. You forecast a 2 percent per annum real growth in your production volumes (and assume oil prices will stay flat; i.e., remain unchanged). You forecast the inflation rate to be 3 percent per annum. Suppose that the appropriate nominal discount rate is 5 percent per annum (Rnominal—that is a market rate that by default usually includes inflation indirectly factored in). What is the present value of next year's sales revenue?

Next year's nominal revenue forecast = $100 million * 1.02 * 1.03 = $105.06 million

PV of that revenue forecast is easy to calculate because we have the nominal discount rate:

$$PV(\text{Nominal Cash Flow}) = \$105.06 \text{ million}/1.05 = \$100.057 \text{ million}$$

On the other hand, next year's real revenue forecast = $100 million * 1.02 = $102.00 million

PV of the real revenue forecast is not so straightforward, as we do not have the real discount rate, and we have to calculate it using the formula:

$(1 + Rreal) = (1 + Rnominal)/(1 + \text{inflation rate})$

Hence, Rreal (the real discount rate) $= [(1 + Rnominal)/(1 + \text{inflation rate})] - 1$

$= [(1.05)/(1.03)] - 1$

$= 0.019417$

$= 1.9417\%$:

The real discount factor = 1.019417

PV(Real Cash Flow) = $102 million/1.019417 = $100.057 million

Note the PV of real cash flows is the same as the PV of nominal cash flows providing that the appropriate discount rates are used (Rreal for real cash flows; Rnominal for nominal cash flows).

Important rules that prudent DCF analysts follow are:

- Discount nominal cash flows using nominal discount rates.
- Discount real cash flows using real discount rates.
- Determine whether a quoted discount rate is real or nominal.

Assuming we are using the cash flows and the appropriate discount rate to calculate the Net Present Value (NPV), we need to follow the rule of consistency, which states: *if discount rate R is stated in real terms, real cash flows must be used, and if discount rate R is stated in nominal terms, nominal cash flows must be used.*

A problem arises when arbitrary discount rates are used or where they are supposed to include components addressing risk and inflation as well as the cost of capital in real terms. Although some classic financial theories suggest that it is appropriate to incorporate risk into discount rates, the practical impacts of this are usually to make undesirable adjustments to future cash flows (see Exhibit 10.1), and lead to confusion when incorporating inflation effects. Also in situations of high inflation (say > 4%/year) it often helps to isolate the inflationary impacts on cash flow by working in real terms. On the other hand, in low inflation situations it is often easier to work in nominal terms.

Key formulas to use (and easily applied with spreadsheets) are:

To adjust real cash flows (RealCF) to nominal cash flows (NominalCF), we inflate (compound) it by (n) periods, using the rate of inflation (i) for each period:

$$(\text{NominalCF}) = (\text{RealCF}) * (1 + i)^{\wedge (n)}$$

Similarly, to adjust (NominalCF) to (RealCF), we deflate (discount) it:

$$(\text{RealCF}) = (\text{NominalCF})/(1 + i)^{\wedge (n)}$$

Where n is the number of investment periods.

The relationship between real and nominal rates can be expressed as:

$$(1 + \text{Rnominal}) = (1 + \text{Rreal}) * (1 + i)$$

or:

$$1 + \text{Rnominal} = 1 + \text{Rreal} + i + (\text{Rreal} * i)$$

When inflation is sufficiently low (less than about 2 percent), the real interest rate can be approximated as the nominal interest rate minus the expected inflation rate (i). In such instances the following approximations can be applied without significant error in most cases:

$$\text{Rnominal} \sim \text{Rreal} + i$$

and,

$$\text{Rreal} \sim \text{Rnominal} - i$$

The use of inflation indices to adjust for inflation is relatively straightforward.

To remove inflation (i.e., convert data year, nominal dollars into base year, real dollars):

$$\text{Dollars (base year)} = \text{Dollars (data year)} \times \frac{\text{Inflation Index (base year)}}{\text{Inflation Index (data year)}}$$

To add inflation (i.e., convert base year, real dollars into data year, nominal dollars):

$$\text{Dollars (data year)} = \text{Dollars (base year)} \times \frac{\text{Inflation Index (data year)}}{\text{Inflation Index (base year)}}$$

For instance, assume that the base year for a DCF analysis is 2012. If an oil facility cost $100,000 to build in 2002, how much would it have cost in base year 2012 dollars (all else being equal)?

The answer based on the cost index would be:

$$\$100,000 \text{ (data year 2002)} \times \frac{205 \text{ (index value 2012)}}{103 \text{ (index value 2002)}}$$
$$\text{or } \$199,029 \text{ base year 2012 dollars}$$

Similarly, a base year dollar can be converted to an equivalent amount of purchasing power for any other year based on the dollars (data year) formula stated above. Historical inflation index data can be used to adjust for inflation in years prior to and including the present.

In the oil and gas industry, it is often useful to be able to express price forecasts in both nominal and real terms distinguishing real growth from growth plus inflation (e.g., Exhibit 10.2).

HURDLE RATES AND MINIMUM ACCEPTABLE RATES OF RETURN

Although discounted cash flow calculations form the cornerstone of energy DCF analysis, there is often uncertainty as to what discount rate should be used by a specific organization to calculate present values. Different organizations may have different criteria for selecting the discount rates they apply in DCF analysis. Commonly used discount rates are:

- Cost of capital (WACC or other methods) providing a guide to the minimum discount rate to apply.
- Prevailing interest rates available for bank deposits or money market.
- Values above cost of capital to represent expectations of just the equity investors.
- Values above the cost of capital to incorporate adjustments for risk (not recommended by this author).
- A hurdle rate or minimum acceptable rate of return (MARR) that reflects average or generic returns that can be achieved by alternative investments available to an organization or in a specific region.

It is important to justify MARR or hurdle rates. Many companies mislead themselves by applying invalid discount rates (either unrealistically high or low) to adjust cash flows in their economic evaluations. Considerations such as risk, inflation, and interest paid need to be included in the cash flow calculation but not

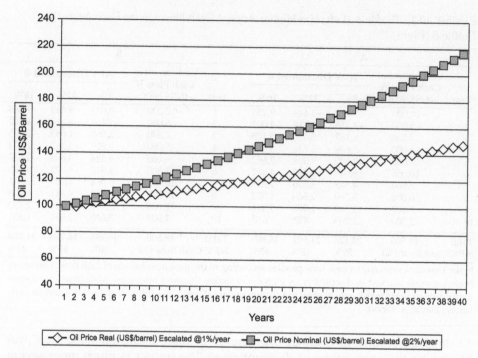

Exhibit 10.2   Example of an Oil Price Forecast
This displays both real escalation (lower curve) and nominal terms, which includes both real growth and inflation (upper curve).
The price trends shown are for illustrative purposes only and do not reflect the author's view of actual future oil prices.
Source: David A. Wood.

in the form of the discount factor, which can distort calculated present values. The trends illustrated in Exhibit 10.3 reveal that an increase in discount rate to account for risk preferentially penalizes the later years in the cash flow. Let us assume that an organization's cost of capital is 8 percent per year, which it uses as a discount rate for DCF analysis low-risk projects. However, the organization increases the discount rate to 12 percent and 16 percent for medium-risk and high-risk project DCF analysis. As already explained, discount rates are designed to adjust for time value and will reduce cash flows from many years in the future to quite low values in present value terms. Most risks affect cash flow in all future periods in a similar way, not primarily impacting those periods far into the future.

Exhibit 10.3 considers two cash flow profiles—A and B—undiscounted and discounted at three different rates. The "cash flow" column is undiscounted (i.e., zero discount rate applied). Increasing the discount rate to compensate for perceived higher risk reduces the NPV by an amount that will vary depending upon the timing of the cash flow, which usually does not correspond to the level of risk associated with each of a number of projects. Cash flow profile A and cash flow profile B both sum to the same total undiscounted value in real terms, but cash flow profile A has higher annual cash flows in the early years of the profile, whereas cash flow profile B has higher annual cash flow values in the later years of the 10-year profile.

Exhibit 10.3 Profile A (Left) Has Higher Annual Cash Flows in the Early Years than Profile B (Right).

	A					B			
	Undiscounted Cash Flow A	NPV Discounted @				Undiscounted Cash Flow B	NPV Discounted @		
Year	(US$ 000)	8%	12%	16%	Year	(US$ 000)	8%	12%	16%
1	−10,000	−9,623	−9,449	−9,285	1	−10,000	−9,623	−9,449	−9,285
2	−5,000	−4,455	−4,218	−4,002	2	−5,000	−4,455	−4,218	−4,002
3	7,500	6,187	5,650	5,175	3	2,500	2,062	1,883	1,725
4	10,000	7,639	6,726	5,948	4	5,000	3,819	3,363	2,974
5	15,000	10,609	9,008	7,692	5	6,000	4,244	3,603	3,077
6	10,000	6,549	5,362	4,421	6	7,500	4,912	4,021	3,315
7	7,500	4,548	3,590	2,858	7	10,000	6,064	4,787	3,811
8	6,000	3,369	2,565	1,971	8	15,000	8,422	6,411	4,928
9	5,000	2,599	1,908	1,416	9	10,000	5,199	3,816	2,832
10	2,500	1,203	852	610	10	7,500	3,610	2,556	1,831
Total	48,500	28,626	21,992	16,805	Total	48,500	24,255	16,773	11,206
NPV/Cash flow (%)		59%	45%	35%	NPV/Cash flow (%)		50%	35%	23%

Note: Discount rates adjust cash flow profiles according to the time distribution of cash flow. This effect becomes more marked as discount rates increase. It makes discount rates unsuitable to use for meaningful adjustment for risk, where most risk factors impact all years of a future cash flow in a similar way.
Source: David A. Wood.

It is interesting to compare the impact of discounting on these two profiles using the same range of discount rates. The impact is much more severe on cash flow profile B for the higher discount rates as indicated by the ratio of NPV@16%/undiscounted cash flow shown in Exhibit 10.3.

Exhibit 10.4 illustrates graphically the impact of adjusting the undiscounted and discounted cash flows from Exhibit 10.3 for a range of risk factors expressed

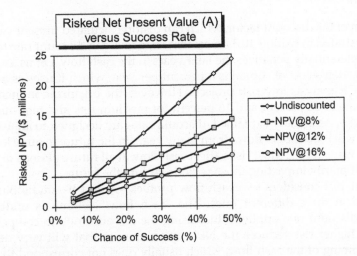

Exhibit 10.4 Doubling the Discount Rate
Doubling the discount rate from 8 to 16 percent does not lead to an easily predictable or meaningful adjustment to either cash flow profile A or B in terms of risk adjustment. (However adjusting the cash flow by a separate risk factor does produce more meaningful outcomes. Halving the chance of success does halve the risk–adjusted NPV.)
Source: David A. Wood.

as percentage chances of success. The risk adjustments in terms of chances of success provide more meaningful outcomes than impact of higher discount rates from a risk perspective.

The relationships illustrated in Exhibits 10.3 and 10.4 reinforce the importance of justifying in detail the discount rates applied for DCF analysis and capital budgeting purposes. The key message here is that it is more transparent to conduct discounting and risk adjustments to cash flows as two separate calculations.

THE NONLINEARITY AND COMPLEXITY OF UNCERTAINTY

Uncertainty is a multifaceted issue for the energy industry (Wood, Lamberson, and Mokhatab 2007) with many facets leading to both risk for loss and opportunity for gain (Exhibit 10.5).

Few would argue that the most important single variable in many energy projects is uncertainty. However, the terms *uncertainty* and *risk* are not well understood or used in a consistent manner.

Risk has come to mean a chance of failure or loss, but it is better considered as a dispersion or range of the possible outcomes. Risk is related to, and is a measure of, the degree of *uncertainty* and does not necessarily reflect a high probability of failure. Risk exposure is a term often used to reflect the degree of uncertainty, and attempts to quantify the penalty of failure and the reward of success.

Because of the common misuse of the term *risk* it is appropriate to assign different meanings to the terms *risk* and *uncertainty*. As used in this chapter, the term *risk* is used to specifically mean a potential for loss. The term *uncertainty* is applied to factors where the outcome is not certain but where there is a potential for loss or gain with varying probabilities, often not easy to quantify, associated with specific outcomes.

In the upstream petroleum industry, the resource uncertainty is associated with the presence of oil and gas in a specific drilling prospect (a discrete uncertainty; it is either there or it is not) and the volume of resource should a discovery be made (a continuous uncertainty; with a range of possible resource volumes associated with different probabilities forming a frequency distribution—commonly lognormal in nature). However, upstream petroleum projects are exposed to numerous other uncertainties in addition to the resource uncertainty (sometimes termed *below-ground* uncertainty), which can collectively be referred to as *above-ground* uncertainties (Exhibit 10.5). The potential for loss or gain associated with many of the above-ground uncertainties identified in Exhibit 10.5 is less clear-cut than the uncertainties associated with a single well result. Other energy sectors have a similar spectrum of above-ground uncertainties, but their resource uncertainties differ from the petroleum sector; for instance, in the case of hydro, ocean, solar, and wind energy projects, a key resource uncertainty is climatic; that is, possible future changes to climate could either increase or decrease the availability and consistent performance of these resources.

Risk and opportunity management should start at the concept and planning stages of an energy project and continue throughout its life. Risk is any potential threat or occurrence that may prevent the project achieving its defined business

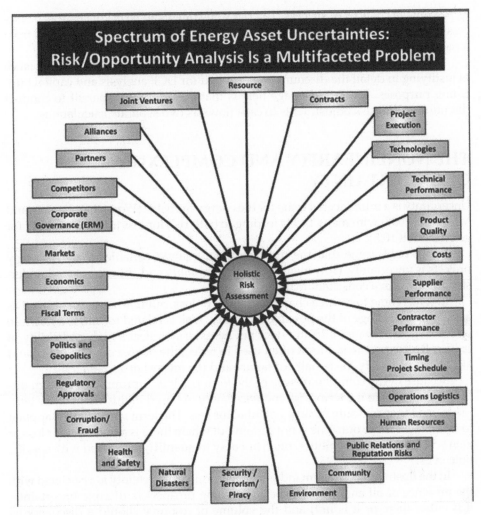

Exhibit 10.5 Spectrum of Uncertainties Impacting the Oil and Gas Industry
(These uncertainties need to be assessed in a systematic and Integrated way to provide a holistic assessment.)
Source: David A. Wood.

objectives (time, cost, quality, delivery); that is, negative impact potential. Opportunity, on the other hand is the possibility that the project may go better than planned (time, cost, quality, fiscal terms, regulatory approvals, synergy with other projects, etc., etc.); that is, positive impact potential.

Risk (uncertainty) management objectives for energy projects are to ensure:

- Risks and opportunities are identified and evaluated using systematic, holistic, and repeatable methods.
- Significant risks once identified are mitigated prior to the project's being sanctioned.
- Contingency plans are formulated for low-probability, but potentially high-impact extreme/catastrophic events.

- Opportunities are evaluated for potential exploitation without delay.
- Where possible, individual uncertainties are quantified.
- Certain uncertainties (e.g., political and community) are difficult to quantify with meaningful precision, and the best that can usually be achieved involves a certain amount of subjective assessment.
- Deriving an overall risk/opportunity adjustment factor from a holistic analysis of all uncertainties involved in a project/asset is desirable, but difficult, as individual risk and opportunity exposures do not combine in a linear manner.
- DCF analysis is adjusted for uncertainty associated with investment decision making using an uncertainty adjustment factor, which is recognized to be, at least in part, subjectively derived.
- Fiscal designs impact the net values of projects to governments and investors, and uncertainty analysis of energy projects helps to determine the government–investor division of profits, and potential fiscal incentives to investors (e.g., tax credits) appropriate for the risk and opportunity exposure undertaken by investors (Exhibit 10.6).
- For renewable energy projects, fiscal designs often incorporate subsidies as well as tax incentives to attract investors to participate in high-cost energy options. Uncertainty analysis can help governments set subsidies at appropriate levels, and investors to assess the attractiveness of the subsidies available.

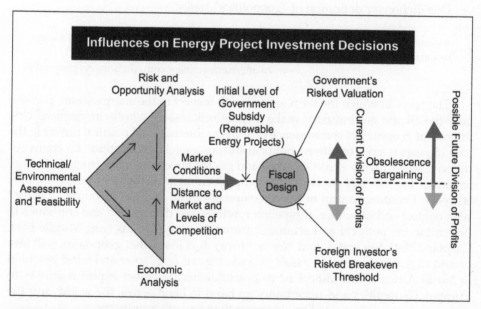

Exhibit 10.6 Uncertainty (Risk and Opportunity) Analysis
Risk and opportunity analysis is a key component in the decision-making process and in establishing appropriate fiscal designs and incentive mechanisms in the energy sector. It is important to factor in the realities of obsolescence bargaining into energy investment decisions.
Source: David A. Wood.

Uncertainty analysis is therefore a key part of the investment decision process in the energy sector. Investment in the energy industry is intimately associated with trade-offs of risk versus reward. Typically for effective investment decisions there needs to be a technical analysis, a DCF analysis, and a risk-opportunity analysis. The results of each analysis should be integrated and often considered in the light of the prevailing fiscal design (and available subsidies in the case of renewable projects) in order to assess whether a project offers appropriate rewards for the risks being taken (Exhibit 10.6).

GEOPOLITICAL RISKS AND OPPORTUNITIES

The meaning of *risk* and its multifaceted nature are discussed above. Many would argue that the world is becoming a riskier place to do business based upon the prevailing dynamic environment of political tensions, price volatility, fiscal instability, resource nationalism, strong competition from cash-rich national (state-owned) companies and sovereign wealth funds, and a risk-averse financial sector. Without an appetite for risk and the vision to see the substantial resource opportunities that exist internationally in the energy sector, few companies venture far into large international projects along the energy supply chains. In addition to the technical, economic, and market risks and opportunity discussed in the previous section, politics and geopolitics provide additional dimensions of uncertainty that are notoriously difficult to predict or quantify. Nevertheless it is important for the petroleum economist to understand the underlying influences driving political trends in a region if realistic risk and opportunity adjustments are to be incorporated into project cash flow analysis.

One dictionary definition of "geopolitics" states:

> A combination of political and geographic factors relating to something (as a state or particular resources)
> —www.merriam-webster.com/dictionary/geopolitics

The ways in which the term is used with respect to the energy sector, particularly the oil and gas industry, make this definition seem wholly inadequate! One important geopolitical consequence of shifts in international political power in the past 15 years is a rise of intense political and commercial competition for control of (or even access to) the world's vast oil and gas resources and infrastructure. Energy resources have in fact reshaped the geopolitical map of the world over the past 60 years. Eventual control of the development of oil and gas resources, together with control and influence in pipeline routings, has determined and continues to determine the political and economic future of many nations (e.g., Middle East, Caspian/Black Sea states, and North Africa). It is likely that geopolitics will also extend to renewable energy assets in some regions (e.g., solar and wind potential in North Africa and Middle East as potential electric power export resources to Europe). Geopolitics and uncertainty go hand in hand across the world, and the energy industry is impacted by this more than any other industry.

Oil remains currently the world's most important and most political commodity. Without oil and to a lesser extent gas and coal, today's industrial society in developed countries would not be possible. Oil and, to a lesser extent, natural gas

are what fuel the engine of modern capitalist countries (OECD nations account for two-thirds of all oil consumed in the world).

Politics, geopolitics, and business are intimately entwined. Politicians establish the legislation, fiscal terms, rules, guidelines, and statutory bodies that control the activities of specific industries in their countries. Geopolitics encompasses the interactions between regional geographical and political issues and their worldwide consequences. Such issues are particularly relevant to the strategies of organizations operating with a global perspective.

These are fundamental influences on business and the economic returns that can be achieved from undertaking a specific venture in a specific country or region. Global businesses now spend huge sums in lobbying politicians worldwide to enact more favorable regulatory and fiscal terms for all sectors of industry. Global businesses also frequently take decisions based upon geopolitical factors that go beyond just the political issues relevant to one specific country.

In major oil and gas export projects, there is often a shift over the life of the project in the bargaining power of the host government of the nation supplying the resource, the transit countries through which the export pipeline passes, and the multinational companies providing the capital investment and technology to develop and exporting the resource. Prior to the field development facilities and pipeline infrastructure being built, the bargaining power is with the multinational companies as the host government lacks the financial, technical, and market power to unlock the resources. However, once the facilities and export infrastructure are built and operating, with the investment sunk by the foreign investors and lenders into the project, the power shifts to the host government and the transit countries, as they have the power to interrupt operations or withhold resources.

In addition, over the life of such projects, often extending for many decades, governments and/or their political persuasions change and often seek greater fiscal returns than originally agreed upon from what have become, as they mature, low risk projects. This means that what were once attractive fiscal terms for the government to initiate the project and secure the inward investment, over time often become "obsolete" and fail to meet the expectations of host and transit nations. The business concept referred to as *obsolescence bargaining* has long recognized (e.g., Jenkins 1986); that is, bargaining power shifts from the investment providers (multinational companies) to investment recipients (host governments) once the investment is in place. The obsolescence usually takes the form of contract renegotiation, increased fiscal take, or in extreme cases asset appropriation or expropriation.

Obsolescence bargaining is not just a phenomenon seen in the developing world. The state of Alaska has introduced a number of increases to the fiscal burden levied on oil investors since the commissioning of the TAPS (Trans-Alaska Pipeline System) in 1977. The ACES (Alaska's Clear and Equitable Share) fiscal system introduced in 2007 significantly increased the fiscal take from incumbent oil producers (Dickinson and Wood 2009a&b). The UK government introduced three increases to the corporation tax levied on North Sea oil producers (termed supplemental corporation tax) between 2002 and 2011, placing increased fiscal burden on an industry in decline producing from mature assets with the main infrastructure investments made many years earlier. In the OECD countries, however, asset expropriation is rare, and tax increases are usually not made on a retrospective

basis. But in the developing world, this is far from the case in the oil and gas sector; both outright expropriations and forced acceptance of onerous fiscal terms by existing investors imposed by pressure from governments (e.g., Algeria, Ecuador, Kazakhstan, Russia, and Venezuela in the past decade) occur more frequently when oil prices rise above former market norms (Wood 2005a&b).

A global mind-set helps to make sense of the geopolitical instability of world and local affairs. Even experienced analysts are often unable to predict major political upheavals, but a global perspective should enable them to recognize such events for what they are earlier than the parochial investor. Such a mind-set also helps investors to interpret the geopolitical implications for the energy industry such that appropriate and informed investment decisions can be taken promptly. The impacts of global and regional events on energy markets occur more quickly in the modern world, partly because of globalization, and partly because of technological advance and diversification. There are no signs of that acceleration of impact from events abating. Advances in media and communications in general continue to cause the world to shrink, so that a wrangle anywhere in the world is immediately reflected in the world's stock markets (e.g., the Arab Spring of 2011). Revolutions, riots, regional tensions, natural disasters, and so on are relayed to TV screens in real time (e.g., earthquake, tsunami, and nuclear power plant failure in Japan in March 2011).

In some cases, global events unfold in television studios. In the energy sector, it is important for multinational organizations (i.e., publicly traded companies and state-owned entities) not just to build a global portfolio of assets but to globalize the mind-set with which decisions are taken to manage those assets. It is usually not enough to just extrapolate from present geopolitical settings and events. It is important to see the coming together of a number of forces, which are gathering momentum and have an ability to reshape the future of entire industries and their constituent organizations. Scenario planning is a technique that helps to develop a global mind-set (Shell 2011).

Fracture lines are breaks in continuity from events, new technologies, or social progress. A fracture line is a break with the past or an interruption in the continuity with the past. Some examples are:

- The formation of OPEC and the period of nationalization of oil resources (1970s)—security of global oil supply has not been the same since that time.
- Global environmental awareness that followed the Chernobyl (Ukraine) nuclear plant accident, Bhopal (India) petrochemical accident, and the Piper Alpha (UK) platform explosion (1980s)—attitudes to the environment and safety of industrial plants have not been the same since that time. The global reactions to the Fukushima nuclear emergency in March 2011 may turn out to be another fracture line impacting the future uptake of nuclear power.
- The World Trade Center terrorist attack (New York) on September 11, 2001—securing industrial plants from global terrorist attack became a higher priority after that event.

Managers and risk analysts should interpret news with a mind-set of trying to identify possible fracture lines and spotting the opportunities and threats implicit in global events. In the energy industry, it is important to develop not just a global

but a future mind-set and to focus on trends and be thinking of the possible shape of things to come, with a variety of options to meet alternative futures. It is a skill to see alternative possibilities and to develop planning scenarios from events; but often scenarios will represent contradictory possibilities.

It is also important to look for the opportunities and threats in all the alternative scenarios considered, and to remember that no one can predict the future with any meaningful certainty or accuracy. Too often, in the commercial environment we are preoccupied with managing the aftermath of what has happened in the past, in dealing with the consequences of events that have already happened (i.e., a reactive strategy). A future mind-set is essential to the successful strategic management of change. Assume you are already there in a future of your choice (i.e., a proactive strategy). You see a future event. It is real, and you are certain that it can be brought about. Such an approach dismisses the "if we get there." Instead you are there and looking back at how you got there. While it is foolish to throw away the past, it is the future that we can affect, and that is why such an approach is helpful. We value energy assets with forward-looking forecasts so future scenarios can and do have a huge impact on the value of our organizations and their assets. It therefore is beneficial to periodically free yourself from the constraints of the present (or past) and engage in uninhibited brainstorming to conceive future scenarios and evaluate the decisions (and regulatory frameworks) required to be successful within such scenarios. Such an approach helps to create an environment in which innovation and creativity can flourish.

As already highlighted, opportunity and risk go hand in hand and are in fact two facets of uncertainty. There are good reasons why many energy organizations (i.e., companies and government entities) now are more rigorous in evaluating—and where possible quantifying—the spectrum of uncertainties (not just geopolitical uncertainties) that their operations as well as their physical assets and financial resources are exposed to. Energy organizations are also keen to calculate their potential financial exposures (i.e., mainly risk for loss rather than opportunity for gain) to extreme risk events related to accidents, natural disasters, terrorist attacks, corporate fraud, and so on. Although such extreme and sometimes catastrophic events occur quite infrequently, they can be devastating for both organizations and communities, if and when they do occur (e.g., Deepwater Horizon/Macondo well blowout in the Gulf of Mexico of April 2010, see BP 2010a; Gulf of Mexico hurricanes of 2005, see Wood & Mokhatab 2006). This recognition, and pressure from tightening regulation, has, together prompted energy companies to develop ever more robust enterprise risk management (ERM) frameworks to integrate these issues more rigorously and systematically (Wood & Randall 2005a&b). The U.S. Securities and Exchange Commission (SEC) tightened regulations following the introduction of the U.S. Sarbanes & Oxley Act (SOX: for an explanation of this legislation see www.soxlaw.com) of 2002 and responding to the scandalous corporate frauds (e.g., Enron, see Healy and Palepu 2003) and poor disclosure performances by some large energy corporations (e.g., Shell's reserves misrepresentation of 2003–2004, see U.S. SEC 2004).

It is now generally recognized that it is very difficult to estimate accurately the likelihood of extreme events occurring. Normal and lognormal distributions of historical data are only adequate in relatively static environments to estimate the probable occurrence of extreme events in the future. In dynamic and quite rapidly

changing environments, such methods of forecasting often underestimate levels of uncertainty, as capital markets and many major international oil and gas projects learned to their cost in 2008. Complex mathematical models claiming to identify and quantify risk exposures, such as many of the Value at Risk (VaR) models popularized in the financial sector and now used widely in the energy sector (e.g., Burger, Graeber, and Schindlmayr 2007) to justify risk exposure of both traded and physical asset portfolios, themselves pose a major threat to the quality of decision making for two main reasons. Firstly, such approaches lead companies and their decision makers to believe they can quantify their risks with unrealistic levels of precision, which often leads to exposures being underestimated and an overconfidence in their ability to manage risk (e.g., the Black Swan effect popularized by Taleb (2007)). Secondly, these approaches encourage decision makers to focus too much of their attention exclusively on the downside risks at the expense of considering and trying to identify and exploit the opportunities that are associated with many uncertain situations.

It is important to consider the bigger picture and not to lose sight of the opportunities. Opportunities, like risks, require careful identification and evaluation, and rarely manifest themselves without efforts being made to seek them out and innovative approaches established to exploit them. Risk managers with a downside mitigation mentality (e.g., the hazard management mandate of many safety, security, and environmental managers within organizations) are rarely equipped or have the vision or time to recognize and manipulate opportunities into projects that are considered achievable. This does not mean that hazard management should be downgraded or replaced with an unconstrained search for opportunity. Quite the contrary, much valuable insight emerges from quantitative risk analysis techniques (e.g., Monte Carlo simulation, real options valuations, and Value at Risk and its derivative techniques), even if the numerical calculations involved are rarely able to provide us with an accurate value or unequivocal decision criteria. Such analysis is clearly required, but not necessarily at the earliest stages of project definition or strategy formation. There is an old saying that numerical analysts should keep in mind at all times, it states that *all models are wrong; the practical question is how wrong they have to be before they cease to be useful?*

Placing a project, asset, portfolio, or nation into an energy industry context using qualitative or semiquantitative techniques to estimate its risks and opportunities in an integrated way is often a more useful starting point from which to approach the first hurdles of the decision-making process. Such an approach is facilitated by a global mind-set, which encourages us to seek out or recognize from a helicopter vision where the opportunities might reside. Adopting such an approach is more likely to enable a risk analyst to conduct the more detailed quantitative analysis focused on upside and downside scenarios that encompass the most probable outcomes and the rare, extreme, but realistically plausible outcomes that might occur at both ends of the probability spectrum.

It helps to begin by grounding opportunity and risk analysis in a global context. What is important in the initial or strategic stages is that risks and opportunities be considered initially together with an integrated, systematic, and rigorous approach that is grounded and presented in a global perspective relevant to the industry. There are several ways in which this can be done. The approach described below, focused on comparative analysis of country risk and opportunity, grounds

the analysis in the context of proved oil reserves at the national level, statistics that are readily available. Although the accuracy of the proved reserves volumes reported at the national level varies by region, and confidence in such numbers is rightly questioned for the unverifiable and unaudited numbers presented by several resource-rich nations, they are useful for distinguishing the resource endowments on the order-of-magnitude scale that is required for global perspectives. Other useful global statistics that could be used include oil and/or gas production volumes, export volumes, and primary energy consumption statistics, depending upon the strategy and type of energy assets being evaluated or pursued. Reserves are used here because many large international organizations (e.g., publicly traded and state-owned) are seeking, as a strategic priority, new international opportunities to increase and diversify their resource bases.

A quick-look analysis that addresses some key uncertainties for the international oil and gas industry was proposed by Wood (2009), and it complements a more rigorous quantitative approach (Wood 2003a&b). Assigning a score to five factors broadly evaluating country risk and to another five factors broadly evaluating country opportunity provides a fast and effective way of systematically evaluating a large number of countries in a rigorous but initially superficial manner.

The five attributes I propose to evaluate for scoping *risk* analysis are focused mainly on political, business, and fiscal risks:

1. Expropriation of assets and political instability.
2. Corruption.
3. High administrative burden (cost and time).
4. Community and labor disputes.
5. Regressive fiscal terms (i.e., those that become tougher on investors as market and asset performance conditions deteriorate).

The five attributes I propose to evaluate for scoping *opportunity* analysis are focused mainly on technical, operational, and financial risks:

1. Access to large petroleum (or other energy) resources and reserves.
2. Low finding and development costs.
3. Ease of operation.
4. Access to equity and/or debt funding.
5. Access to infrastructure and markets to move and sell oil and gas.

Applying a simple scoring system makes the evaluation process quicker and more transparent. I propose a scale of 1 to 5 applied to both risk and opportunity, but extending in different directions from a zero point such that:

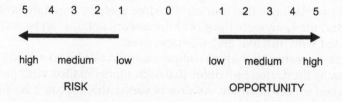

Note that "zero" on the scale proposed is an impossible score implying an attribute with no uncertainty—of either risk or opportunity.

An alternative scoring system is to use negative numbers for risk and positive numbers for opportunity. The proposed, semiquantitative scheme has the advantage of distancing points of high opportunity from those of high risk when cross-plotted graphically. It helps to have a clear verbal description of each score to reduce ambiguity and improve rigor. In this regard, a more precise definition of each number could be:

1 = very low (minimal)
2 = low
3 = moderate
4 = high
5 = very high (extreme)

If a score of 1 to 5 is assigned to each attribute and the scores of all five attributes of opportunity and risk are added separately to yield two scores, those scores can vary between 5 and 25. By subtracting 5 from the sum of the five attribute scores and multiplying that sum by 5 the total risk and opportunity scores are simply manipulated into an index scale from 0 to 100, which is relatively easy to interpret and contrast amongst nations. Clearly detailed knowledge and understanding of the petroleum and energy industry in the nation or region being evaluated is required by the analyst to assign a reliable score to each attribute. To ground this simplistic analysis in a global context, the risk-opportunity indices for a spectrum of significant resource holders can be evaluated and presented graphically with respect to their resource volumes (Exhibit 10.7).

Exhibit 10.7 illustrates an initial risk-opportunity evaluation, based upon my own perceptions and experience of the international oil industry in early 2011. Other analysts might disagree with this comparative analysis, based upon their own experience or perceptions, but at least the method provides the flexibility of being easy to adjust and tailor to the perspectives of specific organizations. The point of the simple scales proposed is that they can be adjusted and updated easily and regularly in response to events, different opinions, changing environments, or re-assessed from different perspectives (e.g., publicly traded versus state-owned entities) in a transparent and rigorous manner. Depending upon whether the analysis is presented in relation to petroleum key performance indicators (e.g., reserves or resources) or broader energy industry metrics (e.g., national primary energy consumption statistics), the analysis provides different global frameworks. Each framework may be more relevant to certain organizations, energy portfolio strategies, or situations.

Having produced the framework, it is relatively easy to highlight the analysis of a region or a country of specific interest (e.g., Region X highlighted in Exhibit 10.7) in relation to that framework. More usefully, the analysis of the region of interest and the analysis of the global framework nations can be easily updated or regrounded with different global perspectives.

Such risk-opportunity analysis comparisons can also be expressed in summary tabular form as illustrated in Exhibit 10.8 or in more detailed form providing the scores assigned to each attribute. As already stated, this approach is simplistic and

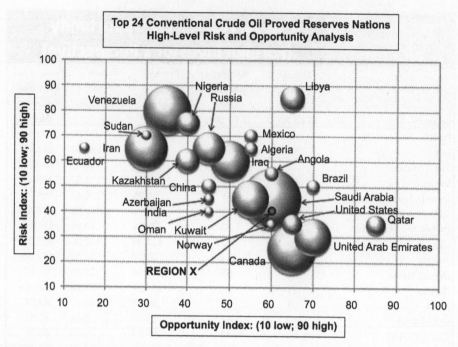

Exhibit 10.7 Risk-Opportunity Indices
These indices evaluate the top proved crude oil reserves holding nations. The diameters of the bubbles are proportional to proved crude oil reserve holdings as reported by BP statistical review of World Energy (BP 2010b).

can only provide a scoping assessment. In many instances, the early stages of the decision-making process can benefit from the rapid and transparent insight such analysis can provide. A much more rigorous in-depth, probability-based risk and opportunity analysis is likely to be required in order to provide a "quantified" risk adjustment for DCF analysis in support of major investment decision making (see Wood (2003a&b) for a multifaceted risk analysis scoring system). I am not suggesting that an in-depth holistic risk analysis be replaced by the approach outlined above, but I am suggesting that this quick-look approach is useful in the context of seeking out opportunities and can complement and help to develop a more in-depth quantitative approach.

It is also important to recognize that the global framework used to ground the risk-opportunity analyses can in some cases itself hide or obscure some opportunities. Again, the oil reserves framework introduced as an example here further illuminates this point. It is appropriate in certain analysis to use proved reserves statistics, as they are the volumes in which the industry by definition believes with the highest levels of confidence. However, from an exploration and future development context it is often the lower-confidence categories of resources (i.e., probable and possible reserves and contingent resources) representing the potential yet to be found in a region that may be more relevant to identifying future opportunities. Hence, it may make more sense for certain oil and/or gas analysis to be grounded in a less accurate contingent resource framework rather than a proved reserves framework.

Ranked by Oil Plus Gas Proved Reserves: (Largest First)	Reserves, Risk & Opportunity (Foreign Investor's Perspective)			
Country	Overall Risk Score (0 to 100)	Overall Opportunity Score (0 to 100)	Proved Gas Reserves tcf	Proved Oil Reserves Gb	Proved Oil Plus Gas Reserves Gboe
Russia	65	45	1567.14	74.20	335.39
Iran	65	30	1045.67	137.62	311.90
Saudi Arabia	45	60	279.67	264.59	311.20
Venezuela	80	35	200.09	172.32	205.67
Canada (incl. oil sands)	25	65	61.95	176.43	186.76
Qatar	35	85	895.76	26.83	176.13
United Arab Emirates	30	70	227.14	97.80	135.66
Iraq	60	50	111.95	115.00	133.66
Kuwait	45	55	63.00	101.50	112.00
United States	35	65	244.66	28.40	69.17
Nigeria	75	40	185.37	37.20	68.09
Libya	85	65	54.38	44.27	53.34
Kazakhstan	60	40	64.36	39.83	50.55
Turkmenistan	60	40	286.17	0.60	48.30
Algeria	65	55	159.06	12.20	38.71
China	50	45	86.71	14.83	29.28
Indonesia	50	40	112.47	4.40	23.15
Australia	30	60	108.66	4.22	22.34
Malaysia	40	55	84.08	5.52	19.53
Norway	35	60	72.25	7.08	19.12

Exhibit 10.8   Summary Quick-Look Risk and Opportunity Indices
The author's analysis (as of March 2011) is for the top 20 barrels of oil equivalent (BOE) nations ranked in descending order of proved BOE reserves holdings, according to BP (2010a).
Gb = billions of barrels; tcf = trillions of cubic feet

CONCLUSION

Discounted cash flow (DCF) analysis requires careful consideration in the energy sector to adjust valuations for the impacts of risks, opportunities, and inflation. This goes way beyond the basic time value analysis of applying a selected discount rate to a forward-looking cash flow profile. Care must be taken to clarify whether cash flows and the discount rates applied to them are expressed in nominal or real terms. Much confusion and distortion result from the practice of adjusting a discount rate to reflect the level of uncertainty of an asset or company being valued. A more realistic approach in practice is to apply a discount rate to adjust future cash flows for time value issues and to separately apply an uncertainty adjustment factor to the cash flow to account for risk and opportunity.

Uncertainty in the energy sector is a multifaceted, nonlinear problem that requires a systematic and holistic approach for meaningful analysis. Some facets of uncertainty are easier to quantify than others. Fiscal and geopolitical risks and opportunities, for example, can only be quantified in a subjective way. However,

both qualitative and quantitative techniques to evaluate such uncertainties can provide useful insight and comparative country analysis that help companies with investment decision making and governments to establish realistic fiscal designs and to tailor fiscal incentives.

DISCUSSION QUESTIONS

1. Should discount factors adjust cash flows for risk?

2. What are the major constraints that oil and gas companies commonly face in making investment decisions?

3. Why does DCF analysis preferentially penalize projects with long-life cash flows (e.g., 20 to 50 years in length)?

4. What type of discount rate should *real* cash flows be discounted with?

5. As well as inflation and risk adjustments, in what kind of oil and gas projects do cash flows also require significant adjustments for currency exchange rates?

6. What alternative terms are used to describe values expressed in nominal terms?

7. In the equation used to calculate present value (PV) from future value (FV), $PV = FV * (1 + d)^{-n}$ what does the exponent n represent?

8. A hurdle rate of return is sometimes also referred to as a MARR. What does the acronym MARR stand for?

9. What does the acronym WACC stand for? And why is it relevant to selecting a discount rate in DCF analysis?

10. If uncertainty analysis suggests that a project has a 70 percent chance of commercial failure, then it has a chance of commercial success of _____?

REFERENCES

BP. 2010a. "Deepwater Horizon Accident Investigation Report." September 8, 2010, 1–192. Available at www.bp.com/sectiongenericarticle.do?categoryId=9036598&contentId=7067574.

BP. 2010b. *Statistical Review of World Energy*. June 2010 Edition. Available at www.bp.com/productlanding.do?categoryId=6929&contentId=7044622.

Brealey, R. A., S. C. Myers, and F. Allen. 2008. *Principles of Corporate Finance*. 9th ed. New York: McGraw-Hill/Irwin.

Burger, Markus, Bernhard Graeber, and Gero Schindlmayr. 2007. *Managing Energy Risk: An Integrated View on Power and Other Energy Markets*. Hoboken, NJ: John Wiley & Sons.

Dickinson, Dan E., and David Wood. 2009a. "Alaska Tax Reform: Intent Met with Oil" (Part 1 of 2). *Oil & Gas Journal*, June 1, 20–26.

Dickinson, Dan E., and David Wood. 2009b. "Alaska Tax Reform: Gas Raises Questions" (Part 2 of 2). *Oil & Gas Journal*, May 25, 20–24.

Guide to the Sarbanes-Oxley Act. 2002. Available at www.soxlaw.com.

Healy, Paul M., Krishna G. Palepu. 2003. "The Fall of Enron" [PDF]. *Journal of Economic Perspectives* 17:2, 3–26.

Jenkins, Barbara. 1986. "Re-examining the "Obsolescing Bargain:" A Study of Canada's National Energy Program." *International Organization* 40, 139–165.

Shell International BV. 2011. "Shell Energy Scenarios to 2050: Signals and Signposts," 1–80. Available at www-static.shell.com/static/aboutshell/downloads/aboutshell/signals_signposts.pdf.

Taleb, Nassim N. 2007. *The Black Swan*. Penguin Books.

U.S. Securities and Exchange Commission. 2004. "Royal Dutch Petroleum Company and the 'Shell' Transport and Trading Company PLC Pay $120 Million to Settle SEC Fraud Case Involving Massive Overstatement of Proved Hydrocarbon Reserves." U.S. Securities and Exchange Commission Press Release 2004-116. August 24, 2004. Available at www.sec.gov/news/press/2004-116.htm.

Wood, David A. 2003a. "E&P Asset & Portfolio Risk Analysis: Addressing a Many-Faceted Problem." *Oil & Gas Journal*, September 29, 49–56.

Wood, David A. 2003b. "More Aspects of E&P Asset and Portfolio Risk Analysis: Linked with Digital Executive Report." *Oil & Gas Journal*, Oct 6, 28–32.

Wood, David A. 2005a. "Long-Term Fiscal, Contractual Stability Proves Elusive, Part 1." *Petroleum Review*, February, 38–42.

Wood, David A. 2005b. "Long-Term Fiscal, Contractual Stability Proves Elusive, Part 2." *Petroleum Review*, April, 44–48.

Wood, David A. 2009. "Integrating High-level Upstream Opportunity & Risk Analysis with Global Perspectives." *Oil & Gas Journal*, February 9, 20–26.

Wood, David A., and Scott Randall. 2005a. "Implementing ERM-1: The Importance of Perspective." *Oil & Gas Journal*, March 21, 18–23.

Wood, David A., and Scott Randall. 2005b. "Implementing ERM-2: The Link with Risk Management." *Oil & Gas Journal*, March 28, 20–26.

Wood, David A., and Saeid Mokhatab. 2006. "US Gas Market Responds to Hurricane Disruptions." *Oil & Gas Journal*, September 25, 18–24.

Wood, David A., Greg Lamberson, and Saeid Mokhatab. 2007. "Project Risk: A Key Consideration for Upstream Project Management." *World Oil* 228:9, 127–130. Available at www.worldoil.com/September-2007-Project-risk-A-key-consideration-for-upstream-energy-project-management.html.

ABOUT THE CONTRIBUTOR

David A. Wood has more than 30 years of international oil and gas experience spanning technical and commercial exploration and production operations, contract evaluation and senior corporate management. Industry experience includes Phillips Petroleum, Amoco (Africa, Europe, and UK), and Canadian independents (South America, Africa, Middle and Far East), including three years based in Colombia and four years based in Dubai. From 1993 to 1998 he was UK Managing Director for Lundin Oil and then of Morrison Petroleum responsible for a broad portfolio of assets and a staff of more than 100. David gained a PhD in geochemistry from Imperial College, London, in 1977.

Wood now works as an independent international consultant and expert witness for governments and a range of international companies. He has published an extensive body of work on diverse energy-related topics including: performance modeling of fiscal terms, political risk, economic analysis, enterprise risk and portfolio simulation, liquefied natural gas, gas to liquids, and gas supply, as well as deepwater exploration and production techniques, corporate performance, portfolio and strategy management, mergers and acquisitions, and negotiation and project management. He is actively involved in diverse professional training, research, and development programes. Wood is Assistant Editor-in-Chief of the *Journal of Natural Gas Science & Engineering*. He can be contacted at www.dwasolutions.com.

CHAPTER 11

Real Options and Applications in the Energy Industry*

BETTY J. SIMKINS
Williams Companies Professor Business and Professor of Finance,
Oklahoma State University

KRIS KEMPER
Assistant Professor, University of Wisconsin–Eau Claire

> One of the strongest arguments that can be made for real options is that it provides
> a framework that bridges the longstanding gap between strategy and finance.
> —Triantis and Borison (2001)

> It's not the strongest of the species that survive, nor the most intelligent, but those
> that are the most responsive to change.
> —Charles R. Darwin (1809–1882)

INTRODUCTION

The globalization of world markets and advances in technology make it imperative
for companies to adapt quickly to the changing marketplace, regardless of whether
they are a local business or global corporation. As Triantis and Borison (2001)
note, real options techniques can bridge the gap between strategy and finance. As
Darwin notes, adaptability is the key to survival and success. While Darwin was
referring to living species, this concept is applicable to all businesses whether they
are public, private, nonprofit, or governmental. Using a real options approach to
address the challenges of a global marketplace leads to better managerial decision
making. Coupled with traditional capital budgeting techniques, it leads to long-
term survival and success of corporations.

What are real options? Real options are option-like opportunities, such as
business decisions and flexibilities, where the underlying assets are real assets;

---

*This chapter is a reprint of Chapter 36, "Real Options in Corporate Finance," in Betty J.
Simkins and Kris Kemper, *Financial Derivatives: Pricing and Risk Management*, Robert W. Kolb
and James A. Overdahl, eds., pp. 559–573, Hoboken, NJ: John Wiley & Sons, 2009.

hence the term *real options*. These opportunities are based on managerial flexibility and are commonly found in the operation of many corporate assets. Examples include: the choice to expand into new markets and product lines when growth opportunities are available in the marketplace; the option to wait until more information is available (such as to delay investment and operating decisions in response to uncertainty in the marketplace); the option to switch between inputs, outputs, or processes (such as a dual-fired power plant that operates on two types of fuel and can switch from one fuel to another); the option to abandon or temporarily shut down operations when losses are being occurred; and hybrid options.

It is important to note that the value of real options is dependent on the skills and expertise of management to "exercise" the real option at the optimal time. With strong managerial oversight, such options can add significant value to the business enterprise and can greatly benefit the strategic success of a firm. Likewise, with poor managerial oversight, these options have little or no value because the options are overlooked or not exercised optimally.

In the remainder of the chapter, we provide a brief history of real options, discuss the differences between financial and real options, describe the types of real options together with examples from the energy industry, list ways real options are valued, and conclude.

A BRIEF HISTORY OF REAL OPTIONS

Until 1973, when Fisher Black and Myron Scholes published their path-breaking paper on pricing options, options valuation was not well developed because there was no well-recognized or accurate method. Black and Scholes's work, which provided the first closed-form solution to options valuation, laid the foundation for the birth of real options as a formal area of study.

While "real option–type" business opportunities have been around for centuries, the official coining of the words *real options* was by Stewart Myers (1977) of MIT when he observed that any capital budgeting decision was in fact a series of embedded "real options" on additional investments. Myers states: "Many corporate assets, particularly growth opportunities, can be viewed as call options. The value of such 'real options' depends on discretionary future investment by the firm" (1977, 147). Prior to this period, real options decisions were based on intuition, ad hoc techniques, or rules of thumb with little quantitative theory behind the decisions. Myers formally introduced the topic as a new area of financial research. For this reason, he is viewed as the father of real options.

Since the 1970s, many articles and books have been written on the subject of real options, and continue to be written. Researchers first applied real options to valuation of oil and gas exploration rights. Oil and gas companies realized that reserves had real options value, even if the costs of developing were unprofitable at the present time, due to the high historical volatility of oil prices. These valuation techniques subsequently led to applications in other industries.

Real options are now recognized as a way of thinking, as a part of the capital budgeting process, as an analytical tool incorporated into software packages such as Crystal Ball, and as an integral component of corporate strategy and decision

making.[1] However, the practice of real options analysis by businesses is still limited and is used most frequently in industries such as energy (oil, gas, and power) and other natural resources, aviation, transportation, pharmaceuticals, and high tech, among others. There is a robust literature on applying real options to capital budgeting decisions in corporate finance.[2] Many businesses do not know about the process/technique/concept.[3]

DISTINCTION BETWEEN FINANCIAL OPTIONS AND REAL OPTIONS

Before discussing the types of real options, it is important to understand the distinction between financial and real options. Financial options give the holder the right, but not the obligation, to engage in a financial transaction at a predetermined price and date. More specifically, a *call option* gives the holder the right to buy the underlying financial asset (such as a share of stock) at some predetermined, or *exercise*, price. A *put option* gives the holder the right to sell the underlying asset at its *exercise* price. Conversely, real options give the holder the ability to acquire an asset using a call option, to divest using a put option, or to "exercise" other flexibilities on real assets. These options give a manager the ability to be flexible and can be viewed as strategic options (i.e., strategic opportunities that arise from owning real assets). In other words, financial options give the holder a right to purchase (sell) a financial asset while real options give the holder the right to purchase (sell) an actual physical or knowledge-based resource. Furthermore, financial options have exact exercise prices and dates, while real options are a function of the resources involved, the owner, and the environment.

To summarize:

Financial Options	Real Options
Right to purchase/sell a financial asset	Right to purchase/sell physical resource
Exact exercise date	Exercise date not specified by contract
Exact exercise price	Exercise price not specified by contract
Value does not depend on who owns it	Value generally depends on who owns it

TYPES OF REAL OPTIONS AND EXAMPLES IN THE ENERGY INDUSTRY

Real options have many useful applications in the energy industry. The existence of derivative securities, such as futures, forwards, and options on oil, petroleum products, natural gas, and power, makes it possible to more fully exploit the flexibility of energy assets, such as oil and gas reserves, natural gas storage facilities, pipelines, fertilizer plants, power plants, and alternative energy projects. (See Chapter 9.) Real options applications in these areas permit the optimization and valuation of the flexibilities embedded in the operation of these energy assets by their owners. Furthermore, the volatility of energy prices adds value to real options applications in the energy industry.

When considering a project, the traditional net present value (NPV) formula is modified to include the value of the real option.[4] In other words, the value of a project with real options features is equal to:

$$Value\ of\ project\ with\ real\ options = NPV + Real\ option\ value \qquad (11.1)$$

Common types of real options and examples in the energy industry are described next. Exhibit 11.1 lists common types of real options together with

Exhibit 11.1 Common Types of Real Options

Types of Real Options	Option Type	Examples in the Energy Industry or Related	Selected References
Option to expand	Call	Southwest Airlines Blended Winglets; replace oil or gas reserves by exploration or acquisition; invest in new data acquisition (seismic data and logs, etc.) for energy exploration	Amram and Kulatilaka (1999); Copeland and Antikarov (2001); Damodaran (2000); Martin, Rogers, and Simkins (2004); Titman and Martin (2008)
Option to wait	Call or put	Explore for oil or gas onshore or offshore; valuing petroleum undeveloped reserves (PUD) reserves; valuing oil sands; carbon capture investments	Damodaran (2000); Dixit and Pindyck (1994); Brennan and Schwartz (1985); McCormack and Sick (2001); Ronn (2005a&b)
Option to switch (inputs, outputs, or processes)	Call or put	Valuing a natural gas power plant; valuing natural gas storage facilities; flexibility of inputs with dual-fired power plants	Amram and Kulatilaka (1999); De Jong and Walet (2005); Kasanen and Trigeorgis (1993a&b); Kulatilaka (1993); Miller and Waller (2003); Ronn (2005a&b); Thompson, Davison, and Rasmussen (2007); Triantis (2000); Trigeorgis (1993a&b)
Option to abandon or temporarily shut down	Put	Production of fertilizer; stripper well abandonment decision	Damodaran (2008); Ronn (2005a&b); Titman and Martin (2008)
Hybrid real options	Call or put and others	Game theory applications in competitive game situations	Dias (2005); Grenadier (2000); Smit and Ankum (1993)

examples and references for additional information. These types of real options are not mutually exclusive because real assets can have multiple option type opportunities embedded in them.

Option to Expand

The option to expand allows a company to enter into a new market or project with caution or to move more aggressively if conditions warrant such action. In this scenario, the firm (holder of the option) has a call option on additional capacity. If conditions are favorable, the call option will be exercised, and additional capital will be invested in the project.

As another application, a firm may have an option to extend the life of an asset at the end of a project. In this situation, the firm has a call option on the asset's future value. In this case, an asset that had been anticipated as being obsolete at the end of a project instead has remaining economic life. The firm has a call option on the asset's future value and may exercise its right to extend the project.

Example: Tertiary Recovery Techniques in Oil and Gas Production
A common application to extend a project's life in the oil and gas industry (an option to expand recoverable reserves) is to use tertiary recovery techniques. Tertiary recovery in oil and gas production begins when secondary oil recovery is not enough to continue adequate production, but only when the oil can still be extracted profitably.[5] Hence, this potential opportunity can be viewed as a call option in which the option premium depends on the cost of the extraction method, and the payoff is based on the current price of crude oil. When prices are high, the option is exercised and previously unprofitable wells are brought back into production.

Option to Wait

Instead of deciding today to invest in a project based on NPV analysis, a firm can wait and learn more before investing. This is also known as the *timing option*. In this situation, the firm has a call option on the value of the project. For example, this type of real option would be valuable when a firm is considering entering into a new line of business, one in which there is not much of a track record. A firm can opt to delay its decision and see if demand is high. If demand is high, the firm can exercise its call option and enter the market. However, if demand is low, the firm can avoid this market altogether without having made any financial investment.

Example: Valuing Petroleum Undeveloped Reserves as Real Options
The market value of oil and gas reserves, especially petroleum undeveloped reserves (PUDs), usually has a greater value than the value calculated using the traditional NPV approach. This is due to the real option opportunities embedded in such assets. Exhibit 11.2 illustrates this concept. Consider PUDs that have a NPV of $100 million if developed now at a cost of $100 million. According to NPV analysis, the value is zero. However, these reserves have positive economic value because the owner (or lease holder) of these reserves has years to wait before losing the right to develop. Hence, these assets have real options value from the flexibility to

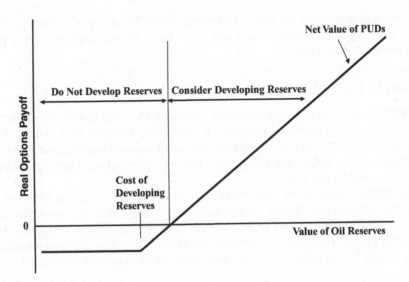

Exhibit 11.2 Value of Petroleum Undeveloped Reserves (PUDs) as a Real Option

expand in the future. This option value can be viewed as a finite-lived American call option, with time to expiration established by ownership of the mineral rights or lease agreement. The real options value is the value of the right (but not obligation) to invest in the PUD during the life of the lease. The value can be modeled as following a geometric Brownian motion, among other techniques.[6]

Option to Vary Production Inputs, Outputs, or Processes

Standard NPV analysis ignores the value of flexibility in projects such as the option to vary production inputs, outputs, or processes. Such flexibilities can greatly enhance the economic value of a project. With flexibility in inputs and outputs, the company has the option in each time period to convert the lowest-cost input into the highest-value output (if there is more than one choice for the input or output). In essence, any company that builds a production system so that it can change easily from one input to another or from one product to another has built a real option component into the asset. The company only needs to exercise the real options in these flexible projects if it is profitable to do so.

With the values of inputs and output commodities fluctuating highly (i.e., high price volatility), the profitability can vary widely from high profits to large losses, especially if input and output prices are not highly correlated. The more volatile this profitability spread, the higher the value of this option and the greater the possible profits. This can be summarized: The more volatile the relationship between the prices of inputs and outputs, the greater the difference between the standard NPV and the true NPV (if inherent real options are exercised and included in the true NPV value).

The next examples describe applications in the energy industry. It is interesting to note that equity prices have exhibited correlations with real options

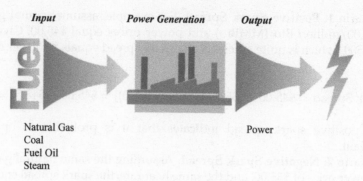

Input   Power Generation   Output

Natural Gas   Power
Coal
Fuel Oil
Steam

Exhibit 11.3 Simple Illustration of the Tolling Concept

valuation. For example, Dawson and Considine (2003) show that the stock price of an electricity-generating company is significantly correlated with the volatility of spark spreads.[7] The real options illustration described next provides more information on this topic.

Example: Valuing a Natural Gas Power Plant: The Tolling Arrangement

The tolling arrangement is an innovative structured deal that has been used by the power industry since the late 1990s. Exhibit 11.3 provides a simple illustration of the tolling concept. Tolling arrangements are the practice of operating a natural gas power plant for a fee under a contract to another party (the real options holder) who provides the input (natural gas fuel) and sells the output (the electric power produced). In other words, the real options holder takes on the market risk by supplying the natural gas used and selling the power produced, and the counterparty owns and operates the power plant with its own employees. This concept has allowed market participants to capitalize on new market opportunities in the deregulation of the power industry. The real options holder has a flexibility option (call option) on operating the power generation asset. Williams Companies and other power companies such as ExxonMobil, Dynegy, and Noram Energy have executed a number of these long-term tolling arrangements since the late 1990s to provide wholesale power in the United States.

This real options investment can be viewed as a portfolio of short-term spread options on the spark spread (i.e., the difference between electricity prices and natural gas prices). Simply put, the power plant can be operated when the spark spread is in the positive and turned off when the spark spread is in the negative.[8] Consider two scenarios: Scenario 1 uses a positive spark spread (i.e., the option is "in the money") and Scenario 2 illustrates a negative spark spread (i.e., the option is "out of the money"). Both scenarios assume an efficient power plant (higher heat rate, which is the thermal efficiency). The formula for the spark spread is:

$$\text{Spark Spread} = \text{Price of Power per MWh} - [\text{Price of Natural Gas per MMBtu} \times (\text{Heat Rate}/1{,}000)] \tag{11.2}$$

Scenario 1: Positive Spark Spread. For example, assume natural gas prices equal \$5.00/million Btu (MMBtu) and power prices equal \$45.00. Given a heat rate of 8,500 (which is quite efficient), the spark spread equals \$2.50 per megawatt (MWh).

$$\text{Spark Spread} = \$45.00 - [\$5.00 \times (8,500/1,000)] = \$45.00 - \$42.50 = 2.50$$

The positive spark spread indicates that it is profitable to operate the power plant.

Scenario 2: Negative Spark Spread. Assuming the same natural gas price, a lower power price of \$35.00, and the same heat rate, the spark spread equals a loss of \$7.50 per MWh:

$$\text{Spark Spread} = \$35.00 - [\$5.00 \times (8,500/1,000)] = \$35.00 - \$42.50 = (\$7.50)$$

The negative spark spread indicates that it is unprofitable to operate the power plant.

Example: Flexibility of Inputs with Dual-Fired Power Plants

As mentioned, production systems that can change easily from one input to another have an embedded real option. Thus, dual-fuel power plants that can use either oil or gas give the operators of these assets the right to switch between fuels whenever it is economical to do so (i.e., the switching option is in the money). For these plants, the owner can be viewed as having a call option on oil and a put option on gas (versus oil only) and the risk increases (decreases) if inputs are positively (negatively) correlated.[9]

Example: Valuing a Natural Gas Storage Facility

Real option analysis can be applied to valuing natural gas storage facilities because for certain types of storage, such as salt dome caverns, there is substantial flexibility in the operations. Using salt caverns, the natural gas can be more easily withdrawn and sold when prices are high (or to take advantage of short-term price spikes) or injected into storage when prices are low. Also, the facilities can be operated to trade around expected future gas prices and can maximize real option opportunities. Such options can be very valuable based on the seasonality and volatility in natural gas prices. Therefore, owners or leasers of storage can buy in cheap seasons and sell in expensive seasons and concurrently trade on derivative contracts on natural gas. A gas storage facility (again ignoring operating characteristics) can be thought of as a series of call and put options of different strikes. Depending on the amount of gas in storage and the characteristics of the facility, the relative influence of the put and call components varies.[10]

Option to Abandon or Temporarily Shutdown

The right to abandon or scale back an investment has value to the firm when its cash flows do not measure up to expectations. Such options allow the firm to shut down a financially harmful project. As illustrated in Exhibit 11.4, the firm (holder of the option) has a put option on the project's value. If the project is not satisfying

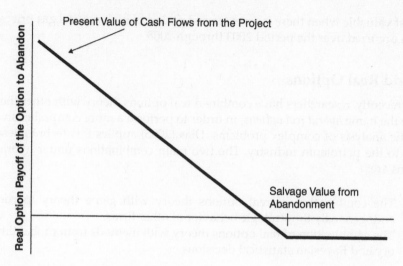

Exhibit 11.4 Option to Abandon a Project

the goal of maximizing shareholder value, the put option can be exercised and the project and its assets divested. With active management throughout the project's life, the choice can be made to shut down in any period when there would be an operating loss (i.e., value of the output is less than the cost to produce).

Example: The Option to Shut Down a Stripper Well

An example of an abandonment option is the decision of whether to shut down a stripper well (an oil well that produces low volumes of oil) that is marginally profitable. Because these wells produce low volumes, frequently less than 1,000 barrels a year, the operating cost per barrel is high, and the profitability is very sensitive to oil prices. When oil prices dropped substantially in 1998, many stripper wells in Oklahoma and Texas became unprofitable and were shut down. This decision can be viewed as permanent because shutting down production may cause the geology to change (oil formation collapse or similar), making these decisions irreversible ones.[11]

Example: Option to Temporarily Shut Down a Fertilizer Plant

Natural gas is the primary feedstock (i.e., input) for nitrogen fertilizer (anhydrous ammonia) and makes up approximately 80 percent of the cost.[12] Furthermore, fertilizer is a world market commodity, impacted by supply and demand around the world. Due to high volatility in both natural gas and fertilizer prices, the real option to temporarily shut down a fertilizer plant has significant value. The option to temporarily shut down a production operation can be viewed as a series of put options because the option to shutdown can be exercised at any time up until the expiration date (life of the plant). The option premium is the expense of terminating operations for a period (such as engineering costs to mothball equipment, associated administrative costs, and subsequent start-up costs or other incremental expenses). The strike price is the difference between fertilizer prices and the cost of operating (approximately 80 percent of which is due to the price of natural gas).[13] This option

is most valuable when there is an extended period of high natural gas prices such as has occurred over the period 2003 through 2008.

Hybrid Real Options

More recently, researchers have combined real options theory with other theories, hence the name *hybrid real options*, in order to perform a more comprehensive and realistic analysis of complex problems. Dias (2005) applies this technique specifically to the petroleum industry. The two main combinations under hybrid real options are:

1. The combination of real options theory with game theory to consider endogenously the strategic behavior of other firms.
2. The combination of real options theory with methods from probability theory and Bayesian statistical decisions.

The models under this technique generate a new way to model technical uncertainty of a project in dynamic real options models. In essence, using hybrid real options, these two combinations can be recombined so as to capture the value of information differences in noncooperative and cooperative games.

For example, in the petroleum industry when using hybrid options, important variables like exploratory chance factor, volume, and quality of a petroleum reserve, can be modeled with the development of a new theory on revelation distribution and measures of learning.[14] Dias (2005) describes the combination of real options theory with the evolutionary computation theory (evolutionary real options) and states they hold great potential in complex applications of optimization under uncertainty. He presents this method to illustrate an application using the genetic algorithms to evolve the decision rule for optimal exercise of a real option.

VALUING REAL OPTIONS

Applying real options valuation to energy assets involves these challenges:

- Modeling of energy prices.
- Modeling of energy demand.
- Understanding the relationships between forward prices and forecast prices.
- Understanding liquidity in derivatives markets.

As discussed earlier, the value of a project with real options features is equal to the project's traditional NPV plus the real option value. How can a real option value be quantified? Just as in NPV analysis, real options valuation involves making a number of assumptions based on uncertainty. But it is this very uncertainty that gives the real options value and the greater the uncertainty, the greater the potential value. It is important to calculate a specific value as a starting point, but remember that the computed value is just an estimate. Next, methods to value real options are described. There is an extensive literature on valuing real options.[15]

Decision Trees

The use of a decision tree seems most in line with the needs of managers, although more sophisticated methods are available. This approach is, in fact, the simplest approach and can be used to examine projects that have embedded options to abandon, expand, contract, defer, or extend.

The basic decision tree can be explained in this way: The project under consideration will have a net investment at time zero. Following this net investment, or cash outflow, the decision maker will assign probabilities to different possible future states of nature. For example, there may be three possible futures states: low demand, medium demand, and high demand. Each future state of nature has a corresponding expected cash inflow. Obviously, cash inflows will be higher when demand is highest, and cash inflows will be lowest when demand is lowest. A finite set of possible states is used for simplicity, and different NPVs are calculated based on the cash flows and the probability of those cash flows, along with an appropriate discount rate. The decision maker is then left with multiple NPVs and their corresponding probabilities. This is an example of a decision tree without any embedded options.

The value of real options is seen when embedded options are introduced into the decision tree. Introducing an option to defer will allow the decision maker to make the initial investment at a time other than today. This will change the cash flows and also can reduce uncertainty. Similarly, options to expand or abort will also impact cash flows and reduce risk while also increasing the expected NPV. The ability of embedded options to increase the expected NPV, while at the same time reducing uncertainty, creates value.

Monte Carlo Simulation

It should be noted that while decision tree analysis is prevalent in capital budgeting decisions that incorporate real options, there is an obvious shortcoming. Decision tree analysis offers only a finite number of possibilities for future states. To incorporate multiple risks and an almost infinite amount of possible future states, a Monte Carlo simulation can be used. The decision maker is then provided with a single measure of volatility for valuing real options. The result of the simulation is a probability distribution in which different outcomes and their likelihoods of occurrence are presented. In this manner, an NPV is calculated that has incorporated many different courses of action in the future—that incorporates the use of real options.

Option Pricing Models

Finally, real options can be valued using the Black-Scholes (B-S) pricing model. Five inputs are needed to price an option (including real options) using B-S:

1. Current price
2. Exercise price
3. Time to maturity
4. Risk-free rate
5. Volatility

Given these inputs, the value (or price) of a real option can be calculated. The difficulty, as with pricing any option, is in quantifying the volatility. Furthermore, modeling energy prices is extremely difficult, and entire books have been written on this topic.[16]

CONCLUSION

The application of real options analysis is more than just another capital budgeting tool; it is a way of thinking. Traditional net present value analysis does not capture the value of real options embedded in projects. The types of real options discussed in the chapter include the option to expand, the option to wait, the option to vary production inputs, outputs, or processes, the option to abandon or temporarily shut down, and hybrid real options. These real options were illustrated using applications in the energy industry. As noted earlier, the value of these real options is dependent on management insight and strategic decision making. If properly valued and exercised, real options add substantial value to projects. Likewise, if these flexibilities are not properly exercised or, worse yet, if they are ignored, the value of real options embedded in projects will not be fully realized.

Real options are still not widely used in practice. Applications are found most commonly in the pharmaceutical and oil and gas exploration industries—two industries characterized by high risk. Two possible reasons that real options analysis is still not widely adopted are the complexity of real options analysis and the lack of corporate incentives to undertake projects justified by this analysis. Clearly, there is still a lack of understanding about real options applications in many industries.

More research is needed on the application of real options. There is still a lack of good empirical work on real options. As Copeland, Weston, and Shastri (2005, 871–872) note:

> Even though there has been a great deal of successful research into the pricing of all types of financial options, there has been much less work on real options.... We note that no one has provided any evidence that real options are priced correctly in the marketplace. Both empirical evidence and experimental evidence are needed.

DISCUSSION QUESTIONS

1. What are real options? Provide examples.
2. Who officially coined the words *real options* and in what year? Give the quote and reference where the words were first introduced.
3. Explain how real options are different from financial options.
4. List and discuss the common types of real options.
5. Describe the common types of real options in the energy industry.
6. What are PUDs, and how can they be valued as real options?
7. What is a tolling arrangement? How is it a type of real options? Explain how real options valuation can be applied to the flexibility of tolling arrangements.
8. How can a natural gas storage facility be value as a real option?
9. List and describe the ways that real options are valued.

10. As the authors point out, real options are still not widely used in practice. Why? Suggest ways that you believe can help companies better understand the benefits of using real options valuation techniques.

NOTES

1. Crystal Ball is produced by Oracle and is a leading spreadsheet-based application for predictive modeling, forecasting, simulation, and optimization.
2. There is a robust literature on applying real options to capital budgeting decisions. Alex Triantis has a searchable database of over 500 practitioner and academic articles on real options. Refer to www.smith.umd.edu/faculty/atriantis/ for more information. Also refer to Dixit and Pindyck (1994), Damodaran (2000 and 2008), and references listed in Exhibit 11.1 of this chapter.
3. The authors have interviewed a number of business professionals and were surprised to learn how many were unfamiliar with the term *real options*.
4. Dixit and Pindyck (1994, chap. 1) present a comparison between the real options approach and the neoclassical investment theory with its variants, such as the Tobin's q or marginal q and the Jorgenson's user cost of capital. Both variants of the neoclassical model rely on the well-known net present value rule.
5. There are three distinct phases of oil recovery: primary, secondary, and tertiary (or enhanced) recovery. Primary recovery can be viewed as the easiest because the natural pressure of the reservoir or gravity drives oil into the wellbore and then artificial lift techniques, such as pumps, can bring the oil to the surface. Some estimates indicate that only about 10 percent of a reservoir's original oil in place is typically produced using primary recovery. Secondary recovery techniques typically involve injecting water or gas to displace oil and result in the recovery of 20 to 40 percent of the original oil in place. After using primary and secondary techniques, some producers utilize several tertiary, or enhanced oil recovery (EOR), techniques, which commonly involve thermal recovery, gas injection, and chemical injection. These techniques can recover 30 to 60 percent, or more, of the reservoir's original oil in place. However, these techniques are much more expensive and depend on the petroleum economics.
6. For more information, see McCormack and Sick (2001), Ronn (2005b), among others.
7. The spark spread represents the theoretical margin for a power plant. If the price of electricity (the output) is higher than the price of fuel (such as natural gas) for a power plant, then the spark spread is positive. Likewise, if the price of electricity is less than the cost of the fuel, the spread is negative.
8. A number of complex factors need to be incorporated into the modeling of this type of real options. Plant physical constraints in the form of start-up costs, ramp-up and ramp-down costs, and maintenance due to wear and tear associated with switching the plant on and off, must be incorporated into the real options valuation analysis. Furthermore, these facilities can run at different capacity usage amounts. A number of articles have been written on this topic. For example, see Leppart (2005), Pilipovic and Wengler (1999), and Price (1997), among others.
9. For more discussion, refer to Kulatilaka (1993) and Ronn (2005a).
10. For more information on valuing real options on natural gas storage, refer to De Jong and Walet (2005); and Thompson, Davison, and Rasmussen (2007), among others.
11. Refer to Titman and Martin (2008, 466–468) for additional discussion on this topic.
12. It takes 34,000 million Btus of natural gas to make 1 ton of anhydrous ammonia.
13. It is important to note that the volatility of natural gas historically has been significantly higher than the volatility of most other commodities, including crude oil and fertilizer. Additionally, natural gas prices have a strong seasonal component.

14. As Dias (2005) notes: "The real options theory is combined with other theories—so the name hybrid real options—in order to perform a more comprehensive and realistic analysis of complex problems that arises from petroleum industry. The two main combinations analyzed here are: (a) the combination of real options theory with game theory—real options games—to consider endogenously the strategic behavior of other firms, especially in the optimal stopping game with positive externalities known as war of attrition, as well as the possibility to change this game by a cooperative bargain game; and (b) the combination of real options theory with methods from probability theory and Bayesian statistical decision—Bayesian real options—generating a new way to model technical uncertainty of a project in dynamic real options models. These two combinations are recombined in order to obtain an adequate solution that captures the value of information differences in non-cooperative and cooperative games." See www.puc-rio.br/marco.ind/abstract.html for the quote in English. The dissertation is in Portuguese.

15. For more information on valuing real options, particularly in the energy industry, refer to references listed in Exhibit 11.1 and also to Amran and Kulatilaka (1999), Kaminski (2005), Ronn (2005a), and Titman and Martin (2008).

16. Risk Books (London) has published a number of excellent books on modeling energy prices and related issues. Refer to http://riskbooks.com/ for more information.

REFERENCES

Amram, M., and N. Kulatilaka. 1999. *Real Options: Managing Strategic Investment in an Uncertain World*. Boston: Harvard Business School Press.

Black, F., and M. Scholes. 1973. "The Pricing of Options and Corporate Liabilities." *Journal of Political Economy* 81:2, 637–654.

Brennan, M. J., and E. S. Schwartz. 1985. "Evaluating Natural Resource Investments," *Journal of Business* 58:2, 135–157.

Copeland, T. E., and V. Antikarov. 2001. *Real Options: A Practitioner's Guide*. New York: Texere.

Copeland, T. E., J. F. Weston, and K. Shastri. 2005. *Financial Theory and Corporate Policy*, 4th ed. Boston: Pearson Education.

Damodaran, A. 2000. "The Promise of Real Options," *Journal of Applied Corporate Finance* 13:2, 28–39.

Damodaran, A. 2008. "The Promise and Peril of Real Options." Working paper. New York University. Available at www.ssrn.com.

Dawson, T., and J. Considine. 2003. "Real Option Valuation and Equity Markets." *Risk* (May), 98–100.

De Jong, C., and K. Walet. 2005. "Gas storage management." In V. Kaminski, ed. *Managing Energy Price Risk: The New Challenges and Solutions*, 631–648. London: Risk Books.

Dias, M. A. G. 2005. "Hybrid Real Options with Applications in Petroleum." PhD diss., Industrial Engineering Department, PUC-Rio, Rio de Janeiro, Brazil.

Dixit, A. K., and R. S. Pindyck. 1994. *Investment under Uncertainty*. Princeton, NJ: Princeton University Press.

Grenadier, S., ed. 2000. *Game Choices: The Intersection of Real Options and Game Theory*. London: Risk Books.

Kaminski, V., ed. 2005. *Managing Energy Price Risk: The New Challenges and Solutions*. London: Risk Books.

Kasanen, E., and L. Trigeorgis. 1993. "Flexibility, synergy, and control." In R. Aggarwal, ed. *Strategic Investment Planning, Capital Budgeting under Uncertainty*, 208–231. Englewood Cliffs, NJ: Prentice-Hall.

Kolb, Robert W., and James A. Overdahl, eds. 2009. *Financial Derivatives: Pricing and Risk Management*. Hoboken, NJ: John Wiley & Sons.

Kulatilaka, N. 1993. "The Value of Flexibility: The Case of Dual-Fuel Industrial Steam Boiler." *Financial Management* 22:3, 271–280.

Leppart, S. 2005. "Valuation and risk management of physical assets." In V. Kaminski, ed. *Managing Energy Price Risk: The New Challenges and Solutions*, 649–682. London: Risk Books.

Martin, A., D. A. Rogers, and B. J. Simkins. 2004. "Southwest Airlines: The Blended Winglet Project." *Case Research Journal* 24 (Summer/Fall), 23–33.

McCormack, J. M., and G. Sick. 2001. "Valuing PUD Reserves: A Practical Application of Real Option Techniques." *Journal of Applied Corporate Finance* 13:4, 110–115.

Miller, K., and H. G. Waller. 2003. "Scenario, Real Options and Integrated Risk Management." *Long Range Planning* 36: 93–107.

Myers, S. 1977. "Determinants of Corporate Borrowing." *Journal of Financial Economics* 5:2, 147–175.

Pilipovic, D., and J. Wengler. 1999. "Basis for Boptions." *Energy & Power Risk Management* (December/January): 28–29.

Price, J. P. 1997. "What's a Power Plant Worth?" *Public Utilities Fortnightly*, September 15, 38–41.

Ronn, E. I. 2005a. "Valuation of oil fields as optimal exercise of the extraction option." In V. Kaminski, ed. *Managing Energy Price Risk: The New Challenges and Solutions*, 609–630. London: Risk Books.

Ronn, E. I., ed. 2005b. *Real Options and Energy Management: Using Options Methodology to Enhance Capital Budgeting Decisions*. London: Risk Books.

Smit, H., and L. Ankum. 1993. "A Real Options and Game-Theoretic Approach to Corporate Investment Strategy under Competition," *Financial Management*, (Autumn): 22:3, 241–250.

Thompson, M., M. Davison, and H. Rasmussen. 2007. "Natural Gas Storage Valuation and Optimization: A Real Options Application." Working paper, University of Western Ontario.

Titman, S., and J. D. Martin. 2008. *Valuation: The Art & Science of Corporate Investment Decisions*. Boston: Pearson Education.

Triantis, A. J. 2000. "Real Options and Corporate Risk Management." *Journal of Applied Corporate Finance* 13:2, 64–73.

Triantis, A. J., and A. Borison. 2001. "Real Options: State of the Practice." *Journal of Applied Corporate Finance* 14:2, 8–24.

Trigeorgis, L. 1993a. "The Nature of Option Interactions and the Valuation of Investments with Multiple Real Options." *Journal of Financial and Quantitative Analysis* 28:1, 1–20.

Trigeorgis, L. 1993b. "Real Options and Interactions with Financial Flexibility." *Financial Management* 22:3, 202–224.

ABOUT THE CONTRIBUTORS

Betty J. Simkins, PhD, is the Williams Companies Professor of Business and a Professor of Finance in the Department of Finance at Oklahoma State University's (OSU) Spears School of Business, where she teaches energy finance, corporate finance, and enterprise risk management, among other courses. Dr. Simkins received her PhD from Case Western Reserve University (CWRU), her MBA from OSU, and her BS in chemical engineering from the University of Arkansas. She has more than 50 publications in academic finance journals and book chapters and has

won awards for her research, most recently in risk management. In addition, Betty has won several teaching awards including the Regents Distinguished Teaching Award. She has taught Energy Finance, a course she created, at both the undergraduate and graduate levels for over 12 years and teaches executive education courses on energy finance for companies around the world. She is also very active in the finance profession and currently serves on the Board of Directors for the Financial Management Association, as co-editor of the *Journal of Applied Finance*, as past president of the Eastern Finance Association, and on the editorial boards of several prestigious finance journals. Prior to academia, she worked in the energy industry for Williams Companies and Conoco (now ConocoPhillips). In addition to being co-editor of this book, in 2010 she co-edited *Enterprise Risk Management: Insights and Analysis on Today's Leading Research and Best Practices*, also published by John Wiley & Sons.

Kris Kemper is an assistant professor at University of Wisconsin—Eau Claire. He received his both his BBA in finance and his MBA from the University of Central Oklahoma and his PhD from Oklahoma State University. Prior to attending Oklahoma State University, Kemper worked for five years in the financial services industry and also spent four years in the United States Air Force. His current research interests include mutual funds, credit ratings, and capital structure.

International Petroleum Fiscal System Design and Analysis

DAVID JOHNSTON
Partner and Managing Director, Daniel Johnston & Co. Inc.

INTRODUCTION

The international petroleum industry is characterized by (1) significantly greater geopotential than the supermature U.S. basins, (2) a diversity of petroleum fiscal/contractual systems, and (3) diverse means by which governments allocate license rights to international oil companies (IOCs). The larger field-size distribution overseas is attractive, but many international oil companies are hesitant to confront strange and complex fiscal systems and governmental relationships.

GEOPOTENTIAL AROUND THE WORLD

By any measure the U.S. basins that are open (unlike those offshore along the East Coast, Florida, and California as well as much of the Alaskan Arctic) are beyond comparison with the rest of the world in terms of exploration and development maturity. There have been almost 4 million wells drilled in the United States and in all of the rest of the world less than a million wells have been drilled. By world standards most of the United States is supermature and field-size distributions overseas are orders of magnitude greater than much of what is available domestically. For example, average discovery size worldwide the past 10 years or so has been around 100 MMBOE—if the giant discoveries are ignored, the average drops to 50 MMBOE. Test rates per well in the various international discoveries worldwide average around 4,000 to 5,000 BOPD for oil discoveries and 20–30 MMCFD for gas discoveries.[1]

Licenses are also larger overseas; average block sizes are around 500,000 acres. Frontier blocks are typically on the order of 3–4 million acres or more.[2] Historically there have been some very large licenses granted but generally speaking these numbers are fairly typical.

Costs in the international sector are unsurprisingly higher but with the economy of scale that comes with larger discoveries the cost per barrel is often quite attractive.

Political/commercial risks take on new dimension overseas, especially with such diverse cultural and social differences that exist. Additionally, the ubiquitous

distrust of oil companies in the United States is also found overseas and sometimes magnified by cultural, economic, and religious dynamics.

Petroleum fiscal/contractual systems or regimes around the world have for many years been classified into two main categories.

1. Royalty/tax (R/T, also called concessions or concessionary systems or licenses)
2. Production sharing contracts (PSCs) and risk service agreements (RSAs)

The basis of this classification is legal based on whether or not title to hydrocarbons transfers to the oil company. Unlike the United States and Canada, the law in other countries grants the state title to all hydrocarbons or mineral rights. Within the framework of various agreements between international oil companies (IOCs) and governments, IOCs can sometimes obtain title to at least a portion of the hydrocarbon production.

While these two categories reflect contracts or systems of fundamentally different styles, there is often substantial variation between contracts or systems within a given category. Some systems are considered to be *hybrids*, which have characteristics of both a royalty/tax system and a PSC. For example many PSCs (like those in Indonesia, Nigeria, Malaysia, India, China, and Russia) also have royalties and/or taxes included in their standard agreements.

From a financial point of view the similarities can easily outweigh the differences between these various categories. From an economic or financial perspective the same objectives[3] can be achieved under all systems.

CONCESSIONS OR LICENSES— ROYALTY/TAX SYSTEMS

A concession or license is an agreement granting an IOC or consortium the exclusive right to explore for and produce hydrocarbons within a specific area (license area or block) for a given time period. In exchange for these rights, the IOC may have paid a signature bonus or a license fee to the host government. The host government's compensation will typically include royalty and tax payments if hydrocarbons are produced. This type of system is used for example in the United States, UK, France, Norway, Australia, Russia, New Zealand, Colombia, South Africa, and Argentina. Nearly half of the countries worldwide use a concessionary (or royalty/tax) system. Within this group of countries, there is considerable diversity with regard to various fiscal devices, royalty and tax rates, number of layers of tax and other features such as incentives (e.g., investment allowances and tax credits).

PRODUCTION SHARING CONTRACTS

Productions sharing contracts or agreements (PSCs or PSAs) give an IOC or consortium (known as the contractor) the right to explore for and produce hydrocarbons within the contract area or block for a specified time period—much the same as an R/T license. The IOC assumes all exploration risks and costs in exchange for a share of the oil and or gas produced.

Under this type of system, as with a license, if the IOC's exploration efforts do not yield a commercial discovery, the IOC is not reimbursed by the host

government. However, in the event of commercial discovery, production is split between the parties according to formulas in the PSC that are either statutory (fixed), negotiated, or secured through competitive bidding.

Unlike a license, the host government typically receives a large share of oil and/or gas, which can be commercialized and monetized according to the host government's development programs and economic needs. These agreements were introduced in Indonesia in the mid-1960s and for many years became the fiscal system of choice for many countries. They are now also used in Malaysia, India, Nigeria, Angola, Trinidad, the Central Asian republics of the former Soviet Union (FSU), Algeria, Egypt, Yemen, Syria, Mongolia, China, and many other countries. Slightly over half of the governments with hydrocarbon production worldwide use PSCs.

It was inevitable that the industry would eventually use PSCs in order to define the contractual relationship between IOCs and government. Production sharing had existed for hundreds of years around the world and in the United States. Many farmers in the United States even now work under arrangements similar to a production sharing contract.

RISK SERVICE CONTRACTS

A risk service contract is a type of agreement whereby an IOC performs exploration and/or production services for the host government within a specified area for a fee. At all times the host government maintains ownership of the hydrocarbons produced, and usually the IOC (contractor) does not acquire any rights to oil and or gas, except where a contractor is paid its fee in kind (oil and or gas) or is given a preferential right to purchase production from the host government.

Pure service agreements are rare between an IOC and a foreign government, but some do exist like the Iranian buy-backs, which are very similar to an engineering procurement and construction (EPC) contract. Other countries that use RSAs include Saudi Arabia, the Philippines, and Kuwait. True pure service agreements ordinarily exist between a service company (Schlumberger or Halliburton) and an IOC. They are quite rare between an IOC and a government.

EVOLUTION AND DEVELOPMENT OF THE INDONESIAN PSCs AND RSAs

Indonesia holds a special place in the industry when it comes to international petroleum exploration and fiscal design. In the 1960s and 1970s, Indonesia was at the center of the international exploration industry. At that time, there were many fewer countries granting exploration rights to foreign companies than there are now. Back then, Southeast Asia was one of the most active and established regions in the international oil patch. Indonesia represented nearly half of all Southeast Asian activity in terms of drilling activity, contracts signed, and production. Almost anyone involved in international exploration in the 1970s and early 1980s had some experience with Indonesia and the Indonesian-type contracts.

The early Indonesian PSCs developed in the mid-1960s were relatively simple. The contractor could recover costs out of gross production (usually with some

limit known as a *cost recovery limit*). This was called *cost oil*. After cost recovery and remaining oil (known then as *equity oil* now called *profit oil*) was shared between the state and the contractor. Unrecovered costs would be carried forward and recovered in later periods depending on production rates and prices. Many countries followed Indonesia's lead but modified their systems to include royalties and income taxes to be paid directly. Indonesia also began including direct taxes in the mid 1970s.

COMPARATIVE ANALYSIS (SERVICE AGREEMENTS—R/T SYSTEMS—PSCs)

From a mechanical point of view there are practically no differences between the various systems. The hierarchy of arithmetic such as (1) generation of production and revenue; followed by (2) royalty or royalty equivalent elements; followed by (3) cost recovery, tax deductions, or reimbursement and so on; and (4) profits-based mechanisms such as profit-oil sharing and/or taxes are for all practical purposes found in almost all systems.

The distinguishing characteristic of each is *where*, *when*, and *if* ownership of the hydrocarbons transfers to the oil company. Numerous variations and twists are found under *both* the royalty/tax (*concessionary*) systems and the *contractual*-based themes (PSCs and RSAs). The taxonomy of petroleum fiscal systems is outlined in Exhibit 12.1.

Key Differences—Transfer of Title of Hydrocarbons

The philosophical differences between the two main families (PSCs and R/Ts) is evident in the contract language and management structure found. With PSCs and RSAs the term *contractor* is used to represent the IOC or consortium of IOCs. The term is used in the same context as the terms *tenant* or *sharecropper*. Key differences include the following:

- With royalty/tax systems title transfers at the wellhead
- The IOC takes title to gross production less royalty oil
- With PSCs title transfers at the export point or *fiscalization point*
- The IOC takes title to cost oil and profit oil
- With Service Agreements title does not transfer

The legal classification of petroleum fiscal regimes is the most common, although secondary to the philosophical directive. Depending upon a nation's philosophical attitude toward their mineral resources, the legal aspects follow.

NUMEROUS SIMILARITIES AMONG FISCAL SYSTEMS

While the differences between the various fiscal/contractual arrangements are extremely important, they become even more important when considering what

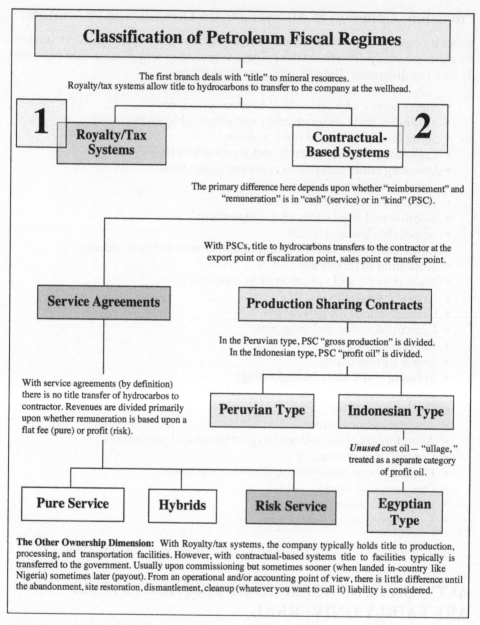

Classification of Petroleum Fiscal Regimes

The first branch deals with "title" to mineral resources.
Royalty/tax systems allow title to hydrocarbons to transfer to the company at the wellhead.

1   **Royalty/Tax Systems**   **Contractual-Based Systems**   **2**

The primary difference here depends upon whether "reimbursement" and
"remuneration" is in "cash" (service) or in "kind" (PSC).

With PSCs, title to hydrocarbons transfers to the contractor at the
export point or fiscalization point, sales point or transfer point.

Service Agreements   **Production Sharing Contracts**

In the Peruvian type, PSC "gross production" is divided.
In the Indonesian type, PSC "profit oil" is divided.

With service agreements (by definition)
there is no title transfer of hydrocarbos to
contractor. Revenues are divided primarily
upon whether remuneration is based upon a
flat fee (pure) or profit (risk).

Peruvian Type   **Indonesian Type**

Unused cost oil— "ullage,"
treated as a separate category
of profit oil.

Pure Service   **Hybrids**   **Risk Service**   **Egyptian Type**

The Other Ownership Dimension: With Royalty/tax systems, the company typically holds title to production, processing, and transportation facilities. However, with contractual-based systems title to facilities typically is transferred to the government. Usually upon commissioning but sometimes sooner (when landed in-country like Nigeria) sometimes later (payout). From an operational and/or accounting point of view, there is little difference until the abandonment, site restoration, dismantlement, cleanup (whatever you want to call it) liability is considered.

Exhibit 12.1   Legal Classification of Petroleum Fiscal Systems

constitutes a modern petroleum agreement between an IOC and a host government. For all practical purposes, it does not matter whether the agreement is a PSC, RSA, or R/T system; as a practical business matter the following issues must be addressed either in the agreement itself or in the petroleum and/or tax laws and regulations of the country.

Provisions Common to All Systems (in One Fashion or Another)

When it comes to treatment of these various elements, the approaches can be similar although many differences exist. There is no reason why there would necessarily be a big difference. The following are similarities:

- Initial license area and relinquishment provisions
- Minimum work program and expenditure obligation
- Term, termination, and force majeure
- Currency exchange controls and repatriation of proceeds
- Investing entity and parent company guarantees
- Fiscal incentives and disincentives
- Health, safety, and environment
- Stability and legal status of the agreement
- Applicable law and forum
- Rules and procedure regarding establishment of commerciality
- Allocation of production
- Measurement and valuation of hydrocarbons
- Non-arms-length sales
- Considerations for natural gas
- Communications and language
- Reports and studies
- Use of infrastructure
- Training and transfer of technology
- Importation and immigration considerations
- Confidentiality
- Assignment of interests
- Abandonment/site restoration provisions and procedures
- Control of operations
- Hydrocarbons ownership and ownership transfer
- Ownership of assets
- Dispute resolution mechanisms
- Export and sale of production

Key distinctions among the various systems are provided in Exhibit 12.2.

ACCOUNTING ASPECTS OF FISCAL SYSTEMS ARE FAIRLY UNIVERSAL

Basic accounting principles are virtually universal across the full range of petroleum fiscal systems. Almost all systems have at least one profits-based mechanism, which could include such things as profit oil sharing as well as special petroleum taxes and/or corporate income taxes. Profit-based mechanisms like these require measurement and accounting for both revenues and/or production as well as the costs associated with exploration, development and operations.

The budget process, procurement practices and regulations, authorization-for-expenditures, reporting requirements, auditing, and the approvals process can be similar from one system to another. Also while there are numerous conventions for

Exhibit 12.2   Fiscal System Comparison

	R/T Systems	PSCs	RSAs
Type of projects	*All types:* Exploration Development EOR	*All types:* Exploration Development EOR	All types but often non-exploration
Ownership of facilities	International oil company	Government NOC	Government NOC
Production facilities title transfer	No transfer	"When landed" or upon commissioning	"When landed" or upon commissioning
IOC ownership of hydrocarbons (lifting entitlement)	Gross production less royalty oil	Cost oil + profit oil	None (may have preferential right to purchase)
Repatriation of service company equipment	Yes	Yes	Yes
IOC lifting entitlement (%)	Typically around 90%	Usually from 50 to 60%	None (by definition)
Hydrocarbon title transfer	At the wellhead	Delivery point Fiscalization point or export point	None
Financial obligation	Contractor 100%	Contractor 100%	Contractor 100%
Government participation	Yes (not common)	Yes (common)	Yes (very common)
Cost recovery limit	No	Usually	Sometimes
Government control	Low typically	High	High
IOC control	High	Low to moderate	Low

capitalizing costs (amortization and/or depreciation) such as straight-line, unit-of-production, and declining-balance, for example, these are found in many systems.

DIVISION OF REVENUES AND PROFITS

The division of profits is a key aspect of any contract. This is determined prior to contract signing like so many elements either through (1) competitive bidding, (2) negotiations, or (3) through statutes (by law: i.e., "fixed terms"). In fact, it is usually the first thing agreed upon. While much of the discussion of the division of profits focuses on "economic" profits (gross revenues less costs associated with obtaining those revenues), timing is everything.

There are four main means by which governments get a piece of the pie (*take*) or as it is commonly called *rent*:[4]

1. Signature bonuses
2. Royalties

3. Profits-based elements (profit oil split and/or taxes)
4. Government participation

The general view is that unless a government is desperately in need of up-front cash it is better off in the long run obtaining its share of production or revenues (or rent) with back-end-loaded elements like profit oil, taxes, or government participation. While the more regressive elements (bonuses and royalties) will ensure that some of the government's take comes sooner (rather than later), the government is likely to end up with less if the system is too heavily front-end loaded (i.e., regressive).

SIGNATURE BONUSES

Nearly half of all countries with hydrocarbon fiscal systems use signature bonuses as part of their system. In the United States, signature bonus bidding is the means by which the federal government allocates licenses. Signature bonuses usually contribute a small part of the overall government take (or rent). For example, in the cash flow model in Exhibit 12.3 a $40 million bonus would amount to just half of 1 percent of gross revenues.

In the following cash flow model and flow diagrams, bonuses are not included. There are many other kinds of bonuses such as those triggered by a discovery, or attainment of commercial status, production startup, commissioning of facilities, or achievement of certain production thresholds such as accumulated production or specified production rates. These other bonuses are also usually relatively insignificant but unlike a signature bonus, which constitutes part of the risk capital, the other bonuses are part of the reward side of the equation.

Signature bonuses can range from as little as $20,000 to over $1 billion. It is difficult to estimate an average, but there are some trends. For example, where signature bonus bidding is the sole criteria for license allocation, bonuses can often be quite large. When bonuses are not the only bid parameter, they are usually smaller: that is, less than $5 MM. There are many famous bonuses such as the $300 MM bonuses each for the first three ultra-deepwater licenses (known as Blocks 31, 32, and 33) in Angola. All other bonuses are typically contingent upon some measure of success, and therefore oil companies usually only hope they will be able to pay these bonuses. Signature bonuses, because they are part of the risk capital, are not popular.

GOVERNMENT PARTICIPATION

One unique element found outside of North America is what is known as government participation (or *government carry* or *government risk-free carry*). Nearly half of the governments worldwide use this option as part of their system. Typical government participation is where a national oil company (NOC) or the equivalent has the right and/or option to take up a working interest in a discovery if it is deemed to be *commercial*. It is not a popular thing with IOCs, but it is a fact of life. In about half of these arrangements, the NOC will reimburse its share of *past costs* at the point at which it *backs-in*. Past costs include all costs incurred from the *effective date* of the agreement to the *commerciality date*. The terms and conditions under which

the NOC can back-in and take up a working interest are usually governed by a *commerciality clause* of a PSC. The other half of the countries that have this option do not reimburse past costs, but they do allow these costs to be cost recovered and/or tax deducted (usually). Typically from the moment the NOC backs-in (at the commerciality point) it pays-its-way or is said to be *heads up* or *straight up* just like any other working interest holder (except that it represents the host government).

Government participation is one of the more dramatic elements of a fiscal system when it comes to such issues as (1) control and (2) technology transfer. Being a working interest partner usually means that the NOC (if that is the participating entity) has better access to data and information and the NOC personnel can attend operating committee meetings and technical committee meetings. It is in meetings like this where significant insight can be gained into IOC decision making as well as industry standards and practices. Also, NOC personnel can gain experience. This can be especially powerful for new governments with little operational capacity or experience in the oil industry.

ROYALTIES AND PROFITS-BASED MECHANISMS

The other two (of the four) main means by which governments get a piece of the pie include royalties and profits-based elements. These are the heart and soul of most arrangements between IOCs and host governments and constitute around 90 percent of the rent received by host governments around the world. The following discussion as well as the detailed economic model and flow diagram (Exhibits 12.3 and 12.4) illustrate where these elements fit in the typical hierarchy of operations that exist when hydrocarbons are sold, revenues are generated, and the pie is divided. The following discussion, flow diagram, and cash flow model are all based on the following assumptions:

Basic Assumptions

Field Size: 100 MMBBLS
Oil Price: $80/BBL
Costs:[5] 20% of Gross Revenues

In order to illustrate how similar the basic systems can be, this discussion compares a PSC with an R/T system, which are similar except for a few things: terminology and one mechanical aspect (the cost recovery limit).

Fiscal System Analysis

PSC Terminology	R/T Terminology
Royalty (10%)	Royalty (10%)
Cost Recovery Limit 60%	No Limit to Tax Deductions
Gvt. Share of P/O (50%)	First Tax (50%)
Income Tax (30%)	Second Layer of Tax (30%)

First—Gross Revenues (or Gross Production)

Fortunately the determination of gross production is relatively easy to measure and/or monitor. Gross revenues, on the other hand can be a bit more daunting

if hydrocarbons are not sold in an arm's-length transaction. In the event of non-arm's-length sales, many PSCs or R/T systems require an artificial measure of price based on a *basket* or *cocktail* of known *marker crudes* adjusted for crude quality.

Second—Royalty

In the language of the industry royalties come right off the top. Royalty determination can be a bit more complicated because often hydrocarbons are typically not sold at the wellhead. Instead they are often sold downstream from the wellhead. So, many governments will allow the contractor (or IOC) to deduct transportation costs associated with getting the hydrocarbons from the point of valuation for royalty determination purposes (the wellhead) to the point of sale. If the government allows the full range of deductions associated with the transportation function, they will consist of three basic components:

1. Capital costs associated with the transportation function (depreciated)
2. Operating costs
3. Cost of capital

Note: Neither the flow diagram nor the economic model (see Exhibits 12.3 and 12.4) have assumed any *netbacking* or deductions for royalty determination purposes.

Third—Cost Recovery and/or Deductions

After royalty payments the IOC is allowed to *recover costs* or take tax deductions. These costs consists of two components:

1. Capital costs (depreciated)
2. Operating costs

It is typically this aspect of a petroleum agreement that will undergo scrutiny by government auditors to ensure that only legitimate costs are included. Almost all systems have specific costs that will not be allowed for cost recovery or allowed as deductions.

In this example, it is assumed that costs as a percentage of gross revenues are 20 percent. A relatively typical percentage for projects during the 1980s and 1990s worldwide was from 30 to 40 percent. For example with an oil price of $20.00/BBL, 30 percent comes to $6.00/BBL, which would likely consist of capital costs on the order of $3.00/BBL and operating costs of around $3.00/BBL. For most conventional developments during these decades, operating costs and capital costs were often about equal (full cycle). Now with higher oil prices, costs have increased significantly. Assuming that costs are equal to 20 percent of gross revenues with $80/BBL crude (in these examples) equates to roughly $8.00/BBL each for Capex and Opex ($16.00/BBL total).

The contractor under a PSC would be reimbursed at this stage (after royalty) with oil called *cost oil*. The contractor would expect to receive cost oil during the life of the contract. During the early years of production, capital costs would represent most of the cost oil. Operating costs would be recovered throughout the life of the

contract. The same is true of an R/T system, but instead of cost recovery or cost oil it would be called *deductions*.

The one truly significant difference between R/T systems and PSCs (mechanically speaking) is that PSCs typically have a cost recovery *limit* (also called *cost recovery ceiling, cost stop, capped cost recovery rate,* and *cost cap*). In the example, PSC cost recovery is limited to 60 percent of gross revenues (i.e., a cost recovery limit of 60 percent). If operating costs and depreciation amount to more than this in any given accounting period, the balance is carried forward and recovered later just like a tax loss carry forward (TLCF). It simply means there is a limit to the amount of deductions that can be taken in any given accounting period for the purpose of determining the profit oil split. PSCs typically allow virtually unlimited carry forward (C/F). From a mechanical point of view, the cost recovery *limit* is the only difference between R/T systems and PSCs.

Note: Many PSCs (nearly half) do not require depreciation for cost recovery purposes. The other half of the world's PSCs do require depreciation. However, almost all PSCs require depreciation for tax calculation purposes.

Fourth—Profit Oil Split or First Layer of Tax

Revenues remaining after royalty and cost recovery are referred to as *profit oil* or profit gas. The analogue in a concessionary system would be taxable income.

In this example, the contractor's *share* of profit oil is 50 percent. This could easily be a service agreement where the contractor would receive a 50 percent share of *revenues* at this stage. Like cost oil, profit oil is denominated in terms of *barrels* and will thus constitute part of each party's *entitlement*. The contractor's entitlement will typically consist of two components: cost oil and profit oil. The government's entitlement will consist of royalty oil and profit oil. Taxes typically do not affect lifting entitlement; they are not based on barrels—they are paid in cash.

Usually it is this aspect of a system that is governed by a sliding scale such as:

> Production-based sliding scales
>> Based upon average daily rates of production
>> Based upon accumulated production
> Payout-based sliding scales *R factors*
> Internal-rate-of-return (ROR)-based sliding scales

These sliding scales are designed to provide the host government a greater share of profits for larger and/or more profitable fields. The example systems used in this paper do not include a sliding scale. Approximately 80 percent of the systems worldwide have some form of sliding scale governing the profits-based rent extraction mechanisms such as profit oil split or special petroleum taxes.

Fifth—Corporate Income Taxes

The tax rate of 30 percent in the flow diagram appears to apply to the profit oil. It is acceptable to do this when thinking in terms of full-cycle economics. On average over the life of a field, the accounting profits subject to ordinary taxes will be equal to the company share of profit oil. However, the profit oil ordinarily does

not constitute the tax base unless it is defined as such, as in the Russian PSCs. In any given accounting period, a company will receive a share of profit oil if there is a cost recovery limit, but the company may not necessarily be in a tax paying position. This is important when considering the royalty effect of the cost recovery limit. (Discussed later under "Effective Royalty Rate.")

There are quite a few PSCs that have the taxes paid for and on behalf of the contractor out of the national oil company's share of profit oil. These are known as *taxes in lieu*. The Egyptian-type PSCs and Philippine RSAs are characterized by this. Some analysts believe that having taxes in lieu offers a more stable agreement because if taxes change it only affects the NOC.

CONTRACTOR AND GOVERNMENT CASH FLOW

Almost all fiscal arrangements (R/T, PSC, or RSA) allow the IOC a means of recovering costs (reimbursement) and receiving a share of profits (remuneration). In the examples used here, the expected capital and operating costs (20% of gross revenues or production) are *recovered* by the contractor once revenue is generated. In addition, the contractor would receive remuneration in the form of after-tax profit oil amounting to 24.5 percent of revenues (or production). Total cash flow generated by the entire project comes to 80 percent of gross revenues (gross revenues less costs: 100% – 20%).

The model shown in Exhibit 12.3 projects government and contractor cash flows, discounted and undiscounted.

For comparison, the flow diagram in Exhibit 12.4 also shows the distribution of production and/or revenues over the life of the project or license. It also depicts the 100 MMBBL scenario found in the "Typical Fiscal System" cash flow in Exhibit 12.3. It honors the accounting operations (arithmetic) that would be expected in any given accounting period, yet this is an analysis of the distribution of all revenues; i.e., full cycle. The flow diagram treats all production or revenues as if they were all generated in a single accounting period. This kind of analysis is a bit abstract, but for analytical purposes it is useful. Every number on a flow diagram like that found in Exhibit 12.4 can represent numbers found in a detailed economic model like Exhibit 12.3.

In the flow diagram and in the economic model, costs as a percentage (%) of gross revenues equals 20 percent. The diagram honors the hierarchy of arithmetic or distribution of production/funds that would be expected in any given accounting period. Each step in the process is discussed in Exhibit 12.4.

GOVERNMENT TAKE

The division of profits is one of the most important and central aspects of any agreement. This may be particularly true of the capital-intensive petroleum exploration business.

Both Exhibit 12.3, the economic model, as well as the back-of-the-envelope example in Exhibit 12.4 show total economic profits or cash flow (which some refer to as *rent*) amount to 80 percent of production (or revenues) (100% revenues – 20% costs). The contractor share of economic profits amounts to 24.5 percent of revenues. Contractor take is 30.6 percent (24.5%/80%). In addition to recovering its

Exhibit 12.3 Typical Fiscal System—Cash Flow Projection—$80.00/BBL 100 MMBBL Field

Year	Annual Oil Production (MBBLS) A	Oil Price ($/BBL) B	Gross Revenues ($M) C	Royalty 10% ($M) D	Net Revenue ($M) E	Capital Costs ($M) F	Opex ($M) G	Depreciation ($M) H	C/R C/F ($M) I	Cost Recovery ($M) J
1	—	$80.00	—	—	—	50,000	—	—	—	—
2	—	$80.00	—	—	—	175,000	—	—	—	—
3	—	$80.00	—	—	—	275,000	—	—	—	—
4	1,172	$80.00	93,760	9,376	84,384	200,000	33,457	140,000	—	56,256
5	11,750	$80.00	940,000	94,000	846,000	125,000	64,663	165,000	677,201	564,000
6	10,693	$80.00	855,440	85,544	769,896	—	61,544	165,000	302,864	364,408
7	9,730	$80.00	778,400	77,840	700,560	—	58,704	165,000	—	58,704
8	8,854	$80.00	708,320	70,832	637,488	—	56,119	165,000	—	56,119
9	8,058	$80.00	644,640	64,464	580,176	—	53,771	25,000	—	53,771
10	7,332	$80.00	586,560	58,656	527,904	—	51,629	—	—	51,629
11	6,672	$80.00	533,760	53,376	480,384	—	49,682	—	—	49,682
12	6,072	$80.00	485,760	48,576	437,184	—	47,912	—	—	47,912
13	5,525	$80.00	442,000	44,200	397,800	—	46,299	—	—	46,299
14	5,028	$80.00	402,240	40,224	362,016	—	44,833	—	—	44,833
15	4,576	$80.00	366,080	36,608	329,472	—	43,499	—	—	43,499
16	4,164	$80.00	333,120	33,312	299,808	—	42,284	—	—	42,284
17	3,789	$80.00	303,120	30,312	272,808	—	41,178	—	—	41,178
18	3,447	$80.00	275,760	27,576	248,184	—	40,169	—	—	40,169
19	3,138	$80.00	251,040	25,104	225,936	—	39,257	—	—	39,257
	100,000		8,000,000	800,000	7,200,000	825,000	775,000	825,000		1,600,000

(Continued)

281

Exhibit 12.3 (Continued)

Yr	Total Profit Oil ($M) K	Gvt. Share 50% ($M) L	IOC Share 50% ($M) M	Tax Loss C/F ($M) O	Taxable Income ($M) P	Income Tax 30% ($M) Q	Contractor Cash Flow ($M) Undiscounted R	12.5% DCF S	Government Cash Flow ($M) Undiscounted T	12.5% DCF U
1	—	—	—	—	—	—	(50,000)	(47,140)	—	—
2	—	—	—	—	—	—	(175,000)	(146,659)	—	—
3	—	—	—	—	—	—	(275,000)	(204,857)	—	—
4	28,128	14,064	14,064	103,137	(103,137)	—	(163,137)	(108,024)	23,440	15,521
5	282,000	141,000	141,000	—	372,200	111,660	403,677	237,601	346,660	204,041
6	405,488	202,744	202,744	—	340,608	102,182	403,425	211,069	390,470	204,291
7	641,857	320,928	320,928	—	155,928	46,778	274,150	127,496	445,547	207,206
8	581,369	290,684	290,684	—	125,684	37,705	252,979	104,578	399,222	165,033
9	526,405	263,202	263,202	—	238,202	71,461	191,742	70,456	399,127	146,661
10	476,275	238,137	238,137	—	238,137	71,441	166,696	54,447	368,234	120,275
11	430,702	215,351	215,351	—	215,351	64,605	150,746	43,767	333,332	96,778
12	389,272	194,636	194,636	—	194,636	58,391	136,245	35,161	301,603	77,836
13	351,501	175,751	175,751	—	175,751	52,725	123,025	28,222	272,676	62,552
14	317,183	158,592	158,592	—	158,592	47,578	111,014	22,637	246,393	50,242

	A	C						T	U
15	285,973	142,986	142,986		100,090	42,896	18,142	222,490	40,327
16	257,524	128,762	128,762		90,133	38,629	14,522	200,703	32,336
17	231,630	115,815	115,815		81,071	34,745	11,610	180,872	25,903
18	208,015	104,008	104,008		72,805	31,202	9,268	162,786	20,723
19	186,679	93,339	93,339		65,338	28,002	7,393	146,445	16,571
	5,600,000	2,800,000	2,696,863	103,137	1,960,000	840,000	489,690	4,440,000	1,486,296

A) Production profile thousands (M) barrels/year
B) Crude price ($/BBL)
C) Gross revenues thousands of dollars ($M)
D) Royalty 10% = (C*.10)
E) Net revenues = (C–D)
F) Capital costs
G) Operating costs (expensed)
H) Depreciation of capital costs (5-year SLD)
I) Cost recovery C/F (if G+H+I > 60% of C)
J) Cost recovery = (G+H+I) up to 60% of C
K) Total profit oil = (C–D–J)
L) Government share P/O 50% = (K * .50)
M) Contractor share P/O 50% = (K–L)
O) TLCF (See Column P)
P) Taxable income = (C–D–G–H–L–O)
Q) Income tax (30%) = [if P > 0, P*.30]
R) Company cash flow = (E–F–G–L–Q)
S) Company cash flow discounted at 12.5%
T) Government cash flow = (D+L+Q)
U) Government cash flow discounted at 12.5%

Exhibit 12.4   Division of Revenues/Production

		Accounting Hierarchy (Full-cycle)	
		PSC Terminology	R/T Terminology
A	100%	Gross production	Gross production
B	−10	Royalty (10%)	Royalty (10%)
C	90	Net production	Net revenues
D	−20	Cost recovery*	Tax deductions
E	70	Profit oil (P/O)	Taxable income
F	−35	Gvt. share of P/O (50%)	First tax (50%)
G	35	IOC share of P/O (50%)	After-tax income
H	−10.5	Income tax (30%)	Second layer of tax (30%)
J	24.5	Contractor (IOC) cash flow	Company (IOC) cash flow
	69.4%	Government take [(B + F + H)/(A − D)]	
	30.6%	Company take [J/(A−D)]	
	80%	Total Cash Flow (A−D) (shared 70.4/30.6% between Gvt. and IOC)	

*It is assumed that costs (Capex and Opex full cycle) equal 20% of gross production or gross revenues.

costs, the company receives another 24.5 percent of gross revenues. Therefore, the contractor's share of gross revenues (or production) is equal to 44.5 percent (20% + 24.5%).

Government take is 70.4 percent [(10% + 35% + 10.5)/80%]. The Exhibit 12.3 summary essentially represents full-cycle economics but also honors the hierarchy of accounting operations that would be expected in a single accounting period. Even though none of the rent extraction mechanisms (royalty, profit oil split, and tax) are actually based on true economic profits, the government take statistic represents the effective tax rate of this system—as if it had a single levy based on true economic profits. This then provides the best means of comparing one system with another, and the government take statistics are widely used. However, the statistic does have weaknesses.[6] Government take can range from as low as 30 percent or so to over 90 percent as illustrated in Exhibit 12.5. Furthermore, the market for acreage and projects is very dynamic with considerable change taking place these days (also depicted in Exhibit 12.5).

EFFECTIVE ROYALTY RATE

While the government take statistic demonstrates how much the government may receive in a project over the life of the license or contract, the effective royalty rate (ERR) provides insight into how and when the government receipts will be received. It is also an excellent measure of how front-end loaded a system is. The ERR statistic represents the minimum share of gross revenues or production a government will receive in any given accounting period for a given project and does not normally include the national oil company (NOC) or oil minister's working interest share of production (if there is one) although for some purposes including this aspect provides useful perspective. The ERR is an important index that adds dimension to the take statistics—it is an important companion statistic.

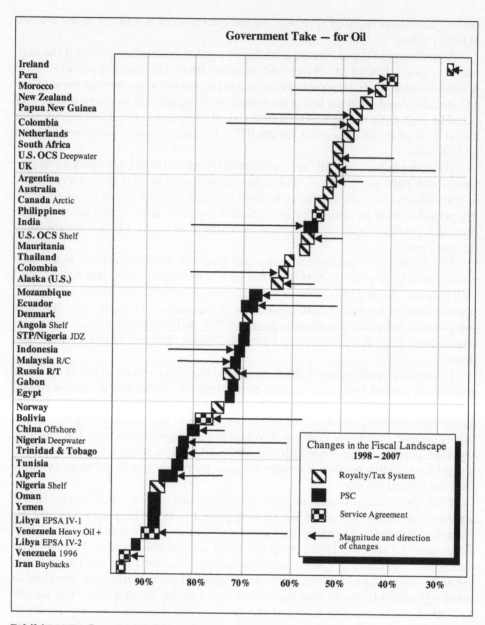

Exhibit 12.5 Government Take

The ERR captures the effect of royalties and/or a cost recovery limit (in combination with the profit oil split) on the distribution of revenue (or production) especially during the early years of production—the capital cost recovery phase.

The world average guaranteed share of revenues (ERR) in any accounting period for a government is around 20 percent (see Johnston 1997). For royalty/tax systems. It is less, around 10 percent or so. and for PSCs it is closer to 30 percent.

Some guaranteed share of revenues for the government is actually in the interest of both parties.

A government could receive nothing in a given accounting period if the contract or system has no royalty or cost recovery limit. This can happen even with profitable fields during the early years of production when substantial exploration and development costs are being recovered—the capital cost recovery phase. This could be politically dangerous for a national oil company, and if it is dangerous for the NOC, it could be dangerous for the IOC—the parties can be fairly well aligned on this issue.

The complement of ERR, access to gross revenues (AGR), provides an important oil company perspective. AGR is the maximum share of revenues a company or consortium can receive relative to their working interest in any given accounting period. It may be limited by government royalties, and/or cost recovery limits and a profit oil split. It is a direct measure of how quickly a company may recover costs.

In a royalty/tax system without a cost recovery limit, the royalty is the only government guarantee. In that case, the ERR *is* the royalty rate, and AGR is limited only by the royalty. In most royalty/tax systems in any given accounting period, there is no limit to the amount of deductions a company may take and companies can be in a non-taxable position. The deductions can create a situation where there is no taxable income. However, this is also true of PSCs with direct taxes.

PSCs with a cost recovery limit guarantee the NOC a share of profit oil every accounting period because a certain percentage of production is always forced through the profit oil split. Thus both royalties and cost recovery limits guarantee the government a share of production or revenues regardless of whether or not true economic profits are generated. While the average royalty with PSCs is only around 5 percent, the average ERR is closer to 30 percent, so the cost recovery limit is significant in this respect. It creates a guarantee nearly five times more dynamic than the typical royalty.

ERR/AGR calculations require a simple assumption—that expenditures and/or deductions in a given accounting period (relative to gross revenues) are virtually unlimited. Therefore cost recovery is at its maximum (*saturation*), and deductions for tax calculation purposes yield zero taxable income. This assumption allows the limits of the system to be tested. Situations like this can occur in the early stages of production, with most fields but particularly with marginal or submarginal fields. It can also occur at the end of the life of a field. The analytical object of the exercise is to test the limits of the system. It is very practical, too, because even for large economically healthy developments the majority of capital costs are incurred for drilling, production, and transportation facilities before production even begins. Therefore, in the early accounting periods when the IOC is anxious to recoup its exploration and development costs, the limits of the system will be experienced—deductions can by far outweigh revenues.

In the example of ERR (Exhibit 12.6), the government is guaranteed a minimum of 25 percent, even though the royalty is only 10 percent. This is because the combination of the cost recovery limit and the profit oil split guarantees the government

Exhibit 12.6 Effective Royalty Rate (ERR) Calculation

		Government Share of Revenues at Saturation (Single Accounting Period)	
		PSC Terminology	**R/T Terminology**
A	100%	Gross production	Gross production
B	−10	Royalty (10%)	Royalty (10%)
C	90	Net production	Net revenues
D	−60	Cost recovery*	
E	30	Profit oil (P/O)	
F	−15	Government 50% Share P/O	
ERR		25% (B + F)	10% (B)

*It is assumed that costs (Capex and Opex "single accounting period") equal 200% of gross production or gross revenues. This happens in early years of production when accumulated past costs (for cost recovery or tax deduction purposes) by far outweigh gross revenues. Early years therefore are often characterized by large cost recovery carry-forwards and/or tax loss carry forwards (TLCFs), and the IOC is in a no-tax-paying position in these early accounting periods.

an additional 15 percent above and beyond the 10 percent royalty. With sufficient deductions (consistent with the key assumption underlying the ERR calculation), the company would pay no tax in that accounting period.

KEEPING COSTS DOWN—THE SAVINGS INDEX

Governments have a keen interest in seeing costs kept as low as possible, but so do IOCs. In this area, there is clear alignment of interests, although there are varying degrees of alignment. And, it can be measured. One must simply ask:

"If costs are reduced by one dollar, who benefits and by how much?"

There are two profits-based fiscal elements in the example "Typical PSC" used here. These elements are the only ones that influence the contractor incentive to keep costs down. If the company saves a dollar, there will be one dollar less cost oil and an extra dollar of profit oil.

The government share of this extra dollar of profit oil is 50 percent. This leaves the company with 50 percent of the profit oil but with a tax rate of 30 percent the contractor will ultimately end up with only 35 percent of the savings. The savings index then is 35 percent or 35¢ on the dollar. This statistic represents, to a large extent, the contractor's incentive to keep costs down. Thus the IOC benefits from keeping costs down and so does the government. From a present value point of view, the IOC benefit is often greater than the undiscounted savings index (of 35 percent in this case) would indicate. Any time there are profits-based mechanisms in a fiscal system, there will likely be an incentive to keep costs down. This index (35¢) is fairly typical—close to world average. It constitutes mathematical proof that with a structure like this (which is so common) there is a mutual incentive to keep costs down, and it is the same for either a PSC or an R/T system. It depends on the profits-based levies, as shown in Exhibit 12.7.

Exhibit 12.7   Effect of Saving a Dollar

		Resulting Division of Revenues (Single Accounting Period or Full Cycle)	
		PSC Terminology	**R/T Terminology**
D	$1.00	Savings	Savings
E	$1.00	Increased P/O	More taxable income
F	−.50	Gvt. Share of P/O (50%)	First Layer of Tax (50%)
G	.50	IOC Profit Oil (P/O)	IOC After-Tax Income
H	−.15	Income Tax (30%)	Second Layer of Tax (30%)
	.35	IOC Share (D − F − H)	IOC Share (D − F − H)

35% Company Savings Incentive (Index).
35¢ on the dollar saved.

Typically, if a dollar is saved, the IOC will end up with about 30 to 40 cents on the dollar. It may not sound like much, but it works. In Indonesia under the old standard oil PSC, the contractor received only about 15 cents on a dollar saved. This is near one end of the savings incentive spectrum; the other end is upwards of 65 to 75 cents on the dollar (United States, UK, and Ireland, for example).

The term *goldplating* often arises in the context of those countries like Indonesia where the savings index is quite low. However, true goldplating is where a company is encouraged to spend *more* than it otherwise would. The more they spend, the more they make. However, this kind of arrangement is extremely rare. Most systems are not that inefficient.

However, if a company receives only 15 cents on a dollar saved the incentive to save is certainly diminished. Why not have a Rolls-Royce for a company car if it only really costs about 15 cents on the dollar? However, the simple calculation above does not account for time-value of money. When this is taken into account an undiscounted index of say 15 percent may easily increase to 35 percent or so. For development costs, this is common. This test is simple, but it requires discounted cash flow analysis. A field development feasibility study can be tested with an extra $10 million in capital costs to see the impact on IOC discounted cash flow.

Almost all petroleum fiscal systems have profits-based rent extraction mechanisms that create this incentive to keep costs down. This is a huge concern of most governments, and that is understandable. However, the concern is usually overblown and misplaced. Companies rarely have the incentive to spend more than they might otherwise spend. However, there is always the incentive to cheat, and that is a different matter altogether.

Cheating can be found in two general areas: (1) on the revenue side (transfer pricing—selling to an affiliate; i.e., non-arm's-length) or (2) the cost side (pretending to spend more than was actually spent or using non-arm's-length service/supply companies). This is an area where contract language, procurement guidelines and rules, laws, and government auditors play an important role.

LIFTING ENTITLEMENT

As mentioned earlier, the IOC lifting entitlement (the hydrocarbons the IOC *takes title to*) often has an influence on the amount of reserves the IOC will *book*. *Booking barrels* is the common term that refers to the proved reserves a company reports to shareholders that it has found or acquired. These *booked barrels* will then influence the IOC finding costs and *reserve replacement ratio*, which stock analysts follow closely. These metrics influence the IOC stock price, and therefore they are very important, and thus *booking barrels* is a big deal. The general rule is: Companies book barrels according to their (legal) *lifting entitlement*. There are however exceptions to this general rule.

The three main exceptions are: (1) Many companies book barrels under service agreements even though (by definition) they do not take title to hydrocarbons. (2) With Egyptian-type contracts where taxes are paid in lieu, companies gross up their actual entitlement and book the reserves they would have been entitled to lift had they paid taxes directly themselves. With these systems the company's taxes are paid "for and on behalf of the contractor" out of the national oil company (NOC) share of profit oil. Thus they book more barrels than they are legally entitled to lift. (3) In some countries the government will exercise its option to take royalty in cash instead of in kind. Therefore the IOC would lift the government's royalty oil as well and would also likely book these barrels, too. Lifting entitlement for a PSC is calculated in Exhibit 12.8.

The components of IOC entitlement for the example PSC and R/T system are shown in Exhibit 12.8. It gets a bit abstract because the components from a cash flow model are in cash (not barrels). However, if contractor cost oil (in $) and profit oil (in $) are divided by gross revenues ($) the percentage will yield the IOC lifting entitlement as a percentage of gross production (%).

Exhibit 12.8 Lifting Entitlement

		Accounting Hierarchy (Full-cycle)	
		PSC Terminology	**R/T Terminology**
A	100%	Gross production	Gross production
B	−10	Royalty (10%)	Royalty (10%)
C	90	Net production	Net revenues
D	−20	Cost recovery*	
E	70	Profit oil (P/O)	
F	−35	Gvt. share of P/O (50%)	
G	35	IOC share of P/O (50%)	
H	−10.5	Income tax (30%)	
J	24.5	Contractor (IOC) cash flow	
IOC Lifting			
	Entitlement	55% (D + G)	90% (A − B)

*It is assumed that costs (Capex and Opex full cycle) equal 20% of gross production or gross revenues.

ALIGNMENT OF INTERESTS

A critical aspect of most agreements (PSCs, SAs, or R/T systems) is the alignment of the various parties' interests. The incentive to keep costs down (discussed earlier) is one aspect of this important subject. In most international negotiations, there is considerable lack of alignment prior to contract signing. Obviously, both the IOC and the government want to get as large a share of profits as possible (within reason). Furthermore, the government would like to ensure it gets a healthy share of production (or revenues) each and every accounting period (i.e., effective royalty rate). Conversely, IOCs would like to see a low ERR. However, if the contract is efficiently and appropriately crafted there should be substantial alignment or mutuality of interests as soon as the contract is signed. Once a contract is signed, then theoretically the issue of such things as (1) division of profits and (2) effective royalty rate are no longer relevant because they are agreed upon. After the agreement is signed, the natural instincts of an IOC are usually well aligned with the host government.

Once a contract is signed the interests of the parties are usually fairly well aligned:

1. The IOC wants to make a significant discovery as soon as possible.
2. The IOC wants to start production quickly.
3. The IOC wants to maximize profitability.
4. The IOC wants to keep costs as low as possible (within reason). (Keeping safety and maximum efficient production rate in mind.)

These issues are consistent with the interests of host governments and NOCs.

INCREMENTAL PRODUCTION CONTRACTS (IPCs)

Most of the science of fiscal system analysis and design has historically involved exploration agreements. More and more non-exploration projects are entering the international market in various forms. Incremental production contracts include enhanced oil recovery (EOR), improved oil recovery (IOR), *rehabilitation* or redevelopment contracts. They have been around for years but not in large numbers. In 1998 China signed their first such contract with Husky Oil. At that time there were three main regions worldwide where these contracts had been used (or attempted) most: the former Soviet Union (FSU), Indonesia (under the JOB-type contracts),[7] and to a lesser extent in the Eastern Bloc countries. However, in the future there will be more and more of such projects. The focus of Project Kuwait (the long-proposed Operating Service Agreement) is for this kind of project. Typically these agreements can be quite similar to exploration agreements, but often negotiations focus on existing (base or primary) production including an assumed decline rate and treatment of any production beyond the projected declining base production (called incremental production). The incremental production will likely be governed by royalties and taxes or a PSC or the equivalent as discussed above. The August 2011 license round in Mexico was for existing fields; that is, non-exploration.

ALLOCATION AND LICENSE PROMOTION

While most of the acreage in the United States is allocated or awarded on the basis of bonus bidding, this is not the case in most of the rest of the world. Just as there is a wide diversity of systems that exist, the means by which governments allocate acreage (or projects) is also diverse. The two main approaches governments use are bid rounds and negotiated terms.

Bid rounds worldwide have many similarities including the process of gazetting (officially announcing), and marketing the acreage or projects on offer. The big differences are in the bid parameters. The potential bid items are diverse and can consist of a number of elements depending on the country and the license round. The potential bid items include:

- Work program
- Signature bonus
- Royalties
- Profit oil/gas split
- Local content (for goods and services)
- Government participation (carry)
- Tax rate (rare)

With typical bidding situations (also referred to as auctions), there is a further variation depending upon whether or not the government uses a *nomination* system or not. A nomination system is where IOCs earmark particular areas or blocks that they would like to see put up for bid in a bid/license round. In the United States federal offshore prior to 1983, a nomination system was used—called the Track Nomination System (TN). After 1983 the system was changed to what is called Area Wide Leasing, and nominations are not considered. Government agencies involved in license/acreage allocation have numerous issues they must consider.

By the 1990s acreage began to take on more of the characteristics of a commodity because more acreage and projects were available than ever before.[8] Over three times more acreage became available than there was 25 years earlier. The Soviet Union became the former Soviet Union (FSU), and much of Africa and the Eastern Bloc countries opened up. With the natural evolution of more aggressive and specific relinquishment provisions in contracts and licenses around the world, the market for acreage or projects is more dynamic and robust. Countries are competing with more than just their neighbors for capital and technology, and they have become much more sophisticated and aware of what the market can bear. Concerns vary depending on the situation, as summarized in Exhibit 12.9.

FIXED, NEGOTIATED, OR BID TERMS

This issue is of huge concern to many governments, and it affects the IOCs as well. Many governments, through legislation, will *fix* the key fiscal terms (such

Exhibit 12.9   Different Situations—Different Considerations

	Enhanced Oil Recovery	Development Projects	Exploration Acreage	Frontier Acreage
Degree of risk	Low	Low	High	Highest
Block size	Field	Smaller	Large	Very large
Acres	4,000 or so	3,000–5,000	1-2 MM+	3-4 MM+
(km²)	(16)	(12–20)	(8,000)	(16,000)
Work Program (s)	1. Feasibility study 2. Pilot program 3. Development	1. Appraisal 2. Development	Exploration program	Exploration program
Focus of negotiations/ analysis	IRR	IRR	Take	Take
Most common allocation strategy	Negotiated deals	Negotiated deals	Competitive bidding	Competitive bidding

as royalties, profit oil share, and taxes). With *fixed* terms, there is no bidding or negotiation of the "terms," and the bid items or negotiable elements will include such things as work program, signature bonus, or local content, either separately or in combination.

Some governments authorize their national oil company or oil minister to negotiate various elements in the system such as the profit oil split as well as bonuses and work programs and other elements. There is of course concern about the greater potential for corruption with negotiated deals relative to a transparent bid round. The problem is that some countries do not have sufficient geological potential to provide for the luxury of having a typical bid round. There are few things more embarrassing for an Energy Ministry or NOC than a failed license round where no bids are received.

There is considerable pressure these days from the World Bank, the International Monetary Fund, and even Tony Blair's Extractive Industry Transparency Initiative (EITI) and other similar initiatives for oil companies and governments to be more transparent and "publish what they pay." With these initiatives, there is a strong push for governments to be more transparent and allocate acreage on the basis of public auctions similar to the highly publicized EPSA IV rounds in Libya in 2005–2007.

The problem is that unless the acreage is particularly interesting, the industry has been relatively unwilling to face the kind of magnified head-on competition that a sealed bid type license round (like Libya) provokes. In many circumstances it is naïve and unrealistic to expect a government to allocate acreage and projects on the basis of sealed bids. There is nothing worse than a failed license round for a NOC official or oil minister.

Allocating licenses through negotiated deals can be fair and efficient. Government officials (Energy Ministry or NOC) become aware of what the market can bear as they entertain various proposals and offers.

KEY CONTRACT PROVISIONS

Work Program

It is typical with agreements (R/Ts, PSCs, or SAs) in the international sector that exploration rights are divided into three phases with separate and distinct work commitments, sometimes with bank guarantees. If the work commitment is fulfilled for a particular phase, then the IOC has the right to enter a subsequent phase, which will trigger another distinct work program.

The work commitment is a critical aspect of international exploration. It is usually measured in terms of (1) wells drilled and/or (2) seismic data acquired, processed, and interpreted. It embodies most of the *risk* of petroleum exploration. The other component of the *risk capital* is the signature bonus if there is one.[9] With most exploration efforts, taxes are never experienced because so many wildcats are dry. There is perhaps only a 10 percent to 15 percent chance of ever getting beyond the work commitment. Negotiators focus a lot of attention on the work commitment.

Crude Pricing

One of the things that governments and/or royalty owners fear most is a thing called *transfer pricing*. In this context it refers to pricing of oil or gas in transactions between associated companies. This is often referred to as non-arm's-length sales. Almost all agreements or petroleum laws either do not allow this, or they may require that the price be market-based by basing prices for oil or gas sales (for royalty and tax calculation purposes) on a quality-adjusted *basket* of crudes or *crude cocktail* of known *marker crudes*, such as Brent, Urals, Minas, Fatah, Saudi Light, and West Texas Intermediate.

Royalty Determination

Just as in the United States there is diversity worldwide with respect to just how many deductions can be taken for royalty calculation purposes. The diversity ranges from situations where no deductions are allowed to fully *net back* to the wellhead including deductions for (1) operating costs, (2) capital costs (depreciated), and (3) cost of capital for the transportation function from the wellhead (point of valuation) to the point of sale. These are the same basic components used for tariff determinations by regulated utilities. The wellhead price then would be the price used for royalty and tax calculation purposes.

Taxes in Lieu

Production sharing systems with taxes in lieu where taxes are paid "for and on behalf of the contractor" out of the national oil company's share of profit oil are common: Egypt, Syria, Oman, Qatar, Trinidad, Philippines, Vietnam, and so on.

With taxes in lieu, companies receive a lower entitlement than they otherwise would if they had paid the taxes directly (in cash). So companies are *grossing-up*

the contractor share of profit oil by dividing by (1 − tax rate), and they are booking this *imputed* entitlement instead of their actual entitlement.

For example, assume in Egypt the statutory tax rate is 40 percent but this tax is paid out of the NOCs share of profit oil (taxes in lieu). Also assume that the contractor (actual) entitlement (of expected proved barrels) is 20 MMBBLS cost oil and 15 MMBBLS profit oil for a total of 35 MMBBLS.

For *booking* purposes the contractor would book the equivalent of 20 MMBBLs of cost oil + 25 MMBBLS *imputed* profit oil [15 MM/(1 − 0.4)] for a total of 45 MMBBLS.

Initially the taxes in lieu approach caused problems in the United States with the tax credit system and potentially created double taxation. This was a huge issue in Indonesia in 1976, and an IRS ruling nearly shut down exploration in Indonesia that year. To get around this, Indonesia issued its then second-generation PSC, which required companies to pay taxes directly. Today it is not such an issue—formalities are required such as the taxes actually being paid and the contractor receiving a tax receipt from the NOC, which is reported to the IRS. Problems with possible double taxation are remote in the United States these days.

Ringfencing

One aspect that American oil companies are typically not familiar with is *ringfencing*. This is a cost-center-based fiscal (or contractual) device that forces contractors or concessionaires to restrict all cost recovery and or tax deductions associated with a given license (or sometimes a given field) to that particular cost center. Essentially if a government ringfences this means that they do not allow consolidation of accounts between licenses or fields (cost centers). The cost centers may be individual licenses or on a field-by-field basis.

For example, with typical ringfencing, exploration expenses in one nonproducing block could not be deducted against income for tax calculation purposes in another block. Under a PSC ringfencing acts in the same way—cost incurred in one ringfenced block cannot be *recovered* from another block outside the ringfence. Most countries use ringfencing.

Ringfencing ordinarily refers to space (i.e., area and/or depth), but it can also be based on time and categories of costs. It can also apply to specific reservoirs or reservoir depths and exploration versus development expenditures.

Stability Provisions

Of all the various political/country/commercial/currency/social risk that exists (there are numerous categories) one of the greatest is the risk that a government might change the rules (taxes or royalties) once a discovery is made—or worse yet—once production begins. In many Western countries it is often believed that the commercial and social risks and the ordinary inconveniences of doing business are minimal. There is mainly the risk of petrofiscal changes (again taxes and/or royalties), which can be decreed or legislated.

In many other (non-OECD) countries a full range of risks and inconveniences exist and are often magnified. Of these risks the one over which

governments usually have greatest control is the risk of changing the rules. The bottom line is that while the government may not have control over many risk elements, it will provide a guarantee or a measure of guarantee against this particular category of risk in order to make its country more competitive. Therefore, many governments will provide stabilizing provisions in their agreements with IOCs. These take various forms but there are three main categories of stabilizing provisions:

1. Freezing clauses
2. Equilibrium clauses
3. Taxes in lieu

Freezing Clauses

In many PSCs (but in few R/T systems) contract language will stipulate that the agreement will be governed by the laws in place (including tax laws) at the time of the agreement—regardless of new laws or changes in the law. This approach is generally considered to be outmoded or at least the old way.

Equilibrium Clauses

Equilibrium clauses are becoming the preferred approach and are considered to be the direction of the future. These also go by other names such as *economic equilibrium* or *intangibility clauses*. Typical language of an equilibrium clause would stipulate for example that if there is "a discriminatory measure" instituted by the government that has a negative financial impact on the contractor, then the profit oil split is adjusted to maintain the economic balance.

Taxes in Lieu

This approach is believed to provide a measure of stability. The general view is that if taxes go up this is already handled in the agreement that the NOC will pay taxes "for and on behalf of the contractor." Some believe that approach is superior to a freezing clause.

There is often other language and elements found in the "definitions" in the agreements that contribute to the provisions intended to stabilize an agreement.

Dispute Resolution Provisions

There is always the potential for disagreements between parties to an agreement. In many countries the parties agree to resolve disputes through international arbitration (instead of the host country courts). Arbitration can be just as costly as ordinary litigation in the courts but usually it is not. And, with arbitration unlike typical court systems, the proceedings can be kept confidential. While there are numerous authorities and/or conventions used, the three main arbitration bodies include UNCITRAL (United Nations Commission on International Trade Law), ICSID (International Center for Settlement of Investment Disputes), and the International Chamber of Commerce (ICC).

CONCLUSION

This chapter provided a primer on fiscal system design and analysis, and exploration acreage allocation from the perspectives of host governments and investors. The design and analysis of international petroleum fiscal systems is relatively new, although many of the principles of fiscal system design date back hundreds of years to early agricultural production sharing. Governments must at once design fiscal systems that maximize revenues and provide investors with incentives to explore for and develop hydrocarbons as efficiently as possible. Investors are looking to recover investments and share in the profits produced—with as little grief as possible.

APPENDIX 12.1

Abbreviations and Acronyms

%	Percentage
¢	Cents
°	Degrees (as in Centigrade)
$	United States dollar
$M	Thousands of dollars
$MM	Millions of dollars
AGR	Access to gross revenues (complement of ERR)
BBL	Barrel
BCF	Billion cubic feet (gas)
BOPD	Barrels of oil per day
Capex	Capital expenditures
C/F	Carry forward (as in CR/CF)
C/R	Cost recovery
C/R C/F	Cost recovery carry forward
DCF	Discounted cash flow
Dev.	Development
DDB	Double declining balance
DMO	Domestic market obligation
EITI	Extractive industries transparency initiative
EOR	Enhanced oil recovery or EOR contract
EPC	Engineering, procurement, and construction
EPSA	Exploration production sharing agreement
EPSA IV	Exploration production sharing agreement fourth generation (2005)
EPSA IV-1	Exploration production sharing agreement fourth generation (April 2005)
EPSA IV-2	Exploration production sharing agreement fourth generation (October 2005)
ERR	Effective royalty rate
FSU	Former Soviet Union
Gvt.	Government
G&A	General and administrative (costs)

IC	Investment Credit
ICC	International Chamber of Commerce
ICSID	International Center for Settlement of Investment Disputes
IDC	Intangible drilling cost
IOC	International oil company
IOR	Improved oil recovery
IPC	Incremental production contracts
IRR	Internal rate of return
IRS	Internal Revenue Service
JDA	Joint Development Area (same as JDZ)
JDZ	Joint Development Zone (as in between countries like the STP/ Nigeria JDZ)
JOA	Joint operating agreement
JOB	Joint operating body
JOC	Joint Operating Committee
JV	Joint venture
JWELB	*Journal of World Energy Law and Business*
km²	Square kilometers
LIBOR	London inter-bank offered rate
M	Thousand
MCF	Thousand cubic feet (gas)
MM	Million
MMBBLS	Million barrels
MMBOE	Million barrels of oil equivalent
MMBOPD	Million barrels of oil per day
MMCFD	Million cubic feet (of gas) per day
N/A	Not available or not applicable
No.	Number
NOC	National oil company
OECD	Organization for Economic Cooperation and Development
Opex	Operating expenditures (operating costs)
P/O	Profit oil
PSA	Production sharing agreement (Same as PSC)
PSC	Production sharing contract (same as PSA)
R Factor	Ratio factor (ratio of cumulative receipts to cumulative expenditures)
ROR	Rate of return (same as IRR) as in "Rate of return systems"
R/C	Receipts divided by costs (from 1998+ vintage Malaysian PSAs)
RSA	Risk service agreement
R/T	Royalty tax
SA	Service agreement
SLD	Straight line decline (depreciation or amortization)
STP/Nigeria	São Tome e Principe/Nigeria
TAC	Technical assistance contract
TCF	Trillion cubic feet (gas)
TLCF	Tax loss carry forward
UNCITRAL	United Nations Commission on International Trade Law
US	United States
US OCS	United Stated Outer Continental Shelf

APPENDIX 12.2

Example Block Sizes Worldwide

Province/Block	Acres	km²
Gulf of Mexico	5,000	20
Qatar RDPSA	24,700	100
United Kingdom	57,600	233
New Zealand (PEP 38719–Swift 1996)	87,840	356
Norway	102,400	415
Venezuela Lasmo Dacion EOR	106,000	429
Equatorial Guinea–grid blocks	125,000	506
Dutch North Sea	134,000	543
São Tome e Principe/Nigeria JDZ (average)	230,000	931
Venezuela—Gulf of Paria West	281,000	1,138
Trinidad Block 27	291,000	1,178
Trinidad Block 89/3 Offshore	311,000	1,259
Oman Conquest	343,300	1,390
MTJDA	370,500	1,500
Venezuela—La Ceiba	430,000	1,741
Turkmenistan Negit-Dag/5	444,600	1,800
Ecuador Block 19 (and others)	494,000	2,000
Bulgaria	500,000	2,024
China Bohai Bay Block 9/18	578,000	2,340
Vietnam Block 04-2	640,000	2,591
Belize	650,000	2,631
Gabon Offshore	700,000	2,834
Nigeria OPL 214 Deepwater	748,000	3,028
Angola Block 17	834,366	3,378
Cambodia	860,000	3,482
China Bohai Bay Block 11/19	934,000	3,781
Chile Onshore	1,235,000	5,000
Angola Block 32	1,405,000	5,688
Uganda	1,450,000	5,870
Cambodia	1,850,000	7,490
Uganda	2,200,000	8,907
Bangladesh Average Onshore	2,220,000	8,989
Greenland Shell 1996	2,340,000	9,474
Malaysia Block F Offshore	2,400,000	9,717
Bangladesh Block 21 Offshore	3,076,000	12,453
Myanmar Blocks M5 and M6 (average)	3,230,000	13,077
Pakistan—Badin Block 1977	4,416,000	17,878
Egypt Block G Central Sinai	4,500,000	18,218
Saudi Area A (Lukoil) 2004	7,400,000	29,960
Saudi Area B (Sinopec) 2004	9,600,000	38,866
New Zealand (PEP 38602—Conoco)	12,000,000	48,583
Saudi Area C (Eni-Repsol) 2004	12,800,000	51,822
Indonesia Northwest Java (NWJ) 1966	14,000,000	56,680
Indonesia Southeast Sumatra (SES) 1966	32,000,000	129,554
Saudi (Total 30%, Shell 40%) Rub Al-Khali 2003	49,400,000	200,000
Sudan (Chevron 1975)	127,500,000	516,194

APPENDIX 12.3

Examples of Contract Duration Worldwide

Province/Block	Exploration Years	Production Years
Abu Dhabi	3 + 2 + 2	33
Ajman	2 + 2 + 2	35
Albania	2 + 3 + 1.5	24
Algeria	5 + 2	15 – 30
Algeria	5 + 2	20 – 25
Australia	6 + 5	42
Belize	8	25
Benin	2 + 2 + 2	25 + 10
Bolivia	30 Max	
Brunei	8	38 + 30
Brunei Offshore	17	40 + 30
Cambodia	3 + 2 + 1	22
Congo Br.	4 + 3 + 3	30
Congo Br.	10	30
Côte d'Ivoire	2 + 2 + 2	25
Czech Rep.	4 + 4	20
Dubai	3 + 2 + 3	35
Ecuador	4 + 2	22
Egypt	8	20
France	5 + 5 + 5	5 + 5 + 5
Gabon	3 + 2 + 2	25
Gabon Deepwater	5 + 3	10 + 5 + 5
Ghana	7	18 (25 Total)
Guyana	4 + 3 + 3	25 + 5
Honduras	4 + 2	20 + 5
Hungary	2 + 2 + 1	25
India	3 + 2 + 2	25 + 5
Indonesia	3	20
Liberia	3 + 3	25 + 10
Madagascar	8	15 + 5
Malaysia	3 + 2 2 + 2 Dev	15
Malaysia R/C	5	29 Total
Netherlands	10	40
Nigeria	3 + 3 + 4	20
Oman	2 + 2 + 2	20 + 10
Peru	7	30
Poland	3 + 3	20 + 5 + 5
Rep. of Guinea	5	21 (Max 25)
Senegal	3 + 2 + 2	25 + 10
South Africa	4 + 3 + 3	as long as is profitable
Syria		20 + 10
Vietnam	3 + 1 + 1	20 (total not to exceed 25)
Zambia	8	25
Average/Typical	3 + 2.5 + 2 (7.5)	25

APPENDIX 12.4

Example Agreements

ANGOLA

Offshore mid-1990s PSC		
Area	4,000–5,000 km^2	(1–1.2 MM acres)
Duration	Exploration	3 years + 1 + 1 + .5 + .5
		4 years + 2 for deepwater
	Production	20 years from date of discovery
Relinquishment	All except development areas after 5 years onshore after 6 years deepwater	
Exploration Obligations	Conoco 1986 $60 MM	4,000 km Seismic + 6 wells
Negotiable	Total 1989 $9 MM	Seismic + 2 wells
Signature Bonus Rentals	$300/km^2 for development areas	
Royalty	None	
Cost Recovery	50% limit	
	40% uplift on development costs	
Depreciation	Exploration costs expensed	
	Development costs 5-year	
	straight-line (was 4 years)	
Profit Oil Split (Typical)	MBOPD	Company
	0 to 25	50–60%
	25 to 50	30
	50 to 100	20
	>100	10
Taxation	In lieu—paid by Sonangol (50%)	
	With economic equilibrium/stability clause	
Ringfencing	For cost recovery	
	Around license for exploration	
	Around field for development	
DM	Pro rata option/right up to 40% of production	
Gvt. Participation	Up to 51% in early contracts (assumed here)	
	After 1997 typically 20% "Heads up"	
Other	Price cap formula government takes 100% above $32/BBL (1991)	

AZERBAIJAN

Onshore REDPSA (April 2003, Gaffney Cline and Assoc. Report to Trade Partners UK)

Area

Duration   Exploration   Typically 10 years
                                 Production   Typically 20 years

Relinquishment

Bonuses   Yes various
Rentals ?

Royalty   Not for new PSCs (12.5% in
                                   some contracts)
                                 Also specific rate royalties for
                                   some government
                                   operations

Cost Recovery Limit   100% OPEX
                                 50% CAPEX *
*Limited to 50% of what is left over after OPEX recovery.
Interest cost recovery at LIBOR + 1%

Profit Oil Split	**"R" Factor Based**	**P/O Split**
(two examples)	0 to 1.00	50/50%
	1.00 to 1.50	55/45%
	1.50 to 1.75	60/40%
	1.75 to 2.25	65/35%
	2.25 to 2.50	70/30%
	2.50 to 2.75	80/20%
	> 2.75	90/10%

"R" = [(Cum. Capex recovered + Interest + Cum. Profit)/Cum. Capex]

Taxation   32% General Tax Rate
                                   (creditable—paid on behalf
                                   of contractor by SOCAR)

Depreciation

Ringfencing   Yes

DMO   Essentially "Base Production"
                                   determined by decline
                                   curve analysis

Gvt. Participation   Yes, ?% SOCAR backs in
                                   when production over 4
                                   Qts is 1.5 times greater than
                                   the year before the
                                   REDPSA was signed.

BANGLADESH

1997 PSC

Area	Designated Blocks	8–10,000 km²
Duration	Exploration	3 years + 2+2 year extensions + 5 years for gas market development phase
	Production approval	20 years for oil from date of development plan 25 years for gas
Relinquishment	25% after 3 years and 25% after 5 years If well is drilled in first phase 1st relinquishment waived	
Exploration Obligations	With seismic options first phase is 2 years not 3	
Bonuses **Negotiable**	Discovery and production bonuses $100K annual training fee $50K contract service fee	
Production Bonus	5,000 BOPD: 10,000 BOPD: 15,000 BOPD: 20,000 BOPD:	US$0.5 MM 1.0 MM 1.5 MM 2.0 MM
Royalty	None	
Cost Recovery **Sliding Scale:**	Up to 20,000 BOPD 20,001 + Interest cost recovery on loans up to 50% of overall project cost	50% Limit 40%
Depreciation	4 Yr SLD	

Profit Oil Split **Negotiated—example**	**Production BOPD**	**Split %**
	Up to 20,000	60/40
	20,000 to 40,000	65/35
	40,000 to 60,000	70/30
	> 60,001	75/25

Taxation	In Lieu paid by Petrobangla 3¢/BBL or 4¢/MCF R&D fee from contractor profit oil or gas
DMO	25% of crude at up to 15% discount from market price
Ringfencing	Yes
Gvt. Participation	None

CHINA

Deepwater PSC—1994/1995

Duration	30 years
Exploration	7 years
Production	15 years + extensions with approval
Relinquishment	25% after Phase I, 25% of remaining after Phase II, Remaining at end of Phase III excluding development areas.

Exploration Obligations and Bonuses

Royalty	Oil	BOPD	Gas	MMCFD
	< 20,000	0%	< 195	0%
	20,001 to 30,000	4%	195 to 338	1%
	30,001 to 40,000	6%	338 to 484	2%
	40,001 to 60,000	8%	> 484	3%
	60,001 to 80,000	10%		
	> 80,001	12.5%		

(BOPD converted from Tons/Year at 7:1)
(MMCFD converted from MM m3/year at 35.3:1)

Pseudo Royalty	5% Consolidated Industrial and Commercial Tax CICT replaced 1/1/94 with 13% VAT for Chinese companies and 5% VAT for foreign companies—but still based on Gross Revenues

Profit Oil Split	BOPD	Gvt/Contractor	
(Negotiable)	Up to 10,000	3/97%	*Some contracts start at 95%
Example Split	10,000 to 20,000	4/96%	
("X" factor)	20,000 to 40,000	6/94%	
	40,000 to 60,000	7/93%	("X" factor) and slide to 45%.
	60,000 to 100,000	25/75%	
	> 100,000	36/64%	

Cost Recovery Limit	50% All costs expensed
Taxation	30% Income Tax (15% in Hainan Province) 10% Surtax Contractors must also pay vehicle and vessel usage, license tax, and individual income tax.
Depreciation	6-year SLD for development costs, exploration costs expensed
Ringfencing	Yes for cost recovery but not for income tax
Gvt. Participation	Up to 51% upon commercial discovery No repayment of past exploration costs.

CÔTE D'IVOIRE

27 June, 1995 Block CI–11 PSC Pluspetrol

Area	335,179 acres			
Exploration Obligations	Phase I	1.5 yrs	1 well;	$4 MM
	Phase II	2 yrs	2 wells;	$8 MM
	Phase III	2 yrs	2 wells;	$8 MM
	Appraisal	2 years for oil discovery 4 for gas + 6 month ext.		
	Exploitation	25 years + option to extend 10 years		

Relinquishment   25% of original after Phase II & Phase III

Bonuses   Signature $300K in vehicles and office equipment

              Production $1, 3, 5, & $10MM @ 10, 20, 30 & 50 MBOPD

Gas 6:1
Royalty   None

Cost Recovery Limit   40%   All costs expensed

     [75% of interest costs and fees are recoverable, bonuses not cost recoverable]

Profit Oil Split

Production* MBOPD	Contractor Share	Production MMCFD (Qtr)	Contractor Share
Up to 10	40%	Up to 75	40%
10 to 20	30	75 to 150	30
20 to 30	20	> 150	?
> 30	10		

*Avg. production rate during quarter

Taxation   Paid by Nat. Oil Co. on behalf of contractor (50%)

Ringfencing   Yes

DMO   10% of contractors crude at 75% of market price

Gvt. Participation   Around B1-8X 40% +

     Outside special area Gvt. carried through exploration 10% + option to purchase 10%

Other   75% Minimum Employment Quota: $100K/yr training > $150K/yr

G&A   During exploratory/appraisal 4% of costs
     Development 3% up to $3MM: 2.5% 3-$6MM: 1.5% > $6MM

INDIA—NELP V

Deepwater licenses	
Bonuses	None
Royalty	12.5% onshore oil
	10.0% onshore gas
	10.0% offshore (oil and gas)
	5.0% offshore > 400 meters for first 7 years
Cost Recovery	90% all costs expensed
Profit Oil/Gas Split	

Investment multiple (slightly similar to an "R" factor)

Cumulative net cash flow/exploration & development costs

Investment Multiple	Government Share
0 to 1.5	10%
1.5 to 2.0	16
2.0 to 2.5	28
2.5 to 3.0	85
3.0 to 3.5	85
> 3.5	85

IM = Accumulated C/O + P/O – Opex – Royalty/(Expl + Dev Costs)

Taxation	35% Corporate Income Tax for Foreign Oil Companies
Depreciation	25% predominantly
Ringfencing	Yes
Gvt. Participation	0%
DMO	"None"

MALAYSIA

R/C PSC Model 1997±

Duration	29 years from effective date; exploration 5 years
	Production 20 years for Oil or expiry of the contract
	20 years + 5 year holding period for gas

Relinquishment   No interim relinquishment

Exploration   Bid items
  Obligations

Bonuses   None

Royalty   10% + 0.5% Research Cess

Profit Oil Split and Cost Recovery

| | | Petronas Share Profit Oil (and Gas) | | | |
| | | Cumulative Production Below THV | | Cumulative Production Above THV | |
Contractor's R/C Ratio	Cost Oil (Gas) Limit	Unutilized C/O Split	Normal P/O Split	Unutilized C/O Split	Normal P/O Split
0 to 1.0	70%	N/A	20%	N/A	60%
1.0 to 1.4	60%	20%	30%	60%	70%
1.4 to 2.0	50%	30%	40%	60%	70%
2.0 to 2.5	30%	40%	50%	60%	70%
2.5 to 3.0	30%	50%	60%	60%	70%
> 3.0	30%	60%	70%	80%	90%

Individual Field Total Hydrocarbon Volume (THV) = 30 MMBBLS or
0.75 TCF

Price Cap Formula   70% of value of contractor P/O or P/G above base price paid to Petronas. Base price is US$25.00/BBL or $1.80/MMBtu increased by 4% commencing on the first anniversary of the effective date. But the Price Cap Formula only kicks-in if the R/C > 1.0.

Taxation	40% Petroleum Income Tax
(Assumed)	20% Duty on profit oil exported (with 50% Export Tax Exemption)
Depreciation	?
Ringfencing	Each license ringfenced
DMO	None
Gvt. Participation	Up to 15% Petronas carried through all expl. expenditures (assumed)

MAURITANIA

PSC with Sonatrach (from Barrows 17 April, 2008)
November 30, 2007, Sonatrach's subsidiary, SIPEX (Sonatrach Int'l. Petroleum E&P BVI)

Blocks 1, 30, 31, 35 in the Taoudenni Basin.

Relinquishment

Bonuses

Royalty	None
Cost Recovery Limit	62% oil
	65% gas

Profit Oil Split

MBOPD	MMCFD	Contractor Share
Up to 25	0 to 150	70%
25 to 75	150 to 450	65
75 to 100	450 to 600	60
> 100	> 600	50

Taxation	27%
Depreciation	G&G & startup 100% assumed
	Most other 20%
	Drilling equipment 33%
	Interest is deductible
Ringfencing	Around the contract area for C/R and Tax purposes
Gvt. Participation	13% at commerciality (ordinary carry) + 7% at 100,000 BOPD
	State reimburses out of up to 50% of its share of production (assumed)

NOC - Ste. Mauritanienne des Hydrocarbures (SMH)

RUSSIA

Royalty/Tax system 2005

Obligations	$50 MM Appraisal
Bonuses Signature	$6 to $20 MM
Rentals	
Payments	
Royalty	16.5% (also known as mineral extraction tax "MET")
Cost Recovery Limit	
Production Sharing	
Taxation	24% Profit tax
Depreciation	Various wells 10–15 years (double-declining balance "DDB")
	Surface facilities 5–7 years (DDB)
	Buildings 30 years (straight-line decline "SL")
	Pipelines 20–25 years at a maximum rate of 5%
	(main pipe: SL only; other pipe: SL or DDB)
Withholding Tax	5%
Asset Tax	2.2% of average annual net book value
Value Added Tax	18% (assumed to be mostly neutralized by VAT creditability)

Export Duty

Tier			Rate
Ural CIF	<	$15/BBL	0
$15/BBL	<Ural CIF<	$20/BBL	35% (Ural CIF − $15)
$20/BBL	<Ural CIF<	$25/BBL	45% (Ural CIF − $20) + $1.75
Ural CIF	>	$25/BBL	65% (Ural CIF − $25) + $4.00

Export Tariff Gas	= 5% of customs value (but not less than 2.50 Eu/000 m^3)
Ringfencing	Yes (assumed)
Gvt. Participation	41%

TURKMENISTAN

Petronas PSC July 2, 1996

Area	Block I Gubkin + Barinov Fields
Duration	26 years from "effective date"
	2.5 years for G and B fields to start up
	Exploration 3+ 2
	Production 20 years (gas is different)
Relinquishment	
Obligations	2,500 km² 2-D 2 W/C wells
	5,500 km² 3-D 2 Appraisal wells
	"Allocate" US$45 MM
Bonuses	"Execution" Bonus $13 MM

Royalties

Oil BOPD	Royalty	Gas 10%
Up to 25,000	3%	
25,000 to 50,000	5	
50,000 to 75,000	7	
75,000 to 100,000	10	
> 100,000	15	

Cost Recovery Ceiling	60% for development fields; 70% for unexplored structures
Depreciation	All costs expensed (assumed)
Production Sharing	

	P/C Ratio	Profit Oil Split
P/C = X/Y		
	0 to 1	35/65%
X = Contractor revenues from sales	1 to 1.5	50/50%
Y = Total Costs	1.5 to 2	60/40%
	2 to 2.5	80/20%
	> 2.5	90/10%

Taxation	25%	TLCF 5 years
Depreciation	5-year SLD	
Ringfencing	Yes for cost recovery not for tax	
Gvt. Participation	None	

DISCUSSION QUESTIONS

1. What are the primary concerns of a host government in designing a petroleum fiscal system?
2. What are the four main means by which governments get their share of profits?
3. What are at least two advantages of royalties?
4. How do governments benefit by participating in projects?
5. What fiscal elements contribute to front-end loading, or the effective royalty rate?
6. Why are governments concerned about front-end loading?
7. How does front-end loading impact the investors?
8. Why are so many fiscal systems regressive?
9. Which fiscal elements are considered progressive?
10. Why is petroleum taxation typically so high compared to other industries?
11. What are the primary concerns of investors?
12. What do investors offer governments—or why don't governments just go it alone?
13. What is the main thing that attracts investors to exploration acreage?
14. What is the primary difference between an exploration and development investment?
15. Name at least five weaknesses of the government take statistic.
16. What is goldplating?
17. Why do most fiscal systems provide investors an inherent incentive to keep costs down?
18. What are the legal distinctions among the various fiscal systems?
19. Discuss the allocation systems with respect to transparency?
20. How would you characterize a fiscal system that aligns the interests of all stakeholders?

NOTES

1. Refer to Johnston (2003).
2. See D. Johnston and D. Johnston (2008).
3. Such as the division of profits and/or division of revenues.
4. Also called *resource rent, economic rent*, and other similar names.
5. This includes both capital expenditures (Capex) and operating costs (Opex) *full-cycle*; that is, over the life of the field.
6. See Johnston (2002).
7. JOB stood for *joint operating body*, a committee that oversaw operations in a 50-50 joint venture between the IOC and Pertamina, the Indonesian NOC for existing fields.
8. This was strongly influenced by the dissolution of the Soviet Union and by World Bank efforts in Africa.
9. Around 40 percent of the countries worldwide include signature bonuses in their fiscal/contractual system.

REFERENCES

Johnston, D. 1997. "Index Useful for Evaluating Petroleum Fiscal Systems." *Oil and Gas Journal*, December 1, 49–51.

Johnston, D. 2002. "Government Take—Not a Perfect Statistic." *Petroleum Accounting and Financial Management Journal* 21:2, 101–108.

Johnston, D. 2003. *International Exploration Economics, Risk and Contract Analysis*. Tulsa, OK: PennWell Books.

Johnston, D. and D. Johnston. 2008. "International Petroleum Fiscal Systems and PSCs." Course Workbook (see Conference Connection at www.cconnection.org).

ABOUT THE CONTRIBUTOR

David Johnston is an engineer from the University of Rochester, Rochester, New York, and an engineering and petroleum industry consultant who has worked and lectured internationally on the subjects of energy and technology. He is a director with Daniel Johnston & Co. Inc. and works with oil companies and governments on upstream exploration, development, enhanced oil recovery, design and analysis of petroleum fiscal systems, and marginal field development contracts worldwide. His work includes contract design, economic/financial analysis, negotiations, and expert witness work. He is also on the Board of Directors of Ahead Energy, an NGO associated with the University of Rochester in New York that works to develop small-scale gas projects and alternative energy applications in Africa.

Johnston teaches courses in "Economic Modeling and Risk Analysis" and "International Petroleum Fiscal System Analysis and Design" at the University of Dundee, and has published two books through the university: *Economic Modeling and Risk Analysis Handbook* and *Maximum Efficient Production Rate*. He has also published *Introduction to Oil Company Financial Analysis* (2006), a best-seller with PennWell Books, and has written a number of articles on the subjects of energy and technology.

CHAPTER 13

Financing Large Energy Projects

STEPHEN V. ARBOGAST
C. T. Bauer College of Business at the University of Houston

PRAVEEN KUMAR
C. T. Bauer College of Business at the University of Houston

INTRODUCTION

This chapter examines the optimal financing of large energy projects, focusing on the oil and gas (O&G) industry.[1] There are two important issues that arise at the very outset. First, how important are large projects in the oil and gas industry, and what are their notable features? Second, and more importantly, why do these projects merit special attention; that is, why can not one simply apply the standard corporate finance framework to finance these projects?

Large projects have historically played an important role in both the upstream (i.e., exploration and productions) and downstream (i.e., refining and production of derivatives) segments of the energy industry. A principal reason for this is that the energy business is a cost business, meaning that in an industry where prices are essentially determined by world commodity markets, the major source of competitive advantage is lower unit costs. Hence, to survive and compete, firms' projects must grow bigger, harvest economies of scale, and drive down the unit costs. This motivation is reinforced by the strategic imperatives of using large capacity and complex technology choices to preempt entry and establish a long-term dominant position in an industry where projects have long gestation times and relatively long horizons. Furthermore, and as we will emphasize below, large projects often allow firms to achieve stronger bargaining positions vis-à-vis lenders and foreign governments, and reduce the cost of capital.

Interestingly, the importance of large projects is only likely to increase in the evolving economic environment for the industry. In a world where new resource plays increasingly reside in challenging physical environments, complexity and difficulty drive up costs. Simultaneously, the energy business remains intensely competitive. Traditional majors and independents vie with old and new state firms. Private equity and diversifying niche players appear as new entrants. One result of this changing but intense competitive landscape is a drive toward ever bigger project scale.

In sum, large-scale energy projects are fundamental to forging a successful competitive strategy. And since cost competition is the fundamental dynamic,

financing large projects at the lowest, risk-adjusted cost is an important component of any successful strategy.

A bit more explanation is needed as to why the words *risk-adjusted* are in front
of *cost* in the previous paragraph. This is done to signal that a successful energy
financing cannot be summed up simply in terms of interest rates and cost of capital. Financing performs other functions for an energy firm's competitive strategy. Many involve mitigating the risks inherent in large projects. For example,
well structured financing may facilitate efficient project execution, lessen political risks, and even help overcome the risk of becoming opportunity constrained.
Thus financing large projects must be viewed in the broader context of energy firm
competitive strategy—where it can be a key enabler of success.

Given its economic importance, there is a surprisingly limited analysis of
project financing in the finance literature, and even this literature rarely examines
the special aspects of large projects (see below). Therefore, we will not only delve
into the salient economic characteristics of large projects in the O&G industry, but
also develop a more general framework for considering the interaction between
large projects and projects versus corporate financing.

The rest of this chapter is organized as follows. The next section sets the stage
by developing some special features of large energy projects and their influence
on the competitive and financing strategies of energy companies. The subsequent
section provides a brief review of the available literature on the financing of large
projects and identifies gaps in light of the special features of these projects in the
energy sector. After that, the next three sections analyze the centralized (or corporate) financing and project financing models in relation to large projects. The final
section concludes with the identification of important issues for future research.

SPECIAL ASPECTS OF LARGE PROJECTS IN THE ENERGY INDUSTRY

The most notable economic characteristic is simply that large energy projects typically require an immense amount of investment capital. For example, new offshore
platforms can cost several billion dollars each, and the latest wave of major refinery
and chemical plant expansions range from $2 to $6 billion. And at the upper end
of the investment capital spectrum resides a project like ExxonMobil's Papua New
Guinea LNG (liquefied natural gas) venture with a price tag of $16.7 billion, which
dwarfs the investment capital needs in almost any large project in any other
industry. Of course, not every energy industry player has access to this kind of
capital.

More generally, the capital requirements for competing in the energy business
are huge and continually increasing. Industry players face a chronic financing challenge. Their objective is not just to raise enough capital to finance the next large-
scale project. Rather, they must maintain ongoing access to sufficient capital to fund
all the projects underpinning a viable competitive strategy.

Narrowing the focus for a moment, it quickly becomes clear that each project of
this size involves *large-bet* risk. Firms must continuously manage the relationship
between the scale of their individual opportunities and the risk that one or more
might turn out badly. The history of the energy business is strewn with the debris of

busted ventures. In northwest Colorado the near–ghost town of Battlement Mesa testifies to an unfortunate Exxon oil shale venture—abandoned after an investment of multiple billions of dollars. BP will incur losses far greater than that when it eventually closes the books on its ill-fated Macondo well.

Among the challenges in energy financing, managing the risk of badly performing large projects ranks just after finding the necessary money to fund the firm's capital program. Given the immensity of this challenge, it is unsurprising that joint ventures are so common across the industry.

The next special characteristic is less obvious. The complexity and scale of large energy projects tend to require multiyear executions. It is not uncommon for a major refinery or chemical plant project to take two to four years from design to start-up. The aforementioned Papua New Guinea LNG project was approved by its sponsors in 2010; first production is expected in 2014.

Several risks flow from this characteristic. The first is that timely funding will not be available. This is especially the case when joint ventures involve teaming up partners of unequal financial strength. If weaker partners fail to supply promised funds, project implementation can be impacted. The challenge of raising large amounts of money can also require energy firms to pursue financing in multiple markets. Should one or more financing effort be delayed or fail, project teams can run out of money. The results can then be disastrous. Long lead-time items may be cancelled, field work disrupted, and project teams demobilized; all of this can result in delays and big cost overruns, consequences that adversely impact expected returns.

Large price tags plus multiyear implementation have another consequence—a longer wait to recover invested capital and begin earning a return. Projects with a mid-teens internal rate of return (IRR) can take 6 to 10 years from first spending to recover invested capital. This reality intensifies the large-bet risk cited above and puts a premium on managing operating period risks.

Unfortunately, the multiyear implementation period makes it difficult to foresee the operating period risks. To give one example, in 1976 Exxon signed a contract to develop a large coal mine in northeast Colombia. The project's coal reserves were proved up, and the project was engineered over the subsequent four years. Meanwhile, oil prices rose above $30/b, and the price of steam coal rose in parallel. Based upon such robust prices, the $2 billion project was approved in 1981. By the time construction was completed in 1984, oil prices were clearly weakening; they crashed below $10/b two years later and stayed below $20/b for the next decade and a half. Exxon never earned its expected return on the mine and ended up divesting the property. This outcome and others like it contributed to a view often expressed by CEO Lee Raymond—"we know one thing—we can't predict prices."

Prices aren't the only risk that the sponsors of large energy projects have trouble predicting. The long implementation timetables make market, environmental, and especially political risks difficult to foresee. Companies such as Conoco and Mobil who responded to Luis Guisti's Venezuelan *abertura* in 1995 could little imagine that they would be dealing with Hugo Chavez when their projects came on stream around 2000.

One more characteristic deserves mention—the risk of operating in emerging-market countries. Energy industry competition was global as early as the beginning of the twentieth century. It is even more so today, when the energy growth

markets are in East Asia and the biggest frontier plays in lands as diverse as Brazil, Kazakhstan, Russia, Ghana, and Iraq. Locations such as these pose acute economic and political risks, ranging from currency devaluation and inconvertibility to expropriation and physical violence. Yet, industry players often conclude they have little choice but to accept such risks. The alternative may be a failure to replace current production with new reserves. This failure can be fatal for firm independence, as such former household names Gulf, Amoco, Arco, Texaco, and Unocal could testify.

For energy companies then, this suite of risks adds another element, risk management, to financing strategy's traditional cost objective. Financing strategy must complement the firm's competitive strategy, both by keeping the cost of new funding low and by mitigating the risks involved in undertaking large energy projects in risky locations. Let us now examine the broad approaches that the energy industry's diverse players use to meet these objectives.

FINANCING OF LARGE PROJECTS: A LITERATURE REVIEW

While the standard corporate financing model—or, for our purposes, the *Centralized Finance Model*—is the standard paradigm for investment financing (see, e.g., Brealey and Myers 2002), *structured financing* of investment projects has been has been historically important and has seen explosive growth recently. Broadly defined, structured finance refers to the transfer of a subset of the firm's assets into a *bankruptcy-remote* special-purpose entity or vehicle; these entities then offer a single or multiple class of securities (see Leland 2007). The two most important illustrations of structured financing are asset securitization and project financing. But from the viewpoint of the energy industry, it is the *Project Finance Model* that is the most relevant alternative to centralized financing.[2]

Project finance typically involves the creation of an independent entity (the project) financed by *nonrecourse debt*; that is, where the cash for debt service comes from the cash flow and assets being funded and not from the other assets of the corporation project sponsors (see, e.g., Bruner, Langohr, and Campbell, 2008; Esty and Christov 2002). Said differently, project finance involves borrowing money to create assets whose operations then generate the cash for servicing the debt.

Taken at face value, project finance appears to have a number of appealing features. Lenders assume a broad range of risks normally associated with equity investment, including that the project sponsors will actually complete the assets they've promised to build. Borrowers, on the other hand, wall off their other assets, including personal wealth, from being attached if the project loan defaults. However, there clearly must be costs of project financing relative to centralized financing; for, if not, firms could easily create value by restructuring themselves as a set of smaller legally separate entities. Yet, if anything, the trend in the energy industry has been toward increasing the size and the scope of the firms, typically through horizontal and vertical integration.

A useful initial framework for analyzing potential value creation by project financing relative to centralized finance is to start with the Modigliani and Miller (1958) world where, in the absence of (1) taxes, (2) bankruptcy and financial distress

costs, (3) transactions costs, (4) imperfect and/or asymmetric information costs, and (5) moral hazard and agency costs, capital structure is irrelevant and hence project financing per se could not create value. In reality, of course all five of these "imperfections" apply to varying degrees and potentially allow project financing to create value.[3] The extent and significance of these imperfections in large projects has not been fully described and appreciated in the literature, and we do so below.

It is important to note, however, that the presence of imperfections does not imply by themselves that the project financing model will be superior to the centralized financing model. For example, it is widely recognized in the literature and industry practice that project financing in general may include additional costs, such as higher legal and administrative fees and transactions costs; increased demand on managerial time, compounded by managerial distraction and organizational compartmentalization; and increased agency costs of monitoring and information disclosure.

Meanwhile, the literature has noted the benefits of project finance in terms of improved risk management in the presence of significant economic costs of distress; amelioration of the underinvestment problem due to debt overhang at the corporate level; and reduction of agency costs problems when large co-mingled cash flows at the corporate level intensify the free cash flow agency problem.[4]

It is not difficult to show that these benefits of project finance are more likely to apply for *large* projects that can have a significant impact on the both the first and the second moments of corporate cash flows, and where the underinvestment costs may be especially important. Yet, as noted by Esty (2004), there is relatively scant attention paid in the academic finance literature to the unique issues raised by financing of large projects. But this gap in the literature appears especially acute with respect to large energy projects. In our analysis below, we emphasize the interface between the special features of these projects (that we highlight above) and the relative costs and benefits of the centralized versus the project finance model.

CENTRALIZED FINANCING OF LARGE ENERGY PROJECTS

The most prominent feature of the Centralized Finance Model in the energy sector is maintenance of a very strong balance sheet and credit rating. From this position of strength, major energy firms raise needed capital at a central location—usually at the parent company or via finance subsidiaries that employ the parent's guarantee. This capital is then pooled and funneled out to the firm's network of operating affiliates. Such capital allocations follow decisions made by the parent's senior management as part of its annual capital budgeting process.

To give some feel for what is meant by the maintenance of strong central credit, consider the financial 2010 metrics shown in Exhibit 13.1 for the leading international oil companies.

The reasons why these firms maintain such debt capacity are many and not widely understood outside the industry. Indeed, from the perspective of minimizing the weighted average cost of capital these firms are often criticized for being "overcapitalized," that is not employing enough debt, losing out on valuable tax deductions and thus having a suboptimized cost of capital. This view does not

Exhibit 13.1 Financial Metrics for Leading International Oil Companies

Company	Equity ($ billion)	Debt-Cash/Equity	Debt Rating
ExxonMobil	152.68	0.027	AAA
Shell	157.80	0.069	AA
BP	103.18	0.137	AA
Chevron	105.81	−0.029	AA
Total	63.43	0.046	AA

Source: Capital IQ, March 31, 2011.

adequately take into account the role that financing strategy plays in firm competitive strategy; it also underestimates the challenge of risk management in a cyclical industry characterized by large capacity and commodity prices that can crash in a very short period of time.[5]

While the relationship between leverage and risk management is discussed widely in the literature, the interaction between leverage and the competitive strategy imperatives confronting energy firms has received little attention. To explicate, textbook corporate finance theory implicitly assumes that projects are marginal; that is, projects comparable to the existing project are readily available. However, in reality this condition must be achieved, not assumed. Indeed, the privately owned energy business has recently been especially challenged in this area; for the past three decades, more and more of the large-scale, undeveloped oil and gas prospects have fallen under the control of governments and state companies.

Large energy companies have responded to this competitive challenge by seeking opportunities globally and bidding for multiple projects simultaneously. This strategy puts a premium on having sufficient financial flexibility to respond to both a sudden surge of successful bidding and a successful acquisition opportunity seeking strategy. Financial flexibility can be usefully interpreted as the ability to borrow or raise substantial capital at relatively short notice without jeopardizing the firm's debt rating or the cost of debt. We will henceforth align the concept of *financial strength* with this notion of financial flexibility. Thus, strong firms are able to buy attractive companies and long-lived reserves when industry conditions are weak and acquisition prices more favorable.[6]

A second nexus between unassailable financial strength and competitive strategy concerns the pursuit of scale economies. Industry leaders have discovered that pushing scale economies has two simultaneous advantages. First, it results in energy projects whose unit costs put severe pressure on the positions of smaller sized firms. Second, the large firms move industry competition onto a frontier that favors their full suite of skills. These firms curry favor with host governments by emphasizing large projects that have a transformative impact on the local society. They also sharply limit the field of competitors who can credibly put themselves forward as alternative project developers. Some examples illustrate this competitive dynamic. The Exxon/Chevron/Petronas consortium, which developed Chad's billion barrels of oil reserves, produced taxes and royalties that more than doubled the government's revenues. The PNG LNG project will increase Papua New Guinea's entire GDP by one-third.

Superior financial strength can also be a competitive differentiator in other ways. Since many of the best opportunities are today controlled by emerging-market governments, joining forces with financially weak state companies is often required. Such governments tend to favor partnering with financially strong private firms as one way to compensate for their state firm's limited funds. This reality is often a two-edged sword for the private firm—a benefit in terms of gaining access to attractive plays but an unwanted complication in terms of ensuing pressures to overfinance its weaker state partner. Leading industry players have developed several means to avoid this over dilemma. One of these, the use of project financing for joint ventures of this type, is discussed further below.

These approaches to competitive strategy require that firms maintain strong credit and ample financing reserves. The potential payoffs for successfully aligning financial structure with competitive structure are substantial. These include industry-leading reserves replacement and entry into projects promising returns well above the cost of capital. There is considerable evidence, on a case-by-case basis, that CEOs of energy companies favor using Centralized Finance to reinforce competitive strategy.

Finally, superior financial strength is essential to bearing the larger risks that large energy projects entail. All of the risks feed into large-bet risk. The ability to accept large-bet risk is clearly related to having sufficient financial strength, not just survive a poor project, but to be able to continue with planned investments. Without this degree of financial flexibility, competitive strategies are perennially exposed to disruption. Firms may plan an investment program, spend millions on lease bonuses, exploration, and front-end engineering, only to have the program suspended by a sudden need to economize. Firms with the financial flexibility to ride through industry price volatility absorb disappointing project outcomes and still implement their strategies end up winning—because they can execute projects more efficiently, spend less capital over time, and capture opportunities when they are available on the best terms.

As we noted above, there is a long literature that has discussed the positive association between risk management and firm value in the presence of economic costs of financial distress and bankruptcy along with other transactions costs and contractual imperfections. However, this literature has not emphasized the link between risk management ability and the successful execution of long-term value-creating competitive strategy in the energy industry.

In sum, long-term competitive advantage for companies in the energy industry essentially resides in:

- A superior ability to access reserves that are increasingly difficult to find independently.
- Using economies of scale and scope to drive down costs per unit.
- Having a relatively lower cost of external financing for the large project size that is necessitated by economies of scale and scope.

Financial strength based on the notion of higher financial flexibility or debt capacity is therefore central to all three drivers of competitive advantage, as we have emphasized above.

While strong credit is the foundation of the Centralized Finance Model, there are other elements to it; these contribute to efficiency, its ability to lower financing costs after tax, and its capacity to mitigate specific project risks. Such contributions complement the considerable assistance provided to competitive strategy just cited. They also compensate for costs that may be incurred by not adopting a more theoretically optimized capital structure.

OPERATING FEATURES OF THE CENTRALIZED FINANCE MODEL

A Centralized Finance Model uses the following six guidelines to finance large energy projects:

1. Use the annual capital budgeting process to calculate the *Gross Consolidated Funding Requirement* for both ongoing operations and capital projects.
2. Require operating affiliates, both domestic and foreign, to remit all cash not strictly needed for operations to either the parent company or to financing affiliates controlled by the parent company's finance function.
3. Compute the *Net Consolidated Funding Requirement* by netting the Gross Requirement against all internal cash flow centralized per step 2.
4. Raise external finance for the Net Requirement using the parent's credit rating. Organize this financing into the most cost-efficient number of transactions while considering opportunities across the full range of international capital markets.
5. Develop an internal finance system to lend money and/or contribute capital to those operating affiliates and ventures that have funding needs.
6. Determine whether intercompany funding is extended as loans or capital injections, taking into account considerations of tax optimization and risk mitigation.

Using these guidelines to build a Centralized Finance System results in an organization characterized by a strong parent treasury function that is closely aligned with the tax department; the system also will have domestic and foreign financing affiliates (FINCOs), and an extensive network of intercompany financing facilities (I/C loans and deposits). A simple schematic of this system for a U.S. energy firm appears in Exhibit 13.2.

Note that the cash generated by U.S. operations and dividends from controlled foreign companies (CFCs) is centralized at the parent company. Other foreign cash generation that is not remitted home is deposited in foreign FINCOs controlled by the parent. The firm then calculates its Net Funding Requirement. Funds to meet this requirement, which are then raised at the parent company level. Capital structure for the entire company is also managed at this level and is expressed by the parent's decisions to raise debt or equity.

Foreign operations that need financing are first funded from the cash deposited in foreign FINCOs. Any remaining foreign needs and all domestic requirements are then met via capital injections or intercompany (I/C) loans from the parent or the parent's domestic FINCOs. Capital structure decisions for all foreign and domestic

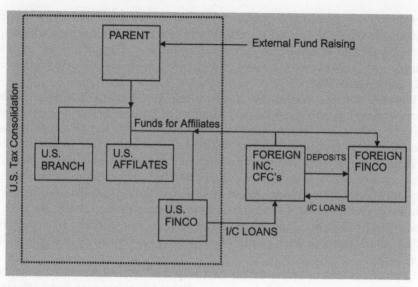

Exhibit 13.2 Centralized Finance System

affiliates are made by the parent and adjusted by managing the mix of loans and capital directed through the intercompany system. Exhibit 13.3 is an example of this system in action for a foreign affiliate needing $150 million.

Benefits of Centralized Finance for Large Projects

By employing this system energy firms are able to raise debt finance for large projects at the lowest after-tax cost and mitigate several important risks. Regarding

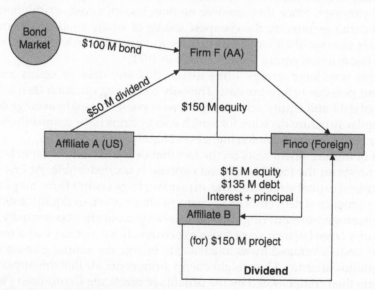

Exhibit 13.3 Intercompany System

the cost objective, employing the parent's credit or guarantee assures that the firm's strongest credit rating is used to raise all external debt. On this basis *all* company borrowing should achieve the lowest before-tax cost. Borrowings by individual affiliates with weaker credit are eliminated; so too are borrowings in smaller, more costly capital markets.

Working with a consolidated Net Funding Requirement, the parent is able to organize financing into the minimum number of transactions and to optimize the timing of new issues. Transactions fees are thus minimized as are penalties for financing into unfavorable markets. Instead, the parent is able to operate opportunistically. The parent surveys global capital markets for favorable moments and special opportunities. Many financing opportunities are available for strong energy companies; examples include export credits, subsidized government investment facilities, pollution-control funding, and vessel construction loans. Because cash at the parent company level is fungible, a new project in Brazil may actually be funded out of proceeds from pollution control bonds issued for a facility in Beaumont, Texas.

Centralized cash operations also give the parent control over deployment of all internal cash generation. Affiliates are not allowed to retain cash unless the parent consents. This prevents retained earnings from disappearing into numerous local projects peripheral to the firm's overall strategy. This is an invaluable control benefit of a Centralized Finance System. Because of the energy industry's enormous scale, organizations populated by hundreds of affiliated entities are common. At last count, ExxonMobil operated in over 200 countries. In such far-flung organizations, keeping the attention and allegiance of local management is a constant challenge. The rigorous centralization of all internal cash, when combined with capital budgeting requiring parental approval of large projects, contributes greatly to this objective; having to ask for capital helps assure that suborganizations pay attention to shareholder interests and to the parent's overall strategy.

Control over internal cash generation also gives the parent control over all retained earnings. Since they involve no new issuance costs or dilution effects, retained earnings provide the cheapest source of equity funding. Major energy companies manage their capital structures to target this outcome. For example, Exxon's last external equity issue occurred in 1971.

In this way large energy firms assure that any debt or equity raised has the lowest possible before-tax cost. The only remaining question then is whether the mix of debt and equity achieves the lowest possible weight average cost. This is the capital structure decision for which energy firms have frequently been criticized for maintaining too much higher-cost equity.

Part of this argument rests on the fact that debt is usually cheaper before-tax, and part rests on the fact that interest expense is tax deductible. At first glance a suboptimized capital structure looks expensive; large energy firms may be judged to incur normalized debt costs of 3–4 percent after-tax versus equity costs in the 8–10 percent range. Surrendering approximately 5 percent after-tax annually on some portion of a large balance sheet looks expensive. If we assume that a major firm might be underleveraged by as much as $10 billion, the annual give-up amounts to $500 million after-tax. How might energy firms conclude that this apparent give-up is more than compensated by the benefits of practicing Centralized Finance?

The first response to this question involves Centralized Finance's role as an enabler of new opportunity capture. Traditional capital structure and cost of capital theory is generic; it is intended to apply to all industries and abstracts away key differences among industry strategic situations. Thus, it fails to take into account the contribution to specific industry strategy, which an otherwise suboptimal capital structure may make.

This is especially the case with the energy industry. Here one encounters the predominance of large projects, a constrained new opportunity environment, and the frequent need to work with financially weak partners—these conditions all put a premium on unquestioned financial flexibility. The strong credit at the foundation of Centralized Finance is thus considered essential to gaining entry to Qatari gas, Kashagan, Gorgon, Sahkalin, and similar mammoth frontier opportunities.

The behavior of major energy firms suggests that managements view this contribution to firm strategy as more than compensating for any apparent capital structure suboptimization. Note that all of the firms listed in Exhibit 13.1 carry credit ratings of AA or better. The industry leader, ExxonMobil, has been AAA rated since the 1930s.

The second response involves Centralized Finance's role in risk mitigation. We have already noted how strong central credit mitigates the energy industry's large-bet risks. Less obvious are the roles Centralized Finance plays in reducing the distress costs of troubled ventures and in enhancing the capacity to remit cash from high-risk locations.

As regards venture distress costs, encumbering specific operations with external debt subjects them to restrictive covenants, liens, and default provisions. Should projects experience distress, which these provisions may trigger, this can expose the assets to being seized as collateral. Even if the debt is renegotiated, such restructurings are expensive and disruptive. Management attention is diverted from running the business, and strategy takes a back seat to generating cash. With Centralized Finance all of this risk goes away. When an operation is financed with intercompany debt, the parent is also the banker. In that role, the parent can still maintain focus on long-term value maximization. Parents can capitalize intercompany loans, reschedule amortizations, and forgive interest as necessity warrants—all without the frictions and costs associated with third party restructuring.

As for remittance risks, intercompany financing offers two benefits: (1) It allows the firm to maximize the loan funding for high-risk ventures (without increasing the risk of losing the assets via default), and (2) it allows the parent to offer flexible loan terms, especially easy prepayment.

Together these conditions maximize the ability of risky ventures to remit cash. The use of intercompany debt allows cash to be remitted to parents as principal repayments; regular payments of intercompany loan principal are seldom challenged. By way of contrast, equity injections can produce blocked cash, as many locations only permit dividends to be paid out of earnings. Other cash distributions can then require a time-consuming and politically sensitive decapitalization. Cash generated from depreciation can thus accumulate; such blocked cash is then exposed to local conditions, including changing tax rates, devaluation, and expropriation. Saudi Arabia and many Latin American countries have these kinds of remittance constraints.

When ready prepayment rights are added to the intercompany loan terms, affiliates gain an extra degree of remittance freedom; should they see political or devaluation risks intensifying, they may concentrate all available cash and even borrow locally to pay down their intercompany loan before emergency conditions hit.

Finally, Centralized Finance lowers the cost of capital via tax optimization. This feature speaks directly to the criticism that this system suboptimizes the capital structure and sacrifices tax deductions. Centralized Finance overcomes this objection by using its internal financing system to (1) maximize *internal leverage* and (2) arbitrage tax rates across different jurisdictions.

Internal leverage refers to the amount of debt created on affiliate balance sheets via the parent extending intercompany loans. This leverage is invisible to outside observers; for accounting purposes it is netted out in consolidation and never appears in published financial statements. Yet the debt is a real obligation owed by the affiliate to the parent. More important, it generates interest expenses that are tax deductible in the local jurisdiction.

A simple example illustrates this concept. Parent X uses $200 million of internal cash generation to extend an intercompany loan to its Japanese affiliate. Interest of 6 percent p.a. is charged on the loan; this generates $12 million per year of deductible interest expense for the Japanese affiliate. As the affiliate is in a tax-paying position at a 40 percent marginal rate, it reduces its Japanese tax bill by $4.8 million equivalent ($12 M × 40%). At the same time, the Parent X FINCO used to extend the loan receives $12 M of interest income. This FINCO is located in a jurisdiction with a 10 percent tax rate; thus it incurs $1.2 million per year in taxes payable.

When Parent X consolidates its annual results, neither the affiliate's loan payable nor the FINCO's loan receivable appears on the balance sheet. The Japanese affiliate's net income reflects its interest paid on the loan and its local tax shield. The FINCO's income after-tax is also consolidated into Parent X's net income. The net effect of these entries becomes the difference in tax results in the two jurisdictions; that is, $4.8 million lower taxes in Japan less $1.2 million higher taxes in the FINCO location, for a net $3.6 million savings. Exhibit 13.4 illustrates the Japan case before and after the intercompany (I/C) loan.

This example shows the two effects of internal leverage at work. First, the parent company is able to target an affiliate with a high marginal tax rate to be the recipients of high amounts of intercompany debt. Second, the parent can extend these loans from jurisdictions with low or a zero marginal tax on the loan interest income. The effects are highly beneficial. Affiliate before-tax income that would otherwise be exposed to high tax rates is converted into interest income flowing into a much lower tax jurisdiction.

Leveraging up a high-tax affiliate is more difficult to achieve without the use of the Centralized Finance intercompany network. Local affiliates can borrow, but local lenders are more expensive and likely to balk at allowing the affiliate a high leverage ratio; local lenders will also try to restrict profit and other remittances to the parent. A parent lender will impose no such restrictions. Should the affiliate's high leverage result in solvency issues, the parent can always capitalize or restructure the loan. Finally, there is no possibility of tax arbitrage when an affiliate simply borrows in the local market.

Exhibit 13.4 Japanese Company's Income Statement before and after the Intercompany Loan

$ M	Before I/C loan	After I/C loan
Japan EBIT	100	100
Interest @ 6%	—	(12)
Taxes Payable @ 40%	(40)	(35.2)
Japan Net Income	60	52.8
FINCO EBIT	—	12
Taxes Payable @ 10%	—	(1.2)
FINCO Net Income	—	10.8
Combined Japan/FINCO Net Income	60	63.6
Consolidated Parent X gain	—	3.6

The value of employing internal leverage is especially high in the energy industry. Over time many host governments have imposed high marginal tax rates on oil/gas producers. For example, Norway's marginal tax rate tops out at 80 percent. Numerous other producing countries have highly progressive systems with similar top rates. For energy companies who are able to leverage up their affiliates and route the interest income to a low-tax jurisdiction, the arbitrage gain can be large indeed.

Because intercompany loans do not appear in consolidated financial statements, it is difficult to assess how much internal leverage the major energy companies employ. Nevertheless, the scale of their producing operations in high-tax locations gives some idea of the potential savings available, and suggests a conclusion that these companies make extensive use of internal leverage. As a consequence, the net arbitrage savings must also be material. Such savings constitute a major offset to any tax deductions foregone through the underleveraging of the parent's capital structure.

A final word is needed as to how parents manage to make loans that incur little or no taxes. This is a complex area that involves the specific incorporation and tax situation of individual companies. Yet a few general comments can be made. First, it is clear that numerous opportunities exist. Some companies are able to establish FINCOs in tax haven locations and not see any of the income realized there be subject to tax in the parent's home location. Where home jurisdictions do tax foreign income, tax credit systems often provide credits that can shield foreign-source interest income from further taxation. Finally, more than a few jurisdictions use moderate tax rates (e.g., 10–15%) and favorable tax treaties to encourage financial subsidiaries to locate there. Examples include Singapore, Hong Kong, and the Netherlands.

Summary: Centralized Financing and Large Energy Projects

Thus far we have seen that industry competition drives energy companies to pursue large projects on a global basis. These large-scale projects offer opportunities to achieve industry-leading cost positions, replace reserves, and earn above-average returns. To pursue these advantages however, energy firms have to accept the special risks which large energy projects entail. Foremost among these is large-bet risk. This is followed by a variety of risks posed by the long execution times characteristic of large energy ventures. Finally, a suite of location risks must be faced in a world where the best geologic prospects increasingly reside in problematic political-economic environments. All of these location risks feedback on and compound the risks of making large bets on projects with long development times.

To compete successfully in this world, major energy firms have found it valuable to maintain a very strong financial posture and use this strong credit operate a Centralized Finance System. This financial strategy enables major firms to differentiate themselves from many weaker competitors and achieve greater access to attractive energy plays. This Centralized Finance System is also highly effective in lowering the firm's after-tax cost of capital. Its efficient workings insure that the marginal cost of both debt and equity is the lowest possible; it also employs an extensive system of tax-optimized internal leverage to compensate for the lower leveraging that a visibly strong parent balance sheet requires.

Finally, a Centralized Finance System is very effective at mitigating some of the risks associated with large projects. It is especially effective at enabling energy firms to work more effectively with financially weak local partners. It also makes a major contribution to facilitating cash remittances to the parent company from risky jurisdictions.

Not every energy firm has the financial strength to employ a Centralized Finance System. For those firms without a super-strong balance sheet, an alternative exists. This alternative can be called the *Project Finance System*. It addresses the same issues posed by large energy projects—opportunity capture and risk management—in an entirely different way.

PROJECT FINANCING OF LARGE ENERGY PROJECTS

In the energy industry, project finance is a technique that has existed since the 1930s and has acquired a wider range of applications over time. Developed as a way for cash-starved entrepreneurs to fund ventures, project finance has matured into a system for financing rapid growth, partnering with stronger firms, and rejuvenating mature operations.

Of course lenders have much to say about the final terms of any project financing. Successive waves of project loan defaults taught lenders to require more security. Many oil/gas project loans defaulted when oil prices collapsed in the 1980s. Bankers were handed the keys of partly completed independent power projects (IPPs) shortly after 2000. Since then, lenders typically require partial or full sponsor guarantees that the project will be completed along with contracts with suppliers and customers that provide some assurance that costs and revenues will be predictable. This has led to a modified definition—*project finance* today refers to borrowing where debt service is provided primarily from sources other than

the project sponsors. This definition embraces not only the cash flow and assets being financed, but also such contractual protections as *ship or pay* and *take or pay* provisions. It also leaves room for sponsors to supply limited support, such as a completion guarantee. Project financing of this type is referred to as *limited recourse financing*.

How then does this type of finance become a Project Finance System? The answer depends on two ingredients: (1) the project sponsor's ability to pick mostly attractive projects and (2) the sponsor's ability to walk away from failed projects with only limited losses.

When these conditions prevail, the following systematic approach becomes possible:

- Sponsors invest only a limited amount of equity in each attractive project. The rest of the necessary capital comes from project debt.
- When the project succeeds, it pays off the project loan and provides a high return on equity; this generates cash equity investments in new projects, and builds a base of paid-up assets that provide a foundation for long-term expansion.
- Cash generation from these successful projects is recycled into a growing number of attractive projects; sponsors continue to employ project loans while limiting their equity at risk in each venture.
- When the occasional disappointing project materializes, sponsors make careful decisions about whether to invest any more equity or walk away. The option to walk away means that losses from truly failed projects can be capped.
- As its scale of operations grows, the investor can make a decision to migrate toward a Centralized Finance System; this would involve securing a parent credit rating and funding projects using the consolidated balance sheet. Project financing may still be used in specific situations where the project's risks make this advisable.

An example of this system in action illustrates its power to fuel growth and help emerging companies compete. The poster child for successful use of a Project Finance System is the Saudi Arabian Basic Industries Corporation (SABIC).

In the 1970s the Kingdom of Saudi Arabia (KSA) decided to diversify its oil-based economy. It also felt it was wasting a valuable resource by flaring the natural gas that was produced along with oil. Yet the KSA did not have much domestic demand for natural gas. The KSA's solution was to build an export-oriented petrochemical industry. SABIC was founded for that purpose. To provide SABIC with cost advantage, the KSA directed its state oil firm, Aramco, to supply it with chemical feedstocks (ethane and propane) at a very low cost. Initially this gas was priced below $40/ton when comparable feeds on the U.S. Gulf Coast went for $100 to $200/ton.

Armed with this cost advantage, SABIC invited international companies to become partners in its various petrochemical ventures. Shell, Mobil, Exxon, and Idemitsu were among the companies that responded. SABIC insisted on project financing each venture. Initial sources of project funds included Saudi state

development funds and the international project finance banks. Arab banks in Persian Gulf countries later joined the program.

The results were dramatic. SABIC was able to build world-scale plants from the start. Its partners brought engineering and operating skills to assure that the plants were competitive with anything operating elsewhere. The combination of big, efficient plants and cheap feedstock made the ventures exports highly competitive. SABIC's profitability grew, allowing it to rapidly expand its plants, production, and revenues. Eventually SABIC stopped inviting partners into new projects, choosing to develop plants on its own. It then began acquiring foreign operations, including the Dutch company DSM and General Electric's plastics business. Throughout it has continued to employ project financing on a venture-by-venture basis. Today, SABIC and ExxonMobil are recognized as the industry cost leaders in commodity petrochemicals. SABIC now enjoys the option to transition towards Centralized Finance.

The SABIC story illustrates how project financing can help a start-up company grow into a global leader. It also shows that a Project Finance System can be effectively applied to large energy-related projects. Let us now consider in more detail how a Project Finance System addresses the competitive challenges and risks inherent in large energy projects.

Project Financing and Competitive Strategy

Earlier on we discussed how large energy projects are related to creating leading low-cost operations and competitive advantage. The large price tags associated with such projects obviously disadvantage financially weaker firms. These same firms are also ill suited to bear the outsized risks that large energy projects carry. How then does a Project Finance System work to overcome these disadvantages and enable smaller energy players to compete?

The first answer to this question is that a Project Finance System minimizes the amount of equity funds that smaller players must invest in each project. Consequently, a sponsor with a finite amount of cash can fund many more projects using a Project Finance System than would be possible otherwise. Assuming the projects are successful, this allows a sponsor to capture high returns on equity and compound its funds available for reinvestment at a rapid rate. Over time this approach can enable sponsors to invest in individual large-scale projects and to grow the assets rapidly. In this way, a firm like SABIC can transform itself from a start-up to a global player operating world-scale plants.

The second answer is related to the first. By minimizing the amount of sponsor funds invested in each project, a project financing system also minimizes the sponsor's exposure to individual project risks. Assuming the financing is truly nonrecourse, the sponsor should lose no more than its equity from a failed bet. In many cases that equity stake will amount to 30 percent or less of the project's capital cost. Project financing also involves many structural features that mitigate specific project risks. It can be especially effective at minimizing remittance risks and can provide unique protections against a range of political risks. These project finance attributes will be discussed in more detail below. For now the point to emphasize is this—a project financing system allows smaller energy players to minimize their investment stake exposed to large project risk; it then goes on to mitigate specific

Exhibit 13.5 De-Levered Project Economics

Year	0	1–10	Residual
Capital	(100)		10
EBITDA		15.8	
Less: DA		(10)	
EBIT		5.8	
Less: interest expense		0	
Less: taxes @ 35%		(2)	
Net income (NI)		3.8	
Net cash flow (NI + DA)		13.8	
NPV@ 8% = –3.1			
IRR = 7.3%			

commercial and location risks through structural features embedded in the loan's terms and conditions.

At this point it is necessary to provide more details about how a type of financing that reduces project risk can also elevate investor returns. This requires a discussion of what is known as *leveraged economics*. Most energy players, and virtually all large ones, evaluate projects on the basis of *de-levered economics*. This approach reflects the full cost of a project and projects future cash flows without any impacts from financing; that is no payments of interest or principal. The project's net cash flows are then discounted at the firm's weighted average cost of capital (WACC). If a positive Net Present Value results, the project's economics justify proceeding with the project. This approach has been the energy industry's basic evaluation tool for some 50 years. An example of this approach for a "marginal" project appears in Exhibit 13.5.

Avoiding financing effects in these economics allows an apples-to-apples comparison among energy projects with different economic lives, cash flow profiles, and locations. The effects of debt financing are confined to the WACC, which provides the discount rate. The implicit assumption is that the firm raises capital using a Centralized System backed by all its assets. If a firm wants a further refinement to reflect the fact that different business lines have different capacities to support debt, it can use multiple WACCs and discount rates.

The use of project financing restructures this approach. Project financing legally encumbers specific assets in favor of the project lenders. By extension, a sponsor's other assets are legally protected. This new situation allows project economics to be reconfigured. Specific debt financing can be assigned to the specific assets being financed. The sponsor's *investment at risk* is also limited to its equity invested into the project. Effecting these changes transforms de-levered project economics into *leveraged economics*.

Four changes are necessary to convert de-levered to leveraged economics. First, upfront project capital costs are reduced to only the sponsor's equity invested in the project. Second, the project loan that funds the remaining capital cost must be paid back. A repayment schedule is assumed, and project cash flows are duly debited to fund principal amortization. Third, cash flows are also debited for interest

Exhibit 13.6 Leveraged Project

Year	0	1–7	8	9	10	Residual Value
Capital	(40)					10
EBITDA		15.8	15.8	15.8	15.8	
Less: DA		(10)	(10)	(10)	(10)	
EBIT		5.8	5.8	5.8	5.8	
Less: interest expense		(3.6)	(3.6)	(2.4)	(1.2)	
Less: taxes @ 35%		(.8)	(.8)	(1.2)	(1.6)	
Debt repayment			(20)	(20)	(20)	
Net cash flow	(40)	11.4	(8.6)	(7.8)	(7.0)	10

NPV@ 8% = \$11.5
IRR = 18% on equity

expense on the outstanding project loan balance. Finally, income taxes are recomputed to reflect the deductibility of interest. This lowers taxes and is a credit to project cash flows.

The net effect of these changes is usually positive for a project's cash flow profile. Significant upfront capital is deferred for years until it is paid out as loan amortization. The project's tax bill is substantially reduced. For these credits, the project incurs interest expense. Unless the loan interest rate is exceptionally expensive, this trade-off substantially improves the cash flow profile. This can be seen by transforming the previous de-levered economic example to leveraged economics as is shown in Exhibit 13.6. An unexceptional project loan equal to 60 percent of project costs and bearing interest at 6 percent is assumed.

The results of this financial restructuring are eye catching. Without changing the underlying project economics, the Net Present Value has been elevated from a negative to a substantial positive number. The IRR of the sponsor's equity has jumped to 18 percent.

A remaining question concerns the discount rate to use for leveraged economics. In the example above, the sponsor's WACC of 8 percent continues to be employed. This is defensible on the grounds that the sponsor raises its equity away from the project using some mix of debt and equity. The result is a *double leveraging* effect, whereby debt is employed both at the sponsor and project levels. Many sponsors value this effect and finance projects and leveraged buyouts in exactly this fashion. Other, possibly more conservative approaches are to use the sponsor's cost of equity as the discount rate or compute a project cost of capital. Typically these approaches raise the discount rate. Some practitioners also argue for adding a financial risk premium to compensate for leveraging the project capital structure. In most cases these adjustments do not change the basic answer—leveraged economics showing substantially improved returns on equity versus de-levered returns on total capital costs. In fact, higher discount rates can end up improving returns if the project is highly leveraged and the repayment of principal sufficiently deferred.

Large Project Risks and a Project Finance System

For obvious reasons large project risks are more threatening to financially weaker energy companies. However, skillful employment of a Project Finance System can mitigate these risks in a surprising number of ways.

This strategy begins with careful legal segregation of the assets being project financed. So long as the loan terms are crafted to be nonrecourse after project completion, sponsors only expose a finite amount of equity to each project's operating and commercial risks. Even if one or more big projects fail to perform, the sponsors' other, successful ventures should proceed unaffected.

Second, weaker players can combine project financing with joint ventures of their largest opportunities. The joint venture can be with strong players who bring execution and operating skills to the project; this allows the weaker player to preserve his capabilities for more digestible, 100 percent–owned opportunities. Using project financing in joint venture situations also limits the amount of equity interest a sponsor must *sell down*. A simple example will illustrate the point. Assume that a sponsor has a $1 billion opportunity but only $200 million to invest. Using only its own funds, it would have to divest 80 percent of the venture to other parties. However, using project financing to fund 60 percent of costs, the required equity drops to $400 million. The sponsor can then retain a 50 percent interest and possibly a lead operating role with its $200 million.

Project finance loan structures can also solve remittance concerns. This is especially the case for export projects in risky locations. Loans for these ventures typically establish *offshore accounts* and *cash waterfalls*. The former refers to bank accounts set up in a secure banking center (e.g., New York or London), to which all export customers are instructed to direct their payments. The latter refers to the written, irrevocable instructions to the bank as to how cash received is to be paid out. Lenders rank near the top, usually right after operating costs and taxes. What matters for sponsors, however, is that their project's revenues are kept in hard currency and in a safe location. Inconvertibility, devaluation, and other risks are thus mitigated.

Project financing can also be very helpful on the large project political risks that characterize many frontier locations. Project financing brings three forms of benefits in such situations:

1. *Stake reduction*: the project loan reduces the amount of funds that the major firm puts at risk.
2. *Arbitrary Act Deterrence*: the project loan is made by specific lenders whom the host country is eager not to offend with unreliable behavior.
3. *Terms clarification*: the project loan terms clarify ambiguities that the host country might later exploit while providing for dispute resolution in a neutral location.

The first of these has been touched on before. The second deserves some explanation. Energy companies have observed that certain lenders, most especially export credit agencies (ECAs) and multilateral agencies (MLAs), such as the World Bank, bring a degree of political protection to projects they finance. Host countries value these credit sources and try to keep their lines to future funding open.

Increasingly, energy firms strive to include some of these entities in the lending groups funding their risky projects.

Terms clarification is perhaps the most underrated of project financing's means for mitigating political risk. Frequently host governments and state companies prefer to leave critical deal terms ambiguous. Then, once the project is completed, they interpret the vague provisions to their advantage. Foreign investors, especially those of modest size, can find themselves with few means to defend their interests. Project financing introduces a new set of players, the lenders, into the situation. Lenders are usually insistent on clarifying terms that might jeopardize timely payment of interest and principal. Energy companies of all weights have come to value these clarifications, which often align with their interests.

If a Project Finance System can help weaker players compete, elevate their returns, and reduce their project risks, a question arises as to why all energy companies don't employ such a system? Its potential benefits seem almost irresistible. The answer is twofold: (1) project financing also creates risks that can undermine its benefits; and (2) most energy companies, even the biggest practitioners of Centralized Finance, do find it attractive, but only in specific situations. We now turn to these matters.

Pitfalls of a Project Finance System

The pitfalls of a Project Finance System are rooted in the two pre conditions mentioned earlier: (1) the project sponsor's ability to pick mostly attractive projects; and (2) the sponsor's ability to walk away from failed projects with only defined and limited losses. Many sponsors find it difficult to meet both conditions for more than a couple of projects. Meeting them over the extended time span (e.g., 5–10 years) that is required to grow from start-up to world class competitor is much more difficult.

The ability to continuously identify attractive projects is usually rooted in a sustainable competitive advantage. SABIC's example makes the point. From inception, the company gained feedstock costs lower than other global producers. This advantage attracted interest from household-name foreign firms. Their presence addressed weaknesses in SABIC's initial management and operating capabilities; early projects that might have failed under SABIC-only development were instead successful, and SABIC was able to build upon that success.

SABIC-style competitive advantage is hard to achieve let alone sustain. Firms that develop an advantage usually attract imitation and competition. Advantages typically erode unless the originator is dynamic and innovative. In SABIC's case, the KSA provided protection for its competitive advantage. SABIC was given cheap feedstock by government decree, and no other competitor, foreign or domestic, was granted similar supplies. Most private energy companies cannot count on starting up with such a privileged position.

The more common case is that an initial competitive advantage erodes over time. Calpine, the electric power company, is a case in point. Calpine developed a low-cost combined-cycle generation plant model based upon using natural gas. When Calpine developed this model, U.S. natural gas was abundant and cheap. Calpine used a Project Finance System to rapidly grow generating capacity. In 1999 it launched a program to grow capacity from 6,300 MW to 15,000–25,000 MW.

First Boston, a New York investment bank, helped Calpine develop a revolving project finance facility, Calpine Construction Finance Company (CCFC), whereby Calpine's first set of plants would generate the cash to underpin debt financing for the next set.

Over time, however, cheap gas led other power producers and chemical companies to base new facilities on such supplies. The U.S. natural gas surplus disappeared, and prices rose dramatically. Calpine's cost advantage proved ephemeral. When California went into recession post-dotcom and 9/11, electricity prices declined, and Calpine's spark spread margins were compressed. At this point the high fixed charges associated with its project finance loans put multiple loan facilities and plants into default. Calpine, whose stock was priced at $50/share in 2001, went bankrupt and was de-listed by the NYSE in December 2005.

Calpine's story also contains elements of the second project finance pitfall. At the moment when Calpine turned most aggressive, the terms on which it accessed project loans involved increasing recourse. In launching CCFC, Calpine agreed to provide a full completion guarantee for the first four plants. It also promised that Calpine's parent would maintain certain consolidated financial ratios. This meant that if Calpine's parent failed to meet these ratios, lenders could attach the first four plants unless Calpine parent did something to remedy its default. Finally, the term of the financing was only four years. There was no way cash generation from the first four units would pay down all the debt in that limited time span. Calpine was banking on being able to refinance the first loans and attract more CCFC funding for the next generation plants. It needed a strong success story for this to be feasible. If such refinancing proved impossible (as it did), Calpine would have to step up (which it could not) or face loss of the plants (which it only avoided through bankruptcy).

In fact, the project finance landscape is littered with stories of firms who became enamored of project financing, only to learn that it requires care and discipline to use successfully. A firm as famous and competent as Walt Disney discovered this as well. Disney financed Euro Disney with a project finance structure of amazing complexity and skill. The deal was so good for Disney that only a home run performance by the park and hotels would cover the debts owed the project lenders. Unfortunately, the park and hotels underperformed projections, and the loans quickly went into default. It was then that Disney discovered a hard truth—even though the loan terms gave it the legal right to walk away, Disney couldn't actually do so. The damage to the Disney brand and reputation would be too great. Euro Disney's loans and contracts were restructured, and then restructured again, with Disney surrendering many preferential terms and putting up more equity.

Perhaps the most egregious example of a firm fooling itself about project financing is Enron. Early in its history Enron made reasonable use of project finance structures to raise funds for its Gas Bank scheme and for trading natural gas futures. Over time, however, it increasingly had recourse to dubious structures whose principal objective was to disguise the amount of debt Enron had taken on. To complete these repeated trips to the project finance market, Enron was forced to concede more recourse to the parent's balance sheet. For example, in one structure, Whitewing, Enron promised Citibank that it would donate more Enron stock to the structure if the stock price fell below a certain threshold.

These problematic practices had two effects. First, they fooled Enron's management as to the state of its indebtedness. Only at an August 2001 board meeting did CFO Andy Fastow tell the board that Enron had over $35 billion in debt. The financial statements were showing $10 billion. Fastow then told the board not to be concerned because the additional debt was all "nonrecourse to Enron." Unfortunately, it was not. When Enron's stock fell precipitously in fall 2001, the various debt triggers were hit, and Enron was obliged to step up at the worst possible time. Two months later the firm was bankrupt.

These cautionary tales have a common thread. Project financing's allure can be seductive. Over time, users find that their future projects are not as robust as those already funded while lender terms stiffen. Lacking discipline, many overreach and end up in distress. How then can the user of a Project Financing System strike the right balance between growth and discipline?

An Optimized Project Finance System

To make proper use of a Project Finance System, weaker firms must carefully appraise their situation. Several key questions must be answered:

- How robust is the competitive advantage at the heart of the investment program?
- Will this advantage erode or disappear as investments move beyond the immediate set?
- Does the firm have the execution and operating capabilities to support rapid growth?
- Will lender terms stiffen as more deals complete, or will an improving financial situation allow the firm to enter new capital markets on more favorable terms?

If the answer to these questions is mostly negative, as it often is for weaker firms, a hybrid Project Finance System is recommended. This hybrid approach has the following three guidelines:

1. Project finance its most attractive, early projects. Use the cash flow from these successful ventures to build a stronger consolidated financial position.
2. Study the subsequent opportunity set carefully with the following rules in mind:
   a. Attractive projects that may stress execution capability should be joint ventured.
   b. Project-finance only attractive projects whose predictable cash flows allow reasonable loan and nonrecourse terms to be achieved.
   c. Sacrifice growth at the margin rather than undertaking marginal projects on the basis of less favorable project loans.
3. Use success from this second wave of projects to establish an investment-grade credit rating. From there, fund a core budget using a Centralized Financing System. Use project finance at the margin for projects well suited to the technique or whose special partner-risk circumstances favor the use of project loans.

Firms, like SABIC, who enjoy an unusual and enduring competitive advantage, can take a more aggressive approach. However, most start-up private firms in competitive markets would be well advised to adopt the discipline implied in the guidelines above.

To complete the discussion of a Project Finance System, we now turn to how stronger firms incorporate project financing into an overall Centralized Finance System.

Financially Strong Firms, Large Energy Projects, and Project Financing

Even energy companies with the strongest credits have learned the value of integrating project financing into their Centralized Finance Systems. The most common circumstance where they do so involves joint ventures with weaker partners. A second situation involves projects with unusually acute political risks. Since large frontier energy projects increasingly involve both conditions, major energy firms are doing more project financing today than they did 20 years ago. Locations as diverse as Qatar, Nigeria, Azerbaijan and Papua New Guinea have completed their first ever project loans during this period.

The issue that arises with weak partners is known as *overfinancing*. Its most obvious form has the weaker partner asking to be *carried* by the stronger firm. This involves the stronger firm funding not only its share of project expenses but also those of the weaker partner. Typically this overfunding becomes an interest-bearing loan, with the weaker partner directing that the loan be repaid out of its share of project cash flows. In effect, the weaker partner project finances its share of project costs by forcing the stronger partner to be its banker.

Carries are rightly considered by strong partners to be expensive. In essence, the strong partner is taking all project equity risks, for which it receives only its share of the equity returns plus a project loan return on the carry. This results in a negative opportunity cost on the carry equal to the difference between the debt rate received and the equity return foregone. Strong partners typically capitalize this negative return at their WACC and reflect it as a cash flow debit in project economics. Such debits are often large and can kill projects. Carrying a partner is also an unfortunate precedent. It tends to lead current partners to ask for other preferential treatment and encourage potential future partners to expect similar help. For these reasons, strong energy players are justifiably adverse to granting carries.

Project financing can be very helpful for resolving overfinancing situations. At a minimum, it reduces the size of the carry under discussion. Even better, many times it will reduce the weak partner's equity contribution to an affordable sum. A simple example will illustrate. Consider a $1 billion project with a major energy firm and a local state company as 50/50 partners. In a straight carry situation, the state firm would look to finance its $500 million share of project costs by having the major firm fund this amount and its own share. If instead the partners agree on project financing 70 percent of costs, the two partners must only fund the remaining $300 million, or $150 million each. In the best case, the state firm is able to contribute this smaller sum. In the worst case, the carry funding is greatly reduced.

Overfinancing issues arise in many forms. In addition to carry requests, weak partners sometimes simply fail to meet *cash calls* during construction. This can leave strong partners with the unappetizing choice of disrupting construction or advancing the defaulting partner's share. Weak partners also ask for the guarantees to be backstopped by the stronger firm. This can take the form of *joint and several guarantees*, where partners guarantee both their own share of costs and backstop their partner's guarantee. Project financing can help mitigate these risks as well. Lenders are also interested in efficient project execution. Often they will support loan document language that spells out clear penalties for partners who fail to meet cash call obligations. Assuming the stronger partner is smart enough not to concede a joint and several guarantee, lenders will also press to assure that the weaker partner can perform on the guarantees it provides.

Earlier we saw how project financing can enable smaller firms to bear large project risks, including political risk. Major firms also use project financing when faced with acute location and political risks. Here the most dramatic example involved the Chad-Cameroon pipeline. Approximately one billion barrels of crude were discovered in Chad starting in the 1970s. Yet, none of it was produced until the World Bank agreed in 1999 to join a project lending consortium. Chad is a landlocked country; its oil could only reach commercial markets via a 670-mile pipeline built through Cameroon. Private lenders were concerned that the oil production could be held hostage by either Chad or Cameroon shutting down the pipeline. This fear was only overcome when the World Bank and its agency, the IFC joined the pipeline loan consortium. ECAs, including U.S. Export-Import Bank and Coface also participated.

Some things are noteworthy in this deal's structure. Funding was not really the issue; Exxon, Chevron, and Petronas had ample resources to pay for all project costs. The amounts lent by the World Bank/IFC were quite small—less than $100M. It was their presence in the project that was valuable. Second, all the ECA/MLA funds were targeted on the politically vulnerable pipeline. The World Bank's money went specifically to finance pipeline equity stakes for the Chad and Cameroon governments, thus making those governments partners in the project's most politically vulnerable asset. This was designed political deterrence. The results are instructive. The pipeline got built, starting up in 2003. Considerable frictions followed between the World Bank and the Chad government. Eventually, Chad repaid the Bank, but the IFC and the ECAs remain as lenders. Meanwhile, the private investors' deal terms have remained intact, and the pipeline has operated without impediment.

In sum, major energy firms that practice Centralized Finance have learned that project financing can be a valuable component of their system. By avoiding or reducing carry requests, project financing can break partner deadlocks that might cause valuable large energy projects to be canceled. The same holds for mitigating project political risks that otherwise would leave energy resources undeveloped. Major firms still raise the funds they put into these projects in a centralized fashion, and may still route them to the project location using their internal finance system. However, the funds they put at risk are reduced by the use of project loans, by the fact that partners are encouraged to fund their appropriate share of costs, and by the presence of other influential parties in the lending group.

Summary: Project Financing and Large Energy Projects

As we mentioned earlier, relative to its economic importance, there has been only limited attention paid in the literature to project financing as a source of value creation. Our approach has been to present the practice of project financing of large energy projects in a manner that highlights some more general salient aspects of the project finance model.

It is apparent that optimally designed and executed project financing of large energy projects is the solution to a very complex contractual design problem. This contractual design problem is generated by the so-called real-world imperfections relative to the Modigliani-Miller (1958) world: taxation, transactions costs, economic benefits of risk management, imperfect/asymmetric information, and moral hazard/agency conflicts. The analysis of project financing of large energy projects allows one to identify some of the major forces that come into play in using project finance as a value-creating instrument.

Axiomatically, large energy projects have infra-marginal effects on both input and output markets. But the very size of these projects alters, often very substantially, the industry structure and the distribution of competitive advantage among the major players. But it is also the case that these projects exhibit high risks that are difficult to manage using traditional (derivative-based) instruments. As we have repeatedly emphasized above, the energy sector is relatively unique because even the biggest firms cannot control price risk at the market level. The combination of the infra-marginal economic effects with the intrinsically high risk puts a great onus on the project sponsors to create an *option play* in large projects, whereby they can benefit on the upside but can walk away on the downside without significantly damaging the corporate credit rating and financial strength that is central to their long-term competitive advantage. This option play may serve as negotiating leverage vis-à-vis arbitrary government actions or may be triggered in cases of acute deterioration, such as Venezuela's recent actions against ExxonMobil and Conoco Phillips's heavy oil projects. And by allowing a relatively small equity stake to be leveraged into financing a large project, such financing may especially benefit entrants and smaller players to rapidly ramp up scale and learning.

Taking the view that scope of firms is determined through an optimal or cost minimizing *nexus of contracts* (Jensen and Meckling 1976), project financing has additional attractions of reducing the agency risk from moral hazard (or opportunism) of resource owners—such as capital expropriation by resource owners—because a truly nonrecourse financing allows sponsors to put a floor, so to speak, on their equity investment risk. We have provided considerable detail above to explicate the power of properly designed and executed project finance contracts to reduce political risk, which moral hazard really is a particular form of agency risk, albeit one that has been understudied in the literature.

Here we would also emphasize the role that well designed project finance contracts play in addressing imperfect and/or asymmetric information, as when their detailed provisions clarify host government intentions and provide clear remedies for various adverse contingencies. Indeed, a take-away from this formulation is that project financing may be superior to centralized financing because it can reduce through appropriate contract design the moral hazard for opportunistic

behavior by resource owners or other joint venture partners. Another useful perspective from the efficient nexus of contracts formulation is that by creating an entity separate from the corporation, project financing allows companies to avoid disclosing strategic company-wide information, which would be otherwise necessary if there was external financing at the corporate level. This is particularly the case for weaker investors for whom extensive public disclosure can amount to the enumeration of a daunting risk catalogue. To illustrate, consider a weaker credit having to seek additional financing through seasoned equity offers or public debt issue. In such cases, capital market institutions such as the lead underwriters and debt ratings agency have high thresholds of disclosure. In contrast, in project financing the level of disclosure is asset-specific. This can be a substantial source of advantage in negotiating terms that are beneficial to the company.[7]

Of course, and as we have noted above, project financing comes with its own set of pitfalls and risks. In particular, overestimation of competitive advantage can lead to a lemons problem (Akerlof 1970) or adverse selection in project choice, along with the agency costs of monitoring behavior of project partners.

Furthermore and as often happens with contracting imperfections, potential advantages can turn into liabilities (or vice versa) depending on the context. Specifically, we have emphasized an appealing feature of project finance, namely, allowing sponsors to participate in large and potentially high return projects with limited equity investment. But in the presence of moral hazard, the low equity stake can provide low-powered incentives for the sponsors: There is often a fine line between having a limited risk exposure and having too little skin in the game.[8]

FINANCING LARGE ENERGY PROJECTS: SUMMARY AND CONCLUSIONS

Financing large energy projects has become a central feature of energy industry competition. Large projects provide the best means to grow production to meet the demands of a developing world and offset declines from earlier ventures. Only large projects provide the economies of scale and other efficiencies to assure that their sponsors can compete in the low-cost-producer-wins energy business. Yet large projects also bring outsized risks. Energy companies who fail to solve the challenge of undertaking many large projects without suffering large setbacks eventually find that they disappear as independent entities.

Financing is a major challenge in this competitive world. Large amounts of capital must be assured over long planning horizons to succeed in a world where projects can take three to six years to develop and up to a decade to recover the capital invested. Successful energy players must find ways to assure both a ready access to long-term capital and ways to use their financing efforts to mitigate large project risks.

Two approaches have proven successful at performing these feats. The Centralized Finance System is the dominant approach. It combines strong central credit with a sophisticated intercompany financing system and selective use of project financing to provide major companies with a suite of advantages. Low-cost debt and equity, efficient use of internal cash generation, global tax optimization, and enhanced remittances of affiliate cash are its most salient accomplishments.

Project financing can economize a firms' capital, allowing it to do more projects than using only its own resources would allow. Through the use of leveraged economics, firms also can harvest high returns on equity and compete effectively in bidding situations. These considerations are especially attractive for start-up or weaker energy players who have found that a Project Financing System can enable them to commercialize their attractive opportunities and compete with the majors in specific situations. Considerable discipline is required to practice this system successfully. Practitioners who fail to project-finance only economically robust projects and preserve "nonrecourse" loan terms, tend to overreach over time. Financial distress and even bankruptcy can then result.

Ultimately, successful practitioners of both systems end up developing hybrid solutions. Project Finance players strive to build consolidated financial strength and move towards centralized financing. Major firms end up incorporating project finance as a component of their centralized approach. These results suggest that the best-practice financing model for large energy projects uses Centralized Finance for its core investment program, while developing disciplined guidelines for using Project Finance on an exception basis (i.e., as needed).

However, it is transparent from the foregoing discussion that much work remains to be done on a contract-theoretic analysis of centralized versus project financing. We believe we are among the first to indicate the potential usefulness of the nexus-of-contract approach to developing a more rigorous but practicable framework for comparing the relative benefits of the two financing models.[9] Along with the considerations of tax optimization, risk management, and transactions costs minimization, this approach would systematically and rigorously recognize the strengths and weaknesses of the two financing models with respect to the variety of agency conflicts—among the project partners, between lenders and borrowers, and along the internal corporate hierarchy—that are often sufficiently important to change the sign of the realized rate of returns.

DISCUSSION QUESTIONS

1. What are the unique characteristics of large energy projects, and why can't one apply the standard corporate finance framework to finance these projects?

2. Explain how value is created using project financing. Use the Modigliani and Miller (1958) world and the five imperfections to answer the question.

3. What is the Centralized Finance Model? As part of your answer, list and explain the six guidelines to finance large projects.

4. What are the benefits of Centralized Finance for large energy projects?

5. How did SABIC use project financing as a start-up company to become a global leader?

6. A Project Financing System minimizes the amount of equity funds that smaller players must invest in each project. This statement is:
   a. True
   b. False

7. Explain how project financing can reduce project risk and also elevate investor's returns using leveraged economics. Provide an example to illustrate your response.

8. Project Finance loan structures cannot solve remittance concerns. This statement is:
   a. True
   b. False

9. What are the pitfalls of a Project Finance System? Give two examples.

10. To make proper use of a Project Finance System, what key questions must be answered?

11. Financing is a major challenge in this competitive world. Successful energy players must find ways to assure both a ready access to long-term capital and ways to use their financing efforts to mitigate large project risks. What two financing approaches have proven successful at performing these feats? List and describe each.

NOTES

1. Project economics in the regulated power sector, while sharing some of the features emphasized in this chapter (such as large capital requirements and long horizons), are sufficiently different from those in the oil and gas industry to merit a separate treatment.

2. Of course, prior to the financial crisis of 2008 there was explosive growth in asset securitization in the financial services industry, especially the mortgage financing industry.

3. We distinguish between imperfect and asymmetric information: the former refers to a situation where all parties are uncertain about the true distribution of returns whereas in the latter some parties have better information than the others. We also distinguish between the agency costs incurred in principal-agent relationships (such as shareholders and managers) and a moral hazard costs that arise, for example, from opportunistic behavior by project sponsors. Our discussion will indicate that the relative optimality of project financing is influenced by the presence of both imperfect and/or asymmetric information, and by both moral hazard and agency costs.

4. A more general analysis of the role of risk management in raising firm value is provided by, among others, Stulz (1984); Smith and Stulz (1985); and Nance, Smith, and Smithson (1993). The debt overhang problem is discussed in Myers (1977), while Jensen (1986, 1993) emphasizes the free cash flow agency problem.

5. Oil and gas price volatility, whether computed at short or long durations, exceeds by a wide margin the price volatility of stocks and other financial securities (see for example Kumar and Rabinovitch 2011).

6. This was demonstrated most dramatically during the late 1990s. Then, as oil prices plummeted below $10/b, BP bought Amoco and Arco while Exxon acquired Mobil. Press commentary at the time labeled these "mergers of weakness." That characterization was revised during the subsequent decade when oil prices recovered and these firms harvested historic profitability levels.

7. The bargaining advantages that stem from private information have been analyzed extensively in the economics literature (see Osborne and Rubinstein 1994).

8. See Holmstrom (1979) for a definitive analysis of the relationship between effort incentives and share in profit or output.

9. Such an approach has been quite successful, for example, in developing a framework for analyzing the net benefits of various types of loan and bond covenants; see Smith and Warner (1979) and Chava, Kumar, and Warga (2010).

REFERENCES

Akerlof, G. 1970. "The Market for Lemons: Quality Uncertainty and the Market Mechanism." *Quarterly Journal of Economics* 84:3, 488–500.

Brealey, R., and S. Myers. 2002. *Corporate Finance: Capital Investment and Valuation*. New York: McGraw-Hill.

Bruner, R. F., H. Langohr, and A. Campbell. 2008. "Project Financing: An Economic Overview." Darden Case No. UVA-F-1035.

Chava, S., P. Kumar, and A. Warga. 2010. "Managerial Agency and Bond Covenants." *Review of Financial Studies* 23:3, 1120–1148.

Esty, B. 2004. "Why Study Large Projects? An Introduction to Research on Project Financing." *European Financial Management* 10:2, 213–224.

Esty, B., and I. Christov. 2002. "An Overview of the Project Finance Market—2002 Update." Harvard Business School Technical Note.

Holmstrom, B. 1979. "Moral Hazard and Observability." *Bell Journal of Economics* 10:1, 74–91.

Jensen, M. 1986. "Agency Costs of Free Cash Flow, Corporate Finance, and Takeovers." *American Economic Review* 76:2, 323–329.

Jensen, M. 1993. "The Modern Industrial Revolution, Exit, and Failure of Internal Control Systems." *Journal of Finance* 48:3, 831–880.

Jensen, M., and W. Meckling. 1976. "Theory of the Firm: Managerial Behavior, Agency Costs and Ownership Structure." *Journal of Financial Economics* 3:4, 305–360.

Kumar, P., and R. Rabinovitch. 2011. "CEO Entrenchment and Corporate Risk Management." Working paper. University of Houston.

Leland, H. 2007. "Financial Synergies and Optimal Scope of the Firm: Implications for Mergers, Spinoffs, and Structured Finance." *Journal of Finance* 62:2, 765–807.

Modigliani, F., and M. Miller. 1958. "The Cost of Capital, Corporation Finance and the Theory of Investment." *American Economic Review* 48:3, 261–297.

Myers, S. 1977. "Determinants of Corporate Borrowing." *Journal of Financial Economics* 5:2, 147–175.

Nance, D., C. Smith, and C. Smithson. 1993. "On the Determinants of Corporate Hedging." *Journal of Finance* 48:1, 267–284.

Osborne, M., and A. Rubinstein. 1994. *A Course in Game Theory*. Cambridge: MIT Press.

Smith, C., and R. Stulz. 1985. "The Determinants of Firms' Hedging Policies." *Journal of Financial and Quantitative Analysis* 20:4, 391–405.

Smith, C., and J. Warner. 1979. "On Financial Contracting: An Analysis of Bond Covenants." *Journal of Financial Economics* 7:2, 117–161.

Stulz, R. 1984. "Optimal Hedging Policies." *Journal of Financial and Quantitative Analysis* 19:2, 127–140.

Stulz, R. 1996. "Rethinking Risk Management." *Journal of Applied Corporate Finance* 9:3, 8–25.

ABOUT THE CONTRIBUTORS

Praveen Kumar, PhD is the Texas Commerce Bank/Tenneco Professor of Finance and Chair, Department of Finance in the C. T. Bauer College of Business at the University of Houston. He is also the co-founder and executive director of the Global Energy Management Institute at the University of Houston. He is the recipient of the University of Houston Research and Scholarship Excellence Award (at the level of Professor) *and* the University of Houston Teaching Excellence Award. (Both these awards are for the entire UH system.) He also received the Award for Excellence in the Classroom from Carnegie-Mellon University. Dr. Kumar received the AB (Honors) and MPA degrees from Princeton University, and the PhD in Economics from Stanford University. His teaching interests include corporate finance and risk management, real options and project evaluation in the energy industry, carbon trading, security pricing, and financial market microstructure.

Dr. Kumar is very widely published in the top finance, economic, and management journals. His research interests focus on the role of information in financial

markets, organizations, and trading; executive compensation and corporate governance; payout policy; and competitive strategy and industrial organization. His research has been discussed in major business publications like *Business Week*, the *Wall Street Journal*, and *Financial Times*. He has received numerous awards for his research and teaching. Dr. Kumar has taken a leading role in the establishment of the Global Energy Management Institute at the C. T. Bauer College of Business. Most recently, his research in energy finance has focused on the application of real options valuation and risk-management approaches to the development of unconventional sources in oil and gas. He is also a co-instructor in one of the first graduate courses on the practice and future of carbon trading to be offered in business schools. He has also consulted widely with major investment banks, energy corporations, international lending institutions, and regulatory agencies such as the CFTC.

Stephen V. Arbogast served from 1999 to 2004 as the treasurer of ExxonMobil Chemical Company and has over 30 years experience in finance working with Exxon Corporation and ExxonMobil Chemical. While treasurer of Chemicals, Arbogast held positions that included director of Qenos (Australia's sole manufacturer of polyethylene, a joint venture with Orica PLC), director of Dexco (a joint venture with Dow Chemical), and director of Al Jubai Petrochemical Company in Saudi Arabia. Other former positions included vice president of finance for SeaRiver Maritime Inc. (the former Exxon Shipping Company), treasurer for Exxon Capital Corporation, finance and planning manager for Esso Brasileira de Petroleo in Brazil, and treasurer of Esso Central America, Panama, and Mexico.

Currently serving as an Executive Professor of Finance at the C. T. Bauer College of Business, Arbogast's teaching career has focused on international finance, project financing and business ethics. In addition to authoring over 50 case studies based on his experiences at ExxonMobil, he has previously taught at both Fordham University's Graduate School of Business in New York and Rice University's Jesse Jones Graduate School of Management in Houston.

Arbogast has authored articles on the energy industry focusing on the future of the U.S. Gulf Coast refining and petrochemical industries. He also is the author of *Resisting Corporate Corruption, Lessons in Practical Ethics from the Enron Wreckage* (M & M Scrivener Press, 2008). His most recent publication (2009) is "Project Financing & Political Risk Mitigation: The Singular Case of the Chad-Cameroon Pipeline," *Texas Journal of Oil, Gas and Energy Law* 4:2, 269–298.

CHAPTER 14

Financing Bio-Fuels Projects: Case Study Lessons

STEPHEN V. ARBOGAST
C. T. Bauer College of Business at the University of Houston

INTRODUCTION

Bio-fuels projects have been a growing factor in U.S. energy markets for over a decade. Today, corn-based ethanol plants deliver over 12 billion gallons per year into America's gasoline pool. Bio-diesel also exists, though on a much smaller scale. Rapid expansion of domestic bio-fuels manufacturing is now an official U.S. public policy objective. The Energy Independence and Security Act (EISA) of 2007 established aggressive mandates for 2022. By that year the U.S. gasoline pool is required to include 36 billion gallons of assorted bio-fuels. Only 15 billion gallons of corn-based ethanol is incorporated into this mandate. The rest is expected to come from "cellulosic-based bio-fuels (CBFs)" and other "advanced bio-fuels (ABFs)." What exactly are these new bio-fuels, and what is going to determine whether they appear on time or not?

The answers to these questions will greatly depend on whether the likely CBF/ABF developers can attract necessary financing. Access to financing will in turn depend on who the CBF/ABF developers turn out to be and whether public policy provides them with the right help.

When the EISA legislation was written, it was widely expected that CBFs would be the biggest new fuel contributor. CBFs can be produced by enzymatic/fermentation or thermal/chemical approaches. Some 16 billion gallons of such materials were anticipated to help meet the EISA mandates. As for the ABFs, specific expectations here were less defined. Indeed, the terminology *advanced* was suggestive of the reality that nobody knew exactly which of several possibilities might work out.

Four years later it is possible to provide some more definition. U.S. corn ethanol producers should be able to meet the 15-billion-gallon target and have potential to go further. Whether they will be encouraged or allowed to do so will depend upon the complex political reconsideration of corn ethanol now ongoing. As for CBFs, progress here has been slower than expected. In the ABF area a number of possibilities have emerged, but these face years of development before commercialization may be possible.

What has been the cause of this disappointingly slow progress? Generally it can be summarized as follows—breaking down and converting the biomass raw materials has proven more costly and harder to improve than hoped. The enzymatic/fermentation approaches are hard to scale up; the thermal/chemical approaches require technical breakthroughs and new catalysts; they also are capital and energy intensive; this makes them expensive, especially in an era of rising energy prices. As a result, all methods under study are struggling to demonstrate cost-competitiveness with conventional hydrocarbons. Because of this, major energy companies, the ones with the biggest balance sheets and most capacity to bear risk, are lukewarm at best on developing these opportunities.

Assuming this situation doesn't change, that will leave the development of CBFs and ABFs to two other types of players: (1) pure play refiners, forest and food products companies, and biomass firms; and (2) private equity/entrepreneurs. Few, if any, of these players have the financial strength to underwrite the development program and projects entailed in commercializing new bio-fuels. Such conditions will also make financing bio-fuels the final and possibly the biggest hurdle to bringing these alternative fuels to market.

This chapter will examine the development programs involved in commercializing bio-fuels and the financing hurdles that pure players and entrepreneurs will eventually face. To do this, it will draw upon two case studies. The first case study, undertaken by the University of Houston's Global Energy management Institute (GEMI), examines an ABF candidate known as Pyrolysis Oil (Pyoil). This study outlines the projected economics and a decade-long development path for this potential fuel. As such, it provides a good illustration of the efforts and costs investors must contemplate when planning to develop and commercialize an ABF. The second case involves an existing plant, a corn ethanol facility in Hereford, Texas. This project was developed by entrepreneurs and funded mostly via a project finance loan. The plant was built in 2006–2007 but never went into operation. Its lessons and legacy will be instructive regarding what likely ABF developers will face when they eventually take their first generation plants to the financing markets.

Let us now turn to the case of Pyrolysis Oil and specifically to the development plan that will be required to prove it as an ABF.

PYOIL—DEVELOPMENT FROM CONCEPT TO COMMERCIALIZATION

To begin we must introduce Pyrolysis Oil. Pyoil is a dark liquid that visibly resembles crude oil. It can be produced from different types of biomass. GEMI's study focused on making Pyoil from woodchips. The biomass is heated rapidly to over 500 degrees centigrade and then quickly cooled; residence time is less than a second. The biomass first gasifies, and then condenses. Roughly 65–70 percent condenses into liquid Pyoil with the remainder either remaining a gas or solidifying into char. Although Pyoil visually resembles crude oil, chemically it is quite different. The raw Pyoil is a soup of compounds, many of them oxygenated acids. Raw Pyoil typically contains about 35–45 percent oxygen by weight; aldehydes, ketones, acetic acid, and other carboxylic acids are typically present. The material

is thus highly acidic, with a pH of 2.2–3 and a total acid number (TAN) > 80. Energy content tends to average about 65 percent of crude oil.

Because of its highly acidic nature, Pyoil has never been considered a refinery feedstock. The material is highly corrosive to the carbon steel used in refinery reactors and piping. The high oxygen content also will deactivate some existing refinery catalysts. Consequently, Pyoil use as a fuel has been confined to limited cases of being burned in boilers; the largest operating Pyoil plants only process 200 dry tons perday (dt/d) of biomass, yielding ~500 barrels per day (b/d) of raw Pyoil.

As crude oil prices rise through $100 per barrel (/b), interest in alternative refinery feedstocks has intensified. Various research efforts, including those at the National Renewable Energy Laboratories, have experimented with hydrotreating raw Pyoil to remove its oxygen. This work has produced a number of interesting results:

- Pyoil can be hydrotreated to virtual oxygen extinction (< 0.5 percent oxygen by weight). It then resembles a conventional hydrocarbon that produces a reasonable gasoline-blending material. Its heavier fractions lie mostly in the diesel boiling range, but show low cetane numbers.
- Hydrotreating Pyoil to oxygen extinction consumes voracious amounts of hydrogen; cost estimates for just this upgrading step approach $40/b for finished fuel product material (blendstock Pyoil). This cost is approximately 10× the typical cost for refining a crude oil barrel at a Gulf Coast refinery.
- Stopping the hydrotreatment at an earlier level may be more cost efficient, but will require refineries to learn how to handle higher concentrations of oxygenated compounds in their feedstocks.

This work provides an interesting snapshot of a potential ABF in development. Lab work has demonstrated a concept that is viable within a lab context. This is to say that labs can start with woodchips, make raw Pyoil in a small reactor and hydrotreat this material to oxygen extinction using bench-scale equipment. Accomplishing this is a significant first step. It does not, however, demonstrate technical viability or commercial readiness.

For that threshold to be crossed, lab work would have to demonstrate the development of a robust hydrotreating catalyst that can meet industrial operating standards. Typically this means demonstrating uninterrupted operating runs lasting 12 months or more. The Pyoil lab work done to date has not come close to meeting this standard. Because of this, estimating the costs of producing gasoline/diesel from Pyoil is very difficult to do. Large contingencies must be assigned to lab-scale cost estimates, and when this is done Pyoil-based fuels end up with projected costs in the $180 to $200/b range.

Assessing Pyoil Economic Viability with Research and Development

A cost estimate in the $200/b range would appear discouraging enough to cause Pyoil research to be deemphasized. However, it is also possible to assess Pyoil's viability from a different perspective—what would this fuel's production costs look

like at the end of a defined research and development process? More specifically, the question could be phrased: "What would Pyoil's project costs look like if R&D success was achieved in the following areas?"

- Development of a robust upgrading catalyst.
- Development of more economic means of either removing oxygen from Pyoil at the pyrolysis stage and/or tolerating some oxygen content within the refining stage, including such steps as are needed to meet finished fuel product specifications (e.g., octane and cetane).
- Successful scale-up of the pyrolysis and upgrader facilities to harvest economies of scale.

GEMI's case study attempted to answer this question. It estimated that successful scale-up alone could reduce the cost of blendstock Pyoil by $40 to $50/b. A similar level of savings from research on oxygen removal/toleration would bring Pyoil's costs down to levels where commerciality becomes a possibility at today's oil price levels. Further savings from the development of well-situated wood plantations, genetically engineered trees, and the integration of pyrolysis and upgrading facilities with refineries may also be achievable.

These interesting prospects bring us to two dilemmas inherent in developing advanced bio-fuels. These dilemmas can be described as:

1. The extended time and capital intensive R&D path.
2. The first mover cost dilemma.

The first item involves extensive outlays for research, pilot plants, and demonstration plants. These are expensive and require an extended time period (e.g., a decade or more). The second involves the fact that the first commercial plants for this ABF will likely be at a scale significantly smaller than that eventually achieved by a mature industry. This means that first movers will have to make their commercialization decision knowing that their plant's production costs will be higher than those of the mature industry they are helping to create. Depending upon how quickly the industry advances its scale-up, ABF first movers face the threat that their initial plants may become uncompetitive.

Together these two dilemmas form a significant barrier to the development of advanced bio-fuels. To understand this barrier better and how it could be overcome, let us consider the case of these two dilemmas for Pyoil in more detail.

Time and Capital for Pyoil R&D

The GEMI study developed a timeline for a possible Pyoil R&D program. This timeline takes Pyoil from its current *lab proof of concept* status through three stages of development:

Stage I—Technical Viability: where the technology to manufacture and upgrade Pyoil via a continuous industrial process has been demonstrated. To achieve this stage, upgrading catalysts capable of continuous runs for one year or more must be demonstrated, and the Pyoil materials ultimately

produced must meet fuel product specifications without harming engines or refining units.

Stage II—Economic Viability: where sufficient research gains have been made to provide confidence that after scale-up blendstock Pyoil can be produced at costs competitive with existing motor fuels.

Stage III—Industrial Scale-Up: where technologies and processes shown to have worked in the laboratory are tested in pilot plants and then demonstration plants. The aim here is to show that the inevitable operating problems involved in scale-up can be overcome without undermining the technical and economic viability projected from Stages I and II.

GEMI's study estimates that such a program for Pyoil will take approximately 10 years. This estimate assumes that reasonable success is achieved on key program elements and that no major unforeseen problems materialize. It also assumes the availability of adequate funding, especially for a demonstration plant. Exhibit 14.1 provides GEMI's detailed R&D timetable for Pyoil.

This program will be expensive as well as time consuming; the pilot and demonstration plants alone will cost several hundred million dollars. These estimates are based on major energy company experience developing new refining and chemical processes as well as R&D efforts into synthetic fuels (e.g., coal and gas to liquids). Obviously the research expenditures in Stages I and II ($\sim$$5 to $10 million for each phase) are additive to the pilot/demo plant cost estimates.

The magnitude of this program sheds light on the first financing challenge facing ABF development. Such a commitment of time and funds typically requires the strong financial condition characteristic of major energy firms. However, it is unlikely that such firms will be leaders in ABF development. At least three reasons are likely to limit their interest in undertaking such programs.

1. First, the economics of prospective ABFs are not compelling. A decade of expensive R&D is required to produce a possibility of competitive cost with existing fuel products. Even with fairly optimistic assumptions regarding R&D success, projected economic returns are only in the 10–15 percent range. The ultimate manufacturing process will be capital intensive, and thus involve considerable financial risk for first movers.
2. Second, these ABFs compete with the existing businesses of the major energy firms. Those businesses are established and require nothing like the R&D expenditures contemplated for Pyoil. To major energy firms ABF development looks something like spending large sums to cannibalize their existing assets.
3. Third, the core business affected here is refining, and major energy firms are increasingly uncertain about their commitment to the U.S. refining industry. Gasoline demand is widely expected to have peaked. Demand erosion from the entry of higher mileage cars, hybrids, and electric vehicles will only put further pressure on a refining industry suffering from surplus capacity and low returns.

For these reasons, major energy companies are unlikely to be leaders in ABF development. Some may devote limited research dollars to accompany progress

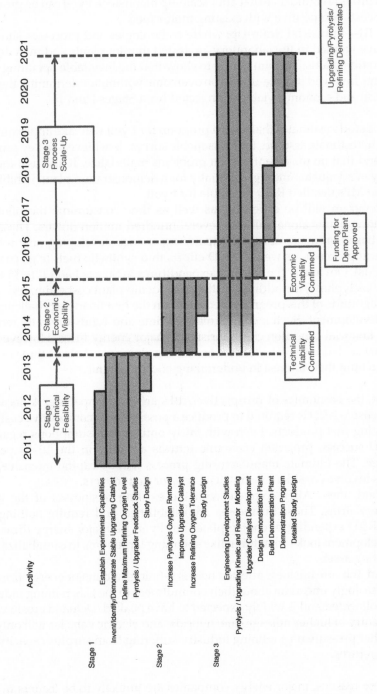

Exhibit 14.1 Conceptual R&D Plan for Bi-O-Crude from Fast Pyrolysis + Hydrotreating of Wood

and assure they obtain early notice of any major, unexpected breakthroughs. Mounting a committed program and spending large sums on demonstration plants is another matter.

This leaves a different set of players as the group most likely to lead ABF development. Foremost among these would be pure play refiners. These firms, by their nature, are committed to the refining business. Developing a new feedstock supply from domestic materials that could provide competitive and more predictable costs versus imported crude oil is strategically interesting to this group. Forest product companies looking for alternative outlets for their resources will share this interest. Entrepreneurs and private equity seeking new opportunities will also take a look.

Unfortunately for the development of ABFs, none of these players has either the research organizations or the throw-away capital that the development program outlined above requires. The hundreds of millions that Pyoil first movers would spend on pilot and demonstration plants will generate no return. That is not a proposition that the group strategically interested in ABFs can afford.

This first economic dilemma is then reinforced by the first mover plant issue.

THE FIRST MOVER PIONEER PLANT ISSUE

Economies of scale are developed and harvested over time. First movers in Pyoil or another ABF will build their first-generation pioneer plants when plant scale up has progressed enough to support commerciality. Subsequent entrants will look for further economies of scale. In a mature energy industry, plant scale can be two to three times the size of initial commercial plants. For example, ethylene catalytic crackers with capacity of 400 thousand tons (kt) annually were once considered industrial scale; today's new crackers boast production of 1 million tons per year (mt/yr). or more.

GEMI's study focused on the eventual development of pyrolysis plants consuming 2 k dry tons per day (t/d) of biomass; these plants would represent about a 10× scale-up of units existing today. Such plants will produce material sufficient to yield about 5 thousand barrels per day (kbd) of blendstock components after upgrading. By constructing a site comprising five such units operating in parallel, a 25 kbd operation would be created. This vision of the first mover Pyoil site thus combines an ambitious scale-up factor from existing facilities with a final product volume approximating the minimum that would interest a refining customer.

A mature Pyoil industry will continue development from this base. Although pyrolysis plants of 2 k dt/d capture a good percentage of likely scale economies, additional scale-up to 5 k dt/d may be possible. Four units of this size operating as parallel trains would permit integrated sites converting 20 k dt/d of biomass into 50 kbd of blendstock products.

The first mover's dilemma can be seen by comparing the projected economics of these two cases. The mature industry case could see unit costs, including a return on capital, in the $80 to $90/b (per barrel) range. The first mover's economics appear to be in the $105 to $120/b range.

This outlook has two effects. First, it delays energy company interest in being a first mover until crude oil prices show a sustainable trend above $120/b. Big industry players will make their decisions on whether to spend sizeable R&D funds on the basis of pioneer plant economics, not those of a later mature industry. Second,

industry players will be careful to determine whether adequate demand will exist for their pioneer plant production over an extended timeframe. At least a decade of full sales and robust margins will be needed to recoup capital and generate an acceptable return. Thus, major firm first movers will be cautious about the possibility of later, larger plants undercutting their pioneer facilities.

Financing Implications of ABF First Movers' Dilemmas

Collectively these issues mean that likely ABF first movers will not have the strong balance sheets needed to fund extended R&D, plus build and then discard pilot/demonstration plants. Without government intervention to favor ABFs in the fuels market, the mounting of a program like the one charted above would appear to be greatly deferred.

Second, even if the government helps to provide adequate incentives for ABF development, likely private sponsors will probably not be capable of funding pioneer plants from their own funds. Most likely, they will be looking to tap the project finance market. Such has been the case for numerous ethanol, wind, and other alternative fuel projects. The use of project loans attracts pure play companies, entrepreneurs, and private equity for several reasons:

1. It allows them to evaluate projects on a leveraged return-on-equity basis. Under the right circumstances leveraged economics give a considerable boost to marginal returns on total capital.
2. It allows them to proceed with projects even though their available funding may constitute less than 50 percent of project costs.
3. It allows them to limit their exposure to losses should the venture prove a failure.

Such benefits do not come with financing complications. To understand these complications, we must first consider what type of incentives the government may employ to encourage ABF development. We may then examine the requirements that project finance lenders are likely to impose on ABF first movers. Insight into these requirements can be gained by studying the results of recent ethanol project loans, especially the case of Panda Ethanol in Hereford, Texas; that project's failure is likely to influence future ABF project lending for some time.

Public Policies to Support ABF Development

For a project to be eligible to attract project financing, the most important requirement is an *adequate and predictable* revenue stream. A high likelihood of such revenue generation enables a project to achieve a leveraged capital structure and post-completion loan terms that are nonrecourse to the sponsor.

An adequate revenue stream means one whose margins provide sufficient cash flow coverage for debt service. While standards vary by industry and location, acceptable projects typically show annual debt service coverage ratios of 1.4–2.0×. The more predictable the revenue stream, the more the required annual coverage can be toward the bottom of the ratio range.

ABF projects will be challenged on both counts. To the extent they must compete with conventional fuel products, ABF economics will be determined relative to crude oil prices. As we have seen, research and development will need to produce cost reductions on the order of 40–50 percent of current cost estimates to render an ABF like Pyoil commercial at today's crude prices. Said differently, Pyoil and other ABFs have a long way to go before private investors conclude that project economics will show robust debt service coverage.

The price volatility inherent in competing with conventional fuel products is even more daunting. In the last three years, investors have seen crude prices peak at $145/b, retreat to $35/b and then recover to over $100/b. With this kind of volatility, they are likely to require a large margin for error before concluding that an ABF is cost competitive with crude-based fuels.

Public policy's principal answers to these dilemmas have been two: (1) renewable fuel standards (RFS) mandating that such fuels must be incorporated into motor fuels and (2) tariffs and tax subsidies to improve the economics of producing corn-based ethanol. For various reasons, neither assures that an ABF like Pyoil will have an adequate and predictable cash flow margin. The RFS mandates are still ambiguous as to whether various ABFs will qualify. Here the example of Pyoil is instructive. The EISA 2007 language seems crafted to include Pyoil; section 201 emends the Clean Air Act definition of "renewable fuels" to include:

- Planted trees and residues from actively managed plantations ... cleared any time prior to December 7, 2007."
- Renewable fuels from facilities built after that date must achieve a 20 percent reduction in Life Cycle Greenhouse Gas emissions (LCGG) vs. fuel replaced.
- To qualify as ABF, the fuel must achieve a 50 percent reduction in LCGG.

However, status as a renewable fuel and also an ABF is conditioned on greenhouse gas emission reductions; here an EPA–approved study methodology has yet to be finalized. Even more important, no methodology has been defined for counting renewable fuel/ABF volumes or for crediting those barrels to a specific segment of the fuel's value chain.

Again Pyoil serves to illustrate these difficulties. Most projected Pyoil value chains involve moving wood chips to a pyrolysis plant producing raw Pyoil. This material is then transported to an upgrader that transforms the material into refinery-grade Pyoil. Then, a refinery co-processes these Pyoil streams with conventional hydrocarbons, attending to octane, cetane, and other fuel quality specifications. Lastly, the co-processed material is blended with other product streams to make finished fuel products. As the Pyoil industry develops, it is possible that the pyrolysis plant, upgrader, and refinery may all be owned by different investors. In that case, who gets credit for producing an ABF? Also, what gets counted volumetrically as the ABF produced—the raw Pyoil, the refinery-grade material, or the blendstock material? At this point, nobody knows. The problem is not helped by the fact that, by the time the material is in blendstock form, it is already fully blended with conventional hydrocarbons.

One cumulative effect of these conditions for financing Pyoil is that neither the EISA RFS mandates nor the existing rules/subsidies applying to ethanol can be assumed to apply to a prospective ABF. No investor can today assume that Pyoil is

an ABF or that anyone knows how to count it. Investors also don't know whether blending Pyoil streams into gasoline directly relieves the requirement to blend in ethanol, or doesn't back out ethanol at all. This means investors cannot assume that it will compete pricewise with ethanol. Consequently, investor economics for Pyoil must be based upon competition with conventional fuel products—taking us back to fundamental issues of adequate and predictable margins in a world driven by crude oil prices.

The good news here is that clarifying the ABF regulations is an act lawmakers and regulators have it in their power to resolve. Doing so would allow investors to make wholly different economic assumptions about fuels like Pyoil, assumptions that would better underpin the costly and time-consuming R&D efforts required. The most useful suite of regulatory clarifications is as follows:

- That blendstock Pyoil meets the EPA's ABF standards for LCGG reductions.
- That for ABF purposes Pyoil barrels shall be counted as they exit the upgrader and be credited to the upgrader's owner based upon an algorithm reflecting standard processing within a model refinery.
- That Pyoil blended into finished product gasoline can be used to meet the ethanol blending requirement in some ratio based upon energy content and/or mileage.

Considerable study and testing is required to provide the basis for these regulatory clarifications. This would be appropriate work for the national laboratories, such as the National Renewable Energy Laboratory (NREL). Putting this work at the front end of planned research will, if it supports the above conclusions, have the effect of promoting and reinforcing private industry research. Private investors would henceforth be able to make the following economic assumptions:

- Pyoil gasoline is a direct substitute for ethanol.
- Pyoil gasoline will thus compete with ethanol for the market defined by RFS mandates.
- Pyoil gasoline will then be priced as an ethanol substitute within this market segment.

Whether the ethanol tax credit survives or not is interesting but not fundamentally critical. What is critical is the regulatory change that would position ABFs to complement corn ethanol within the nation's gasoline pool; this change would greatly clarify ABF pro forma economics. Within EISA 2007's 36-billion-gallon market, ABFs like Pyoil could then develop cost structures based upon corn ethanol; as long as the RFS mandates are secure, ethanol prices will have to settle at levels that allow ethanol producers to earn reasonable returns. ABF producers can then focus on these cost structures, which are a good deal more discoverable and achievable than those for international crude oil.

These regulatory clarifications go some distance to support adequate ABF cash margins. However, price volatility is still an unresolved issue. To examine this issue within the ethanol world and also devise solutions that enable financing, we now turn to look at the Panda Ethanol case study.

Bio-fuels and Project Financing: The Case of Panda Ethanol

In May 2006 Panda Ethanol closed a $188 million financing package to complete funding for a 105 million gallons per year corn ethanol plant. Total costs for the project, to be built in the Texas Panhandle town of Hereford, were estimated to be $260 million. To partially finance the project Panda Energy (PE), a Dallas-based private equity firm with a specialty in industrial energy projects, would provide $72 million in equity. PE's management consisted of individuals drawn from various branches of the energy and power businesses. PE itself had developed 9000 MW of power. This would be its first venture in ethanol.

These basic facts illustrate conditions cited above as likely to characterize development of ABF projects. First, the investors are more likely to be entrepreneurs/private equity than major energy firms. Second, they will risk only a limited amount of money; in this case PE contributed only 28 percent of total project costs. Third, the investor group may have limited, or no, experience with the fuel being produced and the technology to be used. Finally, all three of these characteristics will channel the project towards project financing, a complex web of operating and commercial contracts, and a leveraged, multiple-tier capital structure.

What then happened to Panda Ethanol exemplifies the special risks of using this model to develop new bio-fuels. PE developed an innovative plant design, one that emphasized synergies with the Hereford cattle feedlots. They entered into contracts with reputable ethanol marketers and a plant operator. They were successful in signing Lurgi, the German engineering/contracting firm, to construct the plant on a lump sum, turnkey basis. Arrangements were concluded with corn suppliers and rail logistics providers. Exhibit 14.2 outlines the proposed contract arrangements for the Project.

Finally, on the financing front, PE used its innovative plant concept and web of contracts to attract project financing that was both highly leveraged and had very limited recourse to PE. The project capital structure contained only 28 percent equity. PE gave no completion guarantee. Lurgi backed its construction contract, but capped its potential damages at less than $30 million.

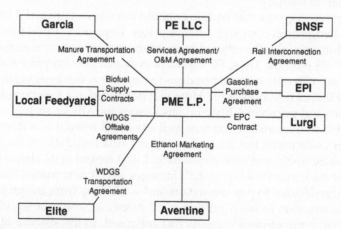

Exhibit 14.2 Proposed Contract Arrangements for the Project

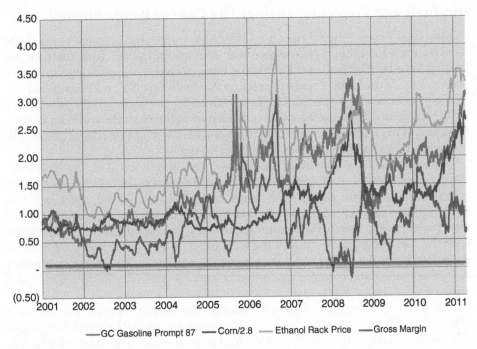

Exhibit 14.3   Corn Ethanol Gross Margins

The leveraged capital structure, limited completion support, and absence of recourse to PE all represented a significant risk shift to the lenders. Within that context one would expect the lenders to demand that PE put in place a meaningful commodity hedging program. A core principal of successful project financing is that pledged cash flow must be both reliable and predictable. For Panda Ethanol to enjoy such a cash flow, the ethanol and corn prices in existence when the project was conceived would either have to remain stable or be hedged. As illustrated by Exhibit 14.3, the price history of Panda Ethanol's key commodities is more one of volatility than of stability.

This history suggests that hedging should have been required. However, it is not easy to hedge both corn and ethanol prices. Depending upon timing and the contract volume sought, the ethanol forward market only offers reasonable liquidity out to 18–48 months. Thus, PE's lenders essentially bet on price stability; they let PE proceed with only general promises to consider active hedging in the future.

Panda Ethanol never got built. How that happened as a function of both completion issues and price volatility contains lessons for ABF financing.

Panda Ethanol's construction was well advanced when it was discovered that one of Lurgi's subcontractors had poured faulty tank foundations. Reconstruction was going to be costly and time consuming. Lurgi looked at its alternative, which was to incur the contracted liquidated damages, and it determined that would be cheaper. Lurgi decided to pay these costs and walk away from the project. PE also looked at its situation to see if putting more money in would be justified. At this moment, 2007, corn/ethanol margins had collapsed. In the absence of any hedging program, PE would be investing more money to bring onstream a plant that

now seemed likely to operate at a loss. PE too decided to walk away. PE's lenders got handed the keys of a mostly completed project. They too determined that it was uneconomic to finish the job. The plant remained in its unfinished state, and the assets, with time, began to deteriorate. Today corn/ethanol margins are again robust; finally an investor, Murphy Oil, has decided to acquire the Hereford site, paying a fraction of original cost.

There are several lessons in this story pertinent to the financing of ABFs. First, the entrepreneurs/private equity players most likely to develop ABFs will try to limit the capital they put at risk; whether this is done as a choice or out of necessity, it will have important consequences. For starters, it will severely restrict their ability to provide financial support to assure project completion. Second, it will limit their capacity to absorb or manage their projects' price volatility risks. Even should the sponsors be willing to implement a robust price hedging effort, such programs require capital in the form of option premiums or margin calls. Looking at Panda Ethanol, it is not hard to observe how the sponsor's desire to economize capital caused it to work hard at minimizing its commitments in all of these areas.

Unfortunately, such an approach is likely to mean that project financing will not be readily available for ABF projects even when their technology has advanced to become commercially-ready. Panda Ethanol's sponsor benefited from the fact that corn ethanol technology was considered proven. This enabled PE to convince its lenders that the Lurgi turnkey contract was a sufficient completion support. That is unlikely to happen for a newly developed ABF technology; project finance lenders typically demand air-tight completion supports from a strong financial entity until three to five industry-scale plants are up and running for several years. Who then will provide such support for the completion of these first three to five plants?

Similar concerns surround the price volatility issue for ABF projects. With the memory of Panda Ethanol and similar projects in mind, project lenders will be more demanding that energy price volatility be hedged. Likely ABF sponsors will not be well equipped to meet that demand. Almost certainly they will not have adequate balance sheets available to offer sponsor price guarantees. As for the less capital-intensive path of financial hedging, commodity futures markets do not currently provide the tenor or liquidity needed to satisfy ABF lender requirements. Gasoline price hedges do exist for tenors longer than five years, but gasoline is not necessarily the marker that ABFs will need to target. Ethanol is more likely to be the key price reference; unfortunately, ethanol forward contracts are only available in depth out to 18–48 months. ABF lenders will be looking for hedges out 6 to 10 years.

As things sit today, the potential ABF industry faces this paradox. Major players with strong balance sheets are unlikely to commercialize these products. This leaves development of the ABF industry dependent upon weaker financial players. These players will want to employ a project financing mode. Unfortunately, the employment of such a financing model requires the establishment of several properly functioning plants to prove the technology and the development of hedge instruments to address commodity price volatility. How will these prerequisites be created given the reluctance of financially strong players to be the pioneers?

Unless some major player achieves a large cost breakthrough on some ABF, one which would turn that fuel's economics much more attractive than currently projected, the answer must come from revised public policy. As a last discussion topic, we now turn to this subject.

Public Policy Revisions to Support ABF Commercialization

Assuming the ABF clarifications cited earlier come into being, the remaining public policy revisions involve financing. More specifically, they involve removing the obstacles that will prevent entrepreneurs/private equity from accessing project financing for their first-generation commercial plants.

Today three forms of public assistance exist to support bio-fuels development:

1. Government equity capital that can be invested alongside private sector funds
2. Government loan guarantees
3. The RFS and ABF mandates, plus the possibility of qualifying for the ethanol tax credit

None of these programs will resolve investor concerns regarding the first-generation ABF plants. The fact that some government equity is available does not mean that private equity will materialize for projects whose returns are inadequate. Government loan guarantees protect lenders but not the equity investors that drive project development and operations. The various mandates and even the ethanol tax credit are helpful, but do not address the risk that price volatility could still overwhelm ABF project economics.

Building government support policies around what is necessary to unblock access to the project financing market is a sounder approach. For one thing, project finance money will only flow to projects characterized by sound economic prospects. Project finance lenders look for projects whose pro forma equity returns look solid—because it is the sponsors' equity return that constitutes the project lender's margin for error. Hence, the project finance market is a good litmus test of economic viability for emerging ABFs. Second, the requirements of project finance lenders direct public policy to resolve more specific and limited problems than do the existing government support programs.

This can be seen by contrasting the loan guarantee program with a more limited program focused on allowing project sponsors to purchase completion guarantees. Such a program would reduce the extent of the government's guarantee to the technical and operating risk of the new plants. The current program is an all-risk program covering the life of the venture. Assuming the project economics are reasonably robust, project lenders are willing to assume many of the operating period risks. What they won't absorb is new technology completion risk.

It is here that the government has a compelling public interest—the final proving of renewables technologies that can provide several public goods, such as GHG reductions, reduced import dependence, and sustainability. Providing completion guarantees for the three to five plants needed to accomplish this "proof" is a much more targeted approach for harvesting these goods than are all-risk loan guarantees.

To take on this completion risk, the government will have to satisfy itself that the project sponsor's technology and design will work. Participating as an equity investor in the sponsor pilot and demonstration plants is one way for the government to accompany the technology's scale-up from the lab. Such an approach can be employed using existing programs; this will also aid the entrepreneurs/private equity players to fund these significant costs of pilot and demonstration plants. The government will also be charging fees for its completion guarantee. Assuming it does proper due diligence, these fees could end up as net revenue for the government.

That leaves price volatility as the remaining impediment to unblocking ABF project financing. At present, the government offers entrepreneurs/private equity players no tool to address this lender concern.

Here it is important to note the strong historical opposition within the government to what are seen as price supports. Much of this opposition appears to reside in the history of farm price supports. These farm programs, born in the 1930s, have proved enormously enduring and expensive. Understandably there is resistance to transporting that model into the energy arena. Outside of farm price supports, the most notable other examples of government volatility-management programs involve some exceptional Department of Defense (DOD) contracts for purchasing aviation fuels. While some contracts continue to be forged on this basis, DOD's experience has not fostered a more general enthusiasm for the approach.

This opposition to government price hedging has been very disruptive to energy public policy. Alternative fuels development has never escaped the shadow to oil price volatility. Synfuels developers (e.g., oil shale, coal to liquids) began development in the late 1970s as oil prices hit $40/b ($160/b in current dollars). By the time first movers were ready to consider building plants, prices had fallen back toward $10/b; plants were abandoned and research mothballed. OPEC is fully aware of this phenomenon and has adeptly influenced oil prices toward levels that raise the risks of commercializing alternative fuels. Though the cartel periodically loses its grip, the combination of oil's natural price volatility and the cartel's efforts has for decades effectively stymied private sector development of alternative fuels.

Distilled to its essence, political opposition to volatility hedging centers on the perception that such programs expose the government to unpredictable and potentially unlimited financial loss. Such would be the case if government volatility hedges were to be focused on insuring consumers against rising fuel prices. If in theory fuel prices can rise to infinite heights, so too can the cost of providing hedges against rising prices. However, getting ABFs off the ground involves insuring producers against falling prices and revenues. Zero sets an absolute floor on price declines and in fact the likely actual floor is well above zero. Moreover, the objective of enabling first movers to achieve economies of scale does not require an open-ended program for all future plants. Rather, it requires a targeted program focused on bringing those first three to five industry-scale plants into existence. In these two ways, the cost of the government providing sale price "floor" protection to ABF first movers can be limited.

A third way also exists to limit the cost of government price hedges. This involves the government designing its hedges to work with existing financial market instruments. This supplementing approach would require an ABF first mover

to buy primary price protection in the commodity futures markets. Supplemental government assistance would focus on managing the basis risk between the purchased futures hedge and the actual commodity price determining the first mover's revenues.

An example of such a basis hedge will illustrate how it limits the government's financial exposure. Assume that an ABF producer has a product that will be priced relative to ethanol. Assume also that current ethanol prices of $2/gallon produce margins sufficient to generate a reasonable return (12–15%) on total capital invested. The producer wants to attract project financing, and the lenders are demanding a hedge program covering the life of their 10-year loan. Unfortunately, ethanol forward contracts are only available in reasonable volume out to 18–48 months. How then can the first mover satisfy the lender's demand for a 10-year hedge?

Such a program could be constructed as follows. The first mover would sell gasoline futures forward for the full 10-year period. Assume for the moment that this could be accomplished at a constant price of $1.80/gallon. The first mover now needs to add basis protection to this basic hedge—that is protection covering the relationship of ethanol to gasoline prices. This is the targeted protection that the government needs to provide. In our example, ethanol is trading at a $0.20/gallon premium to gasoline; this is the basis the first mover must protect. The government here provides a forward basis contract, under which it commits to make up the difference if the spread between ethanol and gasoline prices narrows to less than $0.20/gallon. Conversely, if the spread widens out, the first mover pays the government all excess over $0.20/gallon. Assuming the link to ethanol is solid, these measures collectively lock the first mover's future ABF sales at a $2.00/gallon price.

This can be seen by imagining a moment five years into the project life. At this moment, gasoline prices have now risen to $2.25/gallon while ethanol prices have only risen to $2.30/gallon. Under the hedge just described, the first mover will sell his ABF production at the market's ethanol price of $2.30/gallon. It then would owe $0.45/gallon ($2.25 – $1.80) on its gasoline futures contract while receiving $0.15/gallon from the government on its basis hedge ($0.20 hedge – 0.05 actual). The first mover's economics thus remain at $2.00/gallon, the level needed to pay lenders and assure an investment return:

	$/g
First mover's current sale price	$2.30
FM owes on gasoline forward contract	(0.45)
FM receives on ethanol/gasoline basis hedge	0.15
First mover Net Price	$2.00

Exhibit 14.4 shows the construction of this hedge position in Moment 1 and Exhibit 14.5 its economic flows in Moment 2.

A hedge program designed along these lines can provide the price and revenue assurance needed to unlock project finance market for ABF first movers. To assure a full margin hedge, these first movers would have to take other actions to manage potential raw material price volatility. This could be accomplished via contract terms set with individual suppliers or by backwards integration into raw material

Moment 1—Revenue Hedge Structure

- Current Ethanol Price: $2.00/gallon
- Forward Gasoline Price: $1.80/gallon average
- Ethanol/Gasoline "Basis" Spread: $0.20/gallon
- ABF sales priced off spot ethanol
- ABF Plant loan tenor: 8 years

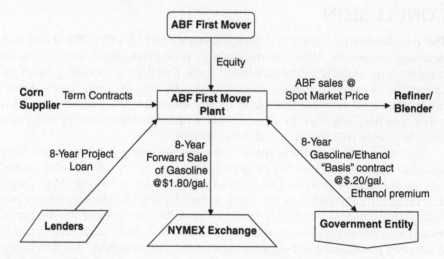

Exhibit 14.4 ABF First Mover—Government Commodity Price Basis Hedge

Moment 2—Payment Flows

- Current Ethanol Price: $2.30/gallon.
- Current Gasoline Price: $2.25/gallon.

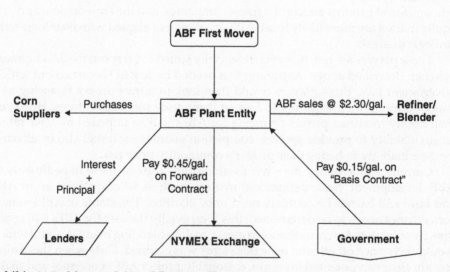

Exhibit 14.5 Moment 2: Year 5 Payment Flows

production. Both ought to be feasible steps. As for the government, providing such basis hedges limits its exposure to the general direction of fuel prices; instead it simply helps ABF first movers manage the key interfuel price relationship. Focusing only on this and limiting the program only to first mover plants should greatly limit the government's financial exposure and assuage political opposition to such a price support program.

CONCLUSION

The development of advanced biofuels envisioned in EISA 2007 faces several daunting challenges. ABF economic viability is uncertain; their destiny, which is to compete with existing petroleum-based fuels, threatens the existing downstream operations of major integrated oil companies. Finally, their regulatory status has major undefined features that could greatly influence ABF economic viability in either direction. Together these conditions temper the enthusiasm of major energy firms to pursue ABF research and development.

Unfortunately, it is these major firms whose strong balance sheets are best suited to finance the extended R&D programs needed for ABF development. The case of one ABF, Pyrolysis Oil, showed the need for a 10-year R&D program; this program culminates in the need to build pilot and demonstration plants. Such plants will cost hundreds of millions of dollars and are essentially discarded once the scale-up experience and lessons have been harvested. From there first-generation plants must be built keeping in mind the knowledge that later competitor plants will be even larger in scale and lower in unit costs. Finally, this extensive program must be carried out in the face of all the economic and price cyclicality that characterizes energy markets.

For all of these reasons, the private firms most able to fund and sustain such a program are unlikely to do so. Unless oil prices rise to levels showing large premiums versus projected ABF costs and give evidence of remaining there indefinitely, major energy company interest in ABF development is likely to be tepid. Pure play refiners, forest product and agribusiness companies, and the entrepreneur/private equity market are more likely to see ABF development aligned with their long-term strategic interests.

These players are not, however, financially suited to carry out the development program described above. Assuming that needed basic R&D is carried out within government labs, these players would then look to attract project financing as a way of limiting their exposure to loss on these risky pioneer ventures. However, their ability to attract project financing for ABFs will be impeded by their reluctance/inability to provide sponsor completion guarantees; it will also be affected by their inability to hedge their project's commodity price risk.

Current public policy does not meaningfully address these impediments to ABF development. Basic definitional matters, such as what qualifies as an ABF and how will barrels be counted, need to be clarified. The status of ABFs versus corn ethanol needs to be determined; this is especially the case for ABFs that could directly substitute for corn ethanol to meet gasoline-blending mandates, and which would then price off ethanol once this status was clarified. Only when these matters are clear can potential investors reasonably project ABF economics and make decisions about what might be worth developing.

Existing government programs also do not focus on the problems likely to block ABF access to project financing. Targeted programs to provide project completion support and commodity price hedges would go far to remedy these problems. Adopting such programs for ABF first movers could effectively aid the construction of first-generation ABF plants while minimizing the government resources required to do so.

Building the first three to five ABF plants should lay the basis for private sector development of a mature industry. Once these plants demonstrate their staying power, major companies will consider whether they are missing out on both future growth and what may eventually become the basis for future industry competition.

DISCUSSION QUESTIONS

1. What are the new bio-fuels? What factors will impact bio-fuel projects and determine when, or if, they will contribute significantly to future energy needs?
2. Describe the development programs involved in commercializing bio-fuels.
3. Describe how a basic hedge works when an ABF first mover buys price protection in the commodity futures market.
4. Describe the barriers to developing ABF and how they affect commercialization and what has been done by industry and government.

ABOUT THE CONTRIBUTOR

Stephen V. Arbogast served from 1999 to 2004 as the Treasurer of ExxonMobil Chemical Company and has over 30 years experience in finance working with Exxon Corporation and ExxonMobil Chemical. While treasurer of Chemicals, Arbogast held positions that included director of Qenos (Australia's sole manufacturer of polyethylene, a joint venture with Orica PLC), director of Dexco (a joint venture with Dow Chemical), and director of Al Jubai Petrochemical Company in Saudi Arabia. Other former positions included vice president of finance for SeaRiver Maritime Inc. (the former Exxon Shipping Company), treasurer for Exxon Capital Corporation, finance and planning manager for Esso Brasileira de Petroleo in Brazil, and treasurer of Esso Central America, Panama, and Mexico.

Currently serving as an Executive Professor of Finance at the C. T. Bauer College of Business, Arbogast's teaching career has focused on international finance, project financing, and business ethics. In addition to authoring over 50 case studies based on his experiences at ExxonMobil, he has previously taught at both Fordham University's Graduate School of Business in New York and Rice University's Jesse Jones Graduate School of Management in Houston.

Arbogast has authored articles on the energy industry focusing on the future of the U.S. Gulf Coast refining and petrochemical industries. He also is the author of *Resisting Corporate Corruption, Lessons in Practical Ethics from the Enron Wreckage* (M & M Scrivener Press, 2008). His most recent publication (2009) is "Project Financing & Political Risk Mitigation: The Singular Case of the Chad-Cameroon Pipeline", *Texas Journal of Oil, Gas and Energy Law,* 4:2, 269–298.

Energy Risk Management and Related Topics

Energy Risk Management
and Related Topics

CHAPTER 15

Energy Derivatives and Markets*

CRAIG PIRRONG
Professor, University of Houston

MOHSEN MOLLAGHOLAMALI
PhD Student, Oklahoma State University

INTRODUCTION

Energy derivatives are a relatively new financial product, but have been growing rapidly during since their introduction in the 1970s. Large quantities of energy derivatives are traded on exchanges in the over-the-counter (OTC) market. Moreover, in the 2000s there has been a notable influx of energy trading by financial institutions and portfolio investors that increasingly view commodities in general, and energy in particular, as a distinct asset class that exhibits a low (and indeed, negative) correlation with traditional equity and fixed-income investments, and therefore improves portfolio risk-return characteristics through the effects of diversification. Commodities are also viewed as an inflation hedge. This development, which has occurred in parallel with a four-fold increase in oil prices since 2003, has sparked intense criticism of energy derivatives trading.

PRODUCTS: AN OVERVIEW

Energy derivatives are traded on a variety of energy products. The largest single category consists of derivatives on petroleum and petroleum derivatives. Petroleum derivatives include contracts on crude oil, with sweet crudes (West Texas Intermediate and Brent) being by far the dominant products; middle distillates, including heating oil, gasoil, and jet fuel; and gasoline. In addition, derivatives are traded on natural gas and various gas liquids (such as propane) and electricity. Although not properly an energy product, derivatives on emissions (such as sulfur dioxide and carbon dioxide) are also traded; since these emissions are often the result of energy production or consumption (e.g., the generation of

---

*This chapter is based largely on Chapter 9, "Energy Derivatives," in Robert W. Kolb and James A. Overdahl, eds., *Financial Derivatives: Pricing and Risk Management*, 125–133 (Hoboken, NJ: John Wiley & Sons, 2009), but has been expanded and updated.

electricity produces SO_2 and CO_2), emissions derivatives are often bought and sold by energy trading desks.

All types of standard derivatives are traded on energy products. Standardized futures contracts are traded on exchanges, most notably the New York Mercantile Exchange and ICE Futures, a division of the Intercontinental Exchange (ICE). Energy futures contracts have been introduced by the Shanghai Futures Exchange, the Dubai Mercantile Exchange, the Hong Kong Futures Exchange, and the Singapore Mercantile Exchange have announced efforts to introduce energy futures contracts. Exhibit 15.1 shows the major exchanges in the world that are either specialized in energy derivatives or offer them as part of their product basket.

In addition, options on futures contracts are traded on these exchanges. Furthermore, there is extensive trading in OTC energy derivatives instruments. These include vanilla forward contracts and swaps, basis and differential swaps, and options and swaptions. These are primarily cash-settled instruments, with final settlement prices based on exchange settlement prices or prices reported in industry publications. Exhibit 15.2 lists different categories of underlying energy commodities that are covered in the NYMEX exchange. As can be seen from the exhibit, there might be different kinds of contracts for each underlying commodity.

Some energy products, such as natural gas, are costly to transport relative to value, and hence for these products there are often numerous local markets. So-called basis contracts have developed to facilitate hedging and price discovery for these local markets. These contracts have payoffs that are equal to the difference between prices in two different markets. The most common example of such contracts have payoffs equal to the difference between the price of natural gas at the Henry Hub (the delivery point for NYMEX natural gas futures) and the price in another market (such as the Chicago City Gate). Settlement prices in these contracts are typically based on indices reported in trade publications such as *Inside FERC* or *Natural Gas Daily*. These publications collect and average prices for cash transactions; *Inside FERC* reports prices on contracts for delivery of gas ratably over a contract month entered into by buyers and sellers during the "bid week" prior to the delivery month, whereas *Natural Gas Daily* reports cash prices on transactions for delivery the following day.

HISTORY

Futures contracts were traded on oil in the United States during the nineteenth century, especially in the aftermath of the first Pennsylvania oil boom. Numerous oil futures exchanges came and went during this period (Weiner 1992). The development of the Standard Oil monopoly and the pervasive move to vertical integration in the industry undermined the need for futures trading, and energy derivatives trading largely disappeared in the late nineteenth century and remained largely moribund until the 1970s (although there were attempts to trade oil futures in the 1930s).

The New York Cotton Exchange (NYCE) introduced first modern exchange-traded energy contract, on propane, in 1971. The NYMEX introduced the first widely-traded energy futures contract (on heating oil) in 1974.

Exhibit 15.1 Major Energy Derivative Exchanges around the World

Exchange	Abbreviation	Location	Product Types	Website:
Anglo-Dutch Energy Exchange	APX-ENDEX	Amsterdam, NL	Energy	www.apxendex.com
Australian Securities Exchange	ASX	Sydney, AU	Agricultural, electricity, thermal coal & natural gas	www.asx.com.au
Chicago Board of Trade (CME Group)	CBOT	Chicago, USA	Grains, ethanol, treasuries, equity index, metals	www.cmegroup.com
Chicago Climate Exchange	CCX	Chicago, USA	Emissions	www.theice.com/ccx
Climex	CLIMEX	Amsterdam, NL	Emissions	www.climex.com
Dalian Commodity Exchange	DCE	Dalian, CN	Agricultural, plastics, energy, agri commodities	www.dce.com.cn
Dubai Mercantile Exchange	DME	Dubai, UAE	Energy	www.dubaimerc.com
Energy Exchange Austria	EXAA	Europe	Emissions	www.exaa.at
European Energy Exchange	DME EEX	Leipzig, DE	Energy, emissions	www.eex.com
Houston Street Exchange		New Hampshire, USA	Crude oil, distillates	www.houstonstreet.com
Indian Commodity Exchange Limited	ICEX	India	Energy, precious metals, base metals, agricultural	www.icexindia.com
Intercontinental Exchange	ICE	Atlanta, USA	Energy, emissions, agricultural, biofuels	www.theice.com
Nadex Exchange		Chicago, USA	Energy, industrial metals	www.nadex.com
New York Mercantile Exchange(CME Group)	NYMEX	New York, USA	Energy, precious metals, industrial metals	www.cmegroup.com/company/nymex.html
Tokyo Commodity Exchange	TOCOM	Tokyo, JP	Energy, precious metals, industrial metals, agricultural	www.tocom.or.jp
U.S. Futures Exchange	USFE	Chicago, USA	Energy	www.usfe.org

Exhibit 15.2 Different Categories of Energy on Which Derivatives Are Traded on the NYMEX Exchange

Category	Examples of Contracts
Crude oil	Light Sweet Crude Oil (WTI) Futures (options on futures), Western Canadian Select (WCS) Crude Oil Futures
Ethanol	New York Harbor Ethanol Futures
Natural gas	Henry Hub Natural Gas Futures (options on futures), Henry Hub Natural Gas Look-Alike Last Day Financial Futures
Electricity	PJM Western Hub Peak Calendar-Month Real-Time LMP Swap Futures, PJM Western Hub 50 MW Peak Calendar-Month Real-Time LMP Swap Futures
Refined products	Heating Oil Futures (options on futures), RBOB Gasoline Futures, New York Harbor Ultra-Low Sulfur Diesel (ULSD) Futures,
Coal	Central Appalachian Coal Futures
Other	UxC Uranium U3O8 Swap Futures

Source: www.cmegroup.com/trading/energy.

Developments during the 1970s, notably the decade's oil shocks and the abrogation of long-term "equity" oil contracts between producing nations and major oil companies, disrupted traditional oil marketing methods and encouraged the development of an oil spot market. This, in turn, created a need for energy derivatives contracts to facilitate risk management and price discovery. In short order, exchanges introduced a variety of futures contracts on petroleum products. NYCE introduced a crude oil contract in 1974, and the Chicago Board of Trade and the NYMEX launched crude contracts in 1983. NYMEX soon gained the lead in this market, and although other exchanges launched oil contracts in the 1980s, NYMEX maintained its dominance and extended it with the introduction of gasoline futures in 1984.

Outside the United States, the United Kingdom's International Petroleum Exchange (IPE, since acquired by ICE and now operating as ICE Futures) began trading gasoil futures in 1980, and introduced its Brent crude oil futures contract in 1988.

Deregulation of transportation and prices in the United States during the 1980s laid the foundation for natural gas futures trading. NYMEX launched the successful Henry Hub natural gas futures contract in 1990. IPE launched a natural gas futures contract for delivery into the UK grid in 1997.

Deregulation was also the impetus for the introduction of futures contracts on electricity. NYMEX began trading California-based electricity futures contracts in 1996 (when the state was in the process of a major regulatory restructuring), and added contracts for midwestern and Eastern markets two years later. IPE introduced UK electricity futures in 2004, and on the Continent the European Electricity Exchange commenced trading futures in 2001. Nordpool began trading futures on Scandinavian electricity in the 1990s, and the Amsterdam Power Exchange was created in 1999.

Development of OTC trading in the energy complex paralleled that of exchange trading, with crude oil and refined products trading developing first, followed by natural gas and then electricity.

PETROLEUM DERIVATIVES: DETAILS

There are two dominant crude oil futures contracts, West Texas Intermediate traded on NYMEX and Brent traded on ICE Futures (the successor to the IPE). Both contracts are for light, sweet (i.e., low sulfur) crude oils. Such crudes are the most valuable, but represent a smaller and smaller fraction of world crude oil production.

The WTI contract is a delivery-settled contract, calling for delivery of 1000 barrels of crude oil in Cushing, Oklahoma (a major storage and transportation hub.) ICE Futures also trades a cash-settled WTI contract, with contract settlement price tied to the NYMEX price. Brent is also delivery settled, but with a cash-settlement option, with the cash-settlement index based on transactions prices for 21-day Brent, Forties, Osberg, and Ekofisk (BFOE) cargoes. However, WTI is not the only benchmark contract in the world, and there are some other popular crude oil futures contracts in other exchanges in the world. For example, the Dubai Mercantile Exchange (DME) Oman Crude Oil Futures Contract is the Asian crude oil pricing benchmark, which is traded on the CME Group's electronic platform CME Globex and cleared through CME ClearPort.

Trading volume in these contracts has grown dramatically in recent years. For instance, NYMEX crude oil average daily volume was 107,579 contracts in 1988, 254,162 contracts in 1998, and 1,173,458 by June of 2008. As can be seen from Exhibit 15.3, the prices of the crude oil futures have also been volatile in the last three

Exhibit 15.3 Historical Crude Oil Futures Daily Prices from April 1983 until April 2012, NYMEX Exchange

Source: Energy Information Administration, EIA.

decades. The price of crude oil futures reached a historic high of $145.29 in July of 2008. No one can argue about the importance of crude oil for the world's economy. Hence it has a very active trading market with huge volumes. WTI futures traded in NYMEX is also the most liquid and active form of crude oil trading. Therefore, this futures contract, because of its liquidity and price transparency characteristics, is used as the world's most important pricing benchmark.

WTI and Brent futures are the primary beacons of price discovery in the oil market. Many physical oil trades are quoted based on one of these futures instruments, with physical transactions executed at differentials to the futures prices. Since sweet crudes are becoming progressively less representative of world oil production, there is a perceived need for a pricing benchmark based on heavier, sourer crude. Despite several attempts to introduce such contracts, WTI and Brent have retained their dominance due to the difficulty of shifting liquidity to new contracts. Exhibit 15.4 lists the product specification for Light Sweet Crude Oil (WTI) Futures in NYMEX.

NYMEX's most important refined product futures—for heating oil and gasoline—are settled by physical delivery of 42,000 gallons of product in New York Harbor (a major refining center). Gasoline futures contract specifications have changed throughout the years due to changes in American environmental regulations. ICE Futures gasoil is settled by delivery in barges in Amsterdam, Antwerp, and Rotterdam.

Spread trading in petroleum futures is quite common. For instance, a *crack spread* trade involves the simultaneous purchase of a crude oil futures contract and the sale of gasoline and/or heating oil futures contracts. Such trades can be used to hedge or speculate on refining margins.

Both NYMEX and IPE were originally floor-based exchanges. IPE switched all trading to an electronic platform in 2005, and NYMEX entered into an agreement with the Chicago Mercantile Exchange to trade NYMEX petroleum futures contracts on the GLOBEX system in 2006. Although NYMEX continues to trade crude and refined products on its New York floor, over 80 percent of volume in these products is traded electronically on GLOBEX.

Large volumes of crude oil forwards, swaps, and options are traded in the OTC market. Most swaps and forwards are cash settled, with NYMEX WTI futures prices being an important source of settlement prices for these contracts. In addition, there is extensive OTC paper trading of Brent crude, or more recently, BFOE contracts. Twenty-one-day BFOE contracts call for delivery of crude oil in a 21-day window of a particular month. Once the loading date for a particular cargo is set, the contract becomes a *dated BFOE* contract. Like most exchange-traded futures contracts, 21-day Brent contracts are liquidated—*rung out*—prior to delivery. In addition, contracts-for-differences, with payoffs based on the difference between dated BFOE and 21-day BFOE are widely traded; these CFDs are essentially swaps.

NATURAL GAS DERIVATIVES: DETAILS

The main NYMEX natural gas futures contract is settled by delivery of 10,000 million British thermal units (MMBtu) of natural gas ratably throughout the contract

Exhibit 15.4 NYMEX Light Sweet Crude Oil (WTI) Futures Specifications

Product Symbol	CL
Venue	CME Globex, CME ClearPort, Open Outcry (New York).
Trading unit	1,000 U.S. Barrels (42,000 gallons).
Trading hours	Open outcry trading conducted between 10 am till 2:30 pm. NYMEX ACCESS on Mon–Thu begins at 3:15 pm and concludes 9 am the following day. Sunday ACCESS begins at 7 pm (all times are New York).
Trading months	30 consecutive months plus long-dated futures initially listed 36, 48, 60, 72, and 84 months prior to delivery. Additionally, calendar strips can be executed (during open outcry trading hours) at an average differential to the previous day's settlement prices for periods of 2 to 30 consecutive months in a single transaction.
Price quotation	Dollars and cents per barrel.
Minimum price fluctuation	$0.01 per barrel (i.e., $10 per contract).
Maximum Daily price fluctuation	Initially $3.00 per barrel for all but the first two months, rising to $6.00 per barrel if the previous settlement price of any back month is at the $3.00 limit. If $7.50 per barrel movement in either of the two front months, then the limit for all months becomes $7.50 per barrel in the direction of the price movement.
Last trading day	Trading stops at close of business on the 3rd business day prior to the 25th calendar day of the month proceeding the delivery month. If 25th is a nonbusiness, then trading stops on 3rd business day prior to last business day preceding the 25th.
Delivery	FOB seller's facility, Cushing, OK, at any pipeline or storage facility with access to pipeline, by in-tank transfer, in-line transfer, book-out, interfacility transfer.
Delivery period	Deliveries are ratable over the course of the month and must be initiated on or after the first calendar day and completed by the last calendar day of the delivery month.
Alternative delivery procedure	Available to buyers and sellers matched by the Exchange after termination of spot month contract. If buyer and seller agree to the contract specifications, they may proceed and must notify the Exchange. Exchange of Futures for Physicals (EFP) Commercial buyer or seller may exchange a futures position for a physical position by notifying the Exchange. EFPs may be used to initiate or liquidate a futures position.
Deliverable grades	Specific domestic crudes with 0.42% sulfur or less, and not less than 37 degree API gravity nor more than 42 degree API gravity; including WTI, Low Sweet Mix, NM Sweet, North TX Sweet, OK Sweet, South TX Sweet. Specific foreign crudes not less than 34 degree API nor more than 42 degree API; including Brent, Forties, and Osenberg Blend for which the seller will receive a 30 cent per barrel discount; Bonny Light and Cusiana (a 15 cent premium); and Qua Iboe (a 5 cent premium).
Inspection	Will be conducted according to pipeline practices. Buyer or seller may appoint an inspector, and the requesting party will cover the cost and notify the other party.
Position limits	20,000 contracts for all months combined, but not to exceed 1,000 in the last 3 days of trading in the spot month or 10,000 in any one month.
Margin requirements	Margins are required for open futures positions.

Source: www.cmegroup.com/trading/energy/crude-oil/light-sweet-crude_contract_specifications .html.

Exhibit 15.5   NYMEX Henry Hub Natural Gas Options Contract Specification

Underlying Futures	Henry Hub Natural Gas Futures (NG)
Product symbol	LN.
Venue	CME Globex, CME ClearPort, Open Outcry (New York).
Contract unit	On expiration of a call option, the value will be the difference between the settlement price of the underlying Henry Hub Natural Gas Futures and the strike price multiplied by 10,000 MMBtu, or zero, whichever is greater. On exercise of a put option, the value will be the difference between the strike price and the settlement price of the underlying Henry Hub Natural Gas Futures multiplied by 10,000 MMBtu, or zero, whichever is greater.
Price quotation	U.S. dollars and cents per MMBtu.
Option style	European.
Minimum fluctuation	$0.0001 per MMBtu.
Expiration of trading	Trading ends at the close of business on the business day immediately preceding the expiration of the underlying futures contract.
Listed contracts	Consecutive months for the balance of the current year plus 5 additional years.
Strike prices	One hundred strike prices in increments of $0.01 per MMBtu above and below the at-the-money strike price, for a total of at least 201 strike prices. Strike price boundaries are adjusted according to price movements of underlying futures contract.
Settlement type	Financial.
Exchange rule	These contracts are listed with, and subject to, the rules and regulations of NYMEX.

Source: www.cmegroup.com/trading/energy/natural-gas/natural-gas_contract_specifications.html.

month at the Henry Hub in Louisiana. NYMEX natural gas basis contracts are settled financially based on the difference between a price index quoted for a particular location, and the final settlement price of the NYMEX Henry Hub natural gas contract. For example, the Chicago City Gate settlement is set equal to *Natural Gas Intelligence* (an industry publication) Chicago City Gate index price minus the final settlement price of the Exchange Henry Hub natural gas futures contract for the corresponding month on the last trading day.

Other popular and interesting natural gas derivatives are options on natural gas futures. Exhibit 15.5 shows the contract specification for Henry Hub Natural Gas Options. As can be seen from the exhibit, the underlying of this European option contract is Henry Hub Natural Gas Futures, and it is settled financially. Although this contract is traded in NYMEX and other exchanges, natural gas options on futures could also be created by individual counterparties and traded in OTC market.

NYMEX also trades index swaps, which have payoffs equal to the difference between the average of a daily price during a particular month at a particular location, and a monthly forward price at that location. For example, the Chicago City Gate Index Swap settlement is set equal to the average of the *Platts Gas Daily*

price at the Chicago City Gate during the contract month minus the bidweek price provided by *Natural Gas Intelligence* Chicago City Gate index price. (Bidweek is a period during which buyers and sellers contract for physical natural gas to be delivered in the following calendar month.)

The ICE Futures natural gas contract is also delivery settled, with shorts making delivery ratably throughout the contract month into the British national pipeline grid.

NYMEX Henry Hub natural gas contracts are traded both on the floor, and on the GLOBEX system, with the bulk of the volume traded on the latter. The basis swap and index swap contracts are traded on the NYMEX ClearPort system, or on the OTC market and cleared through NYMEX. ICE Futures natural gas contracts are traded electronically.

Natural gas trading volumes have increased steadily since the introduction of the Henry Hub contract in 1990. In 1991, the average daily trading volume for this contract was 1,654 lots. By 2001, this volume had grown to 47,457 lots per day. By mid-2008, trading volume averaged 153,329 contracts each day. On March 29, 2012, Henry Hub Natural Gas trading volumes surged to 824,316 contracts, a 48 percent increase over the previous record of 557,179 set on January 17, 2012, and a 170 percent increase over the average daily volume of 305,017 contracts in 2011.

Henry Hub swaps, basis swaps, index swaps, and natural gas options and swaptions are also traded extensively in the OTC market. These contracts are traded via voice brokers, and on the Intercontinental Exchange's electronic system.

ELECTRICITY DERIVATIVES: DETAILS

The first generation of U.S. electricity futures contracts were settled by delivery of a fixed quantity of electricity in each "peak" hour during the delivery month. These contracts never garnered significant trading volumes, and eventually became dormant.

In the late 1990s and early 2000s, as part of the ongoing industry restructuring process, major Independent System Operators established centralized real-time markets for electricity in large parts of the United States. These ISOs include PJM (originally operating a market in Pennsylvania, New Jersey, and Maryland, but now extended to encompass most of the Midwest as well), NYISO (New York), and NEISO (New England). These ISOs collect bids from generators indicating the prices at which they are willing to produce power and use these bids to determine the marginal price to generate the electricity demanded in the ISO control region.

New NYMEX futures contracts utilize these real-time prices established by the ISOs to settle futures contracts. For instance, the final settlement price for the NYMEX PJM peak futures contract for a particular contract month is the average of real time prices at 111 pricing points in the western part of the PJM region during the peak hours of that month.

Volumes of exchange-traded electricity futures contracts have been modest. This reflects the nature of electricity. Although electricity spot prices are highly volatile, electricity forward prices are much less so because (a) the lack of storability attenuates the connections between spot and forward prices, and (b) most of the important shocks that drive electricity spot prices (e.g., weather) are highly

transitory. Moreover, there is evidence that suggests that (a) there are substantial hedging imbalances, with long hedgers predominating, and (b) it is difficult for speculators to trade electricity (Bessembinder-Lemmon 2002; Pirrong and Jermakyan 2008).

Electricity swaps (with the floating leg of the payoff typically based on ISO spot prices) are traded via voice brokers, and on the ICE electronic platform.

PRICING

Energy derivatives exhibit distinctive pricing behaviors. Moreover, standard cost-of-carry models do a poor job of characterizing energy forward curves. This is almost self-evident for electricity; because it cannot be stored, carry is infinitely costly, and the cost-of-carry model is therefore inapplicable. Even for ostensibly storable energy commodities, however, the cost of carry model performs badly.

Crude oil is an exhaustible resource, and according to the standard pricing theory (Hotelling 1931) its price should rise at the rate of interest over time. This, in turn, should lead to contango in the forward market (with deferred futures prices exceeding nearby prices). However, crude oil has historically been in backwardation (with nearby prices exceeding deferred prices) about 60 percent of the trading days from 1983 to 2007. The main periods of contango have occurred when prices were very low, as during the Asian economic crisis of 1998. The one exception to this is the late-2005-to-2007 period, when the crude forward curve was in contango even when prices were at (then) historically high levels.

Various theories attempt to explain the prevalence of backwardation in oil futures. Litzenberger and Rabinowitz (1995) argue that since the owner of an oil well has the real option to determine the timing of extraction, price uncertainty generates option time value that induces the owner to defer production if the futures price is above the spot price by the cost of carry; the forward premium compensates for the deferral of the receipt of revenue from sale, and the owner retains the option to sell at more favorable prices in the future. The only way to induce current production, according to Litzenberger and Rabinowitz, is for the market to trade below full carry, and perhaps in backwardation. The deviation from full carry must be sufficient to offset the effect of the option value associated with deferring production. Litzenberger and Rabinowitz document that, consistent with this theory, deviations from full carry are larger when output is high and when volatility is high.

Other explanations of crude oil forward price curves include applications of the standard convenience yield version of the theory of storage (Pindyck 1994), and modifications of the dynamic programming version of the theory of storage (Pirrong 2008).

In the convenience yield version, inventories of a commodity such as crude generate a stream of benefits accruing to the inventory holder. This functions as an implicit dividend that the owner of the spot captures but the holder of the futures does not, which depresses the futures price relative to the spot price.

In the dynamic programming version, storage is used to smooth out the effects of demand and supply shocks; inventories rise when demand is unexpectedly low (or supply is unexpectedly high), and fall when the reverse is true. Forward

curves adjust to provide the incentive for agents to do the right thing; the market moves toward full carry in low demand/high supply states in order to reward storage, and shifts into backwardation in high demand/low supply states to punish holder's inventory, thereby inducing them to liquidate their holdings. In the standard variant of this theory, the volatilities of demand and supply shocks are constant. This variant of the model cannot readily account for phenomenon like that observed in 2005–2007, when both inventories and prices were high. Pirrong (2008) modifies the standard model to allow for stochastic fundamental volatility. This modified model can account for simultaneously high prices and inventories. Positive shocks to fundamental volatility induce agents to hold additional precautionary inventories. For inventories to increase, prices must rise to reduce consumption and increase output.

Other storable energy commodities, notably heating oil, gasoline, and natural gas, exhibit seasonality in their forward curves. This, in turn, reflects the highly seasonal demand in the demand for these commodities.

Electricity forward prices also show substantial seasonality (Eydeland and Wolniac 2004). The seasonal peaks depend on the markets. In the U.S. South, Midwest, and West, for instance, forward prices are highest for summer delivery months (July and August), lowest in the "shoulder" months (April and October), and exhibit a smaller seasonal peak in winter months (notably December and January). In contrast, in European (especially Nordic) markets, and in the U.S. Northeast, the largest peaks correspond to the winter months.

Energy commodities also exhibit rich relationships. For instance, the *crack spread* is a measure of the profitability of refining crude oil into the products individuals actually consume to power vehicles or heat homes. Thus, the relationship between crude oil, heating oil, and gasoline prices varies to reflect the economics of transforming the input (crude) into the output (refined products). As an example, a cold snap tends to increase the demand for heating oil, the demand for refining capacity, and indirectly, the demand for crude oil (the demand for crude being derived from the demand for refined products). Thus, this weather shock tends to cause the price of heating oil to rise, the price of crude to rise, and the crack spread to increase (due to the increase in the demand for refining capacity). That is, the price of refined products rises relative to the demand for crude oil. Interestingly, the shock to heating oil demand tends to cause the gasoline price to fall because due to the fact that heating oil and gasoline must be produced in (roughly) fixed proportions, increasing heating oil output also increases gasoline output, which has a depressing effect on price.

Economic fundamentals can also induce interesting relationships between other commodities. In electricity, the *spark spread* between the price of power and the price of fuel (such as natural gas) used to generate it reflects the demand and supply for electricity. Although shocks to electricity demand move electricity and fuel prices in the same direction, power prices tend to move more. Moreover, Pirrong and Jermakyan (2008) demonstrates that the correlation between power and fuel prices is time varying; correlations are high when the demand for power is low, and power prices are low, and correlations are low when the demand for power is high and power prices are high. This occurs because when demand is high, prices reflect the scarcity value of generating capacity, which does not depend on fuel prices; but when demand is low, prices are driven primarily

by the marginal cost of generation, which is determined primarily by the price of fuel.

Energy prices exhibit higher volatilities than virtually any other commodity or commodity class (Duffie, Gray, and Hoang 2004). For instance, the annualized volatility of front month crude oil over the 1992–2004 period was 36 percent, while the volatility of natural gas during the same period was 52. In contrast, gold volatility was 16 percent, soybean volatility 21 percent, and copper volatility 24 percent. Energy price volatilities are time varying (Duffie, Gray, and Hoang 2004). Moreover, there is evidence (at least from crude oil) that prices are more volatile when the market is in backwardation than when it is not, and that the correlation between spot and futures prices is lower when the market is in backwardation than when it is not (Pirrong 1995). These findings are consistent with the dynamic programming version of the theory of storage.

CLEARING

Energy derivatives are one product where clearing has made extensive penetration into the OTC market, especially in the natural gas market, and especially for gas basis swaps. Both NYMEX and ICE clear OTC energy products. The robust growth in energy clearing is attributable in large part to the severe credit problems experienced in the energy trading sector following the implosion of merchant energy firms such as Enron, Dynegy, Williams, and Mirant.

The NYMEX and ICE OTC clearing models differ. NYMEX clears deals executed either on its ClearPort trading system, as well as deals executed with voice brokers or on a principal-to-principal basis. In contrast, ICE clears deals executed on its trading platform. NYMEX clears transactions through its own clearing subsidiary. Until September 2008, ICE cleared through the London Clearing House Ltd. (LCH), but has since shifted its OTC clearing to its own clearing subsidiary. Moreover, NYMEX clears via a mechanism called Exchange of Futures for Swaps (EFS) whereby each counterparty's swap position is exchanged for an equivalent position in a look-alike futures contract; ICE deals remain OTC subsequent to clearing.

Clearing volume on NYMEX has risen from less than 30,000 contracts per day in January 2004 to over 400,000 contracts per day in June 2008.

RECENT DEVELOPMENTS

The dramatic rise in oil prices during 2007–2008 focused considerable attention on oil derivatives trading. Speculation in oil futures and swaps was widely blamed for contributing to the rapid price increases, with some commentators opining that as much as $70 per barrel of the price of oil (out of a total price of around $140/barrel) was attributable to the effects of speculation. These concerns led to myriad legislative proposals in the United States Congress to constrain speculation, none of which have been enacted as of the time this is being written in March 2012.

Relatedly, the breadth of participation in energy markets has increased markedly in recent years, with the entry of banks, investment banks, hedge funds,

and portfolio investors (including pension funds) into the energy market. Many portfolio investors participate in the energy derivatives markets through the purchase of, or less frequently, the sale of, OTC contracts with payoffs tied to commodity indices, such as the S&P Goldman Sachs Commodity Index (S&P GSCI) or the Commodity Research Bureau Commodity Index. In turn, financial institutions that make markets in these OTC contracts lay off some of the risks they incur through the futures markets. Energy represents a large fraction of these indices. For instance, in December 2011 energy represented 70.5 percent of the S&P GSCI, with oil alone accounting for approximately 51.4 percent of the total index value The predominance of long-only index investors has been widely cited as a source of increased demand for oil that has contributed to higher energy prices. This belief, in turn, has spurred legislative proposals (none enacted as of the writing of this entry) to restrict commodity index investments by financial institutions.

These antispeculation and anti-index arguments and legislative efforts echo earlier criticisms of derivatives trading in grain, and share the same conceptual deficiencies. Most notably, most speculators never take delivery of physical energy, and offset their derivatives positions prior to delivery; indeed, speculators using OTC contracts, and index investors, do not even have the contractual right to take delivery. Hence, these participants do not contribute any demand for physical energy. Moreover, there is no evidence of physical market distortions (such as, the accumulation of large inventories in the hands of speculators) that would accompany price distortions. It should also be noted that an interagency task force of the U.S. government attributed the large rise in oil prices in 2007–2008 to economic fundamentals, rather than speculation, as did the International Energy Agency (Interagency Task Force 2008; International Energy Agency 2008).

DISCUSSION QUESTIONS

1. Are energy derivatives a relatively new product? What are the largest types of energy derivatives? In other words, which category is the single largest?

2. Energy derivatives are traded on what commodities?

3. What are basis contracts?

4. Which exchange had the first modern exchange-traded energy futures contract. Also list the year and commodity.

5. In what year was the NYMEX Henry Hub natural gas futures contract launched? What year did IPE launch a similar contract in the UK?

6. Are there derivative contracts on electricity? If so, where?

7. What are the two dominant crude oil futures contracts for crude oil? What are the two primary oils that futures contracts are traded upon?

8. What are the two most important refined product futures traded on the NYMEX?

9. What crude oil contracts are traded on the OTC markets?

10. Describe the natural gas derivatives contracts traded, and list where they are traded. Give a few details about the NYMEX contract.

11. Describe the electricity derivatives contracts traded and list where they are traded. Give a few details about the NYMEX contract.

REFERENCES

Bessembinder, Hendrik, and Michael Lemmon. 2002. "Equilibrium Pricing and Optimal Hedging in Electricity Forward Markets." *Journal of Finance* 57:3, 1347–1382.

Duffie, Darrell, Stephen Gray, and Phillip Hoang. 2004. "Volatility in Energy Prices." In Vince Kaminski, ed. *Managing Energy Price Risk,* 539–571. London: Risk Books.

Eyedeland, Alexander, and Krzysztof Wolniac. 2004. "Power Forward Curves." In Vince Kaminski, ed. *Managing Energy Price Risk.* London: Risk Books.

Hotelling, Harold. 1931. "The Economics of Exhaustible Resources." *Journal of Political Economy* 39:2, 137–175.

Interagency Task Force on Commodity Markets. 2008. "Interim Report on Crude Oil."

International Energy Agency. 2008. "Oil Market Report."

Kolb, Robert W., and James A. Overdahl, eds. 2009. *Financial Derivatives: Pricing and Risk Management.* Hoboken, NJ: John Wiley & Sons.

Litzenberger, Robert, and Nir Rabinowitz. 1995. "Backwardation in Oil Futures Markets: Theory and Empirical Evidence." *Journal of Finance* 50:5, 1517–1545.

Pindyck, Robert. 1994. "Inventories and the Short Run Dynamics of Commodity Prices." *Rand Journal of Economics* 25:1, 141–159.

Pirrong, Craig. 1997. "Metallgesellschaft: A Prudent Hedger Ruined, or a Wildcatter on NYMEX?" *Journal of Futures Markets* 17:5, 543–578.

Pirrong, Craig. 2008. "Stochastic Fundamental Volatility, Speculation, and Commodity Storage." Working paper, Bauer College of Business, University of Houston.

Pirrong, Craig, and Martin Jermakyan. 2008. "The Price of Power: The Valuation of Power and Weather Derivatives," *Journal of Banking and Finance* 32:12, 2520–2529.

Pirrong, Craig. 2009. "Energy Derivatives." In Robert W. Kobl and James A. Overdahl, eds. *Financial Derivatives: Pricing and Risk Management*, 125–133. Hoboken, NJ: John Wiley & Sons.

Weiner, Robert. 1992. "Origins of Futures Trading: The Oil Exchanges in the 19th Century." Cahiers du GREEN 92-09. Université Laval.

ABOUT THE CONTRIBUTORS

Craig Pirrong is a professor of finance, and energy markets director for the Global Energy Management Institute at the C. T. Bauer College of Business of the University of Houston. He was previously Watson Family Professor of Commodity and Financial Risk Management at Oklahoma State University, and a faculty member at the University of Michigan, the University of Chicago, and Washington University. Pirrong's research focuses on the organization of financial exchanges, derivatives clearing, competition between exchanges, commodity markets, the relation between markets fundamentals and commodity price dynamics, and the implications of this relation for the pricing of commodity derivatives. He has published 30 articles in professional publications, is the author of three books, and has consulted widely, primarily on commodity and market manipulation–related issues. He holds a BA in economics, an MBA, and a PhD in business economics from the University of Chicago.

Mohsen Mollagholamali is a PhD student in business finance at Oklahoma State University. He holds a BA in journalism, an MBA from Multimedia University in Malaysia, and a MS degree in quantitative financial economics from Oklahoma State University. His interests are financial engineering, derivative pricing, and energy markets.

CHAPTER 16

Introduction to Energy
Risk Management

IVILINA POPOVA
Associate Professor of Finance, Texas State University San Marcos

BETTY J. SIMKINS
Williams Companies Professor of Business and Professor of Finance, Oklahoma
State University

If we had no liquid capital markets that enable savers to diversify their risks, if
investors were limited to owning just one stock, the great innovative enterprises
that define our age—companies like Microsoft, Merck, DuPont, Alcoa, Boeing, and
McDonald's—might never had come into being. The capacity to manage risk, and
with it the appetite to take risk and make forward-looking choices, are key elements
of the energy that drives the economic system forward.
—Peter L. Bernstein, *Against the Gods: The Remarkable Story of Risk* (1996)

If we don't hedge jet fuel price risk, we are speculating. It is our fiduciary duty to
try and hedge this risk.
—Scott Topping in 2003 (previously vice president treasurer at Southwest
Airlines, now chief financial officer, Hawaiian Airlines)

INTRODUCTION

Historical Overview of the Oil and Gas Industry Formation

Use of petroleum products have been documented since the sixth century B.C. In
450 B.C., Herodotus described oil pits near Babylon and in 325 B.C., Alexander
the Great used flaming torches of petroleum products to scare his enemies. However, not until the early 1800s did the actual drilling and production of oil happen. In 1859, one of the first wells that produced oil was drilled by Colonel Edwin
Drake in Titusville, Pennsylvania, which established the foundation of the modern
petroleum industry (see Exhibit 16.1).

On August 27, 1859, Colonel Drake's efforts were rewarded when the drillbit
slipped six inches beyond the bottom of the drilled hole. It had found a crevice.
The next day, August 28, crude oil started rising through the hole. Oil was pumped
into a washtub! Several years later, in 1863, J. D. Rockefeller founded an oil refining
company in Cleveland, and by 1872 he controlled 25 percent of the market share. In

Exhibit 16.1   Colonel Edwin Drake, Credited as Being the First Driller in the United States
Source: Drake Well Museum.

1901, Captain Anthony Lucas drilled near Beaumont in East Texas and established the beginning of the Texas oil industry.

Since the middle 1800s, the oil and gas industry has grown tremendously, and now oil and gas companies operate in different segments: upstream, midstream, and downstream. Companies that include significant upstream and downstream activities are known as integrated oil companies. Around 1951, the U.S. State Department suggested the creation of a consortium of major oil companies in response to actions by Iran. The following seven companies, called the Seven Sisters, belonged to this consortium:

1. Anglo-Persian Oil Company (United Kingdom, subsequently became Anglo-Iranian Oil Company and then changed its name to British Petroleum. After the acquisition of Amoco and Atlantic Richfield, the name was shortened to BP).
2. Gulf Oil (United States).
3. Royal Dutch Shell (Netherlands/United Kingdom).
4. Standard Oil of California (Socal) (United States; now known as Chevron).
5. Standard Oil of New Jersey (Esso) (United States; later Exxon and now known as ExxonMobil after the acquisition of Mobil in 1999).
6. Standard Oil Co. of New York (Socony) (United States; later become Mobil).
7. Texaco (United States; acquired by Chevron in 2001).

Currently, the very largest of the integrated companies are known as *supermajors* and include ExxonMobil, Gazprom, Royal Dutch Shell, Chevron, Total S.A., and BP. The most influential national oil and gas companies, known as the New Seven Sisters as coined by the *Financial Times*, include China National Petroleum Corporation (China), Gazprom (Russia), National Iranian Oil Company (Iran), Petrobras (Brazil), PDVSA (Venezuela), Petronas (Malaysia), and Saudi Aramco (Saudi Arabia).

The Emergence of Risk Management and Derivatives Exchanges

In Book I of *Politics*, Aristotle described an option as "a financial device which involves a principle of universal application." Derivatives today are well-known instruments used for management of risk (hedging) and also speculation. Basically, derivatives are financial instruments (contracts) that do not represent ownership rights in any asset. Rather, they derive (hence the name *derivative*) their value from the underlying commodity or other assets. The first most notable use of such contracts is usually associated with the Dutch Tulip mania in the 1600s. Forward contracts on tulip bulbs were traded at that time. The first futures contracts can be traced back to Japan around 1650 when futures on rice were traded in Osaka.

Since the early 1980s, derivatives in energy commodities have been an explosive area of innovation and are now used extensively for managing risk. During this period, corporate risk management (the management of unpredictable events that would have adverse consequences for the firm) arose as a major area of development for firms and a rapidly growing branch of research by academics. Major reasons for the need of energy derivatives is energy industry deregulation, supply price shocks, geopolitics, and resulting volatility, which led to the innovation of new risk management tools.

The history of modern risk management began with futures trading in the midwestern United States. In the early 1800s, it began in the area of grain trade (Simkins and Ramirez 2008). Simkins and Ramirez on page 578 state: "This history is tied closely to the development of commerce in Chicago, a city strategically located at the base of the Great Lakes and close to the farmlands of the Midwest. Problems of supply and demand, transportation and storage led to the logical development of futures markets in Chicago." As grain trade expanded in Chicago, the Chicago Board of Trade (CBOT) was formed in 1848. During the early years, forward contracts (then called, "to arrive" contracts) were used. However, forward contracts had drawbacks because they were not standardized according to quality or delivery time, thus creating problems for merchants and traders. In 1865, the CBOT formalized grain trading by developing the futures contract—which was standardized as to quality, quantity, and time and place of delivery for the commodity being traded. A margining system (which required traders to deposit funds with the exchange or an exchange representative to guarantee contract performance) was also initiated that same year to eliminate the problem of buyers and sellers not fulfilling their contracts. Trading in other agricultural commodities quickly followed: the New York Cotton Exchange was established in 1870, the New Orleans Cotton Exchange began around 1882, among others.

The Chicago market model became the global standard for futures contracts and exchanges. To regulate trading in the U.S. futures markets, the Commodity Futures Trading Act of 1974 created the Commodity Futures Trading Commission (CFTC). The CFTC has broad regulatory powers over all futures trading and related exchange activities in the United States. One of the biggest innovations in the futures markets in the late 1900s was financial futures. Another catalyst was the rapid increase in exchange rate risk with the Bretton Woods system's collapse in 1971. Also, high inflation from the late 1960s to the early 1980s created substantial interest rate risk. The first financial futures contract was devised by the Chicago Mercantile Exchange (CME), which opened the International Monetary Market in

1972, and introduced a standardized contract in currency futures. An interest rate futures contract followed in 1975. Interest in financial futures spread, and markets were opened in Australia (1979), London (1982), and other world centers in the mid-1980s. By 1982, another market innovation, options on futures, was launched by the CBOT on Treasury Bond futures, and later adopted by other exchanges. In 1982, futures contracts were introduced on equities with the introduction of the CME Standard & Poors 500 futures contract. The first equity futures contract in Europe was the *Financial Times* Stock Exchange futures contract, introduced by the London International Futures Exchange in 1984.

In 1973, the first oil price shock hit the world when the Organization of Petroleum Exporting Countries (OPEC) cut back production and increased oil prices, resulting in prices rising from $3 to $12 per barrel over a one-year period, shattering consuming countries' complacency about oil supply and prices. Financial risks quickly emerged as a top concern in risk management, and the need for tools to manage risk, and the mathematics to value the tools, became a top priority. Within a few years, institutions and entire industries that utilized these tools emerged and the word *derivatives* became a commonplace term.

Exhibit 16.2, "Evolution of Energy Risk Management Tools," illustrates the innovation in energy derivatives that developed in response to the 1970s price shocks, price deregulation in the natural gas markets, and an overall rapid increase in energy price volatility. The percentage change (y-axis) is for the U.S. crude oil composite acquisition cost by refiners. This price series is available from the Energy Information Administration (EIA). The New York Mercantile Exchange (NYMEX, which is the world's largest futures exchange) heating oil contract, the world's first successful energy futures contract, was introduced in 1978. A futures contract on light, sweet crude oil (WTI, West Texas Intermediate) was launched by the

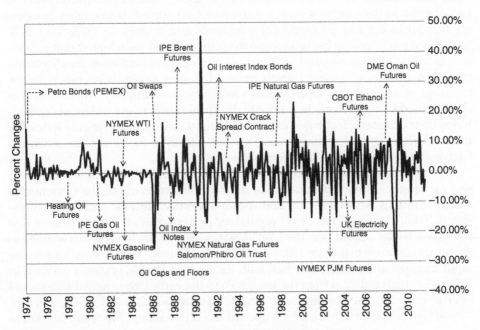

Exhibit 16.2 Evolution of Energy Risk Management Instruments

NYMEX in 1983 and is currently the most actively traded futures contract based on a physical commodity in the world (New York Mercantile Exchange 2002). The International Petroleum Exchange (IPE) was founded in London in 1980 and launched the Gas Oil futures contract in 1981 and the Brent Crude futures in 1988. A futures contract on natural gas was launched by the NYMEX in 1990 and by the IPE in 1997. In the late 1990s, the NYMEX launched a futures contract on electricity, but the long-term viability of an exchange-traded electricity contract is still uncertain. In 1990, the Salomon Phibro Oil Trust was introduced. At the time, this derivative represented a sort of popular projection of the 1995 oil price, and four units of the trust represent one barrel of West Texas Intermediate oil (Wald 1990).

During this same period, a revolutionary mathematical breakthrough gave derivative markets one of the tools needed to value and manage price risk. In 1973, Fisher Black and Myron Scholes published their pathbreaking paper for option pricing in the *Journal of Political Economy*, and their model, the Black-Scholes Option Pricing Model, quickly transformed risk management globally. In 1997, Myron Scholes and Robert Merton were co-recipients of the Nobel Prize in Economics for "a new method to determine the value of derivatives,"[1] For more information on energy derivative markets, see Chapter 15, "Energy Derivatives and Markets."

RISK MANAGEMENT AND TYPES OF RISK

The concept of risk appeared as a rigorous subject during the Renaissance when the theory of probability was discovered. The word *risk* derives from the Italian word *risicare*, which means "to dare." In this sense, risk is a choice. The actions and decisions that we dare to make will have implications about the possible future outcomes. But what is risk management? The scientist who developed the Saturn 5 rocket that launched the first Apollo mission to the moon put it this way: "You want a valve that does not leak and you try everything possible to develop one. But the real world provides you with a leaky valve. You have to determine how much leaking you can tolerate" (obituary of Arthur Rudolph, *New York Times*, January 3, 1996).

There are many types of risks.

- *Credit risk/default risk:* Risk associated with the ability of customers and vendors to pay or deliver.
- *Demand risks:* Those associated with the demand for a firm's products or services.
- *Enterprise risk management:* This deals with managing all of the various risks across the firm from an enterprise-wide view.[2]
- *Environmental risk:* Risk associated with polluting the environment.
- *Event risks:* Risk associated with particular types of events, such as fire, flood, or theft.
- *Financial risks:* Those that result from financial transactions.
- *Input risks:* Those associated with a firm's input costs.
- *Legal or liability risks:* Risk connected with product, service, or employee liability.
- *Liquidity risk:* Risk associated with the inability to buy or sell commodities at quoted prices.

- *Market or Price risk:* Risk associated with unexpected changes in the market price of commodities.
- *Operational risk:* Risk associated with the performance or availability of physical or managerial systems.
- *Personnel risk:* Risks that result from human actions.
- *Political risk:* Risk due to new regulations, expropriation, etc.
- *Property risks:* Those associated with loss of a firm's productive assets.
- *Reputation risk:* Risk associated with the firm's business reputation.
- *Speculative risks:* Those that offer the chance of a gain as well as a loss. This is not a hedge.

Market risk and price risk, specifically for energy, are the focus of this chapter. As discussed in Chapter 17, the five steps of risk management are:

- Step 1. Set the hedging objective.
- Step 2. Establish the hedging level.
- Step 3. Execute the hedging strategy.
- Step 4. Constantly monitor and reassess exposure.
- Step 5. Quantify the final outcome.

Why Do Firms Hedge and How Does Hedging Increase Firm Value?

Hedging is a form of risk management. The phrase "to hedge a bet" dates from 1672 according to the Oxford English Dictionary and means "to secure oneself against loss." The verb *to hedge* derives from the noun *hedge*; that is, a fence made from a row of bushes or trees. These hedges were normally made from the spiny hawthorn, which makes an impenetrable hedge when laid. To hedge a piece of land was to limit it in terms of size and this gave rise to the meaning "secure, limited risk."[3] A modern definition of *hedge* as a verb from the Merriam-Webster Dictionary is: "to protect oneself from losing or failing by a counterbalancing action." In the context of energy finance, users of energy want to hedge themselves against increases in the price of energy, and producers of energy want to hedge themselves against decreases in the price of energy.

The article "Why Hedge: Some Evidence from Oil and Gas Producers" (Haushalter 2001) states firms hedge for two reasons, the first being that management is risk averse, meaning that management wants to reduce the likelihood that they may lose their jobs if the price of a major input/output changes unfavorably. The second reason stated is that hedging can reduce the likelihood that a company will incur financial distress and therefore increase the ability to fund profitable capital projects.

As the article "Energy Derivatives and the Transformation of the U.S. Corporate Energy Sector" states "derivative markets help enable companies to take the risks that they want to take in part by getting rid of the risks that they don't want to take . . . allowing them to concentrate more on their core competence. So, if they can reduce or eliminate that price risk, then shareholders should feel better about that" (Chew, 2001, p. 60). By transferring the risk of business processes that firms

do not have any insight into or control over, a firm is able to concentrate its efforts on those competencies that they are best at, increasing the overall effectiveness and efficiency of the firm.

Energy companies have different exposures to risk. For integrated companies, many of the risks they face are considered to be hedged naturally and offset each other. However, this is not necessarily true because with global operations, many outputs will not be available in the same location where the input is needed, along with other problems. On the other hand, if there is a disruption in oil or gas production, an integrated company may have sufficient storage facilities to handle this problem. An independent production company may need to hedge against a disruption.

Consumers of energy such as airlines and utilities may need to hedge against increases in energy prices because these are inputs into their business. Research has shown that hedging input price risk can increase firm value (see Carter, Rogers, and Simkins 2006; Smithson and Simkins 2005).

What are the ways that risk management can add value to the firm? Risk management allows firms to:

- Have greater debt capacity, which has a larger tax shield of interest payments.
- Lower cost of capital.
- Prevent underinvestment so that the firm can make optimal capital expenditures (capital budget) without having to unexpectedly raise external capital in years that would have had low cash flow due to volatility.
- Avoid costs of financial distress.
- Utilize comparative advantage in hedging relative to hedging ability of investors.
- Minimize negative tax effects due to convexity in the tax code.

Energy Price Volatility

Volatility is usually defined as the annualized standard deviation of commodity price returns. Energy prices quickly became the most volatile of all commodities as illustrated in Exhibit 16.3, "Annual Volatilities of Commodities, Equities, Interest Rates, and Exchange Rates as Represented by WTI Crude Oil, S&P 500 Index, U.S. Treasury Bond, and Eurodollar." Over the four-year period 2007–2010, it is clear that crude oil has the greatest price volatility, followed by equities, interest rates, and currencies (four-year average volatilities of 44.0%, 25.6%, 25.4%, and 11.4%, respectively).

ENERGY DERIVATIVES AND IMPORTANT TERMINOLOGY

Forwards and Futures

A forward contract is an agreement to buy or sell the underlying commodity at a fixed price in the future. These contracts require physical delivery and are

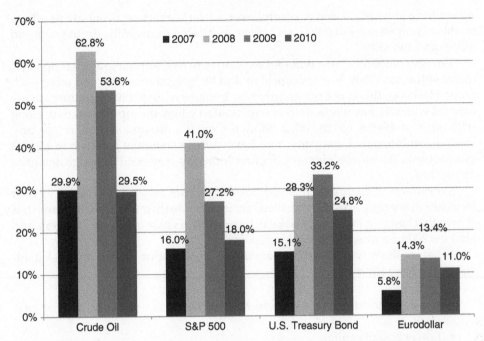

Exhibit 16.3　Annual Volatilities of Commodities, Equities, Interest Rates, and Exchange Rates as Represented by WTI Crude Oil, S&P 500 Index, U.S. Treasury Bond, and Eurodollar

traded over the counter (OTC). For example, assume that in December 2012, Party A agrees to buy and Counterparty B agrees to sell 50,000 barrels of crude oil at Chicago in January 2014 for a price of $80 per barrel. The contract quantity is 50,000 barrels, the delivery date is January 2014, the delivery place is Chicago, and the forward price is $80 per barrel.

A future contract is an agreement to buy or sell the underlying commodity for a certain price (futures price) at a certain time (expiration date). These contracts are standardized, may not require physical delivery, and are traded on organized exchanges. The party that has agreed to buy has what is termed a "long position." The party that has agreed to sell has a "short position." For example, on July 25, 2012, one can enter into an agreement to buy 1,000 barrels of oil (Light Sweet Crude, WTI, one contract) for June 2013 delivery at $90.90 per barrel. The spot price of WTI on June 25 is $88.81 per barrel. Information on current NYMEX futures contracts is available at www.cmegroup.com/trading/energy/crude-oil/light-sweet-crude.html.

Spot Price, Forward Price, Futures Price, Prompt Month, Open Interest, and Volume

Before proceeding further, it is necessary to cover some terminology. The *spot price* (also referred to as the cash price) of an asset is the price established today for delivery of the asset today (or within 24 hours). The *forward price* of an asset is the price established today for delivery of the asset on a designated future date. If this is the price on a futures contract, it is referred to as the *futures price*. In other words, the spot price is the price for immediate delivery, while the forward/futures

Exhibit 16.4 Example of a Hedge Using the NYMEX Crude Oil Futures Contract

Cash Price (i.e., Spot Price)	Futures Price	Basis (Cash price minus futures price)
July 24, 2012, cash price $88.81 per Bbl	$88.41 per Bbl	$0.40 per Bbl
January 2, 2015, cash price of $96.10	$95.50 per Bbl	$0.60 per Bbl
	$7.09 per Bbl	$0.20 basis loss
Result:		
	Cash purchase price of crude oil $96.10 per Bbl	
	Minus crude oil futures gain −$7.09 per Bbl	
	Net purchase price of crude oil $89.01 per Bbl	

price is the price for future delivery. The *prompt month* futures contract refers to the nearest month of delivery for which NYMEX futures prices are published during the trading month. *Open interest* is the total number of contracts outstanding, and *volume of trading* is the number of trades in one day.

Futures contracts are settled daily which means that at the end of every trading day, the last traded price (settlement) is used to value the investor's position. Futures exchanges require each customer to post an initial margin in their account in the form of cash or other collateral when the contract is originated. The margin account is marked to market at the end of each trading day according to that day's price movements. All outstanding contract positions are adjusted to the settlement price set by the exchange after trading ends. Forward contracts may not require either counterparty to post collateral.

Over 99 percent of futures contracts are closed out before maturity by entering into an offsetting trade—if the investor is long one contract, he must sell one contract to close the long position. This is known as *financial settlement*. If a futures contract is not closed out before maturity, it is usually settled by delivering the assets underlying the contract. This is known as physical settlement. When there are alternatives about what is delivered, where it is delivered, and when it is delivered, the party with the short position chooses. As discussed in Chapter 15, there are futures contracts on crude oil, natural gas, and heating oil traded on the NYMEX, among others.

Exhibit 16.4, "Example of a Hedge Using the NYMEX Crude Oil Futures Contract," shows how a futures hedge is applied to a purchaser of crude oil (such as a refiner). On July 24, 2012, a crude oil purchasing director wants to hedge his crude oil purchase planned for January 2015.

He buys a January 2015 futures contract on the NYMEX at $88.41 per barrel (contract size is for 1,000 barrels). On the same day, the crude oil spot price is $88.81 per barrel (Bbl). The director closes out this futures contract on January 2, 2015, at $95.50 per barrel. As shown, the director has made a profit of $7.09 per barrel (95.50 minus 88.41) on the futures contract. In essence, the hedger bought a futures contract (a long hedge) in July 2012 and then sold back the futures contract in January 2, 2015, to offset the position. The spot price of crude oil on January 2 is $96.10 per barrel. Without the futures hedge, the director would have paid $7.09 per barrel more for the fuel (cash price − net purchase price of crude oil with

futures = \$96.10 − \$89.01). However, by using the futures contract and purchasing crude oil in the spot market, the gain of \$7.09 on the futures offsets the \$7.29 per barrel increase in the crude oil spot price. As a result, the director's net cost of crude oil is \$89.01 per barrel (i.e., \$96.10 spot price in January 2015 minus the futures hedging gain of \$7.09 per barrel). See the calculations in Exhibit 16.4.

In summary, many participants in the futures markets are hedgers. They want to reduce a particular risk they face. They can take either long or short positions on futures contracts depending on their exposure. A long futures hedge is appropriate when you know you will purchase an asset in the future and want to lock in the price. A short futures hedge is appropriate when you know you will sell an asset in the future and want to lock in the price. For more examples of hedging using futures, see Chapter 17, "Risks in Trading Energy Commodities," and NYMEX's *A Guide to Energy Hedging*, which is available on their website for free.

Example: Chemical Company Hedging High Density Polyethylene (HDPE) Prices

The NYMEX has a futures contract on high density polyethylene (HDPE), and one contract covers 47,000 pounds. As discussed in Chapter 5, chemical companies use HDPE to make various plastics such as bottles and crates. On July 27, 2012, a chemical company could purchase (go long one futures contract) that matures in December 12, 2012, and lock in a price of \$0.58 per pound. This contract would be marked to market each day, but effectively the company has locked in this price for the volume hedged.

MORE CONCEPTS AND TERMINOLOGY

Basic risk: The term *basis risk* is used to describe the risk that the value of the commodity being hedged may not change in tandem with the value of the derivative contract used to hedge the price risk. In an ideal hedge, the hedge would match the underlying position in every respect. However, in actuality, basis risk is a high concern, even if the derivatives contract is for the exact same commodity being hedged. Basic risk often takes three different forms: *product basis risk* (such as when the derivatives contract is not for the same commodity, known as a cross-hedge), *time basis risk* (timing difference), and *locational basis risk* (the futures contract is for a different delivery point from the hedger's exposure).

Contango and backwardation and how they impact hedging: Futures prices for different deliveries for various commodities may have diverse behaviors. In some cases, prices may increase as the delivery time increases. In this case we say that the market is in *contango* as illustrated in Exhibit 16.5. The term originated in nineteenth-century England and means "continue" or "contingent." If markets are in contango, there is a financial incentive to purchase the commodity in an earlier period for use in later periods if the storage costs are less than the price increases. For example, an energy user hedging input price risk might choose to lease additional fuel tanks as its hedging strategy rather than hedge in the commodity markets (only if the carrying costs of this storage is less than the time basis between months). Often, such a strategy is too expensive because storage is typically costly relative to the time basis for energy commodities such as crude oil and jet fuel.

Owners of natural gas storage facilities can use excess capacity both to manage the price risk that often exists between months and to make additional income.

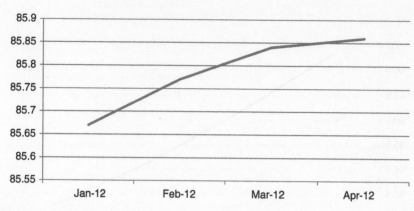

Exhibit 16.5 Markets in Contango

In contango markets, owners of underground natural gas storage facilities with excess capacity can arbitrage the situation if they can store natural gas for less than the difference between the prices (such as purchase the nearby futures contract, the prompt month contract, and sell futures contracts for the future months. The storage facility can then take delivery of the natural gas on the nearby contract and deliver it against the distant contract, earning an arbitrage profit equal to the difference between the sale and purchase of the futures contracts less the facility's cost of storage. For more discussion on storage arbitrage, refer to Chapter 17.

During 2008 and 2009, the crude oil market was in contango, yet world economies were in a tailspin. On December 10, 2009, the WTI spot price was $43.53 per barrel but the futures contract for delivery in December 2010 was $55.60 (a 30% higher price for one year later). Some companies and institutions took advantage of the situation. At the time, there were 161 tankers at sea storing 141 million barrels of oil, which is enough to supply the entire United States for one week (Energy Intelligence Research 2011).

Backwardation is a market situation where prices are progressively lower in distant delivery months as shown for crude oil futures in Exhibit 16.6. When markets are in backwardation, a hedging strategy using futures contracts may be useful. This lack of storability is one reason that crude oil markets tend to exhibit backwardation.

Mean reversion: Mean reversion, also known as regression to the mean, was first discovered by Francis Galton in 1875. Galton was an amateur mathematician who was the first cousin of Charles Darwin. This behavior of some commodity prices indicates they may change but eventually go back to a "mean level" that may be time varying as well. As prices get further from the long-term mean view of the market (whether above or below), there is greater price pressure to move back towards the mean over time. Energy commodity prices for crude oil and natural gas have exhibited this behavior as evidenced by observing futures curves. See Exhibit 16.7, "Example of Mean Reversion for Crude Oil Futures Contracts." This exhibit shows the futures curve at three different points in time, exactly one year apart. Note how the current prices are further apart but at 36 months out, the prices converge around $87 per barrel.

Head and shoulder pattern for the natural gas futures curve: Exhibit 16.8 illustrates the head and shoulder pattern that can be seen in the natural gas futures curve.

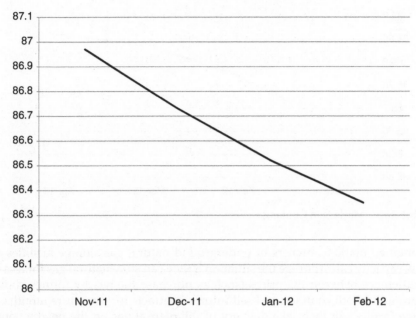

Exhibit 16.6 Markets in Backwardation

Because of the seasonality of natural gas prices (higher prices in winter, which cause the head, and lower prices in summer, which cause the shoulder), we observe this pattern. Note the parallel shift in the futures curve at three different points in time a year apart.

Calls and Puts

An option contract confers the right to buy (if it is a *call*) or sell (if it is a *put*) an asset for a predetermined price on (or before) a specified future date. The contract

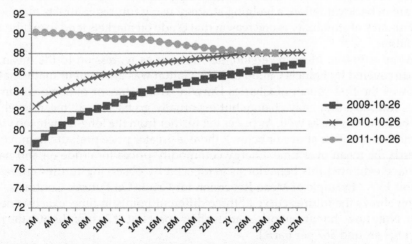

Exhibit 16.7 Example of Mean Reversion for Crude Oil Futures Contracts

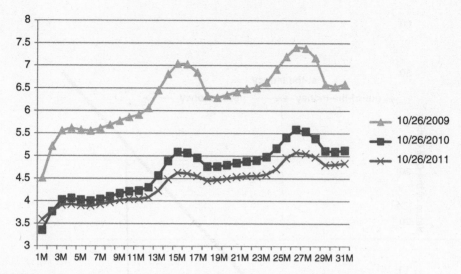

Exhibit 16.8 Head and Shoulder Pattern for the Natural Gas Futures Curve

price is the *strike* or *exercise* price. The specified date is the *expiration* date. The asset (e.g., commodity) on which an option is written is the *underlying asset*. The holder will exercise an option contract only if it is profitable to do so.

More formally, a call option is an option contract that gives the holder the right to buy a certain quantity (such as a 1000 barrels of crude oil or 10,000 MMBtu of natural gas) of an underlying security from the writer of the option, at a specified price (the strike price) up to a specified date (the expiration date). A put option contract gives the holder the right to sell a certain quantity of an underlying security to the writer of the option, at a specified price (strike price) up to a specified date (expiration date).

As a result, the risk profile of option contracts is asymmetric (one-sided). Exhibit 16.9 illustrates the payoff diagram for a call option buyer, and Exhibit 16.10 illustrates the payoff for a put option buyer. For every buyer of a contract, there is a seller of the contract, and they have the opposite payoff diagrams. This is shown in Exhibit 16.11.

As shown in Exhibit 16.12, the value of the option (the premium) is determined by the intrinsic value (which is the difference between the strike price and the underlying price) and the time value remaining in the option. As shown in the exhibit, a call option is *in-the-money* when the asset price is greater than the strike price, *at-the-money* when the asset price is the same as the strike price, and *out-of-the-money* when the asset prices is less than the strike price.

The intrinsic value of a call option = Max (S – X, 0). Likewise, the intrinsic value of a put option is = Max (X – S, 0), where S is the asset's value and X is the strike price.

It should be clear that:

- Calls can be purchased to *cap* prices if the expectation is that prices will rise.
- Puts can be purchased to establish a *floor* under prices if the expectation is that prices will fall.

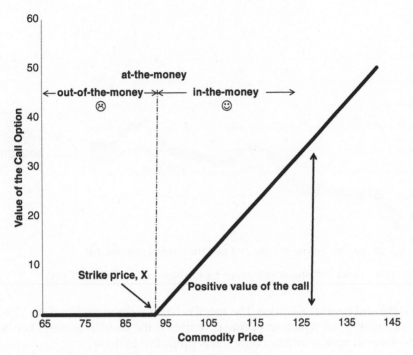

Exhibit 16.9   The Payoff Diagram for a Call Option Buyer

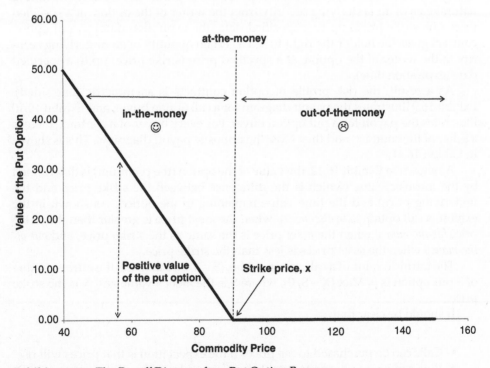

Exhibit 16.10   The Payoff Diagram for a Put Option Buyer

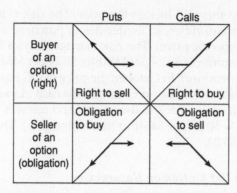

Exhibit 16.11   Opposite Payoff Diagrams for Buyers and Sellers of Options

Exercise Style: Options are distinguished as to whether or not *early exercise* is permitted. An option that can be exercised only on the maturity date is called a *European option.* An option that can be exercised on or any time prior to maturity is called an *American option.*

Example: Purchase a Call Option on Natural Gas

In June, a natural gas risk manager is concerned about rising prices during the coming winter months. He could buy the November 2012 NG futures contract trading

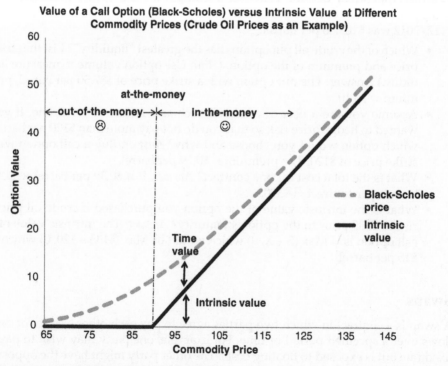

Exhibit 16.12   The Value of the Call Option

at $5 per MMBtu, but this will lock in the price. The risk manager wants to take advantage of any price declines, so he decides to purchase a call option (i.e., the right to buy gas at a specific price). The risk manager buys a November $5.00 call option and pays a premium of $0.24 per MMBtu; $5.24 per MMBtu is the breakeven price (including the premium). In October, the price of NG has risen to $6/MMBtu when the physical gas needs to be purchased in the cash market. The risk manager decides to sell the call option back to the market and receives a premium of $1.00. He has $1.00 – $0.24 = $0.76 per MMBtu (net hedge gain). The effective purchase price = $6 – $0.76 = $5.24.

Example: Purchase a Put Option on Natural Gas

A hedger should purchase a put in order to set a floor under prices. For example, if the October natural gas (NG) futures price is $5/MMBtu and the hedger wants to lock in this price but still benefit from any rise in prices in the month of October, she will purchase an October NG put option instead with a strike of $5 for a $0.27 option premium. When the hedger sells the physical NG in September for $4.60/MMBtu (which turns out to be the cash market price at that time), she then sells the put option for a $.40 premium ($5.00 – 4.60 estimated premium) = $.40 less the premium paid of $0.27 = $.13 net gain. The net sales price of gas is $4.60 cash price + 0.13 hedging gain = $4.73 per MMBtu total received.

Example Using the NYMEX Calls and Puts on Crude Oil is Shown in the Appendix

(See the Appendix.) Use the Prior Settle column for the option premium. The strike price is listed in cents per barrel and the closing spot price for crude oil on 3/17/2012 was $107.06 per barrel.

- Which of the crude oil put options has the greatest "liquidity"? List the strike price and premium of the option. (*Hint*: Use option volume to measure liquidity.) Answer: The put option with a strike price of $87.50 per barrel, premium = $0.10.
- Assume you are a user of crude oil such as a refiner or an airline. If you wanted to hedge price risk so that you do not pay more than $120 per barrel, which option would you choose and why? *Answer*: Buy a call option with strike price of $120. The premium is $0.39 per barrel.
- What is the total cost for one contract? *Answer*: It is $0.39 per barrel × 1,000 barrels per contract = $390.
- What is the intrinsic value of the option you purchased if crude oil prices rise to $135 prior to the option's maturity? *Answer*: The intrinsic value of a call option is = Max (S – X, 0) which would be Max ($135 – 120, 0) which is $15 per barrel.

Swaps

A swap is a contract in which two parties agree to pay each other a series of cash flows over a specified period of time. For example, one party may wish to pay a fixed rate but is exposed to floating costs. The other party might have the opposite situation. This is illustrated for an airline in the following graphic.

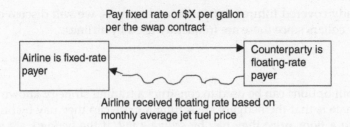

Pay fixed rate of $X per gallon per the swap contract

Airline is fixed-rate payer → Counterparty is floating-rate payer

Airline received floating rate based on monthly average jet fuel price

Example 1: Using a Plain Vanilla Jet Fuel Swap Arranged in the OTC Market

In the above illustration, an airline enters into a swap position. Typically, the airline pays a fixed price and receives a floating price, both indexed to expected jet fuel use during each monthly settlement period. The volume of fuel hedged is negotiated because this is a customized contract. During the life of the swap contract, the airline buys jet fuel in the cash market, as usual, but the swap contract makes up the difference when prices rise and removes the difference when prices decline. The result for the airline is a fixed price for the period covered. The fixed-rate payment is set based on market conditions when the swap contract is initiated. The floating price of jet fuel is commonly based on Platt's New York Harbor jet fuel price and is calculated monthly using daily prices for the month. The net monthly payment (or cost) to the fixed-rate payer is the floating rate minus the fixed rate. For example, if the floating rate for a month averages 280 cents per gallon and the fixed rate is 270 cents per gallon, then the floating rate payer makes a 10 cents per gallon payment that month to the airline. If the size of the contract is 100,000 gallons, a payment of $10,000 is made to the airline (i.e., $0.10 × 100,000).

Example 2: Using the NYMEX New York Harbor Heating Oil Calendar Swap

The NYMEX New York Heating Oil Calendar Swap lets hedgers arrange positions in the heating oil market as far forward as 36 months. The price settlement of the contract is based on the arithmetic average of the NYMEX New York Harbor heating oil futures nearby month settlement price for each business day during the contract month. The swap contract is for 42,000 gallons—the same size as the NYMEX heating oil futures contract. Consider an 18-month swap currently trading with a fixed-price of $2.7716 per gallon. Suppose the futures average daily price for the month was $2.88. The hedger who is long the futures contract (such as a trucking company using the heating oil contract to hedge diesel) will receive a payment from the counterparty of $4,552.80 [i.e., (2.88 – 2.7716) × 42,000]. The trucking company would purchase diesel in the spot market. Assuming the basis has not changed between heating oil and diesel (i.e., the high correlation between heating oil and diesel remains unchanged), the gain on the futures contract will be offset by the higher cash price of diesel fuel. As a result, the trucking company effectively pays a fixed price for diesel over the period of the swap contract.

Hedging Strategies

A recent survey (Osipovich 2012) indicated that airlines use the following hedges most commonly, in order from most frequently used to less frequently used: swaps, call options, costless collars, three-way collars, futures, and forwards. Since we

have already covered futures, forwards, and options, we will discuss collars and three-way collars since these are frequently used by airlines.

Collars

Call and put options can be used to construct a trading strategy known as a *collar*. The rationale is that the hedgers are setting a price cap they pay by buying a call and setting a floor price they pay by *selling a put*, if the hedgers are wanting to manage price risk for a commodity they are going to buy (i.e., input price risk such as for a refiner or airline). Similarly, the hedger would *buy a put* and *sell a call* if he wanted to hedge output price risk (such as for a producer). This strategy allows hedgers to reduce hedging cost with premium income. Both options expire in the same month and the collar sets a band around prices; that is, floor and ceiling. The advantage is the flexibility, too. Futures lock you into a price; however, the collars allows flexibility within the range. When choosing the options, be sure you can defend the range selected for the collar. To summarize:

- Collar strategy to hedge input price risk = buy a call and sell a put
- Collar strategy to hedge output price risk = buy a put and sell a call

Example of Collar Using the NYMEX Calls and Puts on Crude Oil in the Appendix

Apache Corporation, an independent oil and gas exploration and production company, decides to hedge part of their crude oil production. Management has decided to lock in a minimum price of $100.00 they receive for 1,000,000 barrels of production. To offset the cost of the hedge, they will use a collar strategy, and management agrees to let $125 per barrel be the most they receive on the volume hedged. Construct a collar hedging strategy using the Appendix. What options should they buy? State the total cost of the hedge. *Answer:* Apache will buy a put option with a strike price of $100 (premium paid of $0.85 per barrel) and sell a call option with a strike price of $125 (premium received of $0.26). The net premium paid is $0.85 − 0.26 = $0.59 per barrel. Exhibit 16.13 illustrates the total amount that Apache will receive on the crude oil hedged, including the collar payoff for buying a put option and selling a call option. As shown, a floor of $100 per barrel and a ceiling of $125 per barrel are established so the risk is collared. When the price of crude oil is between $100 and $125, Apache will receive the market price for crude oil and both options are out-of-the-money. To hedge a 1,000,000 barrels of production, Apache will need to purchase 1,000 contracts of both the calls and puts (since one contract is for 1,000 barrels) with a total net premium of $0.59 × 1,000 = $59,000.

Zero-Cost and Premium Collars

A zero-cost collar, also known as a costless collar, is established (for a company like Apache) by buying a protective put while selling an out-of-the-money call with a strike price at which the premium received is equal to the premium of the protective put purchased. Hence, the net premium for this strategy is zero. If the zero-cost collar is for a firm hedging the input, similar to the plain collar, the hedger would buy a call and sell a put with the same premiums. A premium collar occurs when

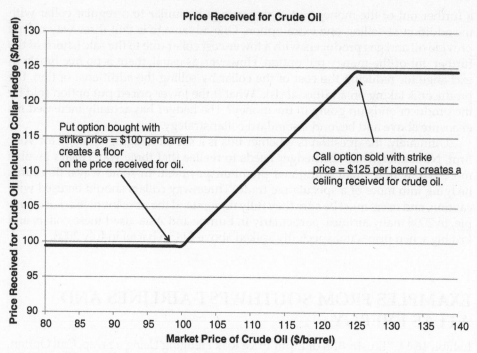

Exhibit 16.13 Total Amount Received for Crude Oil Including the Collar Hedge

the option being sold does not completely offset the option premium paid and results in a net cost (premium) to the hedging strategy.

Do not let the name *zero-cost collar* fool you. It is only zero-cost at the time of initiation. If the option sold goes in the money, the firm will owe money to the buyer of the option contract. There are no free lunches in the derivatives world.

Example of Zero-Cost Collar Using the NYMEX Calls and Puts on Crude Oil in the Appendix

Use the Prior Settle column for the option premium. The strike price is listed as cents per barrel. The spot closing price on crude oil on 3/17/2012 was $107.06 per Bbl. Assume Devon Energy is constructing a collar hedge to lock in a sales price of $97 for crude oil. What type of option should they buy? Be sure to state the type, strike price, and premium. [*Answer:* Buy a put option with strike price = $97. Option premium is $0.49.] Is it possible to construct a zero-cost collar for the company? If so, what type of option do they sell and what is the premium? [*Answer:* Yes; sell a call option with strike price = $118. The call option premium received is $0.49 which offsets the put premium paid.]

Three-Way Collars

In recent years, three-way collars have become popular hedging instruments, as evidenced by the survey results mentioned earlier. Here is how the strategy would work for an oil producer. The producer would buy a put, sell a call, and then sell

a further out-of-the-money put. This strategy is similar to a regular collar with the addition of selling one extra option. One advantage is that three-way collars provide oil and gas producers with a lower-cost collar due to the sale (short) of the further out-of-the-money put option. However, as usual, there is no free lunch. In exchange for reducing the cost of the collar by selling the additional option, the producer is taking on additional risk. What if the lower priced put option sold by the producer ends up going in the money? The hedger has actually increased his exposure above and beyond a standard collar strategy.

Ultimately, the question is whether this is a sound hedging strategy for your firm. No matter what, the hedger needs to realize that three-way collars involve more risk with a small additional premium payment. In some ways, this turns hedging into more of a speculative trade. Three-way collars should be used with caution, and users must be sure they fully understand the risks involved. For example, in 2008 many airlines, particularly in Europe and Asia, used these collars and lost big when prices unexpectedly spiked above $145 a barrel in July 2008.

EXAMPLES FROM SOUTHWEST AIRLINES AND ATLAS ENERGY

Exhibit 16.14, "Illustration of Input Price Risk Hedging Using a Swap, Call Option, and Premium Collar," provides a representation of how airlines such as Southwest Airlines look at the hedging payoffs for a swap, call option, and premium collar. The price hedged on all contract illustrated is for $1.20 per gallon except the premium collar also utilizes selling a put option with a strike price of $1.00. Note how a swap locks in the price of $1.20 without any flexibility. The call option gives the best protection and flexibility but costs more. The premium collar gives the upside

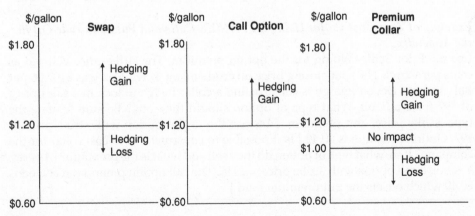

Exhibit 16.14 Illustration of Input Price Risk Hedging Using a Swap, Call Option, and Premium Collar.
Note: The hedge price on all contracts illustrated is for $1.20 per gallon. The premium collar is for buying a call option with strike price of $1.20 and selling a put option with strike price of $1.00.

Exhibit 16.15 Atlas Energy, L.P. Announces Natural Gas and Oil Hedge Positions

April 11, 2011 09:05 AM Eastern Daylight Time
PHILADELPHIA–(BUSINESS WIRE)–Atlas Energy, L.P. (NYSE: AHD) ("Atlas")
announced today that it has established new hedge positions for its future natural gas &
oil production through 2013. Atlas executed a combination of fixed-price swap and
costless collar positions to protect its future production from movement in commodity
prices. The crude oil hedges are intended to protect Atlas' condensate and natural
gas liquids production.
The following is a summary of the newly established hedge positions:

Year Hedge	Instrument	Volume Hedged (mcf/Bbl)[1][2]	Price per mcf/Bbl[1]
Natural Gas Hedges:			
2011[3]	Swap	4,629,080	$4.58
2011	Collar	1,602,373	$3.84–$5.72
2012	Swap	5,459,941	$5.11
2012	Collar	1,899,110	$4.35–$6.20
2013	Swap	3,086,053	$5.40
2013	Collar	3,086,053	$4.85–$6.19
Crude Oil Hedges:			
2011[3]	Collar	45,000	$90.00–$125.31
2012	Collar	60,000	$90.00–$117.91
2013	Collar	60,000	$90.00–$116.40

(1) The abbreviation "mcf" represents thousand cubic feet of gas; "Bbl" represents barrels of oil.
(2) Costless collar prices represent the floor and ceiling price established in the collar position. Also, for
natural gas hedges, price includes an estimated positive basis differential and Btu (British thermal unit)
adjustment.
(3) Reflects hedges covering the last nine months of 2011.
Atlas Energy, L.P. (NYSE: AHD) is a master limited partnership which owns an interest in over 8,500
producing natural gas and oil wells, representing over 185 Bcfe of net proved developed reserves. Additionally, AHD owns and operates the general partner of Atlas Pipeline Partners, L.P. (NYSE: APL),
through which it owns a 2% general partner interest, all the incentive distribution rights and approximately 5.75 million common limited partner units of APL. For more information, please visit our website at www.atlasenergy.com, or contact Investor Relations at InvestorRelations@atlasenergy.com.
Source: http://www.businesswire.com/news/home/20110411006085/en/

price protection similar to the call option only strategy but also involves giving up
some of the downside benefit due to the put option that is sold.

Exhibit 16.15, "Atlas Energy, L.P. Announces Natural Gas and Oil Hedge Positions," provides a very interesting example of how Atlas Energy manages energy
price risk. Many energy companies employ similar strategies. Which of the derivatives contracts does Atlas Energy use that we have covered in this chapter?

OTHER EXAMPLES OF HEDGING CONTRACTS

Basis Contracts: A variety of basis contracts are available in OTC markets to hedge
locational, product, and even temporal differences between exchange-traded standard contracts and the particular circumstances of contract users. The simplest is
a basis swap, in which the difference between two locations, such as a gas price in
Tennessee and the Henry Hub price are exchanged.

Crack Spread Contracts: Refiners' profits are tied directly to the spread, or difference, between the price of crude oil and the prices of refined products. One way in which a refiner could ensure a given spread would be to buy crude oil futures and sell product futures. Another would be to buy crude oil call options and sell product put options. In 1994, the NYMEX launched the *crack spread contract*. The crack spread contract helps refiners to lock in a crude oil price and heating oil and unleaded gasoline prices simultaneously in order to establish a fixed refining margin. One type of crack spread contract bundles the purchase of three crude oil futures (30,000 barrels) with the sale a month later of two unleaded gasoline futures (20,000 barrels) and one heating oil future (10,000 barrels). The 3-2-1 ratio approximates the real-world ratio of refinery output—2 barrels of unleaded gasoline and 1 barrel of heating oil from 3 barrels of crude oil. There are also options on the crack spread.

Calendar Spread Options: NYMEX offers calendar spread options on crude oil, heating oil, and unleaded gasoline. Buying a call on the calendar spread options contract will represent a long position (purchase) in the prompt months of the futures contract and a short position (sale) in the further months of the contract. These types of contracts are useful to storage facilities such as for crude oil or natural gas.

Volumetric Production Payment Contracts: A volumetric production payment contract (VPP) is both a prepaid swap and a synthetic loan. Unlike a normal swap, where the differences between the fixed and variable payments are periodically settled in cash, the buyer (usually a producer) is paid the present value of the fixed payments in advance. In exchange, the seller receives an agreed-upon amount of natural gas or other product over time. These deals typically last for three to five years.

OTHER IMPORTANT ISSUES

Hedging and FAS 133: FAS 133 is a requirement by the Financial Accounting Standards Board for the disclosure of any derivative transaction entered into by a corporation and includes how hedging should be treated in the income statement and balance sheet. From a strictly theoretical point of view, accounting disclosure requirements should have no effect on a firm's hedging strategy. However, one can find many examples of situations in which changes in accounting policy have caused firms to change business behaviors. A concern voiced by heavy users of derivatives is that, by introducing unrealized gains and losses from derivative instruments that fail to qualify for hedge accounting, FAS 133 would cause more volatility in reported earnings. In such cases, firms may be discouraged from entering into cross-hedges that may be subject to significant levels of basis risk.

The Dodd-Frank Act: The Dodd-Frank Act was passed in passed in 2010 and was aimed to clean up the OTC derivatives market after certain instruments such as credit default swaps were implicated in the global financial crisis. Although the law is not directly aimed at commodities markets such as energy, it may impact some industry players in the energy derivatives markets. Recent CFTC decisions appear to be favorable to providers of energy such as utilities and industrials. For example, a recent decision put the interests of consumers first by allowing utilities

to continue hedging against commodity price volatility in a cost-effective manner. While addressing the Dodd-Frank Act is beyond the scope of this chapter, the reader should be aware of this still-evolving area.

CONCLUSION

Managing energy price risk is a complex yet very crucial area of risk management. Since the 1980s, there has been a proliferation of new energy derivatives to manage the risk, both on the organized exchanges and in the over-the-counter markets. This chapter provides an introduction to energy risk management and describes basic hedging instruments used in energy risk management.

As a final caveat, management must keep the following core concepts in mind when developing a hedging strategy. First, it is management's responsibility to fully understand the key risks of the hedging strategy selected. This includes fully understanding the hedging instruments being used and being able to internally value the positions. A firm should never undertake any hedging strategy when it does not completely understand the hedging risks involved. Second, management should assess the interrelationships between market risks, liquidity risks, and basis risk in their hedging strategy. Scenario and what-if analysis should be undertaken so that they are fully aware of potential problems. No hedge is perfect. And finally, the manager should communicate these risks to upper management and the board of directors when applicable. There have been many situations where this was not properly handled and in some cases, it caused the firm to go bankrupt. Refer to the next chapter, Chapter 17, "Risks in Trading Energy Commodities," for more discussion of best practices and common pitfalls in risk management.

APPENDIX

CRUDE OIL CALL OPTIONS FOR NYMEX WTI CRUDE OIL

Prices are for March 17, 2012. The spot price for WTI crude oil was at $107.06 per bbl.

FOR EXERCISES IN THIS CHAPTER, USE THE PRIOR SETTLE PRICE AS THE OPTION PREMIUM.

Strike Price	Type	Last	Change	Prior Settle	High	Low	Volume
9350	CALL	—	—	14.33	—	—	734
9400	CALL	—	—	13.86	—	—	100
9450	CALL	—	—	13.39	—	—	399
9500	CALL	—	—	12.92	—	—	728
9550	CALL	—	—	12.45	—	—	434
9600	CALL	—	—	11.99	—	—	100
9650	CALL	—	—	11.52	—	—	761
9700	CALL	—	—	11.07	—	—	347
9750	CALL	—	—	10.62	—	—	759
9800	CALL	—	—	10.17	—	—	724
9850	CALL	—	—	9.73	—	—	217
9900	CALL	—	—	9.29	—	—	485

(Continued)

Strike Price	Type	Last	Change	Prior Settle	High	Low	Volume
9950	CALL	—	—	8.86	—	—	630
10000	CALL	—	—	8.43	—	—	576
10050	CALL	—	—	8.01	—	—	578
10100	CALL	—	—	7.6	—	—	405
10150	CALL	—	—	7.19	—	—	705
10200	CALL	—	—	6.79	—	—	746
10250	CALL	—	—	6.4	—	—	268
10300	CALL	—	—	6.01	—	—	441
10350	CALL	—	—	5.65	—	—	345
10400	CALL	—	—	5.3	—	—	456
10450	CALL	—	—	4.95	—	—	137
10500	CALL	—	—	4.62	—	—	582
10550	CALL	—	—	4.3	—	—	484
10600	CALL	—	—	3.98	—	—	536
10650	CALL	3.6	−0.09	3.69	3.6	3.6	826
10700	CALL	—	—	3.4	—	—	3543
10750	CALL	—	—	3.13	—	—	1279
10800	CALL	2.95 b	0.08	2.87	2.95 b	—	1598
10850	CALL	—	—	2.63	—	—	4228
10900	CALL	2.48 b	0.07	2.41	2.48 b	—	2395
10950	CALL	—	—	2.19	—	—	1343
11000	CALL	2.08 b	0.07	2.01	2.08 b	—	3620
11050	CALL	—	—	1.83	—	—	2857
11100	CALL	1.71 b	0.05	1.66	1.71 b	—	1187
11150	CALL	—	—	1.51	—	—	2295
11200	CALL	1.45	0.08	1.37	1.45	1.45	4290
11250	CALL	—	—	1.24	—	—	1314
11300	CALL	1.15 b	0.02	1.13	1.15 b	—	312
11350	CALL	—	—	1.03	—	—	2421
11400	CALL	0.96 b	0.02	0.94	0.96 b	—	860
11450	CALL	—	—	0.86	—	—	2155
11500	CALL	0.83 b	0.04	0.79	0.83 b	—	639
11550	CALL	—	—	0.72	—	—	1472
11600	CALL	0.67 b	0.01	0.66	0.67 b	—	1674
11650	CALL	—	—	0.62	—	—	2461
11700	CALL	—	—	0.57	—	—	4697
11750	CALL	—	—	0.53	—	—	3285
11800	CALL	—	—	0.49	—	—	4238
11850	CALL	—	—	0.46	—	—	1207
11900	CALL	0.44 b	0.01	0.43	0.44 b	—	4096
11950	CALL	—	—	0.41	—	—	3829
12000	CALL	—	—	0.39	—	—	2516
12050	CALL	—	—	0.37	—	—	342
12100	CALL	—	—	0.35	—	—	656
12150	CALL	—	—	0.34	—	—	1984
12200	CALL	—	—	0.32	—	—	2042
12250	CALL	—	—	0.31	—	—	855
12300	CALL	—	—	0.3	—	—	315

Strike Price	Type	Last	Change	Prior Settle	High	Low	Volume
12350	CALL	—	—	0.29	—	—	1058
12400	CALL	—	—	0.28	—	—	113
12450	CALL	—	—	0.27	—	—	2442
12500	CALL	—	—	0.26	—	—	2036
12600	CALL	—	—	0.25	—	—	1874
12700	CALL	—	—	0.24	—	—	625
12800	CALL	—	—	0.23	—	—	669
12900	CALL	—	—	0.22	—	—	503
12950	CALL	—	—	0.21	—	—	128
13000	CALL	0.22	0.01	0.21	0.22	0.22	968
13050	CALL	—	—	0.2	—	—	649
13100	CALL	—	—	0.19	—	—	1761
13200	CALL	—	—	0.18	—	—	221
13300	CALL	—	—	0.17	—	—	742
13400	CALL	—	—	0.16	—	—	864
13500	CALL	—	—	0.15	—	—	2185
13650	CALL	—	—	0.16	—	—	2160
13700	CALL	—	—	0.14	—	—	1509
13800	CALL	—	—	0.13	—	—	146
13950	CALL	—	—	0.14	—	—	267
14000	CALL	0.13 a	0.01	0.12	0.16	0.13 a	1215
14200	CALL	—	—	0.11	—	—	2201
14250	CALL	—	—	0.12	—	—	755
14500	CALL	0.08	−0.02	0.1	0.08	0.08	473
14700	CALL	—	—	0.09	—	—	291
15000	CALL	0.07	0	0.07	0.08 b	0.07	1569
15500	CALL	—	—	0.06	—	—	2229
15700	CALL	—	—	0.05	—	—	888
16000	CALL	0.04	0	0.04	0.04	0.04	1758

CRUDE OIL PUT OPTIONS FOR NYMEX WTI CRUDE OIL

Prices are for March 17, 2012. The spot price for WTI crude oil was at $107.06 per Bbl.

FOR EXERCISES IN THIS CHAPTER, USE THE PRIOR SETTLE PRICE AS THE OPTION PREMIUM.

Strike Price	Type	Last	Change	Prior Settle	High	Low	Volume
8100	PUT	—	—	0.04	—	—	198
8150	PUT	—	—	0.05	—	—	332
8200	PUT	0.04	−0.01	0.05	0.04	0.04	483
8250	PUT	—	—	0.05	—	—	895
8300	PUT	—	—	0.06	—	—	810
8350	PUT	—	—	0.06	—	—	120

(Continued)

Strike Price	Type	Last	Change	Prior Settle	High	Low	Volume
8400	PUT	—	—	0.07	—	—	386
8450	PUT	—	—	0.07	—	—	140
8500	PUT	—	—	0.07	—	—	2622
8550	PUT	—	—	0.08	—	—	1255
8600	PUT	—	—	0.08	—	—	1912
8650	PUT	—	—	0.09	—	—	2653
8700	PUT	—	—	0.1	—	—	3740
8750	PUT	—	—	0.1	—	—	3967
8800	PUT	—	—	0.11	—	—	3722
8850	PUT	—	—	0.12	—	—	709
8900	PUT	—	—	0.13	—	—	2118
8950	PUT	—	—	0.13	—	—	3612
9000	PUT	—	—	0.14	—	—	528
9050	PUT	—	—	0.15	—	—	548
9100	PUT	—	—	0.17	—	—	1535
9150	PUT	—	—	0.18	—	—	163
9200	PUT	—	—	0.2	—	—	862
9250	PUT	—	—	0.21	—	—	1885
9300	PUT	—	—	0.24	—	—	2512
9350	PUT	—	—	0.26	—	—	680
9400	PUT	—	—	0.28	—	—	1863
9450	PUT	—	—	0.31	—	—	1013
9500	PUT	0.33 a	−0.01	0.34	—	0.33 a	991
9550	PUT	—	—	0.37	—	—	2844
9600	PUT	0.39 a	−0.02	0.41	—	0.39 a	2210
9650	PUT	—	—	0.45	—	—	1848
9700	PUT	0.47 a	−0.02	0.49	—	0.47 a	2976
9750	PUT	—	—	0.54	—	—	1529
9800	PUT	0.56 a	−0.03	0.59	—	0.56 a	3438
9850	PUT	—	—	0.65	—	—	1980
9900	PUT	0.67 a	−0.04	0.71	—	0.67 a	2091
9950	PUT	—	—	0.78	—	—	2647
10000	PUT	0.79 a	−0.06	0.85	—	0.79 a	1378
10050	PUT	—	—	0.93	—	—	469
10100	PUT	0.96 a	−0.06	1.02	—	0.96 a	3180
10150	PUT	—	—	1.11	—	—	1120
10200	PUT	1.14 a	−0.07	1.21	—	1.14 a	2775
10250	PUT	—	—	1.32	—	—	2629
10300	PUT	1.37 a	−0.07	1.44	—	1.37 a	3427
10350	PUT	—	—	1.57	—	—	2632
10400	PUT	1.63 a	−0.09	1.72	—	1.63 a	235
10450	PUT	—	—	1.87	—	—	2413
10500	PUT	1.9	−0.14	2.04	1.9	1.9	174
10550	PUT	—	—	2.22	—	—	3460
10600	PUT	2.29 a	−0.12	2.41	—	2.29 a	436
10650	PUT	—	—	2.61	—	—	831
10700	PUT	2.7	−0.12	2.82	2.7	2.7	1417

Strike Price	Type	Last	Change	Prior Settle	High	Low	Volume
10750	PUT	—	—	3.05	—	—	3377
10800	PUT	3.15 a	−0.14	3.29	—	3.15 a	2469
10850	PUT	—	—	3.55	—	—	3055
10900	PUT	—	—	3.83	—	—	2679
10950	PUT	—	—	4.11	—	—	1698
11000	PUT	—	—	4.42	—	—	1245
11050	PUT	—	—	4.75	—	—	1240
11100	PUT	—	—	5.08	—	—	1010
11150	PUT	—	—	5.43	—	—	1555
11200	PUT	—	—	5.79	—	—	3321
11250	PUT	—	—	6.16	—	—	1675
11300	PUT	—	—	6.55	—	—	2822
11350	PUT	—	—	6.94	—	—	2137
11400	PUT	—	—	7.36	—	—	630
11450	PUT	—	—	7.77	—	—	1808
11500	PUT	—	—	8.21	—	—	2851
11550	PUT	—	—	8.63	—	—	467
11600	PUT	—	—	9.08	—	—	656
11650	PUT	—	—	9.53	—	—	313
11700	PUT	—	—	9.98	—	—	461
11750	PUT	—	—	10.45	—	—	367
11800	PUT	—	—	10.91	—	—	341
11850	PUT	—	—	11.37	—	—	127
11900	PUT	—	—	11.85	—	—	808
11950	PUT	—	—	12.32	—	—	864
12000	PUT	—	—	12.8	—	—	641
12050	PUT	—	—	13.29	—	—	457
12100	PUT	—	—	13.77	—	—	461
12150	PUT	—	—	14.26	—	—	504
12200	PUT	—	—	14.75	—	—	476
12250	PUT	—	—	15.24	—	—	610
12300	PUT	—	—	15.73	—	—	883
12350	PUT	—	—	16.21	—	—	171
12400	PUT	—	—	16.7	—	—	201
12450	PUT	—	—	17.19	—	—	76
12500	PUT	—	—	17.69	—	—	272
12550	PUT	—	—	18.17	—	—	674
12600	PUT	—	—	18.66	—	—	635
12650	PUT	—	—	19.15	—	—	777
12700	PUT	—	—	19.65	—	—	630
12750	PUT	—	—	20.13	—	—	483
12800	PUT	—	—	20.63	—	—	887
12850	PUT	—	—	21.12	—	—	418
12900	PUT	—	—	21.62	—	—	586
12950	PUT	—	—	22.12	—	—	526

DISCUSSION QUESTIONS

1. Which of the following illustrations is the best example of a commodity market that is in backwardation?

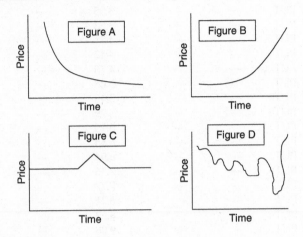

2. Which if the preceding figures is the best example of a commodity market that is in contango (i.e., exhibits the cost-of-carry relationship)?
   a. Figure A
   b. Figure B
   c. Figure C
   d. Figure D
   e. None of the above

3. _____ is the liquidation of a purchase of futures through the sale of an equal number of contracts of the same delivery month, or the covering of a sale of futures contracts through the purchase of an equal number of contracts of the same delivery month.
   a. A hedger
   b. An upset
   c. An offset
   d. A forward contract
   e. A margin

4. _____ is one who has sold futures contracts and has not yet offset that position.
   a. A hedger
   b. A speculator
   c. A short
   d. A futures contract
   e. A long
   f. I don't know! ☺

5. Futures prices are discovered by:
   a. Bids and offers
   b. Officers and directors of the exchange
   c. Written and sealed bids
   d. The Board of Trade Clearing Service Provider
   e. Warren Buffett

6. A zero-cost collar is completely costless during the hedging period.
   a. True
   b. False

7. A farmer with wheat in the fields and who uses the futures market to protect a profit is an example of:
   a. A long hedge
   b. A short hedge
   c. Selling futures to guard against a potential loss
   d. Both a and c
   e. Both b and c

8. To hedge, an airline wants price protection from increasing prices. If they want to use energy options, they do the following:
   a. Buy a call option
   b. Sell a call option
   c. Buy a put option
   d. Sell a put option
   e. All of the above

9. To hedge, an E&P company wants price protection from falling prices. They decide to buy a put to protect from falling prices. But they want a lower cost of hedging and decide to construct a collar strategy. What other option do they use?
   a. Buy a call option
   b. Sell a call option
   c. Buy a put option
   d. Sell a put option
   e. All of the above

10. Jet Fuel Cross-Hedge Using the NYMEX Heating Oil Futures Contract

    On January 6, 2000, Justin Ross, a fuel purchasing director at Cowboy Airlines, wants to hedge his September jet fuel consumption at current prices. Justin wants to hedge a total of 168,000 gallons (40,000 barrels). He buys a September New York Harbor heating oil futures contract on the NYMEX at 70.28 cents per gallon (one contract size is for 42,000 gallons). On the same day, the New York jet fuel spot price is 81.28 cents per gallon. The director closes out this futures contract on August 29, 2000, at 66.59 cents per gallon. The spot price of NY jet fuel on August 29 is 69.99 cents per gallon.

    Complete the worksheet following and answer all of the questions.
    a.

Cash Price (i.e., Spot Price)	Futures Price	Basis
January 6 cash price _____ cents/gallon		
August 29 cash price _____ cents/gallon		
	_____ cents/gallon gain	_____ cents/gallon basis loss

> Result:
> Cash purchase price of jet fuel _____ cents/gallon
> Minus heating oil futures gain _____ cents/gallon
> Net purchase price of jet fuel _____ cents/gallon

   b. Is this a long hedge or short hedge?
   c. Did the basis strengthen or weaken between January 6 and August 29?
   d. Did the basis change benefit the hedger (i.e., was the basis change a gain to benefit the hedger or a loss to harm the hedger)?

11. Collar hedge: Using the NYMEX Crude Oil Call and Put information in the Appendix, answer the following questions.
    a. Lauren Simkins E&P wishes to construct a collarhedging strategy. Lauren Simkins, the CEO, tells you she wants you to construct a hedge to protect the firm from declining crude oil prices for upcoming production. The CEO states that you are to buy a put option that gives crude oil price protection for a minimum of $100 per barrel. She tells you to sell an offsetting call so that your total hedging strategy costs no more than 50 cents total per barrel (i.e., total premium paid on the put minus the premium received on the call is no more than 50 cents net paid per collar). Which call and which put did you select? Pick the best collar. List the collar below and tell the total cost of the collar strategy:
    b. Is it possible to construct a zero-cost collar (at least within one cent net paid per barrel) on the collar hedging strategy? Is so, which call option did you sell?
    c. Why do firms use collar hedging strategies?
    d. If you were a refiner using a collar strategy, how would you hedge to have price protection? Explain the hedging strategy

12. These questions are to be answered using the NYMEX Calls and Puts on Crude Oil provided in the Appendix. The spot closing price on crude oil on 3/17/2012 was $107.06 per Bbl. (Use the Prior Settle price for the option premium.)
    a. Which of the crude oil call options has the greatest liquidity? List the strike price and premium of the option. (Hint: Use option volume to measure liquidity.)
    b. Assume you are a user of crude oil such as a refiner or airline. If you wanted to hedge price risk so that you do not pay more than $115 per barrel, which option would you choose and why?
    c. If you buy the option in Question B and prices rise to $120 at the option expiration, how much would you make or lose per barrel including the option premium?
       What would be your overall profit for one contract, taking into account the option premium?
       Remember that one option contract is for 1000 barrels.
       What if oil prices dropped to $90 for the option you bought in Question B? How much would you make or lose, including the option premium?
    d. Valero Refining Company, another client of yours, is constructing a collar hedge to lock in a maximum price to pay for crude oil of $118.00 that they pay.
       • What type of option should they buy? Be sure to state the type, strike price, and premium.
       • Is this possible to construct a zero-cost collar for the company? If so, what type of option do they sell and what is the premium?
       • If crude oil prices rise to $135, how much will they make or lose on the collar strategy above, on a per barrel basis (and state whether profit or loss)? If crude oil prices fall to $70, how much will they make or pay out on the option collar on a per barrel basis? If they buy the crude oil in the cash market, how much will be the net amount they pay for crude oil (assume it is a perfect hedge) on a per barrel basis?

13. What the five steps of risk management? List and explain each step.

NOTES

1. See Nobelprize.org, http://nobelprize.org/nobel_prizes/economics/laureates/1997/ index.html (announcing Robert C. Merton and Myron S. Scholes as co-recipients of the 1997 Nobel Prize in Economic Sciences "for a new method to determine the value of

derivatives"). Fisher Black would have also received the prize but he passed away in 1995.
2. For more information on enterprise risk management, refer to Fraser and Simkins (2010).
3. http://www.phrases.org.uk/meanings/hedge-your-bets.html.

REFERENCES

Bernstein, Peter L. 1996. *Against the Gods: The Remarkable Story of Risk.* John Wiley & Sons, Inc.: Hoboken, NJ.

Black, Fischer, and Myron Scholes. 1973. The Pricing of Options and Corporate Liabilities. *Journal of Political Economy* 81:3, 637–654.

Carter, David A., Daniel A. Rogers, and Betty J. Simkins. 2006. "Does Hedging Affect Firm Value? Evidence from the U.S. Airline Industry." *Financial Management* 35:1, 53–86.

Chew, Don, ed. 2001 "Energy Derivatives and the Transformation of the U.S. Corporate Energy Sector." *Journal of Applied Corporate Finance* 13:4, 50–75.

Energy Information Administration. 2002. *Derivatives and Risk Management in the Petroleum, Natural Gas, and Electricity Industries.* Washington DC: U.S. Department of Energy.

Energy Intelligence Research. 2011. *Energy Fundamentals: Understanding the Oil & Gas Industries*, 5th ed. New York: Energy Intelligence.

Fraser, John R. S., and Betty J. Simkins, eds. 2010. *Enterprise Risk Management: Today's Leading Research and Best Practices for Tomorrow's Executives.* Hoboken, NJ: John Wiley & Sons, Inc.

Haushalter, G. D. 2000. "Financing Policy, Basis Risk, and Corporate Hedging: Evidence from Oil and Gas Producers." *Journal of Finance* 55:1, 107–152.

Haushalter, G. D. 2001. "Why Hedge? Some Evidence from Oil and Gas Producers." *Journal of Applied Corporate Finance.* 13:4, 87–92.

Haushalter, G. D. 2001. "Why Hedge? Some Evidence from Oil and Gas Producers." *Journal of Applied Corporate Finance* 13:4, 92.

Kaminski, Vincent, ed. 2005. *Managing Energy Price Risk: The New Challenges and Solutions*, 3rd ed. London: Risk Books.

New York Mercantile Exchange. 2002. *A Guide to Energy Hedging.* New York: Self.

Obituary of Arthur Rudolph. 1996. *New York Times*, January 3.

Osipovich, Alexander. 2012. "Airline Hedging Falling Short of Best Practices." *Energy Risk*, May 3.

Simkins, Betty J., and Steven A. Ramirez. 2008. "Enterprise Wide Risk Management and Corporate Governance." *Loyola University Chicago Law Journal* 39:3, 571–594.

Smithson, Charles, and Betty J. Simkins. 2005. "Does Risk Management Add Value? A Survey of the Evidence." *Journal of Applied Corporate Finance* 17:3, 8–17.

Wald, Matthew L. 1990. "Market Place; A Way of Betting on a '95 Oil Price." *New York Times*, December 10.

ABOUT THE CONTRIBUTORS

Ivilina Popova, PhD, is an associate professor at Texas State University—San Marcos where she currently teaches Portfolio Management and Derivatives, Investment Analysis, and Portfolio Theory. She received her PhD in operations research from Case Western Reserve University. Her areas of expertise are option pricing theory, risk management, and derivatives valuation, among other areas. She has previously worked at Seattle University and Purdue University. In addition, Dr. Popova has worked on Wall Street for Deutsche Bank, among other industry firms. Ivilina has published in many journals including the *Journal of Banking*

and Finance, International Journal of Finance and Economics, Journal of Derivatives and Hedge Funds, Journal of Alternative Investments, and *Journal of Trading.*

Betty J. Simkins, PhD, is the Williams Companies Professor of Business and a professor of finance in the Department of Finance at Oklahoma State University's (OSU) Spears School of Business, where she teaches energy finance, corporate finance, and enterprise risk management, among other courses. Dr. Simkins received her PhD from Case Western Reserve University (CWRU), her MBA from OSU, and her BS in chemical engineering from the University of Arkansas. She has more than 50 publications in academic finance journals and book chapters and has won awards for her research, most recently in risk management. In addition, Betty has won several teaching awards including the Regents Distinguished Teaching Award. She has taught Energy Finance, a course she created, at both the undergraduate and graduate levels for over 12 years and teaches executive education courses on energy finance for companies around the world. She is also very active in the finance profession and currently serves on the board of directors for the Financial Management Association, as co-editor of the *Journal of Applied Finance*, as past president of the Eastern Finance Association, and on the editorial boards of several prestigious finance journals. Prior to academia, she worked in the energy industry for Williams Companies and Conoco (now ConocoPhillips). In addition to being co-editor of this book, in 2010 she co-edited *Enterprise Risk Management: Insights and Analysis on Today's Leading Research and Best Practices*, also published by John Wiley & Sons.

CHAPTER 17

Risks in Trading Energy Commodities

DIVYA KRISHNAN
Senior Financial Analyst at Laureate Education Inc.

INTRODUCTION

There has been high volatility in the energy industry over the past few years especially with regard to commodity prices. The key factors that drive energy price volatility are structural and are likely to have a long-term impact. Furthermore, significant events such as natural disasters, political uncertainty, and corporate misconduct have spurred instability in the energy markets.

In an efficient market, the magnitude of the change in price is influenced by the size of the demand-supply imbalance to be corrected. This applies to both the short term and long term. Increasing volatility and complexity of the energy commodities have made it an attractive market for financial players including hedge funds. There has been a significant surge in trading mechanisms globally. Along with these factors, there are many sources of risks faced within a corporation such as:

- **Price Risk:** The risk of loss from changes in market price.
- **Basis Risk:** Different price movements in different commodities due to quality differences, timing or delivery, and locational differences.
- **Credit Risk:** Risk of default due to bankruptcy, broken contracts, etc.
- **Operational Risk:** Risk of transportation delays, off-spec cargoes, etc.
- **Exchange Rate Risk:** Risk due to fluctuations in currency movements.
- **Interest Rate Risk:** Risk due to increased funding costs etc.
- **Weather Risk:** Fluctuations in volume and hence profitability, due to weather events such as flooding and hurricanes.

Corporations use various hedging strategies to minimize or eliminate their exposure to the risks listed above. The goal of hedging is not to make a profit but to eliminate unwanted risk, which may be done by locking in a profit. Let us consider an example. We have produced 100,000 barrels (bbls) of gasoline to sell into the current highly priced market. Due to unforeseen circumstances, we cannot sell the barrels for another month, and we fear that the market prices will drop in that

time. Our target market is New York, so we shall sell the RBOB futures today to lock in the current market values.

Reformulated Gasoline Blendstock for Oxygen Blending (RBOB) refers to unleaded gas. The NYMEX RBOB future is an outright gasoline contract between a buyer and seller.

Sell (short) NYMEX RBOB futures for current market value	**$125.00 per bbl**
Buy (long) the physical gasoline barrel at market value	**$120.00 per bbl**

Here, we have locked in a profit of $5/bbl. Assuming a 100 percent correlation between the physical and financial markets, we will make a profit of $5/bbl regardless of whether the market moves up or down.

In case of a $5 up move:

Sold NYMEX at $125	Buy back at $130	Futures lose $5/bbl	} *$5 profit/bbl*
Long physical at $120	Sell at $125	Physical gains $5/bbl	

In case of a $5 down move:

Sold NYMEX at $125	Buy back at $120	Futures gain $5/bbl	} *$5 profit/bbl*
Long physical at $120	Sell at $115	Physical loses $5/bbl	

This is a very simple example to show how hedging strategies can work. While the example shows how to lock in a margin, we can also participate in upward price movements and protect ourselves from decrease in prices. In this chapter, I will focus on price and basis risks and demonstrate how hedging strategies can be effectively employed to mitigate these risks.

PRICE RISK

There has been a significant increase in commodity prices, especially in oil and natural gas in recent years. This volatility is reflected in the fluctuations in gasoline (Exhibit 17.1) and electricity prices.[1] Price behavior is influenced by cost, market structure, and various macroeconomic factors that dictate the demand-supply scenario.

As of November 2011, the prospects for the world economy are relatively better. Global imbalances will remain an issue as long as unemployment remains high. On the other hand, Asian equity markets are gaining strength, and some of the recent economic releases for Asia suggest a strong momentum. The sudden demand growth in the Asian economies, especially China and India, has resulted in a resource scarcity. Many middle-income and emerging countries are also growing rapidly as a result of better economic policies and financial stability. As a result, production costs are spiking, resulting in an increase in commodity prices.

One key factor driving price that is monitored closely is the inverse relationship of commodity price to the value of the U.S. dollar. One of the main reasons for the impact of the dollar on commodity prices is that commodities are priced in

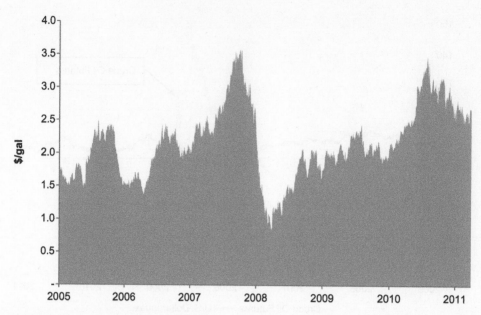

Exhibit 17.1   Gasoline Prices ($/gallon)
Source: Bloomberg Markets API.

dollars. When the value of the dollar drops, it will take more dollars to buy commodities. The relationship between crude futures and the U.S. dollar index[2] is a good example (Exhibit 17.2) to illustrate this.

However, there exist long lead and lag times in this relationship, and hence it takes some time for the inflation factor to start trickling down. Of late, the weakening dollar has served to mask a larger systemic weakness in the market.

Absolute prices of energy products are no longer driven solely by the fundamental factors; the influence of the flow of funds across a wide range of commodities will drive absolute movement and will result in continued volatility. It has been widely noted that the huge capital inflow from hedge funds, financial trades, and other long-term investors is invested in energy (oil) futures to reap a quick profit rather than to hedge risk.[3] This in turn is creating artificial demand and driving up the price for consumers.

The major fluctuations in the oil market, at least in the short term, seem to be totally divorced from actual supply-and-demand fundamentals. Therefore, it is imperative to cap the total value of speculative positions in any commodity market. This would help regulate the number of pure speculators in the market against businesses who buy futures to hedge their risk. Recent reports illustrate this.[4]

BASIS RISK

The biggest expense for an airline company is aviation fuel (jet fuel). Their ideal goal would be to hedge the risk of higher fuel prices. Due to the lack of active jet fuel markets, these companies hedge their risk using derivatives on crude oil. Jet

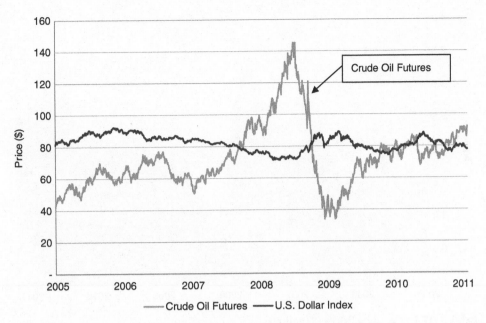

Exhibit 17.2 Inverse Relationship between Crude Futures and U.S. $ Index
Source: Bloomberg Markets API.

fuel is refined from crude oil, so theoretically their prices should move together. However, this relationship does not always hold and the risk associated with this imperfect correlation is called *basis risk*.

Basis risk is therefore the risk in price changes between a futures/forward market and a cash/spot market. There are three types of basis risk in the energy industry:

1. *Locational Basis Risk:* Risk due to difference in the delivery location of the underlying asset and the hedge contract. Consider, a natural gas producer in Alberta, Canada, hedging with NYMEX futures. The producer is still exposed to the basis risk between Henry Hub (the pricing point for NYMEX natural gas futures contracts) and the spot market in Alberta.
2. *Quality Basis Risk:* Risk due to difference in the quality of the underlying asset and the hedge. For example, a person trying to hedge jet fuel with heating oil is exposed to quality basis risk.
3. *Calendar Basis Risk:* Risk due to difference in maturity period of the underlying asset and the hedge. For example, hedging gasoline to be delivered in August with an October futures contract.

The basis (futures price minus spot price) might increase or decrease depending on storage and handling costs, interest rates, transportation costs from the current location to the futures delivery point, supply-demand balance in the spot market, and other cash flows generated by the underlying asset. Hedging helps to reduce the exposure to basis risk but does not eliminate it completely. Quite often,

people trade on the spread between the underlying asset in the spot market and futures contract and this is known as *basis trading*.

When there is a physical asset involved, there is a cost of carry. Cost of carry is the cost incurred while holding or carrying a position and includes interest on the securities, storage, inventory shrinkage, and insurance. Speculators trade on the cost of carry using the spread between the futures and the underlying spot asset.

Supply and demand factors determine the shape of the futures curve. Factors such as cost of carry, interest rates, and so on affect demand and supply. The futures curve also moves up or down as market participants keep changing their view of the future expected spot price. Ultimately, futures converge to spot, and basis converges to zero upon maturity of the futures contract.

- A positive basis indicates that the futures price is higher than the expected future spot price and hence, a positive cost of carry; this implies that markets are in *contango*. The futures price will therefore decrease with time to converge to the expected spot price and benefit speculators who are *net short*.
- A negative basis indicates that the futures price is lower than the expected future spot price and hence a negative basis; this implies that markets are in *backwardation*. Speculators who are *net long* prefer this market, as they want prices to increase.

For example, consider a futures contract purchased on September 19, 2011, that is due to expire in six months. Assume that the expected future spot price is $100. If the price of the futures contract is $120 today, the futures price is more than the expected future spot price and hence a contango. In six months, the futures price must drop (unless the expected future spot price changes), so this is a perfect time to short the contract!

Oil futures contracts are delivered every month. The back months are usually priced slightly higher reflecting the cost of carry, indicating a contango market. However, this market can also be in backwardation. For example, in the event of a natural disaster such as a hurricane, supply tends to get disrupted and prices of commodities (such as natural gas) spike upward. Buyers who need natural gas immediately would be willing to pay the high price, but for investors in the futures market this is good news. They make profits by rolling the futures (sell and buy new contracts) at a discount as the expiring contracts trade at a premium to the back-dated contracts being purchased. What ultimately profit or hurts the speculator is any unexpected change in the basis!

Exhibit 17.3 shows the forward curves for West Texas Intermediate (WTI) crude and Brent crude respectively. WTI as the name suggests is Texas crude traded on the CME while Brent is North Sea crude traded on ICE.[5] WTI is in contango while Brent is in backwardation. This means a trader/hedger would get a premium by rolling forward month to month short WTI futures or long Brent futures.

ARBITRAGE

Arbitrage is the simultaneous purchase and sale of the same securities or commodities in different markets to take advantage of unequal prices, the profit being

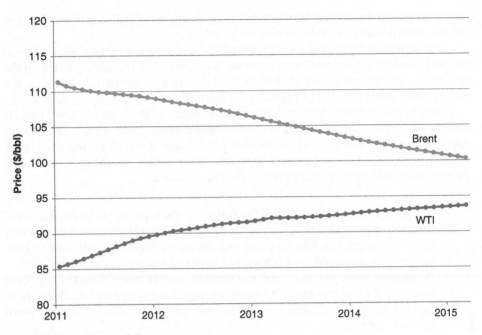

Exhibit 17.3 Forward Curves
Source: CME (NYMEX forward contract prices).

the difference in market prices. Arbitrageurs take advantage of such a situation by buying at a lower price in one market and selling at a higher in another market.

A riskless arbitrage situation assumes perfect futures market, no taxes, no transaction costs, and short selling of the commodity. For example, consider the contango situation described above in WTI markets. If an investor bought 10 WTI contracts for $96.50/bbl and sold them in the forward market at $104.50/bbl, the investor would make a gross profit of $8/bbl before storage, transportation, and other miscellaneous costs.

Price imbalances may occur due to locational differences, structural disparity between exchanges, differences in contract expiration dates, demand supply disruptions, or even market perceptions. Therefore, multiple factors need to be considered to see whether there is an open product arbitrage, such as price differentials, transportation costs, insurance, tolls/port charges/import duties, differences in product specifications, and so forth.

One of the key factors for arbitrage economics is transportation cost. An arbitrage is considered open only if the price differentials are wide enough to offset the transportation costs. For example, refiners choose between competing crudes from across the globe on a daily basis. This crude arbitrage is mainly affected by the value of the end products that can be extracted from the different crudes. There exists a difference (spread) in crude prices at Cushing, OK (WTI) and North Sea (Brent) as discussed previously. The key factors to be considered in this case are:

- Transportation costs from the North Sea to U.S. Gulf Coast.
- Seaway Pipeline tariffs.

- Premium for quality differences—Brent contains around 0.37 percent sulfur compared to WTI, which has only 0.24 percent sulfur (the lower the sulfur, the sweeter the crude).
- Approximate transportation period is 30–35 days. This means that today's Brent prices should be compared with WTI prices in 30–35 days, hence the WTI prices need to be adjusted for this market structure effect.

Two of the most common arbitrage (arb) situations in commodities are storage arbs and the existence of an open product arb to or from key markets.

Storage Arb

The presence of a storage arb is determined by:

1. Price of the physical commodity in the cash market
2. Futures price of the physical commodity
3. Storage and transportation costs

A storage arb exists if the cash price plus storage and associated costs are less than the futures price; then we can get paid to store the commodity and sell it out in the future. The solid lines in Exhibit 17.4 show the forward curve minus the cash price at a given point in time. The larger shaded area is the storage cost and gray area is the cost of money over time. If for example, we had purchased spot distillates in August, stored till February and simultaneously sold February futures, we could have made $0.15 per gallon.

If at the time of delivery, the spot market is trading above the NYMEX, we can buy the futures and sell the product in the spot market. On the other hand, if the

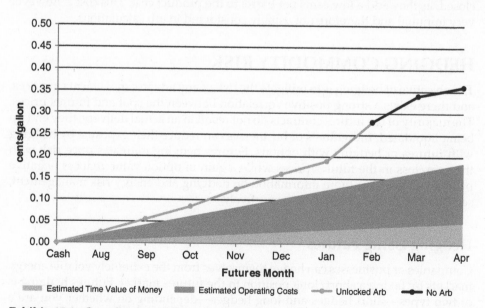

Exhibit 17.4   Open Product Arb
Source: U.S. Energy Information Administration (EIA).

spot is trading below the NYMEX, we need to deliver the product to NYMEX to realize the full potential of the trade.

Consider moving gasoline from northwest Europe to New York Harbor (NYH). This would involve availability of ships, docking space, offloading capacity, and more. The presence of an arbitrage situation can be determined by examining three components:

1. Price of gasoline in Europe
2. Price of gasoline in New York
3. Freight cost from Europe to New York and other costs

European gasoline is quoted in metric tons while NYH gasoline is quoted in gallons. Converting to equivalent units (1 metric ton = 358 gallons), we have

$$\text{European gasoline ARB} = \text{NYH gasoline price} \\ - \left(\text{European gasoline price} + \frac{Freight}{358}\right)$$

This arb averaged around 14.50 cents/gal in 2011 with a range of 8–25 cents/gal. In October 2011, certain refinery-related announcements caused a rally in the NYMEX RBOB prices. This created an arbitrage opportunity for European exports of gasoline, despite low consumption levels in the United States.

A positive arb number indicates open arb while a negative arb numbers indicates closed arb. Other costs, such as port charges, cost of spill insurance, product loss cost, and so forth, are also used in determining whether an arb is open or closed, as they add a few cents per barrel to the product cost. This cost is however very minimal and therefore not usually considered in arb calculations.

HEDGING COMMODITY RISK

The objective of hedging is to mitigate the risk of any adverse movements in prices, and there exists a strong positive correlation between the spot and futures prices. The majority of the futures contracts do not result in an actual delivery; they end up being liquidated. Individuals or businesses can reduce their exposure by hedging with futures or hedging with options. Futures hedging mitigates price risk with the gain/loss in the futures prices while a gain in option value reduces negative price risk. (*Note:* For more information on hedging and energy risk management, see Chapter 19 and Chapter 16, respectively.)

Hedging Using Futures

Companies or businesses can hedge themselves from the extremely volatile energy markets by taking a short/long position in the futures market. Futures hedging is of two types—short hedges and long hedges—depending on whether you are a net consumer (i.e., use a long hedge position) or producer (i.e., use a short hedge position).

Short Hedges

A short hedge protects the commodity producer/owner from the risk of falling prices. It implies shorting a derivative contract to hedge the asset held in the long position. The producer has therefore eliminated the risk of price change by locking in a floor and ceiling price, subjecting themselves to a basis risk. Short hedges work well if the basis improves (decrease in spot price) as seen in the example below.

An oil refiner has entered into a contract to sell 420,000 gallons of regular unleaded gasoline to be delivered in December 2011. The parties agreed to use the futures settlement price on the delivery day as the sale price. The contract was entered into in September 2011; the spot price at that time was $3.55/gallon and the futures price for delivery in 3 months was $3.58/gallon. Based on historical seasonality trends, the refiner feels that gasoline prices will dip in the winter months and so she enters into a short position for 10 contracts (1 contract = 42,000 gallons) at $3.58/gallon.

As expected, gasoline prices fell to $3.00/gal on the delivery date, and the refiner has to sell the gasoline at this price according to the sales contract. The refiner also buys back the future contract at $3.00/gal to close her short position. Assume that the transaction involves no commissions. The proceeds from this sale can be summarized as follows:

Gain from sale of gasoline	$3.00 * 420,000	$1,260,000
Gain on the futures	(3.58 − 3.00) * 420,000	$ 243,600
Net Gain		$1,503,600

This is equivalent to selling 10 contracts at $3.5800/gallon.

Long Hedges

A long hedge protects the commodity consumer/buyer from the risk of increasing prices. The long hedger therefore buys futures to hedge his position as he benefits from a decline in basis (increase in spot price).

A power company has to buy 500,000 MMBtu of natural gas in three months. The spot price of natural gas in March 2011 was $3.95/MMBtu, and the futures price for delivery in three months was $3.98/MMBtu. The company wanted to hedge against an increase in natural gas prices and decided to take a long position at $3.98/MMBtu for 50 contracts (1 contract = 10,000 MMBtu).

Three months later, natural gas prices rose almost 11 percent, and the spot price on the delivery day was $4.38/MMBtu. Since the company entered into the long hedge position at $3.98/MMBtu, they had a futures gain. The transaction details are recorded here:

Purchase price of natural gas	$4.38 * 500,000	$2,190,000
Gain on the futures	(4.38 − 3.98) * 500,000	$ 200,000
Net Payable		$1,990,000

This is equivalent to buying 50 contracts at $3.98/MMBtu.

Hedging Using Options

Option hedges are analogous to insurance policies; we pay a premium to mitigate the risk and execute the option when prices move against us. Options provide you the right but not the obligation to take a particular position on the underlying futures. There are two types of options—put and call.

A *put* option sets the floor price for the commodity. This gives the option holder the right but not the obligation to take a short position in the futures at a certain strike price for a premium. The difference between the strike price and the premium is the profit for the option holder.

A *call* option sets the ceiling price for the commodity. This gives the option holder the right but not the obligation to take a long position in the futures at a certain strike price for a premium. The difference between the strike price and the premium is the maximum price paid by the option holder for the commodity.

The option holder has the right to exercise the option or let it expire or offset it by transferring the rights to a third party.

BEST PRACTICES AND COMMON PITFALLS IN RISK MANAGEMENT

The risk management function has progressed to become a core business area mainly driven by investors and the board, not just to hedge against losses but also to gain a competitive advantage. The hedging process in most corporations is usually a five-pronged approach as shown in Exhibit 17.5 below. The idea is to leverage analytical expertise to establish short, medium, and long-term points of view and thereby support the decision-making activities of other corporate functions.

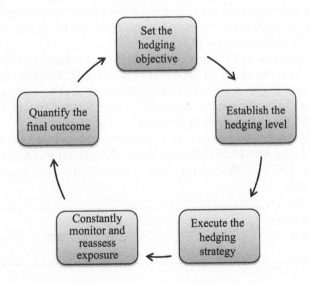

Exhibit 17.5 Hedging Process

Best Practices

The risk management process involves establishing the strategic and organizational context such as nature of the business, inherent risks in the business, and so forth along with risk awareness. Organizations need a systematic way to ensure that all their significant exposures are being captured in the decision-making process. The entire process has now shifted from simply responding to threats to meeting the expectation of investors and stakeholders and improving the reputation of the organization. Some of the best practices include:

- Creating risk awareness by educating the organization, especially the senior management, on practical aspects of risk management.
- Identifying and analyzing current exposures—financial, operational, political, and reputational.
- Assessing the risk appetite and its likelihood, magnitude, and impact.
- Defining the tolerance level based on past experiences and operational requirements.
- Examining the financial instruments/derivatives available in the market to mitigate exposure to the identified risks.
- Measuring the likelihood and impact of the risk.
- Setting strong controls and governance.

Most organizations have a risk management committee that defines their risk appetite. This is usually a corporate function at a central level that consolidates the risk across different business units and implements the risk management strategy. They are in turn supported by a mid-office function that keeps track of policy compliance and risk reporting. The key function of this committee is to establish guidelines, limits, and triggers for routine risk exposures.

The key task of the risk management infrastructure is to monitor price risk, basis risk, and any kind of operational risk across the different business units. Price risk exposure for example can be mitigated by purchasing hedging instruments such as options or swaps or by structuring contracts that cap the company's exposure to increasing prices. Most of the companies maintain a book structure that helps identify, measure, and monitor risk-return of individual activities as well as for providing information across business units. The risk assessment and mitigation functions are integrated with performance review mechanisms such as bonus metrics.

Organizations with effective risk management models and tools perceive risk as an uncertain event that can be identified, measured, monitored, mitigated, and eventually leveraged. The concept of risk is not new to the energy industry and the oil sector in particular. The development of enterprise-wide risk management (ERM) strategies has become important. However, there exist many unexplored risks providing an opportunity for organizations to design strategies that cover a wider spectrum and thereby gain a competitive edge.

Common Pitfalls

Some of the conventional risk-management techniques taught in classrooms are not applicable in the real world. In fact, no forecasting model predicted the impact

of the 2008 economic crisis. This is a perfect example of a Black Swan event—events with a low-probability and high-impact that are almost impossible to forecast. The complex environment in which we live increases the incidence of such events and makes forecasting them even more difficult.

One of the key mistakes made by energy companies is to consider hedging as a source of revenue. Hedging should only be used as a tool to protect against a fall in prices and thereby provide a revenue certainty. Most of the slip-ups in these companies are a result of a poor hedging policy and/or absence of a hedging strategy. Hedging decisions should never be based on the companies' point of view regarding the future prices. All this in turn can be attributed to the lack of clarity in governance.

Organizations tend to overlook the volatility in today's market and economic factors. The current uncertainty in the economic situation demands a more systematic and pragmatic risk management approach. The absence of a risk management committee to clearly delineate and communicate the individual roles and responsibilities, set hedging goals and objectives, and monitor them on a constant basis leads to a highly disorganized hedging process and lack of transparency in communicating the strategies to the stakeholders.

Performance measurement is vital in determining the effectiveness of the hedging strategy. Therefore, it is important to define certain key performance indicators (KPIs) that have an impact on the company's bottom line (such as liquidity, EBITDA, etc.). The choice of KPIs is critical and should be closely linked to the objectives of the hedging strategy.

Exotic hedge strategies can prove to be disastrous if they are not structured well. Costless collars are not always the best hedging tools. If not hedged dynamically, they can lead a company to bankruptcy. For example, in late December 2010 a crude oil producer expected Brent prices to decline, when the prompt contract was trading in the $85 range. So, the producer entered into a costless collar: $77 put option (floor) and $97 call option (ceiling) for 2011. Dated Brent prices averaged around $112/bbl in 2011, meaning the producer had $15/bbl on the table, and also tied up a line of credit until the positions expired at the end of the year. A better hedge would have been the purchase of an outright put option or a three-way option such as the purchase of an additional call option with a higher strike price to mitigate the exposure of being short the $97 call option.

There has been a considerable increase in investment in emerging assets and unconventional resources. Energy companies need to plan carefully, develop strategies for effective capital management, and be prepared to adapt to industry and economic changes quickly.

DISCUSSION QUESTIONS

1. An oil refiner has entered into a contract to sell 210,000 gallons of heating oil to be delivered in August 2012. The futures settlement price on the delivery day has been agreed to be the sale price. The contract was entered into in March 2012; the spot price at that time was $3.70/gallon, and the futures price for delivery in five months was $3.80/gallon. The refiner feels that heating oil prices will drop and enters into a short position for five contracts at $3.80/gallon. Heating oil prices dropped to $3.25/gallon, so the refiner also buys back the future contract at $3.25/gallon to close her short position. Assume that

the transaction involves no commissions. What sort of a hedge is this? Also, summarize the proceeds from this sale.

2. ABC Gas Inc. is a distributor who buys unleaded gasoline at current prices from refiners and sells or delivers to large users such as gas stations. ABC Gas Inc. offers its clients fixed-price contracts but soon realizes that it is exposed to price risk. Which of the following could be the main reason for the price risk exposure?
   a. The price of gasoline changes when there are changes in either the supply of or demand for gasoline.
   b. ABC Gas Inc. has offered its clients fixed-price sales contracts, and because it doesn't own the gasoline it has sold, the firm runs a risk that gasoline prices will rise.
   c. Distributors are often exposed to price risk.
   d. Gasoline distribution is a risky business.

3. An increase in basis will _____ a long hedge and _____ a short hedge.
   a. hurt / benefit
   b. hurt / hurt
   c. benefit / hurt
   d. benefit / benefit

4. A trader who has a _____ position in crude futures believes the price of crude will _____ in the future.
   a. short / increase
   b. long / increase
   c. long / stay the same
   d. none of the above

5. A trader is long 10 gasoline futures contracts that expire in April. To close his position before the delivery date the trader must.
   a. buy 10 May gasoline futures contracts.
   b. buy 10 April gasoline futures contracts.
   c. sell 10 April gasoline futures contracts.
   d. sell 10 May gasoline futures contracts.

6. A crude oil producer has 2 MMbbls crude and believes the market to be undersupplied. A refiner wants 2 MMbbls crude available on December 12. He has bought 2000 December NYMEX Crude futures contracts at $95 anticipating that the price of crude is going to rise between November and December. The producer agrees to sell 2MMbbls crude at the December Crude Futures Contract settlement price for that day's settlement. The crude oil will be delivered on December 9. Assume settlement price of $95.35. The refiner's long futures position will be exchanged for this physical supply. What would be the profit to the refiner?

NOTES

1. *CME Market Data.*
2. The U.S. dollar index measures the performance of the U.S. dollar against a basket of currencies: euro (EUR), Japanese yen (JPY), pound sterling (GBP), Canadian dollar (CAD), Swiss franc (CHF) and Swedish krona (SEK).
3. United States Senate Committee, "Financial Speculation in Commodity Markets," May 2008; Committee of Homeland Security and Governmental Affairs, "The Role of Market Speculation in Rising Oil and Gas Prices," June 2006.
4. United States Senate Permanent Subcommittee on Investigations, "Excessive Speculation in the Wheat Market," June 2009; Edward Miller, "Speculation in Agricultural Commodities," October 2011; K. B. Medlock and A. M. Jaffe, "Who Is in the Oil Futures Market and How Has It Changed," August 2009.

Americans for Financial Reform, "Establish Position Limits for Derivatives Market," March 2011.
5. CME Group, available at www.cmegroup.com. IntercontinentalExchange (ICE), available at www.theice.com, operates leading regulated exchanges, trading platforms, and clearing houses serving global markets for agricultural, credit, currency, emissions, energy, and equity index markets.

REFERENCES

Americans for Financial Reform. 2011. "Establish Position Limits for Derivatives Market," available at ourfinancialsecurity.org. March.
Committee of Homeland Security and Governmental Affairs. 2006. *The Role of Market Speculation in Rising Oil and Gas Prices,* June.
Medlock K. B., and A. M. Jaffe. 2009. "Who Is in the Oil Futures Market and How Has It Changed," Working Paper, Rice University.
Miller, Edward. 2011. *Speculation in Agricultural Commodities,* available at. globalresearch.org.
United States Senate Committee. 2008. *Financial Speculation in Commodity Markets,* May.
United States Senate Permanent Subcommittee on Investigations. 2009. *Excessive Speculation in the Wheat Market,* June.

ABOUT THE CONTRIBUTOR

Divya Krishnan is a senior financial analyst at Laureate Education Inc. Prior to that she worked as a market risk analyst at Citgo Petroleum where she supported the financial trading and hedging activity through fundamental analysis. Krishnan obtained her Master's degree in quantitative financial economics from Oklahoma State University. Her areas of expertise include quantitative risk modeling and corporate finance.

CHAPTER 18

Carbon Management and Environmental Issues

EVGENIA GOLUBEVA
RRT Assistant Professor of Finance and Adjunct Lecturer in Energy Management,
University of Oklahoma

INTRODUCTION

Carbon management may sound like a topic from the past right now. After all, hasn't the cap-and-trade legislation in the United States run aground, haven't the climate exchanges closed and emission allowance contracts been delisted, haven't the international talks about the succession to Kyoto, expiring in 2012, stalled? However, as bleak as the picture may look nowadays, the point is that the issue of global warming and other no-less-significant environmental issues are still there and need to be addressed. The efforts of the international community, the public pressure, the regulatory developments—all those taken together shape the profile of environmental risks and opportunities that businesses in all industries will continue to face with increasing intensity. To understand the nature of the issues and the related uncertainties, costs, benefits, risks, and opportunities is important regardless of the regulatory status *du jour*. This chapter's humble objective is to provide an overview of these issues and discuss the past and the present challenges and realities.

COST OF CLEAN AIR

As this chapter is being written, news is piling in pertaining to the global destiny of the highly controversial carbon cap-and-trade issue. Will we ever have carbon cap and trade in the United States? Is the scheme sustainable around the world? Shall we see a successor to the Kyoto protocol? What is the regulators' role? What are the environmental costs, risks, and opportunities? Would these opportunities have existed in the absence of regulation? Does shareholder activism matter? Clearly, these are way too many questions to be addressed in detail in just one chapter. This chapter, therefore, attempts to provide just an overview of the carbon management and environmental issues.

Let us begin with a simple problem. Suppose a new natural gas–fired power plant is being built. There are two options: to install a carbon capture technology to reduce emissions, or not. Estimated life of the plant is 30 years. The discount rate

Exhibit 18.1 Information about the Two Technologies: Electricity Production Capacity, in kW; the Plant Utilization Rate in Percent; and Two Coefficients, C1 and C2, Used in the Cost Calculations

Technology	Capacity, kW	Utilization Rate	C1 (EPA)	C2 (EPA)	VC, $/kWh (excl. heat)	Heat Input, Btu/kWh	Fuel Cost, $/MMBtu
Carbon capture and storage (CCS)	560,360	75%		0.018	0.001	6,179	$6
No CCS	481,890	75%	1,172	0.014	0.003	7,813	$6

Source: EPA.

VC: Variable Cost; Heat Input: Heat in Btu, Needed to Produce One Kwh of Electricity; Fuel Cost: Price of Natural Gas per Million Btu.

for the project is 10 percent. The information about the two technologies (carbon capture and no carbon capture) is in Exhibit 18.1.[1]

Here are the calculations we shall need to compute the various costs associated with both technologies.

$$\text{Capital cost, } \$ = C1 \cdot \text{Capacity}$$
$$\text{Fixed cost, } \$ = C2 \cdot C1 \cdot \text{Capacity} \cdot \text{Utilization rate}$$
$$\text{Capital cost, } \$/\text{year} = \text{Capital cost} \cdot \text{Annuity (10\%, 30 yr)}$$
$$\text{Fixed cost, } \$/\text{year} = \text{Fixed cost} \cdot \text{Annuity (10\% , 30 yr)}$$
$$\text{Fuel cost, } \$/\text{kWh} = \text{Heat input} \cdot \text{Fuel Price}/1{,}000{,}000$$
$$\text{Annual generation, kWh} = \text{Capacity} \cdot 365 \cdot 24 \cdot \text{Utilization rate}$$

Performing these calculations results in the following information on the annual capital cost, fixed cost, variable cost, and fuel cost, summarized in Exhibit 18.2.

Let us now calculate the price that the utility company should charge its customers just in order to break even within one year. To break even, price per kWh should be:

$$\text{No CCS: } 186{,}986{,}810/3{,}681{,}565{,}000 = \$.05079$$
$$\text{CCS: } 217{,}566{,}719/3{,}166{,}017{,}000 = \$.06871$$

We observe a difference of $.0187, or about 35 percent. That's quite an electricity price increase, from the viewpoint of the consumer! What does this increase buy in terms of saving the environment? Let us look at the amount of carbon dioxide actually emitted from each plant within one year (EPA):

$$\text{No CCS: } 0.40 \text{ tons/MWh} = 1{,}472{,}626 \text{ tons/year}$$
$$\text{CCS: } 0.05 \text{ tons/MWh} = 158{,}301 \text{ tons/year}$$

Exhibit 18.2 Capital, Fixed, Variable, and Fuel Costs on an Annual Basis, Resulting from the Two Alternative Technologies

Technology	Capital Cost, $/year	Fixed Cost, $/year	Variable Cost, $/kWh	Fuel Cost, $/ kWh	Annual Gen., MWh	Total Cost, $/year
No CCS	32,931,182	777,342	.001	.040314	3,681,565	186,986,810
CCS	59,910,916	1,134,230	.003	.046878	3,166,017	217,566,719

We observe a difference of 1,314,325 tons, or nearly 90 percent. This is a substantial environmental benefit! Now let's see what the price is per ton of carbon dioxide emission saved:

$$(217,566,719 - 186,986,810)/(1,472,626 - 158,301) = \text{approx. } \$24/\text{ton}$$

Obviously, that's a lot of money. How about an example of an existing coal plant switching to natural gas in order to reduce emissions? Let us assume also that a cap-and-trade system is in place for carbon allowances, and that a plant that anticipates an excessive emission (over the target allocated) can buy allowances in the market from another plant, which anticipates lower-than-target emissions. Let P be the price of one allowance (it is one allowance per ton of emissions). It can be shown that the marginal cost of generating electricity by burning fuel is calculated as follows:[2]

$$FC_i = \text{fuel cost}$$
$$\eta_i = \text{plant net thermal efficiency}$$
$$EF_i = \text{emission factor}$$
$$EC = \text{emission cost}$$

Writing this equation for both coal and natural gas, and equating the marginal costs for the two fuels, we can solve for the breakeven emission cost, EC.

If $EC^* > P => $ Use Coal, buy allowances in the market

If $EC^* < P => $ Use Gas

$$EC^* = \frac{\eta_{coal} \cdot FC_{gas} - \eta_{gas} \cdot FC_{coal}}{\eta_{gas} \cdot EF_{coal} - \eta_{coal} \cdot EF_{gas}}$$

Let us use data from the U.S. EPA (Exhibit 18.3) to calculate this hypothetical breakeven price. Again, the data does not come from one and the same power plant. The data for coal is from one plant and the data for natural gas from another. However, the two plants are similar otherwise. Our calculations lead us to the breakeven price of $12.86 per ton of carbon emissions. In other words, should a cap-and-trade market exist for carbon allowances, a price anywhere above this level would induce the plant to implement a fuel switch. That's lower than $24 but still significant.

Let us now turn to another way of reducing emissions: electricity generation using alternative sources of energy. Exhibit 18.4 shows a rough comparison of costs spent to generate one MWh of electricity from alternative/renewable energy

Exhibit 18.3 Data from the EPA on Fuel Costs, Net Thermal Efficiency, and Carbon Dioxide Emission Factor, from an Existing Power Plant That Uses Coal; and Another Existing Power Plant That Uses Natural Gas

Fuel	FC, $/MWh	η, %	EF, tons/MWh
Coal	21	.37	.94
Natural gas	40	.51	.40

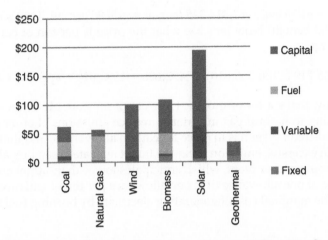

Exhibit 18.4 Comparison of Average Costs from Alternative Electricity Sources
Source: U.S. Environmental Protection Agency (EPA) and author calculations.

sources. The exhibit was generated from the EPA data for 2007, by averaging across many types of power plant designs and technologies (otherwise, the exhibit would become too big to fit on the page!), and there is arguably much more data available for coal and natural gas plants than for the other types. But this rough comparison provides an idea of the feasibility of various energy alternatives. Clearly, we can see that no alternative energy beats coal and natural gas when it comes to the cheapest fuel choice. One exception is geothermal energy; however, one cannot rely on it as a base load fuel.

In addition, every alternative energy source has its own problems. For example, geothermal energy has limited availability, equipment subject to frequent breakdowns, and potential for releasing toxic elements such as lead, arsenic, or mercury. Wind has issues of intermittence, transmission lines, land use, and noise, as well as harm caused to migratory birds. Solar is equally problematic in terms of intermittence, harm to wildlife and land use, to say nothing of its very high cost. Tidal suffers from the same issues of intermittence and harm to wildlife. Biomass has low heat generation capacity compared to fossil fuels and potentially releases harmful toxic elements such as heavy metals. Nuclear fusion is years from being developed.

The conclusion is that there is no single cheap way of saving the environment!

ROLE OF REGULATION?

It sure is nice to live in a clean environment. According to the U.S. Environmental Protection agency statistics cited in Bradley and Fulmer (2004), between 1970 and 2002, aggregate emission reductions were reduced by 48 percent. At the same time, the following all increased: GDP (164%), vehicle miles (155%), energy usage (42%), and population (38%). Apparently, society recognizes the importance of unpolluted air. For contrast, what is the situation in developing countries? Here is a quote (admittedly old now as it dates back to 1996), which paints quite an

opposite picture: "horrific smog despite being located in countries with far less industry than the United States. Millions of cars, trucks, and buses with no smog controls cram the streets; hundreds of uncontrolled factories belch smoke and pollutants."[3] Clearly no one would like to live in such an environment who had a choice!

However, the problem is old: clean air is a common good. It is impossible to write a set of contracts that would make sure that every pollutant of air bears the consequences proportional to its contribution to the overall pollution. Hence, this is one of those areas where regulation is needed. This being said, of course, most economists would agree that the situation with air pollution observed in many developing countries is due not so much to the lack of proper regulation as it is to poverty: when people are battling mortality and hunger, air pollution is probably the last worry on their minds. But, holding the level of economic development fixed, the argument still applies that regulation can make a difference, sometimes positive, sometimes not.

Here is a recent example of where a regulation may lead to quite undesirable consequences!

A city trader accused the European commission tonight of running a "Mickey Mouse" carbon-trading scheme after some traders lost heavily on the market owing to a botched trading statement…. The commission said on its website this morning that the EU's climate change committee had voted to ban the most common type of carbon "offsets" from 1 January 2013, amid concerns that these offsets were being abused…. Half an hour later the EC rescinded the statement, but not before the price of carbon had risen to a three-month high at €11.84 a unit, with more than 1.5m units traded. A huge sell-off then followed that bought the price back to €10.56 …. Three hours after that, the commission put out a third statement which said that offset credits for the substances in question, which include HFC 23 and nitrous oxide—both potent greenhouse gases—would be banned from 2013, but not until May of that year…. The setback is not just a problem for the ETS; it is also an embarrassment for European governments that have been encouraging a skeptical US and other countries to follow their lead. (Macalister 2011)

There are success stories, however, as far as regulation goes. One such success story is the sulfur dioxide cap-and-trade scheme, which has in fact resulted in very tangible environmental benefits.

SO₂ and Cap-and-Trade: A Success Story

The regulation over SO_2 emissions was initiated in order to control the problem of acid rain prevalent in the 1980s and 1990s. The allowance trading program was within the 1990 Clean Air Act Amendments (CAAA). The program was instituted in two phases. The first phase (1995–1999) included a set of 263 high-emitting power plants, required in aggregate to emit less than 5.7 million tons per year, which is equivalent to emission reduction of about 40 percent. The second phase (2000–present) included all fossil-fueled power plants larger than 25 megawatts (3572 units) and required to reduce emissions to about 9 million tons annually by 2010.

The important part about the regulation is that it is a cap-and-trade program. In essence, a cap-and-trade program performs the following:

1. Sets the overall emission limit.
2. Allocates emission allowances to each emitter. One allowance gives its owner the right to emit one ton of the pollutant (in this case, SO_2).
3. Allows for a free trade of the allowances. The owner can sell allowances if it anticipates emissions lower than its target, or buy some otherwise. It may also *bank* the allowances for future use.

Arguably, a scheme that provides for free trade of emission allowances would lead to emission reduction at the lowest cost to the society. For example, in the hypothetical exercise above we have calculated the total cost of reducing carbon emissions by a ton, by switching to a carbon capture technology, which was about $24. What if the plant could "hire" another plant to reduce emissions on its behalf, which could do so at a lower cost, and pay that plant a price lower than $24 per ton? That would reduce the total cost to society of reducing overall emissions.

The EPA distributes allowances at the beginning of every year (about 9 million tons per year through 2030). All allowances are tracked by the EPA registry. There is a $2000 per ton penalty for exceeding an allowance, which essentially caps the allowance price at that level. About 3 percent of all allowances are auctioned by EPA to establish a benchmark price; the auction proceeds are given to the units to which the allowances would have otherwise been allocated, on a prorated basis. The owner of the allowances can use, bank, or trade them. The trading can be done between plants; through brokers (most of the volume); and in the EPA auction. Anybody, including individual traders, may trade. Many traders are environmental groups, which purchase the allowances to keep them away from the polluting plants and thereby inducing them to reduce emissions. Hedge funds are also attracted to allowances as they may provide diversification and better risk-return tradeoff due to their low correlation with equity market returns.

For an allowance trader, it is important to understand the driving factors behind allowance market prices. The long-term factors affect both the supply and the demand of the allowances. For example, various state and federal regulatory developments would be one such factor. The appearance of new technologies, the access to cheaper sources of energy, or the installation of power lines would be examples of long-term factors affecting demand. The short-term factors affect primarily demand and include economic activity and industrial production, weather (heating and cooling degree days), prices of lower-emitting fuels (natural gas), short-term disruptions in the availability of alternative power generation (nuclear, etc.), and the amount of allowances in the allowance bank.

As an example, suppose that a new regulation appears that essentially makes it easier for plants to use low-sulfur coal as the primary generation fuel. Such a regulation would be a bearish factor for the allowance prices because it reduces the cost of environmental compliance. On the other hand, suppose that the price of natural gas, which is a lower-emitting fuel, goes up. This would increase the cost of compliance by fuel switching and hence would raise allowance prices. Or take the current regulatory uncertainty pertaining to carbon cap and trade. Should such a regulation pass, it would make the prices of more environmentally friendly fuels rise; which would increase the cost of reducing sulfur dioxide as well, thereby

producing a side effect on SO_2 allowance prices. Hence, an allowance trader needs to keep all of these fundamentals in mind!

A recent example of a sharp price effect resulting from a regulatory controversy was the vacation of the CAIR rule (Clean Air Interstate Rule of 2005, intending to use cap-and-trade for SO_2 and NOx). The Court of Appeals for the District of Columbia vacated CAIR on July 11, 2008 (subsequently reinstated in December of that year). Industry reacted with concern, since substantial investments were in place for implementation of CAIR, and also since additional regulation by the EPA was anticipated. SO_2 emissions allowance prices fell from \$315 to \$115 in one day. NOx allowances fell from nearly \$5,000 to just above \$1,000 per ton in a short time.

The regulatory uncertainty surrounding first CAIR and then the destiny of carbon cap-and-trade in this country and around the world, coupled with the low price of natural gas, have led to the price of SO_2 allowances hovering around quite low levels these days (single digits now), compared to around \$60 per ton at the end of 2009 and historical highs of over \$700 per ton in 2007! This high historical volatility potentially makes it attractive to hedge allowance price risk using futures contracts.

Has the program been successful in achieving environmental benefits? Exhibit 18.5 shows the EPA data for the sulfur deposition before and after; the difference is striking.[4]

Carbon Cap and Trade: Kyoto and the EU

The situation with carbon is very different from that with SO_2. Carbon dioxide potentially causes global warming, although scientists' opinions differ on its precise effects. It is not a local health issue, but a global issue and needs to be addressed through global solutions.

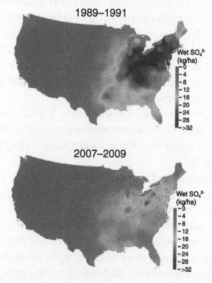

Exhibit 18.5 Annual Mean Wet Sulfate Deposition, EPA report 2009
Source: U.S. Environmental Protection Agency (EPA).

Here is a very brief history of the events pertaining to carbon regulation. In December 1992, at the United Nations Framework Convention on Climate Change (UNFCCC) Earth Summit in Rio de Janeiro, the initial policy framework agreement was signed by 166 countries. Between 1992 and 1997, the parties to the UNFCCC advanced the international negotiations. At that time, the United States pulled out of the process and so far stands against Kyoto ratification. In December 1997 the parties signed the Kyoto Protocol, providing a mechanism to reduce emissions of six greenhouse gases (GHG) to safe levels. A total of 39 countries undertook legally binding obligations under Article 3 of the Protocol to reduce GHG emissions by an average of 5 percent compared to 1990 levels during 2008–2012. Finally, in January 2005, following the ratification of the Kyoto Protocol by Russia, the Protocol became an enforceable, legally binding international climate accord. On February 16, 2005, the Kyoto Protocol entered into legal force.

Under the protocol, all countries are classified into two groups. Annex-B countries are the developed countries which have accepted legally binding targets and are signatory to the Kyoto Protocol. Non-Annex-B countries are the developing countries that may have ratified the Protocol or are in the process of moving legislation for ratification but have not accepted any binding targets. The Protocol has been ratified by 119 non-Annex-B countries.

The European Union Emissions Trading Scheme (the EU ETS) provides for allowance trading under a cap-and-trade mechanism. Within each participating country, the National Allocation Plan (NAP) allocates reduction targets on the eligible participants. The NAP is submitted to the EU Commission. Each installation is allocated the rights to emit so many tons of CO_2 equivalent. The market is designed to be short. In other words, the total amount of allowances is below the business as usual (BAU) level—the amount of emissions that would be emitted based on business-as-usual operation of the underlying eligible asset. The degree of market short is, clearly, one of the price drivers. There are two major types of allowances: the allowances that are met through reducing carbon emissions in an Annex-B country (EUA); and the certified emission reductions (CER) that are credited to an Annex-B unit for investing in an emission-reduction or sequestration project in a non-Annex-B country, under the so-called clean development mechanism (CDM). CERs have been eligible for crediting since 2000 and have a lifetime beyond 2012. CERs are in many ways attractive trading instruments: they have a long life, and they are also highly volatile, being originated in high-risk developing countries (the latter factor attracting traders).

Another trading instrument is carbon offsets. These are achieved via investing in projects such as reforestation, renewable energy, or methane capture. The carbon offsets generated by these investments count toward emission compliance by generating carbon credits.

The major price drivers in the carbon credit market are familiar: regulatory developments and policy; abatement technologies; allocations; and supply of credits from other markets. One very important factor, of course, is the price of low-emitting fuels such as natural gas. However, it is only one of the many factors. Exhibit 18.6 shows the correlation between the price of natural gas and the price of EUA. The correlation in the early part of the graph, when both the price of natural gas and the price of allowances were sliding, is quite apparent. However, it essentially fell apart later due to the dominating role of the regulatory uncertainties in the formation of the allowance price.

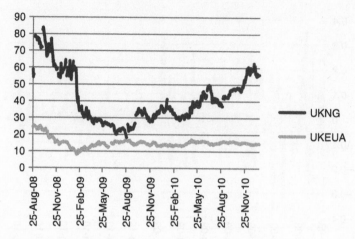

Exhibit 18.6   Correlation between the Price of Natural Gas and the Price of EUA
Source: Intercontinental Exchange (ICE).

The current instruments trading on the European Climate Exchange (ECX) include:

- EUA futures: One lot of 1000 emission allowances, each emission allowance being an entitlement to emit one ton of carbon dioxide equivalent gas.
- CER futures: One lot of 1000 certified emission reduction units (CER).
- EUA and CER Options: The underlying contract is the December Future of the relevant year. For example, the underlying contract for the March 11 option is the December 11 Future.
- EUA/CER spreads.
- Calendar spreads.

Exhibit 18.7 shows the time series for the EUA/CER spread daily return over 2008–2010. As you can see, the spread is quite volatile, reflecting the different factors that drive the relative pricing of the two credit mechanisms.

Carbon Cap and Trade: The United States

At this time, not much is to be said for carbon cap and trade in the United States. There is no federal carbon cap-and-trade system in the United States. This country has never ratified the Kyoto protocol, and it does not appear likely at this moment that the United States will be a part of a major international accord that is to replace Kyoto in the years to come, provided such an accord follows. Instead, there have been regional initiatives. The Regional Greenhouse Gas Initiative (RGGI) was the first mandatory cap-and-trade scheme in this country and included GHG emitters in 10 mid-Atlantic and northeastern states. The initiative began in 2008 by holding the first credit auction. The reduction goals were to reduce 10 percent of emissions by 2018. The Western Climate Initiative (WCI) included 11 western states and Canadian provinces.

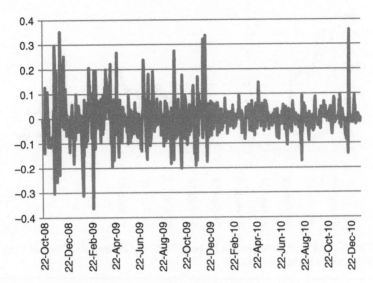

Exhibit 18.7   The Daily Return on the EUA-CER Spread
Source: Intercontinental Exchange (ICE).

Until recently, carbon credits were trading on the Chicago Climate Exchange (CCX) and Chicago Climate Futures Exchange (CCFE). Members of CCX represented many industries: energy, utilities, financials, transportation, telecommunication, information technology, and so on. The product traded on the CCX was the CFI contract, representing 100 metric tons of CO_2 equivalents. CFI contracts were based on both allowances and offsets. However, Exhibit 18.8 shows the collapse in the prices of the CFI vintages on the CCX following the regulatory uncertainty surrounding cap and trade. This, along with several other reasons, has led to the CCX decision to discontinue trading the CFI. The exchange has subsequently ceased to

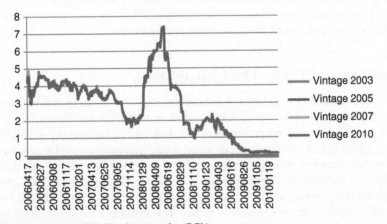

Exhibit 18.8   Price of CFI, Trading on the CCX
Source: Chicago Climate Exchange (CCX).

exist; its trading platform has been acquired by Intercontinental Exchange (ICE) in 2010. A similar fate occurred to the Chicago Climate Futures Exchange (CCFE). As of February 28, 2012, all contracts on CCFE have been delisted.

So is carbon trade in the United States dead? Let us recall that the Waxman-Markey act (H.R. 2454, The American Clean Energy and Security Act of 2009) did pass the House Energy and Commerce Committee on May 21, 2010, by a vote 33–25. True, in June 2010 it died in the Senate. However, there is clear evidence of a substantial concern regarding climate change in this country, despite the lack of explicit federal regulation. There is a possibility of a regulatory move toward carbon emission reduction—through the Environmental Protection Agency. On March 27, 2012, the EPA proposed the first Clean Air Act standard for carbon pollution from future power plants. If the EPA is successful (which, at the time this chapter is being written, remains unclear) in its attempts to regulate carbon emissions, then a cap-and-trade scheme might actually be a less costly solution.

Many U.S. states have adopted Renewable Portfolio Standards[5] requiring the state's energy portfolio to have a certain percentage of energy from renewable sources such as wind and solar, within approximately a 10-year period (the precise requirements, energy types, and time frame vary from state to state). The renewable energy generators that supply power into the grid get paid by the consumer in return for the Renewable Energy Certificates (REC). One REC represents proof that 1 MWh of electricity purchased by its owner was generated from an eligible renewable source. The REC is also a traded commodity.

International Developments

What about the rest of the world? Quite honestly, the picture looks bleak at the moment. Recently, the ETS prices nearly fell through the floor due to the over-allocation of allowances to influential industries, the weak economy, and the poor regulatory prospects. In other countries things are not very promising. South Korea delayed presenting emission trading laws to the parliament. Canada's Senate failed to pass a climate bill. Australia postponed carbon legislation. Japan is struggling to set up a cap-and-trade market. The international negotiations in Copenhagen and Cancun, which were intended to develop an accord to replace the Kyoto agreement (expiring in 2012) stalled. According to one report, $1.7 trillion dollars is to be invested globally into renewable energy over the next decade, which is "$546 bn short of the investments which more proactive government policies on climate change by the G20 countries would bring about globally."[6]

Exhibit 18.9 shows the performance, since 2006, of the Barclays Global Carbon Index, which is an important indicator to many constituents including institutional investors, banks, and money managers, of the performance of the most liquid carbon credits globally. Having invested in that index in 2006, an investor would have hardly made any return over the period ending in 2010.

That being said, let us look at China and India. While these countries have not ratified Kyoto (one of the big reasons the United States won't do so, and one of the strongest arguments against the Waxman-Markey Act), they nevertheless are making substantial progress in terms of developing emission reduction technology as well as alternative and renewable energy sources. China, in fact, was the world's biggest investor in clean energy in 2010. It is expected to triple spending

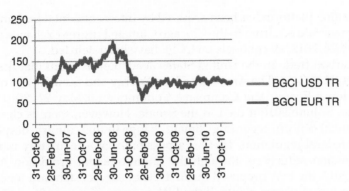

Exhibit 18.9 Barclays Global Carbon Index, United States and Europe
Source: https://ecommerce.barcap.com/indices/index.dxml.

over the next decade to over $90bn per year by 2020, more than 50 percent going to wind power. Chinese spending is forecast to be almost twice that of the United States over the decade. China will spend 5 trillion yuan (US$750 billion) on the energy plan that aims to reduce emissions by 1.2 billion tons annually. [7] India by 2020 is forecast to rise to third place in green investment by the end of the decade. Well, Kyoto or not, these countries recognize the importance of reducing carbon emissions, and—what's especially important—they recognize the importance of investing in clean and renewable energy *technology*.

ENVIRONMENTAL RISKS AND OPPORTUNITIES

So where does this all leave businesses, investors, and lenders? One thing is for sure: the regulatory environment has been, and is going to be, shaping corporate policies and management plans around the globe to a substantial degree. Environmental concerns, both physical and regulatory, present both risks and opportunities.

It is perhaps easier to think of risks arising from the need to be environmentally conscious rather than opportunities. Being environmentally friendly involves additional projects, technologies, and costs, many of which are still being developed and piloted and are, therefore, subject to multiple uncertainties. For example, take the carbon capture and sequestration technology implemented by a power plant. The capture is a chemical process. Post-combustion, flue gas is scrubbed with the amine solution, the amine-CO_2 complex is decomposed by heat, and CO_2 is extracted. Pre-combustion, synthetic gas plus steam is chemically converted into CO_2 plus hydrogen, then hydrogen is burned and CO_2 removed with a solvent and compressed. The technology is now used worldwide by many companies, and it has support of many organizations. Nevertheless, it is still a new technology meaning that the unexpected processes may lead to unforeseen cost of equipment intensity (capital costs), maintenance (operating costs), parasitic energy losses (a huge problem with carbon capture), and so on. The other part, the sequestration, is a process of injecting the captured CO_2 underground, either in storage for industrial use, or into an oil field for enhanced recovery, or simply into a porous and permeable geologic formation (the main method). The sequestration is risky as well since

it presents possibilities of corrosion, leakage, water contamination, or even seismic activity, again meaning unexpected costs.

The risks above are physical risks. How about regulatory risks? Suppose a power plant decides to invest in CCS technology. Looking at our example in the beginning of this chapter, this is a nontrivial investment! Can the plant pass the cost, at least partly, to the consumer in the form of a rate increase? Can the plant obtain government subsidies? Can the plant find interested business partners who, in turn, base their investment decisions on regulatory developments? Can the plant recover some of the costs in the form of carbon credits? If so, how much cost? Finally, can the plant be sure that this investment is going to ensure its environmental compliance one, two, five, ten years down the road? All these are regulatory matters, and the answer to each one of these questions is, "maybe."

Both physical and regulatory risks play an important role in securing project financing, which is very substantial in the energy industry. For example, a lender is concerned about the borrower's potential loss of cash flow due to lawsuits, clean-up orders, and so forth. There is also a physical risk of loss of property value or liquidity, due to potential contamination. The lender, therefore, is going to build certain protective covenants that shield it from environmental risks. In October 2002, the World Bank private sector development arm, the International Finance Corp. (IFC) made a decision to develop an industry framework for evaluating and managing environmental (and social) risks in project financing. As a result, the set of Equator Principles (EP) was worked out, in which financial institutions would participate voluntarily. The key was that these institutions would not lend to borrowers unable to comply with the adopted set of environmental policies. All borrowers would be required to provide the lender with environmental reviews and management plans. In addition, all borrowers would be categorized into one of three groups. Category A projects would have a substantial environmental impact. Category B projects would have a smaller impact (perhaps localized, more easily mitigated or reversible). Category C projects would have little impact. Depending on the category, the borrower would need to provide the lender with certain documents addressing the impact and the alternative ways of managing it. In addition, the lender might perform a detailed analysis of the borrower's project, including site inspection, document review, or even laboratory analysis. In the absence of compliance with the adopted principles, the lender would declare the borrower in default and demand an immediate repayment!

We see that risks are plentiful. What about opportunities? These are, in essence, investment opportunities that are justified by regulatory developments, as well as those justified by physical factors brought about by climate change and other environmental conditions. These include carbon capture and storage (CCS); energy efficiency improvements; using natural gas instead of coal; converting carbon to cleaner energy; alternative energy R&D; bio-fuels research; and renewable power generation, among others. These may prove to be beneficial in the long term. However, currently most of these represent a substantial cost to the business (remember our example at the beginning of this chapter!) with lingering uncertainty of whether these costs would be recouped. Most of these investments are being made with the help of government subsidies or simply in the hope that the emerging environmental regulation will, at the end of the day, justify these costs.

While investment opportunities arise, just like risks, from both physical and regulatory factors, it is clear that these *opportunities are mostly perceived by businesses as regulatory.* It is the regulation that entices firms to seek environmental investment opportunities, meaning that absent regulation those opportunities would not have been sought. For statistics, let us turn to the Carbon Disclosure Project (CDP).[8] This organization originated in 2003, acting on behalf of institutional investors (475 investors in 2009, with $55 trillion in funds under management). The CDP reports are published in more than 20 countries. The project challenges companies to disclose carbon emissions, both the amount and the risks and opportunities related to climate change. The number of voluntarily reporting companies increased from 235 in 2003 to 2456 in 2009.

Many of the S&P 500 firms respond to the project's survey. What do we observe? In 2010 compared to 2009, 70 percent (66%) responded to the CDP survey; 54 percent (50%) reported on GHG emissions in annual corporate reporting; and 59 percent (52%) disclosed emissions in their CDP reports. These statistics are in fact quite encouraging and provide evidence of the rising environmental awareness of firms. Here is more encouraging data: 68 percent have Board responsibility for climate change; 65 percent have emission reduction plans; and 61 percent engage with policy makers on climate change.

What about risks and opportunities? CDP tells us that of the reporting S&P 500 firms, 70 percent see regulatory risks and 70 percent see physical risks. On the opportunities side, however, 77 percent see regulatory opportunities; while *only 52 percent* see physical opportunities! As summarized by one of the reporting firms, "*regulations* increase the value of any technology that has a primary or secondary benefit in the reduction or avoidance of GHG emissions" (the author's italics). How about physical investment opportunities resulting from climate change? The answer is far less clear.

What about the energy sector? Key industries within the sector are oil, gas & consumable fuels, and energy equipment & services. An interesting statistic is the percentage of reporting firms setting emission-reduction targets. Exhibit 18.10

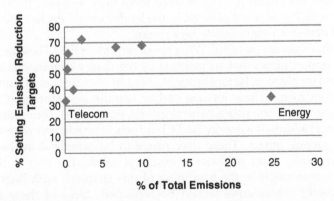

Exhibit 18.10 Sectors Reporting for the CDP, by Relative Emissions and the Percentage of Firms Setting Emission Reduction Standards
Source: CDP S&P 500 Report 2010.

shows this percentage for several industries reporting for the CDP. The energy sector stands out as the main emitter in the group (utilities are not included in the picture), representing about 25 percent of total emissions. However, the percentage of energy firms setting explicit reduction targets is only about 35 percent. Only Telecom is below that figure, but Telecom produces almost no emissions at all in comparison. Clearly not that many firms in the energy sector pursue the opportunities arising from the investments aimed at emission reduction!

That being said, of course, energy firms do make use of the opportunities! This is evident from their responses to the survey. From earning carbon credits by participating in international projects, to installing CCS, to working on bio-fuels and renewable energy research, to building clean power plants ... work is definitely underway! The point is that it is, for the most part, these are for the most part *regulatory* opportunities.

Does environmental awareness increase shareholder value? A related question is: Does environmental awareness increase shareholder value because of regulation? Research suggests that the answer to the first question is "maybe." However, the answer to the second question seems to be "yes." Kim and Lyon (2011), using an event study of CDP reporting, conclude the following: "First, we find no systematic evidence that CDP participation, in and of itself, directly increased share prices. This suggests that participation was not entirely voluntary, but was the result of pressure from shareholders, regulators, and the institutional investors involved in the CDP. Second, we find that CDP participants were treated better by investors when exogenous events caused the likelihood of climate change regulation to rise." (page 22.) In other words, should regulatory costs of environmental compliance increase, investors react positively to evidence of better preparedness of firms.

All of this evidence and all these statistics, although not abundant, suggest that investors do care about the risks and opportunities presented by the environment and that businesses, driven partly by shareholder activism, are accounting for these risks and opportunities in their plans.

It is common practice these days for companies to prepare annual Corporate Responsibility Reports, which include, among the many important areas of corporate responsibility (such as health, safety, and community development), environmental responsibility. It is clear that the shareholders of these firms want to see a responsible attitude toward preserving the environment and that the environmental stewardship has borne a significant impact on a company's reputation and on its ability to do business, to access various geographical regions, and to perform operations globally—especially in countries with keen environmental awareness—as well as to raise capital. Cap and trade or not, the public and regulatory pressure toward better environmental stewardship has become an undeniable reality today.

CONCLUSION

It is difficult to encompass the entire spectrum of energy-related environmental issues in one brief chapter. However, the following are the key points. Environmental regulation is a reality, and even though the specific debate regarding carbon cap and trade has run aground at present, significant international efforts are

underway, and are likely to continue, in assuring further development of technologies that mitigate the human carbon footprint. Furthermore, environmental
awareness is not just a concern of the regulators. Investors and lenders are also
increasingly aware of the environmental impact of their companies and projects,
and they directly consider this impact when making investment and lending decisions. All companies, especially those with significant international presence, have
to take environmental regulation into account when assessing their risks and
opportunities.

DISCUSSION QUESTIONS

Use the following information to answer Questions 1 through 6:

Suppose it costs Plant A $20 per ton to reduce CO_2 emissions. Plant B, however, can
reduce emissions at a lower cost of $15 per ton. Plant A has been allocated the same amount
of allowances as Plant B, equal to 1 million tons. This means that the emissions of each
plant are capped at 1 million tons. Plant A is a bigger pollutant and would have to reduce
emissions by 20 percent to meet the allocation. Plant B uses a cleaner technology and needs
to cut the emissions by 10 percent to meet the allocation.

1. How much would each plant have emitted without the cap?

2. What is the overall percentage reduction of emissions to society if both plants meet the
   allocation?

3. What is the total cost to the society of reducing emissions, if there is no cap and trade?

4. What is the cost to society of reducing emissions in the presence of cap and trade, assuming that the price of one allowance is $17.50 per ton and that 125,000 can be traded? What
   is the total saving to society with cap and trade?

5. What is the cost to Plant B of "hiring" Plant A to reduce emissions on its behalf?

6. How are the "savings to society" split between the two plants? Need your answer hold
   in general?

   Open-ended discussion questions:

7. What potential issues do you see with the cap-and-trade system despite the apparent
   cost savings of emission reduction that it provides?

8. What makes carbon so different from SO_2? Why did the United States implement the
   SO_2 cap and trade successfully but cannot follow suit for CO_2 emissions?

9. How does the global concern about climate change affect risks and opportunities faced
   by businesses today?

10. How does public pressure shape corporate attitudes toward environmental steward-
    ship? How is this relationship affected by regulation?

NOTES

1. The data for this example is from the EPA Greenhouse Gas Mitigation Strategies Database
   for the Electric Utility/Power Industry Sector, available at www.epa.gov/airquality/
   ghgsettlement.html.
2. This example is borrowed from an online presentation by Philipp Koenig, Electricity
   Policy Research Group, University of Cambridge, available at www.eprg.group.cam.
   ac.uk/wp-content/uploads/2010/10/101025-Koenig.pdf.
3. Ehrlich and Ehrlich (1996). The quote and the EPA statistics in the section are found in
   Bradley and Fulmer (2004).

4. www.epa.gov/airmarkets/progress/ARP09_4.html.
5. Detailed information about the states and the state requirements can be obtained from the U.S. Department of Energy at http://apps1.eere.energy.gov/states/maps/renewable_portfolio_states.cfm.
6. www.businessgreen.com/bg/news/1930722/global-investment-renewables-total-usd17-trillion-2020.
7. www.pikeresearch.com/blog/articles/is-carbon-legislation-really-dead-not-outside-the-u-s.
8. www.cdproject.net/CDPResults/CDP-2010-SP500.pdf.

REFERENCES

Bradley, Robert L., Jr., and Richard W. Fulmer. 2004. *Energy: The Master Resource*. Dubuque, Iowa: Kendall/Hunt Publishing Company.

Carbon Disclosure Project. Standard & Poor's Reports 2009 and 2010.

Chicago Climate Futures Exchange. 2004. "The Sulphur Dioxide Emission Allowance Trading Program: Market Architecture, Market Dynamics and Pricing." Chicago: Self.

Ehrlich, Paul, and Anne Ehrlich. 1996. *Betrayal of Science and Reason*. Washington, DC: Island Press.

Kim, Eun-Hee, and Thomas Lyon. 2011. "When Does Institutional Investor Activism Increase Shareholder Value? The Carbon Disclosure Project." *B.E. Journal of Economic Analysis & Policy* 11:1. Available at www.bepress.com/bejeap/vol11/iss1/art50.

Macalister, Terry. 2011."Traders Condemn EU's 'Mickey Mouse' Carbon Market after Botched Trading Statement." *Guardian* [UK], January 21.

ABOUT THE CONTRIBUTOR

Dr. Evgenia Golubeva is an RRT assistant professor of finance and adjunct lecturer in energy management at the Michael F. Price College of Business, University of Oklahoma. She received her undergraduate degree in oil and gas exploration geophysics from Moscow State Academy of Oil and Gas in 1992 in Russia. Upon graduation, she worked in the oil and gas industry for several years before coming to the United States. She earned her MBA in 1997 and a PhD in finance in 2002 from the University of Utah. Since then she has been teaching at the University of Oklahoma. Her research has been published in the *Review of Financial Studies* and the *Journal of Financial Markets*. Dr. Golubeva has been heavily involved in energy-related activities at the College of Business and in coordinating the undergraduate program in finance.

CHAPTER 19

Hedging and Value in the U.S. Airline Industry*

DAVID A. CARTER
Oklahoma State University

DANIEL A. ROGERS
Portland State University

BETTY J. SIMKINS
Oklahoma State University

If we don't do anything, we are speculating. It is our fiduciary duty to hedge fuel
price risk.

—Scott Topping, Vice President Treasurer, Southwest Airlines
(April 29, 2003, in a presentation at Oklahoma State University)

INTRODUCTION

In the past few years, a growing number of companies have devoted major
resources to implementing risk management programs designed to hedge financial risks, such as interest rate, currency, and commodity price risk. Because of the
increasing reliance on such programs, it is important to ask the question: "Does
hedging add value to corporations?"[1] And if it does, the obvious follow-up question is: "How does it add value?"

Finance theorists have proposed a number of ways that hedging and, more
generally, risk management can increase corporate market values. Stated briefly,
risk management has the potential to add value by (1) reducing corporate income
taxes; (2) reducing the probability and expected costs of financial distress; and
(3) preserving management's ability and incentives to carry out all positive-NPV
(net present value) projects (incentives that can otherwise be distorted by the pressure for near-term cash flow faced by financially troubled firms).[2]

---

*This article is a reprint of "Hedging and Value in the US Airline Industry" (Carter, Rogers,
and Simkins 2006) published in the *Journal of Applied Corporate Finance*.

To answer the questions of whether hedging adds value and, if so, how, we conducted a study of the fuel price hedging of 28 airlines over the period from 1992 to 2003 as published in *Financial Management* in 2006.[3] The aim of this chapter is to summarize and evaluate the practical import of the findings of that study.

We chose to investigate the relation between hedging and value in the airline industry for a number of reasons. First, the industry is by and large competitive and remarkably homogeneous. Second, by studying airlines, we were able to focus on the hedging of a single, volatile input commodity—jet fuel—that represents a major economic expense for the industry. Although fuel costs have historically been a distant second to labor costs, the two have almost converged in recent years.[4] Third, jet fuel prices are not only highly volatile (our estimate of annualized jet fuel price volatility during 1992–2003 was about 27 percent, as compared to about 10 percent for major currencies),[5] but the *levels of volatility* are themselves highly variable. The notable variation in both price and volatility levels during the period we studied allowed us to examine more closely the source of potential value from hedging, and how that value is reflected under different price conditions. Fourth, fuel price increases cannot be easily passed through to customers (see Box A) because of competitive pressures in the airline industry. Fifth, and finally, airlines face significant "costs" associated with financial trouble. Perhaps most important, airlines facing a sharp downturn in operating cash flow are likely, especially when faced with a material probability of default, to underinvest in their future, making cutbacks in discretionary expenditures on everything from advertising to maintenance.[6] Hedging fuel costs, as the results of our study suggest, can help the airlines manage this potential underinvestment problem while also limiting other costs of financial trouble.

Box A: Competition, Fuel Costs, and Consumer Prices

"Fuel prices are an external factor that airlines cannot control. What can they do to react and minimize the damage? A comparison with other modes of transportation is revealing. Fuel represents a roughly comparable proportion of expenses for railroads and many trucking companies (in the mid-teens percent range), but they have not been hurt by higher fuel prices to nearly the same degree.

Part of the difference is due to more active hedging programs by these freight transportation companies, but most is due to the fact that many of their contracts with corporate customers allow them to pass through higher fuel costs in the form of surcharges. Airlines have tried repeatedly to raise fares in response to high fuel costs, but with little success. [T]he problem comes back to a lack of pricing power in a very competitive market."

Philip Baggaley, Managing Director, Standard & Poor's, Testimony before the U.S. House of Representatives Committee on Transportation and Infrastructure, June 3, 2004.

SOME BACKGROUND ON THE COMPANIES

We analyzed all publicly held U.S. passenger airline companies (SIC codes 4512 and 4513) for which information was available for at least two years during the period 1992–2003. That fuel price risk is a major risk factor for the airlines is clear from the disclosures about their hedging programs that appear in many of their annual financial statements. At the same time, a number of other airlines that say nothing about hedging *future* jet fuel purchases draw attention to their use of other risk-management tactics, such as fuel pass-through agreements with major carriers or charter arrangements that allow for fuel costs to be passed along to the organization chartering the flight.[7]

Exhibit 19.1 provides descriptive data on our sample of 28 airlines. The second and third columns list the airline classification (major carrier, national carrier, or regional/commuter) and the years for which information about the airline was available.[8] As shown in the fourth column of Exhibit 19.1, fuel costs averaged about 13.75 percent of operating expenses for all years, with a range of 8.5 percent (for Mesaba Holdings) to 18.8 percent (Airtran Holdings). The last three columns in the exhibit report three pieces of information about the companies' fuel hedging programs: (1) the calendar years in which fuel hedges were in place at the fiscal year-end; (2) the maximum maturity of the hedge (expressed in years); and (3) the percentage of next year's fuel requirements hedged.

The major airlines, as can be seen in the exhibit, are much more likely to hedge future jet fuel purchases than the smaller firms. Only AMR and Southwest Airlines had hedges in place at the end of every year for which we have data. But other fairly regular and extensive hedgers included Continental, Delta, Alaska Air, and JetBlue. Of the 28 airlines, 18 (or 64%) reported hedging jet fuel in at least one year.

But among those airlines that hedged, there was considerable variation in the amount of fuel hedged. While the average percentage of next year's fuel consumption hedged was only about 15 percent, some airlines—notably Southwest—have often hedged up to 80 percent of the next year's fuel requirements. And in an interesting development, a few major airlines such as Southwest and AMR have been increasing the maximum length of hedging horizons in recent years.

But, as the case of Delta Air Lines makes clear, fuel hedging is not a panacea. For much of our sample period, Delta maintained fairly high levels of fuel hedging. At the end of 2002, the company had hedged 65 percent of its fuel requirements for 2003, and this level was fairly representative of its hedging policy from 1998 through 2003. But Delta drastically increased its leverage in the post-9/11 environment, perhaps in the belief the industry downturn would be short-lived. By the end of 2003, Delta's long-term debt as a percentage of total assets had grown to 48 percent (up from 27% at the end of 2000), with about $1 billion coming due in 2004. Meanwhile, during the years 2001–2003, Delta reported operating losses of almost $3 billion while servicing $1.9 billion of interest expense. Delta's S&P credit rating declined steadily from BBB– before September 11, 2001, to BB– by the end of 2003. By March of 2004, its credit rating had been cut further to B–. In February of 2004, Delta liquidated its existing fuel hedge contracts to raise $83 million of cash, leaving the company completely exposed to further price shocks.

Exhibit 19.1 Fuel Usage and Derivatives Hedging by Sample Airlines (1992–2003)

Airline	Airline Classification	Sample Years	Jet Fuel as a Percentage of Operating Expenses (Average Over Sample Period)	Years Jet Fuel Hedged	Maximum Maturity of Hedge (Years)	Average Percentage of Next Year Hedged
Airtran Holdings	National	1993–2003	18.84%	1999–2003	1.0	14%
Alaska Air Group	Major	1992–2003	13.92%	1992–1996, 2000–2003	3.0	22%
America West Holdings	Major	1992–2003	13.30%	1997–2003	<1.0	11%
AMR Corp	Major	1992–2003	11.97%	1992–2003	3.0	28%
Amtran	National	1992–2003	18.44%	1998–2001	0.75	3%
Atlantic Coast Airlines	National	1994–2003	12.73%	1997–2000	1.0	5%
CCAir	Regional	1994–1998	8.69%	None		
Comair Holdings	National	1994–1999	10.19%	None		
Continental Airlines	Major	1992–2003	15.14%	1992–1993, 1996–2002	1.0	18%
Delta Air Lines	Major	1992–2003	12.20%	1996–2003	3.0	34%
Express Jet Holdings	National	2002–2003	11.62%	None		
Frontier Airlines	National	1994–2003	15.58%	2002–2003	2.0	2%
Great Lakes Aviation	National	1994–2003	15.28%	None		
Hawaiian Airlines	National	1994–2002	17.11%	1997–2002	2.0	8%
JetBlue Airways	National	2002–2003	16.07%	2002–2003	1.25	43%
Mesa Air Group	National	1994–2003	15.09%	None		
Mesaba Holdings	National	1993–2003	8.45%	None		
Midway Airlines	National	1995–2000	12.52%	None		
Midwest Express Holdings	National	1994–2003	16.53%	1997–2002	0.75	4%
Northwest Airlines	Major	1992–2003	13.57%	1997–2002	1.0	11%
SkyWest	National	1994–2003	12.20%	None		
Southwest Airlines	Major	1992–2003	14.51%	1992–2003	6.0	43%
Tower Air	National	1994–1998	18.36%	1998	N/A	0%
TransWorld Airlines (TWA)	Major	1994–1999	13.00%	1998–1999	2.0	1%
UAL Corp	Major	1992–2003	12.30%	1995–2003	1.0	19%
US Airways Group	Major	1992–2003	9.69%	1994–1997, 2000–2003	2.0	12%
Vanguard Airlines	Regional	1995–2001	17.61%	None		
World Airways	National	1994–2003	9.97%	None		
Average			13.75%			15%

Box B: Southwest Airlines: An Example of a Successful Hedging Program

Southwest Airlines is both the most active hedger of fuel costs and the most profitable among U.S. airlines. At the end of 2005, Southwest posted a profit for its 33rd consecutive year. This success is unprecedented in an industry that has collectively failed to turn a profit for the past five years. Southwest attributes much of that success to its fuel hedging program. As they point out in their 2005 10K report: "This performance was driven primarily by strong revenue growth, as the Company grew capacity, and effective cost control measures, including a successful fuel hedge program." And, in the words of Scott Topping, Southwest's Vice President and Treasurer, "Fuel hedging will continue to play a strategic role in the industry and be a potential source of competitive advantage."

In 2005, Southwest's fuel costs totaled $1.342 billion and represented 19.8 percent of operating expenses. Their fuel hedging program resulted in an estimated reduction of "Fuel and oil expense" during 2005 of $892 million. The airline paid an average of $1.03 per gallon after hedging gains and used 1.3 billion gallons of fuel for the year. The following insert summarizes Southwest's hedging program objectives, commodities used and instruments considered, and other considerations.

Hedging Program Objectives

- Strategically manage the second largest expense category on P&L statement
- Integral to unit cost management & competitive advantage
- Manage upside risk and participate on the downside (requires an investment)
- Be opportunistic

Commodities Used in Hedging

- Crude Oil, Heating Oil, Unleaded Gasoline, and Jet Fuel
- Considerations in choice of commodities include expected performance of the hedge, basis risk, liquidity, and accounting issues (i.e., FAS 133)

Hedging Instruments Considered

- Swaps—no initial cost but highest risk
- Differential swaps—restructure hedge to manage basis risk
- Collars—can be structured at no cost or premium collars; carries a moderate risk (premium collars are often used)
- Call options—highest cost, lowest risk, and can create synthetically (swap plus put option)

(Continued)

Box B (Continued)

Examples of Protection at $1.20 per Gallon Using Swap, Call Option, and Collar

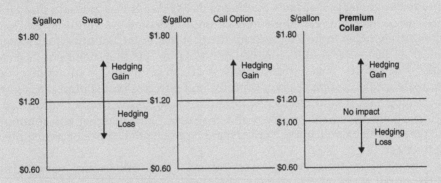

Considerations in Hedging and Operations

- Point in commodity price cycle—swaps look more favorable at low prices, collars in the mid range, and options at high prices
- Uncertainty beyond fundamentals
- Cost/budget
- Other portfolio management objectives or market opportunities (example: volatility)
- Counterparties—prefer OTC trading and counterparties must be investment grade
- FAS 133—goal is to maintain hedge accounting without sacrificing opportunity

HEDGING AND VALUE IN THE AIRLINE INDUSTRY

To investigate whether and how the jet fuel hedging activities of airlines affect their values, we estimated the empirical relationships between a number of measures of the extent of a firm's jet fuel hedging activities and a widely used measure of value added called Tobin's Q ratio. Tobin's Q, in brief, is the ratio of the firm's market value to its replacement cost—and we used the following simplified version:

Market value of equity + Liquidation value of preferred stock

+ Book values of long-term debt and current liabilities

− Current assets + Book value of inventory/Total assets.[9]

We used a number of different measures of fuel hedging activity, including the percentage of next year's fuel requirements hedged and a fuel hedging "indicator" variable (that received a value of 1 if the airline hedges its jet fuel exposure and 0 if it

does not). In addition to variables measuring hedging behavior, we also included several other control variables in our analysis, including firm size (measured by the natural logarithm of total assets), a dividend indicator, long-term debt-to-asset ratio, cash flow-to-sales ratio, capital expenditures-to-sales ratio, advertising-to-sales ratio, S&P credit rating score, and Altman's Z-score.[10] We also included indicator variables to proxy for the possible effects on firm value of other risk management techniques, such as fuel pass-through agreements, charter operations, and interest-rate or foreign-exchange hedging. [11] Finally, we included the ratio of cash to sales as a measure of liquidity, since excess cash can serve as a partial substitute for hedging and risk management.[12]

Exhibit 19.2 summarizes the results of our analysis of the relation between Tobin's Q and fuel hedging, as measured by the percentage of next year's fuel requirements hedged. We tested this relationship using three different models.[13] Our results when using Models 1 and 2 provide evidence of a link between hedging and value for airlines. The estimated coefficients for the percentage of next year's fuel requirements hedged were 0.348 for Model 1 and 0.332 for Model 2 (both statistically significant at the 10% level). In the case of Model 1, the coefficient of 0.348 can be interpreted as saying that an airline that hedges 100 percent of its jet fuel requirements would be expected to command a value premium of almost 35 percent over an airline that hedges none of its jet fuel requirements. For those airlines in our sample that hedged, the average percentage of next year's fuel requirements hedged was 29.4 percent. Thus, our findings suggest that an average hedging airline exhibits a value premium of around 10 percent (0.35 × 29.4%).[14]

Models 1 and 2 are concerned with the relation between *levels* of hedging activity and *levels* of value. Another way of estimating the value consequences of hedging is to measure the *change* in values when companies change their hedging policies. Our results using Model 3 show that changes in jet fuel hedging are positively related to changes in the value of the firm. The estimated coefficient for a change in the percentage of next year's fuel requirements hedged was 0.188 (which was also statistically significant at the 10% level). This result implies that a change from a policy of no hedging to the average level of hedging (for hedging firms) of 29.4 percent is associated with an increase in value of approximately 5.5 percent (0.188 × 29.4%).[15]

Exhibit 19.2 Regression Analysis of the Relation between Firm Value and Jet Fuel Hedging Behavior for Airlines (1992–2003)[a]

Panel A. Relation Between Value and Jet Fuel Hedging

	Constant	Firm Size	Percentage of Next Year's Fuel Req'ts Hedged	LTD to Asset Ratio	R^2	Wald X^2
Model 1 Pooled OLS Dep. Var. = ln(Q) (n = 228)	−0.085 (0.908)	−0.174*** (0.003)	0.348* (0.069)	0.710* (0.074)	0.463	—
Model 2 FGLS Dep. Var. = ln(Q) (n = 228)	−0.557 (0.179)	−0.115*** (0.000)	0.332*** (0.005)	0.819*** (0.000)	—	340.97***

Panel B. Relation Between the Change in Value and the Change in Jet Fuel Hedging

	Constant	Δ Firm Size	Δ Percentage of Next Year's Fuel Req'ts Hedged	Δ LTD to Asset Ratio	R^2	Wald X^2
Model 3 Pooled OLS Dep. Var. = Δln(Q) (n = 200)	−0.164 (0.341)	−0.298** (0.049)	0.188* (0.068)	0.897*** (0.006)	0.439	—

[a]Models 1 and 3 were estimated with OLS using robust standard errors that account for the clustered sample. Model 2 was estimated using time-series feasible generalized least squares with heteroskedastically consistent standard errors. Control variables listed in the text and year dummy variables were included in all regressions, but not reported. p-values are reported in parentheses below the coefficients.
*Indicates significance at the 10 percent level.
**Indicates significance at the 5 percent level.
***Indicates significance at the 1 percent level.

Box C: Lufthansa Airlines: An Example of a Successful Hedging Program by an International Airline

A successful fuel-hedging program is simply one that accomplishes its hedge objectives, like systematic reduction of risk, catastrophe insurance or budget protection.

—Helmut Fredrich, General Manager of Corporate
Fuel Management, Lufthansa[16]

German airline Lufthansa is not new to risk management. The company began hedging jet fuel price risk in 1990 and was one of the first airlines to do so. In 1997, Lufthansa became fully privatized and listed its shares on the stock market when the German government sold off its remaining stake in the company. In 2003, *Energy Risk* named Lufthansa as the "Energy Risk Manager of the Year—End User."

In 2005, fuel consumption accounted for approximately 14 percent of operating expenses. Like Southwest, Lufthansa has also hedged its fuel cost risk with option structures, including collars, as well as swaps.

Commodities Used in Hedging

- Crude oil, gasoil, kerosene

Hedging Instruments Considered

- Swaps including differential swaps
- Crack spreads
- Collars
- Options

Example of Lufthansa's Current Hedging Policy: Medium-Term Crude Oil Hedging Combined with Short-Term Crack-Hedging[17]

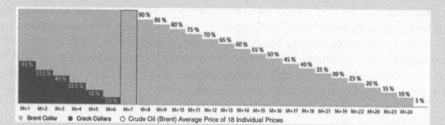

(Continued)

Box C *(Continued)*

Lufthansa hedges up to 90 percent of its planned fuel requirements on a revolving basis over a period of 24 months ahead. As the exhibit above illustrates, beginning 24 months into the future (see M+24 in exhibit), they start hedging 5 percent of their requirements using Brent Crude Oil Collars each month, incrementally increasing the level to 90 percent at seven months into the future (see M+7 in exhibit). To minimize basis risk (i.e., the price difference between crude oil and kerosene, which is the crack spread), Lufthansa also hedges using crack collars. A crack collar is a collar option strategy where option positions are on the crack spread. Since hedging crack is expensive, Lufthansa has modified its hedging approach to combine its hedging of crude oil with its short-term hedging of crack. Lufthansa starts implementing the crack hedging strategy six months ahead (see M+6 in exhibit) at a monthly rate of 7.5 percent. As a result, 45 percent of basis risk is hedged using crack collars by the time the fuel is used (see M+1).

Accounting rules are also an important concern. As Helmut Fredrich states, "We have to follow the IASB (International Accounting Standards Board) rules, to make sure our instruments are seen as just hedges and not trading. But as we go more towards the U.S. GAAP regulations, it is more difficult to stay within the rules, especially if you want to do more intelligent hedges."[18]

HOW DOES HEDGING ADD VALUE FOR AIRLINES?

Having found evidence that hedging adds value for airlines, we now ask, "How?" In his recent book on *Risk Management and Derivatives* (2003),[19] René Stulz offered a variation on the M&M (Modigliani and Miller) irrelevance proposition that he called the "risk management irrelevance proposition." Like the famous M&M theorems, Stulz's proposition says that, under a set of artificial conditions known as *perfect financial markets* (i.e., no asymmetric information, no taxes, and no transactions (including bankruptcy) costs), hedging should not affect the value of the firm.

But in the real world, where most if not all the assumptions of perfect financial markets are violated, the question becomes: "Under what conditions might hedging add value?" As mentioned earlier, the ways in which hedging can add value can be reduced to three main categories: (1) reducing taxes, (2) reducing the costs associated with reorganizing financially troubled companies, and (3) preserving (or strengthening) managers' incentives to invest in the company's future. In what follows, we briefly describe how airline hedging of jet fuel price risk might affect firm value in the context of risk management theory.

Preserving Managers' Normal Investment Incentives

In a paper published in the *Journal of Financial and Quantitative Analysis* in 1984, Cliff Smith and Stulz himself argued that one of the most important benefits of corporate risk management was its role in limiting the probability and costs of financial distress. Such costs can take the form of direct, out-of-pocket costs, such

as the costs of reorganizing a company that defaults. Or they can be indirect, such as the tougher terms exacted by the suppliers and employees—not to mention the reluctance of consumers—when dealing with financially troubled companies. But potentially the greatest of these indirect costs, at least for companies with significant growth opportunities, is the tendency of managers to underinvest when facing pressure to meet interest payments (and analysts' forecasts). Risk management, by helping to ensure a minimal level of cash flow or capital, can preserve management's incentives and ability to invest in all positive-NPV projects.[20]

In a 1993 article in the *Journal of Finance*, Ken Froot, David Scharfstein, and Jeremy Stein proposed an interesting variation on this argument that maintained that the value of hedging is likely to depend heavily on the *correlation* between a company's investment opportunities and the cash flow effects associated with hedgeable risks.[21] For example, if an airline's investment opportunities tend to dry up when jet fuel prices are high and operating cash flow (in the absence of hedging) is down, then the case for hedging is relatively weak; the firm doesn't really need much excess capital under those circumstances. On the other hand, if investment opportunities are greatest when industry cash flows are depressed by high fuel costs, the case for hedging becomes much clearer. In this event, hedging ensures that the firm will have sufficient capital for investment at a time when raising outside capital would likely be very expensive.

In support of this version of the underinvestment hypothesis, our study provides evidence that investment by the airline industry was *not negatively* correlated with jet fuel costs, as one might expect—and, indeed, was positive during parts of the period we studied.[22] That is to say, investment opportunities and, as discussed later, actual airline capital spending was greater in periods when fuel prices were high or rising. Consistent with our findings, other studies have shown that periods of economic downturn result in failure and/or asset sales by financially weak airlines. In such cases, the more profitable airlines may be in a position to buy the assets at fire sale prices.[23]

Box D: Hedging and Investment Behavior: The Case of Southwest and ATA Managing Other Costs of Financial Distress

---

A recent example that illustrates the investment behavior discussed above occurred after ATA's (formerly known as Amtran) Chapter 11 bankruptcy filing on October 27, 2004. Rising jet fuel prices contributed to ATA's deteriorating financial condition as spot prices for Gulf Coast jet fuel rose from below $1.00 per gallon at the start of 2004 to an average of more than $1.50 per gallon during October 2004—a 10-month period during which ATA was not hedged against fuel price increases. At the time of its bankruptcy filing, ATA announced that Airtran had agreed to purchase its Chicago Midway operation along with some additional gates and landing slots at other airports for $87.5 million in cash. In contrast to ATA, Airtran had hedged about 29 percent of its 2004 fuel commitments hedged by the end of 2003, and it increased its

(Continued)

Box D (Continued)

hedged position to 35 percent during the first quarter of 2004. However, the Midway operation was to be put up for auction, and even at the time of the bankruptcy filing, it was speculated that other bidders would emerge.

Southwest Airlines ultimately won the bidding for ATA's Chicago Midway property with a $117 million bid on December 17, 2004. Southwest had over 80 percent of its 2004 fuel commitments hedged at the end of 2003; and in its 2005 10-K filing, the airline reported that its gains from fuel hedging amounted to $455 million during 2004. Thus, one interpretation of these events is that Southwest's fuel hedging provided the cash flow that gave management the confidence to bid aggressively for the distressed ATA assets.

Managing Other Costs of Financial Distress

In addition to its role in managing the corporate underinvestment problem, hedging can also be used to manage other costs associated with financial distress, everything from the fees incurred in reorganizing debt claims to the higher costs of attracting and keeping concerned suppliers, customers, and employees. But this raises an interesting question about the real underlying objectives of airline hedging. If the fundamental purpose of hedging is really to preserve value by avoiding a costly reorganization and reassuring creditors, then we might expect the smaller, and more highly leveraged, airlines to be the most active hedgers. To the extent that there are major costs associated with financial distress, such costs would likely represent a higher percentage of firm value for the smaller airlines. On the other hand, if the main purpose of hedging is to enable the strongest airlines to buttress their already strong strategic positions by acquiring assets at fire-sale prices, then it may make sense that the most consistent hedgers would also be the largest, most successful operators. (And, as discussed below, to the extent that hedging and strategic risk management require an upfront investment in "learning," the largest most successful firms are also likely to be the first, if not the main, users.)

In order to investigate the extent of financial distress costs in the industry, we began by examining the airlines' credit ratings and how they have changed over time. For the period 1988–2004, Exhibit 19.3 reports the median S&P ratings of the senior debt of the 15 sample airlines with ratings reported in the Compustat database. As shown in the exhibit, in 1988 six airlines had investment-grade ratings. During the next 17 years, three airlines filed Chapter 11, and one was purchased after filing bankruptcy. As of this writing, only one airline had an investment-grade credit rating—Southwest. And as these credit ratings suggest, the airline industry's access to external capital markets has been diminishing over time.

One major reason for this decline in ratings can be seen in Exhibit 19.4, which shows the heightened volatility of airline profit margins. Moreover, there is a clear negative correlation between operating profits (not including hedging gains or losses) and jet fuel prices.[24] The combination of volatile cash flow and limited access to capital (especially during weak industry conditions) might provide an incentive for airlines to protect cash flow against a spike in fuel prices.

Exhibit 19.3 S&P Credit Ratings for Senior Debt of Sample Airlines

Airline	Median Rating (1988–2004)	May 2004 Rating
Airtran Holdings	B–	B–
Alaska Air Group	BB+	BB–
America West	B+	B–
AMR	BBB–	B–
Amtran	B	CCC
Atlantic Coast Airlines	B	B–
Continental Airlines	B+	B
Delta Air Lines	BBB–	B–
Midway Airlines	B–	Bankrupt
Northwest Airlines	BB	B+
Southwest Airlines	A–	A
Tower Air	CCC	Bankrupt
Trans World Airlines	CCC	Purchased by AMR
UAL	BB+	Bankrupt
US Airways Group	B+	CCC+

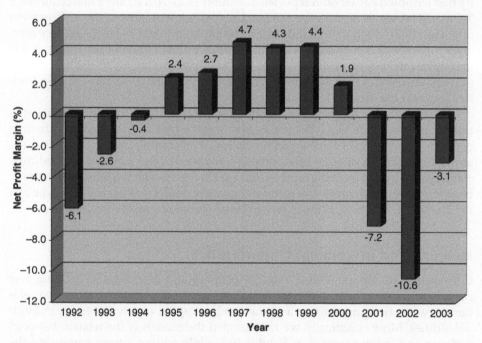

Exhibit 19.4 Net Profit Margin (%) of the U.S. Airline Industry from 1992 to 2003
Source: Air Transport Association Economic Report.

More Evidence on How Fuel Hedging Adds Value

In an additional effort to determine the motives for airline hedging, we conducted a series of multivariate regressions designed to test the relation of the percentage of jet fuel requirements hedged with a number of other potentially important variables, the results of which are summarized in Exhibit 19.5.[25] One of the variables was the credit ratings themselves. As reported in Exhibit 19.5, the airlines with the higher credit ratings (i.e., the lower S&P credit-rating numbers), and those with the least debt (when counting operating leases as debt) as a percentage of book value of total assets hedged the largest proportions of their future fuel requirements. And as we also noted earlier—and as shown in Exhibit 19.5—it is also the larger airlines that tend to hedge a larger percentage of their fuel requirements.

Both of these results are somewhat surprising, at least to the extent that one expects smaller, riskier airlines to have the highest expected costs of financial distress (as a percentage of firm value). But there are at least two possible explanations. One is that the smaller airlines have lacked either the resources to invest in acquiring a hedging capability or the strategic foresight to make that kind of investment. A second, and more intriguing possibility, is that the larger, stronger airlines actually have larger costs of financial distress (even as a percentage of firm value) in the form of more growth opportunities that could be lost as a result of high leverage and financial risk. Recall the positive relation between Tobin's Q and hedging activity that we noted earlier (and reported in Exhibit 19.2). To the extent that an airline's Tobin's Q serves as a proxy for the market's assessment of its value from growth opportunities (which is the standard interpretation of Tobin's Q in the finance literature), this result is consistent with the underinvestment hypothesis. That is, if it is mainly just the largest airlines that are able to buy distressed assets during periods of weak industry cash flows, then such firms may also have the most to gain from hedging and the most to lose from high leverage.

For the smaller airlines, it's true that the probability of getting into financial trouble may be quite high. But it also may well be true that the financial distress costs for such organizations are relatively low. For example, to the extent that the airlines are able to operate efficiently in Chapter 11 (and the stay on creditors' claims provided by the bankruptcy court may have a stabilizing effect), there may be relatively little disruption of normal operating routines. What is likely to be lost in Chapter 11, however, is the ability to invest in major growth opportunities.

Hedging and Investment Opportunities

Consistent with the possibility that the primary aim of airlines in hedging fuel costs is to protect their ability to invest, our study also found a strong correlation between hedging activity and the level of capital expenditures for individual airlines. More specifically, we re-estimated the models of the relation between hedging and value reported in Exhibit 19.2 while adding a term measuring the interaction between airline hedging and capex.

While the results of this test (reported in Exhibit 19.6) show no significant relation between firm value and fuel hedging, the coefficient on the interaction of capital expenditures and hedging was positive (e.g., 1.825 in Model 1) and statistically significant in both models. Moreover, it seems plausible to interpret this result as saying that, for those airlines that hedge future fuel purchases, the higher capital

Exhibit 19.5 Random Effects Tobit Regression Analysis of the Relation between Amount of Jet Fuel Hedged and Underinvestment Hypothesis Variable for Airlines (1992–2003)[a]

	Tobin's Q	Long-Term Debt-to-Assets	Ln(Assets)	Credit Rating
Model 1	0.1367**	−0.0848	0.0532*	−0.0226***
No adjustments for operating leases	(0.017)	(0.579)	(0.056)	(0.000)
Dep. Var. = Amt. of fuel hedged (n = 215)				
Model 2	0.2249***	−0.2729**	0.0492**	−0.0214***
Adjustments for operating leases	(0.007)	(0.043)	(0.032)	(0.000)
Dep. Var. = Amt. of fuel hedged (n = 206)				

[a]The dependent variable in each regression is the percentage of next year's jet fuel requirements hedged as of the end of the fiscal year. The results shown above are a subset of the full regressions and are taken from Table V on page 69 of our *Financial Management* article entitled, "Does Hedging Affect Firm Value? Evidence from the US Airline Industry."

*Indicates significance at the 10 percent level.
**Indicates significance at the 5 percent level.
***Indicates significance at the 1 percent level.

Exhibit 19.6 Regression Analysis of the Relation between Firm Value and the Interaction between Capital Expenditures and Jet Fuel Hedging Behavior for Airlines (1992–2003)[a]

	Constant	Firm Size	Percentage of Next Year's Fuel Req'ts Hedged	Percentage of Next Year's Fuel Req'ts Hedged X Capital Exp.	R^2	Wald X^2
Model 1 Pooled OLS Dep. Var. = ln(Q) (n = 228)	−0.048 (0.947)	−0.174*** (0.003)	0.036 (0.889)	1.825* (0.063)	0.469	—
Model 2 FGLS Dep. Var. = ln(Q) (n = 228)	−0.438 (0.269)	−0.125*** (0.000)	0.060 (0.707)	1.772*** (0.003)	—	572.25***

[a]Model 1 was estimated with OLS using robust standard errors that account for the clustered sample. Model 2 was estimated using time-series feasible generalized least squares with heteroskedastically consistent standard errors. Control variables listed in the text and year dummy variables were included in all regressions, but not reported; p-values are reported in parentheses below the coefficients.

*Indicates significance at the 10 percent level.
**Indicates significance at the 5 percent level.
***Indicates significance at the 1 percent level.

spending made possible in part by hedging is an important contributor to the higher firm value.

To interpret the value premium associated with hedging for the average hedging airline, we used the estimated coefficients for the percentage of next year's fuel requirements hedged (0.036) and the interaction between hedging and capital expenditures (1.825) along with the average level of capital expenditures-to-sales (11.7%) and average hedge ratio for hedgers (29.4%). Using these values, the average hedging airline is expected to be valued around 7 percent higher than a non-hedging airline [(1.825 × 0.117 × 0.294) + (0.036 × 0.294)]. This hedging premium consists of two components. The first term in parentheses corresponds to the portion of the hedging premium associated with capital expenditures, and accounts for approximately 86 percent of the total. The second term is the hedging premium associated only with hedging, which suggests that most of the value premium (86% in this case) is due to investment opportunities.

While not a direct test that jet fuel hedging reduces underinvestment for airlines, this finding does suggest that investors place a higher value on capital spending by hedgers than nonhedgers. In other words, investors may believe that hedgers are able to invest more and such investment tends to be value adding. One explanation for such investor behavior is that hedging makes future capital spending less vulnerable to future increases in jet fuel prices. In such cases, investors view today's capital expenditures as a more reliable proxy for tomorrow's.

THE HEDGING PREMIUM OVER TIME

Prior research has shown the hedging value premium for companies with foreign currency exposure is highest during years in which the U.S. dollar appreciates.[26] This suggests, as might be expected, that the market places higher values on companies that hedge during periods when the hedging instruments produce positive payoffs.

As part of our study, we investigated whether the jet fuel hedging premium changes over time by re-estimating Models 1 and 2 from Exhibit 19.2 and including a term that interacts the percentage of next year's fuel requirements hedged with year indicator variables. As reported in Panel A of Exhibit 19.7, our results show an increase in the hedging premiums over the time period studied. The largest hedging premiums occurred in 2002 in both models, a year in which fuel prices were both high and volatile. (In addition, the premiums are statistically significant in both models for 2002 and 2003.)

Moreover, as shown in Exhibit 19.8, we classified jet fuel prices into four different regimes—(1) low prices and volatility (1992–1996), (2) declining prices (1997–1998), (3) increasing prices (1999–2000), and (4) high prices and volatility (2002–2003)—and then estimated hedging value premiums during each of these periods. As reported in Panel B of Exhibit 19.7, we found that the premium value for hedging generally increased over these four time periods, with the highest premiums occurring in 2002–2003, the period covered by our study that experienced the highest prices and volatility. And if we were to create a fifth period running from 2004 to October 2006—a period in which the level and volatility of fuel costs have continued to rise—our best guess is that the hedging value premium would have continued to grow along with them.

Exhibit 19.7   Jet Fuel Hedging Premium over Time (1992–2003)[a]

	Estimated Coefficients on the Percentage of Next Year's Fuel Req'ts Hedged X Year (or Regime) Indicator Variable	
	Model 1 Pooled OLS Dep. Var. = ln(Q)	Model 2 FGLS Dep. Var. = ln(Q)
Panel A. Hedging Premiums by Year		
1994	−0.027	−0.294
1995	−0.768	−0.834
1996	0.509	0.299
1997	0.087	0.185
1998	0.111	0.307*
1999	0.249	0.252
2000	0.632	0.606**
2001	0.337	0.428*
2002	1.191**	0.936***
2003	0.575*	0.467**
Panel B. Hedging Premiums by Fuel Price Regime		
1992–1996 (low prices & volatility)	−0.290	−0.129
1997–1998 (declining prices)	0.049	0.135
1999–2000 (increasing prices)	0.257	0.134
2002–2003 (high prices & volatility)	0.772**	0.713***

[a]Model 1 was estimated with OLS using robust standard errors that account for the clustered sample. Model 2 was estimated using time-series feasible generalized least squares with heteroskedastically consistent standard errors. Control variables listed in the text and year dummy variables were included in all regressions, but not reported.
*Indicates significance at the 10 percent level.
**Indicates significance at the 5 percent level.
***Indicates significance at the 1 percent level.

CONCLUSION

In response to the question posed at the beginning of the article: "Does hedging add value to corporations?" our response is a definite "yes" for the 28 airlines in our sample. Those airlines that hedge their fuel costs have Tobin's Q ratios that are 5–10 percent higher than those of airlines that choose not to hedge. Our results also suggest that the main source of value added by hedging is its role in preserving the firm's ability to take advantage of investment opportunities that arise when fuel prices are high and airline operating cash flows and values are down. Specifically, we find that the value premium associated with hedging increases with the level of the firm's capital investment.[27]

We also find that the more active hedgers of fuel costs among the airlines are the larger firms with the least debt and highest credit ratings. This result is somewhat surprising, at least to the extent the smaller airlines might be expected to have larger financial distress costs (as a percentage of firm value), and hence greater motive to hedge. One explanation is that the smaller airlines have lacked either sufficient resources or the strategic foresight to acquire a derivatives

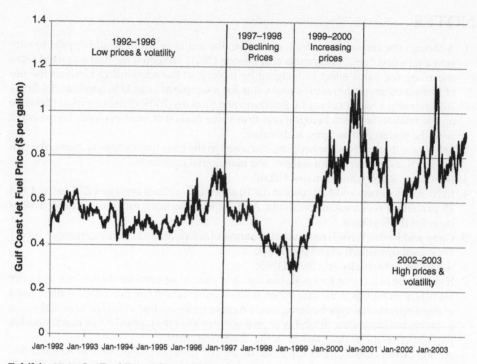

Exhibit 19.8   Jet Fuel Prices from 1992 to 2003
Source: Energy Information Administration. Spot prices are for U.S. Gulf Coast.

hedging capability. A second possibility, however—one that is consistent with our main findings—is that the largest airlines also have highest costs of financial distress (even as a percentage of firm value) in the form of more growth opportunities that could be lost as a result of high leverage and financial risk. Conventional wisdom says it is mainly just the largest airlines that are able to buy distressed assets during periods of weak industry cash flows—and to the extent this is so, such firms may also have the most to gain from hedging.

DISCUSSION QUESTIONS

1. Based on research evidence provided in the chapter, does fuel hedging add value for airlines? If so, how much value (i.e., the hedging premium), on average, is there?

2. What measure is used to examine the value of airlines in this research? Also, how is fuel hedging activity measured?

3. How does hedging add value for firms according to the research discussed in the chapter? List and describe the ways.

4. What is the underinvestment hypothesis, and how would hedging add value under this hypothesis? Give examples for the airline industry.

5. List and describe hedging instruments considered by Southwest Airlines.

6. How does Lufthansa Airlines hedge fuel price risk?

7. Does the hedging premium vary over time? Explain.

8. Explain how the authors examine motives for airline hedging by using multivariate regressions. What do they find?

NOTES

1. Although the answer is far from definitive, the initial evidence would appear to support a guarded "yes." Allayannis and Weston (2001) presented the first empirical work regarding the value effect of hedging by looking at the relationship between the use of foreign currency derivatives and value for a sample of large U.S. nonfinancial firms. Additionally, a recent survey by Smithson and Simkins (2005) of the empirical literature on the relation between hedging and firm value finds that most evidence is consistent with the notion that hedging adds value.

2. Other possible motives for hedging discussed in the literature include reducing the cost of capital, asymmetric information, and managerial incentives.

3. See Carter, Rogers, and Simkins (2006).

4. In 2005, labor costs and fuel costs at the 10 major U.S. airlines averaged 27.5 percent and 25 percent of revenues, respectively. And for some airlines, fuel costs exceeded labor costs for the first time.

5. Guay and Kothari (2003) report that the annualized volatility of major currencies is only 11 percent (measured over 1988–1997).

6. See Froot, Scharfstein, and Stein (1993).

7. It should be noted that fuel pass-through and charter agreements do not lock in a price for future jet fuel, as is the case when airlines hedge future fuel purchases. Rather, users of these operational-type hedging mechanisms experience higher fuel costs as fuel prices increase, but have some flexibility to pass some or all of the higher jet fuel cost to another party, such as the partner airline or the chartering client.

8. Airline carrier classifications are based on the Air Transport Association of America definitions. Major carriers are defined as an airline with annual revenue of more than $1 billion, and national carriers are airlines with annual revenues between $100 million and $1 billion. Regional carriers are airlines with annual revenues of less than $100 million whose service generally is limited to a particular geographic region.

9. Because of data limitation, we used a simple approximation of Tobin's Q rather than a more rigorous construction. See Chung and Pruitt (1994). Prior research by DaDalt, Donaldson, and Garner (2003) has documented that a simple Q calculation is preferable in most empirical applications because of the ease of computation, data availability, and because the simple approximation is highly correlated with more rigorous calculations.

10. Altman's Z-score is a measure of the likelihood of bankruptcy. A score above 3.0 indicates that bankruptcy is unlikely, while a score below 1.8 indicates bankruptcy is likely.

11. See Footnote 7.

12. Prior research notes that airlines with greater liquidity demonstrated less stock price sensitivity in response to the September 11, 2001, attacks. See Carter and Simkins (2004).

13. We used pooled ordinary least squares regression (OLS) with robust standard errors to estimate Models 1 and 3 and a feasible generalized least squares regression (FGLS) with heteroskedastically consistent standard errors to estimate Model 2. Model 3 differs from Model 1 in that we used changes in our variables to explore the effect of changes in jet fuel hedging behavior on the change in firm value. We also included year dummy variables in all regressions. Because all airlines did not operate in all years of our sample, we had a total of 251 firm-year observations.

14. We also estimated the same models using Tobin's Q, total assets, leverage, and capital expenditures adjusted for operating leases. While not shown in this article, the results continue to suggest a statistically significant hedging premium.

15. In a simple analysis of stock returns (i.e., not controlling for size or other factors), hedgers outperformed nonhedgers in 7 of the 10 years we studied. Furthermore, for two of the years that the hedgers did not outperform nonhedgers (2001–2002), the weaker performance of hedging airlines was most likely due to other factors other than hedging. The

stock market heavily punished large airlines (almost all of which hedge) in the post 9/11 period since they were more likely targets of terrorist attacks.

16. *Source:* "Energy Risk Manager of the Year—End User," *Energy Risk* 7:12 (2003).
17. *Source:* Lufthansa Investor Relations public documents on hedging and other public sources.
18. See "Energy Risk Manager of the Year—End User," previously cited.
19. See Stulz (2003).
20. See Smith and Stulz (1984).
21. See Froot, Scharfstein, Stein (1993).
22. Carter, Rogers, and Simkins (2006, 61–63).
23. See Pulvino (1998 and 1999).
24. The Pearson Correlation Coefficient over the period 1992–2003 is –42 percent.
25. Exhibit 19.5 reports a subset of the results from the complete random effects Tobit regressions reported in our *Financial Management* article. For the complete set of results and discussion, see pp. 66–71 of that article.
26. See Allayannis and Weston (2001).
27. Interpreted more broadly, our study provides evidence that the use of commodity hedging by commodity *users* increases firm value. This is in contrast to other studies that have found little or no value gain from hedging by commodity *producers*. For an example of the latter, see Jin and Jorion (2006).

REFERENCES

Allayannis, George, and James Weston. 2001. "The Use of Foreign Currency Derivatives and Firm Market Value." *Review of Financial Studies* 14:1, 243–276.

Carter, David, Daniel Rogers, and Betty Simkins. 2006." Hedging and Value in the U.S. Airline Industry." *Journal of Applied Corporate Finance* 18:4, 21–33.

Carter, David, Daniel Rogers, and Betty Simkins. 2006. "Does Hedging Affect Firm Value? Evidence from the U.S. Airline Industry." *Financial Management* 35:2, 53–86.

Carter, David, and Betty Simkins. 2004. "The Market's Reaction to Unexpected Catastrophic Events: The Case of Airline Stock Returns and the September 11th Attacks." *Quarterly Review of Economics and Finance* 44:4, 539–558.

Chung, Kee, and Stephen Pruitt. 1994. "A Simple Approximation of Tobin's Q." *Financial Management* 23:3, 70–74.

DaDalt, Peter, Jeffrey Donaldson, and Jacqueline Garner. 2003. "Will Any Q Do?" *Journal of Financial Research* 26:4, 535–551.

Froot, Kenneth, David Scharfstein, and Jeremy Stein. 1993. "Risk Management: Coordinating Corporate Investment and Financing Policies." *Journal of Finance* 48:5, 1629–1658.

Guay, Wayne, and S. P. Kothari. 2003. "How Much Do Firms Hedge With Derivatives?" *Journal of Financial Economics* 70:3, 423–461.

Jin, Yanbo, and Philippe Jorion. 2006. "Firm Value and Hedging: Evidence from U.S. Oil and Gas Producers." *Journal of Finance* 61:2, 893–919.

Pulvino, Todd C. 1998. "Do Asset Fire Sales Exist? An Empirical Investigation of Commercial Aircraft Transactions." *Journal of Finance* 53:3, 939–978.

Pulvino, Todd C. 1999. "Effects of Bankruptcy Court Protection on Asset Sales." *Journal of Financial Economics* 52:2, 151–186.

Smith Jr., Clifford, and René Stulz. 1984. "The Determinants of Firms' Hedging Policies." *Journal of Financial and Quantitative Analysis* 20:4, 391–405.

Smithson, Charles, and Betty Simkins. 2005. "Does Risk Management Add Value? A Survey of The Evidence." *Journal of Applied Corporate Finance* 17:3, 8–17.

Stulz, René M. 2003. *Risk Management & Derivatives.* South-Western/Thomson Publishing: Mason, Ohio.

ABOUT THE CONTRIBUTORS

David A. Carter, PhD, is associate professor of finance in the Spears School of Business, Oklahoma State University. He has a BS degree in chemical engineering from Brigham Young University, an MBA from Utah State University, and a PhD in finance from the University of Georgia. Dr. Carter was a faculty member of the University of North Carolina–Wilmington (1996–1998) prior to joining the faculty at Oklahoma State University (OSU) in 1998. While at OSU, Dr. Carter has won several teaching awards including the 2004 Greiner Teaching Award and the 2004 Regent's Distinguished Teaching Award. He is also an adjunct associate professor for the University of Iowa's Tippie College of Business where he teaches in the college's Italy MBA program. Dr. Carter's current research interests include corporate risk management, commercial bank management, and corporate governance. He has published many papers in leading academic journals. Dr. Carter has been quoted in *The Economist*, the *Wall Street Journal*, and *USA Today* in articles related to hedging in the airline industry. Prior to getting his PhD, Dr. Carter worked in industry for Westinghouse Electric Corporation, at the Idaho National Engineering Laboratory, where he was an instructor for the U.S. Navy's nuclear propulsion program, and Questar Corporation (an energy company located in Salt Lake City, Utah).

Daniel A. Rogers is an associate professor at Portland State University. He received his PhD from the University of Utah and has also been on the faculty at Northeastern University. Before working on his doctorate, Rogers held professional and management positions with a national airline and a petroleum products distributor. Rogers conducts research in the areas of corporate hedging, managerial incentives, and executive compensation. His published work includes articles in *Journal of Finance, Journal of Banking and Finance, Financial Management, Journal of Futures Markets,* and *Journal of Applied Corporate Finance*.

Betty J. Simkins, PhD, is the Williams Companies Professor of Business and a professor of finance in the Department of Finance at Oklahoma State University's Spears School of Business where she teaches energy finance, corporate finance, and enterprise risk management, among other courses. Dr. Simkins received her PhD from Case Western Reserve University (CWRU), her MBA from OSU, and her BS in chemical engineering from the University of Arkansas. She has more than 40 publications in academic finance journals and has won awards for her research, most recently in risk management. In addition, Dr. Simkins has won several teaching awards including the Regents Distinguished Teaching Award. She is also very active in the finance profession and currently serves on the board of directors for the Financial Management Association, as co-editor of the *Journal of Applied Finance*, as past president of the Eastern Finance Association, and on the editorial boards of several prestigious finance journals. Prior to academia, she worked in the corporate world for Williams Companies and Conoco (now ConocoPhillips). In addition to being co-editor of this book, in 2010 she co-edited *Enterprise Risk Management: Insights and Analysis on Today's Leading Research and Best Practices*, also published by John Wiley & Sons.

PART FOUR

Case Studies

CHAPTER 20

PKO Resources, Inc.: Valuing a Producing Oil and Gas Property*

JOHN D. MARTIN
Carr P. Collins Chair and Professor of Finance, Baylor University

J. DOUGLAS RAMSEY
Vice President—Finance for EXCO Resources, Inc.

SHERIDAN TITMAN
McAllister Centennial Chair in Financial Services
at the University of Texas at Austin

INTRODUCTION

Pete Carvey, CFO for the PKO Resources of McKinney, Texas, sat at his desk puzzling over the analysis just presented to him regarding an acquisition his firm was considering. The property consisted of a block of producing oil and gas wells in the Salinas Valley region of south Louisiana. PKO's engineers had performed their due diligence of the property and made estimates of production volumes extended through the projected economic lives of the wells.

Although this project seemed like hundreds of others that he had analyzed, Pete was bothered by three things: First, the purchase price that had been quoted to PKO seemed very high in light of prices that PKO had observed in recent months. Second, the typical reserve mix for properties that PKO considered was weighted very heavily on proved reserve categories (i.e., proved developed producing, proved developed nonproducing, and proved undeveloped). The engineers had told Pete that the Salinas field had substantial prospects for unproved reserves (typically referred to as *probable reserves*). In the past PKO had simply ignored the unproved category[1] when evaluating an acquisition, but in this instance it appeared the firm would have to place some value on the unproved reserves if it were to have any chance of winning the bid.

---

*Salinas is not the name of the acquisition property, and the facts and figures have been altered but the setting is based on an actual acquisition candidate.

The final thing that bothered Pete related to the fact that PKO had lost out in all its recent competitive bidding situations. This caused Pete to question the firm's standard approach to arriving at its bid prices. PKO's standard approach is largely static but the firm engages in a number of what-if or scenario analyses before arriving at a final number.

There are two key sources of uncertainty involved in oil and gas production: price and volume risk. PKO's approach to the former is to hedge about 80 percent of its estimated production for five years such that the price of future sales was locked in today.[2] Consequently, when estimating future prices for oil and gas, the company used the forward price curve for a period of five years, after which time they simply assumed a flat price curve for all future years. The firm relied on its engineering staff to control volume risk although Pete realized it was impossible to be spot on with the production estimates, no matter how good the engineers were. In fact, as a precaution PKO's banks typically restricted the firm's ability to hedge more than 80 percent of its production since the banks did not want the company left exposed to commodity price risk on any amount by which the firm fell short of expected production.

THE COMPANY

PKO Resources is an independent oil and natural gas company located in McKinney, Texas. The firm engages in the acquisition, development, and exploration of onshore oil and natural gas properties in North America. Its principal operations are located in Colorado, Louisiana, New Mexico, Oklahoma, Texas, and West Virginia. As of December 31, 2006, the company's proved reserves were approximately 1.45 trillion cubic feet equivalent, and it had interests in 9,764 gross productive wells, including 879 gross productive oil wells and 9,007 gross productive gas wells.

PKO has been aggressively involved in the acquisition of producing oil and gas properties since its inception. The goal is to build value for the firm's shareholders by enhancing the value of its acquisitions through strict price discipline when buying properties, improving control over operations, aggressive property development, and exercising strong cost control.

PKO was known in the industry for its finance-savvy management team. The CEO had a finance background and approached the oil and gas business from the perspective of a financial buyer rather than that of a petroleum engineer, which was more common in the industry. Consequently, PKO's day-to-day operations were dominated by discussions of acquisition candidates, cash flow forecasts, and project valuations.

When Pete's staff evaluated a prospective acquisition, they followed a highly disciplined approach. First, the engineering staff made very detailed projections of production volumes and lifting costs for each producing well in the property. These projections were carried out for the entire productive life of each well. Second, oil and gas price estimates were obtained from the forward price curve out five years and then assumed to remain constant thereafter. The firm used different rates of interest to discount future cash flows that corresponded to the

different categories of reserves. For example, for proved developed and producing reserves the firm used a 10 percent discount rate, proved developed but nonproducing reserves were valued using a discount rate of 12 percent, and proved and not developed reserves were discounted using 15 percent. Typically, the firm did not consider lower-category reserves (i.e., probable and possible reserves) when valuing a property; however, when they did they would use discount rates as high as 20–25 percent.

Salinas Valley Property

The Salinas Valley property is being sold by the Karas Production Company of New Iberia, Louisiana. Karas owns a two-thirds interest in the property, and members of the Karas family own the remaining third but do not wish to sell at this time. Exhibit 20.1 contains production volume estimates for the entire field spanning the period 2008 through 2032. Panels a–c detail the quantities of reserves corresponding to proved developed and producing reserves, proved undeveloped reserves, and probable reserves. In addition, Exhibit 20.1 provides PKO's estimates of operating costs, taxes, and required investments to produce the Salinas properties, as well as the firm's discount rates for each category.

The initial valuations indicated that the value of the three reserve categories is $75,859,848. This total includes the probable reserve category, which does not appear to be worth pursuing since the exploration and development costs in the first three years more than offset the value of the estimated reserves. In fact, based on PKO's best estimate, fully developing and producing these properties would actually cost more to develop than the reserves would be worth, resulting in a negative value of ($2,806,566). However, this estimate assumes that PKO would have no flexibility in shutting down exploration and development should the initial efforts not prove promising. Pete was well aware that the firm had no commitment to continue exploration and development expenditures beyond year 2 if the results of the initial efforts in year 1 was not promising. This led Pete to a conversation with the firm's chief engineer, who indicated that the oil and gas volumes reported in Exhibit 20.1 were indeed the expected volumes; however, the actual volumes might be zero or as much as two-and-a-half times the expected. The engineer further confided that they would know which of these scenarios was correct only after two years of exploration.

After seeing the negative value for the probable reserve category Pete wondered if the company's analysis was correct. In an effort to get a better handle on the potential value of these reserves Pete asked the project's lead analyst to construct a simulation model to value the reserves. Exhibit 20.2 contains a description of the sources of randomness that the analyst suggested be included in the model. Pete also questioned the analyst about using such a high discount rate (25%) to discount the project cash flows since the company had the option to shut down production after two years if the reserves were insufficient to make production economic. It seemed to Pete that a lot of the risk of the project was effectively eliminated where the firm could stop exploration and production after two years if the prospects were not good.

Exhibit 20.1 Project Cash Flow Forecast

Panel A. Proved Developed and Producing Reserves

Year	Gross Production of Oil (MBBLS)	Gas (MMCF)	Net Production of Oil (MBBLS)	Gas (MMCF)	Forward Prices Oil $/BBL	Gas $/MCF	Total Net Sales (M$)	Taxes Severance (M$)	Ad Valorem (M$)	Operating Expenses (M$)	Depletion Allowance (M$)	Net New Investment (M$)	Net Cash Flows (M$)
2008	16.428	1,225.73	10.957	817.559	$80.751	$6.360	$6,084.504	$230.603	$134.468	$147.501	$912.676	$—	$ 3,941.193
2009	15.404	1,184.54	10.275	790.087	79.550	6.285	5,783.050	219.178	127.805	140.657	867.458	—	3,745.627
2010	13.717	1,069.80	9.149	713.553	78.221	6.144	5,099.734	193.280	112.704	126.251	764.960	—	3,301.610
2011	11.356	886.89	7.574	591.554	77.918	5.982	4,128.864	156.484	91.248	104.602	619.330	—	2,671.510
2012	9.846	769.71	6.567	513.397	75.822	5.975	3,565.489	135.132	78.797	90.743	534.823	—	2,306.719
2013	8.777	686.65	5.854	457.992	75.822	5.975	3,180.385	120.537	70.287	80.925	477.058	—	2,057.584
2014	7.971	623.95	5.317	416.177	75.822	5.975	2,889.775	109.522	63.864	73.518	433.466	—	1,869.579
2015	7.336	574.56	4.893	383.234	75.822	5.975	2,660.826	100.845	58.804	67.682	399.124	—	1,721.465
2016	6.819	534.26	4.548	356.353	75.822	5.975	2,474.071	93.767	54.677	62.925	371.111	—	1,600.645
2017	5.599	443.50	3.735	295.818	75.822	5.975	2,050.688	77.721	45.320	51.990	307.603	—	1,326.838
2018	4.934	392.25	3.291	261.633	75.822	5.975	1,812.787	68.705	40.063	45.909	271.918	—	1,172.943
2019	4.348	346.92	2.900	231.399	75.822	5.975	1,602.487	60.734	35.415	40.539	240.373	—	1,036.899
2020	3.831	306.83	2.555	204.659	75.822	5.975	1,416.586	53.689	31.307	35.798	212.488	—	916.636
2021	3.376	271.38	2.252	181.008	75.822	5.975	1,252.253	47.460	27.675	31.611	187.838	—	810.323
2022	2.975	240.02	1.984	160.091	75.822	5.975	1,106.986	41.955	24.464	27.914	166.048	—	716.341
2023	2.621	212.28	1.748	141.591	75.822	5.975	978.572	37.088	21.626	24.649	146.786	—	633.260
2024	2.310	187.75	1.541	125.229	75.822	5.975	865.056	32.786	19.118	21.767	129.758	—	559.816
2025	2.035	166.05	1.358	110.758	75.822	5.975	764.709	28.982	16.900	19.221	114.706	—	494.890
2026	1.793	146.86	1.196	97.958	75.822	5.975	676.003	25.621	14.940	16.973	101.400	—	437.495
2027	1.580	129.89	1.054	86.638	75.822	5.975	597.588	22.649	13.207	14.988	89.638	—	386.757
2028	1.393	114.88	0.929	76.627	75.822	5.975	528.270	20.021	11.675	13.236	79.241	—	341.904
2029	1.227	101.61	0.818	67.772	75.822	5.975	466.994	17.699	10.321	11.688	70.049	—	302.253
2030	1.081	89.87	0.721	59.940	75.822	5.975	412.825	15.646	9.123	10.321	61.924	—	267.201
2031	0.953	79.48	0.636	53.013	75.822	5.975	364.941	13.831	8.065	9.114	54.741	—	236.214
2032	0.840	70.30	0.560	46.887	75.822	5.975	322.611	12.227	7.130	8.049	48.392	—	208.821

Present Value (2008–2032) $18,549.198

Legend:
Ownership Interest: 67%
Discount Rate: 10%
Severance Tax Rate: 3.79%
Income Tax Rate: 35%
Ad Valorem Tax Rate: 2.21%
Depletion Allowance: 15% of Net Revenues

Operating Expenses:
Per barrel: $6.00
Per mmcf: $0.10

470

Panel B. Proved but Undeveloped Reserves

Year	Gross Production of Oil (MBBLS)	Gross Production of Gas (MMCF)	Net Production of Oil (MBBLS)	Net Production of Gas (MMCF)	Forward Prices Oil $/BBL	Forward Prices Gas $/MCF	Total Net Sales (M$)	Taxes Severance (M$)	Taxes Ad Valorem (M$)	Operating Expenses (M$)	Depletion Allowance (M$)	Net New Investment (M$)	Net Cash Flows (M$)
2008	27.156	4,246.32	18.113	2,832.296	80.751	6.360	19,476.050	738.142	430.421	391.908	2,921.408	30,297.425	(17,629.806)
2009	94.302	11,778.57	62.899	7,856.308	79.550	6.285	54,380.547	2,061.023	1,201.810	1,163.027	8,157.082	57,691.125	(22,365.600)
2010	167.485	16,010.02	111.712	10,678.685	78.221	6.144	74,348.106	2,817.793	1,643.093	1,738.144	11,152.216	27,258.803	20,941.372
2011	137.303	13,239.63	91.581	8,830.836	77.918	5.982	59,961.905	2,272.556	1,325.158	1,432.572	8,994.286	—	38,853.552
2012	112.561	10,948.64	75.078	7,302.741	75.822	5.975	49,326.446	1,869.472	1,090.114	1,180.743	7,398.967	—	31,960.614
2013	92.277	9,054.08	61.549	6,039.068	75.822	5.975	40,750.177	1,544.432	900.579	973.199	6,112.527	—	26,405.163
2014	75.648	7,487.35	50.457	4,994.063	75.822	5.975	33,665.302	1,275.915	744.003	802.150	5,049.795	—	21,815.530
2015	62.016	6,191.73	41.365	4,129.886	75.822	5.975	27,812.424	1,054.091	614.655	661.177	4,171.864	—	18,023.778
2016	50.841	5,120.31	33.911	3,415.247	75.822	5.975	22,977.271	870.839	507.798	544.988	3,446.591	—	14,891.177
2017	41.679	4,234.29	27.800	2,824.269	75.822	5.975	18,982.846	719.450	419.521	449.226	2,847.427	—	12,303.122
2018	34.168	3,501.58	22.790	2,335.555	75.822	5.975	15,682.939	594.383	346.593	370.296	2,352.441	—	10,164.937
2019	28.011	2,895.67	18.683	1,931.409	75.822	5.975	12,956.771	491.062	286.345	305.241	1,943.516	—	8,398.411
2020	22.963	2,394.60	15.316	1,597.196	75.822	5.975	10,704.573	405.703	236.571	251.618	1,605.686	—	6,938.932
2021	18.825	1,980.23	12.556	1,320.816	75.822	5.975	8,843.925	335.185	195.451	207.420	1,326.589	—	5,733.121
2022	15.433	1,637.57	10.294	1,092.261	75.822	5.975	7,306.745	276.926	161.479	170.988	1,096.012	—	4,736.883
2023	12.652	1,354.21	8.439	903.255	75.822	5.975	6,036.788	228.794	133.413	140.958	905.518	—	3,913.787
2024	10.372	1,119.87	6.918	746.955	75.822	5.975	4,987.594	189.030	110.226	116.204	748.139	—	3,233.736
2025	8.503	926.09	5.671	617.701	75.822	5.975	4,120.779	156.178	91.069	95.798	618.117	—	2,671.868
2026	6.971	765.84	4.649	510.814	75.822	5.975	3,404.635	129.036	75.242	78.978	510.695	—	2,207.640
2027	5.714	633.32	3.812	422.422	75.822	5.975	2,812.969	106.612	62.167	65.111	421.945	—	1,824.083
2028	4.685	523.73	3.125	349.326	75.822	5.975	2,324.140	88.085	51.364	53.681	348.621	—	1,507.175
2029	3.840	433.10	2.562	288.878	75.822	5.975	1,920.272	72.778	42.438	44.257	288.041	—	1,245.333
2030	3.148	358.16	2.100	238.890	75.822	5.975	1,586.595	60.132	35.064	36.489	237.989	—	1,028.988
2031	2.581	296.18	1.722	197.553	75.822	5.975	1,310.909	49.683	28.971	30.085	196.636	—	850.233
2032	2.116	244.93	1.411	163.368	75.822	5.975	1,083.133	41.051	23.937	24.805	162.470	-	702.536

Present Value (2008–2032) $ 60,121.216

Legend:
Ownership Interest: 67%
Discount Rate: 15%
Severance Tax Rate: 3.79%
Income Tax Rate: 35%
Ad Valorem Tax Rate: 2.21%
Depletion Allowance: 15% of Net Revenues

Operating Expenses:
Per barrel: $6.00
Per mmcf: $0.10

(Continued)

Exhibit 20.1 (*Continued*)

Panel C. Probable Reserves

Year	Gross Production of Oil (MBBLS)	Gross Production of Gas (MMCF)	Net Production of Oil (MBBLS)	Net Production of Gas (MMCF)	Forward Prices Oil $/BBL	Forward Prices Gas $/MCF	Total Net Sales (M$)	Taxes Severance (M$)	Taxes Ad Valorem (M$)	Operating Expenses (M$)	Depletion Allowance (M$)	Net New Investment (M$)	Net Cash Flows (M$)
2008	—	—	—	—	$80.751	$6.360	$ —	$ —	$ —	$ —	$ —	$1,344.822	$(1,344.822)
2009	—	—	—	—	79.550	6.285	—	—	—	—	—	3,103.590	$(3,103.590)
2010	53.488	37.442	35.676	24.974	78.221	6.144	2,944.090	111.581	65.064	$216.556	441.614	5,479.210	$(3,666.568)
2011	51.353	35.947	34.252	23.977	77.918	5.982	2,812.311	106.587	62.152	$207.912	421.847	—	$ 1,730.825
2012	42.749	29.924	28.514	19.959	75.822	5.975	2,281.214	86.458	50.415	$173.077	342.182	—	$ 1,401.085
2013	35.588	24.912	23.737	16.616	75.822	5.975	1,899.084	71.975	41.970	$144.085	284.863	—	$ 1,166.387
2014	29.629	20.947	19.763	13.972	75.822	5.975	1,581.916	59.955	34.960	$119.972	237.287	—	$ 971.619
2015	24.668	17.268	16.454	11.518	75.822	5.975	1,316.360	49.890	29.092	$ 99.873	197.454	—	$ 808.487
2016	20.540	14.378	13.700	9.590	75.822	5.975	1,096.076	41.541	24.223	$ 83.160	164.411	—	$ 673.192
2017	19.250	13.210	12.840	8.811	75.822	5.975	1,026.182	38.892	22.679	$ 77.920	153.927	—	$ 630.224
2018	18.399	12.788	12.272	8.530	75.822	5.975	981.485	37.198	21.691	$ 74.487	147.223	—	$ 602.798
2019	15.655	10.864	10.442	7.246	75.822	5.975	835.043	31.648	18.454	$ 63.378	125.256	—	$ 512.856
2020	13.321	9.229	8.885	6.156	75.822	5.975	710.451	26.926	15.701	$ 53.925	106.568	—	$ 436.333
2021	11.334	7.840	7.560	5.229	75.822	5.975	604.449	22.909	13.358	$ 45.882	90.667	—	$ 371.229
2022	9.644	6.660	6.432	4.442	75.822	5.975	514.263	19.491	11.365	$ 39.039	77.139	—	$ 315.838
2023	8.206	5.658	5.473	3.774	75.822	5.975	437.533	16.583	9.669	$ 33.216	65.630	—	$ 268.713
2024	6.982	4.806	4.657	3.206	75.822	5.975	372.252	14.108	8.227	$ 28.262	55.838	—	$ 228.619
2025	5.941	4.083	3.962	2.723	5.822	5.975	316.710	12.003	6.999	$ 24.047	47.507	—	$ 194.507
2026	5.055	3.469	3.371	2.314	75.822	5.975	269.456	10.212	5.955	$ 20.460	40.418	—	$ 165.485
2027	4.301	2.947	2.869	1.965	75.822	5.975	229.252	8.689	5.066	$ 17.409	34.388	—	$ 140.793
2028	3.659	2.503	2.441	1.670	75.822	5.975	195.047	7.392	4.311	$ 14.812	29.257	—	$ 119.786
2029	3.114	2.126	2.077	1.418	75.822	5.975	165.946	6.289	3.667	$ 12.603	24.892	—	$ 101.913

2030	2.649	1.806	1.767	1.205	75.822	5.975	141.186	5.351	3.120	$ 10.723	21.178	—	$ 86.707
2031	2.254	1.535	1.504	1.024	75.822	5.975	120.121	4.553	2.655	$ 9.124	18.018	—	$ 73.770
2032	1.918	1.304	1.279	0.870	75.822	5.975	102.198	3.873	2.259	$ 7.763	15.330	—	$ 62.763

Present Value (2008–2032) $(2,806.566)

Legend:

Ownership Interest: 67%

Discount Rate: 25%

Severance Tax Rate: 3.79%

Income Tax Rate: 35%

Ad Valorem Tax Rate: 2.21%

Depletion Allowance: 15% of Net Revenues

Operating Expenses:

Per barrel: $6.00

Per mmcf: $0.10

Terminology:

Gross production—total production from the property.

Net production—PKO's share of production (2/3rds).

Forward prices—from the forward price curve for years 2008–2012 and assumed to be flat thereafter.

Severance taxes—3.79% of net sales revenues.

Ad valorem taxes—2.21% of net sales revenues.

Operating expenses—estimated lifting costs for annual production. The cost per barrel of oil is estimated at $6.00 while the cost per mcf of natural gas is $0.10.

Depletion allowance—based on 15% percent of revenues.

Net new investment—drilling and development cost.

Net cash flow—after-tax income plus depletion allowance minus net new investment.

Present value (2008–2032)—present value of net cash flows for these years discounted using 10% for proven developed and producing reserves, 15% for proved but undeveloped reserves, and 25% for probable reserves.

Exhibit 20.2 Simulation Parameters

Oil and gas prices	Assume that oil and gas prices are sold forward for 2010–2012 using the prices reported in Exhibit 20.1. Beginning in 2013 and extending through to 2032 prices are assumed to follow geometric Brownian motion (see the appendix for an explanation of this method for describing the evolution of random oil and gas prices over time). The mean rate of change in both oil and gas prices is assumed to be zero and the standard deviation in annual price changes for oil is $0.25 and $0.35 for natural gas.
Oil and gas volumes	At the end of 2009 and at the conclusion of the second year of exploration and development, the volume of oil and gas volumes will become known. However, today (in 2007) the volumes are unknown and can best be described by a uniform distribution with maximum value equal to 2.5 times the expected volumes listed in Exhibit 20.1 and a minimum equal to 0 times the expected volume.
Operating expenses	The operating expenses per barrel of oil and per mmcf of gas have most likely values of $6.00 and $0.10, respectively. The maximum operating costs for oil and gas are $9.00 per barrel of oil and $0.13 per mmcf for gas, while the corresponding minimum values are $3.00 per barrel of oil and $0.07 per mmcf of gas. Once determined, these operating expenses remain constant over the life of the property.

APPENDIX

Simulating Oil Prices Using Geometric Brownian Motion

We will assume that oil prices are lognormally distributed. This means that the logarithm of the oil price at any time is a normally distributed random variable. To define oil prices using this model, we need the following definitions:

- P_0 = price of oil now (time = 0), which is known or observed.
- t = any future time measured in years.
- P_t = price of the oil in year t. This is a random variable, and its value is not known until time t.
- Z = a standard normal random variable with mean zero and standard deviation 1.
- μ = mean percentage growth rate (per year) in the price of oil expressed as a decimal.
- σ = standard deviation of the growth rate of the oil price (per year) expressed as a decimal.

We can now express the price of oil at some future period, t, as follows:

$$P_t = P_{0e}^{[\mu-.5\sigma^2]t+\sigma Z\sqrt{t}} \tag{20.1}$$

Note, however, that you need to simulate a sequence of oil prices beginning with the price one year hence, followed by the price two years hence, and so forth.

In this instance the time interval t is always one year. Consequently, the oil price at the end of year 1 is found by solving the following equation:

$$P_1 = P_{0e}^{[\mu - .5\sigma^2] + \sigma Z} \tag{20.1a}$$

where t no longer appears in the model since it equals one. Similarly, the price for year 2 is found as follows:

$$P_2 = P_{1e}^{[\mu - .5\sigma^2] + \sigma Z} \tag{20.1b}$$

where P_1 is the simulated price from (1a).

To implement the Brownian motion price process requires estimates of its two parameters: μ_{annual} and σ_{annual}. These estimates can be derived from historical prices where those prices are thought to be reflective of the distribution of future prices. Finally, Z = a normally distributed random variable with mean zero and standard deviation of one.

DISCUSSION QUESTIONS

1. Construct a spreadsheet model to calculate the cash flows for the proposed E&P acquisition of the proved developed and producing reserve category. Be careful to link your model's cells. That is, once a number has been coded in your spreadsheet always refer to that cell location for all future uses of that number (if you type the same number in your spreadsheet more than once, your model is not fully linked). Include in your model an estimate of the present value of the estimated future project cash flows for each reserve category.

2. Use your spreadsheet model from question 1 above and the "goal seek" function to answer the following questions:
   - If PKO anticipates having to pay $80 million for the entire property, what percent change in the price per barrel of oil would it take to produce a zero NPV?
   - What percent change in anticipated production volumes would be required to produce a zero NPV for the property? You may assume that volumes shift for all future years by a constant percent.

3. In analyzing the values of all three reserve categories, PKO uses forward prices for oil and gas for a period of five years and rolls this hedge year-to-year such that five years of production is assumed to be hedged at all times. This practice effectively eliminates price risk from the project cash flows for the period of the hedge. How should this fact impact the choice of discount rates?

4. Construct a simulation model to explore the value of the probable reserves. Incorporate the sources of uncertainty included in Exhibit 20.2 and incorporate consideration for the option to shut down development at the end of year 2 should the project prove to be unprofitable.

NOTES

1. Unproved reserves are categorized as probable and possible reserves.
2. PKO hedged out five years of production. They did not hedge further into the future because of market limitations; however, they kept a full five years of hedged production using a rolling hedge.

ABOUT THE CONTRIBUTORS

John D. Martin holds the Carr P. Collins Chair in Finance in the Hankamer School of Business at Baylor University, where he teaches in the Baylor EMBA programs and has three times been selected as the outstanding teacher. Martin joined the Baylor faculty in 1998 after spending 17 years on the faculty of the University of Texas at Austin. Over his career he has published over 50 articles in the leading finance journals including papers in the *Journal of Finance*, *Journal of Financial Economics*, *Journal of Financial and Quantitative Analysis*, *Journal of Monetary Economics*, and *Management Science*. Copies of his recent papers can be seen at http://papers.ssrn.com/sol3/cf_dev/AbsByAuth.cfm?per_id=17247. His recent research has spanned issues related to the economics of unconventional energy sources (both wind and shale gas), the hidden cost of venture capital, and managed versus unmanaged changes in capital structures. Martin is also coauthor of several books including *Financial Management: Principles and Practice*, 11th ed. (Prentice Hall); *Foundations of Finance*, 7th ed. (Prentice Hall); *Theory of Finance* (Dryden Press); *Financial Analysis*, 3rd ed. (McGraw Hill); *Valuation: The Art & Science of Corporate Investment Decisions*, 2nd ed. (Prentice Hall); and *Value Based Management with Social Responsibility*, 2nd ed. (Oxford University Press).

J. Douglas Ramsey, PhD, is the Vice President-Finance, treasurer, and Special Assistant to the Chairman at Exco Partners GP LP LLC, and treasurer and vice president at EXCO Resources, Inc. Dr. Ramsey was previously employed as financial planning manager by Coda Energy, Inc.

Sheridan Titman, PhD holds the Walter W. Mcallister Centennial Chair in Financial Services and is a professor of finance in the Department of Finance at the McCombs School of Business, at the University of Texas at Austin (UT). He is also the director of the Energy Management and Innovation Center at UT. His research interests include both investments and corporate finance, and he has published and consulted in both of these areas. He currently blogs on energy policy from a financial economist's perspective. Having co-authored a leading advanced corporate finance textbook entitled *Financial Markets and Corporate Strategy*, Dr. Titman has served on the editorial boards of leading academic journals. He is a past director of the American Finance Association and a current director of both the Asia Pacific Finance Association and the Western Finance Association. Professor Titman holds a BS from the University of Colorado and an MS and PhD from Carnegie-Mellon University. He has served on the faculties of UCLA, the Hong Kong University of Science and Technology, and Boston College. He has also worked in Washington. DC, as special assistant to the assistant secretary of the Treasury for Economic Policy. He is a research associate of the National Bureau of Economic Research.

Financial Analysis of the Purchase of a Hybrid Consumer Vehicle

DON M. CHANCE
James C. Flores Endowed Chair of MBA Studies and Professor of Finance
at the E. J. Ourso College of Business at Louisiana State University

PRATIK DHAR
Senior Business Systems Analyst at the Shaw Group Inc.

BETTY J. SIMKINS
Williams Companies Professor of Business and Professor of Finance at Oklahoma
State University's Spears School of Business

INTRODUCTION

Hybrid vehicles combine many of the best features of standard combustion engine vehicles with the use of electricity. For purposes of this chapter, we are defining hybrid vehicles as gasoline-electric hybrids and henceforth, refer to them as hybrids in the discussion. Natural gas vehicles and dual-fuel vehicles are not included in this chapter.

The principal advantage of hybrids is the considerable improvement in gas mileage, with the secondary benefit being a lower level of emissions. Nonetheless, hybrid vehicles are more costly, and the majority of consumers have clearly indicated a reluctance to pay the additional price of a hybrid to save money. Anecdotal evidence suggests that many owners of hybrid vehicles make their purchases based on environmental and social factors.

There are numerous articles on the issue of whether hybrids are worth their additional cost.[1] Views are strong, indeed passionate, on both sides of the issue. Yet, there has apparently been no published financial analysis on whether the additional cost of a hybrid vehicle is justified by the savings in fuel costs. Of course, the environmental and social costs of traditional engines cannot truly be weighed, but a financial analysis can at least isolate one factor, the pure fuel costs savings, leaving the individual or company with a clearer picture of what a hybrid truly costs.

Then, if a hybrid cannot be justified on a pure financial basis, an individual or company who purchases such a car will at least know that the reason is not financial.[2]

HYBRID VEHICLES: CHARACTERISTICS, PROS, AND CONS

A traditional combustion engine vehicle burns some form of fossil fuel. Its range is limited only by the vehicle's fuel efficiency (miles per gallon) and the size of its fuel tank, an attractive feature of the combustion engine vehicle. Fuel has generally been in plentiful supply, though occasionally costly, but this supply is constrained by the amount of fossil fuels contained within the earth's surface. Hence, without development of new fuel sources, the concept of a combustion engine vehicle has a finite life, though this point is clearly not in the near future. Larger vehicles, while normally carrying larger fuel tanks, almost always have larger engines and consume more fuel for a given driving distance. Thus, combustion engines consume a limited resource. Of course, with this consumption comes the emission of harmful pollutants.

Electric vehicles have existed, in concept if not in practice, for about as long as have combustion vehicles but have never been commercially successful. Electric vehicles operate off of batteries, which must be periodically recharged, though they can draw energy from the motor itself. This process, similar to how an alternator charges itself from the engine and provides battery power to the lights, radio, and other devices, can, however, slow the car down. Also, some electric vehicles emit almost no pollution but light hybrids do emit some pollution.[3] Thus, the electric vehicle has many advantages and disadvantages in relation to the combustion engine vehicle.

For all of their advantages, pure electric vehicles have never been able to overcome the inconvenience of being unable to travel very far, usually no more than 100 miles, without recharging. Hybrid vehicles attempt to overcome this disadvantage by blending both an electric motor and a combustion engine. A major advantage of a hybrid is that the combustion engine can be much smaller than in a traditional vehicle. A smaller engine is lighter and operates more efficiently. Therefore, a smaller engine can take a car a far greater distance for a given amount of fuel. Of course, a disadvantage of a smaller engine is that it has less power required for such situations as rapid acceleration or steep inclines. Larger engines are designed for these situations, even though they occur somewhat infrequently, but large engines still remain popular among drivers. Hybrids also have the ability to use the electric motor to slow down the car, rather than use the brake, which results in wasted energy and are also able to use more efficient tires that save some energy. In addition, hybrids are often made out of lighter materials, both to save on fuel and also because they have a lot less power and must be lighter.

Most importantly, however, hybrids use the more efficient energy source whenever they can. Combustion engines operate most efficiently at constant speeds. Hence, a hybrid will generally use the combustion engine on the highway and the battery-operated motor during stop-and-go traffic, though there are some exceptions. Even during highway driving, hybrids draw on both the motor and the engine in the most efficient manner possible. As noted, hybrids emit far less

pollution than combustion engines, a result due to a number of factors, the most obvious of which is that the combustion engine is not in use at all times.

A major downside of a hybrid is that it is virtually always more expensive than a combustion vehicle and sometimes considerably more expensive. As we show later, markups over standard vehicles vary from less than 2 percent to more than 40 percent.[4] It is unclear whether the difference in price is due to the pure cost of the additional features or due to the perceived ability of the manufacturer to extract a greater premium from the buyer's desire to reduce his or her carbon footprint and to save on fuel consumption. This is a point we address. While it is impossible to determine what is a reasonable price a person might pay for reducing pollution, it is not difficult to determine whether the additional cost of the hybrid is offset by fuel savings. If it is not, then we have an estimate of what informed consumers are willing to pay to reduce their environmental footprint from the use of their automobiles.

FINANCIAL ANALYSIS OF THE PURCHASE OF A HYBRID: A CASE STUDY OF THE CHEVROLET MALIBU

Students of finance learn that a capital investment decision, sometimes known as a capital budgeting decision, should be made using the concept of net present value or NPV. The NPV of a capital investment decision is basically defined as the present value of the expected cash inflows from a capital investment less the initial outlay for the investment. The present value of the expected cash inflows is determined by discounting the expected cash inflows at an appropriate opportunity cost that reflects the time value of money, expected inflation, and the risk of the cash flows. This discount rate should be one that would be applicable in well-functioning capital markets for investments with comparable risk, because such an investment alternative reflects the decision maker's opportunity cost. If the computed NPV is positive, the investment should be undertaken because the value of the expected cash to be received exceeds the value of the expected cash to be paid, including the upfront cost and any residual cost or financial benefit.[5] For purposes of this paper, we will not use the term NPV, but refer to this concept as the *value* of a hybrid vehicle, which it should be remembered is the marginal value over that of the standard version of the same vehicle.

With the exception of immediate, upfront cash flows, most of the data used in such an analysis are estimates. The more uncertainty associated with estimates, the higher the discount rate that should be used. With a higher discount rate, the value will be lower, and hence it will be more difficult to justify the investment, which is consistent with the notion of risk-averse decision makers.

Common capital investment problems encountered in finance texts and in practice involve a single decision: go or no-go. Should a new product be launched? Should a factory be built? Should a machine be purchased? Other decisions involve the replacement of one asset with another. In that case, the new asset requires an outlay, and only the incremental cash generated or saved by the new asset relative to the old is compared to this outlay. Yet another type of decision is the case of mutual exclusivity. Two investments can accomplish the same objective, but

only one can be chosen. Analysis can either proceed by finding the value of one investment and comparing it independently to the value of the other or by conducting a relative valuation comparison. One investment, usually the less expensive, is defined as the base, and the other is defined as the increment. Assuming the value of the base is positive, a positive value to the incremental cash flows from the second investment leads to the conclusion that the additional investment is worthwhile and, therefore, the second investment is the one chosen.

Though, in reality, many investments do not directly generate cash inflows and no particular cash inflows are necessarily attributed to a particular asset, typical analyses in finance textbooks associate a particular investment with the generation of specific incremental cash flows. For example, a firm might purchase a piece of equipment that will be used to manufacture a product to be sold. Though cash from sales will be generated, the firm might be considering two alternative machines with which to produce the product. Assuming no difference in quality of the product, sales should be the same regardless of the machine. Hence, the decision of which machine to use would be based on costs only. As is commonly the case, one machine may well cost more, but it may have lower operating costs.

It is the incremental analysis of operating costs in comparison to a typically higher purchase price of the unit itself that is the essence of the hybrid vehicle purchase decision. We will assume that the consumer is in need of a vehicle and has narrowed the choice to two cars, one a hybrid and the other a standard version of the same vehicle.[6] Although we conduct the analysis with a set of all hybrids vehicles that have corresponding standard versions, we illustrate the analysis using a 2009 Chevrolet Malibu.[7]

To undertake this analysis, we need certain information for both cars. We need the purchase price and estimates of mileage and resale values. We then need to make an assumption about the life of the vehicle, the number of miles driven each year, operating costs and maintenance, and the distribution of miles in the city relative to the highway. We also need a discount rate to apply to the estimated future cash flows and a price for gasoline.

Price information and mileage estimates on the cars were obtained from Kelly Blue Book (www.kbb.com). Resale values are obtained using a depreciation calculator at www.carprice.com.[8] Operating costs and maintenance, other than fuel, are assumed to be the same.[9] We assume a five-year life and 12,000 miles driven per year.[10] We assume that 60 percent of the miles are in the city. We use a discount rate of 4 percent, reflecting the fact that while there is some uncertainty, it is much lower than that associated with analysis of corporate cash flows and stock values. The price of gasoline at the time of the analysis was $3.50. We will vary some of these inputs. We make no considerations for financing costs, as financial theory argues that financing should be separated from the decision of which assets to hold. Moreover, given our concern only with the relative value of the hybrid, there are unlikely to be any differences attributable to financing.

Exhibit 21.1 presents the analysis for the Chevy Malibu, which we will walk though here. The standard Chevy Malibu costs $21,192, while the hybrid costs $25,192. We estimate the resale value of the hybrid after 5 years at $9,179, and the resale value of the standard after 5 years at $7,749. The standard vehicle is rated at 22 mpg in the city and 30 mpg on the highway. The hybrid is rated at 26 mpg in the city and 34 mpg on the highway. The analysis compares the incremental

Exhibit 21.1 Inputs for Analysis of 2009 Chevrolet Malibu Hybrid Purchase

	Hybrid	Standard
Purchase price	$25,192	$21,192
Resale value (after 5 years)	$9,179	$7,749
City mileage	26	22
Highway mileage	34	30
Value of hybrid over standard	−$1,747	

	Present Value of Yearly Cash Flows		
Year	PV of Hybrid	PV of Standard	PV Difference (PV Hybrid–PV Standard)
0	−$25,192	−$21,192	−$4,000
1	−$1,407	−$1,640	$233
2	−$1,353	−$1,577	$224
3	−$1,301	−$1,516	$215
4	−$1,251	−$1,458	$207
5	$6,342	$4,967	$1,375
Total	−$24,162	−$22,415	−$1,747

cost and differential resale value of the hybrid to the incremental gasoline savings. At 12,000 miles with 60 percent in the city, we assume 7,200 city miles and 4,800 highway miles. For the hybrid, at mileage of 26/34 (city/highway), 276.92 gallons would be consumed in city driving and 141.18 in highway driving. For the standard, at mileage of 22/30, 327.27 gallons would be consumed in city driving and 160 in highway driving. At $3.50 a gallon, annual fuel costs would be $1,463 for the hybrid and $1,705 for the standard for a difference of $242 a year. The residual resale value difference is $1,430 in favor of the hybrid.

The value calculation is as follows:

$$-\$4,000 + \$242\left((1 - (1.04)^{-5})/(0.04)\right) + (\$9,179 - \$7,749)(1.04)^{-5} = -\$1,747$$

Based on these assumptions, we see that the value of the purchase of a 2009 Chevrolet Malibu hybrid is approximately −$1,747.[11] Nonetheless, any capital investment analysis should recognize that the inputs are just estimates and could vary widely. Exhibit 21.2 shows four graphs depicting the value of the hybrid investment for the Chevy Malibu by varying the discount rate, the price of gasoline, annual miles driven, and the city/total miles distribution. There is no discount rate low enough to result in a breakeven, but a gasoline price of more than $9.20 or driving at least 31,443 miles per year do result in an advantage for the hybrid. The ratio of highway to city miles is, by definition, between 0 percent and 100 percent, and there is no ratio within that range that results in an advantage to the hybrid. The hybrid advantage is greatest with more city miles, however, which is a result of the fact that when driving at a high speed on a highway, the vehicle operates with its standard combustion engine. This latter point is an important factor in understanding the advantages and disadvantages of hybrid vehicles. The hybrid

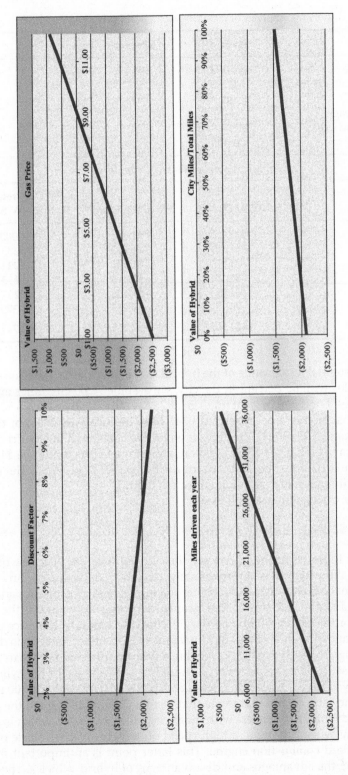

Exhibit 21.2 Sensitivity Analysis of Purchase of Hybrid Chevrolet Malibu

gets better gas mileage but to take maximum advantage of that fact, one would naturally think that more miles should be driven. For most consumers, however, greater mileage is accumulated primarily by highway driving, such as commuting from a suburb to a city or from a city to a city or by taking many long trips. Thus, the main advantage of a hybrid is lost when you need it to justify the price premium.

This analysis was conducted for 14 other 2009 vehicles that exist in both standard and hybrid versions. We now look at these results.

ANALYSIS OF 14 HYBRID AND STANDARD COUNTERPARTS

Exhibit 21.3 lists the input information for the 14 other vehicles that are produced in both hybrid and standard versions. It is interesting to note that while all of the standard vehicles obtain better mileage on the highway than in the city, some hybrids get better mileage in the city. For example, the hybrid Ford Escape, Mercury Mariner (2WD and 4WD), Nissan Altima, and Toyota Highlander all perform better in the city, and the Chevrolet Tahoe 4WD performs equally in the city and highway, while the Tahoe 2WD has only a slight edge on the highway.

Exhibit 21.4 provides the values and breakevens of hybrid purchases of these 14 vehicles. We see that the hybrid advantage appears only in very large SUV-type vehicles. For all vehicles except the Chevrolet Tahoe and GMC Yukon, the value of the hybrid purchase is negative, ranging from –$1,271 for the Honda Civic to –$3,880 for the Ford Escape 4WD. Moreover, the breakeven gas price for all of these 10 vehicles is at least $5.30, and the ratio of city miles to total miles is more than 100 percent. The breakeven total miles vary from around 18,000 to as much as

Exhibit 21.3 Inputs for Other Vehicles

	Purchase Price		Highway/City Mileage		Resale Value	
	Hybrid	Standard	Hybrid	Standard	Hybrid	Standard
Chevrolet Tahoe 2WD	$49,349	$48,595	22/21	20/14	$9,272	$6,616
Chevrolet Tahoe 4WD	$52,042	$51,331	20/20	20/14	$9,778	$7,349
Ford Escape 2WD	$30,370	$21,926	31/34	28/20	$10,876	$7,981
Ford Escape 4WD	$32,120	$23,602	27/29	25/19	$11,510	$8,614
GMC Yukon 2WD	$51,870	$49,552	22/21	19/12	$18,786	$18,067
GMC Yukon 4WD	$54,680	$52,458	20/20	19/12	$19,804	$19,152
Honda Civic	$23,834	$16,636	45/40	36/25	$13,646	$8,988
Mercury Mariner 2WD	$30,170	$22,357	31/34	28/20	$11,037	$8,343
Mercury Mariner 4WD	$31,903	$24,014	27/29	25/19	$11,671	$8,977
Nissan Altima	$26,525	$19,977	33/35	31/23	$9,480	$7,847
Saturn Aura	$26,910	$23,325	34/26	33/22	$9,264	$7,966
Saturn Vue	$28,855	$23,256	32/25	26/19	$4,739	$3,995
Toyota Camry	$26,870	$20,368	34/33	31/21	$14,623	$11,375
Toyota Highlander	$35,445	$29,795	25/27	23/17	$12,634	$10,733

Exhibit 21.4 Values and Breaks of Hybrid Purchase for 14 Vehicles

Vehicle (all 2009)	Value of Hybrid Purchase	Breakeven Points		
		Gas Price	Miles Driven per Year	City Miles/ Total Miles
Chevrolet Tahoe 2WD	$4,440	< $0.00	< 0	< 0%
Chevrolet Tahoe 4WD	$3,690	< $0.00	< 0	< 0%
Ford Escape 2WD	−$3,498	$8.30	28,334	> 100%
Ford Escape 4WD	−$3,880	$9.50	32,625	> 100%
GMC Yukon 2WD	$2,816	$1.30	4,562	7%
GMC Yukon 4WD	$2,250	$1.50	5,140	21%
Honda Civic	−$1,271	$5.60	19,270	> 100%
Mercury Mariner 2WD	$3,030	$7.60	26,158	> 100%
Mercury Mariner 4WD	−$3,417	$8.80	30,160	> 100%
Nissan Altima	−$3,387	$10.00	34,349	> 100%
Saturn Aura	−$1,667	$10.40	35,497	> 100%
Saturn Vue	−$3,032	$8.90	30,595	> 100%
Toyota Camry	−$1,677	$6.20	21,336	> 100%
Toyota Highlander	−$1,383	$5.30	18,136	> 100%

35,000, which is a relatively large number of miles for a consumer, but nonetheless, does suggest that a consumer who drives a lot could benefit from a hybrid.[12] Embedded within the assumption that leads to the breakeven mileage is a 60 percent versus 40 percent division of city to highway driving. It seems likely that most consumers who drive an unusually large number of miles probably do so because of highway driving, where the combustion engine takes over.

The real advantage of hybrids comes in with the large SUVs. A hybrid SUV can be economically justified at any level of gas price, any number of miles driven, and at a very low ratio of city to total miles.[13] The Toyota Highlander, also an SUV albeit a smaller one, does show a negative hybrid value, but its breakeven gas price and miles are the lowest of the other vehicles. Thus, it is clear that hybrids offer the greatest advantage with large vehicles.

The reason for the hybrid advantage for SUVs is not necessarily the marginal improvements in fuel efficiency. It may well be the pricing. Exhibit 21.5 illustrates the percentage markups of the 15 vehicles examined in this study. Note the tremendous difference in the markups on the two Chevrolet Tahoe and GMC Yukons in comparison to the other much smaller vehicles. The large SUV markups range from 1 percent to under 5 percent, while the other vehicle markups range from 15 percent to 43 percent.

This type of pattern is inconsistent with the efficiency advantage of the hybrid. We compute a blended fuel efficiency ratio by determining the average gas mileage based on 60 percent city driving and 40 percent highway driving. Then we compute the percentage difference between the hybrid blended mileage and the standard blended mileage. The results are illustrated in Exhibit 21.6. A number such as 30 percent means that the hybrid blended mileage is 30 percent higher than the standard mileage. Clearly the SUV-type vehicles do not have a lower degree of fuel efficiency, corresponding to their smaller markups. There is a modest Pearson

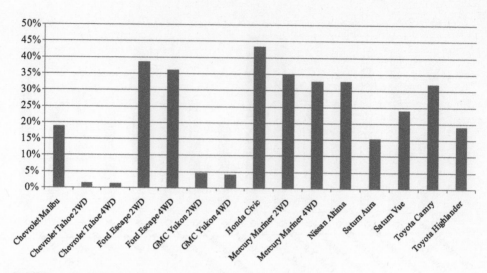

Exhibit 21.5   Relative Markups of Hybrid over Standard Version

correlation of 0.33 and a Spearman rank correlation of 0.46, but squaring these values reveals that only a small percentage of the pricing variation is accounted for by fuel efficiency.[14]

Blended mileage captures only the instantaneous advantage of a hybrid. Another dimension of efficiency is reflected in fuel consumption over a common driving distance. In other words, a vehicle may have only a slight advantage at a

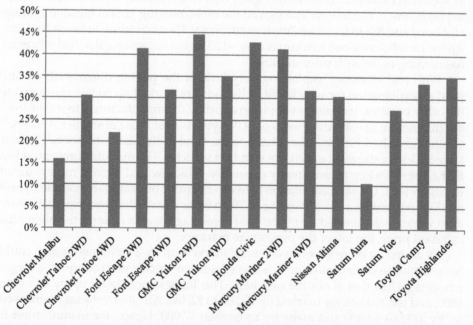

Exhibit 21.6   Relative Differences in Fuel Efficiency of Hybrid over Standard Vehicles

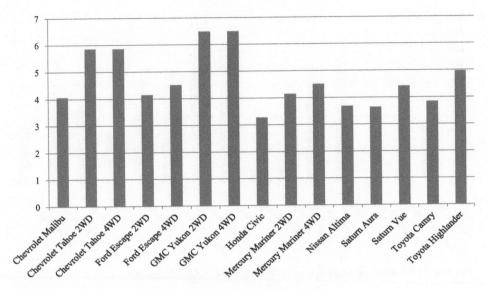

Exhibit 21.7   Fuel Consumption Efficiency of Hybrid Vehicles

given instance but over a common driving distance, that advantage can be magnified. To address this concern, we calculate a new measure called fuel consumption efficiency, which is simply the number of gallons of fuel required to drive 100 miles, broken down as 60 percent in the city and 40 percent on the highway. The results, as shown in Exhibit 21.7, are only slightly different with only a few vehicles changing positions.[15] The Saturn Vue moved the most, ranking 12th in blended mileage efficiency and 8th in fuel consumption efficiency. The correlation between fuel consumption efficiency and markup is only –0.23, again suggesting that fuel efficiency has nothing to do with price markup.

With fuel efficiency explaining very little of the pricing differential, we still need an explanation for why the SUV hybrids are marked up so low compared to the other vehicles. It could be simply an effort by the manufacturers to set the pricing differential to encourage sales of SUV hybrids over those of smaller vehicles.[16] On the other hand it could be related to the level of the standard price. The four large SUVs are the most expensive standard vehicles. The manufacturer could feel that a large markup on an already expensive vehicle would make it more difficult to sell. Indeed, the rank correlation between the price of a standard and the hybrid markup percentage is a very strong –0.79. In other words, the most expensive standard vehicles are marked up by the least percentage, and in general, the higher the standard price, the lower the percentage markup.

Of course, a more expensive vehicle marked up by a small percentage could have the same dollar markup as a less expensive vehicle marked up by a larger percentage, but that is not the case here. The Tahoes are marked up by less than $800, and the Yukons are marked up $2,200 to $2,400. All other vehicles are marked up by at least $3,500 and many by more than $7,000. Hence, the manufacturer is clearly concerned about markup of an already-expensive vehicle.

CONCLUSION

We examine the relative efficiency and pricing differential of 15 hybrid vehicles in comparison to their standard versions and find a few limited circumstances in which a hybrid is advisable on pure financial grounds. To understand the reason, we must first recall that hybrids do not necessarily perform more efficiently than standard vehicles. A hybrid's mileage advantage is primarily in the high traffic, stop-and-go environment of a city. On the highway, the combustion engine takes over. For the average consumer, a large number of miles driven is typically obtained by highway driving. Hence, the hybrid is at an automatic disadvantage from the start. Its modest advantage in mileage must be coupled with high mileage. High mileage is, however, primarily through highway driving, in which case the hybrid's combustion engine takes over.

Examining the cost differential (both initial and resale value) and mileage differential, we find that hybrids can rarely be justified for the typical consumer driving an average-size vehicle. The number of miles required to be driven and the combination of city and highway driving required for the hybrid to have its advantage simply are not there for most consumers. Businesses such as taxis and delivery services, however, could accumulate enough city miles to justify a hybrid purchase. For consumers, the real advantage of the hybrid comes with the large-SUV type vehicles, but this result is not due to efficiency. The hybrid versions of these vehicles are no more efficient than are the hybrid versions of smaller vehicles. The advantage lies in the relatively small markups over the standard vehicles. These markups do not appear related to any particular preference the manufacturer has in promoting hybrid versions of large SUVs. In their standard versions, these vehicles are already very expensive. The markup is nothing more than the manufacturer's reluctance to take an already-expensive vehicle and push its price up significantly higher.

In addition to environmental considerations, hybrids can also offer some nonpecuniary advantages such as the ability to drive in an HOV lane, designated hybrid parking spots, and possibly lower insurance costs. In general, hybrids also help reduce our nation's dependency on other countries for fossil fuels and thus indirectly improve national security. In making a decision of whether to purchase a hybrid, these factors can be weighed against the pure financial considerations as documented in this paper.

DISCUSSION QUESTIONS

1. Which of the cars are justified based on economic analysis at current gasoline prices, based on driving 12,000 miles per year? List and explain.

2. Select four of the cars to compare and contrast on their economic justification. For these four cars, state at what gasoline price each is justified. Use "goal seek" in Excel or another method to calculate.

3. Under what conditions can you justify a hybrid based on the spreadsheet analysis?

4. List other advantages and disadvantages of a hybrid car that may not be considered in this economic analysis.

5. Explore the Excel spreadsheet and discuss your general observations about the analysis involved in determining the economics of hybrids.

6. Select a hybrid car that has the best economics and compute the payback period.

7. How are maintenance costs affected by driving a hybrid as compared to a normal car?

8. Repeat the analysis for a current or next year's hybrid vehicle of your choice. Is the car justified based on your economic analysis assuming 12,000 miles are driven per year?

NOTES

1. See, for example, *Consumer Reports* (2008), Lave and MacLean (2008), and the related editorial responses in *IEEE Spectrum*, May, 2001.

2. While it is well known that many people buy hybrids because they feel a moral obligation to reduce their carbon footprint, a study by Heffner, Kurani, and Turrentine (2005) reveals that for many consumers, a hybrid vehicle is used to project an image of social responsibility. In other words, many consumers not only want to reduce the amount of pollution they produce but also make sure that others known they are doing so.

3. Full hybrid is often used when the vehicle can launch forward at low speeds without consuming any gasoline. Examples include Toyota, Lexus, and Ford hybrids. The Honda hybrids cannot do this. Some General Motors hybrids are full hybrids, and others are not. Mild hybrid cars are able to move from a complete stop only if the internal combustion engine is engaged, and use the electric motor primarily to assist the gas engine when extra power is needed. All hybrids, both full and mild, require use of the gas engine when reaching higher speeds around 25 mph or more. This, of course, depends on how the car is driven.

4. Henceforth, we will refer to a vehicle with a traditional combustion engine as a *standard* vehicle.

5. The terminology of *net present value* and its formal definition are perhaps unfortunate misnomers, having survived partially out of entrenchment in the long history of finance textbooks. The so-called NPV is actually the value generated by undertaking the investment. To define this concept as the present value of the expected cash inflows minus the initial outlay, as is so standard, is not sufficiently general. Many projects do not have an initial outlay, many have outlays spread over multiple years, and some have special termination cash flows. Similarly, many projects have initial inflows followed by outflows later. While standard analysis properly handles all of these cash flows by merely keeping their signs correct, the overall practice would be more broadly and accurately defined as simply the process of valuation. Moreover, most finance textbooks seem to have changed little over the years and have failed to keep up with a rapidly changing economy. Machines and factories are the most common examples given of capital investment decisions, but they seem oddly displaced in this modern service-oriented economy. Finally, it should be noted that reference to the process as capital *budgeting* seems misplaced as well. A budget implies a financial constraint, which seems appropriate only in the context of limited or rationed capital. Finance textbooks show why capital should not be rationed: if NPV is positive, the marginal cost of additional capital is more than covered. In this article, we will simply refer to the so-called capital budget process as determining the *value* of a hybrid vehicle purchase.

6. The most successful hybrid vehicle, the Toyota Prius, is not available in a standard version. Thus, such a comparison is not undertaken in this study, though the methodology used here could be applied to the comparison of a Prius to any other standard vehicle.

7. The Malibu is considered a "mild hybrid," which means it uses the gasoline engine for powering most of the time, unlike the Prius or Toyota Camry Hybrid.

8. www.carprice.com/depreciation-calculator.

9. See Anderson (2009), who finds that while early-year hybrids were more expensive to repair, in more recent years, repair costs are nearly the same. See also www.hybridcars.com/cars.html#maintain, which states that "Maintaining a hybrid doesn't cost any more than a conventional car, and may even cost less due to decreased

wear and tear on the engine and braking system." Moreover, the motor and battery require virtually no maintenance at all. See also http://ask.cars.com/2007/12/hybrid-maintena.html. These articles suggest that maintenance is very similar and should be similar in cost. Numerous other sources state that hybrids are no more costly to maintain and operate than are standard combustion engine vehicles.

10. This estimate is obtained from the EPA web site, www.epa.gov/oms/climate/420f05004.htm, and represents the average number of miles driven per year by a passenger car in the United States.

11. Although it has pros and cons, the payback method is a commonly used evaluative technique in practice. For the Chevy Malibu under these assumptions, the payback is 17 years, far more than the likely life of the car.

12. Recall that EPA data show that the average consumer drives 12,000 miles a year. Thus, if 18,000 miles is required to justify a hybrid, as for the Toyota Highlander, the consumer would need to drive 50% more than average. Clearly there are some consumers who do so, but probably not many. Most of the remaining non-SUV vehicles require at least twice and in several cases almost three times the average.

13. The miles driven figure of "< 0" for the two Chevrolet Tahoe models means that the hybrid value is positive at all levels of miles driven. It moves toward zero at low levels of miles and would be theoretically zero at negative miles, though clearly the concept of negative miles is meaningless. The city to total miles ratio of "< 0%" means that the value turns negative at negative city miles, another meaningless concept. In short, at all ranges of miles driven and breakdowns between city and highway miles the value of the hybrid purchase is positive. For the Yukon, the value is negative only below 7% and 21% (2WD and 4WD). It should be noted that driving more will reduce resale value so there is some tradeoff here.

14. The only other factor that could account for differences in pricing is resale value, but this variable is influenced so heavily by the initial price that its connection to differences in the initial price is likely to be meaningless. The hybrid markup is unlikely to be set by the manufacturers because of the hybrid's advantage in resale value.

15. Blended mileage $0.6m_c + 0.4m_h$ whereas fuel consumption efficiency is $60/m_c + 40/m_h$. A difference arises from the simple fact that a weighted average of two numbers is not the inverse of the weighted average of the inverse of two numbers.

16. The Alternative Motor Fuels Act (AMFA) enacted in 1988 provides Corporate Average Fuel Economy (CAFE) incentives for the manufacture of vehicles that use alternative fuels exclusively or in conjunction with gasoline or diesel fuel. In order to provide incentives for producing alternative fuel vehicles, manufacturers gain CAFE credits by manufacturing these vehicles, which allows them to raise their overall fleet fuel economy levels to comply with the CAFE standards. This provides another incentive for manufacturers to have a lower markup on hybrids. See National Highway Traffic Safety Administration (2011a&b).

REFERENCES

Anderson, Michael T. 2009. "What Drives Hybrid Repair Costs?" *Audatex Directions* 4: Winter, 4–8.

Consumer Reports. 2008. "Which Hybrids Save You Money?" October, 40–43.

Heffner, Reid R., Kenneth S. Kurani, and Thomas S. Turrentine. 2005. "Effects of Vehicle Image in Gasoline-Hybrid Electric Vehicles." Research Paper. Institute of Transportation Studies. University of California, Davis.

IEEE Spectrum (editorial responses). 2001. May, 79–84.

Lave, Lester B., and Heather MacLean. 2001. "Are Hybrid Vehicles Worth It?" *IEEE Spectrum*, March, 47–50.

National Highway Traffic Safety Administration. 2011a. "Report to Congress on Effects of the Alternative Motor Fuels Act CAFE Incentives Policy." Available at www.nhtsa.gov/

Laws+&+Regulations/CAFE+-+Fuel+Economy/Report+to+Congress+on+Effects+of+
the+Alternative+Motor+Fuels+Act+CAFE+Incentives+Policy. Retrieved February 22,
2011.

National Highway Traffic Safety Administration. 2011b. "The Corporate Average
Fuel Economy Program (CAFE)—Background: AMFA CAFE Credits." Available at
www.nhtsa.gov/cars/rules/rulings/cafe/alternativefuels/background.htm. Retrieved
February 22, 2011.

ABOUT THE CONTRIBUTORS

Don M. Chance, PhD, CFA, holds the James C. Flores Endowed Chair of MBA
Studies and is professor of finance at the E. J. Ourso College of Business at
Louisiana State University (LSU). He previously held the William H. Wright, Jr.
Endowed Chair for Financial Services at LSU, and the First Union Professorship
in Financial Risk Management at Virginia Tech. Prior to his academic career, he
worked for a large southeastern bank. Professor Chance has had numerous articles
published in academic and practitioner journals and has authored three books: *An
Introduction to Derivatives and Risk Management*, 9th ed., co-authored with Robert
Brooks; *Essays in Derivatives: Risk Transfer Tools and Topics Made Easy*, 2nd ed.; and
Analysis of Derivatives for the CFA Program. His recent research examines asset allocation and investment performance measurement, executive stock options, the risk
aversion of high-level executives, human aspects of risk management, corporations who accept blame and blame others, dividends as options, risk management
in sports, and the economic efficiency of hybrid vehicles. He is often quoted in the
media on matters related to derivatives and risk management as well as financial
markets and the economy in general. He has extensive experience conducting professional training programs, and his consulting practice (Omega Risk Advisors,
LLC) serves companies, organizations, and law firms. He is also involved in the
development and writing of the derivatives curriculum in the CFA program.

Pratik Dhar is a business systems analyst at the The Shaw Group Inc. in Baton
Rouge, Louisiana. He obtained his MBA from Louisiana State University.

Betty J. Simkins, PhD, is the Williams Companies Professor of Business and a
professor of finance in the Department of Finance at Oklahoma State University's
Spears School of Business where she teaches energy finance, corporate finance, and
enterprise risk management, among other courses. Betty received her PhD from
Case Western Reserve University (CWRU). She has more than 40 publications in
academic finance journals and has won awards for her research, most recently
in risk management. In addition, Dr. Simkins has won several teaching awards
including the Regents Distinguished Teaching Award. She is also very active in
the finance profession and currently serves on the board of directors for the Financial Management Association, as co-editor of the *Journal of Applied Finance*, as past
president of the Eastern Finance Association, and on the editorial boards of several
prestigious finance journals. Prior to academia, she worked in the corporate world
for Williams Companies and Conoco (now ConocoPhillips). In addition to being
co-editor of this book, in 2010 she co-edited *Enterprise Risk Management: Insights
and Analysis on Today's Leading Research and Best Practices*, also published by John
Wiley & Sons.

CHAPTER 22

ExxonMobil Corp.'s Acquisition of XTO Energy, Inc.

An Exercise in Valuation

ALLISSA A. LEE
Visiting Assistant Professor of Finance, Oklahoma State University

BETTY J. SIMKINS
Williams Companies Professor of Business and Professor of Finance, Oklahoma State University

INTRODUCTION

Mergers have long been a commonplace event in the corporate landscape. At times they are on the forefront of daily news media, sometimes not. Industries sometimes see merger waves where there is a multitude of mergers occurring. The oil and gas industry is no exception, having seen its fair share of merger waves as well. Two waves have been noted in recent history: 1980–1985 and 1998–2001.[1] The merger under consideration here did not occur in a merger wave. However, in an effort to tap into unconventional energy resources, ExxonMobil sought to acquire XTO Energy, Inc. at a 25 percent premium, a deal valued at $41 billion. It represents the largest acquisition in the industry in nearly five years. The deal was formally announced in December of 2009 and finalized in June of 2010.

Here we will be focusing on valuation. Was XTO worth the $41 billion offered by ExxonMobil? There are many different methods by which to value firms in the industry; often other industry firms are used as benchmarks in the valuation process. Several methods will be explored here. There are five questions to be addressed specifically; they include: (1) What should the acquisition price for XTO shares have been? (2) Which comparable firm is the best comparison firm for XTO? (3) Why did ExxonMobil want to acquire XTO? (4) Based on the analysis, did ExxonMobil overpay for XTO or get a bargain? (5) What additional information could help with this analysis?

The remainder of the case will be structured as follows: First, we will discuss industry characteristics followed by possible motivations for acquisition. Next, the terms of the deal will be discussed. Last, valuation and case summarization will be presented.

INDUSTRY CHARACTERISTICS

In this section, industry characteristics will be discussed. In any valuation exercise, it is important to understand the environment in which the firm operates. Economic conditions can affect different industry sectors and the firms within them differently.

The energy industry is highly competitive. There are many players in the industry; all are vying for market share, prestige, and, of course, resources. There are several subsectors within the industry. According to the Industry Classification Benchmark,[2] there are six subsectors within the oil and gas industry. Exhibit 22.1 provides a list of the subsectors and their definitions.

ExxonMobil belongs to the integrated oil and gas subsector while XTO is an exploration and production firm. The Dow Jones Oil and Gas Index (Index Symbol: DJUSEN), presented in Exhibit 22.2, shows a significant decline from mid-2008 through early 2009. The trend has since reversed, and some of its losses have been regained. Exhibit 22.3 gives the historical performance of the Dow Jones E&P Index (Index Symbol: DJSOEP). As you can see, there was a substantial decline, from mid-2008 through 2009, to less than 4,000. The index has had a sizeable rebound since, nearly doubling. Dow Jones uses industry classifications and definitions from the Industry Classification Benchmark as previously defined.

This acquisition was a major shale gas play for ExxonMobil because XTO had sizeable resources in shale gas. According to David Rosenthal, ExxonMobil vice president of investor relations, the additional acreage resulted in ExxonMobil controlling the "largest unconventional portfolio in the industry." The addition of

Exhibit 22.1   Industry Subsector Classifications

Subsector	Definition
Exploration & Production	Companies engaged in the exploration for and drilling, production, refining, and supply of oil and gas products.
Integrated Oil & Gas	Integrated oil and gas companies engaged in the exploration for and drilling, production, refining, distribution, and retail sales of oil and gas products.
Oil Equipment, Services, & Distribution	Suppliers of equipment and services to oil fields and offshore platforms, such as drilling, exploration, seismic-information services, and platform construction.
Pipelines	Operators of pipelines carrying oil, gas, or other forms of fuel. Excludes pipeline operators that derive the majority of their revenues from direct sales to end users, which are classified under Gas Distribution.
Renewable Energy Equipment	Companies that develop or manufacture renewable energy equipment utilizing sources such as solar, wind, tidal, geothermal, hydro, and waves.
Alternative Fuels	Companies that produce alternative fuels such as ethanol, methanol, hydrogen, and bio-fuels that are mainly used to power vehicles, and companies that are involved in the production of vehicle fuel cells and/or the development of alternative fueling infrastructure.

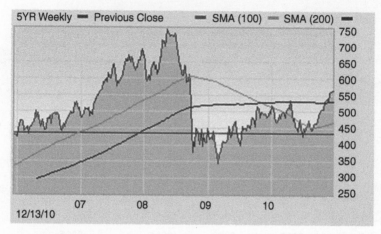

Exhibit 22.2 DJ Oil & Gas Index (5-year chart)
Source: www.djindexes.com/sectors.

shale gas to ExxonMobil's reserves is supported by the recent energy forecast by the U.S. Energy Information Administration (EIA), part of the U.S. Department of Energy (DOE). Their forecasts indicate that shale gas is going to become an increasingly important source of natural gas for the United States (see Exhibit 22.4).

MOTIVATIONS FOR ACQUISITION

Following the announcement of the merger, Representative Edward Markey, Chairman of the House Energy and Commerce Committee's electricity subcommittee, made known plans to convene a hearing regarding the merger. Rep. Markey

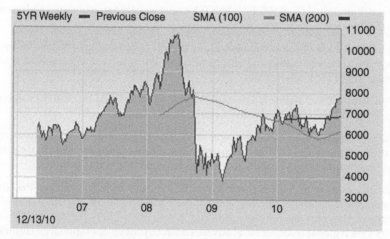

Exhibit 22.3 DJ Exploration & Production Index (5-year chart)
Source: www.djindexes.com/sectors.

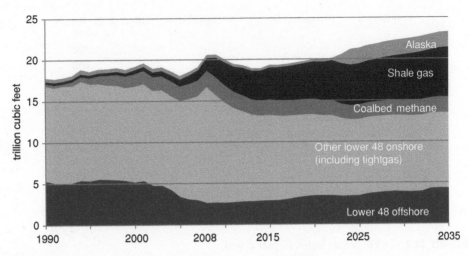

Exhibit 22.4   Natural Gas Production by Source, 1990–2035
Source: www.eia.doe.gov/oiaf/aeo/gas.html (Figure 73). Data obtained through www.eia.doe.gov/oiaf/archive/aeo10/graphic_data.html.

noted several potential issues including industry competition and the environment. In January 2010, the subcommittee did in fact convene a hearing. ExxonMobil President and CEO Rex W. Tillerson testified. In that testimony he addresses ExxonMobil's motivation for acquiring XTO Energy. His testimony is as follows (see Securities and Exchange Form 425 filed by ExxonMobil, January 20, 2010):

> Americans face a critical challenge: continuing to develop affordable, reliable and secure energy supplies needed to grow our economy and create jobs, while also continuing to improve the environmental aspects of energy production and use.
>
> The combination of ExxonMobil and XTO is an important step towards addressing this challenge.
>
> The development of our combined resources will create the opportunity for more jobs and investment in the production of cleaner-burning natural gas spread across many parts of the United States.
>
> It will support our nation's economic recovery, strengthen our nation's energy security, and help meet our nation's environmental goals.
>
> At ExxonMobil, we focus on the long-term. The global scale of our industry, the volatility of the world commodity market in which we compete, and the decades-long timeframes of our projects requires us to plan far into the future.
>
> Our agreement with XTO is consistent with this approach. It combines the complementary strengths of our two companies—XTO's technical expertise and substantial unconventional natural gas resource base in the United States, and ExxonMobil's own global resource base, advanced R&D, proven operational capabilities, global scale and financial capacity.

It will better position us to meet Americans' long-term needs for affordable, reliable, cleaner-burning natural gas.

Enabling a strong and growing U.S. economy requires meeting Americans' total energy needs—including fuels to power their businesses, heat their homes, and generate electricity.

Increases in domestic natural gas supplies could meet an increasingly important share of these needs. This is due in large part to important technologies pioneered by ExxonMobil, XTO and others which enable us to unlock enormous supplies of unconventional natural gas in the United States.

With recent advances in extended reach horizontal drilling, combined with the time-tested technology of hydraulic fracturing—a process in use for more than 60 years—we can now find and produce unconventional natural gas supplies miles below the surface in a safe, efficient and environmentally responsible manner.

Thanks to innovations such as these, unconventional natural gas is projected to meet most of America's domestic natural gas demand by 2030, representing a substantial change in the overall energy profile of the United States.

In the five-year span ending in 2008, the U.S. Energy Information Administration estimates that U.S. total proven natural gas reserves increased by about 30 percent to 245 trillion cubic feet, or the equivalent of about 41 billion barrels of oil.

In an eighteen-month span ending in mid-2008, natural gas production in the United States increased over 13 percent, to 57 billion cubic feet per day. That increase is equivalent to all of the natural gas production in the United Kingdom.

And total U.S. natural gas resource estimates have increased 35 percent in the last two years. From this, Americans can now count on nearly a century of domestic natural gas supply at current rates of consumption.

In addition to its domestic abundance, natural gas holds several other advantages for Americans.

It is the cleanest burning of the fossil fuels, emitting up to 60 percent less carbon dioxide than the current leading fuel source used to meet Americans' electricity needs.

Natural gas production is also responsible for significant economic activity, job creation and revenues for local, state and federal governments in the United States.

In 2008, it contributed $385 billion to our nation's economy and supported more than 2.8 million American jobs. More than 622,000 of these jobs were through direct employment—representing a 20 percent increase since 2006. Significant job growth occurred in many states, including Arkansas, Colorado, North Dakota, South Dakota, Utah and Pennsylvania.

Discovering, developing and delivering cleaner-burning natural gas is integral to the work of the U.S. oil and gas industry, which in 2007 alone contributed more than $1 trillion to our nation's economy and supported more than 9 million American jobs.

The challenge Americans face is significant. To reverse our nation's economic difficulties, meet our energy needs, and reach our environmental goals, we must all do our part.

Governments help by upholding stable tax and regulatory policies which encourage competition on a level playing field.

Consumers help by using energy efficiently.

And industry helps by taking the risk to develop new energy technologies and new, cleaner-burning energy resources, such as unconventional natural gas.

In my view, the combination of XTO and ExxonMobil will enable us to more effectively play our part in addressing the challenge our nation faces, and will help create the integrated solutions that provide Americans with the energy supplies, the energy security, the environmental protection, and the economic growth they expect and deserve.

TERMS OF THE DEAL

The Boards of Directors of both ExxonMobil and XTO Energy, Inc. reached an agreement for the acquisition in December of 2009.[3] ExxonMobil issued a press release announcing the acquisition as well as the terms of the deal on December 14, 2009. At that time, approval by stockholders of XTO and regulators was still outstanding. ExxonMobil announced on June 25, 2010, that the merger had been completed.

This acquisition was a stock-only transaction. ExxonMobil agreed to pay $41 billion for XTO. In the deal, ExxonMobil would issue 0.7098 shares of their common stock for each common share of XTO. The value of the acquisition is based on the closing prices of both companies as of December 11, 2009. XTO shareholders received a 25 percent premium for their shares.

Additionally, ExxonMobil agreed to assume $10 billion of XTO debt. XTO will continue to operate as a wholly-owned subsidiary of ExxonMobil. Further, ExxonMobil committed to create a "new upstream organization to manage global development and production of unconventional resources, enabling the rapid development and deployment of technologies and operating practices to increase production and maximize resource value," after the merger was complete. XTO maintained its name and offices in Fort Worth, Texas (see ExxonMobil 2009).

VALUATION

The exploration and production (E&P) industry uses the method of multiples or market-based comparables in valuation and the ratio of enterprise value (EV) to EBITDAX (earnings before interest, taxes, depreciation and amortization, and exploration expenses)[4] are used as benchmarks in E&P firm valuation.[5] Additionally, the P/E ratio will be employed as a valuation metric. First, comparable firms will be discussed, and then income statement and balance sheet information for all of the firms will be presented. This will be followed by the valuation calculations and analysis.

Comparable Firms

Five comparable companies have been selected to benchmark against XTO.[6] XTO represents an acquisition based on its holdings of shale gas. Therefore, firms that

also had substantial holdings in shale gas were the primary firms under consideration. The firms selected were Chesapeake Energy, Apache Corporation, Southwestern Energy Company, Anadarko Petroleum Corporation, and Continental Resources, Inc. A brief discussion of each firm is provided below.

Chesapeake Energy is one of the largest producers of natural gas and the most active driller of new wells in the United States. Its assets are primarily found in the Big Four natural gas shale plays: the Barnett Shale of north-central Texas, the Haynesville Shale of east Texas and northwestern Louisiana, the Fayetteville Shale of central Arkansas, and the Marcellus Shale of the northern Appalachian Basin. Its strategy is focused on discovering, acquiring, and developing conventional and unconventional natural gas reserves in these areas. Chesapeake also has considerable assets in other plays, both conventional and unconventional, in the Anadarko Basin, Arkoma Basin, Appalachian Basin, Permian Basin, Delaware Basin, south Texas, Texas Gulf Coast, and east Texas regions of the United States. As of December 31, 2008, the company had proved and undeveloped reserves of 12,051,249 million cubic feet of natural gas equivalent, including 11,327,455 million cubic feet of natural gas and 120,632 thousand barrels of oil.

Apache is involved in the exploration, development, and production of natural gas, natural gas liquids, and crude oil. The company has exploration and production operations in seven regions: Canada, Egypt, the North Sea, Australia, Argentina, and the Gulf Coast and central regions in the United States. It also currently has exploration operations in Chile. Globally, Apache owns a gross of 39 million acres that provide ample growth opportunity. As of December 31, 2008, Apache had an interest in 24,982 productive gas and oil wells. As of the mentioned date, it had approximately 2,400.6 million cubic feet of proven reserves.

Southwestern Energy Company is an independent oil and gas firm. They are involved in exploration, development, and production of natural gas and crude oil. Their operations are primarily based in the United States. Their exploration and production activities of unconventional gas reservoirs as well as traditional drilling operations are ongoing in Arkansas, Oklahoma, Texas, and Pennsylvania. Their midstream services group markets their own gas production as well as that of other outside parties. Further, they are engaged in the transportation of natural gas. As of December 31, 2008, they had 2,185 billion cubic feet in proven oil and gas reserves.

Anadarko Petroleum is one of the largest independent oil and natural gas exploration and production companies in the world. The company operates in 12 major U.S. onshore natural gas plays, is the largest independent deepwater producer in the Gulf of Mexico, and has operations in Alaska, Algeria, Brazil, China, Indonesia, Mozambique, and West Africa. As of December 31, 2008, Anadarko had proven reserves of 8.1 trillion cubic feet (Tcf) of natural gas and 0.9 billion barrels of crude oil, condensate, and NGLs. The company also had an interest in 4,219 oil wells and 26,583 gas wells as of the mentioned date.

Continental Resources engages in the exploration and production of oil and natural gas. It operates in the Rocky Mountain, midcontinent, and Gulf Coast regions of the United States. The company focuses their exploration on large new or developing plays that provide significant opportunity to acquire undeveloped acreage for future drilling. As of December 31, 2008, Continental had proven reserves of 159.3 million barrels of oil equivalent.

Income Statement and Balance Sheet Data

Exhibit 22.5 contains income statement data for 2008 year-end for XTO and the comparable firms. Exhibits 22.6 and 22.7 contain selected balance sheet data and other selected financial data, respectively. The information from these exhibits will be the basis for our valuation of XTO.

Valuation Calculations

Now that we have the necessary data, we can begin our valuation of XTO. First, we will look at the methods of multiples approach which includes the $\frac{EV}{EBITDA}$, $\frac{EV}{EBITDAX}$, and P/E ratios. EBITDA and EBITDAX are defined in endnote 5 of this chapter. Refer to Titman and Martin (2007) for more discussion on relative valuation. We will perform this analysis in five steps:

1. Compute Enterprise Value (EV) for each firm
2. Compute $\frac{EV}{EBITDA}$ for each firm
3. Compute $\frac{EV}{EBITDAX}$ for each firm
4. Compute P/E ratio for each firm
5. Compute the average multiples for the comparable firms in addition to individually, to compute an average value for XTO based on all Comps
6. Compare the results

Step 1: We need to calculate the EV. EV is computed as follows: interest-bearing debt (ST & LT) plus common equity (price × shares outstanding) less cash, cash equivalents, and short-term investments. The result is the Enterprise Value of the firm. All of the information required is contained in Exhibits 22.5, 22.6 and 22.7. The complete calculations are provided in Exhibit 22.8.

Example: Interest-bearing debt for Chesapeake Energy ($14,361,000) is obtained by adding short/current long-term debt ($66,000) to long-term debt ($14,295,000). Then, we multiply their share price ($25.88) by the number of shares outstanding ($607.3 million) to get common equity of $15,716,924. Next, cash and cash equivalents and short-term investments are summed, $1,749,000 and $1,082,000, respectively, yielding $2,831,000. Last, we add the interest-bearing debt ($14,361,000) and common equity ($15,716,294) together and subtract out cash and cash equivalents and short-term investments ($2,831,000). This results in our Enterprise Value of $27,246,924 (in thousands of dollars).

Steps 2–4: We can pull the remaining data from Exhibits 22.5, 22.6, and 22.7 and compute our ratios and average ratios as shown in Exhibit 22.9. Recall that the P/E ratio (multiple) is simply price per share divided by earnings per share.

Steps 5 and 6: A comparison of XTO to the other firms, indicates that XTO is similar to Chesapeake with regard to $\frac{EV}{EBITDA}$. The Anadarko Petroleum Corporation (APC) seems to be the most similar when considering the $\frac{EV}{EBITDAX}$ and P/E multiples.

Next, we will calculate the equity value per share using the information in Exhibit 22.9. We will do this in three different ways: (a) we will base our calculation on EBITDA for XTO, (b) EBITDAX for XTO, and (c) the P/E multiple of XTO.

Exhibit 22.5 Selected Income Statement Data (values are in thousands)

	Chesapeake Energy Corp.	Apache Corp.	Southwestern Energy Company	Anadarko Petroleum Corp.	Continental Resources, Inc.	XTO Energy Inc.
Ticker	CHK	APA	SWN	APC	CLR	XTO
PERIOD ENDING	31-Dec-08	31-Dec-08	31-Dec-08	31-Dec-08	31-Dec-08	31-Dec-08
Total revenue	11,629,000	12,389,750	2,311,552	15,723,000	960,490	7,695,000
Cost of revenue	4,821,000	2,066,116	879,145	3,826,000	218,593	1,131,000
Gross profit	6,808,000	10,323,634	1,432,407	11,897,000	741,897	6,564,000
Operating expenses						
Selling, general, and administrative	377,000	1,273,601	131,231	2,318,000	35,719	1,085,000
Depreciation, depletion, and amortization	2,144,000	7,850,260	414,408	3,194,000	93,630	2,025,000
Others	3,014,000	101,346	—	223,000	301,818	(54,000)
Operating income or loss	1,273,000	1,098,427	1,765,913	6,162,000	529,323	3,508,000
Income from continuing operation						
Total other income/expenses (net)	227,000	23,947	61,668	(74,000)	1,395	—
Earnings before interest and taxes	1,500,000	1,122,374	947,849	6,088,000	530,718	3,508,000
Interest expenses	314,000	189,982	28,904	742,000	12,188	(482,000)
Income before tax	1,186,000	932,392	918,945	5,346,000	518,530	3,026,000
Income tax	463,000	220,438	350,999	2,148,000	197,580	1,114,000
Net income from continuing operations	723,000	711,954	567,946	3,198,000	320,950	1,912,000
Nonrecurring events						
Effect of accounting changes and earnings, discontinued operations	—	—	—	63,000	—	—
Net income	723,000	711,954	567,946	3,261,000	320,950	1,912,000
Preferred stock and other adjustments	100,000	(5,680)	—	1,000	—	—
Net income applicable to common shares	623,000	706,274	567,946	3,260,000	320,950	1,912,000

Exhibit 22.6   Selected Balance Sheet Data (values are in thousands)

Firm	Chesapeake Energy Corp.	Apache Corp.	Southwestern Energy Company	Anadarko Petroleum Corp.	Continental Resources, Inc.	XTO Energy Inc.
Ticker	CHK	APA	SWN	APC	CLR	XTO
PERIOD ENDING	31-Dec-08	31-Dec-08	31-Dec-08	31-Dec-08	31-Dec-08	31-Dec-08
Assets						
Current assets						
Cash and cash equivalents	1,749,000	1,181,450	196,277	2,360,000	5,229	25,000
Short-term investments	1,082,000	946,279	343,320	—	—	2,735,000
Net receivables	1,324,000	1,450,356	251,557	1,687,000	247,889	1,274,000
Inventory	58,000	498,567	50,377	420,000	22,210	—
Other current assets	79,000	374,322	44,734	908,000	2,367	224,000
Total current assets	4,292,000	4,450,974	889,265	5,375,000	277,695	4,258,000
Long-term investment	705,000	—		—	—	1,023,000
Property, plant, and equipment	33,145,000	23,958,517	3,713,607	37,047,000	1,935,143	31,281,000
Goodwill	—	189,252		5,282,000	—	1,447,000
Other assets	302,000	13,880	157,286	1,088,000	3,041	245,000
Deferred long-term asset charges	—	573,862		131,000	—	
Total assets	38,444,000	29,186,485	4,760,158	48,923,000	2,215,879	38,254,000

Liabilities						
Current liabilities						
Accounts payable	3,555,000	1,954,919	710,004	4,064,000	398,847	2,865,000
Short/Current long-term debt	66,000	112,598	72,099	1,472,000	—	35,000
Other current liabilities	—	547,711	10,758	—	4,747	30,000
Total current liabilities	3,621,000	2,615,228	792,861	5,536,000	403,594	2,930,000
Long-term debt	14,295,000	4,816,688	680,134	10,867,000	376,400	11,959,000
Other liabilities	468,000	5,245,848	47,493	3,751,000	41,425	818,000
Deferred long-term liability charges	3,763,000	—	721,707	9,974,000	445,752	5,200,000
Total liabilities	22,147,000	12,677,764	2,252,328	30,128,000	1,267,171	20,907,000
Stockholders' equity						
Preferred stock	505,000	98,387	—	—	—	—
Common stock	6,000	214,221	3,436	47,000	1,696	6,000
Retained earnings	4,694,000	11,929,827	1,449,977	14,061,000	526,958	6,588,000
Treasury stock	(10,000)	(228,304)	(4,740)	(686,000)	—	(147,000)
Capital surplus	10,835,000	4,472,826	811,492	5,696,000	420,054	8,315,000
Other stockholders' equity	267,000	21,764	247,665	(323,000)	—	2,585,000
Total stockholders' equity	16,297,000	16,508,721	2,507,830	18,795,000	948,708	17,347,000
Total liabilities and stockholders' equity	38,444,000	29,186,485	4,760,158	48,923,000	2,215,879	38,254,000

Exhibit 22.7 Other Selected Financial Data (values are in thousands)

Firm	Chesapeake Energy Corp.	Apache Corp.	South-western Energy Company	Anadarko Petroleum Corp.	Continental Resources, Inc.	XTO Energy Inc.
Ticker	CHK	APA	SWN	APC	CLR	XTO
PERIOD ENDING	31-Dec-08	31-Dec-08	31-Dec-08	31-Dec-08	31-Dec-08	31-Dec-08
Exploration expenses (thousands)	$ 5,789,000	$ 5,425,207	$ 1,805,358	$ 1,031,000	$ 634,300	$ 3,700,000
Shares outstanding (millions)	607.30	334.71	346.20	491.50	169.56	579.53
Year-end 2008 closing price	$ 25.88	$ 103.17	$ 28.97	$ 62.42	$ 42.89	$ 46.53
Market capitalization (millions)	$ 15,716.92	$ 34,532.03	$ 10,029.41	$ 30,679.43	$ 7,272.43	$ 26,965.53

Exhibit 22.8 Enterprise Value Calculations (values are in thousands)

Firm	CHK	APA	SWN	APC	CLR	XTO Actual
Interest-bearing debt (ST&LT)	$ 14,361,000	$ 4,929,286	$ 752,233	$ 12,339,000	$ 376,400	$11,994,000
Common equity (price x shares outstanding)	$ 15,716,924	$ 34,532,031	$ 10,029,414	$ 30,679,430	$ 7,272,428	$26,965,531
Less: Cash and cash equivalents & short-term investments	$ 2,831,000	$ 2,127,729	$ 539,597	$ 2,360,000	$ 5,229	$2,760,000
Equals: Enterprise value	$ 27,246,924	$ 37,333,588	$ 10,242,050	$ 40,658,430	$ 7,643,599	$36,199,531

Exhibit 22.9 Method of Multiples Results (values are in thousands)

Firm	CHK	APA	SWN	APC	CLR	Average	XTO Actual
Enterprise Value (EV)	27,246,924	37,333,588	10,242,050	40,658,430	7,643,599	24,624,918	36,199,531
EBITDA	3,644,000	8,972,634	1,362,257	9,282,000	624,348	4,777,048	5,533,000
EBITDAX	9,433,000	14,397,841	3,167,615	10,313,000	1,258,648	7,714,021	9,233,000
EV/EBITDA Multiple	7.48	4.16	7.52	4.38	12.24	7.16	6.54
EV/EBITDAX Multiple	2.89	2.59	3.23	3.94	6.07	3.75	3.92
P/E Multiple	21.74	48.50	17.66	9.41	22.66	23.99	14.10

EBITDA EV–Based Equity Value per Share Calculation

Multiply EBITDA for XTO by the average $\frac{EV}{EBITDA}$ multiple for the comparable firms and also for each firm individually. Then, add XTO's cash and cash equivalents as well as short-term investments to the number just calculated. Next, subtract out XTO's interest-bearing debt. The total of these calculations is the equity value. Last, simply divide by the shares outstanding to obtain equity value per share. The calculations are reflected in Exhibit 22.10. As shown, the range of values is from $23.79 using APA as the comparable to $100.95 using CLR as the comparable. The valuation based on the average EV/EBITDA multiple is $51.52 per share.

EBITDAX EV–Based Equity Value per Share Calculation

This calculation is done much the same as above, but instead of using EBITDA for XTO we use EBITDAX. Otherwise, the computations are the same. The results are given in Exhibit 22.11.

P/E Multiple–Based Equity Value per Share Calculation

Here, we will simply multiply each firm's P/E multiple by XTO's net income per share. The results are in Exhibit 22.12.

ANALYSIS

The closing prices of ExxonMobil and XTO Energy were $72.83 and $41.49, respectively, on December 11, 2009. The acquisition price, as discussed previously, was based on these prices. Each XTO share was exchanged for 0.7098 shares of Exxon-Mobil stock. At this exchange rate, XTO shareholders were paid $51.69 per share of their stock or about a 25 percent premium.

Based on the results of the EBITDA-based equity value share price computation, given in Exhibit 22.10, the price paid by ExxonMobil appears to be on target. The results of the EBITDAX and P/E based equity values are not nearly as close. Exhibit 22.11 reports the EBITDAX equity valuation computations. Other than CLR, the analysis suggests a price of less than $51.69. The P/E valuations are reported in Exhibit 22.12. The results of this exhibit, for the most part, suggest a higher acquisition price. In fact, only the valuation using Anadarko Petroleum suggests a price below $51.69.

CONCLUSION

The goal of this case study was to lay out a road map for valuing acquisitions. The basic approach to analyzing a takeover in the energy industry (particularly oil and gas) was presented. Selecting comparable firms, reviewing takeover motivations as well as methods of analysis were discussed.

To summarize the discussion, we go back to our original five questions

1. What should the price have been for XTO?

    Obviously, the appropriate price for ExxonMobil's acquisition of XTO Energy is somewhat subjective. However, it should be based on sound fundamental analysis of the firm as well as the industry and economic

Exhibit 22.10   Equity Value for XTO Based on EBITDA Using Comps (values are in thousands $)

Firm	CHK	APA	SWN	APC	CLR	XTO Valuation Based on Average Multiple of Comps
Enterprise value (EBITDA based)	41,371,359	23,021,862	41,599,539	24,236,489	67,737,921	39,593,434
Plus: Cash & cash equivalents & short-term investments	2,760,000	2,760,000	2,760,000	2,760,000	2,760,000	2,760,000
Less: Interest-bearing debt	11,994,000	11,994,000	11,994,000	11,994,000	11,994,000	11,994,000
Equity value	32,137,359	13,787,862	32,365,539	15,002,489	58,503,921	30,359,434
Equity value per share	*$55.45*	*$23.79*	*$55.85*	*$25.89*	*$100.95*	*$51.52*

Exhibit 22.11 Equity Value for XTO based on EBITDAX Using Comps (values are in thousands $)

Firm	CHK	APA	SWN	APC	CLR	XTO Valuation Based on Average Multiple of Comps
Enterprise value (EBITDAX based)	26,669,230	23,941,160	29,853,643	36,400,590	56,070,763	34,587,077
Plus: Cash & cash equivalents & short-term investments	2,760,000	2,760,000	2,760,000	2,760,000	2,760,000	2,760,000
Less: Interest-bearing debt	11,994,000	11,994,000	11,994,000	11,994,000	11,994,000	11,994,000
Equity value	17,435,230	14,707,160	20,619,643	27,166,590	46,836,763	23,057,077
Equity value per share	*$30.09*	*$25.38*	*$35.58*	*$46.88*	*$80.82*	*$45.79*

Exhibit 22.12   Equity Value Based on the P/E Multiple Method for XTO using Comps

Firm	CHK	APA	SWN	APC	CLR	Value Based on Comps
Equity value per share based on P/E multiple	$71.72	$160.02	$58.26	$31.04	$74.76	$84.38

conditions. Certainly, very little support exists for a higher purchase price; however there is some basis for a lower price. Taken together, it would appear the price ExxonMobil paid for XTO was fairly close to the appropriate price.

2. Which of the comparable firms is the best comparison firm for XTO?

The oil and gas industry has many players, big and small. The comparable firms were selected largely based on the similarity of their holdings (resources) to XTO. Five comparable firms were selected and most likely any of them would make a good comparable firm. Different firms emerge as the best candidate, however, when different measures are examined. In terms of revenue, gross profit, total assets, and $\frac{EV}{EBITDA}$, Chesapeake Energy is the clear standout as far as comparability is concerned. However, Apache is the most similar in terms of net income. Anadarko leads the comparability race when the focus is on market capitalization and $\frac{EV}{EBITDAX}$, and the P/E multiples.

3. Why did ExxonMobil want to acquire XTO?

XTO is a significant shale gas play. This appears to have been ExxonMobil's singular objective in their acquisition of XTO. Comments made by ExxonMobil's president and vice president of investor relations support this claim. Additionally, the DOE's prediction that shale gas is going to become increasingly important in the energy landscape gives credence to ExxonMobil's move.

4. Based on the analysis of comparable firms, did ExxonMobil overpay for XTO or get a bargain?

In this case, the most appropriate answer is: neither. While cheaper is better is generally the mantra followed in business, it does not appear that ExxonMobil substantially overpaid for XTO.

5. What additional information could help with this analysis?

There is a plethora of information that could be useful such as expected growth rates and the extent of the synergies gained in the acquisition. Also, the expected expense of the planned expansion at the XTO location to support commitments promised by ExxonMobil (see "Terms of the Deal") could be useful. Further reflection is left for in-class discussions and the student.

APPENDIX

Case Follow-Up

According to Isabel Ordonez of Dow Jones, the market has been somewhat critical of ExxonMobil's acquisition of XTO.[7] This is due mainly to the size of the stake

they have placed in gas. Gas is considerably cheaper than oil. Ordonez suggested that industry analysts are watching for indications that this purchase is adding to ExxonMobil earnings.

Statements from David Rosenthal, ExxonMobil Vice President for Investor Relations, indicated that they are happy with the acquisition of XTO. In fact, XTO added around $120 million to fourth-quarter 2010 earnings. Of course, this is a very small addition (a little more than 1%) to the firm's overall earnings, which were reported at $9.25 billion. Excluding hedging effects, the earnings contributed by XTO dwindles to a mere $36 million (<0.5% of ExxonMobil's overall earnings).

DISCUSSION QUESTIONS

1. What additional information would be helpful in analyzing this acquisition?

2. Would other methods of analysis be more appropriate? If so, why? Should the analysis here be augmented with other methods of analysis? If so, why? Are there differences in the energy industry that make it unique to the point that special valuation techniques are necessary? Explain.

3. Does the information contained in the case follow-up section change any of your opinions about the acquisition?

4. In this acquisition, ExxonMobil assumed a significant amount of debt. They assumed $10 billion in XTO debt. What affect might this have on ExxonMobil in the long run? What affect does this have on their debt ratio or debt capacity? Will this affect their ability to access the capital markets and borrow in the future?

5. Exhibits 22.2 and 22.3 depict significant decreases in the index values since mid-2008. What might be the effect on the results presented here if the index values returned to near those mid-2008 levels due to increases in oil prices?

6. Recently, oil company executives have touted supply shortages similar to those seen in the 1970s for various reasons. Also, unrest in countries with significant oil reserves and production can be a problem. What effects might these types of events have on firms like ExxonMobil, Chesapeake, and others in the future?

NOTES

1. See Weston (2002) for a description of these particular merger waves.
2. Source: www.icbenchmark.com/docs/Structure_Defs_English.pdf.
3. All information contained in this section was obtained from the ExxonMobil News Release dated December 14, 2009.
4. EBITDAX is defined as earnings before interest, taxes, depreciation and amortization, and exploration expenses. EBITDAX is different from EBITDA because exploration expenses are added back in addition to depreciation and amortization.
5. Valuation methods were described well by Titman and Martin (2007). Please see their excellent book for additional information regarding valuation techniques.
6. Note, Devon Energy would have been an excellent candidate for a comparable firm. However, Devon had negative operating income as well as net income. This would have made the analysis much more complex. Therefore, Devon was excluded from the comparable firm candidate pool.
7. Isabel Ordonez, Dow Jones Newswires. Available at www.nasdaq.com/aspx/stock-market-news-story.aspx?storyid=201101311317dowjonesdjonline000245&title=exxon-mobil-xto-contributed-120-million-to-its-4q-profits.

REFERENCES

Dow Jones. 2010. Dow Jones Sector Indexes. Available at www.djindexes.com/sectors.

ExxonMobil, ExxonMobil Media Relations. 2009. "ExxonMobil Corporation and XTO Energy Inc. Announce Agreement" [press release]. Available at www.exxonmobil .com/Corporate/Files/news_release_20091214.pdf.

Industry Classification Benchmark. 2008. "Industry Structure and Definitions." Available at www.icbenchmark.com/docs/Structure_Defs_English.pdf.

ExxonMobil. 2010. "Securities and Exchange Commission filing Form 425." January 20, 2010, Available at www.sec.gov/Archives/edgar/data/34088/000095010310000142/dp16220_ 425.htm.

Ordonez, I. 2011. "ExxonMobil: XTO Contributed $120 Million to Its 4Q Profits." Available at www.nasdaq.com/aspx/stock-market-news-story.aspx?storyid=201101311317 dowjonesdjonline000245&title=exxon-mobil-xto-contributed-120-million-to-its-4q-profits.

Titman, S., and J. Martin. 2007. *Valuation: The Art and Science of Corporate Investment Decisions.* Reading, MA: Addison-Wesley.

U.S. Energy Information Administration. 2010. The Annual Energy Outlook 2010. Available at www.eia.doe.gov/oiaf/aeo/gas.html and www.eia.doe.gov/oiaf/archive/ aeo10/graphic_data.html.

Weston, F. 2002. "The Exxon-Mobil Merger: An Archetype." *Journal of Applied Finance* 12:1, 69–88.

ABOUT THE CONTRIBUTORS

Allissa A. Lee, PhD, is a visiting assistant professor of Finance at the Spears School of Business at Oklahoma State University. Previously, she was a visiting assistant professor of finance at the McCoy College of Business Administration at Texas State University—San Marcos. Dr. Lee has authored several academic publications including in the *Journal of Banking and Finance* and presented at various academic conferences. Her research interests include mergers and acquisitions, corporate, banking, real estate, and journal citations, among others. She earned her PhD in finance from Oklahoma State University. Prior to academia, Allissa worked in the banking and mortgage industry for MidFirst Bank.

Betty J. Simkins, PhD, is the Williams Companies Professor of Business and a professor of finance in the Department of Finance at Oklahoma State University's (OSU) Spears School of Business where she teaches energy finance, corporate finance, and enterprise risk management, among other courses. Dr. Simkins received her PhD from Case Western Reserve University (CWRU), her MBA from OSU, and her BS in chemical engineering from the University of Arkansas. She has more than 50 publications in academic finance journals and book chapters and has won awards for her research, most recently in risk management. In addition, Betty has won several teaching awards including the Regents Distinguished Teaching Award. She has taught Energy Finance, a course she created, at both the undergraduate and graduate levels for over 12 years and teaches executive education courses on energy finance for companies around the world. She is also very active in the finance profession and currently serves on the board of directors for the Financial Management Association, as co-editor of the *Journal of Applied Finance*,

as past president of the Eastern Finance Association, and on the editorial boards of several prestigious finance journals. Prior to academia, she worked in the energy industry for Williams Companies and Conoco (now ConocoPhillips). In addition to being co-editor of this book, in 2010 she co-edited *Enterprise Risk Management: Insights and Analysis on Today's Leading Research and Best Practices*, also published by John Wiley & Sons.

CHAPTER 23

Southwest Airlines*

The Blended Winglet Project

AARON MARTIN
Sempra Energy Inc.

DANIEL A. ROGERS
Associate Professor, Portland State University

BETTY J. SIMKINS
Professor, Oklahoma State University

INTRODUCTION

On a sunny Tuesday morning in the spring of 2002, Scott Topping, the director of corporate finance at Southwest Airlines, sat in Dallas traffic on I-35 on his way into the office. Because of the delay, he decided to check his voicemail. The final message was from a sales representative with Aviation Partners Boeing (APB) making a sales pitch for its Blended Winglet product. Scott vaguely recalled brushing off a similar proposal from Boeing several years earlier. At that time, the achievable cost savings from installing the Winglets were clearly not sufficient to warrant the high asking price. As Scott continued to listen, he heard "and over the last couple of years our efficiencies have improved dramatically and with the economies of scale that we have achieved, with the right volume, we are willing to offer you a price half of what we offered you in 1999." This comment piqued Scott's interest. As a low-fare airline, Southwest constantly strived to find ways to maintain its cost structure below that of its competition. Could these "Winglets" provide a new avenue to further lower its already-low operating costs? For the next 5 miles, which took approximately 30 minutes in the morning Dallas rush hour traffic, Scott began

*This case study was first published in 2004 and is reprinted by permission from the *Journal of Case Research*. The teaching note for the case is available from the authors upon request. We thank Scott Topping, Laura Wright, Dale Stolzer, Brian Gleason, and Ken Buller at Southwest Airlines for their time and expertise, which has made the development of this case a possibility. We appreciate the valuable suggestions provided by the editor, David W. Rosenthal, the associate editor, Steven M. Dawson, and the anonymous reviewers. We also thank David A. Carter for his valuable insights.

to run through some numbers in his head. But, of course, before a decision could be made, there were many other people he would have to consult.

BACKGROUND

Participants in the U.S. airline industry have struggled financially since the industry's deregulation in 1978. Southwest Airlines represented a significant exception. Since its inception in 1971, Southwest has exhibited continuous profitability and delivered solid returns to its shareholders. Being the fourth-largest domestic carrier in terms of customers boarded, Southwest had developed a system that no other airline had been able to match, making it the only airline to consistently turn a profit. Refer to the Appendix for a fact sheet on Southwest Airlines.

Southwest managed to differentiate itself from the competition by focusing on being the lowest-cost provider in the industry, allowing it to offer low fares. Southwest strived to find efficiencies in managing all of its costs. In recent years, the company had been particularly successful in reducing its jet fuel expense. Southwest managed its fuel costs in two ways: hedging and fuel savings projects. "Southwest, the industry's low-cost provider, is keen on finding innovative ways to keep our operating costs in check so we can continue to provide low fares to millions more Americans," said Laura Wright, Southwest's vice president of finance.[1] One example of an innovative project that Southwest was presented with was the decision as to whether to install a technology known as the Blended Winglet. This technology offered a possible avenue for Southwest Airlines to gain additional efficiencies in its operations.

The Blended Winglet system was developed and tested by Aviation Partners Boeing (APB), a joint venture between Aviation Partners Inc. and the Boeing Company. The carbon-graphite Winglets allowed an airplane to extend its range, carry greater payload, and save on fuel. From an operating economics point of view, the main purpose of the Winglet was to reduce turbulence, leading to higher efficiency. The Winglet accomplished this by increasing the spread of the wing's trailing edge and creating more lift at the wingtips. As pointed out by APB, "The blended winglet allows for the chord distribution to change smoothly from the wingtip to the winglet, which optimizes the distribution of the span load lift and minimizes any aerodynamic interference or airflow separation."[2] As marketed by APB, the Blended Winglet was approximately 8-feet high, added about 5 feet to the aircraft's total wingspan, took about 4–5 days to install, decreased fuel usage by 4–6 percent and advertised several additional operating features. The increased wingspan was expected to allow each of Southwest's aircraft to fly up to 115 nautical miles further and reduce fuel burn, saving Southwest an expected 178,500 gallons of jet fuel per airplane per year. The Blended Winglet, simply put, was a more efficient and aerodynamic means of increasing the wingspan of the aircraft. Exhibit 23.1 illustrates a diagram of a Boeing 737-700 aircraft outfitted with the blended Winglets.

Decision Process for the Blended Winglets Project

Scott knew that the project was at least feasible at this point, particularly because he had conducted a rough study back in 1999 when Boeing first approached the airline. He was also aware that other airlines operating Boeing 737-700 aircraft,

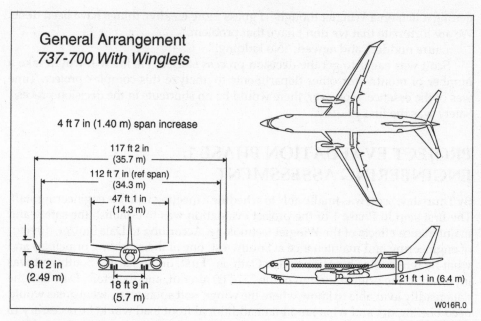

General Arrangement
737-700 With Winglets

4 ft 7 in (1.40 m) span increase

117 ft 2 in
(35.7 m)

112 ft 7 in (ref span)
(34.3 m)

47 ft 1 in
(14.3 m)

8 ft 2 in
(2.49 m)

18 ft 9 in
(5.7 m)

21 ft 1 in (6.4 m)

W016R.0

Exhibit 23.1 Blended Winglets on a Boeing 737-700

such as WestJet in Canada, were giving the Winglet technology careful consideration. At this point, the next step was to have other departments verify costs and benefits, and give clearance before the project could proceed. Most importantly, the Maintenance Engineering Department and the Flight Operations Department would have to give first approval. Then, the Facilities Department needed to verify that the airline's facilities could accommodate the aircraft with the blended Winglets. If the project made it though these steps, then the Finance Department could calculate a more definitive value of the project using all the data provided by the other departments. If the project passed this next to last hurdle, then it would have one final (albeit, critical) hurdle—a formal presentation to the Executive Planning Committee who would make the final project decision—"go" or "no go."

Scott thought to himself that this was probably the most exciting project he had analyzed in his entire career. Scott had worked at Southwest since 1995 and was promoted to director of corporate finance in 2001. The Blended Winglets project was exciting to Scott because first and foremost, it would help the airline fulfill its mission to be the low-cost provider in the domestic airline industry. Furthermore, this was a great project because it involved all major departments of the airline and, if successful, it would help the company maintain its competitive advantage over other higher-cost competitors. After a recent meeting about the project, Laura said, "Scott, if the project economics work out, this will be another way for us to extend our competitive cost advantage."

Scott replied, "You know Laura, I can't agree with you more. Several of our competitors are facing possible bankruptcy and can't commit capital to a project like this even if it makes sense financially. I am hearing that there is an effort underway to offer financing for Winglets. That may be the only way to grow the market for this product in today's environment. I'm not sure how a lender would go about

getting a lien on a Winglet though—I guess more creative things have been done. We are fortunate that we don't have that problem."

Laura nodded, and agreed: "No kidding!"

Scott was eager to get the decision process started. He knew it would take a number of months for other departments to analyze this complex project. Time was of the essence. However, there would be no shortcuts in the decision process. Safety was the first priority.

PROJECT EVALUATION PHASE 1: ENGINEERING ASSESSMENT

By Thursday, Scott was finally able to schedule a meeting with his engineering staff. The first step in Phase 1 of the project evaluation was to establish the safety and maintenance effects of the Winglet technology. According to Dale Stolzer, director of engineering and maintenance at Southwest, one of their guiding principles and what he refers to as his Hippocratic Oath, is "First, do no harm." Southwest was involved in the original design of the 737-700 aircraft, and therefore, Dale had the data readily available to know where the wings' soft spots were, what areas would need beefing up, and what amount of additional front load would be necessary to offset the additional weight (340 lbs.) of the Winglets in order to reduce flutter.[3] Personnel in Dale's department then looked at the short- and long-term effects of the Winglets and looked to see if they would cause an increase in wear on other areas of the aircraft, which would in turn increase maintenance costs. Dale told Scott that there would be no additional maintenance costs on the engine, but that the aircraft would require, overall, an estimated $210,000 in repair costs per incidental damage to the Winglets. Dale assumed that 1 percent of Southwest's aircraft, per year, would incur that cost. In addition to maintenance costs, Scott wanted to know how much downtime would be experienced for each existing aircraft to allow for the installation of the Winglets. Scott knew that any increase in soft maintenance, which is any maintenance required over and above the already scheduled hard maintenance (i.e., planned maintenance), could cause a significant interruption in the company's revenue stream. Aircraft are required by the FAA to undergo routine maintenance evaluations to ensure the safety of the aircraft. Southwest's hard maintenance takes an aircraft out of pay for four to five days. With much time and effort, Southwest's maintenance department was able to allow for the installation of the $700,000 Winglet, at an installation cost of $56,000, during its hard maintenance schedules. In other words, the aircraft could be scheduled at each maintenance facility so that the Winglet installation coincides with regular maintenance. As a result, each aircraft was only expected to experience downtime of the aircraft for one extra day at $5,000/day, rather than the proposed Winglet installation time of four to five days.

PROJECT EVALUATION PHASE 2: FLIGHT OPERATIONS ASSESSMENT

While waiting for the analysis from Engineering, Scott met with Brian Gleason, director of flight operations, to verify the cost savings data that APB had

advertised. Brian knew that the longer the flight, the greater the fuel savings, and therefore, based his analysis on an average fuel savings. Brian's department generated data suggesting that the fuel savings result from reduced drag. In addition to fuel savings, Brian's engineering analyses showed that the increased lift capability that the Winglets allowed would increase the amount of payload per flight. The total weight of a 737-700 flight could not exceed 154,500 lbs. The aircraft itself, empty, weighs 86,000 lbs. There is a 43,000 lb. fuel capacity with a minimum contingency requirement of 5,000 lbs. and the weight of a passenger is figured at an average of 190 lbs. Therefore, increased payload can be realized in one of two ways: more cargo (passengers, baggage, mail, etc.) or more fuel. For example, a Southwest flight from Dallas to Las Vegas equipped with the Blended Winglet technology can carry up to 5,000 more pounds of fuel (there are 6.7 lbs/gal of jet fuel). From Southwest's perspective, the principal advantage of additional fuel-carrying capacity was that additional nonstop markets became feasible for the airline. Nevertheless, Scott did not believe that he could attach a quantifiable benefit to such options. According to the manufacturer, the additional lift capability provided by the Winglet would cause Southwest's restricted runways to be less restricted. Brian estimated these savings at $500 per aircraft per year.

PROJECT EVALUATION PHASE 3: FACILITIES ASSESSMENT

After Scott did a preliminary cash flow analysis based on the analyses from Engineering and Flight Operations, he then proceeded with Phase 3 of the evaluation process, which constituted meeting with his director of facilities, Ken Buller, to see if the increased wingspan caused by the Blended Winglet technology was feasible from a facilities point of view. One would think that this would be the logical first step in the process; however, due to the complexity of reconfiguring an airport terminal, Scott knew that it was not. This had been an issue as long as Southwest had been in the industry.

When Ken and Scott met, Ken immediately became fascinated and intrigued with this project. Ken had been with Southwest Airlines for many years and was planning to retire soon. This project made him excited and at the same time, presented a tremendous challenge for him and his department. Five years before, in 1997, the total wingspan of their aircraft had been 95 feet, and Ken thought it would always be this way. Their goal at Southwest had always been to try to keep terminals and ramps as small as possible. Then with the integration of the 737–700 into its fleet, the wingspan increased to 112'7". Then if the Winglets were added, the total wingspan would be increased to 117'2". Ken knew that Southwest had approximately 320 gates throughout their system, and every single gate would need to be scrutinized. Furthermore, he would need approval from every airport for implementation of changes, and getting this approval always involved politics. Ken knew he had a lot of work ahead and immediately got started on his part of the project analysis.

There were three major integrated factors influencing the reconfiguring of an airport terminal: fixed ramps, spread distances, and underground fueling tanks. First, ramp locations were driven by the terminal design. In many cases, the ramps

were mobile and therefore could be moved as needed. However, there were minimum passing spreads (which were different for each airport Southwest occupies) that also control where the aircraft could park.

Given Southwest's current route structure, Ken's department needed to assess the effect of the added wingspan on each of the 59 airports Southwest utilized. Before the Winglet technology, Southwest sought a 20′ parking spread and a 15′ passing spread. If the Winglets were installed, the goal would be a 17′ parking spread and a 12′ passing spread. As an example of these issues, 12 gates to which Southwest had rights were unable to accommodate a 737-700 series aircraft. With the addition of the Blended Winglets, there would likely be an additional three gates that would not accommodate the jets. Ken suggested that it would cost $300,000 per jet bridge if it became necessary to move fixed ramps. In addition to ramp flexibility and spread, the location of the underground fueling tanks also played a part. The aircraft must park directly over these filling points so that it may be refueled. If the aircraft is moved, the fuel hole may be too far away to fuel the aircraft. In turn, either the fuel hole would have to be moved, which cost $40,000 for every 10 feet the fuel hole was moved, or an alternate fuel source would have to be sought. And to make matters even more difficult, this was not simply a decision made by Ken Buller; it was a process that required 10 different signoffs (document available upon request). After extensive discussions with individuals working at airports throughout Southwest's system, Ken estimated that the necessary facilities modifications could be achieved for about $1,200 per aircraft.

PROJECT EVALUATION PHASE 4: FINANCE DEPARTMENT ASSESSMENT

If the Blended Winglet project made it through the three evaluation phases, it would then go back to the finance department. The finance department calculated the *official value* of all capital projects. The first step was for Scott and his boss, Laura Wright, to complete a Project Authorization Request (PAR). This form was required for all business cases. It specified the desired Internal Rate of Return, identified all possible risks, outlined the necessary resources, and explained why the project was being done. Once the form was completed, it would go to the Capital Spending Committee, who met once a month. The project would be flagged as green, yellow, or red, depending on the priority of the project. If the Capital Spending Committee approved the PAR, Scott and Laura were then required to give a formal presentation to the Executive Planning Committee (EPC), who had the final vote.

Other Project Analysis Information

Southwest's finance department used the Capital Asset Pricing Model (CAPM) to estimate its cost of equity. Additionally, the staff assumed a market risk premium of 5 percent in its capital budgeting analysis. Finally, they required long-term projects to provide higher rates of return: approximately a 5 percent premium over the company's weighted average cost of capital.[4]

Scott expected the Blended Winglet project to have a life of at least 20 years, at the end of which the Winglets were anticipated to have a salvage value of

Exhibit 23.2   Depreciation Schedule

MACRS table (Year):	Normal Table	Normal Table × 50%	Year 1[a] Additional 50%	Total Depreciation (modified table)
1	14.29%	7.15%	50.00%	57.15%
2	24.49%	12.25%		12.25%
3	17.49%	8.75%		8.75%
4	12.49%	6.25%		6.25%
5	8.93%	4.47%		4.47%
6	8.92%	4.46%		4.46%
7	8.93%	4.47%		4.47%
8	4.46%	2.23%		2.23%

[a]Job Creation and Worker Assistance Act of 2002. The additional depreciation was valid until December 31, 2004.

15 percent. Over the life of the project, costs other than fuel were expected to escalate at a 3 percent rate, and Scott assumed the price of jet fuel at $0.80 per gallon.

Scott and Laura noted additional benefits to the project. The Blended Winglet project qualified for accelerated tax write-off benefits under the Job Creation and Worker Assistance Act of 2002. With a marginal tax rate of 39 percent, and using a 7-year depreciation schedule (see Exhibit 23.2), the Job Creation and Worker Assistance Act of 2002 allowed for an additional 50 percent of the project to be depreciated in the first year.

To assess the sensitivity of the project's value, Scott's staff projected the cash flow effects of the Blended Winglets project assuming different fuel prices, fuel burn rates, and costs of capital. Finally, the numbers had been crunched thoroughly and the Finance Team was ready to present the analysis. Scott also prepared some discussion to highlight potential risks and benefits not incorporated into the quantitative analysis.

APPENDIX

Southwest Airlines Fact Sheet

Updated December 18, 2003

Leadership

> Jim Parker—Vice Chairman of the Board and CEO
> Colleen Barrett— President, Chief Operating Officer, and Corporate Secretary
> Herbert, "Herb" D. Kelleher—Chairman of the Board and Chairman of the Executive Committee of Southwest Airlines

Headquarters

> P.O. Box 36611, 2702 Love Field Drive, Dallas, TX 75235

About the Company

The airline began service June 18, 1971, with flights to Houston, Dallas, and San Antonio. Southwest is the fourth largest U.S. airline (in terms of domestic Customers carried annually). Year-end results for 2002 marked Southwest Airlines' 30th consecutive year of profitability. Southwest became a major airline in 1989 when it exceeded the billion-dollar revenue mark. Southwest is the United States' only major shorthaul, low-fare, high-frequency, point-to-point carrier.

Daily Departures: Nearly 2,800 flights a day.
Employees: More than 34,000 total employees throughout the Southwest system.
Stock: Common stock is traded under the symbol "LUV" on the NYSE.

2002 Financial Statistics

- Net income: $241 million
- Total passengers carried: 63 million
- Total RPMs: 45.4 billion
- Passenger load factor: 65.9 percent
- Total operating revenue: $5.5 billion

Cities Served by Southwest

Southwest flies to 58 cities (59 airports) in 30 states.

Albany	Indianapolis	Orlando
Albuquerque	Long Island/Islip	Phoenix
Amarillo	Jackson	Portland
Austin	Jacksonville	Providence
Baltimore/Washington	Kansas City	Raleigh-Durham
Birmingham	Las Vegas	Reno
Boise	Little Rock	Sacramento
Buffalo	Los Angeles (LAX)	St. Louis
Burbank	Louisville	Salt Lake City
Chicago (Midway)	Lubbock	San Antonio
Cleveland	Manchester	San Diego
Columbus	Midland/Odessa	San Jose
Corpus Christi	Nashville	Seattle/Tacoma
Dallas (Love Field)	New Orleans	Spokane
Detroit (Metro)	Norfolk	Tampa
El Paso	Oakland	Tucson
Ft. Lauderdale/Hollywood	Oklahoma City	Tulsa
Harlingen/South Padre Island	Omaha	West Palm Beach
Hartford/Springfield	Ontario	
Houston (Hobby & Intercontinental)	Orange County	

Philadelphia will become Southwest's 60th airport (31st state) in May 2004.

Fleet

Southwest currently operates 385 Boeing 737 jets (as of September 30, 2003).

TYPE	NUMBER	SEATS
737-200	24	122
737-300	194	137
737-500	25	122
737-700*	142	137

- The Company's fleet has an average age of about 9.5 years.
- The average aircraft trip length is 537 miles with an average duration of about one and one-half hours for 2002.
- Southwest aircraft fly an average of about 7 flights per day, or about 11 hours per day.
- Southwest was the launch customer for the Boeing 737-700 in 1997. Southwest was also a launch customer for the Boeing 737-500 and -300 series aircraft.
- Southwest is updating its traditional gold, red, and orange paint scheme by adding canyon blue. All new aircraft will have the updated colors and interior. Existing aircraft will be retrofitted over time.
- *Performance-enhancing Blended Winglets will be added to the current and future fleet of 737-700s.

Southwest Airlines' Top Ten Airports (as of October 5, 2003)

Cities	Daily Departures	Number of Gates	Nonstop Cities Served	Established
Phoenix	183	23	38	1982
Las Vegas	182	19	43	1982
Baltimore/Washington	159	19	35	1993
Houston Hobby	141	17	22	1971
Chicago Midway	134	16	29	1985
Dallas (Love Field)	130	14	13	1971
Oakland	122	12	18	1989
Los Angeles (LAX)	114	12	19	1982
Nashville	86	10	28	1986
San Diego	80	10	14	1982

Fun Facts

- Southwest received 243,657 resumes and hired 5,042 new employees in 2002.
- In 2002 Southwest served 32.8 million cans of soda and juices; 11.7 million cans of water; 9.9 million alcoholic beverages; 4.7 million bags of pretzels;

162.4 million bags of peanuts; 10.2 million snack packs; and 36.4 million other snacks.

- Southwest purchased 1.1 billion gallons of jet fuel in 2002.
- In 2002 Southwest moved 214,704,547 pounds of cargo and mail.
- The shortest daily Southwest flight is between Austin (AUS) and Houston (HOU) (152 miles). The longest daily Southwest flight is between Baltimore/Washington (BWI) and San Jose (SJC) (2,438 miles).
- Southwest has approximately 1,000 married couples. In other words, approximately 2,000 Southwest employees have spouses who also work for the Company.

Southwest Airlines Distinctions and Recognitions

For a complete list, see www.southwest.com/about_swa/press/factsheet.html.

- Southwest's average passenger airfare is $87.16, and the average passenger trip length is about 744 miles.
- Southwest has ranked number one in fewest customer complaints for the last twelve consecutive years as published in the Department of Transportation's Air Travel Consumer Report.
- The airline began the first profit-sharing plan in the U.S. airline industry in 1974. Through this plan, employees own at least 10 percent of the Company stock.
- The airline is approximately 81 percent unionized.
- Southwest Airlines is a member of the *Fortune* 500.
- The Ronald McDonald House program, cornerstone of the Ronald McDonald Children's Charities, is the primary corporate charity of Southwest Airlines. Annually, the Company sponsors the Southwest Airlines LUV Classic golf tournaments whose proceeds benefit the Ronald McDonald Houses and have totaled more than $6 million for the past 18 years.
- For the eighth year in a row, *Fortune* magazine has recognized Southwest Airlines in its annual survey of corporate reputations. This year, *Fortune* listed Southwest Airlines as number two among America's Top Ten most admired corporations. In 2003, as in 2002, 2001, 2000, 1999, 1998, 1997, and 1996, Southwest also was named the most admired airline.
- Southwest Airlines has been named a charter member of the International Airline Passengers Association's Honor Roll of Airlines among the World's Safest Airlines. Southwest also has been recognized as one of the world's safest airlines by *Conde Nast Traveler*.
- On May 20, 2003, the *Wall Street Journal* reported Southwest Airlines ranked first among airlines for the highest customer service satisfaction according to a survey by the American Customer Satisfaction Index for the first quarter of 2003.
- *Fortune* has ranked Southwest Airlines in the top five of the Best Companies to Work for in America. Southwest ranked first in 1997 and 1998, second in 1999, and fourth in 2000. Southwest has chosen not to participate since.

- *Air Transport World* magazine selected Southwest Airlines as its "Airline of the Year" for 2003. The editors praised Southwest for being profitable for 30 consecutive years, while providing affordable fares for millions of passengers.

DISCUSSION QUESTIONS

1. Estimate Southwest's expected future cash flows from the Blended Winglet project, as well as the initial cash outflow.

2. Using publicly available data sources, determine what rate of return should be used to discount the expected cash flows and document your methodology for determining the rate. Comment on Southwest's use of a discount rate that is 5 percent greater than its cost of capital.

3. Calculate the net present value (NPV), internal rate of return (IRR), and modified internal rate of return (MIRR) of the Blended Winglet project assuming the incremental cash flows suggested in the case.

4. How sensitive is the Blended Winglet project's NPV to changing assumptions regarding expected future fuel costs and the firm's cost of capital?

5. (Optional for instructors who cover real options in capital budgeting.) Are real options implicit in the Blended Winglet project? How would you incorporate the value of real options into the capital budgeting decision?

NOTES

1. This quote is from a private interview of Laura Wright in 2002.
2. The *chord* (which is an aerodynamic term) is a straight line joining the trailing (back) and leading (front) edges of an airfoil section. The airfoil section is the surface of the wing designed to aid in lifting. Chord distribution refers to how the chord changes over the installed length of the Blended Winglet. Basically, the design of the Winglet and chord distribution reduces drag and improves aircraft performance.
3. Soft spots on the wings are areas more prone to stress.
4. For an excellent article on the cost of capital, refer to Robert F. Bruner, Kenneth M. Eades, Robert S. Harris, and Robert C. Higgins, 1998, "Best Practices in Estimating the Cost of Capital: Survey and Synthesis, *Financial Practice and Education* 8 (Spring/Summer): 13–28. Additionally, Aswath Damodaran *Corporate Finance: Theory and Practice*, 2nd edition, Hoboken, NJ: John Wiley & Sons, 2007, Chapter 7, provides an excellent practical guide to estimating a firm's cost of capital.

ABOUT THE CONTRIBUTORS

Aaron Martin received his BS in finance and Master's in business administration from Oklahoma State University. He works in the energy industry for Sempra Energy, San Diego, California.

Daniel A. Rogers, PhD, has taught courses in valuation (including real estate valuation), corporate finance, and derivative securities at Portland State University, Northeastern University, Massey University, and University of Utah. He has published research in the areas of corporate risk management and derivatives usage, managerial incentives arising from compensation, and stock option repricing. His

published work includes articles in the *Journal of Finance, Journal of Banking and Finance, Financial Management, Journal of Applied Corporate Finance,* and *Journal of Futures Markets.* Prior to his life as an academic, Dr. Rogers held management positions with a national airline and a petroleum products distributor during which he purchased jet and diesel fuel, and managed the price risk associated with these commodities. Dr. Rogers has a BA in business administration from Washington State University, an MBA from Tulane University, and a PhD (finance) from the University of Utah.

Betty J. Simkins, PhD, is the Williams Companies Professor of Business and a Professor of Finance in the Department of Finance at Oklahoma State University's (OSU) Spears School of Business, where she teaches energy finance, corporate finance, and enterprise risk management, among other courses. Dr. Simkins received her PhD from Case Western Reserve University (CWRU), her MBA from OSU, and her BS in chemical engineering from the University of Arkansas. She has more than 50 publications in academic finance journals and book chapters and has won awards for her research, most recently in risk management. In addition, Betty has won several teaching awards including the Regents Distinguished Teaching Award. She has taught Energy Finance, a course she created, at both the undergraduate and graduate levels for over 12 years and teaches executive education courses on energy finance for companies around the world. She is also very active in the finance profession and currently serves on the Board of Directors for the Financial Management Association, as co-editor of the *Journal of Applied Finance,* as past president of the Eastern Finance Association, and on the editorial boards of several prestigious finance journals. Prior to academia, she worked in the energy industry for Williams Companies and Conoco (now ConocoPhillips). In addition to being co-editor of this book, in 2010 she co-edited *Enterprise Risk Management: Insights and Analysis on Today's Leading Research and Best Practices,* also published by John Wiley & Sons.

CHAPTER 24

Wind Energy Power Company, Inc. (A)

Analyzing a Wind Energy Investment

JOHN D. MARTIN
Baylor University

J. DOUGLAS RAMSEY
EXCO Resources, Inc.

SHERIDAN TITMAN
University of Texas at Austin

WIND ENERGY POWER COMPANY, INC. (A)

In the summer of 2008, the prices for fossil fuels were at record levels with gasoline prices reaching $4 a gallon in many parts of the country. The effects of rising fuel costs were not limited to transportation, however. Fossil fuels are widely used in the generation of electricity and the effects of the price increases were causing the price of electric power to increase too. In the United States, approximately 22 percent of all electric power is produced using natural gas. Although natural gas plants are relatively inexpensive to construct, their fuel cost makes the power produced in these plants more costly than either coal or nuclear.

Paralleling the rising cost of fossil fuels is a growing concern by many people that the use of fossil fuels for power generation is an important contributor to global warming as well as atmospheric pollution. In fact, some 29 states and 3 Canadian provinces have statutes that promote the development of renewable energy power plants such as wind and solar. Since natural gas is the most expensive fuel currently being used to generate electricity, the cost of power generation using this fuel is the standard typically used to assess the economic viability of renewable energy sources.

The Wind Energy Power Company (TWEPCO) was formed in 2007 by Bill Garner, a former energy company executive; retired attorney Jim Hale; and Gary Patterson, formerly a member of the Texas Utilities wind energy group. The three partners felt that the time for wind-powered energy generation was at hand and they announced in June 2008 their intention to build a wind farm capable of producing 2,500 megawatts of power generation capability near Vernon, Texas. This

site was selected for its wind potential as well as its proximity to the statewide energy grid called ERCOT (Energy Reliability Council of Texas).

TWEPCO's founders planned to launch the construction of the wind power facility by November 1, 2008; however, by October three factors had changed, which dramatically altered the economics of wind energy:

1. The price of natural gas had fallen from around $13 per MMBtu in July to around $6 per MMBtu. This decline reduced the attractiveness of alternative energy sources such as wind.
2. The growing demand for wind turbines combined with rapidly rising prices for the basic raw materials used to build the turbines, such as steel and copper, had pushed the cost of new turbines up dramatically.
3. The financial crisis accompanying the collapse of the credit markets that peaked in 2008 was sure to increase the cost of all forms of new financing. Investor tolerance for risk and financial leverage was at its lowest point in decades if not since the Great Depression.

The three business partners met at their offices on Preston Lane in Dallas, Texas, on the morning of October 15, 2008, to discuss what they should do, for each of them knew that the wind energy plan was in jeopardy. The initial financing arrangements had already been made with a consortium of banks as well as a group of equity partners to purchase the wind turbines and begin construction. The terms of the financing, however, were not set. Moreover, the tightening conditions in both the public and private capital markets meant that the cost of capital for the investment was going to increase, the only thing the partners did not know was just how much. In addition, an order had been placed for the turbines accompanied by a nonrefundable deposit of 5 percent of their cost, and the firm had entered into binding three-year land lease agreements calling for annual payments of $6,000 per wind turbine per year.

Never one to mince his words, Jim Hale offered this opening comment to kick off the meeting: "It seems to me that the gods have conspired against us and that we ought to consider pulling the plug."

Bill Garner responded almost immediately, "Hold on just a minute, Jim, we've got a lot invested here, and I think this oil price thing is going to correct itself in time. I still think we need to stay the course and begin installing our wind turbines as scheduled. In fact, we have invested a lot of money getting the land leases signed and are obligated to honor those leases for three years if we ever want to make this investment."

Gary interjected, "I agree with Jim's sentiment but don't think we should just walk away right now. After all, we've tied up the location with leases that are good for three years even if we don't develop them. Why not continue paying for the leases and put the orders on hold for the turbines? Can't we work out something with the manufacturer to delay delivery or something?"

ELECTRIC POWER GENERATION AND THE POTENTIAL FOR WIND ENERGY

In the fall of 2008 roughly half of all electricity produced in the United States was generated by coal-fired plants (48%), another 19 percent came from nuclear plants,

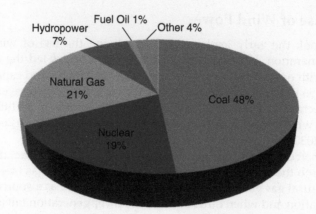

Exhibit 24.1 U.S. Electric Power Industry Net Generation, Year to Date through September 2008
Source: www.eia.doe.gov/cneaf/electricity/epm/epm_sum.html.

and 21 percent from natural gas fired plants (see Exhibit 24.1). The remainder of U.S. power production came from hydropower (7%), fuel oil (1%), and other energy sources including renewable energy sources (4%). However, rising oil prices which reached $140 per barrel in the summer of 2008, combined with growing concerns about the environment and global warming produced a boom in the demand for alternative sources of energy with wind leading the parade.

Wind energy generation was a very minor component of total U.S. power generation in 2008. However, wind energy generation had experienced several years of growth and the projected rapid expansion in wind power for the future, as Exhibit 24.2 illustrates. Installed wind power doubled in the three years between 2003 and 2006 and doubled again in the two year period 2006 to 2008. Based on this trend the American Wind Energy Association (AWEA) stated that the United States is "ahead of the curve for contributing 20 percent of the U.S. electric power supply by 2030 as envisioned by the U.S. Department of Energy."[1]

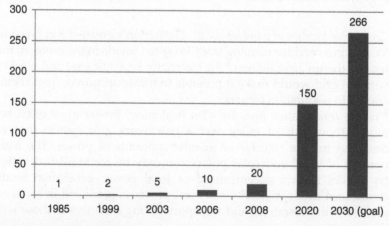

Exhibit 24.2 Wind Power Forecast
Source: American Wind Energy Association (AWEA) and Emerging Energy Research.

The Promise of Wind Power

Europeans took the early lead in commercializing the use of wind power for electricity generation. However, by 2008 the United States led the world in total generation with over 20,000 mega watts (MW) of installed wind capacity that produces about 56 billion kilowatt hours (kWh) of electrical power every year which is enough electricity to power 5.3 million American homes. In addition, the rate of expansion of wind power was dramatic with projections reaching 266 gigawatts of capacity by 2030.

The 20 percent projected contribution of wind power generation is almost exactly equal to the current power generated using natural gas (see Exhibit 24.1). Although natural gas generation will probably be needed as a source of peak load power generation and when other sources of power generation fail (e.g., when the wind does not blow where wind turbines are located), the need for natural gas generation as a base load power source would surely decline with the development of wind power generation capability.

Factors Limiting the Development of Wind Power

Although wind generation has proven itself to be economically viable in Europe where Denmark, for example, generates 20 percent of its electricity using wind turbines, the case for U.S. wind energy has some legitimate problems. The most critical limitations relate to the transmission problems arising out of the limitations of the electrical grid in the United States and the cost per kWh of producing electricity with wind power.[2]

Transmission Grid Issues
The electrical grid in the United States consists largely of a patchwork of local and regional transmission lines. This means that the existing grid was not built to transmit large amounts of power across great distances as would be required by the full development of the wind power potential. Specifically, the full development of wind and solar power generation would benefit greatly from the existence of a national grid for three reasons:

- *Geographic location of wind resources.* The nation's greatest wind resources are located in a corridor running from Texas to Canada in the center of the country, yet the greatest demand for electricity is on the east and west coast. A national grid would make it possible to transport power from remote generators to population centers.
- *Existing transmission lines are often inadequate.* Power must often be transmitted thousands of miles over a patchwork grid system that was not designed for the transfer of massive amounts of power. The full development of wind and solar power can only be accomplished if the country moves from a decentralized or local power generation model to a centralized model whereby electrical power is produced in areas with the greatest wind resources and transported long distances to those who need the power.

- *Wind is an intermittent source of energy.* When the wind does not blow in a particular region of the country, a national grid would allow wind generation in other parts of the country to pick up the slack.

If the cost of connecting to the grid and upgrading the grid to handle the long-distance transfer of power is allocated to the cost of installing wind power generation, it would dramatically reduce the economic viability of this source of renewable electric power.

Uncertain Public Policy

Public policies at the federal level are critical to the full development of wind energy for at least two reasons:

1. *Support for the development of a national transmission grid.* The full build-out of a national transmission grid is not only expensive but will require public policy support from the federal government as the grid, like interstate pipelines, crosses multiple state lines.
2. *Continuation of federal subsidies for alternative energy production.* Moreover, wind power generation is currently subsidized by government in two ways: renewable energy credits and production tax credits. The sale of renewable energy credits is worth just under 1 cent per kWh while the production tax credit pays producers $0.02 per kWh. Both these subsidies are subject to the whim of public policy. For example, since the production tax credit was initiated in 1992 it has been discontinued for short periods of time on two occasions before being reinstated.

Cost Competitiveness of Wind Generation

In the electric power industry the cost per kWh is commonly used to compare the relative costs of alternative plant configurations and fuel sources.[3] To analyze the attractiveness of wind generation, Gary Patterson, who has extensive experience with wind power generation from his previous position with Texas Utilities, has prepared a basic discounted cash flow model that compares the cost per kWh of producing electricity from wind compared to the three primary sources of electric power production: coal, natural gas, and nuclear. The resulting cost estimates are found in Exhibit 24.3, and the assumptions underlying this analysis are found in Appendix A.

The cost estimates underlying the cost per kWh found in Panel A of Exhibit 24.3 reflect estimates made in July of 2008. Gary explained to the other partners that these estimates indicate that both coal-fired and nuclear plants have a lower cost per kWh to produce electricity than either wind or natural gas. However, he went on to say, these cost estimates do not incorporate consideration for the production tax credit of $0.02 per kWh or the sale of renewable energy credits, which are estimated to be slightly less than $0.01 per kWh. The net result, he explained, is that for comparison purposes the cost of wind generation was estimated to be about $0.0572 in July 2008, which was very competitive with all the alternatives and much less expensive than natural gas.

Panel B of Exhibit 24.3 provides revised cost per kWh costs for the natural gas–fired plant in light of the decline in the cost of natural gas from a high of

Exhibit 24.3 The Cost of Generating Electricity per kWh: Wind, Natural Gas, Coal and Nuclear

Panel A. Analysis Based on Costs of Fuel in July 2008

Breakdown of annualized cost per kWh	Wind Turbines	Gas Plant	Coal Plant	Nuclear Plant
Capital Cost per kWh	0.0746	0.0105	0.0286	0.0439
O&M, Admin, Property Taxes, and Insurance Cost per kWh	0.0114	0.0026	0.0108	0.0210
Land Lease Cost per kWh	0.0012	NA	NA	NA
Decommissioning Costs per kWh	NA	NA	NA	0.0014
Fuel Cost	NA	0.0887	0.0139	0.0040
Annualized Costs per kWh	$ 0.0872	$ 0.1018	$ 0.0533	$ 0.0703

Panel B. Analysis Based on the Costs of Fuel in November 2008

Breakdown of annualized cost per kWh	Wind Turbines	Gas Plant	Coal Plant	Nuclear Plant
Capital Cost per kWh	0.0746	0.0105	0.0286	0.0439
O&M, Admin, Property Taxes, and Insurance Cost per kWh	0.0114	0.0026	0.0108	0.0210
Land Lease Cost per kWh	0.0012	NA	NA	NA
Decommissioning Costs per kWh	NA	NA	NA	0.0014
Fuel Cost per kWh	NA	0.0410	0.0139	0.0040
Annualized Costs per kWh	$ 0.0872	$ 0.0541	$ 0.0533	$ 0.0703

Capital Cost per kWh—incorporates consideration for the initial cost of acquiring and installing generation capacity net of the depreciation tax savings.
O&M, Admin, Property Taxes, and Insurance Cost per kWh—includes the operating and maintenance, property taxes, and cost of insurance for the generation capacity.
Land Lease Cost per kWh—the cost of leasing land for the location of wind turbines.
Decommissioning Costs per kWh—the cost of decommissioning nuclear power plants at the end of their productive life. Although these plants were originally commissioned for 20 to 30 years, many of them continue to operate under an extension of their charter.
Fuel Cost per kWh—only applicable for non-renewable energy sources.

$13 per MMBtu in July to about $6 in November 2008. Fuel cost per kWh drops from $0.0887 in July to only $0.0410 in November, which pushes the cost per kWh down to only $0.0541, which is less than the cost of wind generation, even after adjusting for the $0.03 per kWh subsidy for wind power generation. Gary also pointed out that this result only reflects the changed cost of natural gas and specifically did not incorporate consideration for any increase in the capital costs associated with the purchase wind turbines that occurred between July and November. For example, if the cost of wind turbines rose by 10 percent from July to November, the cost per kWh from wind generation would increase to $0.0953. Adjusting this cost for the government subsidies would still make the cost per kWh $0.0653 which is not competitive with either gas or coal fired generation.

It is apparent from the cost of natural gas is a critical determinant of the economic viability of wind power generation. The prices of coal and nuclear fuel did not change much from July to November 2008 so no adjustments to these costs were made in Panel B of Exhibit 24.3. However, coal prices per MMBtu did rise over the last year, rising about 22 percent (from $1.78 per MMBtu in 2007 to $2.18 in July 2008). Nonetheless, the July 2008 price is used in the computation of the cost per kWh found in Exhibit 24.3.

SPARK SPREADS: COMPARING THE PRICE OF ELECTRICITY AND COST OF NATURAL GAS

For natural gas–fired plants, the cost of natural gas is the key determinant of the cost per kWh. However, both natural gas prices and electricity prices are driven by market forces, and both are highly volatile. Given the significance of the natural gas price in determining the profitability of its use in electrical power generation, the electric power industry has defined a measure of gross profit for gas-fired plants called the spark spread. The spark spread reflects the difference in the price of electric power per kWh and the fuel cost incurred in producing it per kWh. Consequently, the spark spread is a crude measure of the profitability of natural gas–fired generation.

To make a direct comparison between the price of electricity and the cost of fuel, the electric power generation industry converts the cost of fuel from the cost per MMBtu to the cost per MWh using the heat rate of natural gas, which indicates the relationship between the volume of gas consumed in the production of a MWh of electrical power. The resulting relationship between the price of electricity and the cost of natural gas is captured in the spark spread.[4] Specifically, the spark spread is defined as follows:

$$\begin{matrix} \text{Spark} \\ \text{spread} \end{matrix} = \left(\begin{matrix} \text{Price of} \\ \text{electricity per MWh} \end{matrix} \right) - \left(\begin{matrix} \text{Cost of fuel} \\ \text{used per MWh} \end{matrix} \right)$$

where

$$\begin{matrix} \text{Cost of fuel} \\ \text{used per MWh} \end{matrix} = \left(\begin{matrix} \text{Cost of} \\ \text{fuel} \end{matrix} \times \begin{matrix} \text{Heat} \\ \text{rate} \end{matrix} \right)$$

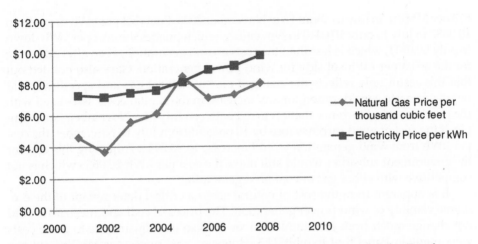

Exhibit 24.4   Price of Electricity per kWh and the Cost per Thousand Cubic Feet for Natural Gas
Source: Energy Information Administration. Data accessed January 13, 2009.

and the heat rate is the ratio of MMBtu of natural gas required to produce a MWh of electrical power. As such, the heat rate reflects the efficiency of natural gas used as well as the plant in which it is being used. The spark spread for a natural gas–fired plant would be computed as follows:

$$\begin{matrix} \text{Spark} \\ \text{spread} \end{matrix} = \left(\begin{matrix} \text{Price of} \\ \text{electricity per MWh} \end{matrix} \right) - (\$/\text{MMBtu} \times \text{MMBtu}/\text{MWh})$$

Exhibit 24.4 documents the relationship between the price of electricity per kWh and the cost of natural gas per thousand cubic feet. The two series cannot be compared directly, of course, since they do not reflect the same units of measure (\$/MMBtu for gas prices versus \$/MWh for electrical power). What we do see is that the price of electricity and the cost of natural gas are positively related.

TWEPCO's DISCOUNTED CASH FLOW ANALYSIS

TWEPCO analyzed the wind generation investment using accepted discounted cash flow analysis. This included the use of both the internal rate of return and net present value metrics.

In Exhibit 24.5, the estimated project net present value (NPV) for the proposed wind turbine investment is presented alongside of a similar analysis of natural gas, coal, and nuclear power generation. Once again, the two panels in the exhibit correspond to July and October prices for natural gas. Under the July higher prices for natural gas, the NPV of the gas-fired plant is very negative, which reflects that fact that the price per kWh received from the plant is $0.10 while the cost per kWh to produce power is $0.1018.

Exhibit 24.5 The NPV of a 2,500 MW Power Plant Based on Wind, Natural Gas, Coal and Nuclear Power

Panel A. Analysis Based on $6 per MMBtu Cost of Natural Gas in July 2008

	Wind Turbines	Gas Plant	Coal Plant	Nuclear Plant
Total kWh Produced Annually	5,475,000,000	17,520,000,000	17,520,000,000	17,520,000,000
Rate of Return (IRR)	11.43%	−2.46%	17.63%	11.79%
Net Present Value (NPV)	$ 571,496,060	$ (3,805,099,843)	$ 4,215,643,235	$ 1,402,348,242
Cost per kWh to Produce Electricity	$ 0.0872	$ 0.1018	$ 0.0533	$ 0.0703

Panel B. Analysis Based on $13 per MMBtu Cost of Natural Gas in November 2008

	Wind Turbines	Gas Plant	Coal Plant	Nuclear Plant
Total kWh Produced Annually	5,475,000,000	17,520,000,000	17,520,000,000	17,520,000,000
Rate of Return (IRR)	11.43%	26.60%	17.63%	11.79%
Net Present Value (NPV)	$ 571,496,060	$ 4,085,397,250	$ 4,215,643,235	$ 1,402,348,242

Note the dramatic differences in the total kWh produced by the wind plant versus the other alternatives found in Exhibit 24.3. The source of this difference relates to the different utilization rates for wind and the other types of plants. In this analysis, wind is assumed to have a 25 percent utilization rate, which means that the total kWh produced annually is 25 percent of the maximum output of the plant multiplied by the number of hours in the year. The alternative plants are assumed to be utilized 80 percent of the time, which accounts for the much higher level of output.

Another potentially important attribute of wind generation compared to natural gas is capital intensity. Since wind power generation has no fuel cost component and most of the capital cost is incurred at the time the turbines are installed, wind power generation investments are very capital intensive compared to natural gas–fired plants and coal plants. Roughly 75 percent of the total cost of power from wind generation is incurred in the installation phase whereas the analogous cost for a natural gas fired plant can be as little as 40 percent. This means that the costs of wind generation are not nearly so responsive to changes in discount rates as are the costs of natural gas generation where a larger fraction of the total costs are spread out over time.

APPENDIX 24.1
Model Assumptions

Model Parameters	Wind Turbines	Gas Plant	Coal Plant	Nuclear Plant
Rated Power (MW)	2,500	2,500	2,500	2,500
Capacity Utilization Factor	25.0%	80.0%	80.0%	80.0%
Power Output (kWh/year)*	5,475,000,000	17,520,000,000	17,520,000,000	17,520,000,000
Average Price of Electricity ($/kWh) Today	$ 0.10	$ 0.10	$ 0.10	$ 0.10
Nominal Electricity Escalation Rate (%/year)	2.00%	2.00%	2.00%	2.00%
Cost of Installed Power Generation per kW	$ 1,730	$ 780	$ 2,120	$ 3,260
Total Installed Cost*	$4,325,000,000	$ 1,950,000,000	$ 5,300,000,000	$ 8,150,000,000
Depreciable life of Equipment	30	30	30	30
Marginal Effective Tax Rate	35.00%	35.00%	35.00%	35.00%
Operating and Maintenance Expense Variable cost /kWh	$0.0015	$ 0.0015	$ 0.0015	$ 0.0000
Fixed cost (per wind turbine or) per kW per year	$ 10,000.00	$ 30.00	$ 60.00	$ 150.00
Property Taxes and Insurance (% installed cost)	1.0%	1.0%	1.0%	1.0%
Administrative and General Expenses /kW	$ 5.00	$ 5.00	$ 5.00	$ 5.00
Nuclear Plant Decommissioning Cost/kW	$ 0.00	$ 0.00	$ 0.00	$ 15.00
Nominal O&M Cost Escalation Rate (%/year)	2.00%	2.00%	2.00%	2.00%
Fuel Rate ($/MMBtu) Base Rates	NA	$ 6.00	$ 2.18	$ 0.60
Fuel Cost Adjustment Factor	NA	1.00	1.00	1.00
Fuel Rate ($/MMBtu)	NA	$ 6.00	$ 2.18	$ 0.60
Heat Rate (Btu/kWh)	NA	10,500	9,800	10,200
Cost of Capital	10.00%	10.00%	10.00%	10.00%
Wind Turbine Output (MW)	1.5	NA	NA	NA
Annual Lease Rate per Wind Turbine	$ 6,000	NA	NA	NA
Total Annual Land Lease Cost*	$ 10,000,000	NA	NA	NA

*Computations.

APPENDIX 24.2

Free Cash Flow Computations

Revenue	2008	2009	2038
Power Output (kWh/year)		$ 5,475,000,000	$ 5,475,000,000
Price of Electricity plus			
Subsidies ($/kWh) (B)		0.132	0.211
Total Revenue		$ 722,700,000	$ 1,155,970,467
Expenses			
Operating and Maintenance Costs		$ (25,376,750)	$ (45,065,167)
Property Taxes and Insurance		(43,250,000)	(76,805,283)
Administrative and General Expense		(12,500,000)	(22,198,059)
Land Lease Costs		(10,000,000)	(10,000,000)
Fuel Costs		–	–
Depreciation Expense		(144,166,667)	(144,166,667)
Total Expenses		(235,293,417)	(298,235,175)
Earnings before Taxes		$ 487,406,583	$ 857,735,292
Less Taxes		(170,592,304)	(300,207,352)
Net Operating Profit after Taxes		$ 316,814,279	$ 557,527,940
plus: Depreciation Expense		144,166,667	144,166,667
less: Capital Expenditures	$ 4,325,000,000	–	–
less: Increase in Net working Capital		–	–
Free Cash-Flow (FCF)	$ (4,325,000,000)	$ 460,980,946	$ 701,694,607
Cumulative Net Cash-Flow	$ (4,325,000,000)	$ (3,864,019,054)	$ 12,783,281,818

APPENDIX 24.3

Technical Note—The Cost of Producing Electric Power

It is customary in the electric power industry to evaluate alternative power plant configurations using a single number, the cost per kWh to produce electricity. The procedure used to make this comparison can be thought of as the annualized cost of electric power per kWh or, as it is sometimes referred to, the levelized cost per kWh. The purpose of this technical note is to explain how the annual cost per kWh is calculated for alternative power sources including wind, fossil fuels, and nuclear.

We proceed as follows: First we define the annual cost per kWh as the annualized cost of power generation per unit of power or kWh. The computation entails calculating the present value of the annual cost per kWh of power generation over

the life of a power plant, and converting this present value to its annual annuity equivalent. The result is an annual annuity equivalent cost of power per kWh. We then investigate the method used to estimate the cost per kWh in practice where the kWh output is assumed to be constant for all years of plant operation. Furthermore, industry practice entails decomposing the total cost per kWh into multiple component costs.

Annual Cost per kWh

The process used to evaluate this cost can be thought of as a two-step process. First, we calculate the present value of the annual cost of power per kWh over the life of the plant as follows:

$$\text{Present value of annual} \atop \text{costs of power per kWh} = \sum_{t=1}^{N}\left(\frac{\text{Annual cost of power}_t/\text{annual kWh}_t}{\left(1 + \dfrac{\text{Cost of}}{\text{capital}}\right)^t}\right) \quad (24.1a)$$

Note that in this formulation we calculate the present value of the annual cost of power per kWh for each year of the N years of plant operation. This allows the actual output to vary from year to year. In practice, the annual kWh output is assumed to be constant for all years, since the analyst is dealing with forecasts of future output.

In step two we annualize or annuitize the present value of the annual costs over the N-year life of the plant under consideration. Specifically, we calculate the annuity equivalent of the present value of the annual costs per kWh as follows:

$$\text{Annualized cost} \atop \text{per kWh} = \frac{\begin{array}{c}\text{Present value of annual}\\ \text{costs of power per kWh}\end{array}}{\sum_{t=1}^{N}\dfrac{1}{\left(1 + \dfrac{\text{Cost of}}{\text{capital}}\right)^t}} \quad (24.1b)$$

The annualized cost per kWh then becomes our estimate of the cost of producing power using a particular plant configuration.

Industry Method for Calculating the Cost of Energy

As we pointed out earlier, the annual production of power is typically assumed to be constant such that instead of annualizing the present value of the annual costs per kWh as was done in equation (24.1b) above, industry practice annualizes or annuitizes the present value of the total annual costs and then divides this annuity by the kWh of power produced each year (assumed to be constant). The components vary in important ways for alternative classes of fuel sources.

Cost Per KWh for Wind Energy

For wind energy the total cost of producing power is broken down into the three cost components shown in equation (24.2), which is the method recommended by the National Renewable Energy Laboratory (part of the DOE):

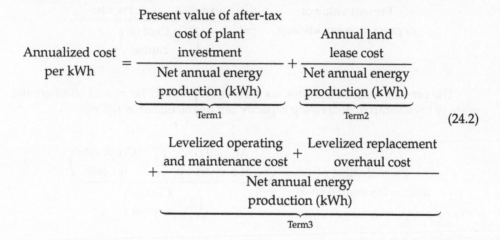

$$
\underset{\text{per kWh}}{\text{Annualized cost}} = \underbrace{\frac{\substack{\text{Present value of after-tax} \\ \text{cost of plant} \\ \text{investment}}}{\substack{\text{Net annual energy} \\ \text{production (kWh)}}}}_{\text{Term1}} + \underbrace{\frac{\substack{\text{Annual land} \\ \text{lease cost}}}{\substack{\text{Net annual energy} \\ \text{production (kWh)}}}}_{\text{Term2}}
$$

$$
+ \underbrace{\frac{\substack{\text{Levelized operating} \\ \text{and maintenance cost}} + \substack{\text{Levelized replacement} \\ \text{overhaul cost}}}{\substack{\text{Net annual energy} \\ \text{production (kWh)}}}}_{\text{Term3}}
$$

(24.2)

There are two key differences in this formulation and the one found in equation (24.1b):

1. The net annual energy production measured in kWh found in equation (24.2) is assumed to be constant for all years.
2. The annualized cost per kWh produced is calculated individually for three component costs—capital (Term 1), land lease costs (Term 2), and operating and maintenance plus replacement/overhaul costs (Term 3).

The capital cost in Term 1 is estimated using a fixed-charge rate that incorporates construction financing, financing fees, return on debt and equity, depreciation, income tax, property tax, and insurance. The capital cost per year is equal to the product of the fixed-charge rate multiplied by the initial investment in the plant.

To see how the various components of the cost of the plant investment impact the fixed charge rate in Term 1 we define the total cost of owning the plant (found in the numerator of Term 1 above) as follows:

$$
\substack{\text{Present value of after-tax} \\ \text{cost of plant} \\ \text{investment}} = -\left(\substack{\text{Initial capital} \\ \text{cost}}\right) + \left(\substack{\text{Present value of} \\ \text{depreciation tax savings}}\right)
$$

(24.3)

$$
- \left(\substack{\text{Present value of insurance,} \\ \text{property taxes, and other} \\ \text{costs after-taxes}}\right)
$$

The initial capital cost is the total cost of acquiring the generating capacity (plant). The present value of the depreciation tax savings can be calculated as follows:

$$\text{Present value of depreciation tax savings} = \sum_{t=1}^{N} \frac{\text{Depreciation expense}_t \times \text{Corporate tax rate}}{\left(1 + \dfrac{\text{Cost of capital}}{}\right)^t}$$

The present value of the after-tax insurance, property taxes, and other annual costs of ownership of generating capacity can be calculated as follows:

$$\text{Present value of after} - \text{tax annual costs} = \sum_{t=1}^{N} \frac{\text{Annual costs of ownership}_t \left(1 - \dfrac{\text{Corporate tax rate}}{}\right)}{\left(1 + \dfrac{\text{Cost of capital}}{}\right)^t}$$

The annual costs of ownership include such things as insurance and property taxes.

$$\text{Annualized (levelized) capital cost per kWh} = \left[\frac{\text{Present value of after-tax cost of plant investment}}{\sum_{t=1}^{N} \dfrac{1}{\left(1 + \dfrac{\text{Cost of capital}}{}\right)^t}} \right] \div \text{Net annual energy production (kWh)} \quad (24.4)$$

Therefore, the capital cost per kWh is equal to the sum of the initial capital investment, the present value of depreciation tax savings, and present value of the annual costs of owning generating capacity divided by the net annual energy production in kWh.

It is common practice to reduce equation (24.4) down to the product of a Fixed Investment Factor multiplied by the initial investment in plant and equipment. That is,

$$\text{Annualized (levelized) capital cost per kWh} = - \left(\text{Initial capital cost} \right) \times \left(\text{Fixed investment factor} \right)$$

The Fixed Investment Factor can be defined as follows where both depreciation and the other annual costs of ownership are assumed to be constant proportions

of the initial capital cost equal to a_1 and a_2, respectively; that is,

Fixed Investment
Factor

$$
= \frac{1 + a_1 \left(\frac{\text{Corporate}}{\text{Tax Rate}} \right) \left(\sum_{t=1}^{N} \frac{1}{\left(1 + \frac{\text{Cost of}}{\text{Capital}} \right)^t} \right) - a_2 \left(1 - \frac{\text{Corporate}}{\text{Tax Rate}} \right) \left(\sum_{t=1}^{N} \frac{1}{\left(1 + \frac{\text{Cost of}}{\text{Capital}} \right)^t} \right)}{\text{Net Annual Energy Production (kWh)}}
$$

Fuel Costs for Fossil Fuel and Nuclear Plants

To apply equation (24.2) to the analysis of plants that require fuel such as fossil fuel or nuclear, requires that we add a term to incorporate consideration for the cost of fuel. The fuel cost per kWh is typically analyzed as the product of two factors: the fuel rate factor and the heat rate of the fuel source; that is,

$$
\frac{\text{Fuel rate}}{\text{factor}} = \frac{\text{Fuel cost}}{\text{MMBtu}}
$$

For example, the cost of natural gas per million Btu on December 3, 2008, was $6.74. This price had been as high as $13.00 earlier in the year and is highly volatile. The second determinant of the cost of fuel per kWh is the heat rate, which is defined as follows:

$$
\text{Heat rate} = \frac{\text{Btu}}{\text{kWh}}
$$

The heat rate for a particular fuel source equals the number of Btus required to produce one kWh where Btu is a measure of the heat value or energy content of a fuel source. The heat rate is measured using British thermal units or Btus. For example, the heat rate natural gas is 10,500 Btus per kWh, coal is 9,800 Btu/kWh; and nuclear is 10,200 Btu/kWh.

We can estimate the fuel cost per kWh by multiplying the fuel cost factor and the heat rate for that fuel source; that is,

$$
\frac{\text{Fuel cost}}{\text{per kWh}} = \frac{\text{Fuel cost}}{\text{MMBtu}} \times \frac{\text{Btu}}{\text{kWh}}
$$

To illustrate consider the fuel cost per kWh for natural gas where the fuel cost factor is $6.74 per million Btu and the heat rate for natural gas is 10,500 Btu per kWh:

$$
\frac{\text{Fuel cost}}{\text{per kWh}} = \frac{\$6.74}{1{,}000{,}000 \text{ Btu}} \times \frac{10{,}500 \text{ Btu}}{\text{kWh}} = \$0.071
$$

Thus, the fuel cost per Btu for natural gas is 7.1 cents per kWh. Since the heat rate is constant for a given fuel source, variation in the fuel cost per kWh is driven by variation in the market price of the fuel source. The lower price of coal per MMBtu and nuclear make their fuel cost per kWh much lower than that of natural gas as we see below:

Fuel Type	Fuel Cost / MMBtu*	Heat rate/kWh	Fuel Cost / kWh
Natural Gas	$6.74	10,500	$0.071
Coal	$2.18	9,800	$0.021
Nuclear	$0.60	10,200	$0.006

*All fuel costs are based on December 3, 2008 prices.

Of course, there is no fuel cost for wind power, but the cost of fuel for nuclear is very low as well.

We can now complete the calculation of the annualized cost per kWh by adding the following term for the cost of fuel:

$$\text{Annualized (levelized) cost of fuel} = \frac{\sum_{t=1}^{N} \dfrac{\dfrac{\text{Fuel cost}}{\text{per kWh}_t} \times \dfrac{\text{kWh}}{\text{produced}}}{\left(1 + \dfrac{\text{Cost of}}{\text{capital}}\right)^t}}{\sum_{t=1}^{N} \dfrac{1}{\left(1 + \dfrac{\text{Cost of}}{\text{capital}}\right)^t}} \qquad (24.5)$$

Note that in this calculation the fuel cost per kWh is allowed to vary for each year. The forward price curve provides a source of future prices out several years. However, it is unclear whether forward fuel prices are actually used in this type of analysis or whether a constant cost of fuel based on current fuel prices is substituted for all future years.

Spark Spreads and Dark Spreads

The spark spread is the difference in the price of electrical power per kWh and the cost of fuel required to produce that power. As such it represents gross income per MWh. Specifically, the spark spread is calculated as follows:

$$\frac{\text{Spark}}{\text{spread}} = \left(\frac{\text{Price of}}{\text{electricity per MWh}}\right) - \left(\frac{\text{Cost of fuel}}{\text{used per MWh}}\right)$$

Where

$$\frac{\text{Cost of fuel}}{\text{used per MWh}} = \left(\frac{\text{Cost of}}{\text{fuel}} \times \frac{\text{Heat}}{\text{rate}}\right)$$

and heat rate is the ratio of fuel quantity measured in MMBtu for natural gas to electrical power produced by the fuel used in the power plant measured in MWh. As such, the heat rate reflects the efficiency of natural gas used as well as the plant in which it is being used. The spark spread for a natural gas–fired plant the spark spread would be computed as follows:

$$\text{Spark spread} = \left(\text{Price of electricity per MWh} \right) - (\$/\text{MMBtu} \times \text{MMBtu/Mwh})$$

The dark spread refers to the gross profit of a coal-fired plant where the cost of fuel reflects both the cost of coal and its heat rate.

DISCUSSION QUESTIONS

1. Is wind power generation economically viable under the conditions observed in July 2008? What about in October 2008?
2. Discuss the importance of capital intensity on the risk and value of investments in general and on wind generation in particular.
3. What are TWEPCO's options at this point? What would you recommend that the company do with regard to the wind generation project? Specifically, should TWEPCO proceed with the investment in wind power generation or not? Explain?

NOTES

1. http://earth2tech.com/2008/09/03/us-now-the-world-leader-in-wind-electricity-generation/.
2. Refer to Chapter 4, "Sustainable Energy: Myths and Realities," for more discussion on the costs of different power sources.
3. See the accompanying technical note at the end of this chapter titled "Appendix C: Technical Note—The Cost of Producing Electric Power" for a discussion that contains a brief description of how the cost per kWh is computed.
4. See the accompanying Technical Note, Appendix C, on the cost of producing electrical power and the spark spread.

ABOUT THE CONTRIBUTORS

John D. Martin holds the Carr P. Collins Chair in Finance in the Hankamer School of Business at Baylor University, where he teaches in the Baylor EMBA programs and has three times been selected as the outstanding teacher. Martin joined the Baylor faculty in 1998 after spending 17 years on the faculty of the University of Texas at Austin. Over his career he has published more than 50 articles in the leading finance journals including papers in the *Journal of Finance, Journal of Financial Economics, Journal of Financial and Quantitative Analysis, Journal of Monetary Economics*, and *Management Science*. Copies of his recent papers can be seen at http://papers.ssrn.com/sol3/cf_dev/AbsByAuth.cfm?per_id=17247. His recent research has spanned issues related to the economics of unconventional energy sources (both wind and shale gas), the hidden cost of venture capital, and managed versus unmanaged changes in capital structures. He is also co-author

of several books including *Financial Management: Principles and Practice*, 11th ed. (Prentice Hall); *Foundations of Finance*, 7th ed. (Prentice Hall); *Theory of Finance* (Dryden Press); *Financial Analysis*, 3rd ed. (McGraw Hill); *Valuation: The Art & Science of Corporate Investment Decisions*, 2nd ed. (Prentice Hall); and *Value Based Management with Social Responsibility*, 2nd ed. (Oxford University Press).

J. Douglas Ramsey, PhD, is the Vice President-Finance, Treasurer, and Special Assistant to the Chairman at EXCO Resources, Inc. Dr. Ramsey was previously employed as a financial planning manager of Coda Energy, Inc.

Sheridan Titman, PhD, holds the Walter W. McAllister Centennial Chair in Financial Services and is a Professor of finance in the Department of Finance at the McCombs School of Business, at the University of Texas at Austin (UT). He is also the director of the Energy Management and Innovation Center at UT. His research interests include both investments and corporate finance, and he has published and consulted in both of these areas. He currently blogs on energy policy from a financial economist's perspective. Having co-authored a leading advanced corporate finance textbook entitled *Financial Markets and Corporate Strategy*, he has served on the editorial boards of leading academic journals. He is a past director of the American Finance Association and a current director of both the Asia Pacific Finance Association and the Western Finance Association. Dr. Titman holds a BS from the University of Colorado and an MS and PhD from Carnegie Mellon University. He has served on the faculties of UCLA, the Hong Kong University of Science and Technology, and Boston College. He has also worked in Washington, DC, as special assistant to the Assistant Secretary of the Treasury for Economic Policy. He is a research associate of the National Bureau of Economic Research.

CHAPTER 25

A Case Study on Risk Management: Lessons from the Collapse of Amaranth Advisors LLC

LUDWIG CHINCARINI
Associate Professor, University of San Francisco, San Francisco, CA

INTRODUCTION

In September 2006, a large-sized hedge fund named Amaranth Advisors LLC lost $4.942 billion in natural gas futures trading and was forced to close their hedge fund.[1] Although Amaranth Advisors was not exclusively an energy trading fund, the energy portion of their portfolio had slowly grown to represent 80 percent of the performance attribution of the fund (United States Senate 2007a and 2007b). Their collapse was not entirely unforeseeable or unavoidable. Amaranth had amassed very large positions on both the New York Mercantile Exchange (NYMEX) and the Intercontinental Exchange (ICE) in natural gas futures, swaps, and options. The trades consisted mainly of buying and selling natural gas futures contracts with a variety of maturity dates. Their trades were very risky from both a market risk perspective and a liquidity perspective.

Since the collapse of Amaranth, several authors have attempted to understand what positions and risk levels Amaranth was engaged in to cause such a dramatic collapse (Chincarini 2006; Till 2006). Chincarini (2006) used the information from newspapers, CEO statements, and actual natural gas futures data to quantify the nature of the most likely trades that were made at Amaranth. That paper hypothesized that Amaranth had engaged in a short-summer, long-winter natural gas trade primarily using natural gas futures. Based on these backward-engineered positions, the paper examined both the market and liquidity risk of Amaranth's positions prior to its collapse.

On June 25, 2007, the Committee of Homeland Security and Government Affairs released a document containing a detailed investigation of the Amaranth scandal entitled "Excessive Speculation in the Natural Gas Markets." The U.S. Senate Permanent Subcommittee on Investigations used its subpoena power to analyze the trading records at the NYMEX (New York Mercantile Exchange) the ICE (Intercontinental Exchange), as well as the trades of Amaranth and other traders.

It also conducted numerous interviews of natural gas market participants, including natural gas traders, producers, suppliers, and hedge fund managers, as well as exchange officials, regulators, and energy market experts.

In this chapter, we make extensive use of the Amaranth trading positions derived from the actual Amaranth trading data. This data was obtained under subpoena by the Senate Subcommittee. We also discuss the risks associated with the trades Amaranth made and what risk managers should do to avoid these risks in the future. The rest of the chapter is as follows: The section titled Background discusses the background of the firm Amaranth Advisors LLCand also describes the natural gas futures market and details the basics of typical spread trades to help the reader appreciate the more complicated Amaranth trading strategies; "Amaranth's Trading Strategy discusses Amaranth's actual trading positions on August 31, 2006, and in other periods; The Risks of Amaranth's Strategies analyzes the market and liquidity risks inherent in Amaranth's natural gas positions; Five Lessons for Regulators and Hedge Funds discusses lessons for regulators and risk managers, and the last section provides a conclusion.

BACKGROUND

Amaranth Advisors, LLC

Amaranth Advisors LLC was a hedge fund operating in Greenwich, Connecticut.[2] The hedge fund was launched in 2000 as a multistrategy hedge fund, but had by 2005–2006 generated over 80 percent of their profits from energy trading (United States Senate 2007a and 2007b see also Exhibit 25.12). This section provides a very brief summary of Amaranth.

The Management

The management consisted of several seasoned professionals. The most relevant to the natural gas futures disaster was Mr. Brian Hunter. Hunter joined Amaranth in 2004.[3] He was hired by Mr. Maounis and Mr. Arora, a former Enron trader who had established Amaranth's energy and commodities trading desk. Prior to this, Brian Hunter had worked at TransCanada Corporation, a Calgary pipeline company, where he began getting a name for himself in energy trading. While there, he was able to find mispricing in energy options, which helped the firm make profits. After this, Hunter moved to Wall Street to work for Deutsche Bank on the energy desk. While there, his positions in natural gas futures caused large fluctuations in profit and loss.

In the summer of 2005, Hunter threatened to leave Amaranth, partly because he disliked his compensation structure and did not wish to report to Arora. Maounis reacted by allowing Hunter to trade a book separate from Arora. Also, his share of the operating profits eventually were increased from 7.5 percent to 15 percent. Hunter made a name for himself on Wall Street when he helped Amaranth make $1 billion in profits in 2005. Due to his trading success in 2005, Hunter was rumored to have been compensated between $75 million and $100 million. Late in 2005, Hunter was also allowed to return to his hometown of Calgary and trade from there. Eventually, his four other natural gas traders migrated from Greenwich to Calgary.[4]

The Strategies and Fund Structure

Amaranth began as a multistrategy hedge fund, but by 2006 had become dominated by its energy portfolio. The principal fund, with $8.394 billion of capital at the end of August 2006, was the Amaranth LLC fund. The multistrategy portfolio consisted of trades in the following areas: Energy Arbitrage and Other Commodities, Convertible Bond Arbitrage, Merger Arbitrage, Credit Arbitrage, Volatility Arbitrage, Long/Short Equity, and Statistical Arbitrage. Amaranth's exposure to these various strategies changed dramatically over the years prior to September 2006. For example, at Amaranth's inception, 60 percent was devoted to convertible arbitrage, whereas by September 2006 only 2 percent was devoted to this strategy. Also, over 86 percent of their performance in 2006 was due to energy and commodity-related trades. In addition to this, Amaranth had no stop limits and no concentration limits, which allowed the fund to concentrate more towards energy by the end of August 2006. Also there were no leverage restrictions within the firm. Style drift was evident with this multistrategy fund.[5]

Amaranth's capital came from a variety of investors. About 60 percent came from fund-of-funds, about 7 percent from insurance companies, 6 percent from retirement and benefit programs, 6 percent from high net worth individuals, 5 percent from financial institutions, 2 percent from endowments, and 3 percent was insider capital.

Minimum investments in Amaranth were $5 million. The management fee was 1.5 percent, and the incentive fee was 20 percent. A high water mark was also employed.[6]

Risk Management and Liquidity Management

The Chief Risk Officer of Amaranth had a goal of building a robust risk management system. Amaranth was unusual in terms of risk management in that it had a risk manager for each trading book that would sit with the risk takers on the trading desk. This was believed to be more effective at understanding and managing risk.[7] Most of these risk officers had advanced degrees.

The risk group produced daily position and profit and loss (P&L) information, Greek sensitivites (i.e., delta, gamma, vega, and rho), leverage reports, concentrations, premium at risk, and industry exposures. The daily risk report also contained the following three items:

1. Daily value-at-risk (VaR) and stress reports. The VaR contained various confidence levels, including one standard deviation (SD) at 68 percent and 4 SD at 99.99 percent over a 20-day period. The stress reports included scenarios of increasing credit spreads by 50 percent, contracting volatility by 30 percent over 1 month and 15 percent for 3 months, 7 percent for 6 months, and 3 percent for 12 months, interest rate changes of 1.1 times the current yield curve. Each strategy was stressed separately, although they intended to build a more general stress test that would consolidate all positions.
2. All long and short positions were broken down. In particular, the risk report listed the top 5 and top 10 long and short positions.
3. A liquidity report that contained positions and their respective volumes for each strategy was used to constrain the size of each strategy.

The risk managers also calculated expected losses for the individual positions. The firm had no formal stop-losses or concentration limits. Amaranth took several steps to ensure adequate liquidity for their positions. These steps are listed on the more detailed version of this section on the FMA website.

Events in September

The price movements of natural gas futures in September 2006 were quite different from those in past years. Exhibit 25.1 shows a timeline of the events in September and leading up to September. Historically, a spread trade strategy in natural gas futures had done quite well. Exhibit 25.2 shows the average returns of different maturity futures contracts in the month of September from 1990 through 2005. The x-axis plots the contract months forward. Thus, in this particular graph, "1" represents the returns for the nearest October futures during September, "2" represents the returns for the nearest November contract in September, and so on. One can see that generally winter month returns are higher than non–winter month returns and that natural gas prices have tended to rise on average in September for the first 36 months out. Some of the near contracts had returns as high as 5.73 percent on average in September.

In September 2006, the natural gas futures market behaved entirely differently from the way it had historically. Exhibit 25.3 shows the behavior of natural gas futures returns in September 2006. One can see, from this figure, the dramatic negative returns in September, which were as low as –27 percent for front-month contracts.[8] One can also see that the negative returns were less for non–winter months. That is, although returns were severely negative for most natural gas futures contracts, they were worse for winter months through the maturity spectrum. For example, for the first year out the contract months 2 through 6 did poorly, representing the contracts for November 2006 through March 2007, while in months 7 through 13 the negative returns are less severe for the months April 2007 through October 2007. This pattern is seen for contracts in future years as well. This pattern would not bode well for a strategy that is long winter and short non-winter months.

Exhibit 25.4 shows the profit and loss (P/L) of Amaranth's natural gas futures equivalent positions on a daily basis in September 2006. Exhibit 25.4A shows the daily P/L, while Exhibit 25.4B shows the cumulative P/L starting at zero on August 31, 2006. The daily P/L is computed using Amaranth's actual daily positions from August 31, 2006, through September 15, 2006. After September 15, 2006, no data on their positions was available, and the daily P/L was computed assuming Amaranth maintained their September 15, 2006, natural gas positions.

As shown in Exhibit 25.4B, from August 31, 2006, to September 7, 2006, Amaranth had lost about $199.5 million on their natural gas positions. This soon deteriorated very quickly. By the close of business on September 20, they had lost about $3.774 billion on their natural gas futures positions. Margin calls on these losses eventually led Amaranth to sell the energy portfolio to Citadel and J.P. Morgan with the final transfer occurring on September 21, 2006.

If one computes the losses of Amaranth's natural gas positions from August 31, 2006, through September 21, 2006, assuming the positions were not altered during the period, the losses amount to about $3.295 billion. The actual losses computed in

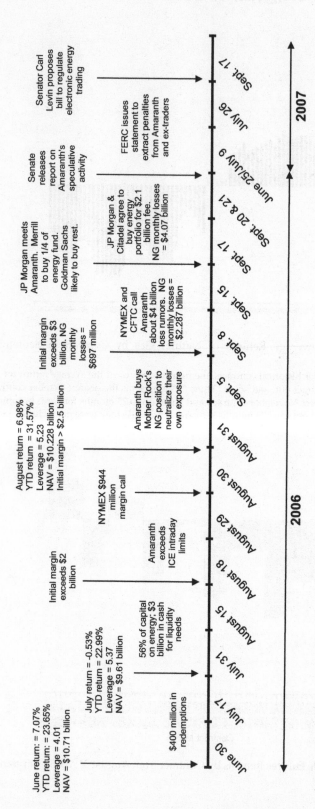

Exhibit 25.1 Timeline of the Amaranth Collapse

Note: On the NYMEX, Amaranth held positions in outright natural gas futures contracts from October 2006 maturity to December 2011 maturity. Amaranth also had a significant amount of positions in call and put options on the underlying natural gas futures contracts with NYMEX. They also had natural gas swap contracts through the Clearport system of NYMEX. They had a combination of regular swaps and penultimate swaps, the latter of which expire one day prior to the former, but are otherwise identical. The rest of their positions consisted of natural gas swap contracts on ICE, some of which were electronically traded and cleared positions on ICE, while others were off-exchange contracts, but later cleared through ICE. Among the trades entered on ICE, some of the swap contracts were in individual contract months (e.g., October 2006), while others were in calendar strips (e.g., November through March). All of these different types of instruments were converted to NYMEX futures equivalent value (NYMEX FEQ).

547

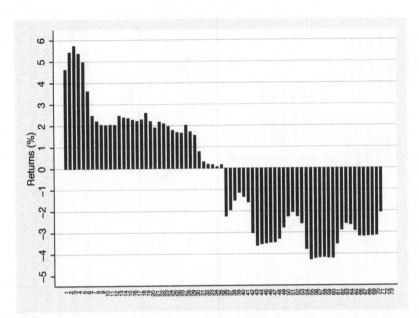

Exhibit 25.2 Historical Average Returns of Natural Gas by Contract in September (1990–2005)

Note: Since these returns are for historical contracts, the numbers represent the average return for the first contract out, second contract out, and so on. Thus, "1" represents the nearest October contract, while "2" represents the nearest November contract, and so on up to 73 months forward. In some of the earlier years, contracts did not exist 73 months forward; in this case they were not included in the averages.

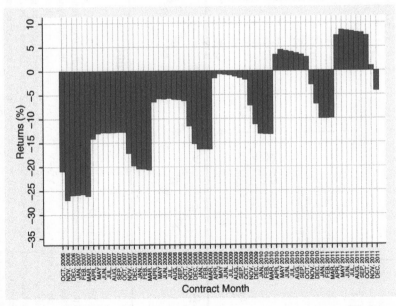

Exhibit 25.3 Natural Gas Futures Returns by Contract from August 31, 2006 – September 21, 2006

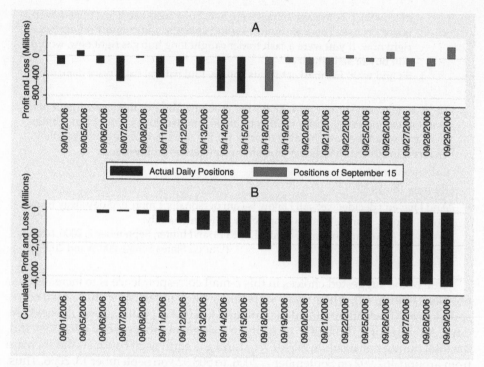

Exhibit 25.4 The Profit and Loss of Amaranth's Natural Gas Positions in September
Note: Losses each day are computed based upon the actual positions Amaranth had at the close of the prior day. From September 18, **2006,** onward, the positions of Amaranth were not available, thus the returns are computed assuming Amaranth maintained the positions they had at the close of business on September 15, 2006.

Exhibit 25.4 total $4.071 billion.[9] This difference between the losses indicates that the trades that Amaranth executed between August 31, 2006, and September 15, 2006, served to increase their losses by an additional $775.5 million. In fact, these additional losses were probably not accidental or random. That is, given the losses up to September 7, 2007, the Amaranth energy traders may have exercised their "free option" of limited downside liability if things went wrong by increasing the bets in response to troubled times. Correspondence from an Amaranth trader to Brian Hunter indicates a line of reasoning along this path:

Tell me if I am wrong, but we have three choices here.

1. Shut down and start energy fund, lose 0.3 to 1.0 getting out, and have great future potential. However, if we lose that, who is going to want in on the energy fund? If h/j drops to 1.50 or worse, the deferred positions are all going to get obliterated too.[10]
2. Jump back in and help this market out. Risk losing some investors due to risk profile, but manage along until we get the proper catalyst to exit positions. Start energy fund when we can later. Without the market's ability to absorb some xh or even some back length right now this market in a world

of trouble.[11] 2 days ago things were fine, but it feels like it just tipped over-
board on risk. There is comfort selling spreads, and comfort selling price
right now. If you were a cash trader caught long hub gas right now, would
you buy or sell January?

3. Sit and wait. Let market take its course, find natural fixed price demand.

There is not catalyst right now. That's the problem. You exit this size without one
(without exiting every positions in your book), and we got a big problem. Things
were fine when we were holding the risk for the market, b/c we could handle it.
That risk in 30 other hands is a much more dangerous proposition.

Calhoun think #2

Rummy thinks #3

And I haven't decided yet. All I know is I am personally 1 more bad day away from
stopping out...can't afford to drop below 30 for my family.
        —Amaranth Trader Shane Lee to Brian Hunter, September 7, 2006 16:54
                                (United States Senate 2007a and 2007b)

One of the suggested choices in this e-mail correspondence is to increase their
positions (choice #2), which some were suggesting. In fact, after this e-mail correspondence, Amaranth modified their natural gas future positions over the next few
days. Although it is difficult to quantify in a single number exactly what they did,
the total number of absolute NYMEX natural gas equivalent contracts did increase
from around 462,992 on September 7, 2006, to 508,923 on September 13, 2006. Thus,
the additional losses of Amaranth in these days were partly due to increasing the
actual exposure to natural gas futures contracts, partly due to modifying the positions across the maturity spectrum and partly due to the movement of the options
and other positions in the Amaranth portfolio.[12]

Natural Gas Spread Trades

Amaranth's collapse was mainly due to losses in the trading of natural gas. To
understand the Amaranth collapse, one needs to understand the mechanics of trading natural gas futures, options, and swaps.

Trading Natural Gas

In this section, I discuss some basic features of trading natural gas futures on the
NYMEX and ICE exchanges. Traders in natural gas futures have several options.
The largest exchange for trading natural gas futures is the NYMEX, which has
futures contracts of consecutive delivery months up to five years out. They also
have options on all of the futures contracts, as well as spread options that pay off
on the difference between futures contract prices of two different months. The initial margin requirement on futures contracts vary by type of trader (nonmember
customer, member customer, and clearing member and customer) and also vary by
time to maturity of the contract. Contracts closer to delivery have stricter margin
requirements. To give a flavor of the margin differences as a percentage of notional
value, on August 31, 2006, $12,150 was required for each October 2006 contract
(Tier 1), which had a futures value of $60,480, thus, representing about 20 percent of
the future's notional position. The March 2007 contract had a margin requirement
of $7,425 (Tier 5) with a notional value of $104,830 or 7.08 percent. The expiration

of the contracts is usually a few days before the end of the prior month, and there are conventions for the last trading day of each contract, which can be obtained from NYMEX.

In addition to NYMEX, traders can use the ICE, which is a virtually unregulated exchange but performs very similar functions. ICE is the leading exchange for the trading of energy commodity swaps in natural gas and electricity. "The ICE natural gas swap and the NYMEX natural gas futures contract perform the same economic functions. The ICE swap contract even provides that its final settlement price will equal the final settlement price of NYMEX futures contract for the same month, which means that the final price for the two financial instruments will always be identical" (United States Senate, 2007a, 29). Traders also can use the ICE trading screen to enter into bilateral, noncleared transactions rather than cleared transactions (i.e., over-the-counter, OTC, transactions with other parties to buy or sell natural gas). One major difference between NYMEX and ICE is that ICE has "...no legal obligation to monitor trading, no legal obligation to prevent manipulation or price distortion, and no legal obligation to ensure that trading is fair and orderly..." (United States Senate, 2007a, 41), due to its status as an electronic trading facility. In addition, the Commodity Futures Trading Commission (CFTC) has no authority or obligation to monitor trading on ICE.

The Natural Gas Futures Spread Trade

A popular type of trade in natural gas futures is to short one contract, while going long another contract. This type of trade has several attractive features. First, the trade as a whole will have less risk to the direction of natural gas futures prices—in a sense, hedge-like in nature. Second, by shorting one contract and being long another contract, an entity will reduce their overall net position and hence may allow for greater positions on the exchange without causing a trader to hit position limits.[13] NYMEX's control system will investigate any position with a size greater than the position limit in that contract. However, if the entity is questioned by NYMEX about the position, an offsetting position in another contract may be an acceptable reason for NYMEX to allow the trade in excess of the position limit. Third, if the trade is done as a spread position, then the actual margin requirements from NYMEX are lower allowing greater leverage possibilities. Even if position limits are reached, by being short one contract and long another contract, the entity will have a better story of why they have such large positions (i.e., the position is naturally hedged) and may be allowed to engage in such positions on the exchange. Fourth, spread positions allow for more sophisticated hedge fund–like trades.

A simple example of a spread position may illustrate the point: Suppose on July 31, 2006, a trader wished to short one contract and go long another contract. Suppose the trader chose to short the March 2007 contract and go long the April 2007 contract. The closing prices on July 31, 2006, for the March and April contract were $11.461 and $8.851 respectively. The notional value of this position would equal $114,610 short and $88,510 long.[14] The position is "hedged" in the sense that if natural gas futures prices rise or fall, one position's loss will be partly offset by the other's gain. However, the position is focusing on a spread bet. That is, a bet that the March futures contracts will have a lower return than the April futures contracts. In the month of August 2006, this was actually the case. By August 31, 2006, the price for March and April 2007 futures contracts was $10.483 and $8.343

respectively. Thus, if the position were closed out on August 31, 2006, by buying March 2007 futures (covering the short position) and selling back (offsetting the long position) April 2007 futures, the net profit would have been $4,700 on this simple spread position. The return of these positions will depend on the leverage employed. Notice that even though natural gas prices dropped, the spread position still made profits.

On July 31, 2006, these natural gas futures contracts represented the Tier 5 futures contracts on the NYMEX for margin calculation.[15] For a nonmember customer, this would require an initial margin on each of the March and April contracts of $7,425. Thus, for an initial capital outlay of $14,850, the return on this investment would have been 31.6 percent ($\frac{4,700}{14,850}$). This is one of the advantages of leverage; big returns for little initial capital outlay.

The Natural Gas Spread Trade with Options

The previous section discussed one way a natural gas futures trader can engage in a calendar spread trade using natural gas futures contracts on the NYMEX. In addition to this, a trader could use NYMEX natural gas options, which are options whose value depends on the underlying natural gas futures contract. There are both call and put options, and they are available for selling or purchasing.[16] Thus, the trader could also make a calendar spread trade using options.

In addition to straight call and put options, the NYMEX also has calendar spread options available for trading. These are options on the difference in price between two natural gas futures contracts of different months. For example, an IBK07 call option is a call option on the price differential between the May 2007 natural gas futures contract and a short position in the July 2007 natural gas futures contract.

Natural Gas Swaps

Finally, using the NYMEX ClearPort trading platform, traders can transact in natural gas swaps and natural gas penultimate swaps, which are based upon the final price of the natural gas futures contracts, but are one-fourth the size.

A trader could also do such a spread trade using the ICE. The ICE allows for trading of natural gas swaps that are based on the settlement prices of the NYMEX natural gas futures contracts.[17] The ICE swaps are, for all practical purposes, identical in behavior and risk to the NYMEX natural gas futures contracts.

All of the positions and types of trades we discussed in this and the preceding sections were employed by Amaranth. In fact, Amaranth's collapse was due to a large variety of these type of trades that they made on NYMEX and ICE in both futures, swaps, and options. In the next section, we focus on the Amaranth trades in detail.

AMARANTH'S TRADING STRATEGY

The Basic Strategy

The Permanent Subcommittee on Investigations report (United States Senate 2007a) provided a detailed account of Amaranth's natural gas positions on a daily

basis throughout 2006. Amaranth's positions in natural gas involved trades in various types of contracts, including futures, swaps, and options. Their trades also amounted to a collection of many spread trades whose return depended on the movement of natural gas futures price all the way out until 2011. It is difficult to classify a large group of trades into one simplified strategy, but for the most part, the complex combination of instruments and spread trades could be summarized as a general bet that winter natural gas prices would rise, while non-winter natural gas prices would increase to a lesser degree, referred to as the long winter, short non-winter spread trade (Chincarini 2006, 2007a, 2007b).

Amaranth's positions in natural gas consisted of a variety of actual instruments. The vast majority of positions were traded on the NYMEX and ICE. On the NYMEX, Amaranth held positions in outright natural gas futures contracts from October 2006 maturity to December 2011 maturity. Amaranth also had a significant amount of positions in call and put options on the underlying natural gas futures contracts with NYMEX. They also had natural gas swap contracts through the ClearPort system of NYMEX. They had a combination of regular swaps and penultimate swaps, the latter of which expire one day prior to the former, but are otherwise identical.[18] The rest of their positions consisted of natural gas swap contracts on ICE, some of which were electronically traded and cleared positions on ICE, while others were off-exchange contracts, but later cleared through ICE. Among the trades entered on ICE, some of the swap contracts were in individual contract months (e.g., October 2006), while others were in calendar strips (e.g., November through March). Due to the difficulty of understanding Amaranth's positions when divided among so many types of securities, it is useful to convert all of the securities into the NYMEX futures equivalent value (NYMEX FEQ). For the swap contracts, this is quite easy to do, since the swaps are essentially the same as the NYMEX natural gas futures contract, but one-fourth the size. Thus, one swap contract is worth one-fourth of a NYMEX natural gas futures contract. The option contracts are more complicated, but can be translated by adjusting the position for the delta of the option.[19] Once these conversions have been made, we can aggregate the entire Amaranth position in terms of NYMEX natural gas futures equivalents.[20] Exhibit 25.5 shows the positions of Amaranth in the various instruments as NYMEX natural gas futures equivalents on August 31, 2006.

For example, on August 31, 2006, Amaranth had a net position of October 2006 NYMEX natural gas futures equivalent contracts of –94,441. That is, the combined position of NYMEX natural gas futures, options, and swaps and ICE swaps was equivalent to a short position in 94,441 NYMEX natural gas futures contracts. In fact, many of the outright positions on the October 2006 were short (i.e., 64,711 NYMEX natural gas futures contracts, 21,703 and 5,307 NYMEX swap contracts, and 87,625 ICE swaps), but some positions had a long exposure (i.e., 43,523 NYMEX options and 41,381 off-exchange ICE swaps). For October, ICE swap contracts represented the largest component of the trade at 33.16 percent of the position.

For the entire period, looking at all contract months in which they had positions, the averages are shown in the last row of Exhibit 25.5. On average, 28.40 percent of the monthly exposures were through NYMEX natural gas futures contracts, 14.82 percent in NYMEX options, 34.61 percent in NYMEX swaps, 10.21 percent in ICE swaps, and the remaining 11.96 percent in ICE off-exchange swaps.

Exhibit 25.5 Natural Gas Positions of Amaranth on August 31, 2006

Contract	NYMEX Contracts				ICE Contracts		Total
	Futures	Options	Swaps (NN)	Swaps (NP)	ICE Swaps	ICE Off-Exchange	
Oct-06							
FEQ	−64711	43523	−21703	−5307	−87625	41381	−94441
Percent	24.49	16.47	8.21	2.01	33.16	15.66	100
Nov-06							
FEQ	−336	6431	17451	−442	85597	−49453	59247
Percent	0.21	4.03	10.93	0.28	53.60	30.96	100
Dec-06							
FEQ	−7308	−2430	−8154	−449	28711	−38127	−27757
Percent	8.58	2.85	9.57	0.53	33.71	44.76	100
Average							
Percent	28.40	14.82	32.61	2.00	10.21	11.96	100

Note: On the NYMEX, Amaranth held positions in outright natural gas futures contracts from October 2006 maturity to December 2011 maturity. Amaranth also had a significant amount of positions in call and put options on the underlying natural gas futures contracts with NYMEX. They also had natural gas swap contracts through the Clearport system of NYMEX. They had a combination of regular swaps and penultimate swaps, the latter of which expire one day prior to the former, but are otherwise identical. The rest of their positions consisted of natural gas swap contracts on ICE, some of which were electronically traded and cleared positions on ICE, while others were off-exchange contracts, but later cleared through ICE. Among the trades entered on ICE, some of the swap contracts were in individual contract months (e.g., October 2006), while others were in calendar strips (e.g., November through March). All of these different types of instruments were converted to NYMEX futures equivalent value (NYMEX FEQ).

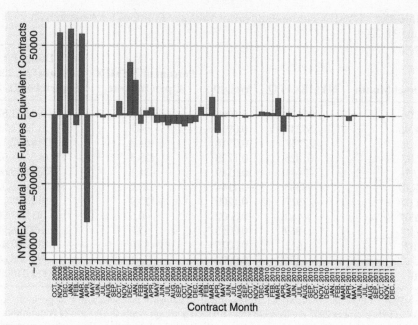

Exhibit 25.6 Amaranth NYMEX FEQ Positions on August 31, 2006

Note: NYMEX FEQ refers to NYMEX futures equivalent values of positions. Only the positions for contracts out to September 2007 are listed in this table. For a table of all of their positions in natural gas on August 31, 2006, see the expanded version of this table on the *JAF* website. Weight represents the weight of Amaranth's exposure in that particular contract as a percentage of the total absolute dollar volume of all contracts. That is, for each contract, the absolute value of Amaranth's positions are multiplied by the price for that contract on August 31, 2006, and 10,000. The percentage for each contract of each contract is the total dollar value of their position in that contract divided by the sum of the total dollar value of all of the contracts. The Dollar P/L represents the profit and loss of Amaranth in each position assuming no changes were made to the holdings. That is, it is simply Dollar P/L = NYMEX FEQ $(P_{t+1} - P_t)$, where P_t is the contracts price on August 31, 2006, and P_{t+1} is the contract's price on September 21, 2006.

Amaranth's actual positions in natural gas future equivalents on August 31, 2006, are depicted in Exhibit 25.6 and Exhibit 25.7. This graph is identical to the graph produced in the appendix of the Senate Subcommittee's report. It contains the Amaranth positions on each contract month in NYMEX natural gas futures equivalents. Before the data on Amaranth's positions were publicly available, Chincarini (2006, 2007b) postulated that Amaranth's position was a long winter, short non-winter position. Although the figure seems to indicate this, it is worth examining the issue further.[21] For the purposes of this analysis, we follow Chincarini (2007a) and define winter contract months to be November, December, January, February, and March. All other months will be considered non-winter months.

Exhibit 25.8 presents additional measures of the August 31, 2006, positions of Amaranth in natural gas. The total dollar value of natural gas futures positions by Amaranth in winter months equaled $23,489,626,234. That is, the notional value of all winter contract months was almost $23 billion across all exchanges and instruments. The total dollar value of non-winter positions was −$15.863 billion. This is

Exhibit 25.7 NYMEX Futures Equivalent Values of Positions for Amaranth on August 31, 2006

Contract Month	NYMEX FEQ	Weight	Percent of NYMEX Open Interest	Dollar P/L (August 31, 2006— September 21, 2006)
OCT.06	−94441	0.1068	−80.8	$1,196,571,821
NOV.06	59247	0.0911	84.1	$(1,313,512,297)
DEC.06	−27757	0.0518	−54.3	$718,082,127
JAN.07	61825	0.1228	125.5	$(1,698,345,675)
FEB.07	−7464	0.0149	−24.1	$204,658,602
MAR.07	58365	0.1144	73.2	$(1,597,458,370)
APR.07	−77527	0.1209	−123.9	$912,497,139
MAY.07	−140	0.0002	−0.6	$1,491,906
JUN.07	869	0.0013	5.7	$(9,226,529)
JUL.07	−1612	0.0025	−13.9	$17,362,443
AUG.07	406	0.0006	3.1	$(4,408,604)
SEP.07	−1128	0.0018	−9.6	$12,318,357

Note: NYMEX FEQ refers to NYMEX futures equivalent values of positions. Only the positions for contracts out to September 2007 are listed in this table. Weight represents the weight of Amaranth's exposure in that particular contract as a percentage of the total absolute dollar volume of all contracts. That is, for each contract, the absolute value of Amaranth's positions are multiplied by the price for that contract on August 31, 2006, and 10,000. The percentage for each contract of each contract is the total dollar value of their position in that contract divided by the sum of the total dollar value of all of the contracts. The Dollar P/L represents the profit and loss of Amaranth in each position assuming no changes were made to the holdings. That is, it is simply Dollar P/L = NYMEX FEQ $(P_{t+1} - P_t)$, where P_t is the contracts price on August 31, 2006, and P_{t+1} is the contract's price on September 21, 2006.

consistent with a long winter, short non-winter position. Of all the contract months out until December, 2011, 35 of those months are non-winter months, while 27 are winter months.

Another way to measure whether Amaranth's strategy was long winter and short non-winter is to find the percentage of winter months in which they had long positions versus short positions. For winter months, Amaranth had a long position 63 percent of the time, while for non-winter months, Amaranth had a short position 69.44 percent of the time. This is again consistent with a long winter, short non-winter strategy. And within the winter months, they had an equivalent of $28.812 billion long and $5.322 billion equivalent short positions. For the non-winter months, they had an equivalent $17.626 billion of short positions and $1.762 billion of long positions.

Thus, although not every winter contract was held long and not every non-winter month was held short, the Amaranth actual positions on August 31, 2006, seemed to be consistent with a long winter and short non-winter spread trade in natural gas using a combination of NYMEX futures, swaps, and options, as well as ICE natural gas swaps.

It's clear that on August 31, 2006, Amaranth was engaged in a natural gas futures position that was long winter and short non-winter. Next we examine whether or not they had a similar trade in prior months. In order to examine the general position of Amaranth, we look at their position three months prior to

Exhibit 25.8 Amaranth Positions in Winter and Non-Winter Months

	Total Dollar Value						Correct Sign (%)	
Trade Date	Winter-Longs	Winter-Shorts	W. Total (Net)	Non-Winter-Longs	Non-Winter-Shorts	N.W. Total (Net)	Winter	Non-Winter
Jan-31-06	4,258,305,934	(4,207,665,123)	50,640,811	1,435,236,076	(2,186,529,127)	(751,293,051)	64.29	50.00
Feb-28-06	6,747,057,844	(2,581,042,631)	4,166,015,213	1,107,062,004	(4,459,247,449)	(3,352,185,445)	77.78	50.00
Mar-31-06	8,139,116,076	(1,823,491,062)	6,315,625,014	1,414,829,338	(5,252,719,674)	(3,837,890,336)	70.37	51.22
Apr-28-06	11,676,812,614	(3,236,275,580)	8,440,537,034	1,927,180,168	(6,202,124,031)	(4,274,943,863)	70.37	57.50
May-31-06	17,101,267,975	(4,524,524,915)	12,576,743,060	2,782,321,098	(11,225,510,296)	(8,443,189,198)	70.37	48.72
Jun-30-06	20,229,114,833	(5,357,498,215)	14,871,616,618	3,222,527,838	(11,998,686,079)	(8,776,158,242)	66.67	47.37
Jul-31-06	28,568,081,397	(2,432,009,020)	26,136,072,377	1,198,034,025	(19,426,414,857)	(18,228,380,831)	62.96	56.76
Aug-31-06	28,812,493,335	(5,322,867,101)	23,489,626,234	1,762,963,323	(17,626,398,609)	(15,863,435,286)	62.96	69.44

Note: For this table, winter months are defined to be November, December, January, February, and March. Non-winter months are all other months. For each day listed, Winter-Longs represented the total dollar value of the long positions in winter months, Winter-Shorts represent the total dollar value of the short positions in winter months, W. Total represents the sum of the two, Non-Winter-Longs represents total dollar value of the long positions in non-winter months, Non-Winter-Shorts represents the total dollar value of the short positions in non-winter months, and N.W. Total represents the sum of the two. Correct Sign (%) represents the number of Winter (Non-Winter) months in which the position is long (short) regardless of size.

August 31, 2006. The NYMEX natural gas futures equivalents of Amaranth's natural gas positions on May 31, 2006, are depicted in Exhibit 25.8. The total absolute dollar value of winter month contracts was $12.577 billion, while the non-winter months was $8.443 billion. Of the winter month contracts, 48.7 percent were held long, while 70.4 percent of the non-winter months were held short. The total value of long positions in winter months was $17.101 billion, while short positions were $4.525 billion; for non-winter it was $2.782 billion and $11.226 billion respectively. Although not a perfectly consistent winter/non-winter spread trade, the general position of the trade is long winter and short non-winter on May 31, 2006.

The natural gas positions of Amaranth on other days during the summer are of a similar nature to those on May 31, 2006, and August 31, 2006 (see Exhibit 25.8). Thus, even months prior to August 31, 2006, Amaranth had engaged in a long winter, short non-winter spread trade in natural gas.

The Rationale for the Strategy

In the previous section, we concluded that Amaranth's primary trading strategy consisted of a spread trade that was primarily long winter natural gas contract months and short non-winter natural gas contract months. Chincarini (2007a, 2007b) noted that such a spread trade had performed well on average since 1990. That is, a long winter, short non-winter spread trade in proportion to the open interest on NYMEX tended to do very well in September. It is not clear whether the Amaranth natural gas traders actually backtested the strategy or whether they used experience combined with their own trader instinct.[22] If one backtests the Amaranth strategy of August 31, 2006, on past years, one finds that the strategy produced a significantly positive average return of 0.74 percent per month or 8.96 percent on an annualized basis with relatively small losses in down years (see Exhibit 25.3).

One might naturally ask if there is some potential reason explaining this historical pattern. More specifically, one might ask if there is a justifiable reason for a trade that is long winter and short non-winter to earn an excess return. Natural gas is one of the main sources of energy for the United States, fueling nearly one-quarter of the nation's energy consumption. Natural gas is used by individual households, small businesses, and large industries. The total domestic demand for natural gas is highly seasonal; this is mainly because natural gas is the primary heating fuel for homes in the winter months.[23] "During summer months, when supply exceeds demand, natural gas prices fall, and the excess supply is placed into underground storage reservoirs. During the winter, when demand for natural gas exceeds production and prices increase, natural gas is removed from underground storage" (United States Senate 2007a, 17). In many commodity markets, the storage costs of a commodity are priced into futures contracts. Theoretically, the price of a futures contract is given as $F_t = S_t e^{(c+r)(T-t)}$, where S is the spot price of the commodity, c is the continuously compounded storage costs of the commodity, r is the opportunity cost of money or the interest rate, and $T - t$ is the time until the futures contract matures.

Thus, a storage operator might use natural gas futures to *hedge* her exposure. That is, by selling natural gas winter contracts and buying non-winter months, the storage operator will lock-in her profit for storage, which in a perfectly

competitive market should cover interest and storage costs.[24] On the other side of this trade would be the *speculator* who buys winter contracts and shorts non-winter contracts providing liquidity to the natural hedgers. In exchange for taking on this risk, the speculator should receive compensation on average. This might explain the positive average return to this strategy over time. Thus, the excess returns from a long winter, short non-winter trade in September might be a compensation to speculators for supplying liquidity to natural hedgers, which consist of storage operators and natural gas producers.[25]

A quantitative type of trader would have probably backtested the winter-summer spread strategy and found that it produced significant excess returns historically and might have used this as a basis to make such a trade going forward. However, it is difficult to determine if Amaranth's traders had based their strategy on a similar motivation. It is somewhat reassuring to find that the Amaranth strategy generated positive average returns historically. However, in my opinion, the traders were not relying on statistical techniques, but rather were using their instincts and experience in natural gas futures, which was conditioned by this historical pattern. Their view was also influenced by their beliefs about the demand and supply of natural gas in 2006. Interviews with Amaranth traders revealed that they believed that winter natural gas prices would rise throughout 2006. They believed that with increasing domestic demand for natural gas, they expected supply shortages, delivery bottlenecks, and weather-related disruptions to develop during the winter and boost prices. From early 2006, they believed that the fundamentals of supply and demand justified much higher spreads between the natural gas winter and summer prices (United States Senate 2007a, 56).

In addition to this, a lot of their trading around the main position seemed to be driven by typical trader instinct, sentiment, and weather conditions, rather than some well-designed trading strategy. Many of the instant message and e-mail conversations between Brian Hunter and other traders seemed to reveal this.[26] For example, in one e-mail, an Amaranth employee writes to Brian Hunter:

> I think you should sell 15,000 red March April and buy 15,000 (or more) front Mar/Apr. My rationale is not that you should short the reds, just that you're moving risk...not increasing it. Leveraging it to the part of the curve that is undervalued and lightening up on the one that is perhaps fair value.[27]
> —Amaranth Employee, E-mail to Brian Hunter, July 28, 2007
> (United States Senate *2007a* and 2007b)

THE RISKS OF AMARANTH'S STRATEGIES

As was described previously, Amaranth had an apparently sophisticated risk management operation with 12 dedicated risk managers supporting each desk, including a chief risk officer. They used daily VaR and stress reports, so one might naturally ask how they did not foresee the risks they were taking on August 31, 2006. In fact, the CEO of Amaranth stated in a conference call to investors that:

> Although the size of our natural gas positions was large, we believed, based on input from both our trading desk and the stress-testing performed by our energy risk team that the amount of risk capital ascribed to the natural gas portfolio was

sufficient. In September 2006, a series of unusual and unpredictable events caused the Funds' natural gas positions (including spreads) to incur dramatic losses while the market provided no economically viable measure of exiting these positions.

—(Maounis 2007)

It could be that historical measures of natural gas volatility were insufficient to identify the types of events that occurred in September, 2006, or it could be that Amaranth simply ignored the warning signs from risk measurement systems. Or, it might be that market risk was not the principal risk of the positions, but it was rather liquidity risk. In this section, we take the actual Amaranth positions in natural gas and attempt to construct both market risk and liquidity risk measures using only data up to August 31, 2006, to examine whether or not the risks of the Amaranth portfolio could have been obtained from basic risk measurement tools. In particular, we examine three sources of risk for Amaranth: market risk, liquidity risk, and funding risk. Market risk is the risk that occurs from the volatility of investment returns. Liquidity risk measures the degree of difficulty in exiting a given trading position. Funding risk measures the extent to which they were able to meet margin calls on their natural gas positions.

Market Risk

In order to evaluate Amaranth's market risk on August 31, 2006, simple historical VaR (value-at-risk) measures are constructed for their actual positions. We consider three ways to measure this VaR. The first method is computed by recreating the August 31, 2006, natural gas exposures of Amaranth in other years from 1990 to 2005 (see Exhibit 25.7). Exhibit 25.7 shows the weight of Amaranth's exposure to each contract month of natural gas futures. This weight is computed by taking the absolute value of the notional value of each contract and dividing it by the sum of the absolute notional value of all other contracts. For example, for the October contract month, this was equal to 10.68 percent. For prior years, the weight scheme was kept similar. That is, in each prior year, the weight of the October current year contract was kept at 10.68 percent. The corresponding returns of these positions were computed in every year from the last trading day in August to the last trading day in September. These 16 years of September returns were then used to calculate a sample average and standard deviation of the strategy in September to be used to estimate a VaR for the strategy in September.[28]

The VaR was computed as

$$VaR_t = V_t(\mu - k(\alpha)\sigma) \tag{25.1}$$

where μ represents the average historical return of the strategy in September, σ represents the standard deviation of the historical September returns, V_t represents the notional value of the portfolio positions, and $k(\alpha)$ represents the critical value from the normal distribution for a confidence level $(1-\alpha)$ [i.e., $k(0.025) = 1.96$ for a 97.5 percent confidence interval].

The second method is a modification of the first method to account for non-normally distributed returns. It is the Cornish-Fischer expansion VaR (Cornish and Fisher 1937, Ord and Stuart 1994, and Favre and Galeano 2002). This method

adjusts the VaR calculation taking into account the skewness and kurtosis of the distribution of returns.[29]

The third method is to measure the most recent volatility in natural gas futures over the three months prior to August 31, 2006. Ideally, one would like to recreate the same type of positions in the past as what Amaranth had on August 31, 2006, but there is no obvious way to do this, since a whole host of different contract months are introduced. Instead, the actual positions of Amaranth from May 31, 2006, to August 31, 2006, are used and the daily returns calculated. The VaR for September on August 31, 2006, is then computed as follows:

$$VaR_t = V_t(\mu_d T - k(\alpha)\sigma_d\sqrt{T}) \qquad (25.2)$$

where μ_d represents the daily return of the strategy over the past three months, σ_d represents the standard deviation of daily returns over the last three months, and T represents the number of trading days that Amaranth used for VaR (i.e., 20 days). The confidence levels were chosen to conform closely with the risk reports that Amaranth produced internally on a daily basis (see the Background section).

Exhibit 25.9 shows the potential VaR from the spread positions and different confidence intervals. Suppose we take the 99 percent confidence interval for use with our Method 1 VaR calculation at the end of August 2006. A notional position in the spread trade of $10,228 billion would give us a VaR calculation of −$254.95 million.[30] The actual leveraged position of Amaranth had an estimated VaR of $1.33 billion. This is a sizeable amount of VaR; however, it is not the actual amount they lost in September. The actual amount they lost from August 31, 2006, to

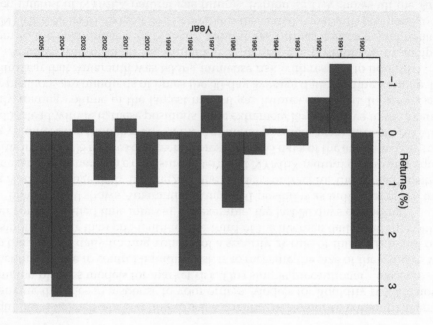

Exhibit 25.9 Historical September Returns (1990–2006) from Positions Similar to Amaranth's Position on August 31, 2006

September 21, 2006, had the positions been held constant was around $3.295 billion which is listed under the column "Actual" in the table.

Prior to that year, the worst lost in September of any year with the same-sized position since the opening of natural gas trading in 1990 would have been –$719.7 million. The average return of the spread position over the prior 16 years was 0.7466 percent with a sample standard deviation of 1.3902 in September. Thus, if Amaranth used a simple risk measurement system as used here, they would have been chasing an average return of $399.6 million (0.7466)x($53,524,979,536) with a potential 99.95 percent VaR of –$2.048 billion.

Thus, they were chasing a 4.13 percent return in September for a "worst-case" scenario of a loss of 21.2 percent.[31] This is, in itself, quite risky, but perhaps part of their philosophy. It should also be noted by looking at Exhibit 25.3 that the historical returns of such a spread trade seemed to look favorable. The strategy provided mainly positive returns with a positively skewed distribution. The largest negative return of the trade was –1.34 percent in 1991 on an unlevered basis.

The other methods show similar results. The Cornish-Fisher VaR is actually smaller reflecting the negative kurtosis of the sample distribution and very slight skewness.[32] The VaR based upon the last three months of Amaranth positions reflected a lower VaR than the historical calculation, but basically near the same magnitude.

It is clear from this exercise that the losses of September were not entirely explained by VaR calculations. The further losses may have come from another source of risk which they failed to manage as well: liquidity risk.

Liquidity Risk

Liquidity is defined as the ability to sell a quantity of a security without adversely changing the price in response to your orders. Models for liquidity risk are not as common place as models for market risk. One simple precautionary measure that practitioners use to control liquidity risk is to measure the size of their trades versus the average daily trading volume of a security. A rule-of-thumb is to not own positions greater than one-tenth to one-third of the average daily trading volume over some specified time interval, for example, the last 30 days of trading.

Exhibit 25.10 shows Amaranth's August 31 positions as multiples of the trailing 30-day average daily trading volume in each contract for the spread position. For example, Amaranth's exposure in terms of NYMEX natural gas futures equivalents in July 2008 futures contracts represented 253 days of the average daily trading volume. Even though many of the Amaranth positions were not with NYMEX, and instead with ICE, these positions were extremely large relative to the average daily trading volume of the largest natural gas futures exchange. In some cases, the positions are hundreds of times the 30-day average daily trading volume. It is quite clear that Amaranth was taking immense risk with respect to liquidity.

Another way of depicting Amaranth's natural gas positions is to compare them to the open interest of NYMEX natural gas futures contracts (abbreviated as NYMEX NGFOI). Exhibit 25.11 compares the actual Amaranth positions to the open interest of NYMEX natural gas futures. Exhibit 25.11A shows all the Amaranth positions (including ICE positions as well) as a percentage of the NYMEX NGFOI. In many contract months, this is greater than 100 percent.[33] Exhibit 25.11B

Exhibit 25.10 Measures of VaR of Amaranth's Natural Gas Position on August 31, 2006

| | Position Size | Confidence Interval | | | Worst | Actual[a] |
		68%	99%	99.95%		
Method 1 (VaR)						
No Leverage[b]	$10.228B	−65.83	−254.95	−391.53	−137.53	−629.97
Leverage	$53.523B	−344.50	−1334.18	−2048.92	−719.71	−3295.50
Method 2 (Cornish-Fisher VaR)						
No Leverage	$10.228B	−126.44	−246.31	−225.14	−137.53	−629.97
Leverage	$53.523B	−661.67	−1288.97	−1178.16	−719.71	−3295.50
Method 3 (Recent Historical VaR)						
No Leverage	$10.228B	−76.27	−224.43	−331.42	−137.53	−629.97
Leverage	$53.523B	−399.12	−1174.44	−1734.37	−719.71	−3295.50

Note: [a]Actual losses represent the losses had Amaranth maintained the positions of August 31, 2006, through the end of trading on September 21, 2006.[b] No leverage computes the VaR based on an investment in natural gas futures equal to the value of the total assets under management by Amaranth on August 31, 2006, of $10.228B. The Leverage row represents the VaR with Amaranth's actual leverage of 5.23 on August 31, 2006. For Methods 1 and 2, the numbers for each confidence level in the table represent the VaR estimates in millions of dollars using the historical mean and volatility of the winter/non-winter spread trade of 0.7466 percent and 1.3902 percent respectively. For Method 3, the VaR estimates are based on the daily mean and standard deviation of Amaranth's natural gas positions for the prior three months. These daily values were 0.0172 percent and 0.2435 percent respectively. The "Worst" column represents the losses of the respective size fund if one uses the worst historical September loss using NYMEX data from 1990 to 2005. The "Actual" column represents the actual loss that occurred for Amaranth from August 31, 2006, to September 21, 2006, assuming no changes were made to the positions held on August 31, 2006.

shows only the positions on NYMEX as a percentage of NYMEX NGFOI. It is still very high and, in some contracts, greater than 100 percent as well. Exhibit 25.11C shows only Amaranth's position in NYMEX natural gas futures as a percentage of NYMEX NGFOI. Even by this very direct measure of Amaranth's positions on the NYMEX exchange, their positions were excessive, representing more than 50 percent of the open interest in many contracts and almost 100 percent in some contracts. In some contracts, Amaranth had positions of nearly 100,000 contracts, which represents roughly 1 trillion cubic feet of natural gas, 23 percent of the amount of natural gas consumed by residential users in 2006, and 5 percent of the total amount of natural gas consumed in the United States in 2006 (Senate Report 64).

Thus, while market risk measures such as VaR indicate that Amaranth may have had a VaR of about −$2.048 billion, their liquidity risk was also very high. Thus, Amaranth was certainly being imprudent with respect to its natural gas futures positions in terms of the size versus the market size. This may have resulted in the extra $1.247 billion losses not accounted for by simple VaR measures.[34]

In addition to these measures showing Amaranth's excessive positions in natural gas, Amaranth was continuously reprimanded by NYMEX for violating trading standards and position limits on NYMEX. The Senate Subcommittee report

discusses these violations in detail (United States Senate 2007a, 90–99). On April 26, 2006, for example, Amaranth violated trading rules on the May 2006 futures contract resulting in a letter from NYMEX and a CFTC investigation. In addition to this, Amaranth exceeded NYMEX position limits virtually every month in 2006 triggering reviews of Amaranth's positions.

Of particular note was an August 8, 2006, complaint by NYMEX officials that Amaranth's position in the September 2006 contract (near-month contract) was too high at 44 percent of the open interest on NYMEX. Exhibit 25.12 shows that Amaranth reduced this short position by the day's close by 5,379 contracts (see the change in NYMEX contracts from the close of August 7 to the close of August 8), but they also increased their similar exposure short position on ICE by 7,778 contracts. Thus, ironically, the request by NYMEX to reduce Amaranth's positions led Amaranth to actually increase their overall September 2006 position. At the same time, they also increased their exposure to the October 2006 contract, a contract that is a close substitute to the September 2006 contract. In particular, they had increased their October 2006 position in NYMEX natural gas futures by 7,655 contracts and their equivalent position on ICE October 2006 contracts by 4,984.

On August 9, 2006, the NYMEX called Amaranth with continued concern about the September 2006 contract and warned that October 2006 was as large as well and they should not simply reduce the September exposure by shifting contracts to the October contract. In fact, by the close of business that day, Amaranth increased their October 2006 position by 17,560 contracts and their ICE positions by 105.75. For September 2006, Amaranth did follow NYMEX instructions by reducing NYMEX

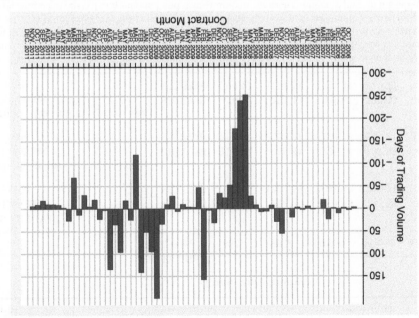

Exhibit 25.11 Amaranth's August 31, 2006, Positions as a Ratio to 30-Day Average Daily Trading Volume

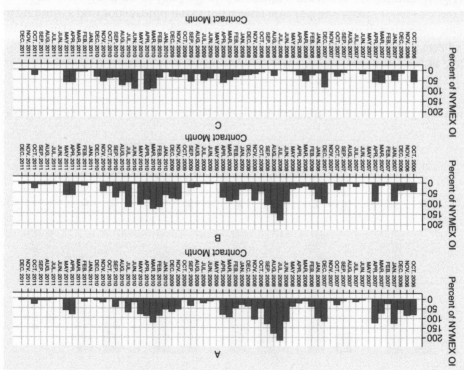

Exhibit 25.12 The Amaranth Positions as a Percentage of NYMEX Open Interest (August 31, 2006)

natural gas positions by a further 24,310, but increased September ICE positions by 4,155.

On August 10, 2006, another call from NYMEX urged Amaranth to reduce the October 2006 position since it represented 63.47 percent of the NYMEX open interest. In response to this call, Amaranth reduced the October 2006 position by 9,216 contracts, but increased their similar October 2006 ICE position by 18,804 contracts. By the end of this three-day session of calls from the NYMEX warning Amaranth of its position size in September and October contracts, Amaranth had actually increased their overall positions from August 7, 2006, to August 11, 2006, in those two contracts by 16,484 (a decrease in September 2006 positions by 23,143 and an increase in October positions by 39,627). See Exhibit 25.13.

The Senate Report highlighted that one of the problems with the current system is that electronic exchanges like ICE are not regulated. Thus, Amaranth was able to shift their exposure and actually increase it by using ICE without the CFTC or any other regulatory body aware of the increasing risk they were taking. In fact, in an instant message conversation on April 25, 2006, Brian Hunter wrote about ICE that "... one thing that's nice is there are no expiration limits like NYMEX clearing" (United States Senate 2007a, 98).

Although NYMEX only uses its position limits as guidelines of whether or not to investigate an entity's position, it is interesting to note how far above these guidelines Amaranth was. The NYMEX guideline is to examine entities with an

amount over 12,000 contracts in any given maturity. One can see from Exhibit 25.12 that Amaranth had exceeded this "guideline" by a substantial amount. Perhaps a quantitative rule would be better than a qualitative rule. With quantitative rules, Amaranth's positions would never have been able to be so large.

The reconstruction of the VaR of Amaranth's positions on August 31, 2006, was high, but cannot entirely explain Amaranth's losses in September 2006 unless one designates the Amaranth collapse as a 5 standard deviation event.[35] It appears Amaranth's traders and senior management were well aware of a VaR number similar to the one produced in this chapter. It seems that they were willing to take this amount of risk given the expected return they hoped to achieve. With regard to their liquidity risk, while the traders were very aware of the size of their positions, it is not clear that senior management in Greenwich really understood the extent of it. First, Amaranth's risk management with regard to liquidity did not explicitly specify position limits as a percentage of volume traded or open interest on the exchanges, so risk of this type may not have been on senior management's radar in an explicit way. Second, Amaranth allowed Brian Hunter and his trading team to move to Calgary without any risk management team (U.S. Federal Regulatory Commission 2007, 18–19). Third, Amaranth was slowly increasing the size of their natural gas positions over the summer of 2006.

It appears that Amaranth's senior management allowed Hunter too much freedom because they had enjoyed his prior success and wanted to believe that he really was "...brilliant..."[36] and also independently..." ... really, really good at taking controlled and measured risk."[37] Even this statement by the CEO reveals problems with their risk management philosophy. It should not be the trader that one is confident about with regards to risk management, but rather the risk manager which is monitoring that trader's risk.

In summation, the energy traders of Amaranth were well aware of the large size of their positions and either did not care (i.e., the free option) or did not realize how perilous a position such as May, they seemed to be aware of the large size of their positions. In interviews by the Senate Subcommittee with

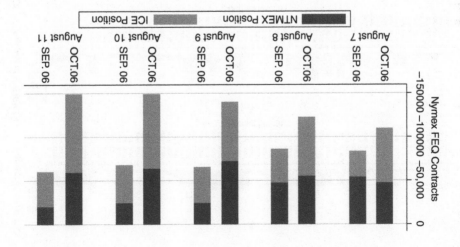

Exhibit 25.13 The Amaranth Positions in Response to NYMEX Position Limit Phone Calls

Amaranth traders, they stated after the losses in May that they were waiting to see if the liquidity in the markets would come back so that they could reduce the size of their winter/summer spread positions at favorable prices.

> We thought about pulling the trigger and taking the loss. We had many discussions about it. We figured we could get out for maybe a billion dollars. But we decided to ride it out and see if the market would come around.
> —Interview with Amaranth trader (United Sates Senate 2007a, 77)

Yet, despite being apparently aware of the liquidity issues with their natural gas positions, they continued to act perilously and actually increased the size of their positions from the end of May to the end of August (the leverage of the natural gas positions with respect to the fund increased from 3.83 to 5.23) perhaps because they ultimately believed that the market was wrong and they were right. In their monthly letter to investors explaining the losses of May, they said "... we believed certain spread relationships remained disconnected from their fundamental value drivers" (United States Senate 2007a, 73).

With respect to management, the senior management in Greenwich knew of the market risk but overlooked the position size by giving too much credit to Hunter, partly out of their own greed.

Funding Risk

Funding risk is related to liquidity risk, but is focused on leverage in particular.[38] Any leveraged position implies that the trader borrowed some of the capital to finance his position. Leverage and funding risk are very much interlinked. For example, if a trader purchases that same futures contract but keeps the remainder funds in cash (e.g., $56,250), the trader will never have funding risk, because although the future contract was purchased on margin, the trader's fund is not levered. Suppose the trader buys 2 contracts, although he only has capital to cover 1 contract. This trader's fund now has a leverage of 2 (notional value of position/cash on-hand plus initial margin). Now there is some funding risk, although it is still low. The trader will be able to meet all margin calls until the position falls by more than 50 percent. Thus, a rule of thumb in this simple example is that a trader will face funding risk anytime the return of his levered position falls by more than $1/L$, where L is the amount of fund leverage. Of course, this is only true in our simplified example where all excess capital is held in cash. It becomes even more complicated when some of this excess capital is invested in other assets.

In Amaranth's case, the leverage of natural gas future equivalents on August 31, 2006, was 5.23 ($53,524,979,537/$10,228,192,000) with respect to just their natural gas exposures. To the extent that they were investing on margin in other markets, their leverage might have been even higher. Amaranth had set aside up to $3 billion of their capital in cash to meet liquidity needs according to Mr. Artie DeRocco in conversations with NYMEX's Michael Christ on August 15, 2006. To the extent that only $3 billion might have been available for margin calls, Amaranth's leverage could have been considered as high as 17.84 ($53,524,979,537/$3,000,000,000). That would imply that even a −5.6 percent return on their futures position would cause them funding problems. On August 31, 2006, Amaranth's initial margin on NYMEX exceeded $2.5 billion. This high margin

requirement was primarily due to the notional size of Amaranth's position. In fact, if we assume that NYMEX required the maximum margin for each NYMEX natural gas equivalent, then Amaranth's positions would require $5,306,512,760.[39] Even the actual margin requirement on that day of $2.5 billion left very little room for adverse returns for Amaranth. Amaranth's daily profit-and-loss from their natural gas positions on September 8, 2006, would have been $697 million. By September 15, the additional margin required would have been $2.287 billion, and by September 21, it would have been $4.07 billion. Clearly, this was unsustainable as Amaranth did not have the cash to meet these margin calls. If we assume that on August 31, 2006, they had exactly $2.5 billion in initial margin, by September 21, 2006, they would have required around $6.57 billion of margin.[40]

What differentiates this sort of risk from other risk is that even if the strategy turned out to be profitable by month-end (which it did not), Amaranth would not have had enough funding in place to hold on to their positions until month-end. Thus, even if Amaranth's trade had been logical from a VaR perspective and a liquidity perspective, it would have not been logical or prudent from a funding risk perspective.

FIVE LESSONS FOR REGULATORS AND HEDGE FUNDS

It is difficult to construct lessons after major crises because often times the specific corrections to certain situations will only cause new crises to occur under different loopholes or conditions. Nevertheless, lessons from other crises have been useful. For example, after the LTCM (Long Term Capital Management) crisis of 1998, hedge funds learned that making sure lines of credit are really lines of credit is extremely important. Hedge funds also learned that stress testing sophisticated trading systems includes the worst-case scenarios, for example when the correlation of seemingly unrelated strategies goes to one.

In the aftermath of the Amaranth collapse, there are five lessons as well.

1. *First, liquidity risk is a real risk that must be accounted for by both exchanges and hedge funds, money managers, or traders.* For exchanges, it means strict concentration limits should be placed on a customer's positions. While NYMEX has soft position limits, they allowed human judgment, conversations with Amaranth, and greed to soften those limits up to a point, where they did not really know the severity of the enormous positions of Amaranth. *By concentration limits,* I refer to limits that are based upon some percentage of the open interest that would be dynamic over time rather than static as position limits are. The limits might also vary by contract maturity. But not only should exchanges consider strict concentration limits, they should also consider quantitative rules for managing these limits rather than ad hoc human judgment. For hedge funds, money managers, and traders, the lesson has long been known—don't own too much of a market in combination with leverage. If prices move adversely against one's levered position, margin calls might require the trader to reverse the positions to acquire cash to make the margin calls. These position reducing trades may make the prices move further adversely and perhaps

cause prices to deteriorate so much that the investor loses more than his capital and goes bankrupt. If a trader limits the concentration of his position in
a certain market, it will help insure that in the case he would like to reduce
or close his position, there will be a sufficient number of other traders to
absorb his selling pressure without moving prices too much.

2. *Transparency across exchanges in the same market may be useful.* In the case of
Amaranth, the NYMEX knew of Amaranth's NYMEX positions, but did not
know of the other positions held with ICE. Although the CFTC oversees
the NYMEX, they had no jurisdiction over ICE, since ICE is an unregulated
energy trading platform. Were there a system held by the CFTC that could
oversee all positions on energy platforms, the excesses of Amaranth could
have been spotted. By forcing Amaranth to hold much more reasonable
positions, Amaranth investors would have ultimately been better off. Also,
the possible manipulation by one entity of security prices would be avoided.
Amaranth's selling of large positions may have caused intense volatility in
natural gas prices causing actual users of natural gas (i.e., households) to
pay high prices, which may have been artificially high due to the excessive positions of Amaranth. In fact, Amaranth and Amaranth traders are
currently being sued over the matter (U.S. Federal Energy Regulatory Commission 2007).

One of the steps to improve transparency in the U.S. markets is a bill
introduced on September 17, 2007, by Senator Carl Levin of Michigan to regulate electronic energy trading facilities by registering with the CFTC (Levin
2007). The bill also proposes to provide trading limits for energy traders
that can be monitored by the CFTC across all energy trading platforms and
exchanges, and requires that large domestic traders of energy report their
trades on foreign exchanges. The bill defines precisely what constitutes an
"energy trading facility" and an "energy commodity".

3. *More standard measures of liquidity risk ought to be devised so that, as with VaR,
traders, risk managers, regulators, and exchanges have a language to communicate
with each other.*

4. *There are lessons for internal risk management.* It might be important to have
risk managers in the same location as traders, rather than thousands of miles
away. It might also help to follow guidelines that many large banks have of
allotting only certain risk capital to certain traders and diversify across the
firm, rather than have one trader, like Hunter, use the majority of the firm's
capital and be responsible for the majority of the firm's performance. After
all, Amaranth was not an energy trading hedge fund, it was a multistrategy
hedge fund. Along that line of thought, one might even consider a different incentive scheme for risk managers. Risk managers are not paid as well
as traders. This causes their voice to be less important in the firm. And of
course, risk managers' bonus also depends on firm profits. Thus, to a certain extent they will also be reluctant to reduce the firm's aggressive trading
activities. They have a free option, too. It is not clear that there is a simple
way to restructure the incentives of risk managers, but it might be worth
thinking about.

5. *Spread positions can lose money and are not "arbitrage positions," especially when
the size of these positions is large.* Spread positions are usually thought of as less

risky than outright positions, since by being long certain contracts and short other contracts, the position is less exposed to the directional volatility of the natural gas market. It should be stressed that these positions have lower risk, but they do have risk. That is, the returns of these positions do exhibit some volatility, even if this volatility is smaller than outright positions. If a trader leverages these spread positions, the volatility increases linearly with the leverage. Thus, for a large enough leverage, the spread position can be as risky as or even riskier than an unleveraged outright position. This is because the spread positions are not arbitrage positions; they are just less volatile positions. Thus, when evaluating spread trades, one should consider the amount of leverage and its effect on actual volatility and not naively assume they have lower risk.

There are critics of the new proposals for regulation in the U.S. natural gas markets. The criticisms fall into four categories. First, there is a camp that believes Amaranth's positions were not too big for the market and that setting strict positions limits will compromise "…the efficient transfer of risk in the market place" (Watkins 2007). Second, some people do not wish there to be multiple regulatory agencies regulating the natural gas futures market. Third, some people worry that regulation will cause business to transfer to overseas markets. Finally, some argue that the regulation will ultimately not work, because market participants will find other loopholes (Watkins 2007).

Each of these criticisms will be discussed in more detail along with my own thoughts with respect to each of them. The first criticism is that position limit constraints will prevent "…legitimate speculation…" and thus make markets less efficient. Also, the critics worry that position limits and laws can become outdated. The first comment assumes the proportion of arbitrageurs is very small in the market place. To the extent that there are many speculators in natural gas, the transfer of risk can still be accomplished—it just will reduce the likelihood that the speculation is in the hands of just one large speculator. While it is true that laws will become outdated, it doesn't mean they are not useful in the short run. In addition, position limits can be made relative so that they do not become outdated quickly. For example, rather than have a limited specific number of contracts for each speculator, an exchange could have that number depend upon some percentage of average daily trading volume or of open interest. Also, regulation could allow exchanges and governing bodies to update position limits as market conditions change.

The second criticism is about the number of regulatory bodies in the natural gas markets. Currently, some market participants, including major investment banks like Goldman Sachs, Morgan Stanley, Merrill Lynch, and J.P. Morgan, are opposed to having both the Federal Energy Regulator Commission (FERC) and the CFTC with authority over the commodities markets. Their argument is that too many regulatory agencies might raise confusion and costs among market participants. While this is certainly a negative, the Levin proposal does not encourage multiple regulatory bodies. It specifies the CFTC as the only regulatory body. However, the reality is that when market participants are perceived to have acted incorrectly, many affected parties may resort to legal action, as the FERC has done with regards to Amaranth, even if they are not explicitly assigned the role of regulator.

The third criticism is that increased regulation will lead market participants to overseas trading venues, such as Singapore. While this is always a possibility,

it could be argued that the increased transparency and minimal standards of the U.S. exchanges may draw people to the U.S. exchanges precisely for these reasons. For example, although listing requirements on the NYSE are more stringent that those of NASDAQ, the NYSE has not gone out of business despite the rise of the NASDAQ. There will, of course, be firms that find it more desirable to go elsewhere.

The fourth criticism is that regulators "...will always be one step behind the innovating and evolving markets" (Watkins 2007). This statement is absolutely true. However, this does not mean that regulatory constraints in cases where market failures or externalities exist are not appropriate. The correct question is whether or not externalities and market failures potentially exist in the market for natural gas. In the end, we must answer this crucial question before deciding whether regulation is a good or a bad thing.

Without regulation, Amaranth was able to acquire enormously large positions on NYMEX and ICE that may have led to a distortion of natural gas prices, which ultimately affected consumers of natural gas.[41] However, even though Amaranth's positions on NYMEX were regulated by the CFTC, they still were extremely large. So it is not clear that the regulation *per se* will solve the problem. The position limits on NYMEX were very loosely enforced and subject to interpretation by NYMEX officials. It is only at late stages of the Amaranth debacle that Amaranth moved substantial positions from NYMEX to the unregulated ICE.

Although this chapter was not primarily concerned with Amaranth's effect on natural gas futures prices, a preliminary investigation was done using data on daily natural gas returns and trades by Amaranth. Some evidence was found that contracts which Amaranth sold led to lower returns than other contracts in which Amaranth was not trading.

CONCLUSION

The collapse of the hedge fund Amaranth Advisors in September of 2006 drew a flurry of attention. There are several reasons why this hedge fund failure attracted such widespread media attention. First, the size and speed at which Amaranth made losses. In less than 12 days, from September 8, 2006, to September 20, 2006, they had lost almost $4 billion. Second, their losses occurred in the natural gas markets. There is some evidence that Amaranth's trading activities in the natural gas markets distorted market prices and ultimately hurt consumers of natural gas. For instance, the Municipal Gas Authority of Georgia (MGAG) complained that its hedging costs with abnormally high winter natural gas prices caused its consumers losses of $18 million during the winter of 2006–2007 (United States Senate 2007a, 115). Third, the failure raised new concerns about risk management and leverage. In particular, it raised questions about how large a position and influence an individual entity should have over a financial market, like the natural gas futures market.

This chapter dealt specifically with examining the actual positions of Amaranth in the natural gas market to understand whether conventional risk measurement tools could have estimated the large risks that caused their collapse in September 2006. The chapter finds that Amaranth's VaR on August 31, 2006, was $1.334 billion and $2.048 billion at the 99 percent and 99.95 percent confidence level. Although large, these numbers of rather low probability events still underestimate

their actual losses in natural gas of $4.071 billion and decrease in their net asset value of $4.942 billion. In fact, the chapter finds that it was the management of their liquidity risk that was vastly irresponsible. Amaranth's NYMEX natural gas futures equivalent positions in certain maturity contracts exceeded 200 percent of the NYMEX natural gas open interest. Their ownership of NYMEX natural gas futures contracts alone was, in certain maturities, close to 100 percent of the open interest. When markets turn against a trader's position, futures exchanges will require additional margin to maintain those positions. Once the trader's cash on hand and borrowing sources are exhausted (funding risk), he can only meet margin calls by selling the underlying assets. If that trader owns a large percentage of that market, he can only sell those assets by forcing the prices even lower and thus creating further losses and further margin calls. This is known as liquidity risk. A combination of liquidity and funding risk ultimately caused Amaranth's collapse.

There are several lessons from the Amaranth debacle that have to be relearned. First, even if a strategy has a positive excess return with low volatility historically, with or without a theoretical justification for the strategy, that strategy can still have negative returns in the future. With leverage, these negative returns are amplified. Second, firms need to manage liquidity risk explicitly. The inability to sell a futures contract at or near the latest quoted price can be related to one's concentration in the security. In Amaranth's case, the concentration was far too high, and there were no natural counterparties when they needed to unwind the positions. Third, exchanges can only adequately manage their position limits if they have disciplined rules for doing so and transparency. Currently, a bill has been introduced by Senator Carl Levin to address the second point and regulate energy trading facilities (Levin 2007). The importance of limiting concentration comes also through the potential for price manipulation which can distort prices and have an unfair income distributional effect. It can also lead to larger uncertainties and less effective decision making by individuals. Amaranth is currently being sued by the FERC for price manipulation in specific instances. Their intent is to penalize Amaranth for unjust profits and civil penalties, in addition to seeking $30 million from Brian Hunter as well (U.S. Federal Regulatory Commission 2007).

DISCUSSION QUESTIONS

1. Describe the natural gas futures spread trade that Amaranth used. Provide a simple example of a spread trade position. (*Note:* Make up your own example.)

2. Describe a natural gas options trade that Amaranth used. Provide a simple example of a position. (*Note:* Make up your own example.)

3. Describe Amaranth's primary trading strategy. Explain how or why they expected it would work.

4. What is liquidity risk?

5. What is a rule of thumb about liquidity risk and trading that the chapter mentions? To answer this question, fill in the blank: Do not own positions greater than —— of the average trading volume over a specified period of time.

6. What is funding risk?

7. What are the five lessons that can be learned from Amaranth's collapse?

NOTES

1. These losses are computed as the actual change in net asset value of the Amaranth funds, including the Amaranth LLC fund, Amaranth Partners fund, and Amaranth Global Equities Master fund from Exhibit #12 of the Senate Subcommittee documents. The value of these funds was $10,228,192,000 on August 31, 2008, and $5,286,050,000 on September 21, 2006. These total net asset values do not include the Amaranth Securities LLC, which had a smaller amount of around $30–50 Million, since the data was not available.

2. Many thanks to Dan Berkovitz for providing the information upon which much of this section is based. This section draws heavily from Exhibit #12 of the Senate Subcommittee Investigations. In addition to their Greenwich office, Amaranth had been working on expanding their operations and had offices in London, Singapore, Houston, and Toronto.

3. Most of this discussion is based upon an article by Ann Davis, "How Giant Bets on Natural Gas Sank Brash Trader," *Wall Street Journal*, September 19, 2006; and FERC Docket No. IN07-26-000.

4. These other natural gas traders on his team were Mr. Matthew Donohoe, Mr. Matthew Calhoun, Mr. Shane Lee, and Mr. Brad Basarowich.

5. Style drift refers to a change in a hedge fund's strategy over time, which may or may not reflect a formal change in policy, hence the "drift." An example would be a Large-Cap hedge fund manager that suddenly has huge small-cap exposure. Most of the time style drift happens inadvertently, but in Amaranth's case, they were clearly increasing energy exposure.

6. A high water mark is a common feature of most hedge funds. It is a level of the fund's net asset value (NAV) at which incentive fees begin to accrue. Typically, the high water mark is the highest NAV received by the client over their investment period. The purpose of the high water mark is to prevent a double counting of incentive fees. For example, if the fund went from 100 to 200 NAV, the hedge fund would obtain a percentage of that appreciation as an incentive fee. However, if the fund dropped to 150 the following year, they would not receive an incentive fee for bringing it from 150 to 200. Their incentive fees would only begin again for gains above 200.

7. One might ask whether this system is indeed optimal. It could perhaps cause risk managers to become more integrated in the trading style and not be as objective in assessing risk. Regardless of one's beliefs in such a system, Amaranth actually strayed from their system in the case of Brian Hunter. When Brian Hunter and his traders moved their trading operations to Calgary, Canada, there was no risk management team on the premises to monitor their actions.

8. Front-month refers to futures contracts with the nearest month to expiration.

9. The reader is reminded that these are losses computed from the Amaranth natural gas futures equivalent positions. The actual change in net asset value of the main Amaranth funds was $4.942 billion. The discrepancy is due to losses from other types of positions not related to natural gas futures trading and slightly due to the discrepancies between the natural gas future equivalent positions and the actual positions.

10. Natural gas futures contracts are denoted by letter symbols on the NYMEX. F = January, G = February, H = March, J = April, K = May, M = June, N = July, Q = August, U = September, V = October, X = November, and Z = December. Thus, the h/j comment is referring to the March-April spread. At the close of business on September 7, 2006, the March contract (H) was trading at $10.073, while the April contract (J) was trading at $8.153. Thus, the h/j spread was $1.92. In this conversation, the trader is worried that the spread may decline to $1.50, which would cause a position short April and long March to lose money.

11. In this discussion, *xh* refers to the November and March natural gas futures contracts. See endnote 10 for more information about contract symbols.

12. As described in (2) of the correspondence, Amaranth may have increased positions to drive up the spread or "manipulate" the price spread so as to temporarily remove the possibility for further margin calls on the existing spread position.

13. That is NYMEX looks not only at individual contract position limits to decide about a particular entity, they also consider net exposure limits. Thus, if a trader is long 10,000 contracts in one contract and short 10,000 contracts in another contract, the net position is 0. This makes the position more feasible with respect to NYMEX acceptability of such a position.

14. Each contract of natural gas is worth 10,000 MMBtu. Natural gas futures prices are quoted in terms of 1MMBtu. Thus, each contract in natural gas futures represents a notional value of $1 \cdot P \cdot 10,000$, where P represents the price of that natural gas futures contract.

15. For more details, see www.nymex.com for margin requirements. Tier 5 represents the 6th through the 16th nearby month. On July 31, 2006, March and April contracts were the 8th and 9th month respectively.

16. Margin is required for short positions or writing options. However, for purchasing options, only the premium is required.

17. Although the ICE calls these instruments "swaps," they are similar to futures contracts.

18. These were created to allow traders access to an instrument that would expire one day before option expiration on natural gas futures contracts.

19. For more on this type of concept, one is referred to any options book or any book on value-at-risk. For example, see Hull (2006), Jorion (2006), or Dowd (1999).

20. The conversion of these positions was done by the NYMEX and the Senate Subcommittee.

21. Although some winter months are actually shorted, the overall positions are smaller.

22. Backtesting a strategy refers to the process of testing a trading strategy on prior time periods. In other words, a trader can do a simulation of her trading strategy on relevant past data in order to gauge the effectiveness.

23. A 2001 EIA survey found that 54 percent of all U.S. households use natural gas as the main heating fuel (United States Senate 2007a and 2007b).

24. Even though this is an overly simplistic description of the real behavior of storage operators, it may help explain some of the reasons why a speculator might choose this side of the trade. Natural gas producers might accentuate the need for speculators as they might continuously short natural gas as a hedge, which might require more liquidity for winter contracts.

25. The forward curve for natural gas futures looks like a sine wave with natural gas futures prices high in winter months and low in non-winter months. Another reason is that there is lower demand for natural gas in summer months and higher demand in winter months.

26. These documents were obtained by subpoena from the Senate Subcommittee and used in the public presentation of the Amaranth case. In particular, they were taken from Exhibit 25.9 of the Senate Subcommittee Investigation documents.

27. In natural gas trading, colors are used to distinguish between contracts of different years. "Front" refers to the contract month closest to the current date. For instance, on July 28, 2007, the "front March" contract would be the March 2008 contract. "Red" refers to the next contract year. Thus, in this case, "red March" contract would refer to the March 2009 contract. "Blue" is also used to denote the contract 2 years out. Thus, if someone referred to the "blue March" contract on this date, it would refer to the March 2010 contract. These colors help traders communicate more easily.

28. The return calculation for the strategy is given by $r_t = \sum_{i=1}^{n} w_{i,t-1} r_{i,t} \phi_{i,t-1}$, where $w_{i,t-1}$ is the weight of contract i on the last trading day of August in any given year, $r_{i,t}$ is the return of natural gas futures contract i from the last trading day in August to the last trading day in September in any given year, and ϕ_i is an indicator variable that equals -1 if Amaranth was long in that particular futures contract and equals -1 if Amaranth was short that particular contract month, and N represents the total number of contract months (e.g., 63 from October 2006 to December 2011). In some years, especially in the early 1990s, there were not as many natural gas futures positions and thus the weights were renormalized so as to be relatively the same between any two contracts. For example, on August 31, 1990, there were only 12 contracts from October 1990 to September 1991. Thus, the weight for October 1990 was -0.1697 and the weight for November 1990 was 0.14483. The relative weight was still -1.172 as in other years.

29. The actual calculation of the Cornish-Fisher VaR is available from the author.

30. This net asset value differs from that in Chincarini (2007b) due to a typo in the earlier paper.

31. This downside percentage is for the 99.99 percent confidence level VaR. It would be much less for the 99 percent VaR at -13.8 percent.

32. It should be noted that the Cornish-Fisher VaR critical values began to decrease when the critical values were extended to a 99.99 percent confidence interval.

33. The reason that the percentage of Amaranth positions is greater than 100 percent is twofold. Firstly, included in this calculation are Amaranth positions on ICE, which thus are additional contracts to what NYMEX has. Secondly, the measure of Amaranth's positions included options, swaps, and other instruments that are not strictly NYMEX natural gas futures contracts, but are natural gas futures equivalents as computed by the Senate Subcommittee and NYMEX. Thus, only in Exhibit 25.12C should percentages not be greater than 100 percent. In Exhibit 25.12C, only Amaranth NYMEX natural gas futures positions are compared to NYMEX natural gas futures open interest.

34. Here we are speaking about the total losses of $3.296 billion that would have resulted had they held their August 31, 2006, positions until September 21, 2006. The actual Amaranth natural gas losses were even higher at $4.071 billion, while the total change in net asset value to the main funds was $4.942 billion. These discrepancies are discussed in more detail in the Background section.

35. This would imply a VaR at a 99.99997 percent confidence level.

36. Unidentified trader's e-mail to Brian Hunter when he was making money in July (United States Senate 2007a, Exhibit #9).

37. Public statement by CEO Maounis about Hunter.

38. For other descriptions of funding risk, see Culp and Miller (1994), Edwards and Canter (2008), and Mello and Parsons (1995).

39. Of course, this is unrealistically high, because it requires many assumptions. The primary assumption is that for every natural gas equivalent held, NYMEX would require the full nonmember initial margin. For spread positions, consisting of two months of contracts, the initial margin requirements are much less per position at $1000 per position. Also some of these positions are for option contracts that might not require margin. Thus, this number represents an upper limit of the total margin required. Finally, this also assumes that the initial margin was calculated as if all positions were constructed on that particular day. To actually reconstruct the exact margin required by Amaranth on that day is not possible without further information that is not available. However, we do know from statements by NYMEX that on August 31, 2006, the actual margin requirement on that day exceeded $2.5 billion.

40. Of course, this is only approximate, as some of the natural gas equivalent positions were options. Also, this would be the total margin on NYMEX and ICE together.

41. A distinction should be made between manipulation of natural gas prices and impacting natural gas prices due to the large size of a trade. The former is illegal according to Sections 6(c), 6(d), and 9(a)(2) of the Act of the CFTC, which authorizes the CFTC to bring enforcement actions against any person who is manipulating or attempting to manipulate or has manipulated or attempted to manipulate the market prices of any commodity in interstate commerce or for future delivery on or subject to the rules of any registered entity. Both price manipulation and price impact are valid concerns for regulators, but one is illegal.

REFERENCES

Chincarini, Ludwig. B. 2006. "The Amaranth Debacle: Failure of Risk Measures or Failure of Risk Management?" Presentation at Georgetown McDonough School of Business, December 5. Available at http://faculty.msb.edu/lbc22/video-clip1.html.

Chincarini, Ludwig. B. 2007a. "The Amaranth Debacle: Failure of Risk Measures or Failure of Risk Management?" April. Available at SSRN: http://ssrn.com/abstract=952607.

Chincarini, Ludwig. B. 2007b. "The Amaranth Debacle: Failure of Risk Measures or Failure of Risk Management?" *Journal of Alternative Investments* 10:3, 91–104.

Cornish, E. A., and R. A. Fisher. 1937. "Moments and Cumulants in the Specification of Distributions." *Review of the International Statistical Institute,* 5, 307–320.

Culp, Christopher, and M. Miller. 1994. "Hedging a Flow of Commodity Deliveries with Futures: Lessons from Metallgesellschaft." *Derivatives Quarterly* 1:1, 1.

Davis, Anne. 2006. "How Giant Bets on Natural Gas Sank Brash Hedge-Fund Trader." *Wall Street Journal,* September 19, A1.

Dowd, Kevin. 1999. *Beyond Value at Risk: The New Science of Risk Management.* New York, John Wiley & Sons.

Edwards, Franklin, and M. S. Canter. 1995. "The Collapse of Metallgesellschaft: Unhedgeable Risks, Poor Hedging Strategy, or Just Bad Luck?" *Journal of Futures Markets* 15:3, 211–264.

Favre, Laurent, and J. A. Galeano. 2002. "Mean-Modified Value-at-Risk Optimization with Hedge Funds." *Journal of Alternative Investments* 5:1, 2–21.

Hull, John. 2006. *Options, Futures, and Other Derivatives.* Upper Saddle River, NJ: Prentice Hall.

Jorion, Phillippe. 2006. *Value at Risk.* New York: McGraw-Hill.

Levin, Carl. 2007. "To Amend the Commodity Exchange Act to Close the Enron Loophole, Prevent Price Manipulation Excessive Speculation in the Trading of Energy Commodities and for Other Purposes." Bill S. 2058. September 17.

Maounis, Nick. 2006. Investor Conference Call. Amaranth Group, Inc. September 22.

Mello, Antonio S., and J. E. Parsons. 1995. "Maturity Structure of a Hedge Matters: Lessons from the Metallgesellschaft Debacle." *Journal of Applied Corporate Finance* 8:1, 106–121.

Ord, Keith, and A. Stuart. 1994. *Kendall's Advanced Theory of Statistics* 1. London: John Wiley & Sons.

Till, Hilary. 2006. "EDHEC Comments on the Amaranth Case: Early Lessons from the Debacle." EDHEC Risk and Management Research Centre.

United States Senate Permanent Subcommittee on Investigations Staff Report. 2007a. "Excessive Speculation in the Natural Gas Market," June 25.

United States Senate Permanent Subcommittee on Investigations Staff Report. 2007b. "Excessive Speculation in the Natural Gas Market Appendix." June 25.

U.S. Federal Energy Regulatory Commission. 2007. "Order to Show Cause and Notice of Proposed Penalties." Docket No. IN07-26-000. July 27.

Watkins, David. 2007. "In the Shadow of Amaranth." *Energy Risk, Special Report on Natural Gas* (December), 28–31.

ABOUT THE CONTRIBUTOR

Ludwig Chincarini, PhD, is an Associate Professor of Finance at the School of Management of the University of San Francisco in San Francisco, California. He received his AB from the University of California at Berkeley and his PhD from the Massachusetts Institute of Technology. He specializes in portfolio management, quantitative equity management, and derivatives. He also was an adjunct professor at the McDonough School of Business at Georgetown University from 2003 to 2008. Dr. Chincarini is the author of the book *Quantitative Equity Portfolio Management* and the author of the new book about the financial crisis entitled *The Crisis of Crowding*. He has over 15 years of experience in the financial industry and was involved with creating the S&P 500 equal-weight ETF, RSP, as well as the first hedge-fund ETFs, including an overall hedge fund exposure (QAI), merger-arbitrage (MNA), market-neutral (QMN), and real return (CPI) ETF. He is responsible for building the first basket trading firm and directly responsible for many of the firm's patents.

Index